A Risk Professional's Survival Guide

The Wiley Finance series contains books written specifically for finance and investment professionals as well as sophisticated individual investors and their financial advisors. Book topics range from portfolio management to e-commerce, risk management, financial engineering, valuation and financial instrument analysis, as well as much more. For a list of available titles, visit our Web site at www.WileyFinance.com.

Founded in 1807, John Wiley & Sons is the oldest independent publishing company in the United States. With offices in North America, Europe, Australia and Asia, Wiley is globally committed to developing and marketing print and electronic products and services for our customers' professional and personal knowledge and understanding.

A Risk Professional's Survival Guide

Applied Best Practices in Risk Management

CLIFFORD ROSSI

WILEY

Library of Congress Cataloging-in-Publication Data:

Rossi, Clifford.
   A risk professional's survival guide : applied best practices in risk management / Clifford Rossi.
      pages cm. — (Wiley finance)
   Includes index.
   ISBN 978-1-118-04595-4 (cloth); ISBN 978-1-118-92237-8 (ebk);
   ISBN 978-1-118-95304-4 (ebk)
   1. Risk management.   I. Title.
   HD61.R667 2014
   658.15'5—dc23
                                                                        2014016949

Printed in the United States of America

10 9 8 7 6 5 4 3 2 1

To Linda; with this adventure astern,
may calm winds carry us toward new horizons.

Contents

Preface

The intent of this book is to provide the next generation of risk leaders, as well as current practitioners of financial risk management, a handy reference of techniques and concepts for identifying, measuring, and mitigating the major risks facing financial institutions. Risk management has evolved over the past decade into a highly quantitative field, drawing on increasingly complex mathematical and statistical concepts to portray a variety of traditional risks such as credit, counterparty, market, and interest rate risk. At the same time, the financial crisis of 2008–2009 laid bare the limitations of sophisticated quantitative analysis. Advances in quantitative risk management will continue; however, risk managers must be mindful of the "art" of risk management, namely judgment and experience that augments the "science" of risk management. Many risk management books focus on the quantitative aspects of the field rather than explore the importance of the qualitative side of risk management. This book is an attempt to bring both perspectives together in a cohesive fashion.

Another feature of this book is to provide readers with a framework for thinking about risk not as a singular outcome, but one that has consequences that may ripple across other parts of the business or risks. Leveraging experience from the crisis and afterward, the book follows the events of SifiBank, a stylized significantly important financial institution that provides the common thread of risk management practices throughout the course of the book. In that regard, this book represents a significant departure from other risk management books in that it is effectively a case study of one large complex commercial bank. To bring that story alive, a synthetic balance sheet is constructed within which specific positions, portfolios and loans are created. This information is then used in a series of Excel/VBA workbooks to provide the reader a hands on companion to the text discussion of key concepts and models.

The structure of the book starts by providing background on SifiBank, an imaginary institution that serves as an example throughout the chapters, and its historical roots, organizational and regulatory structure, competitive landscape, and markets. The reader is then guided through a risk taxonomy and governance discussion followed by a chapter introducing the reader to value-at-risk (VaR) and risk-adjusted performance metrics in light of the importance of such metrics for measuring a broad variety of risks.

Following these foundational chapters, the book delves into specific risk types, with an emphasis on identifying and measuring risk. Following each risk the reader is introduced to techniques and structures for mitigating major risk types. The book also presents chapters on operational, model, regulatory, reputation, and legal risk, all of which are of increasing importance for financial institutions following the financial crisis. Finally, the book ends with a look at integrated risk management and how risk managers should be thinking holistically across risks and the firm in performing their risk assessment.

The book is designed for a variety of readers. Readers with technical backgrounds will be able to delve into details surrounding a number of key quantitative concepts and techniques such as Monte Carlo simulation, Principal Components Analysis, copula methods, and econometric models for estimating default risk, to name a few. The Excel/VBA workbooks will be useful to such readers to reinforce concepts and allow sensitivity analysis to be performed. At the same time, readers with an interest in obtaining a basic understanding of key concepts rather than implementing risk models can review the chapter discussion to gain an overall understanding of a particular risk issue.

At the university level, the book is targeted to advanced undergraduate or graduate students in risk management, business, finance, and insurance. The book provides material for a semester long course in financial risk management or bank management or can be easily adapted for a two-course sequence. End of chapter questions provide students an opportunity to test their understanding of important concepts covered and the Test Bank provided to instructors contains ready-made examinations that can be used directly in class. Further, a set of comprehensive PowerPoint instruction slides is provided for each chapter, tying directly to the material discussed in the chapter.

As a former senior risk executive at several large financial institutions, my staff and I were always looking for useful references on risk management that could help us improve our understanding of applied risk management concepts and methodologies. In that spirit, this book is meant to fill a gap in this field that provides a comprehensive applied reference for risk managers, now and in the future.

Acknowledgments

While my name appears on the cover of this book, this project could not have been completed without the direct and indirect support from a number of people critical to the process. First, and foremost, Jim Thompson, a colleague of mine from a former workplace is credited with putting together the Excel/VBA workbooks contained in this book. Jim's exceptional work, particularly evidenced in the Market Risk, Interest Rate Risk, and Consumer Credit Risk chapters provides readers with user-friendly tools, allowing them to test highly complex risk methodologies easily. These Excel tools bring the story of SifiBank alive and without this material the utility of this book would be severely limited.

Linda Rossi, my wife, not only endured the writing and editing process, but also volunteered her time to take on the role of project manager and jack-of-all-trades in manuscript preparation and version control. Without her assistance and moral support throughout the project, this process would have been significantly more difficult for me.

Finally, a number of people have provided reviews and support along this path. Professor Larry Gordon, from the Robert H. Smith School of Business, University of Maryland, provided guidance and insight on the book-writing process from his own experience, motivating me to take on this project. Likewise, Dean Alex Triantis, Robert H. Smith School of Business, University of Maryland, provided support and an introduction to Bill Falloon at John Wiley & Sons. Bill's support of the concept for the book provided the catalyst for it to become something more than just an idea. Thanks also go out to Meg Freeborn and Vincent Nordhaus whose editorial skills greatly enhanced the end product while keeping me on schedule. Finally, I would like to thank the MS Finance students taking my Corporate Risk Management course at the Robert H. Smith School of Business, University of Maryland, who provided feedback and critical input on the materials during the project.

To all of you go my sincerest thanks for your patience and understanding. Your support enabled the book to come to fruition, and any remaining errors and omissions are solely my own.

About the Author

Dr. Rossi is Professor-of-the-Practice and Executive-in-Residence at the Robert H. Smith School of Business, University of Maryland. Prior to entering academia, Dr. Rossi had nearly 25 years' experience in banking and government, having held senior executive roles in risk management at several of the largest financial services companies.

His most recent position was Managing Director and Chief Risk Officer for Citigroup's Consumer Lending Group. He also served as Chief Credit Officer at Washington Mutual (WaMu) and as Managing Director and Chief Risk Officer at Countrywide Bank. Previous to these assignments, Dr. Rossi held senior risk management positions at Freddie Mac and Fannie Mae. He started his career during the thrift crisis at the U.S. Treasury's Office of Domestic Finance and later at the Office of Thrift Supervision, working on key policy issues affecting depositories. Dr. Rossi was also an adjunct professor in the Finance Department at the Robert H. Smith School of Business for eight years and has numerous academic and nonacademic articles on banking industry topics. Dr. Rossi is frequently quoted on financial policy issues in major newspapers and has appeared on such programs as *Fox News*, Canada's BNN, C-SPAN's *Washington Journal* and CNN's *Situation Room*. He also has a weekly column, *Risk Doctor,* in the *American Banker* on risk and regulatory reform issues. Dr. Rossi serves as an advisor to a number of banks, federal regulatory agencies, private equity investment companies, and hedge funds on banking and regulatory topics, and founded Chesapeake Risk Advisors, LLC, a financial risk management consulting practice. He received his PhD from Cornell University.

CHAPTER 1

Navigating Risk at SifiBank

OVERVIEW

Managing risk at a banking institution is one of the most critical activities carried out by financial firms. Banks could not expect to have much longevity if risk management were ignored or poorly executed. The subprime mortgage crisis of 2008 offers a once-in-a-lifetime case study of how many different types of financial institutions lost sight of the importance of risk management and either went out of business, were forced to merge with healthier firms or had to take a bailout from U.S. taxpayers. And this was not a U.S. phenomenon limited to only the U.S. banking industry: The global financial sector during the 2008–2009 period was in virtual free fall with many experts fearing an economic depression on an unprecedented scale. While many causes have been attributed to the crisis—a number of gaps in regulation, a financial incentive structure that rewarded short-run profitability and production, the interconnectedness of banks and other financial entities comprising the so-called shadow banking sector—nevertheless, at the heart of the crisis was a fundamental lapse in risk management across a great swath of the industry. Particularly problematic was that the largest financial institutions were among the companies where risk management deficiencies were most acute. Given the scale and scope of these global financial behemoths, these gaps in risk management at the institution level would manifest as systemic risk and contribute to one of the worst financial calamities on a global scale. These institutions became the focus of intense scrutiny by regulators after the crisis and have been designated as **systemically important financial institutions**, or **SIFIs** for short.

We begin our journey of risk management by taking one such SIFI (we will refer to it as SifiBank) and following it though its various business functions with the intention of understanding how such firms identify, measure and manage their risks. Risk management is not a separate discipline as is finance or accounting, and in practice every employee of a bank should take an active role in risk management, whether they are in sales and production, trading, operations, or other important areas of the company.

SIFIs are a unique class of financial institution. The term *SIFI* surfaced after the crisis as concerns arose over the size and complexity of some firms to become, in principle and reality, **too-big-to-fail** (**TBTF**). Institutions were designed as SIFIs by U.S. federal regulators and as G-SIFIs by the United Kingdom's Financial Stability Board (FSB) based on their size, complexity of operations, degree of interconnectedness across the financial sector, global reach and substitutability of activities. The largest banking institutions worldwide have found their way onto this list and in addition, regulators have developed a set of criteria to designate other institutions as systematically important, such as insurance companies and nonbank companies.[1]

SifiBank makes an excellent case study for risk management since its far-flung businesses touch on every aspect of financial risk management that most banks would encounter. In fact, one could say that banks are in the business to take *prudent risk*. As will be seen shortly, banks that take zero risk are not going to be profitable enterprises. Similarly, banks taking excessive risk—that is, risk not well understood and outside the firm's capabilities to price and manage that risk and its risk appetite—will eventually be doomed. That's why the term *prudent risk* is critical to understanding the process of risk management.

Thinking of risk management as a process or system in itself is helpful since managing risk effectively entails establishing a feedback loop (Figure 1.1) in which risk tolerance is communicated across the organization;

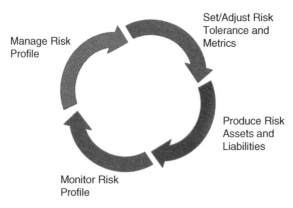

Manage Risk Profile

Set/Adjust Risk Tolerance and Metrics

Produce Risk Assets and Liabilities

Monitor Risk Profile

FIGURE 1.1   Risk Management Feedback Loop

---

[1] A nonbank financial company engages in financial services activities but is not a regulated depository institution such as a commercial bank, thrift or credit union. An insurance company or hedge fund would be examples of nonbank institutions.

expectations are set in terms of how much risk is acceptable for businesses to take (usually expressed in terms of capital allocated to each line of business); there is ongoing measurement and reporting of risks, there are processes and controls for managing risk coming into the firm in the way of transactions, loans, and services; there are techniques and controls for mitigating risk on the books of the firm; and there are methods to adjust the level of risk on an ongoing basis consistent with the above process as well as market and environmental considerations.

Unlike most products of nonfinancial companies, financial products are not physical in nature. Loans, deposits, and investment products for example provide customers with access to credit, enabling them to purchase physical products and services or compensate them for storing their financial assets with the institution. Risk management is an inextricable component of financial product development as a result. The features of financial products such as the term of the loan or deposit, the rate of interest, payment features, and eligibility criteria are effectively levers that the bank uses to manage the risk that the borrower defaults or the bank faces losses from interest rate risk exposure, among others. Consequently, effective risk management requires a deep understanding and appreciation for the business of the bank, the market, its competition, and the regulatory landscape it operates in as well as the structure and organizational dynamics of the firm itself.

FINANCIAL INTERMEDIATION AND PROFIT MAXIMIZATION

At its core, SifiBank, like other commercial banks, engages in profit-maximizing financial intermediation. Profit π_i is defined as:

$$\pi_i = \sum_{i=1}^{n} r_i q_i - \sum_{j=1}^{m} i_j x_j \qquad 1.1$$

where r_i represents the rate on earning assets q for the ith product, and i_j is the cost associated with the jth input x, either financial (e.g., deposits) or real (e.g., personnel).

Financial intermediation refers to the process by which banks take in a variety of liabilities such as deposits and debt and transform them into earning assets. Liabilities for banks are inputs into their production process that are used in creating loans, investments and services to bank customers.

Further, the bank is expected to maximize profit subject to technical conditions underlying a production function, $P(q_1, \ldots q_n, x_1, \ldots x_m) = 0$. In developing their strategic plans for the coming year, banks take into consideration a host of other information in setting their asset targets. These include such factors as relative peer profitability and other indicators of performance, and business structural issues such as product concentrations and competitive conditions, among others. Through the production function whereby the bank as a financial intermediary uses its financial inputs—including various forms of deposits including retail and wholesale sources as well as other funding sources—and nonfinancial inputs such as physical premises and personnel, the bank determines its level and combination of assets to produce, taking into account other external factors as described. As a result, the relationship between bank output and inputs could be described by the following first-order condition of the following simple constant elasticity of substitution (CES) production function[2]:

$$q = C\left(\alpha x_1^{-\rho} + (1-\alpha)x_2^{-\rho}\right)^{-\frac{1}{\rho}}$$

$$\frac{\partial q}{\partial x_1} = \frac{\alpha}{C^\rho}\left[\frac{q}{x_1}\right]^{\rho+1}$$

$$\frac{\partial q}{\partial x_2} = \frac{1-\alpha}{C^\rho}\left[\frac{q}{x_2}\right]^{\rho+1}$$

1.2

To illustrate the link between assets and deposits in this construct, assume the bank has a single asset denoted q in the model above that is produced using two types of deposits; x_1 represents retail deposits and x_2 describes brokered deposits.[3] The relationship described by the CES production function shows that both inputs as factors of production define the level of assets for the firm. In equilibrium, the bank will select a target level of output q that maximizes the expected utility of profit formally described below. The input combinations of x_1 and x_2 are then optimized by their least cost combination in the profit function subject to any technical production constraint such as funding limitations. External factors driving target output for the bank such as peer performance or other metrics could be subsumed within the constant term C of the production function.

---

[2] A constant elasticity of substitution production function exhibits the property that production is a function of a constant relationship between the substitutability between factor inputs such as retail deposits and personnel.

[3] Brokered deposits are a form of wholesale deposit that banks may use to augment their retail branch generated deposit base. They may be purchased in markets from brokers that buy and package these deposits from other institutions.

The profit model can be extended to include the production function as well as to introduce uncertainty (risk) into the decision making process.

$$\pi_i = \sum_{i=1}^{n} r_i q_i - \sum_{j=1}^{m} i_j x_j + \lambda P(q_1, \ldots q_n, x_1, \ldots x_m) \qquad 1.3$$

where λ is a Lagrange multiplier.[4] Introducing output uncertainty into the model, the bank is assumed to maximize expected profit:

$$E(\pi_i) = \sum_{k=1}^{K} \kappa_k \left[r_i q_i - i_j x_j + \lambda P(q_1, \ldots q_n, x_1, \ldots x_m) \right] \qquad 1.4$$

where K_k represents the probability of output q_i. The first-order conditions with respect to output and input are as follows:

$$\frac{\partial E(\pi_i)}{\partial q_i} = \sum_{k=1}^{K} \kappa_k \left[r_i + \lambda P'(q_1, \ldots q_n, x_1 \ldots x_m) \right] = 0 \qquad 1.5$$

$$\frac{\partial E(\pi_i)}{\partial x_j} = \sum_{k=1}^{K} \kappa_k \left[-i_i + \lambda P'(q_1, \ldots q_n, x_1, \ldots x_m) \right] = 0 \qquad 1.6$$

The term $\frac{\partial E(\pi_i)}{\partial X_j}$ represents the input demand function for the jth input x. In this specification, input demands are a function of input prices i as well as the production function. Taking, for example, brokered deposits as an input variable of interest, the change in expected profit for a unit change in the level of brokered deposits would be dependent upon changes in the costs of its inputs as well as the relationship between bank outputs (assets) and inputs (liabilities and other real inputs) as established by the production function P. In other words, changes in profit arising from changes in brokered deposits are driven by underlying structural economic relationships. Taking these theoretical relationships further, we can postulate the relationship between asset growth and risk-taking that figures prominently in policy discussions of brokered deposits. Adapting the profit model above, assume that the bank maximizes the expected utility of profit as follows:

$$\text{MAX } E[U(\pi_i)] = \sum_{k=1}^{K} \kappa_k U(\pi_i) \qquad 1.7$$

---

[4] Lagrange multipliers are used in some types of constrained optimization problems where closed form solutions may be difficult to otherwise obtain.

Setting the derivative of output q equal to zero yields:

$$\frac{dE[U(\pi_i)]}{dq_i} = \sum \kappa_k U'(\pi_i)(r_i + \lambda P') = 0 \qquad 1.8$$

Assuming that the bank utility function follows Neumann-Morgenstern expected conditions, a bank that is risk-neutral would exhibit second-order conditions:

$$\frac{d^2 U}{d\pi^2} = 0 \qquad 1.9$$

In the case that the bank is a risk-taker, it can be shown that the second-order condition must satisfy the following:

$$\frac{d^2 U}{d\pi^2} > 0 \qquad 1.10$$

which implies that $\sum \kappa_k U'(\pi_i)(r_i + \lambda P(q^*)') > 0$, where q^* is the level of bank output that solves the profit maximization problem above. In such situations, q^* is greater than the equilibrium level of q that solves. $\sum \kappa_k U'(\pi_i)(r_i + \lambda P(q^*)') > 0$.

The implication from this result is that risk-taking leads to higher output produced by the bank than if the bank were risk-neutral.[5] With this result we can establish then that asset growth for the bank must be related to the risk appetite of the firm. With the model establishing input demand as a function of input prices and the production function, the model describes how risk-taking at the bank relates to a target level of output. This framework suggests that deposits certainly are a factor of production, but that asset growth and investment in riskier products is driven more by overall risk-taking of the firm rather than fueled by deposit strategies. In this formulation, output is determined by the least cost combination of inputs subject to various constraints on those inputs. The existence of technical constraints on inputs can influence input allocation. For instance, if banks set a target level of assets for the next year that cannot be funded solely with retail deposits due to capacity constraints, then brokered and other wholesale deposits would be used to fill the gap, subject again to profit maximization conditions. With this framework describing the bank's conceptual constrained profit maximization problem, it is instructive to dig deeper into

---

[5] The concept of risk-neutrality is a fundamental concept in financial theory and its treatment in detail is beyond the scope of this book. However, a risk-neutral investor is indifferent between accepting a risky payoff and one that is 100 percent certain to occur.

some of the structural, market and regulatory aspects of banking that affect the way risk management is performed.

SIFIBANK STRUCTURE AND HISTORY

SifiBank is actually made up of a collection of legal vehicles; that is, structural entities of a particular type of financial institution including a commercial bank, thrift, investment company and finance company. As a result, SifiBank is technically a bank holding company, a parent entity formed around the subsidiary banking units. Conceptually, the structure of SifiBank is shown in Figure 1.2. A **bank holding company** was created to oversee the subsidiary companies. Within the holding company structure are a bank holding company that has several commercial banks, a thrift and a finance company.[6] In addition, SifiBank has a capital markets division (SifiInvestment Bank), and asset management and brokerage division and a corporate services unit.

The origins of SifiBank go back 200 years when First National Bank and Trust of Baltimore (FNBTB) was founded by the son of one of the signers of the Declaration of Independence. The bank grew over the next 170 years largely through organic growth as opposed to merger and acquisition. The bank had for nearly two centuries operated under very conservative

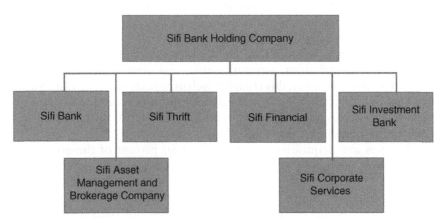

FIGURE 1.2 SifiBank Corporate Structure

---

[6] A finance company is a type of nondepository institution, a firm that does not rely on deposit-gathering activities like a traditional bank and instead is dependent upon capital market financing.

business standards that kept it largely out of financial trouble even during a series of major and minor financial panics, including the Great Depression.

In 1987, the bank underwent a change in CEO and president when the bank itself was bought out by a rival institution with less name brand recognition. That institution recognized the value of FNBTB and embarked on a strategy to opportunistically grow the bank by purchasing weak but well-known thrifts that had large retail footprints in markets complementary to FNBTB. Over this period FNBTB tripled its size in terms of total consolidated assets across all subsidiaries and it was during this period that SifiBank was born. By 2014, total assets of the bank had grown to $1 trillion, making it one of the largest financial institutions in the world and number three by asset size in the United States.

The chairman and CEO of SifiBank was an icon in banking, credited with turning a number of sick banks into financial powerhouses largely based on heavy cost-cutting, and a strategy of creating a financial supermarket that would find broad appeal cutting across different customers and product segments. The theory was that by offering a full service array of products and services to all types of consumers, corporations and even sovereign clients, the bank would be able to diversify its revenue streams and expand its markets better than any peers. While it began as a United States–only institution, by the 1990s it had branched out into several countries in Europe and Asia. Today, revenue from its foreign branches accounts for less than 10 percent of SifiBank's revenues. While the strategy of a "universal" bank lived up to its promise of delivering significant growth for its shareholders, it also came with significant risks. The holding company structure became unwieldy as it established hundreds of subsidiary units to take advantage of tax regulations, accounting rules and other legal benefits from these structures. However, this complex web of various subsidiary organizations led to a fragmentation in management and oversight of the company, making it extremely difficult to get a holistic perspective on the operating units and risks each posed to SifiBank.

Mergers and acquisitions accounted for 80 percent of the growth of SifiBank over the past 30 years. When a prospective acquisition target was identified, SifiBank's M&A team ran the financials to ensure the acquisition had accretive value to the overall firm. Importantly, left out of that financial analysis was the cost of integrating different origination, financial, accounting, servicing, and risk information systems across platforms and subsidiaries. Eventually, SifiBank was forced to maintain 10 different operating systems for financial management and reporting. In some cases it was nearly impossible to roll up a consolidated view of a particular class of assets as data and metrics oftentimes did not align across businesses. For mortgages, SifiBank originated loans primarily from three commercial bank subsidiaries of SifiCommercial Bank, a thrift subsidiary consolidated from several it bought during the thrift crisis and a finance company that catered to subprime borrowers. It used one definition of mortgage default based on the Mortgage Bankers Association definition for its banking entities, but used different definitions for both its thrift and finance company units. Beyond this problem the bank experienced significant difficulties in aggregating its exposures and was plagued by a host of data accuracy and reporting issues. These system issues, while ignored during the M&A decision-making process, had come home to roost for SifiBank. By greatly impairing its ability to understand the kinds of risks it was taking on across the firm in a timely fashion, this infrastructure problem played a major role in limiting the bank's reaction to the growing asset bubble forming in the housing market in the mid-2000s. Something more subtle and pervasive within SifiBank would ultimately result in the near death of the company in the aftermath of the financial crisis of 2008. Specifically, this was the company's focus on growth, the lack of a risk culture, and weak governance during that period.

SIFIBANK ORGANIZATIONAL STRUCTURE AND OVERSIGHT GOVERNANCE

SifiHolding Company is a publicly traded company that was headed by the CEO who also held the title of Chairman of the Board of Directors in the years leading up to the financial crisis. This consolidated power of having both the CEO and chairman titles along with this individual's unique personal stature in the industry afforded him an ability to run SifiBank in a fashion that met with little opposition to the direction he sought for the company.

The board was composed of 10 members, all handpicked by the CEO and all well-known friends or associates. Two members had some related background in financial services—specifically, having been CEOs of an insurance company and investment company—and no one on the board had any direct risk management experience. The board met quarterly for one day each time and in addition to holding a meeting of the full board to review important issues it also broke up into several committee sessions. Among the committees it had were audit, operations and human capital, legal, and finance.

The CEO believed in having a small management team reporting to him and this meant that only the presidents of SifiBank, SifiThrift, SifiFinancial, SifiInvestment Bank, SifiAsset Management, the CFO, General Counsel, General Auditor, and Head of Human Resources had direct access to the

CEO. The CEO had handpicked the presidents as well and all had track records for achieving aggressive product objectives.

At this time the bank had only created the role of Chief Risk Officer two years before the crisis and this was largely a corporate oversight role. In fact at times, the role of the CRO and General Auditor seemed to overlap, creating significant confusion and concern by management that the bank was carrying too many risk oversight staff at a time when margins were thin. The CRO reported into the CFO, leaving an additional layer of management between the senior risk officer of the company and the board. The board did not hold executive sessions with the CRO separate from the CFO or CEO.

Furthermore, risk management activities were spread across the business, operations and audit functions in a decentralized model. As a result, the SifiBank board would pick up risk management issues in piecemeal fashion and only as management decided what was important to elevate to the board. A decentralized risk management function has its own merits over a risk management structure within the corporate center; however, it can lead to a number of governance issues that the firm must understand. In the case of SifiBank, the board of directors delegates development of credit and other major risk policies to the CRO. But since the CRO does not have any responsibility over managing the risk exposure of an individual line of business, a delegation of authority policy would need to be established by the CRO to allow business staff designated to manage risk at the unit level to operate within stated risk objectives. Such a policy would outline the size of deals, loans, and transactions that could be approved by employees, which is oftentimes based on seniority and expertise. By having a small corporate risk office and a large business risk function, it allows an independent review of risk management activities to be conducted by the corporate risk office while allowing the business risk units to be responsible for day-to-day implementation of risk management within each line of business. SifiBank had set up such a structure where each business unit had a CRO who reported directly to each division's president and indirectly to the CRO. The presidents each created their own performance plans for their CROs with input from the corporate CRO (sometimes also referred to as the enterprise CRO). In the years preceding the crisis, SifiBank's CEO gave clear direction to the heads of each business that they had to grow their businesses each year by at least 10 percent. As a result, these objectives were handed down to each executive in the operating units, including the business line CROs. For the business CROs, 85 percent of their performance was based on supporting product and sales within the division and only 15 percent was placed on managing the risk exposure of the unit. This executive compensation structure fueled significant risk-taking by SifiBank in the years leading up to the financial crisis.

Lines of Business

SifiBank operates along a complicated product and institutional structure as depicted in Table 1.1. Due largely to historical arrangements, several business lines cross corporate segments. While SifiBank remains the flagship entity with respect to consumer and commercial banking activities, its thrift and finance company divisions provide specialized consumer and commercial banking oriented in some measure to their unique charters.

Thrifts, or **savings and loans** (S&Ls) as they are sometimes known, are depository institutions like commercial banks and are granted operating charters from the state or federal government that allow them to access cheaper (federally subsidized) deposits. But a major differentiator between commercial banks and thrifts is that a thrift institution must maintain 65 percent of its assets in certain qualifying assets, much of which are mortgage-related. This specialization makes thrifts particularly vulnerable to mortgage market conditions. Moreover, thrifts are especially sensitive to interest rate risk, where losses can be realized due to mismatches between typically shorter-dated funding sources and mortgage loans that have long maturities. This will be examined in more detail in later chapters. SifiThrift Company is regulated by the Office of the Comptroller of the Currency (OCC).

SifiFinance Company had been an independent company prior to its purchase by SifiBank in 1999. As a finance company it did not hold a bank charter, which meant that it had to derive its funding via capital market debt issuance. The lack of subsidized deposits puts finance companies at a competitive disadvantage to commercial banks and thrifts. Balanced against that is the fact that unlike banks and thrifts, finance companies are not subject to safety and soundness regulations. They are subject to various state and federal consumer regulations such as those overseen by the Consumer Financial Protection Bureau (CFPB). However, by focusing on subprime borrowers, SifiFinance Company was able to earn substantial income by charging interest rates and fees significantly above that for prime borrowers. The company traditionally offered small ($500–$1,000) short-term (<1 year) unsecured (i.e., requiring no collateralization) personal loans realizing that the average loss rate on this business was between 12 and 18 percent. Borrowers could be graduated to larger loans, eventually after demonstrated payment ability over time, allowing them to obtain a mortgage loan from SifiFinance Company.

SifiBank, as mentioned earlier, is comprised of several commercial bank subsidiaries. SifiBank, having a federal charter, is technically a national bank, overseen from a safety and soundness perspective by the OCC. The Federal Reserve oversees banks that have state charters and are members of the

TABLE 1.1 SifiBank Business Lines by Corporate Entity

Business Lines	SifiBank	SifiThrift	Sifi Financial	Sifi Capital Markets	Sifi Asset Management	Sifi Corporate Services
Consumer Banking						
Mortgage	✓	✓	✓			
Credit Cards	✓	✓				
Personal Loans			✓			
Auto Loans	✓	✓	✓			
Home Equity Lines of Credit (HELOCs)	✓	✓				
Student Loans	✓	✓				
Retail Deposits and Investment Accounts	✓	✓				
Commercial Banking						
Commercial and Industrial Loans	✓	✓				
Commercial Real Estate	✓	✓				
Investment Banking Services				✓		
Debt and Equity Trading and Services				✓		
Private Equity Services				✓		
Structured Financial Product Services				✓		
Equity and Financial Research				✓		
Brokerage Services					✓	
Asset Management Services					✓	
Treasury and Financial Operations					✓	
Human Capital						✓
Operations						✓
Legal and Audit						✓
Risk Management	✓		✓	✓	✓	✓

Federal Reserve System (FRS) as well as bank holding companies. The Federal Deposit Insurance Corporation (FDIC) oversees state-chartered banks that are nonmembers of the FRS.

SifiBank's lines of business are focused on consumer and commercial customers. The bank offers a full array of consumer loan products as shown in Table 1.1 with credit cards representing one of the larger consumer asset classes. SifiCards is one of the most recognized credit cards in the market, however, a rise in cyberattacks on large retailers and banks has placed the company on guard against this risk. But one of SifiBank's greatest strengths is in its extensive branch network. It operates more than 10,000 retail branch offices across the country, although 75 percent of its network is on the East Coast. The cost of operating branches in an increasingly e-commerce environment has pressured the bank to find ways to reduce its operating efficiency ratio defined as the dollar amount of noninterest expense as a percent of operating revenues. To be more competitive with peer institutions, the bank has waged a cost-cutting campaign for three years and senior management has considered increasing its Internet banking model in an effort to combat higher costs.

Notwithstanding such costs, the branch network represents a significant source of revenue generated from cross-selling of bank products to its customers. On average SifiBank has found that its retail bank customers have about seven products that it obtained from branch operations. That means that when a customer opens up a retail checking or savings account they are marketed for loan and investment products. This compound effect of cross-selling products has boosted revenues even as operating expenses have risen with branch growth.

SifiInvestment Bank was formed to handle all of SifiBank's vast trading and investment activities for its clients and for proprietary trading. The bank trades in virtually all investment types including equities, fixed income, derivatives such as options, futures and swaps, foreign exchange and commodities. When trading for clients it acts as a market maker, bringing buyers and sellers together without taking a position itself.[7] The capital markets group has developed a robust structured finance offering, which features creating, underwriting and investing in various financial instruments with complex cash flow features. Examples of structured financial instruments include mortgage-backed securities and associated resecuritizations, collateralized debt obligations (CDOs), and credit default swaps (CDSs), among

---

[7] There are times when SifiBank takes an offsetting position in order to meet a client's needs when a suitable buyer or seller is not available at that time, however, this tends to be for a very short period of time until it can unwind that position.

others. These types of transactions have a variety of purposes including transfer of different risks such as credit and interest rate risk, tax optimization strategies and obtaining legal and accounting advantages. These often require the establishment of separate legal vehicles apart from the bank to meet certain requirements. Over the years, SifiInvestment Bank has created hundreds of special purpose vehicles (SPVs) for its structured finance activity. The scale and complexity of the business poses significant exposure to SifiBank in terms of counterparty, credit, market, and operational risks.

Five years earlier the capital markets group had established a proprietary trading group that was charged with taking positions in capital markets for profit-making. This type of activity made it a hedge fund within SifiBank and over the years it had performed well for the company, enjoying an annual average return of 18 percent since its inception. The trading group can invest in a wide range of instruments and has focused largely on economic bets since the financial crisis. The company made $1 billion, for example, following the Greek crisis. In the months leading up to the crisis, it took short positions in various sovereign debt instruments of countries that had similar underlying fiscal and monetary problems as Greece. It also was active in shorting various financial stocks during the banking crisis. With the implementation of the **Volcker Rule** banning proprietary trading at federally insured depository institutions, SifiBank faces a decision whether to spin off the hedge fund unit, shrink it to a regulatory allowable size, or change its direction and merge it with other permissible hedging activities.

SifiAsset Management Company had operated as a well-known retail investment company, founded in 1900 until it was bought out by SifiBank as part of the strategic initiative to build a universal bank franchise. SifiAsset Management is focused on advising private retail clients with wealth management services, investments and brokerage activities.

The other unit within SifiBank is the Corporate Division. This group comprises the nonbusiness-oriented activities of the entire company such as finance, accounting, treasury management services, corporate risk management, legal, IT and operations, and human resources. The company over the years adopted a center of excellence model where these activities would emanate from the corporate center for purposes of maintaining consistency and adherence with applicable laws, regulations and accounting rules as well as promoting best practices across the company. Each operating division of SifiBank maintains a cadre of staff performing these functions for its specific business, but these resources have a direct reporting line to their respective corporate offices.

An important function within the Corporate Division is the Treasury Office. This group is responsible for ensuring that SifiBank and its operating subsidiaries have the right mix and level of funding required to meet its activities, on a day-to-day as well as longer term basis. Each day the Corporate Treasurer and her staff face a complex and well-choreographed exercise of determining how much funding is available from its retail deposit network, wholesale deposits, and short-term funding markets, including asset-backed commercial paper (ABCP), and overnight repurchases (repos), which amount to interbank borrowings. It balances its needs for short-term funds with an ability to issue debt and equity at regular intervals in order to best match its asset and liability structure while maintaining a safe cushion of liquidity on hand to meet uncertain events such as unexpected deposit outflows or other disruptions. Thus, one of the Treasury Office's major risks is from liquidity risk. In reporting directly to the Chief Financial Officer (CFO), the Treasurer also has responsibilities for asset-liability management within SifiBank. The CFO and Treasurer also work closely with each business unit CFO to maintain the right level of assets in each subsidiary's portfolio.

For SifiBank and SifiThrift, for example, the bank maintains large **held-for-investment (HFI)** mortgage positions. These are portfolios that the bank and thrift subsidiaries plan on holding for long periods of time. Some mortgages that are originated, however, are designated as **available-for-sale (AFS)**. These assets, for example, might be formed into a pool to be packaged into a mortgage-backed security (MBS) and sold to investors. Different accounting rules apply for assets held for sale than HFI. Accounting principles, for example, require fair value treatment for assets intended for sale. Depending on a number of factors, including how liquid the market is for an asset, fair value could be assessed based on observable market prices, inferences drawn from closely related assets, or even models if no market pricing is available. During the financial crisis SifiBank saw the fair value of their AFS mortgage securities positions fall 50 percent as investors retreated from the market. Meanwhile, the bank's HFI portfolios experienced a much smaller decline limited to its expectation of credit losses forming in the portfolio. In originating loans, the bank engages in a "best execution" assessment that determines the highest price it would be able to obtain for a loan whether that is an HFS or AFS disposition. A detailed financial analysis of the value from retaining or selling the asset is performed.

SifiBank Balance Sheet Composition

At an aggregate level, the variety and composition of SifiBank's balance sheet at the holding company level is illustrated in Tables 1.2 and 1.3. At a glance, Sifibank holds nearly a quarter of its assets in consumer loans, 50 percent of which are in mortgages, with credit cards accounting for another 44 percent. As mentioned before, trends in the economy and housing market will feature prominently in SifiBank's assessment of the credit and interest rate

TABLE 1.2 SifiBank Asset Composition

ASSETS	%	$ Balances
Cash and Deposits with Banks	11	$ 110,000,000,000
Cash and Due from Banks	16	$ 17,600,000,000
Interest Bearing Deposits	84	$ 92,400,000,000
Fed Funds Sold and Securities Borrowed	17	$ 170,000,000,000
Consumer Loans	24	$ 240,000,000,000
Mortgages	50	$ 120,000,000,000
Auto Loans	6	$ 14,400,000,000
Credit Cards	44	$ 105,600,000,000
Commercial Loans	13	$ 130,000,000,000
CRE	50	$ 65,000,000,000
C&I	50	$ 65,000,000,000
Direct Outstandings	50	$ 32,500,000,000
Unfunded Commitments	50	$ 32,500,000,000
Trading Account Assets	18	$ 180,000,000,000
Mortgage-backed Securities	12	$ 21,600,000,000
US Treasuries	8	$ 14,400,000,000
State and Municipal Securities	3	$ 5,400,000,000
Corporate Debt Securities	13	$ 23,400,000,000
Derivatives	21	$ 37,800,000,000
Trading Derivatives		
Interest Rate Contracts		$ 28,350,000,000
Swaps	72	$ 20,412,000,000
Futures and Forwards	9	$ 2,551,500,000
Written Options	9.9	$ 2,806,650,000
Purchased Options	9.1	$ 2,579,850,000
Total Interest Rate Contracts		
Foreign Exchange Contracts		$ 3,402,000,000
Swaps	22	$ 748,440,000
Futures and Forwards	58	$ 1,973,160,000
Written Options	11	$ 374,220,000
Purchased Options	9	$ 306,180,000
Total Foreign Exchange Contracts		

ASSETS	%		$ Balances
Equity Contracts		$	756,000,000
Swaps	7	$	52,920,000
Futures and Forwards	1	$	7,560,000
Written Options	48	$	362,880,000
Purchased Options	44	$	332,640,000
Total Equity Contracts			
Commodity Contracts		$	567,000,000
Swaps	8	$	45,360,000
Futures and Forwards	26	$	147,420,000
Written Options	31	$	175,770,000
Purchased Options	35	$	198,450,000
Total Commodity Contracts			
Credit Derivatives		$	4,725,000,000
Protection Sold	48	$	2,268,000,000
Protection Bought	52	$	2,457,000,000
Total Credit Derivatives			
Foreign Government Securities	27	$	48,600,000,000
Equity Securities	14	$	25,200,000,000
Asset-backed Securities	2	$	3,600,000,000
Investments	17	$	170,000,000,000
Mortgage-backed Securities	19	$	32,300,000,000
US Treasuries	32	$	54,400,000,000
State and Municipal Securities	5	$	8,500,000,000
Corporate Debt Securities	4	$	6,800,000,000
Foreign Government Securities	32	$	54,400,000,000
Equity Securities	3	$	5,100,000,000
Asset-backed Securities	5	$	8,500,000,000
TOTAL ASSETS			$1,000,000,000,000

Note: Subcategory percents add up to 100 percent for each category.

TABLE 1.3 SifiBank Liabilities and Equity

LIABILITIES	%	$ Balances
Deposits		
Demand and Time Core Deposits	55	$ 495,000,000,000
Wholesale and NonCore Deposits	50	$ 247,500,000,000
Time Deposits	50	$ 247,500,000,000
Fed Funds Purchased and Securities Sold	13	$ 117,000,000,000
Trading Account Liabilities	8	$ 72,000,000,000
Derivatives		$ 40,320,000,000
Interest Rate Contracts		$ 30,240,000,000
Swaps	72	$ 21,772,800,000
Futures and Forwards	9	$ 2,721,600,000
Written Options	9.9	$ 2,993,760,000
Purchased Options	9.1	$ 2,751,840,000
Foreign Exchange Contracts		$ 3,628,800,000
Swaps	22	$ 798,336,000
Futures and Forwards	58	$ 2,104,704,000
Written Options	11	$ 399,168,000
Purchased Options	9	$ 326,592,000
Equity Contracts		$ 806,400,000
Swaps	7	$ 56,448,000
Futures and Forwards	1	$ 8,064,000
Written Options	48	$ 387,072,000
Purchased Options	44	$ 354,816,000
Commodity Contracts		$ 604,800,000
Swaps	8	$ 48,384,000
Futures and Forwards	26	$ 157,248,000
Written Options	31	$ 187,488,000
Purchased Options	35	$ 211,680,000
Total Commodity Contracts	100	
Credit Derivatives		$ 5,040,000,000
Protection Sold	48	$ 2,419,200,000
Protection Bought	52	$ 2,620,800,000
Securities Sold Not Purchased		$ 31,680,000,000

LIABILITIES	%	$ Balances
Debt	24	$ 216,000,000,000
Short-term	4	
Commercial Paper		$ 14,400,000,000
Secured Financing-Repurchase Agreements		$ 10,800,000,000
FHLB Advances		$ 10,800,000,000
Long-term	20	
Senior/Subordinated Debt		$108,000,000,000.00
Securitized Debt		$ 18,000,000,000.00
FHLB Borrowings		$ 41,400,000,000.00
Undrawn Lines of Credit		$ 12,600,000,000.00
TOTAL LIABILITIES		$ 900,000,000,000
Total Equity		$ 100,000,000,000

Note: Subcategory percents add up to 100 percent for each category.

risk profile of this portfolio. Commercial lending represents about half the size of the consumer business with commercial and industrial loans (C&I) and commercial real estate (CRE) lending evenly split. The consumer and commercial lending businesses couldn't be more different in many respects. Consumer lending such as the credit card business tends to rely on relatively homogeneous populations to assess risk, which lends itself to intensive data mining analysis. Underwriting for a credit card is more heavily automated than commercial lending which, due to large differences in client, loan size and purpose, among other factors, makes commercial lending a much more manual underwriting process.

The bulk of SifiBank's remaining assets are distributed across its trading and investment units. More than one-fifth of the bank's assets are in a variety of derivatives positions. The bank faces significant risk in the fluctuations of prices in these assets known as market risk. In addition, the vast fixed income and MBS holdings are subject to fluctuations in the value of these securities due to interest rate movements, which expose the firm to considerable interest rate risk. Finally, the bank retains 11 percent of its assets in liquid positions such as cash, and a variety of short-term positions. The bank faces the risk that it does not have sufficient assets that could be sold quickly with little or no price effect in the event of an unforeseen problem such as a bank run. Alternatively it must balance that risk against the reduction in income that it realizes for allocating a sizable portion of its assets to no or low earnings investments.

Turning to the other side of the balance sheet, SifiBank shows liabilities totaling $900 billion against $1 trillion in assets. The difference is the amount of equity in SifiBank, or $100 billion. As will be explained in a later section, not all forms of equity (for example, common and preferred stock, loan loss reserves, and subordinated debt instruments) are created equal in the eyes of the regulator. As a result, SifiBank must comply with a variety of different capital requirements as a regulated depository institution.

The liability structure of SifiBank broadly speaking comprises deposits and nondeposits. Just over half of the bank's liabilities are in deposits and these are evenly split between **retail** (branch-sourced) and **wholesale deposits**. Retail deposits are cheapest since federal deposit insurance backs up each account to a significant level which helps hold funding costs down at banks and thrifts. However, as banks grow, their ability to grow deposits from retail branches may not be able to keep pace with asset generation and so bank treasurers may seek out wholesale deposits that can be procured in open markets. **Brokered deposits** are one such type of wholesale deposit, which allows banks to buy deposits from intermediaries at higher costs than would be the case for retail deposits. Bank regulators for many years have looked at brokered deposits as a source for fueling aggressive risk-taking at some banks that ultimately led to their failure. While such funding sources do need to be carefully evaluated, they can be an important way to augment funding when gaps exist. SifiBank also uses a wide variety of debt instruments of various terms (**tenors**). As previously mentioned, the bank must manage the composition of both its assets and liabilities in order to reduce exposure to interest rate risk. The weighted average life, or better yet the duration of its assets and liabilities, must be in relative balance for the bank to avoid major declines in the bank's **market value of equity** (**MVE**). Since SifiBank has a large portion of its portfolio in mortgages and other longer-dated investments, it needs to extend the life of its liabilities in an effort to accomplish its **asset-liability management** (**ALM**) objectives.

Industry Structure and Competition

Since SifiBank operates in nearly every corner of the traditional banking sector, its competition comes from a variety of different entities. Banking in the United States has undergone significant consolidation for decades as economic forces have driven a large number of banks and thrifts into insolvency or merger precipitated either by economic downturns or weak performance at individual institutions. The nature of bank competition directly influences the risk exposure of SifiBank since its profitability and growth depend on how effectively it can compete in different businesses. To provide some perspective on the overall banking sector, at the end of 2013, there

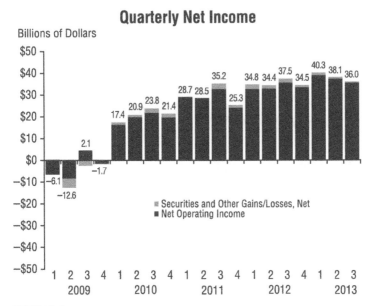

FIGURE 1.3 Bank Net Income over Time
Source: FDIC Quarterly Banking Profile, 2013.

were nearly 7,000 commercial banks and thrift institutions operating in the United States. The industry at that time had a combined asset base of $14.6 trillion. However, 106 firms had assets greater than $10 billion and this group accounted for about 80 percent of the industry's assets, illustrating a high level of concentration among the largest institutions. More astonishing, 36 banking institutions in the United States had assets at or above $50 billion and these firms accounted for 70 percent of all banking assets in the country.

The performance of the banking sector not surprisingly ebbs and flows with regional and general economic conditions as seen in Figure 1.3. The figure shows how in the period immediately following the financial crisis, net income for the sector was negative, driven to a great extent by mounting credit losses taking place around mortgages. With extraordinary measures taken by the Federal Reserve and Treasury Department to support banking, in time net incomes rose and the industry has stabilized since that time. Another way to look at the relative performance of the industry is to compare **net interest margin (NIM)** by bank asset size category (Figure 1.4). Net interest margin is defined as the difference between interest income and expense as a percent of average assets. NIM has steadily declined for banks

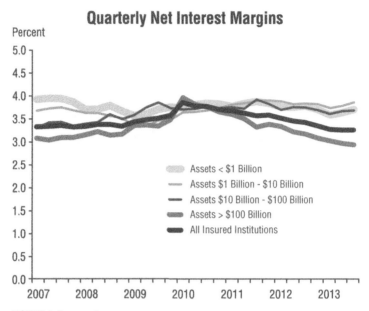

FIGURE 1.4 Bank Net Interest Margins Over Time
Source: FDIC Quarterly Banking Profile, 2013.

since 2010, reflecting lower income from mortgages as interest rates began rising over time and banks started to see erosion in its fixed income sales as interest rates began coming off very low levels after the crisis.

Figure 1.5 provides insight into the extent of damage done to the banking sector during the crisis as reflected in **nonperforming loans** (loans that are 90 days past due or worse). Banks write off (**charge-off**) bad loans as they become apparent and during the crisis, the noncurrent loan rate was five times that of 2006 levels and the charge-off rate was about six times 2006 levels. Since peaking at the end of 2009, credit performance has significantly improved.

SifiBank did not escape the financial crisis and in fact in the months following the failure of Lehman Brothers in September 2008 and both mortgage government sponsored enterprises Fannie Mae and Freddie Mac were placed into conservatorship under their regulator, SifiBank saw its stock price nearly evaporate from a price of $50 to just under $2 per share. Bank management realized that it was in trouble both in terms of liquidity and capital. It had not adequately developed its contingency liquidity plan; a framework for maintaining a level of liquidity that would allow the firm to operate under extreme conditions in which funding dried up and/or became

Noncurrent Loan Rate and Quarterly Net Charge-Off Rate

Percent

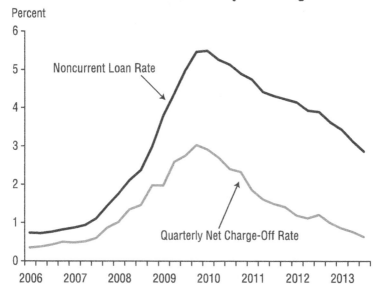

FIGURE 1.5   Bank Trends in Credit Performance
Source: FDIC Quarterly Banking Profile, 2013.

prohibitively expensive, for the crisis that unfolded proved to be devastating to capital markets. The bank suffered several downgrades in the months leading up to receiving this special financing. It had been rated by all three credit rating agencies as AA but by October 2008, it was rated C making it more difficult and costly to raise capital. In October of 2008, the U.S. Treasury offered a financial lifeline to SifiBank in the amount of $250 billion to ensure the company would be able to weather further erosion in financial markets.

SifiBank got into this situation through a combination of errors in the way the company was managed that led it to take oversized risks as well as by way of systemic risk to the entire financial system that created a contagion effect throughout the industry. The degree of interconnectedness of capital markets and financial institutions during the year leading up to the crisis led to a sort of financial flu that spread across the sector like a viral pandemic.

In the years leading up to the crisis, senior management ignored repeated warnings from its enterprise CRO regarding an excessive buildup of mortgage loans and securities in its HFI and AFS portfolios. The bank during that period had compounded their problems by originating a set of brand-new mortgage products that had variable payment terms and other features that while flexible for borrowers often meant that they would likely run into payment shock if and when interest rates rose in the future. There had been no prior experience with such products from which to develop an estimate of credit losses and yet the bank accelerated its production of these loans at the request of senior management.

The bank, as stated earlier, had been under pressure to grow earnings and these new nontraditional mortgages enabled SifiBank to originate mortgages at spreads to Treasuries that were significantly above mortgages originated and sold to Fannie Mae and Freddie Mac. The business line CRO for the bank whose bonus was dependent in part on the success of this program acquiesced to a significant amount of risk layering taking place in credit underwriting on these new loans to the point that significant credit risk was embedded in the products for which the bank was not being appropriately compensated. **Risk layering** occurs when individual risk attributes such as credit score and loan-to-value (LTV) ratio are combined in ways that materially raise the credit risk profile of the loan. For instance, allowing a lower credit score for a low downpayment mortgage raises the likelihood of default for the loan beyond a loan that has both higher FICO and lower LTV (i.e., is less risky). The bank had little historical information on which to base its loan loss reserve or price these new loans and so its models reflected the low level of risk that had been present for the last decade. As a consequence it vastly underestimated the amount of credit risk it was putting on its books.

During this same period, the bank continued to reduce its corporate risk management staff believing that they would be able to save costs by avoiding redundancies with the business risk functions. Moreover, when the products were presented to the board, the CFO and president of the consumer loan division of SifiBank were the corporate officers engaged with the board on this initiative with negligible input from the enterprise CRO. Compounding this problem was the fact that none of the board members had any mortgage or risk background and so little pushback from the board occurred on the potential risks of these products.

Simultaneous to the bank's origination of these loans, SifiInvestment Bank realized that it could expand its structured finance business by selling CDS that had mortgages as the reference asset. Senior management of the capital markets group convinced the board that these new products would be able to serve a wide range of investor appetites and transform credit risk transfer in the mortgage market by allowing CDS buyers to seek credit protection against mortgage defaults while allowing credit investors to participate in mortgage financing without actually originating or owning the loans on balance sheet. For SifiInvestment Bank it could both be involved in creating the CDS for market as well as take positions (i.e., sell CDSs) and create a stable income stream over time from the premiums paid by CDS buyers. With the bank projecting very low defaults looking into the future, it seemed like a sound business decision in 2004. By 2008 SifiInvestment Bank was reeling from losses that it incurred under its CDS program. As mortgage loans defaulted, the bank as seller of CDS protection was forced to cover losses of its counterparties. These losses, as well as those emanating from the bank's retained portfolio, were the primary source of capital erosion for the bank. Had the federal government not stepped in when it did, SifiBank was most likely going to fail within a short period of time.

As these losses were being publicized, creditors and other Wall Street counterparties began pulling back from SifiBank. Lines of credit for the bank were at first being renewed at higher rates but over time access for credit dried up. Spreads on ABCP issued by SifiBank widened to such a degree as to be prohibitive for the company in raising short-term financing. Banks no longer wanted to enter into repo agreements with SifiBank and more concerning, the bank began experiencing considerable withdrawal of deposits in the weeks preceding the announcement of financing from the government.[8]

In order to meet its production targets for its new mortgage program, SifiBank had streamlined a number of its processes and controls in underwriting, closing and servicing loans. Operational efficiencies in mortgage production can mean the difference between becoming a market leader or a follower. SifiBank management pressed hard to place itself as one of the top three mortgage originators in the country before the crisis and to do so meant finding ways to reduce the operational burdens of the loan manufacturing process.

Streamlining bank processes included allowing some loan production staff to bundle closing documents together and sign off with little review of what was being signed. Loan programs allowed many borrowers to avoid having to produce documents verifying their income and employment. Servicing staff was further reduced because, after all, mortgage defaults were expected to remain low. Automation was accelerated in both underwriting and collateral valuation where possible, thus reducing the number of underwriters and property appraisals in the process.

---

[8] A repurchase agreement, or repo, is a sale of securities (such as Treasury instruments) typically over a short window of time (e.g., overnight). The seller buys back the securities at the end of the contractual period and in this manner the seller is in a borrowing position. A reverse repo looks at the repo transaction from the perspective of the buyer of the securities and puts them in an effective lending position.

To no one's surprise, fraud, both internal and external was rampant in these programs and surfaced once loan defaults began rising during the crisis. Counterparties and investors in securities created by SifiBank sued the company for billions of dollars of repurchases based on claims that the loans violated the terms of the contract relating to fraud and misrepresentation. Loan documents went missing during this period and once the deluge of defaults hit the bank, it did not have sufficient servicing resources to handle the caseload. Many borrowers were erroneously foreclosed on as a result, which caught the attention of the media, regulators and litigators. SifiBank faced billions of dollars of legal damages and settlements as state attorneys general and the U.S. Justice Department lodged suits against the bank.

The government's decision to intervene and prop SifiBank up at the beginning of the financial crisis was very difficult. On the one hand, the government realized that there was a reasonable likelihood that not intervening could lead to SifiBank's insolvency. If the third-largest U.S. bank were to fail, it would send shock waves through an already weak financial sector potentially resulting in a cascade of bank failures and precipitating an economic depression. But in saving SifiBank, the government risked not only the ire of the U.S. taxpayer but also created a perverse incentive that if a bank was perceived as too-big-to-fail, it could continue to engage in risky behavior knowing that eventually the company would be bailed out.

The government financing for Sifibank came with several strings attached. The government insisted that the CEO and chairman must be replaced as well as several key members of the executive team and board of directors. The bank was also forced into an agreement in which the U.S. Treasury would receive a large number of warrants, effectively allowing the government to exercise options to buy its stock in SifiBank at a favorable price that it held as part of the agreement. The government would also have greater involvement over key decisions for a period of time until the bank was able to repay its obligation to the government. These events ushered in an unprecedented amount of scrutiny for SifiBank and while the morale of company employees took a massive hit, over time it allowed the bank to remake its tarnished image to the public, investors and employees by reinvigorating the principles that had led the company to greatness in its early years.

Within several months of the ouster of the CEO and chairman, the board hired a new CEO, who had formerly been the enterprise CRO of a major competitor and had 20-plus years of banking experience running commercial bank businesses. With this background SifiBank was well on its way to becoming an industry leader in risk management. On the day the new CEO took office he called for the separation of the combined position of CEO and chairman in order to reduce potential conflicts of interest. He further went on to describe his vision for the bank, which was to be built upon a foundation of strong risk management that would allow the bank to operate prudently in all economic environments while positioning itself to grow its businesses profitably and creating significant value for shareholders, customers and employees. SifiBank was to become a risk-centric organization and one that would be admired by its peers and customers over time. But even with that vision, the bank faced regulatory headwinds that posed a number of challenges for the new management team.

BANK REGULATORY LANDSCAPE

Unlike many other industries, the banking sector is heavily regulated by a patchwork of federal and state regulatory authorities. The larger the institution, the greater the regulatory scrutiny that occurs, and this has only heightened since the financial crisis. As a national bank, SifiBank's primary regulator for safety and soundness of its operation is the OCC. In this capacity, the OCC maintains regular contact with the bank, in fact deploying 75 examiners headed by an examiner-in-charge (EIC). This team actually works onsite at SifiBank and has regular access to management, reports and other information, allowing the examination team to stay abreast of ongoing developments at the bank.

The OCC has a responsibility to ensure the bank operates in a safe and sound fashion and to carry out these responsibilities the OCC conducts periodic standard and as needed targeted examinations. SifiBank receives a 1–5 (best to worst performance) rating each year by the OCC referred to as a **CAMELS** rating, which comprises an assessment of the bank's capital adequacy (C), asset quality (A), management quality (M), earnings (E), liquidity (L), and sensitivity to market risk (S). The OCC has an array of punitive actions that it can take to ensure the bank complies with regulatory standards and policies. The examination process is critically important to SifiBank as the OCC's findings on a particular exam could lead to severe monetary penalties as well as cease and desist orders that could limit the bank's ability to operate in certain ways. The OCC appears at SifiBank's board meetings and provides a summary of their findings and any management required actions (MRAs) they demand from the management team following a major exam.

Since SifiBank has a bank holding company structure it is also overseen from that standpoint by the Federal Reserve Board (FRB). As a BHC, SifiBank is subject to a variety of regulations imposed by the FRB, which will also conduct periodic examinations. After the crisis, one of the more significant requirements imposed on SifiBank was compliance with regular stress tests on its capital, a program known as the Comprehensive Capital Analysis and Review (CCAR). The process requires Sifibank to provide detailed data and analysis on its various positions under a set of FRB established stress scenarios. The FRB conducts this on bank holding companies with assets of $50 billion and greater, although it has added an additional 12 financial institutions to this list of 18 BHCs. This is just one of many regulations imposed by the FRB on SifiBank. In addition, SifiBank enjoys access to the Fed discount window, which provides backup low-cost, short-term funding to the bank.

Another important regulator for SifiBank is the Federal Deposit Insurance Corporation (FDIC) that is charged with overseeing the federally insured deposit insurance fund and resolving institutional failures in addition to its examination of state chartered banking institutions. The FDIC sets deposit insurance premiums for the banking system based on a variety of factors including bank ratings and size, among others. As a result, deposit premiums have a risk-based component to incent the right behavior from institutions. Since the financial crisis the FDIC has an increasing oversight of banks due to changes in legislation known as the **Dodd-Frank Wall Street Reform and Consumer Protection Act (DFA).**

Following the financial crisis, Congress and the Administration came together to pass the most comprehensive legislation to affect the banking industry since the Great Depression: the DFA. The Act touches virtually every aspect of banking and even sets out guidance for regulating nonbank SIFIs. Among key provisions of the Act are regulations regarding derivatives trading such as **over-the-counter** (OTC) transactions, which includes CDS; securities that experienced significant losses during the crisis; a ban on proprietary trading by banks also known as the Volcker Rule; creation of a new Consumer Financial Protection Bureau (CFPB) and associated regulations on the mortgage industry; establishment of the Financial Stability Oversight Council (FSOC) and its analytics agency, the Office of Financial Research (OFR) charged with overseeing the buildup of systemic risk across the entire financial sector; and establishes an orderly liquidation facility for banks, requiring them to create their own "living wills" for how they would liquidate their operations under an insolvency, among other reasons.

The DFA also put the largest financial institutions—that is, those most likely to be too-big-to-fail—under a new set of regulations known as SIFI designation criteria that expose those firms to heightened supervision and other more stringent reporting and capital requirements.

The CFPB has been quick in setting up many new consumer-friendly regulations such as defining what a quality mortgage is, and regulations on fees and interest rates charged to bank and other financial institution customers. In addition to these mandates, the Federal Reserve established a new set of rules on limits on interchange fees that banks could charge for debit transactions. The CFPB in conjunction with the U.S. Justice Department and

Housing and Urban Development (HUD) have elevated their focus on fair lending practices. This increased scrutiny has required banks to redouble their efforts on making sure their lending practices are compliant with various regulations regarding fair lending.

SifiBank is also subject to a set of capital, stress testing, and liquidity requirements (referred to as **Basel III** standards) established by the Basel Committee on Banking Supervision (BCSB) and implemented by the Federal Reserve Board. Large, complex banking institutions such as Sifibank are subject to a number of capital requirements, some of which are risk-based and require considerable data management and analytics to be performed by such banks. Banks that do not meet certain thresholds for well capitalized institutions as determined by the regulatory authorities may be subject to certain limitations on their activities and/or face other regulatory actions such as establishment of capital plans for a bank to raise capital to designated target levels.

Bank regulation requires a substantial commitment of resources and staff by SifiBank. Within the Corporate Division, a unit known as Regulatory Affairs operating under the Legal Department is charged with staying abreast of the various regulations, examination schedules, and other regulatory developments and works with the business units and risk management functions to coordinate responses and analysis to regulatory inquiries and activities. Clearly, SifiBank faces substantial regulatory risk from noncompliance with various local, state and federal regulations. This risk poses yet another important consideration in SifiBank's strategic planning and risk assessment exercises each year. Some banks have taken adversarial positions with bank regulatory agencies that they believe provides an effective check against unnecessary intrusion into bank activities. At times, however, this strategy may backfire against the bank in the event that it needs the regulator to support a particular initiative or temper a regulatory response to an uncovered deficiency. The best course of action is to cultivate a respectful relationship with the regulators that is based on credibility, trust and sound expertise.

SUMMARY

SifiBank's fortunes have ebbed and flowed over time with different management, regulatory, market and economic conditions. The financial crisis of 2008 exposed deficiencies in risk management governance and infrastructure that nearly led to its demise. The company enjoys a second chance at remaking itself into a world class institution known for its risk management expertise by virtue of a government bailout. The bank still faces a dizzying array of financial and regulatory challenges in the post-crisis environment.

Most notably, the regulatory environment is taking a heavy toll on the bank's ability to increase operating revenues while managing expenses. Fees associated with various bank services and products such as debit cards and consumer loans have dampened important income sources for SifiBank. This has incented the bank to look for other products that boost profitability without running afoul of regulatory requirements. Mortgages that lie just outside the CFPB Qualified Mortgage criteria could provide the bank with better spreads than conventional mortgages while exposing the firm to minimal legal risk in the future. However, a product development and design framework that vets the collection of bank risks against each other in a way that meets the bank's objectives would offer the most effective protection. This is where strong risk management practices can make the difference between a sustainable business model and one that experiences a major risk event that puts the entire firm at jeopardy.

Financial risk management is not an exact science despite a revolution over the past two decades to leverage quantitative approaches in measuring and managing risks. A key to successful risk management is knowing the right combination of qualitative controls and quantitative tools to use. The remainder of this book introduces the reader to a complement of key risks faced by SifiBank. While individual risks are examined within specific operating units of SifiBank, it should be understood that these risks span most divisions with variations in exposures based upon the nature of the transactions, and services in place, among other considerations. Further, while most chapters that follow focus on a particular type of risk, as discussed earlier, SifiBank's risk managers must think about risk holistically. Even within an operating unit such as the mortgage group, business risk managers must evaluate tradeoffs between the credit exposure of putting a mortgage on the balance sheet and the interest rate risk exposure and operational risk it creates. Moreover, potential reputation, regulatory and legal risks must be factored in before implementing a product strategy. Some of these risks do not lend themselves to quantification but still expose the firm to lost business, regulatory actions and penalties, and large legal tabs if not carefully accounted for in product development.

QUESTIONS

1. What is a SIFI and how does that relate to the concept of too-big-to-fail?
2. Describe the four elements of the risk management feedback loop.
3. What differentiates banks from nonfinancial corporations?
4. Describe SifiBank's profit-maximizing function.

5. Describe a conceptual model that relates risk-taking to asset generation and firm growth.
6. In a potential merger with another institution, what should SifiBank take into consideration that would mitigate potential risk later?
7. What factors led to the near death of SifiBank after the financial crisis of 2008–2009?
8. What is the Volcker Rule and what impact does it have on banking and financial risk management?
9. What are a few key measures that banks use to monitor their performance?
10. What is systemic risk and how does it affect bank risk?
11. What is risk layering?
12. What is CAMELS?
13. What are some of the key provisions of DFA?

CHAPTER 2

Overview of Financial Risk Management

RISK MANAGEMENT DEFINED

Risk management describes a collection of activities to **identify, measure,** and ultimately **manage** a set of risks. People and organizations confront risks every day: For example, an individual decides to leave a relatively secure job for another with better opportunity and compensation across country, a government faces the threat of terrorist attacks on public transportation, or a bank determines which financial products it should offer to customers. While some risks are fairly mundane and others a matter of life or death at times, the fundamental process for assessing risk entails evaluation of trade-offs of outcomes depending on the course of action taken. The complexity of the risk assessment is a function of the potential impact from a particular set of outcomes; the individual deciding to take a different job is likely to engage in a simpler risk assessment, perhaps drawing up a pros and cons template, while a government facing terrorist threats might establish a rigorous set of quantitative and surveillance tools to gather intelligence and assign likelihoods and possible effects to a range of outcomes.

Regardless of the application or circumstance, each of the assessments above has a common thread, namely, the assessment of risk. But what exactly is risk and is it the same across all of these situations? Risk is fundamentally about quantifying the unknown. Uncertainty by its very nature tends to complicate our thinking about risk because we cannot touch or see it although it is all around us. As human beings have advanced in their application of technology and science to problem solving, a natural evolution to assessing risk using such capabilities has taken place over time. Quantifying uncertainty has taken the discipline of institutional risk management to a new level over the past few decades with the acceleration in computing hardware and software and analytical techniques.

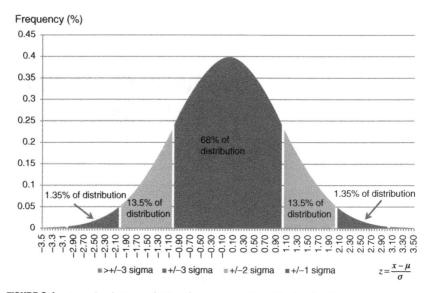

FIGURE 2.1 Standard Normal Distribution and Area Under the Curve

Risk and statistics share common ground as uncertainty may be expressed using standard statistical concepts such as probability. As will be seen later, while statistics provide an intuitive and elegant way to define risk, it nonetheless offers an incomplete way to fully understand risk due to inherent limitations on standard statistical theory and applications that do not always represent actual market behaviors. This does not imply that we should abandon statistical applications for assessing risk, but that a healthy dose of skepticism over accepting a purely analytical assessment of risk is a prerequisite to good risk management. As a starting point, basic statistical theory presents a convenient way of thinking about risk. Figure 2.1 depicts a standard normal probability distribution for some random variable x. The shape of the distribution is defined by two parameters, its mean or central tendency centered on 0 and the standard deviation, σ. If risk can be distilled to a single estimate, standard deviation is perhaps the most generalized depiction of risk, as it measures the degree to which outcomes stray from the expected outcome or mean level. More formally, standard deviation is expressed as shown in Equation 2.1.

$$\sqrt{\sigma_i^2} = \sqrt{\sum_{j=1}^{M} p_j (x_j - \mu)^2} \qquad\qquad 2.1$$

TABLE 2.1 Example Calculation of Standard Deviation of Firm Annual Returns

	x	p		
Year	Return (%)	Probability (%)	$(x-\mu)^2$	$p(x-\mu)^2$
1	25	5.00	188.30	9.41
2	20	10.00	76.08	7.61
3	15	35.00	13.85	4.85
4	14	20.00	7.41	1.48
5	12.5	10.00	1.49	0.15
6	10	8.00	1.63	0.13
7	7	5.00	18.30	0.91
8	0	4.00	127.19	5.09
9	-2	3.00	176.30	5.29
μ	11.3			34.93 Variance
	Total	100.00		5.91 Standard Deviation

where p_i represents the probability of outcome i, and μ is the mean of the variable x. The variable x could reflect the returns from a product or service for a company, the compensation to an employee for a particular job, or the amount of collateral damage from a terrorist attack, for example. Despite the difference in the variable of interest, the one common aspect for all of these risks is that they can be measured by the standard deviation. Further, risks can be managed based on the tolerance for risky outcomes as may be represented by the distance of a specific set of outcomes from their expected level.

To further reinforce the concept of standard deviation as a measure of risk, consider the returns for the firm shown in Table 2.1. There are nine different annual return outcomes representing x in Equation 2.1. The average of these scenarios is 11.3 percent. The deviations of each outcome from that mean $(m\ \mu)$ are shown as $(x-\mu)^2$ and that result is multiplied by each outcome's probability. The sum of these probability-weighted squared deviations represents the variance of the firm's annual returns. Taking the square root of the variance yields the standard deviation of 5.91 percent. That would mean that 68 percent of the firm's potential return outcomes should lie between $(11.3-5.91)$ and $(11.3+5.91)$ or 5.39 and 17.21 percent, respectively.

Take the case of a company that faces whether to engage in a certain business activity or not. The firm obtains a set of historical data from the last several years of returns on similar products provided by other competitors. Suppose now the mean return for the product is 15 percent with a standard deviation of 5 percent. Using the information from the standard normal distribution in Figure 2.1, the company can begin to shape its view of risk. First, the distribution of returns takes on a similar symmetric shape as the standard normal curve shown in Figure 2.1. Under such a distribution, outcomes that deviate significantly from the average come in two forms: some that create very large positive returns above the 15 percent shown on the right-hand side of the distribution, and some that create corresponding returns smaller than 15 percent. The company realizes that returns less than 15 percent (its cost of capital) would drain resources and capital away from the firm, thus destroying shareholder value. In this context, only returns below 15 percent create risk to the company. The company now focuses on the left-hand tail, paying particular attention to how bad returns could be. The distribution's y-axis (vertical) displays the frequency, or percentage of time, that a particular return outcome would be observed. According to the standard normal distribution, approximately 68 percent of the time returns would be between plus and minus 1 standard deviation from the mean. In this case we should find returns between 10 and 20 percent occur about 68 percent of the time. But moving out two or three standard deviations in either direction would capture 95 and 99.7 percent of the occurrences, respectively. However, with the focus only on low-return events, the company only needs to understand the frequency of these occurrences in assessing its project risk. In this example, outcomes that generate returns between 10 and 15 percent occur about 34 percent of the time. If the company were to look at adverse outcomes that are −2 standard deviations away from the mean, then returns between 5 and 15 percent would occur about 47.5 percent of the time. At this point, the company would need to think about what would happen if they were to observe a return of 10 percent versus 5 percent. If, for instance, the company had information to suggest that if returns reached 5 percent it would have to shut down, this would pose an unacceptable level of risk for the firm that it would want to guard against. As a result, it might establish a threshold that it will engage in products where there is a 97.5 percent chance that returns would not fall below 5 percent. Notice that since half of the outcomes fall above a 15 percent return and that 47.5 percent of the outcomes fall between 5 and 15 percent (one half of the 95 percent frequency assuming +/−2 standard deviations from the mean), then the portion of the area under the distribution accounting for returns worse than 5 percent would be 2.5 percent.

Such use of statistics provides risk managers with easy-to-apply metrics of how much risk may exist and how much risk should be tolerated based on other considerations such as the likelihood of insolvency. But blind use of statistics can at times jeopardize the company should actual results begin to vary significantly from historical performance. In such cases formal measures of risk as based on statistical models must be validated regularly and augmented when needed by experience and seasoned judgment. Such considerations bring to mind the need to characterize risk management in situational terms for the existence of uncertainty in any risk management problem implies that circumstances specific to each problem can and will affect outcomes that might not be precisely measured using rigorous analytical methodologies based on historical information.

Situational Risk Management

As the phrase implies, **situational risk management** is a way of assessing risk that takes into account the specific set of circumstances in place at the time of the assessment. It could include the market and economic conditions prevailing at the time, the set of clients or customers of a set of products posing risk, their behavior, business processes, accounting practices, and regulatory and political conditions, among other factors to take into consideration. And complicating the problem a bit more is the need to take these factors into account in projecting potential future outcomes. All of this may seem daunting to the risk manager who is facing how to assess risk based on the unique situation of the particular problem.

If we could teleport back to 2004 into a major mortgage originator's risk management department, it might provide some insights into the nature of situational risk management. Consider the heads of risk management of two large mortgage originators facing whether to expand their mortgage production activities. Both firms face extraordinary pressures on their businesses due to commoditization of prime mortgages that are typically sold to the government-sponsored enterprises Fannie Mae and Freddie Mac. As a result, prices for these loans have squeezed profit margins to a point that other sources of revenue are required for the long-term sustainability of the franchise. As a result, one of the companies, X Bank (a mortgage-specializing thrift) decides that it needs to compete with other major players in loans that feature riskier combinations than they have traditionally originated. X Bank has over time acquired other smaller thrifts and banks focused on mortgage lending and this has led to a number of deficiencies and gaps in the way mortgage loans are underwritten. Fortunately, the economic environment has been extremely favorable, with low interest rates and high home price appreciation contributing to low default rates. These conditions thus have masked any problems that might cause X Bank higher losses for the time being. The other bank, Z Bank faces the same conditions; however, it is more diversified as a commercial bank and in growing organically over time has put in place strong processes and controls for all facets of the underwriting and servicing segments of the mortgage business. Further distinguishing the two firms is their differing reliance on analytic methods and data. X Bank has employed for several years relatively sophisticated data mining and simulation-based techniques to assess risk. Meanwhile Z Bank has just begun to develop risk data warehouses and building modeling capabilities to assess mortgage credit risk. It normally used simple measures of default risk that do not take into consideration possible changes in market conditions that could affect future credit risk outcomes. In its place, Z Bank has come to rely on the expertise of former underwriters put into their Quality Control department. Their job principally has been to perform postorigination reviews of originated mortgages and determine whether there have been any defects in the underwriting process that could pose risk to the firm.

In deciding whether to take on additional credit risk, X Bank relies on what it believes to be its comparative advantage: risk analytics. With losses on riskier segments of their business extraordinarily low, X Bank is satisfied that its estimates of credit risk are stable and reflect the underlying conditions in the market. Given this view, X Bank elects not to build up much of a quality control unit or to integrate their findings into credit-risk discussions. Z Bank, on the other hand, recognizes its limitations in its analytic capabilities and that even if it had such an infrastructure, it would be of limited value since the current environment is completely unlike any seen in recent memory. Consequently, they believe that using analytics exclusively to assess the amount of credit risk in their portfolio would need to be augmented by other factors including input from seasoned underwriters who have experience originating riskier mortgages.

The decision framework that both firms use to determine the amount of product risk each is willing to take on is dependent upon the common and unique set of circumstances (the situation) each bank confronts. X Bank believes it has better information and analytics by which to expand its business and be more competitive against other firms like Z Bank. At the same time, the QC department of Z Bank has concluded that the risks involved in expanding the product underwriting criteria are not sufficiently well understood to warrant taking on what appears to be higher risk. Z Bank management concurs with this conclusion despite the toll on market share this decision will cause, based on an understanding of the limitations of their data and analytics to accurately assess the amount of credit risk that could potentially accumulate should market conditions appreciably change.

By late 2007, the results from X and Z Banks' decisions are clear. In the years following the original decision, the economy stalled, leading to one of the worst housing markets since the Great Depression. With home prices depreciating at double-digit rates and unemployment rising to 10 percent, credit losses on the riskier mortgages grew to levels that were multiples above what X Bank had estimated them to be in 2004. With their loan-loss reserves well understated for this risk and their capital levels weakening,

X Bank experiences a run on its deposits that eventually leads to the closure of the bank by its regulator. In the years leading up to this event, X Bank had become the dominant mortgage originator, but did so at the expense of good risk management practices. Meanwhile, Z Bank largely avoided the mortgage credit meltdown by staying the course with its existing product set. That strategy wound up costing the firm several points of market share, but in the aftermath of the crisis the bank managed to pick up a major mortgage originator and through that combination regained a top-three position in the market while effectively managing its risk exposure.

A lesson from this example is that risk management decisions are highly dependent on the unique situation of the firm and it is essential that risk managers have their pulse on the factors that drive risk-taking. Dissecting the hypothetical case, X Bank risk managers relied too heavily on analytics at the expense of seasoned judgment, which in a period of unusually good credit performance should have signaled a greater emphasis on understanding the processes and controls underlying the underwriting activity. The situation in this case for X bank featured an accommodating economic environment, strong analytic capabilities based on historical information, aggressive management orientation toward market share at the expense of prudent risk-taking, and a limited appreciation for underwriting experience. Z Bank, facing the same economic conditions, came to a different conclusion and set of outcomes as a result. But in several important respects its situation was much different. It recognized its limitations in data and analytics and acknowledged its prowess in understanding the underwriting process and controls required to originate mortgages that could withstand different market conditions. Futhermore it had a management team that embraced its risk manager's recommendations—not an insignificant factor that led to Z Bank's making the right risk decision in the end.

Situational risk management thus is a case-by-case assessment of the factors influencing risk decisions. Figure 2.2 provides a framework for conceptualizing situational risk management. The primary activities of the risk manager of identifying, measuring, and managing the various risks of the company are influenced heavily by a number of internal and external factors at any moment. Clearly market, industry, and political forces establish an economic and regulatory environment that serve as a backdrop to risk management activities. The period leading up to the financial crisis of 2008–2009 was characterized by robust economic growth, relatively relaxed regulatory oversight, and fierce competition among financial institutions. This environment influenced corporate attitudes and perspectives on risk-taking and risk management. With markets and assets performing relatively well during the period, risk outcomes in the form of credit losses and other measures of risk performance were unusually low. Coupled with

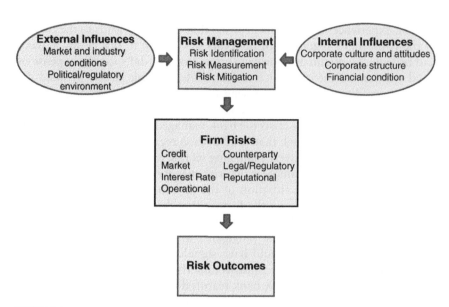

FIGURE 2.2   Situational Risk Management Framework

strong competitive conditions, risk management took on a secondary role to growth and financial performance prime directives. In such an environment, the risk manager faces significant headwinds in outlining a case for maintaining risk discipline when historical measures of risk are low and competition is high. Consider a risk manager's situation in 2005 in establishing a view of mortgage credit risk for X Bank. As shown in Figure 2.3, home prices in the years leading up to 2005 had shown remarkable appreciation at the national level with most markets performing well above the long-term average. Armed with a formidable array of quantitative analytics to estimate expected and unexpected credit losses on the bank's portfolio, the data would suggest that such a strong housing market would lead to low credit losses for the portfolio. Management during such periods can be biased against activities that will raise costs or impede business objectives, as reviewed in more detail in Chapter 3. While a strong risk culture and governance process can significantly mitigate management tendencies to marginalize risk departments, the risk management team must remain vigilant in the performance of its core activities and in regular and objective assessment of future performance. During such times, pressures to accede to business objectives rise, placing countervailing motivations on the risk manager that can influence his interpretation of risk-taking and prospective risk outcomes. Once the crisis began, as unprecedented risks emerged and many financial institutions failed, external conditions promoted a very different climate for risk management, where regulatory oversight of the financial industry stiffened and banks retrenched in an effort to stave off financial collapse as their capital deteriorated under the mounting pressures of large credit losses. In such an environment, greater focus on risk management, in part out of regulatory and financial necessity, becomes of paramount importance. Such vastly different internal and external conditions may introduce a set of tendencies for management, regulators, and risk managers to overreact. In such circumstances, underwriting standards may tighten to abnormal levels, resulting in a procyclical response that exacerbates the market downturn. Risk managers can seize this moment to strengthen not only the firm's risk infrastructure but to shore up any deficiencies in governance and culture that may have been lacking previously.

ELEMENTS OF RISK MANAGEMENT

At its core, risk management is a dynamic and proactive set of processes. To support ongoing risk assessment, the risk management function can be partitioned into three major areas: risk identification, risk measurement, and risk management or mitigation. A complete risk management function must have all three activities in place for it to be possible to actively manage the institution's risks. Since risks and the situation and conditions in which the firm operates are not static, risk managers must constantly be examining emerging trends in the business, economic, and regulatory climate with an eye toward how that might translate into changes in risk exposure for the firm. And as will be seen in later chapters, measurement of risks can and will change as underlying performance adjusts to important risk drivers. Thus, risk management requires ongoing updates and validation of models and assumptions used for estimating the likelihood and amount of risk exposure for the firm. Finally, the actions taken to mitigate risk also depend upon the level of risk relative to established risk tolerances. In a downturn, for instance, when risks may exceed desired risk targets, it will be difficult to engage in meaningful risk transfer strategies such as reinsurance or even asset sales, as market pricing may not be attractive or there may be a lack of interest from capable counterparties to provide insurance or purchase assets. Engaging in risk management activities needs to be well thought out during the product development phase in order to execute agreed-upon actions and to factor in the costs of protecting a segment of the new business against emerging risks outside stated tolerances.

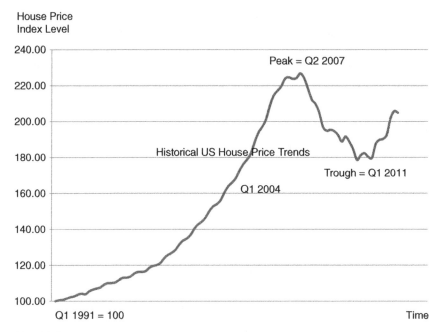

FIGURE 2.3   Historical U.S. House Price Trends
Source: Federal Housing Finance Agency Data, 1991–2013, National House Price Index.

RISK IDENTIFICATION AND TYPOLOGY

Financial institutions confront a myriad of risks, each with their own unique qualities in terms of how they are measured, their effect on firm profitability and capital, and opportunities to mitigate such exposures. The type of risk exposures vary greatly from firm to firm, with the size of the institution, its business complexity, and scope—all key factors in dictating what types of risks the financial firm faces. The exposure to a particular risk type can and will change over time and in this respect, risk identification and measurement is a dynamic process. For instance, during the housing boom preceding the financial crisis of 2008–2009, few firms knew what operational risks lay ahead as issues with mortgage fraud, misrepresentation, and related issues led to huge legal exposures. Establishing a regular assessment of under what conditions risks could escalate not simply within a risk type but in composition across risks is an essential part of the risk management process. Thus it is critical to establish a risk typology to facilitate a discussion of how risk managers must identify the risks to the firm.

Depending on how the firm is structured, the vast majority of risks faced lie within the following risk types:

- Credit
- Market
- Counterparty
- Interest rate
- Operational
- Liquidity
- Insolvency/capital
- Reputational
- Legal/regulatory

Credit risk refers to the exposure associated with losses sustained on assets such as loans and commitments from borrower default on a contractual obligation such as a loan contract or promissory note. The borrower can be an individual as in the case of a consumer mortgage or credit card, a corporation or small business, or even a sovereign nation. The level and variability of credit risk differs with the type of asset and borrower. For example, a portfolio composed of commercial real estate assets tends to be made up of different types of properties with unique characteristics, making credit risk events lumpier than consumer credit exposures such as credit cards, which are more homogeneous in quality and where each credit is relatively small. The methods to measure credit risks will thus differ, however, a common definition of credit risk across asset types is required for aggregating total credit exposure at the firm level.

Market risk captures the losses associated with declines in the trading book of a banking institution. Typically, market risk is of consequence for large institutions that engage in trading of some sort such as equities, fixed income, foreign exchange, and derivatives transactions. For these firms, swings in the valuation of these positions pose risk that can rapidly deplete capital under significant and unusual market conditions. Market risk like credit risk varies by asset type and yet it is essential that the market risk of each asset class be put on a common measurement basis for communicating aggregate market risk exposures.

Interest rate risk affects all financial intermediaries based on the potential mismatch in maturity or duration between assets and liabilities. *Duration* is a common yardstick used in measuring interest rate risk. It may be represented as the time-weighted receipt of cash flows of an asset or liability or as an *interest elasticity* reflecting the sensitivity of an asset or liability's value to small changes in yield. Interest rate risk can affect both the income of the firm as well as its capital position. This is reflected by reinvestment risk, or the exposure a firm has when it has to reinvest cash flows at a different rate than expected due to faster or slower repayment. Reinvestment risk can thus widen or narrow the spread on the difference between interest income and expense (referred to as net interest margin). It can also deplete capital as the market value of equity of the firm is affected by changes in the underlying market values of the firm's assets and liabilities due to changes in interest rates.

Counterparty risk encompasses firm exposures to other companies with which the firm has entered into a particular transaction to buy or sell an asset. This typically arises in situations in which there tends to be a contingent exposure, such as the delivery of an agreed-upon asset at a specific time. A forward contract entailing the purchase of an asset at a future time period for a prearranged price exposes the purchaser of the forward contract to counterparty risk if the other side of the transaction is not able to meet its obligation. During the financial crisis of 2008–2009, counterparty risk exposure was significant for many of the largest financial institutions that had entered into an extensive set of transactions with payoffs contingent on counterparty performance of the obligation. This was particularly acute in the case of companies with large exposures to **credit default swaps (CDS)**, a form of derivative instrument having insurance-like features where a counterparty (seller of the CDS) stood ready to cover defaults associated with underlying collateral in the CDS for a premium.

Operational risk reflects the exposure a firm has to deficiencies predominately associated with people, processes, and technology and remains one of the most difficult areas of bank risk management to assess, given the wide range of issues encompassing this risk type. The nature of these types of exposures are difficult to predict because they tend to be low-frequency events, but once they occur can result in large losses to the firm. Reliable measurement of such risks is thus problematic despite significant strides to enhance analytics in this area. The diffuse nature of what constitutes operational risk across the organization and measurement difficulties thus imposes challenges for the firm and risk managers to maintain vigilance on this as an ongoing exposure that can creep up over time if not well managed and understood by the business.

Another risk type that had a significant role in the financial crisis of 2008–2009 is **liquidity risk**. For a financial institution, liquidity is the lifeblood of the company. With access to borrowing and capital markets at reasonable prices, a bank can find itself quickly in a predicament where it lacks the ability to finance its activities. Such an outcome can lead to a crisis of confidence in the institution, particularly depositories that could be subject to widespread panic as reflected by depositor runs. In 2008, news of continued troubles with mortgages at two of the largest thrift institutions,

IndyMac Bank and Washington Mutual (**WaMu**), led to significant depositor runs that ultimately resulted in both institutions being taken over by the FDIC. Understanding the sources of bank liquidity and their volatility under adverse market and firm conditions is essential.

Bank capital and the risk of insolvency play an important role in risk measurement. Historically, banks are relatively highly leveraged entities, with leverage defined as the ratio of assets to the amount of bank equity. For example, a bank with a 4 percent level of capital to assets would be considered to be levered 25 to 1. A firm holding only 2 percent capital would be twice as levered. Higher leverage can magnify profitability, thus making the firm attractive to investors. However, capital provides a cushion for the bank in the event of an unexpected outcome that could otherwise lead to insolvency. Bank regulatory capital for depository institutions has strengthened over the past several decades in response to various financial crises and enhancements to capital measurement. Evolving over time have been efforts to understand the implications of bank risk-taking from an economic capital perspective. The term *economic capital*, or risk capital, describes the amount of equity required by the bank to sustain unexpected levels of risk exposure to the firm as based on internal assessments of risk rather than regulatory imposed views. A related concept that leverages estimates of economic capital is risk-adjusted performance measurement that can be used to identify profitable opportunities adjusting for risk.

An important risk for financial institutions that had been underestimated by many firms leading up to the recent financial crisis is **model risk**. Model risk emanates from errors generated by analytical tools used to measure and quantify the likelihood and level of risk taken by the bank. Banks may make strategic decisions to deploy capital to certain products or business segments based on model estimates of expected performance, which can be misleading if found to be inaccurate representations of underlying risks. Regulatory agencies such as the Federal Reserve and OCC have provided guidance to depository institutions regarding how models should be validated, however, practices at these firms to understand the risks such tools present vary in their effectiveness. Robust model validation efforts center on understanding the data supporting the analysis, the assumptions entering the model, and the specification or functional form taken to represent a certain type of risk. During the crisis, major assumptions that correlations between assets and geographies would remain static changed abruptly and in ways that the models did not anticipate, given an overreliance on data from abnormally favorable conditions. The end result was significant underestimation of credit losses on mortgage-related exposures.

Other risks that can result from abnormal exposures to the risks mentioned include **reputational, legal,** and **regulatory risks**. Reputational risk stems from adverse publicity surrounding a firm that tarnishes the firm's name and can lead to outflows of deposits, a drop in loan demand, or other negative business outcomes. Excessive risk-taking can become a vicious cycle in which reputational risk results in further pressures on the firm that can amplify other risks. A firm experiencing deposit outflows due to a liquidity crisis may face a deeper crisis as the firm's reputation declines and media attention grows, leading to deposit outflows. In turn, reputational risk and legal and regulatory risks can intersect at various times and be precipitated by another type of risk. An example of this could be a bank that experiences operational risk in the form of a breach in the security of customer private information. Once publicized, media effects can result in an immediate negative effect on the bank's reputation, expose it to customer class action lawsuits, and potentially trigger a regulatory investigation that can lead to various sanctions against the firm. Identifying these sources of risk upfront in discussions regarding product and business development opportunities is an essential ingredient to comprehensive risk management.

By now it should be evident that identification of individual risks presents an incomplete picture of a firm's potential risk exposure. Risks of different types may interact and affect one another in ways that cannot be understood by focusing on an individual risk. Fundamental differences in the drivers of risk types and their measurements further complicate efforts to calculate the interactive effects of various risks. The tendency to manage risks in specific areas such as credit, operational, and market, may not be able to accurately capture other risks that develop from those specific risks. Unfortunately this occurs regardless of the reality that risk intersections are a natural and expected part of the risk management process. Issues to better integrate risk types are addressed in efforts to establish enterprise-wide risk management capabilities, although a more analytically rigorous approach to risk aggregation requires going beyond a simple assessment and aggregation of each risk type by taking into account correlations between risk types.

Another complexity in risk identification is the changing nature of the composition of risk exposure by the firm to individual risk components. For example, a firm may estimate that under a current set of conditions that interest rate risk comprises a third of its total risk exposure as measured by economic capital consumed to that risk, but in a future state it could be eclipsed by credit or operational risk. Stress tests and scenario analysis performed on each risk type can help facilitate discussions of important shifts in risk composition over time, but establishing clear linkages for how specific risks could change is an important part of the identification process.

RISK MEASUREMENT

The second critical activity in risk management surrounds measurement of risk exposures. At the core of this activity is establishing the data needed to build analytic estimates of risk exposures. Quantitative-based models are standard tools in the risk manager's arsenal for estimating expected and unexpected losses, but as experienced in the financial crisis of 2008–2009, models must be augmented with sound judgment and experience. Models are simply tools that provide a useful benchmark for assessing the level of risk exposure within a certain level of confidence. Understanding and appreciating that models themselves pose risks suggests that a delicate balance must be maintained between quantitative and qualitative measures of risk.

In order to measure exposures, risk databases or warehouses must be constructed, leveraging historical information at the transaction, loan, or activity level with details regarding the borrower and available over a window of time representative of the underlying asset or liability of interest. Since the financial crisis, the establishment of Basel III capital requirements, and the enactment of the Dodd-Frank Act, focus on strengthening data management capabilities at financial institutions and supervisory agencies has grown in scope and attention both for measurement of specific risks but also in a broader context for estimating systemic risks across the financial services industry and macroeconomy.

Data for risk analysis can be classified as primary or secondary in nature (Figure 2.4). Primary data essentially refers to information obtained directly about a transaction that would affect its risk profile. Secondary data, by contrast, leverages that information by constructing a set of new data fields that would be useful in explaining some risk. An example of this would be the collection of borrower income and debt burden data for a consumer loan. This would be considered primary data, which could be used to construct a debt-to-income ratio (DTI) that would be used in assessing the default propensity of the borrower. The DTI variable would be considered secondary data or a derived field. Primary data would include information obtained about the transaction including features of the contract, loan or instrument including maturity (tenor), other terms such as price and rate, fees, and collateral features and requirements, if any. Information about a counterparty or channel in which a loan may be originated would be considered part of the primary data collection process. This would include data on the financial health of the counterparty including credit ratings if available, and financial data available in 10-Ks and annual reports as applicable.

Primary and secondary data must be augmented by the actual performance history of a transaction. Performance can be defined in several ways depending on the risk being measured and so building a risk data warehouse

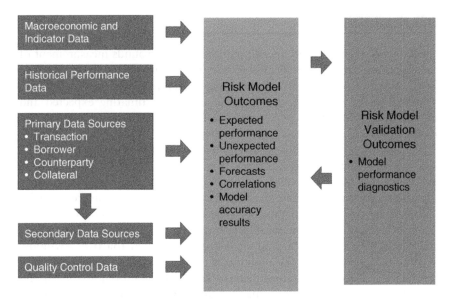

FIGURE 2.4 Risk Data Warehouse Components

with sufficient flexibility to handle multiple definitions of performance is important. For instance, in monitoring credit risk of consumer loans, data on various default states such as 30 days past due, 60 days past due, or the default itself are critical to forming views on the flow of loans working their way through the default pipeline. This allows for more sophisticated measurement of the underlying dynamics of such loans in terms of their "roll" from one delinquency state to another and the factors driving such behavior. Preparing performance data for the risk data warehouse typically involves some further manipulation to put it in a meaningful form for analysis.

Qualitative information about transactions and asset-gathering activities such as quality control information support quantitative data in important ways. For example, quality control units provide invaluable insight into the integrity of loan origination processes and controls. Poor underwriting practices can lead to significant operational risk to an organization, exposing the bank to excessive credit losses and litigation risks downstream. Understanding defects in the process, including the incidence of internal and external fraud, documentation errors, and other signs of process deficiency provides an early warning fact-base, oftentimes well in advance of actual losses. Such information can be incorporated into the risk-analysis reporting dashboard and used to make adjustments to credit policy and tighten operational controls.

Rounding out the risk-data warehouse is macroeconomic and indicator data that may affect a transaction or position's risk. For example, monitoring trends in home prices and interest rates would be vital to understanding mortgage default and prepayment performance. Maintaining such data across both spatial and intertemporal dimensions not only adds an important set of factors that explain performance but facilitates stress-testing and scenario analysis that can yield important insights into the range of risk outcomes for the firm.

In developing a complete risk data warehouse process a number of issues need to be considered. Since risk emanates from the transaction or loan level, capturing data fields at that level of granularity is critical to detecting emerging risks. Designing a data warehouse from the bottom up allows for opportunities to aggregate data into risk segments of interest. The data repository should archive historical transactional and loan information in order to provide sufficient time series to analyze performance over the business cycle. In the years leading up to the financial crisis of 2008–2009, mortgage lenders made decisions based on loan performance during years when the economy was flourishing and house prices were rising. They later found that they had significantly underestimated their credit losses. With the cost of data storage relatively low, efforts to retain a long performance history is a preferred strategy.

It is important that the data be consistent across subportfolios and time. In many instances banks that have acquired other institutions tend to discount the back-end costs of system integration. Making sure portfolios of similar loan types have consistent data can be a struggle for such institutions and impedes their ability to understand risks across the firm in a consistent, timely, and accurate fashion. Protecting the security of customers' private personal information has become a major concern for financial institutions over the years as witnessed by a number of high profile events that have led to the disclosure of sensitive customer information resulting in legal actions and regulatory scrutiny that did not need to happen if these companies had strengthened their information security processes.

Timeliness and accuracy of data are essential ingredients of successful risk analysis. Data that cannot be turned around in time for critical business meetings undermines the credibility of the risk department and, more important, puts management in the difficult position of having to rely on stale information to make risk decisions. Sometimes the schedule for risk and business committees does not take into account the calendar cycle over which data are refreshed. In such cases, risk managers must make the difficult decision to provide the latest information in management reports that have had little time for real analysis over provision of last month's numbers with more refined risk assessment. Such trade-offs are not easy, but at times, concessions to timeliness over analysis can be a preferred course, particularly as conditions change quickly in the market.

Efforts to maintain data accuracy must be deeply rooted in the risk data process. Data errors can occur in a variety of ways: through manual miscoding of information, or transcription errors that occur at either the origination of the loan or consummation of a trade, for example. Missing information is also problematic for analysis and so great care must be given to ensuring critical data fields are populated or can be filled with representative proxies. A more insidious problem happens when product offerings dilute the amount of data available for risk assessment or simply facilitate inaccuracies in secondary data created from primary sources. An example of this comes from the mortgage boom when low-documentation loans became prevalent, allowing borrowers to state their income, assets, or employment without any further verification. Studies after the mortgage crisis have found that borrowers using low documentation loans in many instances overstated their actual incomes by significant percentages in some cases, leading to higher credit losses for banks and investors holding these mortgages. In constructing debt-to-income variables as indicators of a borrower's capacity for loan repayment, the data supplied for income would over time deteriorate as more of these products that were originated begin to erode the accuracy of the DTI variable to predict mortgage default. As borrowers overstated their incomes, it tended to show up as lower DTIs, which historically had been shown to be associated with lower default rates, all else equal. However, since the primary income data were not completely accurate, it gave risk analysts a false indication of the relative risk of low documentation loans compared to fully documented mortgages, leading to significant underestimation of this risk factor. This is also a good example of how quality control units could have helped mitigate these errors through loan file reviews at the time, by uncovering evidence that a sizable percentage of low documentation borrowers were overstating their incomes by significant percentages.

RISK ANALYSIS

Over the past two decades significant strides in computational power and analytical tools have vaulted risk management into one of the more analytically rigorous disciplines. Today the largest and most sophisticated financial institutions leverage these tools as critical inputs to strategic and tactical business decisions. Moreover, regulators are insisting that such firms build out their analytical capabilities, encompassing a wide range of risks. At this time advanced modeling techniques are being applied against traditionally hard-to-quantify risks such as operational risk.

Although risk analytics are an indispensable part of any sound risk management infrastructure, overreliance on models can lead to disaster for the risk manager. As illustrated by the low documentation example given earlier, underwriters and quality control staff had a direct line of sight into the behavior of these borrowers and the degree to which the risk profiles of these loans were being misstated. Hence, as important as analytic models have become to risk management, a balanced approach between analysis and expert judgment is appropriate. Introduction of qualitative assessment into an empirically based model can prevent an otherwise robust model from generating large errors over time. This can be of particular significance when there has been a structural shift in the market or product segment and the period from which data is being drawn for a risk model may not be representative of future outcomes. In such cases, judgmental overrides of the model may be warranted with sufficient documentation about such adjustments.

Risk analysis comprises both backward- and forward-looking assessments. Backward-looking risk analysis entails forming views of the performance of existing transactions, trades, loans, and portfolios to determine if actual performance was in line with modeled expectations at the time the transaction was established. This can be a difficult assignment since it requires archiving earlier versions of models that may have subsequently undergone revision. Nonetheless, the more relevant comparison is to the version of the model in place at the time the transaction was made. Forward-looking analysis by comparison is more challenging than backward-looking analysis since it entails making projections about the future, oftentimes with limited historical experience to guide the analysis. This uncertainty surrounding the outcome can at times serve to undermine the legitimacy of the analysis should the results not be in keeping with intuition or recent experience by senior management.

To better guide prospective risk analysis, market intelligence should be gathered on key macroeconomic drivers of performance, which may in part be derived from proprietary or vendor-supplied forecasts such as interest rates and employment. Each position or transaction will be affected by specific macroeconomic factors and these should be identified and monitored over time for each major category of asset and liability. The set of factors to be included could be lagging, leading, or coincident, depending upon when they are reported and available.

The type of analytic tools to use in measuring risk varies widely depending on the application. If historical databases exist for the institution on positions, statistical models can provide good insight of the relationship of risk drivers to outcomes. Such models can be enhanced to look at a range or distribution of outcomes via techniques such as Monte Carlo simulation, which allows the risk analyst to generate risk distributions that permit analysis of both expected and unexpected risk outcomes. Measures of firm value-at-risk (VaR) for determining market and/or credit risk are commonly developed from such methodologies. These require more technical modeling proficiency and thus are usually deployed in only larger, more complex firms. Other commonly used risk analytics include scenario analysis, which can be used to stress test portfolios under alternative assumptions about performance and economic drivers. Since the financial crisis such techniques have been mandated by bank regulatory agencies for banks to perform on a routine basis. Optimization techniques from the operations research or decision sciences field have increasingly found their way into risk assessment. Trade-offs in risk types such as credit and interest rate risk can be applied using linear optimization techniques and can also be used in optimizing capital allocation across products and business lines. Sometimes complex models are not the solution for a particular need and the risk analyst needs to guard against overengineering a solution for an analysis. For smaller banks with less complicated balance sheets, simpler roll-rate methods for computing loss migration estimates may be more effective than complicated and resource-intensive statistical modeling approaches. Deciding upon what models to use oftentimes comes down to resource availability, time, data availability, and risk measurement issues being addressed by the analysis.

Risk measurement without good benchmarks of performance is of limited value to the risk manager. Understanding whether too much or too little risk exists has to be determined by comparing risk outcomes—either expected or actual—to some tolerance for risk-taking. Risk performance standards also facilitate development of incentive structures for management and staff that adjust for the level of risk taken. In addition, such benchmarks provide the basis for specific risk mitigation actions. For example, in managing the interest-rate risk profile for a bank, the asset-liability management (ALM) committee might establish a target duration gap range between assets and liabilities of .1–.5. Duration gaps outside of this range would warrant some adjustments to the portfolio duration such as by rebalancing assets and liabilities in order to bring it back in within stated ALM policy.

RISK MITIGATION

Risk mitigation describes the process, once risks have been identified, of actions that may be necessary on an ongoing basis to reduce the risk on- and off-balance sheet for the firm consistent with corporate risk appetite. Risk mitigation strategies take on a variety of forms and can be classified as those that can be performed at the front-end of a transaction or loan or that take place after the asset or liability has been booked. Risk policies serve as the principal foundation for managing risks at the front-end of a transaction while other strategies such as default management, risk transfer mechanisms, and dynamic portfolio risk management practices are examples of back-end risk mitigation activities.

Whatever type of risk is being managed requires a set of policies and procedures that articulate the desired risk characteristics of the underlying transactions, loans, or portfolios that the bank believes are consistent with its risk tolerance. Credit policies describe the underwriting process to loan staff both within the firm as well as to external underwriters who may be originating product on behalf of the bank. Collateral valuation policies describe the requirements for determining a satisfactory value of the underlying loan collateral, such as a home. This may entail describing the expectations of an appraiser for conducting the property valuation, required experience, and techniques that can be applied for specific property types, among others. Counterparty credit policies are another type of risk policy that outlines what types of companies a bank will do business with, including descriptions of key risk parameters such as financial condition, past performance, and minimum size, as well as other requirements establishing counterparty eligibility. Asset-liability management (ALM) policies set rules for how much interest rate and liquidity risk the firm is willing to take. These policies may establish risk limits to guide portfolio transactions, such as the purchase or sale of assets and liabilities. For instance, a liquidity management policy may restrict the percentage of liabilities that might come from wholesale versus retail funding sources. Position limits for traders in capital markets divisions can control the level of risk-taking by individuals and should be closely monitored for unusual trading activity, which could indicate fraud.

Once assets and liabilities are brought onto the balance sheet, risks will need to be managed on an ongoing basis to ensure that changes in concentrations or risk exposure remain in line with expectations and risk targets. To accomplish this activity, the risk manager has a number of strategies. As it pertains to loan portfolios, active management of loan servicing staff can yield material benefits in mitigating credit losses gradually. Over time, analytic techniques such as **adaptive control processes** have been able to identify borrower cohorts most likely to slip into various delinquency states and to apply differential treatments to induce repayment. For example, a mortgage borrower who has experienced a 50-point drop in credit score over the past several months but has otherwise been current in the payment might be identified as a higher risk to default over the next six months. If the borrower becomes 30 days past due over that period, it may trigger a call by a customer service representative followed by an automated reminder message for a borrower who has maintained their credit profile and could have forgotten to send in their payment. Unfortunately, during the housing boom, many lenders reduced staffing of their collections and default services functions as loan losses had been very low during the period. Once losses began to appear after 2007, firms had to scramble to reallocate staff, in some cases from underwriting to default activities, or accelerate outside hiring to address significant gaps in these areas to handle immense volumes of delinquent loans that flowed into mortgage servicing departments. Different and increasingly more aggressive treatments may be implemented as loans move into later stage delinquency.

Other risk mitigation actions include dynamic portfolio strategies. These are more likely to be actively managed by the Treasury function of a bank, which may have the responsibility of specific trading activities of the portfolio. The risk management function would ideally establish a set of policies including risk limits that would need to be maintained by the Treasury area. Examples of risk limits might come in the form of product or geographic concentration limits on specific asset types. An example of this would be a hard limit on the percentage of brokered deposits as a percentage of total liabilities that could be used in financing bank activity. Another example could be a limit that no more than 20 percent of all mortgage loans can be concentrated in California. Guidance for setting such limits could be regulatory requirements, risk-based capital allocation, or simple risk-tolerance decisions.

Among the most important and effective ways of managing risk is through a well-designed risk-based **capital allocation** program. Capital allocation planning should accompany the strategic planning process of the firm, but throughout the year, decisions on how to deploy capital to the most economically attractive use as defined by risk capital is an important exercise for the firm. For example, early in the year 20 percent of the firm's capital may have been allocated to the consumer lending division, of which a third was further allocated to the mortgage business. During the year, the mortgage division realizes that competitive and other forces are causing the business to lose market share. In reassessing the business model they believe that they can recoup their lost share (and then some) by redirecting the business into subprime lending that has a much higher margin than prime mortgages but is also subject to higher losses. During these discussions, risk management needs to weigh in on what the risk-adjusted performance of such a product reallocation would mean for the company including how much additional capital subprime loans would require relative to prime. Such product decisions can be addressed within the context of the bank's strategic risk capital allocation framework during the course of the year, when invariably course corrections due to business dynamics become apparent to management. In this way, the business can apply consistent measures throughout the year in allocating their capital.

A variety of strategies are available to the firm, allowing it to transfer risk off its balance sheet. These include asset sales, hedging strategies, and various forms of reinsurance contracts. Selling assets out of the portfolio is a straightforward way of rebalancing the portfolio to maintain a certain risk profile or, during periods of stress, to reduce the financial effect on the firm and its capital. Unfortunately asset sales during stress periods oftentimes are associated with low asset prices, as the market takes into account the losses such assets may generate over time. Managing risks using some combination of the techniques identified above can significantly reduce the chances that the firm may one day be faced with having to sell assets at firesale prices.

Hedging individual assets or liabilities or an entire portfolio from losses is a major strategy used to mitigate risk. Hedging entails identifying suitable hedge instruments that offset the risk of the unhedged position in a way that satisfies the objective of the hedging strategy. Hedging may be used to guard against excessive market and interest-rate risk in fixed-income, equities, foreign exchange, or other financial positions. Even credit risk positions may be hedged, using a variety of structured financial instruments such as senior-subordinated securities that allow investors to buy and sell tranches of a credit risk distribution. A wide variety of derivative instruments can be used in building the hedge strategy and are dependent on a number of issues such as the time horizon for the hedge, policy limits, availability of hedge instruments, and costs, among many others.

Reinsurance has become a commonly used approach to manage risk in the insurance industry where the ability to take on large exposures and then seek reinsurance on portions of these exposures is possible. An example of this includes catastrophic risk, where an insurer seeks coverage of a portion of their risk book for exposures that might be viewed as too large and/or exceeding some level of loss that is outside prescribed policy. Such contracts can be highly customized to fit the specific needs of the buyer of the reinsurance contract. These contracts are also used in banking portfolios like consumer assets where for similar reasons additional protection against losses may be sought. Such contracts can be quite complex at times, establishing at what point the loss distribution losses are absorbed by each counterparty in the transaction. For example, a bank originally expects and reserves for lifetime losses on a pool of loans of 300bps. To protect itself against higher losses, it might seek a counterparty to agree to take any losses that occur on the portfolio in excess of 300bps in return for a premium charged to the bank reflecting the losses on the portion of the portfolio absorbed by the counterparty plus a fair return. More complex arrangements can be constructed that this simple example where the counterparty might limit their losses to some range, for instance 300–800bps and price the premium for that level of risk. The bank would then be responsible for the first 300bps in losses sustained (**first loss position**), the counterparty taking the next 500bps in losses (**mezzanine position**), and the bank coming back to take any losses beyond 800bps (**senior position**).

Securitization is a method of financing various types of assets enabling a loan originator to retain the asset on balance sheet as a security collateralized by the underlying loans but without credit exposure to losses of those loans. The securitization market has been dominated by residential mortgages, commercial mortgages, credit card receivables, and automobile loans, among others. From a risk management perspective, the ability to transform a set of loans with credit risk that may or may not be geographically diversified into a security that reflects a mix of loans where the credit risk is no longer held by the bank but by an investor in the asset-backed security is a valuable financial structuring vehicle. In the years preceding the financial crisis, the advent of further financial engineering to create a dizzying array of derivative products such as collateralized debt obligations (CDOs) and credit default swaps (CDSs) led to an explosion in volume of securitized products, mainly in the residential secondary market. The circumstances under which these products contributed to the crisis are well known; however, the underlying structures remain important tools in managing risks.

SUMMARY

Managing risk at a financial institution is multifaceted and crosses a number of different risk types. As a result, risk managers cannot rely on standard cookbook methods to analyze the risk of their businesses. In fact, a bank in one period can face a much different set of circumstances than in another due to changes in market and economic conditions, management changes, and a host of other issues. As a result, managing risk requires a high degree of situational awareness of current conditions, the culture of the organization for taking risk, competitive forces, and other dynamics that are ever-changing and can lead to different risk outcomes and thus require very different responses to manage risk.

Risks to financial institutions vary in type from credit risk, interest rate, and market risks as classic types tied directly to the risk characteristics of the transaction or portfolio to operational, regulatory, litigation, and reputational risks resulting from breakdowns in process and controls as well as management oversight. The risk manager may be forced to make trade-offs

among risk types, which could be difficult since some risks such as to reputation are difficult to directly quantify. Consider, for example, the case of a
lender with unused home equity lines of credit that finds itself in a credit crisis where such loans are increasingly being drawn by cash-flow-constrained
customers. The risk manager may be able to quantify the likelihood that the
remaining unused lines of credit will be drawn down by less creditworthy
borrowers and thus expose the bank to additional credit losses. By imposing
a set of criteria allowing the bank to freeze the use of any undrawn line of
credit for borrowers with deteriorating credit, the risk manager can effectively mitigate contingent liability later. However, this action is likely to generate some customer backlash if negatively viewed by the public. This could
lead to deposit withdrawals and/or reduction in loan demand. Quantifying
these effects takes more art than science, and against a more fact-based
analysis of the credit effects of the line freeze introduces its own uncertain-
ties into the net impact of a line freeze decision.

The discipline of risk management encompasses three broad sets of
activities: (1) identification, (2) measurement, and (3) mitigation of risk.
Risk managers must conduct an inventory of risks encountered by their
firm and appropriately catalogue them according to each business line. This
inventory allows the risk department to determine resources, design processes and controls, and establish risk appetite and strategies for each risk
in consultation with the business and other relevant areas of the company.
Understanding the ways each risk can adversely affect the firm is a useful thought process for working through potential negative outcomes. This
approach adapts situational awareness to risk management by constantly
challenging current state outcomes against other scenarios that could harm
the institution financially and in other ways. Situational risk management
entails laying out scenarios in which current trends and behavior in the
market, customers, and product offerings could lead to higher risk. Stand-
ing back with the benefit of hindsight, it is easy for armchair risk managers
to second-guess why so many risk professionals did not see and/or heed the
warning signs that a housing bubble was building in the market. Against
the backdrop of benign economic conditions prevailing in the years before
2007 and with the largest, most powerful players in the financial industry
continuing to develop new mortgage products based largely on riskier combinations of attributes but with negligible default exposure, it was difficult
to conceive the confluence of factors that would lead to the worst crisis
since the Great Depression. Nevertheless, the acceleration in home prices
that was outsized by historical standards and continued relaxation of credit
standards were signs that conditions might change. Risk managers are paid
in part based on their ability to paint scenarios where bad outcomes may be
possible and to assign likelihoods to these outcomes. As will be seen in the

chapter on risk governance, risk managers must have the courage of their own convictions to lay out pessimistic views even as the party continues in full swing.

Risk measurement is another critical activity necessary for effective risk management to take place. A wide array of quantitative approaches to measuring market, interest rate, and credit risks have been developed over the past decade, and with advances in computational power and software have vaulted the quant into the realms of stardom among finance and risk professionals. Tempered against their success at evaluating complex risk interactions, quantitative methods actually performed miserably during the boom years, leading many firms to vastly underestimate the level of credit risks building up on their balance sheets. Thus, while such tools remain essential parts of any risk manager's toolkit, they must be handled with a great deal of care. In fact, despite their elegance and ability to boil risk down to a single number at times, there is no substitute for solid judgment, experience, and intuition to challenge model assumptions and outcomes. This is difficult when objectivity remains the hallmark of good risk analytics, however; at times, the limitations of models to project future outcomes must be assessed continuously through the model and product lifecycle.

Finally, once risks have been identified and measured, mitigation strategies must be in place to manage risks to stated tolerances and policy targets. The first line of defense surrounding loan risks takes the form of credit policies. Such policies, along with procedures and control documentation, provide underwriters and other business professionals with the roadmap for what loan features are attractive and must be present in originating a loan. Policies outlining the quality of the underlying loan collateral, the quality of counterparties in a transaction, as well as ALM policies specifying risk limits and thresholds of performance, are the foundation for effective risk management.

Once assets have landed onto the balance sheet, other mitigation strategies may be employed to manage risks to firm tolerances. **Dynamic portfolio management,** whereby assets and liabilities may be bought and sold in amounts and types to maintain interest rate and liquidity risk targets and buffers, can be leveraged for managing credit risk as well. Portfolio limits are an effective way of guarding against adverse risk concentrations and positions in assets or liabilities that may not be consistent with the firm's view of risk. Active account servicing practices can yield large dividends in lower credit losses if applied against good business analytics and judgment regarding borrower tendencies to repay their obligations under adverse situations. Reinsurance and securitization strategies are another way lenders can remove unwanted credit risk from the balance sheet. In the case of reinsurance the lender gives up the credit risk of the loans for which they are seeking protection and in return must assess the level of counterparty risk in the transaction. Thus using financial contracts to transfer risk into the capital markets does not necessarily mean that all risk has been removed. In the case of securitizations, the bank retaining the security still is exposed to market and interest rate risk and must manage them accordingly. Ultimately there is no standard approach to managing bank risk, but instead a collection of activities that are each tailored to the unique circumstances of the bank.

QUESTIONS

1. A bank is in the midst of a highly competitive market environment and over the past few years has created a number of new products to improve its market share. The economy has been booming but there are emerging signs that growth could slow over the next year or so. The risk manager does not have much empirical experience from which to infer the long-term performance of these new products. Management wants risk management to reduce its head count in an effort to reduce expenses and at the same time find ways to bring greater efficiencies to credit underwriting. What concept best describes is a good example of the issues facing this risk manager and why?

2. A portfolio has an expected return of 10 percent and a standard deviation of 3 percent. You know that the 90 percent confidence level is associated with 1.65 standard deviations from the mean and the 95 percent confidence level is associated with 1.96 standard deviations from the mean. What is the worst return you would expect to see with 95 percent confidence?

3. You enter into a CDS contract for $1 billion in which you agree to pay a premium to another institution in order to receive payments that cover the risk of your underlying portfolio. What type of risk do you face?

4. You oversee the risk of a large trading group that specializes in foreign exchange and fixed-income. You notice that over the course of several months, one of your traders has generated $200 million in losses in a 30-day period, well outside the trader's assigned risk limit. After some investigation, you find that the valuation engine used by the trading organization is out-of-date and has a tendency to underestimate the risk of the changes in certain market movements. Three days later the trader vanishes and you find that $10 million of his account is now missing. What kind of risks does this pose to the firm?

5. Your portfolio of $500 million in 30-year Treasuries has declined in value by 3.5 percent as a result of a major rise in interest rates. What type of risk do you face in this instance?

6. How does interest rate risk differ from market risk?

7. You are the risk manager for a $2 billion portfolio of auto loans. The economy over the past five years has been strong and losses on your portfolio have been low. But conditions are changing and you believe that over the next three years, losses could increase substantially to the point of nearly wiping out all the profit made in the past five years. Provide some discussion of how you might mitigate this risk.

8. Your bank has been in the headlines for a number of months as a result of accelerating losses in the credit card division, the largest division of the bank and most recognized by customers. There have been some media reports that the bank may not have enough capital to survive the next six weeks. What risk do you face and what could happen?

9. You are the CEO of your bank and your CRO was recently hired from a competing bank largely because of her technical risk expertise. She is experienced at implementing large-scale highly complex analytical risk solutions for valuation and pricing and has developed a plan to deploy this capability throughout the organization. One of the benefits claimed by the CRO from this initiative is that it will do away with 100 underwriting and QC staff since 90 percent of the underwriting and back-end review can now be automated. How might you react to this proposal?

CHAPTER 3

Risk Governance and Structure

SIFIBANK'S RISK GOVERNANCE—THE EARLY YEARS

SifiBank up until the recent hiring of a Chief Risk Officer (CRO) had operated for its entire existence without a formal risk management structure. Many of the components of a risk management organization existed within the company but were scattered around different business lines and functional areas such as the finance and legal departments. The arrival of the new CRO heralded a new beginning for SifiBank, one that recognized the growing sensitivity of SifiBank's primary regulator to strong risk management practices. In fact, at their last board meeting, the regulators had cited insufficient risk management processes in light of SifiBank's five-year strategic plan calling for double-digit growth across its business divisions.

In order to address the regulatory concerns regarding risk management practices at the bank, the Chairman and CEO of SifiBank instructed the Chief Financial Officer to recruit and hire a CRO who would report to him directly. Upon arriving, the new CRO set about understanding the structure and organizational dynamics of SifiBank in order to determine what structure the new risk organization should take along with the staffing required to accomplish that objective. Aside from the fact that SifiBank's size and business composition represented a significant expansion of responsibility over risk management from the prior position the CRO held at another firm, he was also attracted by the fact that the Chairman and CEO was an icon in the banking industry, having founded the bank just 30 years ago. The Chairman was intimately involved with nearly every facet of the business and his strong presence in management and board meetings was clearly felt by all attending.

The Board, for instance, which was composed of 15 directors, featured 10 who were hand-picked by the Chairman from various associations and from a wide variety of vocations. One director was a Hall of Fame football player the chairman had come to know over time, two headed up their own private equity firms, two were former bankers, and the rest were heads of companies that ranged from consumer products to manufacturing. The board met quarterly for two days each time, meeting as a group as well as in several subcommittees to discuss key business issues. Among the subcommittees established at SifiBank were Human Resources, Finance and Credit, and Audit. Depending on the nature of the issue, risk management topics were distributed between the Finance and Credit and Audit Subcommittees.

Upon arriving, the CFO informed the CRO that one of the first major assignments was to provide the board with an overview of the vision for SifiBank risk management. Given that the board meeting was only a few weeks away, this report to the board was intended as much as anything else to provide a forum for introducing the CRO to the board. At this meeting, the CRO outlined his vision for a two-pronged approach for building the risk management function. This entailed the development of a suite of analytic and data capabilities that would allow the bank to understand its risk across a number of alternative scenarios augmented by risk experts drawn from the business, audit and finance areas predominately. The one thing that struck the CRO at this first meeting was the lack of risk expertise on the board given the scale, scope, and complexity of SifiBank. The board seemed at best mildly interested in what the CRO had to say, but throughout the discussion the chairman and CFO would interject and describe how risk management would enable the bank to meet its aggressive business objectives.

Six months after joining the bank, the CRO had assembled a core team of risk professionals and laid out an organizational structure that featured a centralized risk management department under the CRO's leadership. The department was organized by several functional areas: Consumer and Commercial Credit, Counterparty Risk, Operational Risk, and Market and Interest Rate Risk. The CRO had socialized this proposed plan to the heads of each business line for their feedback and support since a number of risk staff that resided in their areas would be reassigned to the new risk management function. The CRO learned quickly that the risk management organization he envisioned was simply not going to be feasible at SifiBank for a number of reasons. The business heads expressed much concern about losing their risk staff, explaining to the CRO that since the business is compensated for managing financial performance, they require risk professionals to report in to their organization. Compounding issues for the CRO, his manager, the CFO, aligned with the business heads for similar reasons. The CFO had grown up at SifiBank and had come to know the business heads quite well and was one of the two or three senior executives who were close to the chairman. Knowing that the chairman was a couple of years from retirement, the CFO typically aligned his views to those of the chairman, which at this point were to meet the aggressive growth targets the company had set out.

With considerable input from the business heads, the CRO reluctantly reshaped the proposed structure to form a Corporate Risk Oversight group, composed of 150 staff members instead of the larger 700-person team. The other 550 risk staff remained assigned under the business divisions under newly created line of business CROs (BCRO) who reported directly to the business head and not to the CRO. Within SifiBank, the BCROs carried the same corporate title (Managing Director) and level as the CRO, effectively making them peers. With the CRO's arrival, the board modified its charter to delegate credit authority to the CRO. In turn, based on their discretion, the CRO could delegate credit authority to other members of the organization. The CRO had the Risk Oversight team working on a broad **delegation of authority** document that would be based on a combination of risk experience, exposure, and size of transaction, among other criteria. As part of the organizational design, the CRO had been instructed to work with the BCROs to determine what other overlaps between the business risk and risk oversight areas could be realigned or eliminated. The president of the company along with each of the business heads had felt that maintaining two distinct risk functions was inefficient and overly bureaucratic and that a lean risk oversight function that simply observed risk outcomes and reported on them to the board was a desired outcome in light of increasing market competition in banking that made operational efficiency a key objective. In fact, each quarter the CRO and his direct reports were required to meet with each business head and their direct reports, including the BCRO, to justify the Risk Oversight team's personnel and activities. These meetings were an ominous sign for the CRO, who had not previously experienced this kind of attitude toward risk management. Even worse, a number of senior executives had referred to the Risk Oversight group as the "Business Prevention Unit." Clearly many within the company saw little value in the new organization.

Another blow to the CRO came several months after his arrival. SifiBank had a well-established Executive Committee that met monthly and was chaired by the bank's chairman and consisted of the president and their direct reports. The CRO was not a member of this committee and it became problematic that the CFO was not well-versed in formal risk management practices. Thus, it was not clear how effective the CRO would be when expressing his views regarding SifiBank's risk exposure and related risk management activities at the Executive Committee meetings.

These organizational dynamics continued for the next several years with little relief for the beleaguered risk oversight staff. Fortunately for the bank, prevailing economic conditions were favorable across the business lines and the bank's financial performance was strong and its losses among the lowest observed in the past 25 years. Ironically, this environment posed significant challenges to Corporate Risk Oversight and the CRO. As new products were developed to support the business goals, Risk Oversight had sought to establish a variety of controls and review how they performed. The CRO had thus put in place a new Risk Management Committee, composed of the BCROs, the CFO, and other invited senior executives. The Risk Committee provided a forum for reviewing risk exposures, communicating and reviewing the bank's loan loss reserve requirements, and discussing other risk processes and activities. While the CRO chaired these meetings, oftentimes, the bank president and chairman would attend, which tended to steer the discussion toward ways that the risk team could help the business meet their goals.

The fifth year after the CRO's arrival at the bank was marked by a significant set of changes in the market. The CRO had, as part of the board and management reporting process, developed a comprehensive portfolio indicators assessment that drew upon trends and insights on a variety of macroeconomic factors that could provide early warning indicators of how the bank's various portfolios and activities would fare over time. One of these measures was home price appreciation, an important measure given that SifiBank held about 25 percent of its assets in whole loan mortgages or mortgage securities in its held-for-investment (HFI) or securities trading account. The risk team tracked changes of this measure at the national level and local market level on a quarterly basis using vendor supplied data. Over the past five years, home prices had accelerated sharply, but with mortgage losses at historical lows and the economy continuing to show signs of strong growth, such an alarming increase in home prices did not concern the business. The Corporate Risk Oversight group had at least been able to extract one concession from the business by allowing it to impose a soft markets policy on all mortgages in its HFI portfolio. That policy meant that under certain criteria for home price appreciation, the bank would no longer take some mortgage products from specific local markets where abnormally high home price appreciation was observed based on a number of risk attributes. But since SifiBank securitized most of its loan production, this risk control had little effect on the bank's enormous securitization business. By the beginning of the fifth year, several subprime mortgage securities came under scrutiny as defaults on underlying mortgages rose sharply.

Over the past five years, the dynamics at the Board had frustrated the CRO. While the CRO had been able to convince the CFO to allow him to appear at meetings of the Board and provide reports on risk management, the process involved was less than ideal. For instance, the bank had a highly choreographed approach to preparation of board materials.

Weeks in advance of these meetings, the Executive Committee would meet with the General Counsel and the CRO to determine what would be presented each session. While the risk management report was largely the same each quarter, the CRO's comments and observations about the trends in risk exposure were often softened by the Executive Committee, who were concerned about the board's reaction to one executive's (i.e., the CRO's) opinion. Making matters worse, the CRO's report to the board was always done with the CFO and other senior executives present. In other words, the board did not hold separate executive sessions with the CRO only.[1] As a result, while the board received factual information regarding the bank's risk profile, the interpretation of those results was somewhat filtered by the Executive Committee. The fact that not a single board member had any risk management experience at a bank compounded the issue, since probing questions regarding the way the bank managed its risk were far and few between.

By the middle of the fifth year, the mortgage market had continued to spiral downward, leading to an increase in mortgage delinquencies across the country. Since SifiBank was one of the largest originators of mortgages, it came as no surprise that defaults started to pick up. The CRO maintained responsibility over the assessment of the bank's allowance for loan and lease loss reserves (ALLL) that required the bank to make quarterly provisions to that reserve based on losses embedded in the portfolio. At SifiBank this was always a semicontentious activity, even in good years, since adding reserves represented a drag to earnings. Only a few years earlier, the bank had begun originating a new mortgage product for which it had little performance history to use in estimating the reserve. The risk team had adjusted its models for another related product to estimate the new product's risk, which suggested holding a small reserve even at the outset. The CFO, bank chairman, and head of the consumer business challenged these results, pressuring the CRO to modify his estimates. The CRO maintained his position that these were consistent with Generally Accepted Accounting Principles (GAAP) and unless there were empirical findings to the contrary, stood by these estimates. Such periodic showdowns only reinforced management's growing concern about the effectiveness of Corporate Risk Oversight.

Toward the middle of the year, the bank held its monthly Asset-Liability Committee Meeting (ALCO), which featured the entire senior executive

---

[1] An executive session enables the board to hold a private meeting with an officer such as the CRO without other persons of the management team present. In this way it is intended to provide a forum for direct communication about business matters to the board.

team.[2] At these monthly meetings the CRO was to provide a risk management summary, including the provision. At this particular ALCO meeting, the CRO also presented the results of his team's projections for the amount of provisions that would need to be added to the reserve for the third quarter. The number communicated was $200 million greater than had been estimated a month earlier, based on a number of factors, including the fact that with the mortgage securities market having effectively shut down as investors retreated from these instruments, loans that had been in the bank's pipeline and designated for securitization and thus not needing a reserve now had no other outlet and hence would be coming into the portfolio and requiring a reserve. The chairman and CFO became outraged during the meeting that this estimate, which had not been vetted by the CFO ahead of the meeting, had been made available to the rest of the ALCO committee. Within the next several weeks, the chairman, president, and CFO had made a decision that they no longer believed the CRO was aligned with the rest of senior management in the views of bank risk management and that they needed to recruit a new CRO. Before the beginning of the fourth quarter, the CRO was informed that he was being replaced and was asked to leave upon the new CRO's arrival. Despite the fact that the CRO had established credibility with the safety and soundness regulator in the years he had been with SifiBank, the regulators remained silent on the dismissal.

Criteria for Effective Risk Management

Clearly in the years leading up the mortgage crisis, SifiBank risk management experienced a number of challenges to the way it oversaw and managed risks. Although it is hard to say that had SifiBank put in place a strong risk management structure, it would have been able to avoid making business decisions that ultimately led to serious problems afterward, such processes would have enabled the bank to at least better understand what risks it was facing. Effective risk management organizations are those that possess the following qualities:

- A supportive culture for risk management
- An effective risk management team
- Balanced risk management
- Situationally aware risk organization

---

[2] The ALCO meeting brings together senior management on a periodic basis to discuss strategic issues relating to the bank's assets, liabilities and liquidity structure and performance.

A prerequisite for strong risk management is a culture that embraces risk management in all aspects of the company. This is an intangible quality that develops over time, largely as a result of the tone from the top of the organization. Without a cheerleader for risk management, this critical part of the business suffers. In the absence of a supportive culture for risk management, the function and team may wither, much as it did at SifiBank. Thus, the most senior levels of management and the board must make it a priority to build that culture. Unfortunately a number of economic, structural, and behavioral issues can greatly affect the firm's risk DNA. We review a theory of risk governance as part of this shortly.

A supportive culture provides an environment in which a financial institution can thrive, but it does so only if the organization has obtained a certain stature and respect in the industry as a whole. That comes from demonstrating a level of competency in risk management that crosses a number of business activities. Risk management is less a formal discipline, such as accounting or finance, and more an amalgamation of several disciplines. In light of the fact that risk management lies at the heart of financial intermediation, the successful risk organization has intimate knowledge of the business, how it is financed, accounting impacts of various risk decisions, deep operational expertise, and strong analytical and data management capabilities. The risk function cannot afford to be one dimensional if it is to be effective within the organization.

A related concept for risk management is balance. The job of risk management is neither to negate business decisions nor to simply go along with business requests. Risk management is about taking prudent risks, and so balance is of paramount importance. A financial institution will not stay in business long if takes no risk and the same is true if it takes excessive amounts of risk. Striking the right balance in risk outcomes is a major challenge for risk managers and one that is not clear at all times. To better guide the firm through its risk-taking, the risk manager must work with the board and senior management to develop a formal corporate risk vision that broadly lays out the kinds of risks the firm will be allowed to take as well as a maximum level of risk, spelled out quantitatively and qualitatively. This serves as a living document that, together with a strong risk culture and effective risk management can serve as the benchmark test for any risk discussion. Moreover, it should outline clear roles and responsibilities for management regarding risk-taking, including who has authority for taking various levels of risk in the organization. Without clear delegations of authority, risk management can quickly devolve into chaos. The risk vision can also provide a means to establish a common risk lexicon across the company. Going back to establishing quantitative risk tolerances, the firm should apply a common measurement of risk across lines of business and products in order to maintain consistency and establish common terminology across the organization. For instance, the risk vision document may feature estimates of risk or economic capital, framed in terms of risk-adjusted returns.

A final criterion for successful risk management is situational awareness. Risk managers operate in an environment that is constantly in flux. Economic and market conditions rapidly change over time, thus requiring different business and risk responses. Consequently, the risk manager must adapt to these circumstances, learn from them, and modify them as conditions change. This aspect of risk management complicates matters, but is essential for maintaining a readiness to act in the face of uncertainty, which is a major focus for risk management teams. Risk managers must take care not to become complacent over the risks they are managing in the way that SifiBank fell under the mistaken belief that good economic performance in the recent past spelled continued periods of low risk for the future. And, the last risk event is unlikely to be the next risk crisis. Given this, the job of the risk manager is to provide objective views of likely and unexpected poor risk outcomes to management, regardless of what that message may be. In that regard, the CRO acts as the moral compass of the bank.

Once these attributes for strong risk management are in place, an organizational structure best fitting the culture of the firm can be established for risk management. Risk organizations can be structured in widely divergent ways including highly centralized and decentralized models. Oftentimes, a firm will switch out one structure for another, particularly when economic conditions change for the firm. If the firm, for example, is consistently losing market share over time, and if risk management is viewed as a contributing factor, then a centralized organization where all risk resources reports to the CRO could be restructured into a decentralized model where only a core risk oversight group exists at the corporate level and all other resources reports to the business areas. Organizational change can of course go in the other direction, as after a risk event posing significant losses to the firm, a decentralized risk structure may be reconstituted as a highly centralized organization. Ideally, stability within the organization is desirable for maintaining continuity and consistency in the application of risk decisions.

Developing a centralized versus decentralized risk management organization has a number of trade-offs. A centralized risk management structure provides stronger controls over all risk functions than when they are co-located or distributed among business and other units of the enterprise. In such a model, resources from the corporate center can be dedicated to business units, but while serving that area take direction from the corporate risk function. Such models make it easier to establish risk-focused metrics for individual performance agreements and provide greater opportunity for objectivity in risk management discussions with the business. At the same time, a centralized risk management organization may not be nimble enough to respond to business needs and changing market conditions. Moreover, there can be a tendency for myopia to set in around a centralized structure that is more insulated from making tough decisions supporting business initiatives. In some cases, in a centralized model, it may be easier to say no to a business proposal since a centralized risk management function may not be directly accountable in their performance for profit-generating initiatives. That type of incentive structure can be harmful to the firm in greatly limiting otherwise well-controlled business opportunities.

On the other end of the organizational spectrum, a decentralized risk management structure enables the business to have greater access and interaction with risk management professionals. In that way risk management embedded with the business can provide the responsiveness that a centralized organization may not be as capable of providing. However, it may be easier for a decentralized risk management function to become captive to the business, particularly when the risk group shares business objectives for performance management.

There is no clear-cut answer regarding the type of organization structure that best fits a banking organization, and this remains a hot topic for discussion. One approach that can mitigate the problems that both organizational models bring is to create a blended structure. Specifically, both corporate and business risk management groups may be created. The corporate risk office would be responsible for creating, delegating, and monitoring the firm's risk policies and limits and in that capacity would not have any business reporting relationship. The business risk units would report into the business and be deployed against their activities on a day-to-day basis. Business risk officers would maintain a link back to their corporate risk office via a reporting line shared with the business. Whether the line is direct (solid) to corporate risk or indirect (dotted) is a decision point for the firm. In the end, business professionals, including risk management personnel, are incented by pecuniary rewards. Creating a solid line between business and corporate risk offices may limit the degree to which the business risk function responds positively to business requests. Conversely, establishing a solid line to the business can promote an overly aggressive risk management environment. In either situation, the culture of an institution can more than compensate for whatever organizational structure is implemented, so long as expectations are made clear by senior management.

Beyond determining how risk resources are distributed at the corporate and line of business levels is the issue of how audit and risk management functions relate to each other. One thing to keep in mind is that risk management is not audit, and vice versa. Ambiguity between the roles of these two functions can lead to confusion at the least and risk disasters at worst. It is not surprising, however, that the roles in a number of cases became blurred given the relative newness of risk management to banking organizations. For lack of better understanding, some CRO positions have wound up as risk audit functions, with little responsibility over managing risk. In the end, SifiBank's first CRO wound up marginalized due to the poor culture and lack of understanding surrounding the position. Moreover, some CRO functions do not include all risk areas of the organization. For instance, matters relating to legal or regulatory risk may be found in the compliance organization housed in the General Counsel's office. Sometimes this occurs due to personnel and business reasons, however, such structures diffuse responsibility for risk-taking, making it hard to hold a single senior executive responsible for risk outcomes at an enterprise level as well as to consolidate risks within the organization.

Finally, where the CRO reports in the organization is of paramount importance. In the case of SifiBank, the CRO reported to the CFO, which not only removed the CRO one level from the Executive Committee, but in turn reduced the position's stature and introduced potential conflicts between the CRO and his manager. Ideally, the CRO should report to the head of an independent board member that chairs the risk committee of the board. In this way, the board has direct access to the CRO's objectivity, which can be maintained by the reporting relationship. Smaller institutions, say below $1 billion in total assets, may not need to establish such a formal structure as this; nevertheless, it is important to designate one individual as responsible for the company's overall risk management activities.

A Theory of Risk Governance

As was the case with SifiBank, a strong leader can greatly influence risk outcomes. In this section, we bring together a theory that blends formal models of managerial power and executive compensation with cognitive bias borrowed from behavioral finance to describe how management risk-taking evolves and its impact on risk management organizations. Within finance literature, an area of research has emerged that describes situations where a powerful senior chief executive officer imposes significant influence over the organization by virtue of his or her personality. According to this managerial power theory, the executive officer may impose his or her will on a weak board, one that may actually include directors who are close to the CEO. Thus, the CEO enjoys a fair amount of latitude to influence the board in decisions relating to executive compensation structures, including their own. Ideally, an optimal contracting arrangement would minimize *principal-agent* costs between management and shareholders.[3] In this case, the CEO works on behalf of the shareholders who rely on the board and may not completely observe the actions of management. A board that becomes captive or influenced by a strong executive may not be able to minimize these agency costs, thus allowing management to extract rents from shareholders by way of influencing the outcomes of their compensation plans. Structuring incentive compensation plans that have large payouts over short time windows maximizes the executive's utility at the expense of the shareholder. Thus, for a powerful CEO with a short-term horizon it would not be in his best interest financially to design a compensation structure that has long-term risk management objectives.

Potentially influencing the executive's compensation strategy and hence business and risk outcomes are a variety of biases or beliefs held by the executive. These are commonly referred to in behavioral finance as *cognitive biases*. Cognitive biases affect the manager by reinforcing a weak corporate governance structure as demonstrated by the managerial power model. Weak oversight by a board and shareholders enables the executive to design favorable compensation packages, and if their underlying beliefs support this outcome, it can result in behavior that sacrifices prudent long-term risk-taking objectives for short-term profits and market share.

How these biases can affect bank management risk-taking may be observed in the following utility-choice model adapted from financial research first for consumers and then used to describe investor behavior. In the case of executives, we can assume that they are rational and financially motivated to maximize their overall utility, which includes compensation received from the firm. A critical contribution of the work to the expected utility-choice model is in describing asymmetries between gains and losses affecting an individual's risk decision. Specifically, it can be shown how an individual's risk-taking is dependent on prior financial outcomes. In this framework, the standard expected utility model is adapted to represent utility that comes about from changes in the value of an investor's financial wealth. This is described formally as:

$$\text{MAX } E(U) = \theta(I_t) \qquad\qquad 3.1$$

where the term on the right-hand of the expression represents the relationship between incentive compensation (I) in period t, and management utility,

---

[3] The principal-agent problem is an important concept in economics where one party may not act in the best interest of the other party due to differences in information available to them, referred as information asymmetries.

with utility an increasing function of incentive compensation. The effect of firm financial performance such as profitability (p) in a given period t that drives incentive pay as well as risk-taking behavior is related to a historical benchmark in this model designated as $p*_t$. Should management experience gains sometime in the past, the significance of this outcome is that managers become less loss-averse than if prior financial performance has resulted in losses. With this framework in place, it is possible to describe management risk-taking at financial institutions and how it relates to their risk management functions.

Central to the model is the linkage of incentive compensation structure to changes in risk-taking. Incentive compensation, as mentioned earlier, is a function of the firm's corporate governance structure with weaker governance exemplified under the managerial power framework permitting incentive compensation structures that allow for greater risk-taking. In that regard, changes in business management utility are related to θ in the following way: $\dfrac{\partial E[U]}{\partial \theta} > 0$, implying that as a firm's financial performance improves, it raises management utility. Incentive contracts can lead to greater utility as a result of a set of performance measures that do not accurately incorporate a longer-term view of performance adjusting for risk. A focus on short-term profits in a strong market unadjusted for risk, for example, could vastly overstate the firm's performance and unduly reward management. Although the performance metrics of these contracts may lead to favorable compensation outcomes for management in the short-term, they are illusory.

The primary transmission mechanism for this relationship then is the incentive compensation structure. I_t is a function of several factors driving management's "view" of firm performance, which as stated earlier influences management utility. This view of performance is a reflection of the underlying performance metrics embedded in the incentive compensation arrangement. This might include, for example, measures of firm profitability, stock performance (such as price-earnings ratios), market share, and losses, among other possible metrics. Performance metrics established in incentive contracts designed under conditions explained by the managerial power model are related to a set of management cognitive biases well-established in the behavioral economics literature.

One of these behaviors relates to *confirmation biases* that assign greater weight to information supporting a particular view. This bias may be associated with the "house money effect," where prior financial performance influences an individual's risk-taking. In this context, a prior period of sustained favorable financial performance would be a confirming event of future strong performance, thus reducing management's level of loss aversion.

This may also be portrayed as a condition where overconfidence in a particular view or outcome is established merely by the coherence of a story and its conformance with a point of view. Management could be mistakenly lulled into a false sense of security by force of personality coupled with abnormally favorable conditions. Confirmation bias and this "illusion of validity" may be reinforcing biases for managers.

Another bias introduced into this framework is *herd behavior,* which describes a phenomenon where imperfect information regarding a group (e.g., a competitor) leads to decisions where management follows a competitor's strategy at the expense of their own, based on limited information. An example of this would be large mortgage originators such as Countrywide and Washington Mutual following each other's product development movements, which were largely based on relaxed underwriting standards and increased risk layering of existing products. These firms viewed these newer products as having greater expected profitability than existing products based upon formal disclosures of financial performance by competitors of these new products as well as informal information from recently hired employees of competitor firms and other market intelligence. This herd effect could be reinforced by confirmation bias supported by a period of recent past performance reflecting strong house price appreciation, low interest rates and low defaults.

The last bias introduced into this framework is related to the **ambiguity effect**. This bias describes a phenomenon whereby individuals tend to favor decisions based on certain rather than uncertain outcomes. This behavior may be attributed to a general desire to avoid alternatives where information may be incomplete. In the context of risk management, the ambiguity effect has a particular role in defining the effectiveness of risk management. First, since forward-looking estimates of firm risk are probabilistic in nature, this introduces uncertainty into management decisionmaking and performance benchmarks used in incentive contracts. Riskier views could reduce the attractiveness of certain products, and potentially lower the performance of the firm and management compensation in the process.

An example of this would be differences in performance between prime and subprime mortgages. Define the firm's return on equity as net income divided by book, or regulatory capital, where net income equals interest and noninterest revenues less interest and noninterest expenses, of which credit losses are a component. On an ROE basis, applying a 4 percent regulatory capital charge to each loan, and assuming prime and subprime net income of 0.5 and 2 percent respectively, the obvious choice would be to originate subprime loans carrying a 50 percent ROE over a prime loan with an ROE of 12.5 percent. However, if risk management offers a more appropriate performance metric adjusting for the risk of each product relying on risk capital rather than regulatory capital, a different result emerges. Assume that risk management finds that the amount of risk capital that should be deployed against prime loans is 2 percent and for subprime loans it is 10 percent based on the underlying risk characteristics of the borrower, loan, property, and other factors. Using the net income figures from before, the decision would reverse with prime loans preferred (25 percent risk-adjusted return) over subprime (20 percent risk-adjusted return). The overall profitability of the decision declines from before, presumably reflected in bonus outcomes of management.

Compounding the ambiguity effect are data and analytical limitations that can reinforce management decisions to adopt riskier products. This can occur through data and modeling errors rendering risk estimates of limited value in the view of management. Furthermore, confirmation bias and herd effects can also reinforce the ambiguity effect. In the previous example, if risk management establishes that subprime loans have significantly higher risk than previous historical performance suggests and that other competitors continue to originate such products successfully in large volumes, weak governance leading to poor incentive structures augmented by these cognitive biases can neutralize the effectiveness of risk management.

To illustrate these concepts more concretely, consider a manager with a utility function as described earlier such that changes in utility are related to outcomes determined by the incentive compensation structure of that manager, $\theta(I_t)$. Extending the discussion earlier that managers are more sensitive to reductions in compensation (as might be exemplified by low bonus payouts and option grants) than to increases, reflecting their degree of loss aversion, the relationship of interest is as follows:

$$\theta(I_t) = \left\{ \begin{array}{l} \Pi_{t+1} \text{ for } \Pi_{t+1} \geq 0 \\ \delta\, \Pi_{t+1} \text{ for } \Pi_{t+1} < 0 \end{array} \right\} \qquad 3.2$$

where Π_{t+1} represents the gain or loss in firm profitability as described in the incentive compensation contract and $\delta > 1$, reflects the manager's greater sensitivity to losses than gains generally.[4] Thus, since earlier it was shown that $\theta(I_t)$ describes management's level of utility, the above relationship indicates that a kink in management utility occurs due to a change (an increase in risk aversion) when recent losses have occurred.

For this example δ is fixed across scenarios at 1.5, with no loss of generality to the model. In addition, θ is set in three scenarios at 0.5, 1,

---

[4] In other words δ is the risk aversion parameter in the management utility model. Setting $\delta = 1$ thus implies management is neutral with regard to loss aversion.

and 1.5 which differentially affects the manager's utility. In turn, the incentive structure is dependent upon the four cognitive biases: (1) herd behavior ($\overline{H}$), (2) ambiguity bias (A), (3) the house effect ($\overline{HE}$) and (4) the strength of the firm's governance structure (G) reflecting the relative positional power of management according to the managerial power concept. The complete relationship of these cognitive biases to incentive structures can be written formally as:

$$I_t = g(\overline{H}_t, A_t \overline{HE}_t, G_t) \qquad 3.3$$

The ambiguity effect in this model focuses on the estimates of risk presented by the risk management team. One of the issues facing risk managers is their role in providing management with an assessment of uncertain outcomes. Management biases toward tangible outcomes can introduce ambiguity bias that affects the level of risk-taking by management. Furthermore, management takes previous financial performance into account (the house effect) by referencing current performance (e.g., stock price) Π_t against a historical benchmark level Π^*. Thus, cases where $\Pi^* > \Pi_t$ signify situations where past performance has been strong and vice versa. We define this relationship as $\dfrac{\Pi^*}{\Pi_t} = \overline{HE}_t$ in the model with $\overline{HE}_t > 1$ signifying cases where prior performance has been good relative to current outcomes, thus lowering the manager's loss aversion. In a similar fashion, we can relate the firm's performance in a given period to a benchmark of performance of other competitors reflected by a composite performance index of Π_t^C as follows: $\overline{H}_t = \dfrac{\Pi_t^C}{\Pi_t}$. In cases where $\overline{H}_t > 1$, the manager engages in herd behavior since it appears to management that the competition is outperforming the company. Finally, we assume that firm profitability (ROE) ranges from +50 to –50 percent over the general period of interest.

Figure 3.1 presents a summary depiction of the three scenarios across each ROE outcome and utility. It also illustrates how negative return events differentially affect the manager's utility outcomes dependent upon management cognitive biases that affect the level of loss aversion. Consider the baseline scenario where $\theta = 1$. The line segment, as in all three scenarios, is kinked at 0. This scenario illustrates that losses have a greater effect on the manager than gains. In scenario 2, where $\theta = .5$, the manager exhibits less sensitivity to losses than in scenario 1 as cognitive biases and weak corporate governance have lowered the manager's loss aversion. By contrast, scenario 3 ($\theta = 1.5$), the manager exhibits greater loss aversion than the other two scenarios. This outcome could be attributed to a combination of strong governance practices

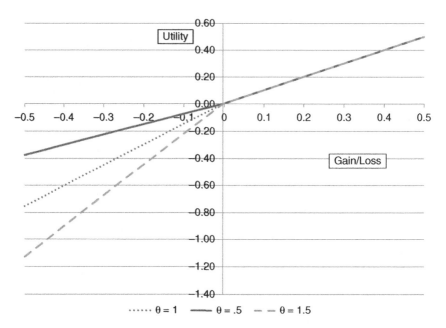

FIGURE 3.1   Cognitive Bias Effects on Management Loss Aversion

and controls that limit the manager's ability to influence their incentive compensation arrangements and supported by cognitive abilities that limit the potential for herd behavior, the house money effect, and ambiguity bias.

Having described the general relationships between governance, incentives and cognitive bias on risk-taking, it is possible to examine how these factors interact with the firm's risk management function. Of particular interest is how data and analytics enter into the process; how the stature and structure of the risk management organization can affect and be affected by management cognitive biases (particularly the case of confirmation bias in the presence of risk management views that are seemingly more conservative than historical performance); and how marginalization of risk management views can affect firm and management outcomes.

Data and analytics are used to construct forward-looking estimates of risk by the risk management team. In the model, these views enter via the ambiguity effect. Formally, this can be expressed as the following:

$$A_t = f\left(D_t|S_t, \ M_t|S_t, \ \frac{E_t}{E_{t+n}}|S_t \right) \qquad\qquad 3.4$$

Where D_t represents the quality of the firm's risk data warehouse, M_t is the quality (accuracy) of the models and analytics deployed to estimate risk, and E_t/E_{t+n} reflects the degree to which forward-looking estimates of risk (E_{t+n}) deviate from actual historical risk outcomes (E_t). This relationship is meant to capture the degree to which risk management estimates of future risk outcomes differ from previous experience. In situations where actual historical performance is significantly better than what the risk management team projects going forward, it raises the potential for ambiguity bias and, in the presence of confirmation bias and the house effect can be a reinforcing negative effect toward risk management. It is expected that both errors and deficiencies in data and models reduce the accuracy of risk estimates and thus management's confidence in those projections, further raising the ambiguity effect. Each of the variables affecting ambiguity bias is conditional on the level of stature in the risk organization, S_t. Stature is defined as the level of impact, value and perceived effectiveness of the risk team by management.

The metrics used to define performance play a critical role in shaping incentive contracts and firm and management performance outcomes. Going back to the earlier example of prime versus subprime loan originations, reliance on ROE versus a risk-adjusted metric can lead to demonstrably different outcomes. In the current model, we capture this effect in the house effect variable (HE) by expressing the general model under two alternative scenarios:

Scenario 1: Non-risk-adjusted $\quad HE_{t,NR} = \dfrac{\Pi^*_{t,NR}}{\Pi_{t,NR}}$

Scenario 2: Risk-adjusted $\quad HE_{t,R} = \dfrac{\Pi^*_{t,R}}{\Pi_{t,R}}$

With these enhancements to the model in place, some general observations regarding the effect on risk management can be offered from some simple examples based upon scenario 2 $(\theta = 0.5)$ from before. Keeping the value of the parameter δ as 1.5, we assume that the stature of the risk management team is high and that it has an endowment of data and models that are of relatively good quality such that D_t and M_t imply no change in θ due to A. Recall that scenario 2 assumed a weak governance structure, and hence poor incentive structures leading to lower loss aversion, all other things being equal. Compare that against a scenario in which the firm's data and models are poor and the stature of the group is low such that together these deficiencies further diminish θ to the level .3. Figure 3.2 compares the outcomes of these two scenarios illustrating the point that the ambiguity effect, reinforced by a lack of stature of risk management can amplify the

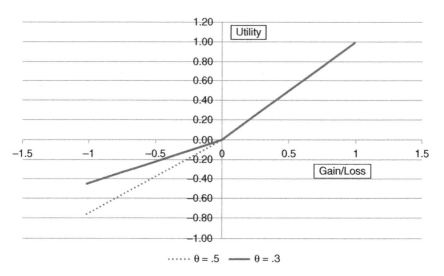

FIGURE 3.2   Effects of Weak Corporate Governance and Risk Infrastructure on Loss Aversion

business manager's risk-taking posture. Stature might be able to limit the ambiguity effect attributed to poor data and modeling outcomes, particularly if such deficiencies have been rare. A similar outcome as depicted in Figure 3.2 could occur due to the actual versus expected outcomes effect on A. That is, should $E_t/E_{t+n} < 1$, it raises A in the same relative manner as a deficiency in data and analytics, thus reinforcing and even amplifying the confirmation and house money effects.

Now consider the impact of applying different performance metrics in the manager's incentive compensation plan. We compare two scenarios: one where risk is not adjusted in the definition of performance (e.g., ROE) and the other where a risk-adjusted metric of performance (e.g., using risk capital instead of regulatory or book capital in the ROE calculation) is applied. Figure 3.3 applies the original scenario 2 ($\theta = .5$) and assumes that the manager applies an ROE metric while the risk team applies a risk-adjusted metric that is closer to actual performance but still is measured with some error.

The results from this scenario suggest that when cognitive biases exist in the presence of weak governance, the tendency would be for management to underestimate risk, which is compounded by application of metrics not adjusted for risk. Although risk-adjusted metrics are not fully accurate either, adjusting for risk results in expected outcomes that are closer to actual performance than management's views.

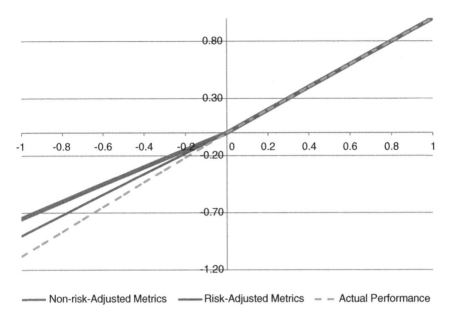

Non-risk-Adjusted Metrics ━━━ Risk-Adjusted Metrics ─ ─ Actual Performance

FIGURE 3.3 Effect of Using Risk-Adjusted Performance Metrics on Loss Aversion

PRESCRIPTIONS FOR STRONG RISK GOVERNANCE

The financial crisis of 2008–2009 taught the financial services industry and regulators a number of painful lessons regarding risk governance. Many of the largest financial institutions manifest weak corporate governance, which inhibited the effectiveness of risk management units during the boom years. In response to the crisis, Congress passed the most expansive set of financial regulatory reforms since the Great Depression. Some of these changes relate to strengthening corporate governance, improving the alignment of executive compensation and risk-taking, and outlining requirements for the largest financial institutions for board risk committees and related activities. As important as these regulatory reforms are we must realize that much of what went wrong with regard to risk governance in the years leading up to the crisis was driven by behavioral responses to economic incentives. In the end, regulation can modify some aspects of behavior, however, it is an incomplete policy prescription at best and in some cases can lead to counterproductive results.

The Federal Reserve has established a number of rules for financial institutions (U.S. banks and bank holding companies) with assets over $50 billion, publicly traded banks with assets over $10 billion and non-bank financial companies that are designated as systemically important.

The requirements call for these institutions to appoint a Chief Risk Officer charged with a number of responsibilities including establishing risk policy limits for each line of business, policies and procedures for risk governance, practices and controls, monitoring adherence with policy limits, establishing delegations of authority for risk-taking, and developing ways to integrate risk management objectives into executive compensation structures. In addition, the rules call for these firms to establish formal standalone board risk committees and set charters and composition requirements for these new structures. The rules call for the chairperson of the risk committee to be an independent board member and at least one member of the risk committee must have expertise in risk management.

These rules address a number of potential issues observed in this chapter relating to incentives and governance. Requirements for an independent chairperson of the risk committee are a way to address weak governance outcomes under the managerial power model. The existence of a risk committee where the CRO has direct access to the committee and even a reporting line to it further strengthens the position and provides some degree of "air cover" to the CRO to remain objective without fear of retaliation. Ultimately, even with such improvements, it will take time for some organizations to embrace risk management as a critical component of the firm's strategic plan.

As for SifiBank, the company suffered a near-death experience in the years following the mortgage crisis, its credit losses mounting, liquidity drying up as word spread over its problems, and its stock price crashing, leading it to raise a significant level of capital while also having to rely on some government assistance for a period. During those few years, the company saw the resignation of its iconic chairman and CEO as well as most of the senior executives who were responsible for the risky behavior that led to massive credit losses. Along the way, a number of board members also tendered their resignation, having been associated with at least tacitly supporting management's actions during the boom years.

These changes led to a fresh attitude in the way risk management was conducted, starting with the new CEO. On day one, the CEO assembled the new executive team and pronounced that risk management would henceforth be the hallmark of her tenure, and introduced the new CRO to the group. SifiBank restructured its board committees in anticipation of the Fed's new rules and established a risk committee chaired by a newly elected member who had been a CRO for a large peer institution of SifiBank for 15 years. SifiBank created a dual reporting structure for the new CRO that was direct (solid line) to the risk committee chairperson and indirect (dotted line) to the CEO for administrative purposes. These changes, along with those of several key management positions within the first year brought about significant change in the company's risk culture across the organization. The CRO was now part of the Executive Committee, not only taking part in the strategic discussions of the company, but viewed as a critical decision maker before any significant product or transaction could move forward. Furthermore, the CRO and his team were sought out by division heads in forming their business strategy and became viewed as indispensable partners to help build a long-term viable franchise.

QUESTIONS

1. What four qualities would you look for in establishing an effective risk management organization?
2. Give an example that describes what *situational risk management* means.
3. What are the advantages and disadvantages of centralized versus decentralized risk management functions?
4. What other structure might address the problems noted in question 3?
5. What are common cognitive biases that can affect senior management at a financial institution? Provide examples of each.
6. Your CEO comes to you armed with the latest earnings results of a major competitor. He shows you that they reported returns on their credit-card division that were close to 25 percent while your bank's returns on this asset class have been hovering around 15 percent. The competitor's credit-card guidelines allow borrowers to have credit scores less than 600 while your program requires a minimum of 720. What message might you provide to your CEO and what type of bias may he be reflecting?
7. Provide a conceptual model relating executive incentive compensation structure to management biases.
8. Using a diagram, illustrate how cognitive biases can affect management decisions and risk-taking.
9. Provide a conceptual model for how data and risk analytics can affect risk-taking by the firm via its impacts on cognitive bias.
10. Use a diagram to show how risk-adjusted performance metrics can affect risk-taking in the management utility model.

CHAPTER 4

Economic Capital, Risk-Adjusted Performance, and Capital Allocation

SIFIBANK'S BUSINESS PROBLEM

As described in Chapter 1, SifiBank Holding Company operates three major business lines: SifiBank, comprised of retail and commercial banking activities; SifiInvestment Bank, conducting trading, sales, and corporate finance activities; and SifiAsset Management and Brokerage. SifiBank's annual strategic planning session is underway and the heads of the three divisions along with the rest of the Executive Committee (EC) including the Chief Risk Officer, CEO, President, and CFO, among others will be reviewing last year's performance of the operating units to gain insight into where the company should deploy its capital for the coming year. A high level summary of how each unit performed is provided in Table 4.1.

SifiBank Holding Company has a required level of capital to total assets of 10 percent. This could be either a regulatory requirement or an internally determined level of capital necessary to maintain some target rating for the company; for example, AA as might be provided by an external rating agency such as S&P. The holding company allocates its capital proportionally among the three business units in this case according to its asset base. Those capital charges are shown in the fourth column of Table 4.1. Due to the fact that the investment bank represents nearly two-thirds of the entire company based on asset size, its capital charge of $65 billion is considerably higher than either of the other operating units. The company computes a return on capital for each unit defined as the ratio of net income to the business unit's capital charge. During the planning meeting, the CEO and CFO call attention to the fact that SifiInvestment Bank and SifiAsset Management & Brokerage exceeded the company hurdle rate of 15 percent. The discussion

TABLE 4.1   Summary Performance for SifiBank Operating Units

Business Unit	Assets ($ Billions)	Net Income ($ Billions)	Capital Charge ($ Billions)	Return on Capital (%)
SifiBank	250	3	25.0	12.00
SifiInvestment Bank	650	25	65.0	38.46
SifiAsset Management & Brokerage	100	2	10.0	20.00

then focused on the drivers of these business results and what the focus for the coming year should be in light of these results, as well as other information brought in to offer a broader view of market and economic trends. Over the past few years the company has increasingly shifted the focus of SifiBank Holding Company toward the investment bank at the expense of its commercial bank and asset management operations, based in part on consistently strong returns of the investment banking business compared to the other two divisions. These results have increased the stature of the head of SifiInvestment Bank, who has been known for years as the "Wizard of Wall Street."

The new CRO is asked what she thinks about the risks to the business plan if additional capital were to be deployed to SifiInvestment Bank while shrinking the other two business units. She comments that the return on capital approach does not take into consideration the underlying risk of the individual business units and therefore is an unfair comparison to make. At this point the head of SifiInvestment Bank sarcastically comments that ROE calculations have been around the industry for decades, and what exactly would the CRO propose in their place?

The CRO has prepared for this question and starts by noting that the past several years of net income for each of the divisions has been marked by abnormally good business and economic environment. Consumers, business, and governments have benefited over the past 10 years from a period of low interest rates, and strong economic and asset growth. As a result, losses in each of the divisions may present an abnormally favorable view of the performance of the businesses. The CRO is gravely concerned that applying the standard ROE approach will misallocate capital and expose the company to massive losses should economic fortunes change.

The fundamental problem the CRO states is that losses in business units not only vary across units, but the likelihood of losses can and will vary substantially, driven by a number of economic and business forces. The key to understanding the risk profile of each business unit is to generate a loss

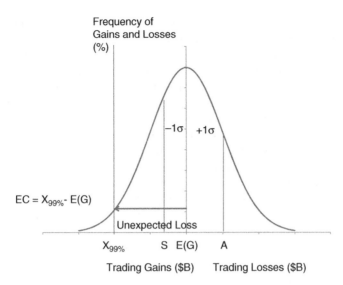

FIGURE 4.1   Illustrative Gain/Loss Distribution for SifiInvestment Bank Portfolio

distribution for each division. A starting point for this discussion is trading losses in SifiInvestment Bank. To make her point, the CRO provides the Executive Committee with Figure 4.1, which shows a hypothetical distribution of losses for SifiInvestment Bank.

The shape of this distribution is symmetrical and centered on a mean level of gains designated as $E(G)$ for expected gains and a standard deviation of X. The distribution depicts the range of possible losses that SifiInvestment Bank's trading portfolio could experience under a wide range of scenarios. The most likely, or expected outcome for the portfolio is an expected gain or loss at $E(G)$. Based on last year's results, the trading portfolio would actually realize a positive gain (denoted A) and thus reflect a better than expected outcome. However, the figure also illustrates what can happen if things go badly for SifiInvestment Bank. There is a 1 percent chance (the 99th percentile of the gain/loss distribution), for instance, that the investment bank could realize a portfolio loss of $X_{99\%}$ over a period of time such as one week. Clearly, such a move is very rare based on the investment bank's experience, but could be devastating should it occur. Note that unexpected losses are defined as losses exceeding expected loss levels. Economic capital is defined as the difference between unexpected losses designated at some percentile level (e.g., 99 percent) and expected loss.

SifiInvestment Bank's trading gains last year were reported as $45 billion against $15 billion in cost to service its debt and an additional $5 billion in operating expenses, resulting in a net income of $25 billion. However, if the bank experienced the 1 percent loss scenario, resulting in a loss of $80 billion, net income for the year would have been –$100 billion (the amount of capital for SifiBank Holding Company), and placing the entire company at risk of insolvency at that point. That would be an unacceptable outcome; however, the Board of Directors would need to consider what is a tolerable risk to the bank should a bad outcome occur. Should the Board determine that the firm on a consolidated basis cannot be exposed to portfolio trading losses of an amount that occur more than 1 percent of the time, then in the case of SifiInvestment Bank the amount of capital that should be charged against this division must be higher than the $65 billion reported in Table 4.1, given the magnitude of the impact that the division would have if this rare portfolio loss were to occur. The head of SifiInvestment Bank remains skeptical of this characterization of trading losses in his business; however, the CRO produces actual historical data over the past 25 years of the investment bank's history and finds that there have been instances of trading losses as high as $80 billion or more about 1 percent of the time. This information catches the attention of the CEO and CFO, who want to know what amount should be charged to SifiInvestment Bank and whether it is possible to assess capital for each business unit in a consistent fashion. The CRO tells them that there is and that the common denominator to establish this allocation is something called economic capital.

ECONOMIC CAPITAL AND VALUE-AT-RISK

The starting point for defining economic capital is a distribution of losses associated with a particular business unit. In the case of SifiInvestment Bank, if it is determined that the bank should hold capital to guard against a 1 percent extreme loss event, then economic capital would be defined as the difference between the 1 percent loss amount and expected loss. This definition of economic capital (sometimes referred to as risk capital), is different from other definitions such as **book capital** or **regulatory capital**. Book capital is simply the difference in the book values of assets and liabilities and thus cannot be used to determine differences in risk, as does economic capital between businesses. Regulatory capital has become much more complex over time under the Basel Agreements, which have defined a set of risk-based capital requirements for financial institutions. Some regulatory capital charges are simple ratios of specific types of capital as a percentage of assets. As a result, these capital ratios also do not appropriately account for risk as much as establish minimum capital levels for a bank. The risk-based capital standards are intended to capture differences in asset risk and

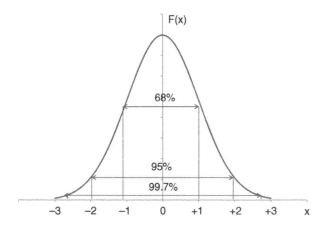

FIGURE 4.2   Standard Normal Distribution

for the largest most sophisticated banks are more aligned with an economic capital definition. Estimates of economic capital can be made leveraging standard statistical measures of mean and standard deviation characterizing the shape of a loss distribution. Since losses vary across the distribution based on their frequency of occurrence, determining what percentage of the time certain high risk events may be observed is critical to the economic capital calculation. To do this requires understanding how to relate loss events to their frequency in the distribution. Using a standard normal distribution (probability density function or pdf) a random variable x is defined as having a mean of 0 and a standard deviation of 1.

The horizontal axis in Figure 4.2 displays different outcomes for x and in this case shows the number of standard deviations away from the mean. Since the area underneath the distribution accounts for 100 percent of all outcomes, the standard deviation (σ) can be used to inform what percentage of the outcomes lie within a certain range around the mean. For the standard normal distribution, approximately 68 percent of all outcomes for x lie between + and –1 standard deviation from the mean of 0. Extending that concept for other values of σ, 95 percent of the outcomes occur within a range of +/–1.96 σ and 99.7 percent occur within +/–3σ of the mean. Conversely, only .3 percent of all outcomes for x occur beyond +/–3σ. An alternative way to describe a statistical outcome is to express it as a level of confidence. For example, we could be 99.7 percent confident of not observing a value of x that lies beyond +/–3σ. In the context of risky outcomes, only those that result in losses are of interest. In that case, if the risk were portfolio trading losses as exhibited for SifiInvestment Bank, only the left-hand tail would be of relevance. That would mean using a one-tailed test of statistical significance. If the level of confidence were set at 95 percent, for example, the number of standard deviations above the mean that cut off the worst 5 percent of losses is not 1.96, but 1.65.

Measurement of unexpected losses took a major step forward when JP Morgan developed and implemented the concept of **value-at-risk (VaR)**. Built to address fluctuations in the valuation of the bank's trading book, VaR allowed senior management to gain a consistent view of the amount of risk exposure over time. Specifically, VaR can be defined as the worst loss (or return) within a specified level of confidence and time period. For a trading book, where prices can fluctuate throughout a trading day, monitoring the fluctuations in value on a daily basis is prudent. Consequently, given the velocity of trading activity in a day, a daily version of VaR, referred to as **daily earnings-at-risk (DEAR)** leverages the basic concepts noted above adjusted for the time period of interest, in this case one day. A generalized form of VaR for market risk applications can be expressed as:

$$VaR_T = [\mu + / - N^{-1}(z)\sigma]\sqrt{T}$$ 4.1

where μ is the mean or expected level of losses or returns, $N^{-1}(z)$ is the **inverse cumulative normal distribution** for a variable z (e.g., 1.65) at a specified level of confidence (e.g., 95 percent), σ is the standard deviation of losses or returns as the case may be and T is the number of days for the time horizon of interest. A couple of points about this expression are worth noting. First, the expected level of losses or returns under a standard normal distribution is 0. More generally, the expression can be modified for normally distributed outcomes where expected values are nonzero. In addition, care must be taken when deciding which tail of the distribution to use. In the case of credit losses, the right-hand tail may be of interest and thus adding the amount $z\sigma$ would be appropriate whereas in the case of portfolio returns, or trading gains, the left-hand tail would be selected, thus deducting this amount from expected returns is correct. At the simplest level, assuming that expected losses to a $100 billion trading portfolio were $2 billion and that historical daily volatility was $1 billion, then a one-day VaR at the 99 percent level of confidence would be:[1]

$$-\$.33B = \$2B - (2.33)(\$1B)$$

In other words, there is a 1 percent chance that in a single day the portfolio could experience a loss of $.33 billion or more. Armed with this

---

[1]For ease of exposition, the factor $N^{-1}(z)$will be referred to as the **volatility adjustment factor**.

information, the management team can have a more informed view of the magnitude of the portfolio's risk to the company.

Two primary methods may be used to calculate VaR: **analytic** and **simulation**. These methods will be explored in more detail in later chapters focusing on different types of risks; however, some basic mechanics of how they work are instructive as they have broad applicability in risk measurement. Analytic VaR measurement involves using historical experience for the firm in developing estimates of mean return or loss and volatility in the VaR calculation. As will be seen in Chapter 10, defining the sensitivity in asset price movements depends on the type of asset being measured. For instance, for fixed income instruments, duration is an appropriate metric, while for equities it would be the volatility of changes in stock price. Determining what data to use in calculating analytic VaR is a critical factor in making sure the estimates accurately represent the portfolio and market conditions being analyzed.

An alternative approach is to generate a number of different scenarios for the portfolio and then look at how losses or returns are distributed. This approach allows the analyst to produce a wide variety of outcomes that can be measured with a certain level of statistical reliability. Monte Carlo simulation techniques have become prevalent in risk management over the years with advances in computing power and data storage. However, such techniques are not without their own issues. Selection of an approach for VaR measurement depends on a number of factors, including the complexity of the portfolio, resources available for the analysis, and data, among others. Use of VaR techniques to measure a wide range of risks has increased over time. Once relegated to understanding market risk of trading portfolios, VaR techniques are increasingly used to measure credit, interest rate, liquidity and even operational risk. While the type of risk differs, the application of statistical principles to VaR measurement is consistent across methods.

Underlying these techniques is the rigid assumption that loss and return distributions are normally distributed. As will be described in more detail in later chapters, oftentimes distributions are found to be nonnormal. Examples include lognormally shaped loss distributions used in measuring credit risk or Poisson distributions used to measure operational losses.[2] The lack of normality may not preclude the use of VaR techniques in these cases, but care must be taken in appreciating the underlying assumptions made in using these models. Further, and more challenging for the risk analyst,

---

[2] Note that the logarithm of a random variable associated with a lognormal distribution is normally distributed.

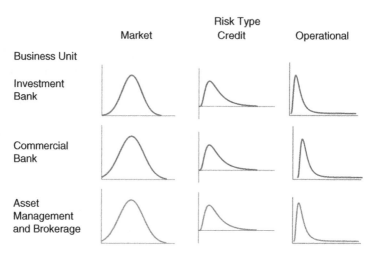

FIGURE 4.3   SifiBank Economic Capital Aggregation by Business Unit and Risk Type

is the need to aggregate estimates of economic capital as it may be derived from VaR models across risk types. If economic capital is the yardstick by which risk is measured in a company, then it must eventually be aggregated across business units and across risks in a consistent way in order to permit management to determine how to optimize the allocation of capital within the organization.

Conceptually, the problem for the enterprise risk group is depicted as in Figure 4.3. The risk profile of each business unit will generate a different set of loss or return distributions, as will be the case for each risk type. The key is understanding the correlations across risk types and business units. Estimating such correlations may be difficult due to data and other limitations, however, diversification benefits may reduce the overall risk to the company in the same way that a portfolio comprised of many stocks reduces risk.

At the simplest level, SifiBank could add up the economic capital estimates across risks and business units without any regard for correlations between risk types. Doing so results in the most conservative estimate of economic capital as it precludes any reduction in economic capital owing to less than perfect correlation among risk types. Since it is unlikely that the distributions across risk types are all normal, standard portfolio theory approaches to estimating an aggregate standard deviation for the institution will result in measurement error. An alternative approach to using the standard deviation for each risk and business unit distribution would be to replace it with the economic capital estimate. The bank's total economic capital thus might be defined as:

$$EC_{bank} = \sqrt{\sum_{i=1}^{n}\sum_{j=1}^{m} EC_{ij}EC_{ji}\rho_{ij}} \qquad 4.2$$

Where EC_{ij} is economic capital for the ith business unit and the jth risk type (defined for the ith unit as $VaR_i - \mu_i$) where μ_i is expected loss and ρ_{ij} is the correlation between business units and risk types. Even this approach may wind up generating some error, if not due to difficulties in developing reasonable correlations, then due to underlying mismeasurement of the statistical relationship between distributions that accompanies this approach. Improvement in the accuracy of aggregate economic capital when distributions are nonnormal requires more advanced statistical methods such as **copulas**.

Copula methods provide the analyst with an approach that combines different variables together such as different sets of losses from such risk types as credit or operational risk (using a multivariate probability distribution) that might not have normal distributions. If the distributions were both normally distributed we could apply the standard correlation methods presumed under a bivariate normal distribution. In the event, however, that one or both of the distributions are not normally distributed, then copulas can provide a solution to this problem. Copulas are defined by distributions such as the Gaussian or Student $-t$ that describe the dependence of a set of random variables.

Conceptually, a copula method works as follows. A variable X that is not normally distributed (e.g., credit losses that may be lognormally distributed) is mapped into another variable Y that has a standard normal distribution as depicted in Figure 4.4. That mapping effectively requires that the percentiles of the X distribution be mapped into the corresponding percentile in the standard normal distribution for Y using the inverse cumulative distribution $N^{-1}(F(X))$, where $F(X)$ is the underlying distribution for variable X. In other words, the 5 percent worst losses of the lognormal credit loss distribution are mapped using the copula method into a corresponding worst 5 percent of the standard normal distribution. The process could be repeated for a second variable K that is also not normally distributed (e.g., operational losses that are distributed according to a Poisson distribution) and it would be mapped into a corresponding variable Z that follows a standard normal distribution. Once completed, the correlation between variables Y and Z can be computed and applied in calculating aggregate economic capital based on standard portfolio volatility methods described above.

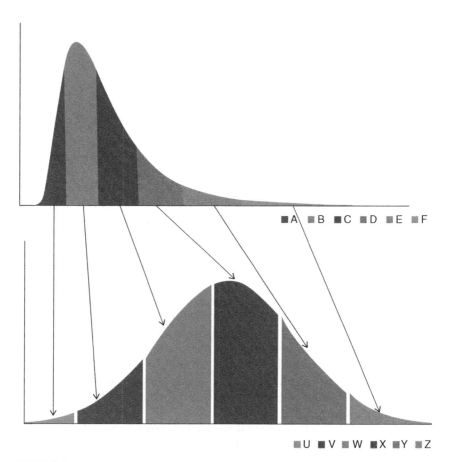

FIGURE 4.4 Conceptual Mapping of a Non-Normally Distributed Variable X to a Standard Normally Distributed Variable Y

To make the copula method more concrete, suppose SifiBank were interested in aggregating the economic capital for credit and operational risk in the SifiMortgage business. Credit losses are lognormally distributed while operational losses follow a Poisson distribution. Credit losses are defined by the variable C and operational losses by the variable O. The functions L_C and P_O describe the lognormal (L_C) and Poisson (P_O) distributions of each loss variable. For operational and credit losses the percentiles associated with different loss outcomes are depicted in Table 4.2 in columns 2 and 3. Columns 4 and 5 take the percentile outcomes for operational and credit losses, respectively, and convert them using the inverse of the standard normal distribution into the comparable part of the standard normal distribution.

TABLE 4.2 Illustrative Use of Copula Method for Aggregating Credit and Operational Losses for SifiMortgage

Credit Loss ($M)	Percentile	Standard Normal Mapping	Operational Loss ($M)	Percentile	Standard Normal Mapping
347	0.05	−1.65	223	0.03	−1.88
482	0.10	−1.28	521	0.08	−1.40
697	0.20	−0.84	912	0.17	−0.95
894	0.30	−0.52	1277	0.30	−0.52
1092	0.40	−0.25	1490	0.45	−0.13
1305	0.50	0	1523	0.60	0.25
1544	0.60	0.25	1303	0.73	0.61
1830	0.70	0.52	1014	0.83	0.95
2205	0.80	0.84	710	0.90	1.28
2790	0.90	1.28	452	0.95	1.65
3324	0.95	1.65	263	0.97	1.88

These results enable the risk manager to "join" the two distributions in a manner that yields the joint probability distribution between credit and operational losses. To do this, one could use the bivariate cumulative normal distribution described as:

$$N_2 = (C, O, \rho_{C,O}) = \frac{1}{2\pi\sqrt{1 - \rho_{C,O}^2}} \iint e^{\left[\frac{-(c^2 - 2\rho_{C,O}CO + O^2)}{2(1 - \rho_{C,O})^2} \right]} dCdO \qquad 4.3$$

where $\rho_{C,O}$ represents the correlation between credit and operational losses. The implementation of Equation 4.3 can be accomplished via approximation methods (which is beyond the scope of this book). Using such a methodology, given the distributions of C and O, one could solve for the correlation, $\rho_{C,O}$ in Equation 4.3. Table 4.2 shows the mapping of credit and operational losses from their respective distributions to the standard normal distribution. Using an approximation method for computing the bivariate normal distribution, the associated probabilities for an outcome where credit and operational losses are less than $1 billion for various correlation assumptions are shown in Table 4.3.

TABLE 4.3 Alternative Joint Probabilities in Credit and Operational Losses

Correlation	Joint Probability
−1	0
−0.5	0.076
0	0.147
0.5	0.219
1	0.302

STRESS TESTING AND SCENARIO ANALYSIS

Where analytic and simulation-based methods can be used to provide the risk analyst insight with a specified level of confidence for an estimate of economic capital defined by VaR less expected loss, other methods to estimate adverse or extreme scenarios have an important role in understanding the firm's ability to withstand such events. **Stress testing** and **scenario analysis** rely more on historical experience to drive the analysis. Scenario analysis, of which stress testing could be considered a subset, requires the analyst to first identify key outcomes of interest to study. It could be credit losses in the consumer portfolio, projections of firm or business unit net income, effects on the value of the trading portfolio due to changes in interest rates, loan loss reserves, or other outcomes tied to the financial performance of the company. **Stress testing** concentrates on assessing the impact of extreme events on outcome variables on- and off-balance sheet. Unlike simulation-based approaches used in determining economic capital, stress testing focuses on a few scenarios of interest. Critical to the analysis is identifying a set of stress factors that directly or indirectly affect the outcome variables. These are usually developed empirically and are included in risk models along with borrower, loan, and other risk attributes of interest. As a result, what may be important to one portfolio, business, or risk type may only have an indirect effect on another. Consider, for example, the risk analysts at SifiMortgage. Having experienced the mortgage crisis of 2008–2009 and suffered massive credit losses, management has decided that it needs to conduct a periodic stress test of mortgage credit losses in its $100 billion loan portfolio. Credit losses are defined by the product of the default rate and loss severity rate once a loan enters default. The risk team has estimated statistical models of default and severity using historical loan level data over the past 10 years, using a number of borrower, loan, property, and risk factors to explain default and loss severity under different time periods. In addition, the team has determined that house price appreciation rates (HPA) are a key driver in determining whether a borrower will eventually default on their loan and what percentage of the loan will be received by SifiMortgage should a loan default. A generalized representation of how HPA affects both variables is shown in Figure 4.5. On average annual national HPA rates have historically been 2–3 percent on a nominal basis. This is shown by the vertical dotted line denoted "Average." The corresponding default and severity rates for the average HPA can be observed from the figure and when combined illustrate the amount of credit losses expected to occur over time. Losses during the

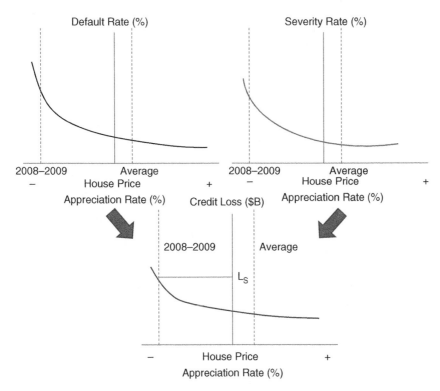

FIGURE 4.5   SifiMortgage Credit Loss Stress Test Relationships

2008–2009 period were the worst on record for the bank and while an extremely unlikely event, it serves as the basis for SifiMortgage's stress test. HPA rates during this actual event fell to 33 percent and are shown as the default and severity rate graphs. Clearly both default rates accelerate as HPA declines and severity rates also exhibit a negative relationship with HPA. This is due to the fact that a reduction in home prices reduces the incentive for the borrower to pay back the loan and if the borrower defaults, the loss severity will be greater since the lender will get back less after selling the home. The combined effect on credit losses shows up as L_S on the bottom graph and are significantly higher than under an average or even worse than average scenario.

In consultation with senior management and with review by the board, a uniform set of stress factors should be developed and applied across the enterprise for stress testing analysis. For example, if SifiMortgage applies a –33 percent house price appreciation scenario to its portfolio, then SifiInvestment Bank should be applying the same HPA scenario to its mortgage securities portfolio. Inconsistencies in the application on scenarios can provide a distorted and misinformed view of potential risks in the company.

Determining the time period of interest over which the stress test is performed is an important decision in stress testing. Stress tests can be developed as static one-time shocks to the bank, or they can be applied over a period of time. For example, SifiMortgage might analyze the one-time effect of an immediate drop in home prices by 33 percent. Care must be taken in developing plausible scenarios in order to avoid implementing tests that have little credibility within and outside the organization. In the above example, an instantaneous drop in home prices of 33 percent may be unrealistic given that changes in home prices occur over months. A more appropriate stress test would be to examine the monthly or quarterly changes in home prices that led to a cumulative decline of 33 percent during the crisis and apply that house price appreciation series to the model. Applying the stress factors in this way may introduce additional complexity to the analysis but would also improve the realism of the test.

Another consideration in stress testing is performing sensitivity analysis on key factors. For example, understanding the differential effect of a range of outcomes may be useful to management and no single economic event may fully represent an extreme scenario for the firm. In the case of SifiMortgage, since the bank holds a large portfolio of mortgages on its balance sheet, it is exposed to both credit and interest rate risk. Specific to mortgages, SifiMortgage is subject to the risk that borrowers decide to prepay their mortgages early if market interest rates drop sufficiently compared to their note rate. When this occurs, the value of the mortgages held by Sifi-Mortgage may decline, offsetting the component of the mortgage that acts

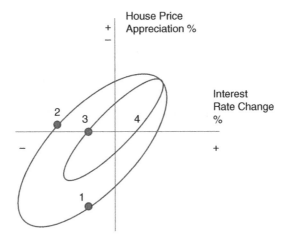

FIGURE 4.6 Alternative Stress Tests for SifiMortgage

like a bond and thus should increase in value as rates drop. In this case, Sifi-Mortgage may consider conducting a range of interest rate and house price appreciation scenarios in combination and perhaps including variables such as unemployment rate and other macroeconomic factors in the analysis. Figure 4.6 illustrates how the bank might think about constructing a set of mortgage stress scenarios across house price and interest rate combinations. Although a stress test is designed to reflect a specific set of stress factors such as house price appreciation rates or interest rate changes, it may be possible for management to gauge the approximate likelihood of its occurrence. The ellipses in Figure 4.6 illustrate a conceptual framework for thinking about the relative likelihood of various scenarios. This might be drawn from actual experience or expert judgment and while not scientific in design may at least help management set some general context for how important each scenario may be. Ellipses closer to the center, for example, would represent events with greater likelihood of occurring, since movements in variables from current levels are smaller. Stress test number 1 could represent a severe drop in home prices coupled with a moderate drop in interest rates as could be reflected in a severe recession similar to that experienced during the financial crisis. Scenario 2, which has the same approximate likelihood, may reflect another severe event but this time interest rates plummet while home price appreciation remains slightly positive.

It is likely in the case of SifiMortgage that prepayment and credit risks have somewhat offsetting effects; however, until the analysis is conducted the extent of any offset is hard to discern. Scenarios 3 and 4 represent more likely outcomes and perhaps softer stress events. An important aspect of stress testing is that while events 1 and 2 may have much larger impacts on SifiMortgage's portfolio, they are nevertheless less likely outcomes. Understanding how the portfolio holds up under more likely but less severe events is also important as it might have business implications for the firm over time.

Best practice risk management would develop both stress testing and probabilistic-based approaches to assess extreme events since each brings its own benefits. While a VaR type of analysis provides management with an ability to estimate the likelihood of extreme events, there are least two issues that limit full reliance on such results. First, and as will be discussed in more detail in later chapters, VaR estimates may not be able to accurately assess extreme events that have not been observed before. The classic example is the 2008–2009 financial crisis. Such an event had not been observed in the data on which VaR models were developed and so in many cases these models were susceptible to fat-tailed risk. **Fat-tailed risk** produces errors in measuring extreme results by underestimating the likelihood of occurrence of such outcomes and their magnitude.

A second aspect of VaR is that because it represents a probabilistic outcome, it is sometimes difficult for management to understand what sort of market and economic events have to occur to generate that event. Statements such as "The greatest amount of losses that could occur over the next year is $10 billion with a 99.7 percent level of confidence" are difficult to relate to a specific type of event. That is where a stress test can complement such analysis to apply specific event stress factors to estimating losses and net income effects.

Another approach at stress testing attempts to map risk ratings to outcomes. Suppose SifiMortgage was interested in providing management with a relative risk rating associated with stress outcomes on its portfolio. One way to do this would be to compare loss outcomes under the stress scenarios with **loss subordination** levels produced by external ratings models.[3] To illustrate the concept, consider Figure 4.7. The risk team takes the loss estimates from the four scenarios and compares them against loss levels associated with rated tranches of comparable quality. An expected level, or baseline loss level is represented to provide management with an idea of how each of the stress scenarios stacks up against a normal level of losses. From this, the risk team may be able to communicate to management how certain events

---

[3] Loss subordination will be examined more closely in the credit hedging chapter, however, it describes the level of losses associated to be borne sequentially by junior (subordinate) holders of credit risk over those in a more senior position.

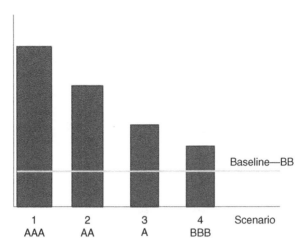

FIGURE 4.7   SifiMortgage Stress Tests Mapped to External Risk Ratings

might be viewed externally as well as based on internal VaR models. For example, if the scenario 1 stress test is mapped (i.e., found to be comparable in loss outcome) to a AAA outcome (associated with a .3 percent likelihood), it might be characterized as having a likelihood of .3 percent consistent with AAA-type events. These relationships may not be precise given a number of alignment issues between stress tests and external rating methodologies, but can be useful constructs in portraying such events.

Another form of stress test that has potential use is the **reverse stress test**. Instead of running a set of specific stress factors against a portfolio and seeing what losses are generated, a reverse stress test seeks to understand the breakpoints for the firm. In other words, it attempts to understand what conditions would place the firm at the brink of insolvency. There are a number of ways banks could attempt to conduct a reverse stress test, but one way that leverages distribution-based approaches at estimating economic capital, as described earlier, provides insights into how this may be performed. A conceptual example is depicted in Figure 4.8.

Suppose a number of factors are built into the economic capital models for each of the major risks: credit, market, and operational. Some examples are shown to the left of these loss distributions. Each could be empirically estimated along with other factors deemed significant in affecting these losses. Using a copula methodology, SifiMortgage generates an aggregated distribution of losses for the business unit and sets a 99 percent VaR confidence interval to define economic capital. Losses in the right-hand tail would be those that technically would result in the business unit having exceeded their

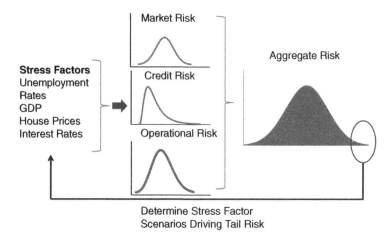

FIGURE 4.8   Reverse Stress Testing Example Leveraging Economic Capital Analysis

capital buffer. Exploring outcomes in this tail further can provide management with an understanding of what stress factors would need to be in order to generate losses of such magnitude as to exceed the level of economic capital of the business unit. Figure 4.9 provides more detail on the results of SifiMortgage's reverse stress test. The top figure depicts the tail of the loss distribution and three of the scenarios (A, B, and C) lying to the right of the economic capital level are selected for further study of extreme loss outcomes. Since the risk team used a Monte Carlo simulation-based methodology to generate the three loss distributions, it examines loss paths that align with the aggregated loss distribution for A, B, and C. Loss amounts are then investigated further individually to determine what stress factor settings have to be in order to generate losses of the magnitude that, when aggregated across risks, lead to the level of losses shown in A, B, and C. Reverse stress testing is not meant to replace existing stress tests or economic capital analysis but is useful in deepening management's understanding of drivers of extreme outcomes.

The financial crisis heightened risk managers' awareness of the importance of systemic risk to understanding loss outcomes for an institution. As liquidity dried up and asset prices tumbled, contagion effects amplified the risks for banking that would otherwise be missing from their stress testing. That is, incorporating potential effects due to widespread market disruption should be a consideration in building robust stress test models. In that case assumptions regarding counterparties, access to financing, reputational issues, and other concerns should be built into the framework. In some cases

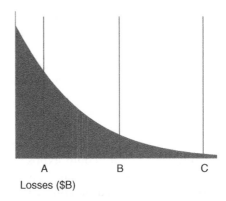

Stress Factor	A	B	C
Unemployment Rate (%)	9.5	10.6	12.5
GDP (%)	−2.0	−3.5	−5.2
Home Price Change (%)	−20.5	−26.3	−36.8
Interest Rate (%) (10-yr Treasury)	2.7	2.3	1.5

FIGURE 4.9   SifiMortgage Reverse Stress Test Outcomes

empirical estimates could be made on some systemic risk factors but the application of judgmentally based risk multipliers are also plausible adjustments to the standard stress testing results.

Proactive stress testing has other advantages for risk managers. Since the crisis, the Federal Reserve Board and other regulators across the globe have imposed stress testing on bank holding companies and subsidiaries to lend transparency into the examination of how well banks may be able to withstand various economic and market shocks. The Federal Reserve Board, for example, requires 18 large bank holding companies to submit to an annual stress test, called the **Comprehensive Capital Analysis and Review** (**CCAR**). The Federal Reserve Board establishes a severely adverse scenario described by a number of macroeconomic factor outcomes over a specified period of time. The Fed requires banks to run these through their own models while also running each bank's data submission through a set of Fed-developed models. Stress testing at the bank level is being conducted at agencies such as the Office of the Comptroller of the Currency (OCC).

Needless to say, stress testing has become a mainstay of bank regulators and expectations are that well-managed risk organizations will have to follow suit with their own tests.

The results from stress testing should be used to guide management in making strategic decisions about the business activity and risk-taking posture of the organization. Stress outcomes can reveal areas requiring management attention—for example, an overconcentration of risk in a single counterparty that under a severe stress scenario may default, imposing significant losses on the bank; or exposures to certain markets such as residential real estate could expose the firm to excessive credit losses under a severe downturn. Management decisions are often made within the context of expected outcomes and over a relatively short period of time. Having the ability to gauge risk on a consolidated basis and under extreme circumstances can now be leveraged in strategic planning discussions.

RISK-ADJUSTED PERFORMANCE MEASUREMENT

Armed with estimates of economic capital, SifiBank is in a much better position to ascertain its risk-adjusted returns across its business units. As presented earlier in this chapter, the bank faces having to determine how best to allocate its scarce capital to their best use. But what does best use really mean? A more realistic measure of a business unit's performance is when its profitability, or net income, is adjusted for the amount of risk capital it uses based on its underlying risk profile. Once such measure is referred to as **risk-adjusted return on capital**, or RaRoC, where capital is defined as economic capital. This can be defined simply as:

$$RaRoC = \frac{NI}{EC} \geq HR \qquad\qquad 4.4$$

$$NI = R - D - O - EL$$

where NI is net income, R represents revenues, D is debt costs, O is operating expense, EL is expected loss, EC is economic capital, and HR is the bank's hurdle rate. A value for RaRoC that meets or exceeds the target return HR is a viable project. An alternative way of expressing risk-adjusted performance is with the **shareholder value-added (SVA)** metric. It basically modifies RaRoC by adjusting for the cost of capital using the HR as the unit measure of capital cost. It may be formally defined as:

$$SVA = NI - HR * EC \geq 0 \qquad\qquad 4.5$$

TABLE 4.4 Economic Capital Impact on SifiBank Holding Company Returns

Business Unit	Assets ($Billions)	Net Income ($Billions)	Capital Charge ($Billions)	Return on Capital (%)	Economic Capital	RaRoC	SVA
SifiBank	250	3	25.0	12.00	17.4	17.24%	0.39
SifiInvestment Bank	650	25	65.0	38.46	226.2	11.05%	−8.93
SifiAsset Management & Brokerage	100	2	10.0	20.00	23.2	8.62%	−1.48

Expressed in this way, a business unit adds shareholder value whenever SVA is positive and destroys shareholder value when it is negative. To gain a better understanding of how these risk-adjusted metrics differ from a traditional ROE measure, we need to first consider how SifiBank should allocate its economic capital across its three business divisions.

SifiBank Holding Company has conducted its assessment of economic capital across each business unit according to the earlier discussion in this chapter aggregating across credit, market and operational risk with the estimates shown in Table 4.4. SifiBank Holding Company has a target rate of return of 15 percent. Applying the above formulas for RaRoC and SVA, the returns to each business unit look very different from the simple ROE calculations using required capital in the denominator of the ROE. In this case, only SifiBank has a risk-adjusted return that exceeds the hurdle rate (and also has a positive SVA). This could lead to a very different strategic conversation at the bank. Based on this information the Investment Bank and Asset Management & Brokerage units are a net drag on the holding company and over time if this persisted might entail significant changes in the structure and operating focus of the holding company. For example, it could lead to these two business units being spun off from the holding company, leaving only SifiBank as the lone operating division. This may be an extreme outcome; however, it illustrates the importance of viewing the performance of each business unit on a risk-adjusted basis. As useful as this may be, it still ignores potential risk diversification effects that may exist between business units. Drawing from portfolio theory, the VaR for SifiBank Holding Company can be defined as the following:

$$VaR_P = \sqrt{\sum_{i=1}^{3} VaR^2_i + \sum_{i=1}^{3}\sum_{j=1}^{3} 2VaR_i VaR_j \rho_{ij}} \qquad 4.6$$

TABLE 4.5   Calculations for SifiBank Holding Company VaR

Business Unit	Unit VaR	Correlation		
		SB	SIB	SAMB
SifiBank	0.070	1	0.25	0.1
SifiInvestment Bank	0.348	0.25	1	0.4
SifiAsset Management & Brokerage	0.232	0.1	0.4	1
Business Unit		Covariances		
		SB	SIB	SAMB
	Weight	0.25	0.65	0.1
SifiBank	0.25	0.005	0.006	0.002
SifiInvestment Bank	0.65	0.006	0.12	0.006
SifiAsset Managment & Brokerage	0.1	0.002	0.032	0.054
Weighted Sum		0.001	0.054	0.001

where ρ_{ij} is the correlation coefficient between business unit i and j.[4] The correlation coefficient can also be used to define the covariance between any two business units as follows:

$$\sigma_{ij} = \rho_{ij}\sigma_i\sigma_j \qquad 4.7$$

where σ_i is the standard deviation of business unit i.

Applying formula 4.6 to SifiBank Holding Company's business units based on the correlation structure among the divisions results in a portfolio at 99 percent VaR of approximately $238 billion. Assuming expected losses are zero for ease of exposition, this would also mean that economic capital is likewise $238 billion. Of course, in general economic capital would be computed as VaR less expected loss. This estimate is obtained by taking the unit VaR for each division (defined as the standard deviation of each division multiplied by 2.33), aggregating across the weighted sums for each division at the bottom of Table 4.5, taking the square root of that result and multiplying it by the portfolio value of $1 trillion.

---

[4] To be more accurate, the correlations might actually exist among different risk types across units and the risk analyst would thus need to compute a matrix of correlations for each combination of risk (i.e., credit, market, operational) and business unit. While this adds to the complexity of the problem, the above example preserves the conceptual portfolio VaR problem.

The fact that the correlations between business units are not perfect (i.e., $\rho = 1$) suggests that there is a risk diversification benefit resulting in lower VaR than in that case. To see this, consider Table 4.6, which preserves the approach as in Table 4.5 to calculate portfolio VaR results in an approximately $267 billion VaR amount, or a $29 billion higher VaR under perfect correlation. When correlations are perfect, the formula for portfolio VaR collapses to the following:

$$VaR_P = \sum_{i=1}^{3} w_i VaR_i \qquad 4.8$$

or, the portfolio's VaR is equal to the weighted average of the business unit VaRs. To confirm this is the case for SifiBank Holding Company (SBHC), applying the weights and unit VaRs above results in:

$267\text{ billion} = (\$250\text{ billion} * .07) + (\$650\text{ billion} * .348) + (\$100\text{ billion} * .232)$

In this example, ignoring the effects of diversification, the allocation of $267 billion in capital would be $17.5 billion ($250B * .07) for SifiBank (SB), $226 billion ($650B * .348) for SifiInvestment Bank (SIB), and $23.2 billion ($100B * .232) for SifiAsset Management & Brokerage (SAMB). At this point the question becomes, how does the holding company allocate

TABLE 4.6 SifiBank Holding Company VaR Assuming Perfect Correlation

| Business Unit | Unit VaR | Correlation | | |
		SB	SIB	SAMB
SifiBank	0.070	1	1	1
SifiInvestment Bank	0.348	1	1	1
SifiAsset Managment & Brokerage	0.232	1	1	1

| Business Unit | | Covariances | | |
		SB	SIB	SAMB
	Weight	0.25	0.65	0.1
SifiBank	0.25	0.005	0.024	0.016
SifiInvestment Bank	0.65	0.024	0.0121	0.081
SifiAsset Management & Brokerage	0.1	0.016	0.081	0.054
Weighted Sum		0.005	0.060	0.006

the capital benefit owing to diversification of $29 billion across the business units fairly? The easiest approach one could take would be to compute the ratios of each division's economic capital to the total capital on an undiversified basis. For example, SifiBank would have a ratio of ($17.5 billion/$267 billion) or 6.5 percent. Applying this ratio to the diversified estimate of economic capital of approximately $238 billion would imply that SifiBank would be allocated $15.6 billion of that amount. But this approach does not take into account the marginal effect on bank economic capital of each division.

A more robust approach requires leveraging a key economic assumption of the SifiBank portfolio referred to as **linear homogeneity**. According to **Euler's Theorem**, the portfolio VaR for SifiBank Holding Company will change by an amount λVaR_P when changes in the size of each business unit exposure (E_i) increase by an amount λ. It can be shown then that the portfolio VaR is the sum of the individual business unit VaRs as follows:

$$VaR_{SBHC} = VaR_{SB} + VaR_{SIB} + VaR_{SAMB} = \frac{\partial VaR_{SBHC}}{\partial E_{SB}} + \frac{\partial VaR_{SBHC}}{\partial E_{SIB}} + \frac{\partial VaR_{SBHC}}{\partial E_{SAMB}}$$

$$4.9$$

where E_i represents the portfolio value in dollars of the ith business unit. Using this relationship, SifiBank Holding Company risk analysts need to compute the sensitivity of the change in VaR at the holding company level for an x percent change in each business unit's exposure. Suppose that changes in SBHC's total VaR for a 1 percent increase in exposures for each business unit holding the other two constant at the same exposure levels are as shown in the third column of Table 4.7. Each of the resulting SBHC VaR results (designated by $\Delta VaR_{SBHC}^{1\%}$) is higher than the original VaR amount of $237.86 billion. The difference between the new level of economic capital and the original level of $238 billion expressed as a ratio to the 1 percent

TABLE 4.7 Capital Allocation for SifiBank Holding Company

Business Unit	Unit VaR	$\Delta VaR^{1\%}{}_{SBHC}$	VaR_P	Capital Allocation $(\Delta VaR^{1\%}{}_{SBHC} - VaR_P)/\Delta E_i$
SifiBank	17.4	238.750	237.855	89.484
SifiInvestment Bank	226.2	238.820	237.855	96.484
SifiAsset Management & Brokerage	23.2	238.375	237.855	51.984
Sum of Unit VaRs	266.8			237.951

TABLE 4.8   Comparison of Absolute and Marginal Capital Allocation Methods

	Absolute Level Method	Marginal Contribution Method
SifiBank	15.5	9.5
SifiInvestment Bank	201.7	134.5
SIM Billion	20.7	94.5
	237.9	238.5

movement in exposure for each division times 100 percent defines the allocation of economic capital and is shown in the last column of Table 4.7.[5] The total VaR is slightly higher than the total portfolio VaR due to the approximation used to derive the incremental impact on portfolio VaR from a 1 percent increase in the exposure of each division. But comparing this marginal method to the absolute method in Table 4.8 shows a distinct difference in how capital is allocated. For example, for SifiBank, the marginal capital allocation method results in a lower assignment of economic capital ($9.5 billion versus $15.5 billion) due to the smaller incremental effect on capital from a 1 percent increase in SifiBank exposure. Contrast that with SIMB that sees a relatively larger allocation under the marginal contribution method, reflecting its incremental risk.

RISK-ADJUSTED PERFORMANCE OPTIMIZATION

Taking the calculations for portfolio VaR one step further, the business head of the equity trading department of SifiInvestment Bank (SIBTD) wants to understand how to better optimize the firm's allocation of capital across its 10 traders based on their RaRoC and economic capital assignments using VaR as the estimate for economic capital for this exercise in keeping with the earlier discussion. Currently SIBTD divides its $100 billion exposure equally across traders so that each trader accounts for 10 percent of the SIB portfolio. The weighted average RaRoC on this portfolio is 18.28 percent with a calculated portfolio VaR of $6.7 billion. However, the head of this unit has been informed by the CFO that the target return for each business unit with few exceptions will be 20 percent and that units that do not meet

---

[5] The calculation takes the 1 percent increase and simply multiplies it by 100 to capture the full effect of the increase on each division.

TABLE 4.9　SIBTD Optimization Inputs

			Correlation Matrix								
Trader	RaRoC	Unit VaR	1	2	3	4	5	6	7	8	9	10
1	0.250	0.151	1.00	0.50	0.65	0.34	0.25	0.50	0.67	0.23	0.32	0.77
2	0.225	0.139	0.50	1.00	0.12	0.56	0.45	0.62	-0.33	0.56	0.32	0.34
3	0.200	0.116	0.65	0.12	1.00	0.26	0.37	0.50	0.45	0.48	0.29	0.36
4	0.193	0.139	0.34	0.56	0.26	1.00	0.45	0.53	-0.40	0.40	0.67	0.48
5	0.210	0.097	0.25	0.45	0.37	0.45	1.00	0.43	0.27	-0.30	0.27	0.39
6	0.185	0.074	0.50	0.62	0.50	0.53	0.43	1.00	0.66	0.68	0.56	-0.43
7	0.180	0.070	0.67	-0.33	0.45	-0.40	0.27	0.66	1.00	0.15	0.23	0.46
8	0.145	0.093	0.23	0.56	0.48	0.40	-0.30	0.68	0.15	1.00	0.56	0.45
9	0.140	0.070	0.32	0.32	0.29	0.48	0.27	0.56	0.23	0.56	1.00	0.25
10	0.100	0.056	0.77	0.34	0.36	0.29	0.39	-0.43	0.46	0.45	0.25	1.00

these objectives will find their capital allocations reduced in the future. As a result, the head of SIBTD seeks out the risk team for the holding company and asks that an optimization model be built using their estimates of risk-adjusted returns and VaR (in this example equivalent to economic capital as expected losses in the portfolio are zero). Table 4.9 displays the key inputs for this exercise.

The optimization model seeks to minimize the amount of VaR (economic capital) allocated to SIBTD subject to meeting a weighted average RaRoC of 20 percent. In addition, it is assumed that all the weights for the 10 traders must sum to 100 percent and must lie between 0 and 100 percent of the SIBTD portfolio exposure. Formally, this can be represented as follows:

$$MIN$$
$$VaR_{SIBTD}$$
$$s.t.$$
$$RaRoC \geq 20\%$$
$$\sum_{i=1}^{10} w_i = 1$$
$$0 \leq w_i \leq 1$$

4.10

TABLE 4.10 SIBTD Trader Performance Statistics

Trader	Exposure ($B)	NI ($M)	ROE	RaRoC
1	4.67	150	32.10	25
2	9.35	225	24.08	23
3	14.02	280	19.97	20
4	6.54	175	26.75	19
5	20.56	295	14.35	21
6	8.41	130	15.46	19
7	11.21	145	12.93	18
8	7.48	178	23.81	15
9	5.61	180	32.10	14
10	12.15	130	10.70	10
	100.00	1,888		

Exposures, net income, ROE, and RaRoC estimates for each trader are found in Table 4.10. Book capital for SIBTD is 10 percent of the unit's total exposure, or $10 billion. The ROEs for each trader reflect an allocation of capital to each trader that is the ratio of their exposure to SIBTD total exposure times SIBTD total capital. Against a return target of 20 percent, traders 1, 2, 4, 8, and 9 meet the company's objectives. However, on a risk-adjusted basis, that changes.

Once estimates of trader RaRoC, VaR (economic capital), and correlations are put into the optimization model, a very different perspective on trading performance is observed. The weighted covariance matrix is shown in Table 4.11 along with the optimized weights for each trader. Based on these results, the optimal VaR for SIBTD is $5.94 billion and it has a weighted RaRoC of 20 percent. Clearly this is a better overall outcome than the current performance ($6.7 billion) based on equal exposures across traders. In fact, according to the optimal portfolio, over 80 percent of SIBTD's portfolio should be allocated to traders 2 and 7. Moreover, the results suggest that the books for four traders would be closed altogether. Since these are model-based results, it would be unlikely that such action would be taken quickly; nevertheless it allows management to understand where weak points in their business lie and can facilitate discussions on how to make changes that can move performance in a better direction.

One question that emerges from such analysis is what happens if a key assumption is changed such as the target RaRoC? Keeping everything else

TABLE 4.11 SIBTD Optimal Portfolio Returns and VaR

Weight	Trader	Covariance Matrix									
		0.014	0.313	0.023	0.018	0.142	0.000	0.490	0.000	0.000	0.000
0.014	1	0.0227	0.0105	0.0114	0.0071	0.0037	0.0056	0.0070	0.0032	0.0034	0.0065
0.313	2	0.0105	0.0194	0.0019	0.0109	0.0061	0.0064	-0.0032	0.0072	0.0031	0.0026
0.023	3	0.0114	0.0019	0.0135	0.0042	0.0042	0.0043	0.0036	0.0052	0.0023	0.0023
0.018	4	0.0071	0.0109	0.0042	0.0194	0.0061	0.0055	-0.0039	0.0052	0.0065	0.0037
0.142	5	0.0037	0.0061	0.0042	0.0061	0.0095	0.0031	0.0018	-0.0027	0.0018	0.0021
0.000	6	0.0056	0.0064	0.0043	0.0055	0.0031	0.0055	0.0034	0.0047	0.0029	-0.0018
0.490	7	0.0070	-0.0032	0.0036	-0.0039	0.0018	0.0034	0.0048	0.0010	0.0011	0.0018
0.000	8	0.0032	0.0072	0.0052	0.0052	-0.0027	0.0047	0.0010	0.0086	0.0036	0.0023
0.000	9	0.0034	0.0031	0.0023	0.0065	0.0018	0.0029	0.0011	0.0000	0.0000	0.0000
0.000	10	0.0065	0.0026	0.0023	0.0037	0.0021	-0.0018	0.0018	0.0023	0.0010	0.0031
1	Sum Covariances	0.0001	0.0018	0.0001	0.0001	0.0006	0.0000	0.0009	0.0000	0.0000	0.0000

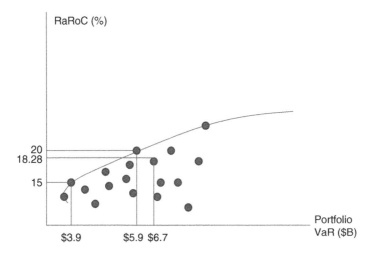

FIGURE 4.10   Conceptual SIBTD RaRoC-VaR Efficient Frontier

the same but changing this target incrementally would generate a RaRoC-VaR efficient frontier. Conceptually, this is depicted in Figure 4.10. Each dot represents a RaRoC-VaR combination and only those that are on the curve would be considered part of the efficient frontier. In other words all dots off the curve and down to the right would be considered inferior outcomes to those on the curve. Moreover, any combination on the curve does not dominate any other appearing on the curve. Finally, the feasible set of RaRoC-VaR combinations exists only at or below the efficient frontier. To gain a better perspective of how such outcomes may impact traders, consider Table 4.12. By varying target RaRoC from 15 to 20 percent, the weights for the 10 traders change considerably. With a much lower hurdle rate established at 15 percent, higher risk (higher VaR) traders either come in with lower weights or none at all. However, as the required return constraint is raised, it requires higher-risk traders to become a larger portion of the business activity, forcing the business to accept higher overall risk as a result. These sort of trade-offs could be examined a bit differently if the objective function were changed from risk minimization to return maximization given a target level of VaR. Portfolio optimization can clearly be a powerful tool in guiding risk and business managers, however, like all models it is highly dependent on accurate inputs and key assumptions.

TABLE 4.12   Alternative RaRoC-VaR Outcomes for SIBTD

	15%	17.5%	20%
SIBTD VaR	0.039	0.047	0.059
SIBTD RaRoC	0.150	0.175	0.200
Trader			Weights
1	0.000	0.000	0.014
2	0.000	0.117	0.313
3	0.000	0.000	0.023
4	0.000	0.122	0.018
5	0.035	0.000	0.142
6	0.542	0.000	0.000
7	0.000	0.580	0.491
8	0.000	0.000	0.000
9	0.000	0.065	0.000
10	0.422	0.116	0.000
Sum of Weights	1.000	1.000	1.000

SUMMARY

This chapter has illustrated the importance of adjusting economic performance for risk. Assessing business performance on the basis of simple ROE measures is likely to give a false impression on the amount of risk being added and with it misstate the true performance of the institution. Developing risk-adjusted measurements such as RaRoC or SVA, however, are not easy exercises. The building blocks for any risk-adjusted performance measure starts with economic capital and this can be defined by VaR estimates less the expected level of losses, returns or value being examined. VaR requires the analyst to develop some sense of the underlying distribution of losses or returns being used as the measure of interest in determining VaR. Such distributions vary by risk type, thus complicating the analyst's ability to combine VaR estimates for a single entity without some computational complexity. VaR has become an industry standard measure for risk as it allows the risk manager to use actual historical experience to generate a distribution of losses with focus on the amount of risk in the tail of the distribution. Understanding the sensitivities of VaR results to key inputs and assumptions is critical as VaR results can and will vary based on how the model is parameterized. Stress testing and conducting scenario analysis on such models is good practice as it allows the analyst an ability to look at unlikely scenarios in more detail to discern any potential anomalies that might exist.

Analysts should take into account risk diversification benefits that may result across risk types and business areas; however, correlations are unlikely to remain constant over time. As a result, care must be taken in updating modeled correlations. Allocation of economic capital is also an important activity once aggregate estimates of capital are developed. Simple methods for allocating capital may not appropriately reflect the incremental risk of one business unit against others. Moreover, allocating capital across business units, taking into account risk diversification benefits, provides a more efficient mechanism for deploying capital.

Finally, portfolio optimization techniques can be used once the analyst has developed robust estimates of RaRoC, economic capital, and business unit/risk correlations. Such capabilities can quickly determine where inefficient allocations of capital are dragging down the performance of the unit. Making significant changes in the business based on such models, however, must be tempered by the stability of the results. Such models are thus better often used to provide directional guidance to the business than as explicit decision-making tools.

QUESTIONS

ExBank has a trading portfolio of $1 billion in various types of fixed-income bonds. The expected return on the portfolio is 10 percent and the variance of returns on this portfolio is 30 percent. The value of the inverse cumulative distribution $N^{-1}(z)$ that accounts for 90 and 95 percent of the standard normal distribution is 1.65 and 1.96, respectively. The board of directors of ExBank would like to set a 95 percent VaR for the bank.

1. What is the DEAR for the trading book of ExBank?
2. What graphics and words would you use to explain what DEAR is for the trading book?
3. Suppose the board asks you to generate a one-week (business) VaR for the trading book. What would your answer be?

Suppose ExBank's risk analysts have estimated that the expected default rate on the commercial loan portfolio are 10 percent. The portfolio currently contains $500 million in commercial loan assets. Estimated recovery rates on the portfolio are 65 percent. The volatility associated with commercial defaults is 6 percent.

4. Using the same $N^{-1}(z)$ as above, compute the 10-day VaR for the worst 2.5 percent of dollar credit losses.
5. What is the risk capital associated with the commercial loan portfolio?
6. What is the difference between economic (or risk) capital and VaR for the commercial portfolio?

Suppose ExBank risk management has estimated VaR for operational, market, and credit risk across all of its operating divisions. Operational risk VaR is estimated at $2 billion, credit risk VaR at $5 billion, and market risk VaR at $3 billion. The risk management team shows a total VaR of $10 billion. Total bank assets are $100 billion.

7. If you were a board member, what issues might you have with this way of reporting VaR?
8. If the underlying distributions were determined to be non-normally distributed, what could you do to improve the calculation of total bank VaR?
9. The risk management team determines that a combination of an extended period of falling house prices for five years resulting in a cumulative decline of 25 percent and a –5 percent GDP scenario results in the bank losses reaching $12 billion and current capital levels at the bank are at $11 billion. What type of analysis has the risk team performed and how do you arrive at this answer?
10. ExBank has an opportunity to deploy $1.125 billion of its capital to two new loan products. The revenues of product 1 and 2 are $60 million and $100 million, respectively. Operating costs of product 1 and 2 are the same at $10 million, both products have identical funding costs of $30 million, and expected losses for product 1 and 2 are $15 million and $45 million, respectively. The bank is required to hold 4 percent capital on products 1 and 2. The bank estimates its economic capital on product 1 to be $25 million and for product 2 to be $90 million. The bank's target hurdle rate is 20 percent. Which product would you recommend the bank invest in and why?
11. How would you characterize the previous question in terms of SVA?
12. ExBank has two operating divisions. Division 1 has a VaR of $5 billion and it has a volatility of 15 percent. Division 2 has a VaR of $8 billion and its volatility is 25 percent. The covariance of Division 1 and 2 is 2.5 percent. What is the VaR for ExBank based on this information?
13. ExBank's VaR for a 5 percent increase in Division 1's exposure becomes $12.5 billion and for a 5 percent increase in Division 2's is $12.1 billion. ExBank portfolio VaR is estimated at $12 billion. How would you allocate capital between the two divisions for this increase in exposure and provide an estimate of total VaR.

CHAPTER 5

Credit Risk Theory

OVERVIEW

One of the major risks that SifiBank faces is from borrowers who default on their obligations to the bank. The financial crisis of 2008–2009 underscores the need to pay close attention to the level of credit risk that, at that time, drove a number of banks with household names such as Countrywide Financial and Washington Mutual out of existence, largely due to excessive amounts of mortgage credit risk on their balance sheets.

Borrowers can be individuals, corporations, or even governments seeking credit. And while the drivers of default for each may differ, the underlying theory of default remains the same. This chapter discusses a theory of default first introduced by Robert Merton and presents the foundation for efforts to measure and manage credit risk exposure. It views default as an embedded put option available to the borrower when circumstances are economically attractive for the borrower to "exercise" their option to default. This option-theoretic framework can be characterized for any type of borrower and used as the basis for default modeling. Credit loss estimates are formed on the basis of combining the borrower's probability of default (or default frequency) with their loss given default (LGD), or loss severity. The Merton default model provides a way to conceptually determine both loss components.

With a basic theory of credit risk established, the remainder of the chapter examines three important approaches to measuring credit risk. Leveraging the Merton model, the first introduces the concept of **credit spreads**, or the additional amount of yield needed on a financial instrument subject to default over a comparable duration risk-free instrument. Credit spreads provide analysts with an important way to extract an estimate of default embedded within the financial contract by observing market prices of underlying assets.

The second area of focus is with regard to credit portfolio management. Over the years a number of techniques have emerged that allow credit managers to look at trade-offs among different types of assets from a credit perspective, drawing on theory first applied to investment management. In addition, key concepts around credit migration, reflecting the dynamics that credit risk is not static over time are reviewed and applied to a simple SifiBank credit portfolio.

Analytic models are then examined, such as the Vasicek default model as a method for generating a distribution of default rates for a portfolio. Finally, a discussion of the importance of counterparty risk to the firm and how to measure counterparty risk completes the introduction to key credit topics.

A Theory of Default

A seminal advancement in credit risk analysis was the work by Robert Merton that presented default in the context of financial options. The Merton model was introduced focusing on corporate defaults, however, to illustrate how adaptable the theory is to a range of credit risks, it is presented in the context of SifiMortgage's need to understand the credit risk profile of its mortgage portfolio in order for it to determine how it can hedge its exposure.

Since the Merton model is predicated on an understanding of option theory a brief overview of options is required. A **financial option** is considered to be a derivative instrument that has some underlying asset, such as a mortgage, that the financial outcome for the buyer and seller of the option is tied to. There are basically two types of option contracts: calls and puts. Options are further divided into **American-** or **European-style options**, where an American option can be exercised at any point up to expiration and a European option may be exercised only at expiration.[1] A **call option** gives the buyer of the option the right, but not the obligation, to purchase the underlying asset whenever the price of the asset exceeds a stated level. That stated price level is referred to as the **exercise** or **strike price**. The contract has a stated **time-to-expiration** associated with it. A more formal expression of the call option's value is as follows:

$$V_C = MAX[0, A - K] - c \qquad 5.1$$

---

[1] Other hybrids between American- and European-style options exist, such as Bermudan options; however, these are beyond the scope of this chapter.

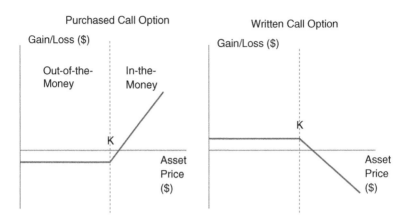

FIGURE 5.1   Call Option Profit Diagrams

where A is the price of the asset, K is the strike price and c is the premium paid by the buyer to the call seller. In the simple case of an equity option on SifiBank, if SifiBank stock is currently priced at $50 and the holder of the call option has a strike price of $40, then the option is considered **in-the-money** and the owner would receive $10 if exercised at that time (the call premium here is assumed to be 0). Conversely, if SifiBank's fortunes were to decline, causing the stock price to fall to $30, then the value of the option (referred to as its **intrinsic value**) would be –$10 and given the above relationship the owner would leave the option unexercised. The graphical depiction of the call option from the perspective of the buyer and seller (**writer of the option**) is shown in Figure 5.1. The figure demonstrates that when the call buyer profits, the writer of the option loses out and vice versa. Note that when the asset price is at or below the strike price for the buyer, the buyer still incurs a loss. That represents the premium (c) paid to the seller of the option for entering the contract and is reflected as a gain for the call writer when the option is out-of-the-money for the buyer.

For a **put option**, the buyer has the right, but not the obligation, to sell the underlying asset to the seller of the option contract. From the put buyer's perspective, this is reflected as:

$$V_p = MAX[0, K - A] - p \qquad 5.2$$

where p represents the put premium and all other terms are defined as before. The profit to a put option for the buyer and writer is shown in Figure 5.2.

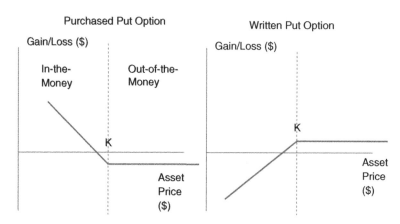

FIGURE 5.2   Put Option Profit Diagrams

In this depiction, the put buyer does better as the price of the underlying asset declines. Assume an investor buys a put option on SifiBank stock with a strike price of $40. If the price of SifiBank declines to $30, the owner of the put option profits by $10. If the stock price, however, were to move to $50 and remain there until expiration at or above the strike price, then the option would expire **out-of-the-money** and go unexercised.

Pricing option premiums was made much easier with the introduction of the **Black-Scholes option pricing model**. Since that model is relied upon in the Merton default model, a brief tour of the main features of the Black-Scholes (BSOP) model is warranted. The math can be a bit daunting, however, the intuition behind BSOP expands on the simple profit formulas depicted above but puts the model on a probabilistic basis. The BSOP formulas for a call and put option are as follows:

$$C = AN(d_1) - N(d_2)Ke^{-rT}$$
$$P = Ke^{-rT}N(-d_2) - AN(-d_1)$$
$$d_1 = \frac{\ln\left(\frac{A}{K}\right) + (r + .5\sigma^2)T}{\sigma\sqrt{T}}$$
$$d_2 = d_1 - \sigma\sqrt{T}$$

5.3

where $N(d_1)$ is the cumulative probability distribution for a standard normal variable with mean μ and standard deviation σ. Other terms

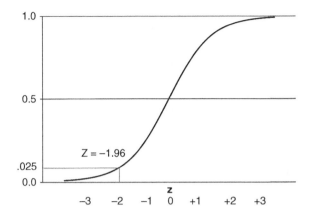

FIGURE 5.3 Cumulative Probability Distribution

include r, the risk-free rate of interest, T, the time to expiration of the option, and σ, the annual standard deviation of the asset's return, continuously compounded.

At the heart of the BSOP model are the $N(d)$ terms for d_1 and d_2. To understand how this relates to the option pricing relationships described earlier, consider Figure 5.3. For a random variable Z, the cumulative probability distribution describes the area under the curve to the left of the probability (bell-shaped) distribution denoted by Z. Assume as shown that $Z = -1.96$ when the mean of the distribution is 0 and its standard deviation is 1. In this case there is a probability of 2.5 percent that Z will have a value that is equal to -1.96 or lower. Applying this to the BSOP option pricing formula, for a call option, as d_1 moves higher, $N(d_1)$ moves toward 1 (or 100 percent of the area under the probability density function). Conversely as d_1 declines, $N(d_1)$ moves toward 0.

For the BSOP model, $N(d_1)$ is interpreted as the probability that the call option expires in-the-money. To see this, assume that d_1 is an extreme value of -6. That would mean that $N(d_1)$ would be very close to 0. Since d_2 is a function of d_1 as defined above, its value would also be very close to zero. In that case, looking back at the BSOP formula for the call option and substituting in for $N(d_1)$ and $N(d_2)$, it can be shown that C would likewise be close to zero, signifying the option has virtually no value. Conversely, if d_1 were $+6$, it would imply a value for $N(d_1)$ close to 1 and likewise $N(d_2)$ would be close to 1. By substitution into the BSOP formula the value of C in the limit would approach $A - K$ on a present value basis, meaning the option expires in-the-money. These relationships also hold for put options.

Applying these concepts to default, in this case a borrower who has taken out a $140,000 mortgage from SifiMortgage on a $200,000 home in Los Angeles, the borrower's equity stake in the home can be thought of as an option in the standard Merton default model. Specifically, the borrower's option may be represented as:

$$E = MAX[0, A_T - L] \qquad 5.4$$

where A_T is the property value of the home at time T and L is the mortgage amount at origination ($t = 0$). Expressed this way, the mortgage, L is equivalent to the strike price and A_T is the asset value. In this form, the borrower's equity is viewed as a call option. The mortgage is in essence a fixed-income security that has two components: a default-free bond less the value of an embedded put option provided to the borrower allowing them to default when economically attractive to do so. This may be represented by the following:

$$B = L - MAX[0, L - A_T] \qquad 5.5$$

Applying the BSOP model to value the mortgage yields the following expression:

$$B = Le^{-rT} - (Le^{-rT} N(-d_2) - A_T N(-d_1)) \qquad 5.6$$

Likewise the borrower's equity value E may be obtained in similar fashion as:

$$E = A_T N(d_1) - Le^{-rT} N(d_2) \qquad 5.7$$

with terms defined as before. In this model, the value of $N(-d_2)$ represents the risk-neutral probability of default for the borrower. The variable d_2 is also referred to as the distance-to-default, a concept we will review shortly. For completeness, $N(-d_2)$ may be defined as:

$$N(-d_2) = 1 - N(d_2) \qquad 5.8$$

In this instance, as the probability that the borrower's equity rises (the call option is in-the-money) increases, that is, $N(d_1)$, so does $N(d_2)$. That implies that $1 - N(d_2)$ is the probability that the borrower exercises their option and defaults on the mortgage.

Once a borrower defaults, how much of the loan is recovered (or conversely, lost) as a percent of its original value completes the credit risk picture in determining expected loss. The LGD is further defined as 1 minus the recovery rate. Using the Merton model framework, the recovery rate, RR, is defined as:

$$RR = \frac{A_T e^{-rT} \dfrac{N(-d_1)}{N(-d_2)}}{L} \qquad 5.9$$

LGD is then defined as 1 – RR.

An important concept that relates to the Merton default model results is the distance-to-default (*DD*). Over some time horizon *T*, an asset's value will vary starting at time 0. At period *t*, a default probability distribution exists such that a loan defaults based on the number of standard deviations below the asset's expected value. Figure 5.4 provides a depiction of the *DD* concept. Assuming a standard normal distribution, asset A's value migrates in this example to some level up or down over time. Based on the Merton model results, in this case default occurs for asset A whenever its value declines 2.25 standard deviations below its expected level by time *t*.

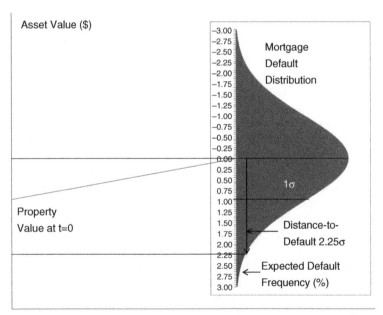

FIGURE 5.4   Distance-to-Default

The area under the distribution and below the volatility factor cutoff of 2.25 accounts for approximately 1.2 percent of all outcomes and implies that there is a 1.2 percent chance that the borrower will default. Distance-to-default can be defined by the following relationship:

$$DD = \frac{\ln A_0 - \ln L + (r - .5\sigma^2)T}{\sigma\sqrt{T}}$$
5.10

where all terms are defined as earlier.

The Merton default model allows one to determine the credit spread of a risky asset. Credit spreads are an important way risk managers can gauge the level of credit risk of an asset or counterparty as it incorporates the expected loss of that asset or counterparty in the yield on risky debt. The yield on risky debt can be defined as the following:

$$y_R - r = \frac{1}{T}\ln\left[\frac{1}{1 - PD * LGD}\right]$$
5.11

where all terms are defined as before.

To understand these concepts better, consider a situation where the SifiMortgage CRO wants to conduct a sensitivity analysis on mortgages in terms of expected loss, default, and LGD using the Merton default model framework. The value of the property is assumed to be $500,000 for all loan scenarios. Three loan amounts are examined: $400,000, $450,000, and $475,000. The associated loan-to-value (LTV) ratios for these scenarios are 80, 90, and 95 percent, respectively. SifiMortgage risk analysts know that the higher the LTV (i.e., the lower the borrower equity stake), the higher the default risk, all else equal. Further, the standard deviation of returns on the property's value is evaluated under three scenarios: 5, 10, and 15 percent. The variations in property value could reflect differences in home prices across geographic areas. For instance, homes in California may exhibit higher home price volatility than similarly situated homes in Indiana. Other assumptions are that the risk-free rate is 2 percent and the time horizon is five years. With these assumptions the Merton model can be used to generate comparative credit risk estimates. Tables 5.1–5.3 present the results from the exercise.

Table 5.1 shows a set of PD and LGD results for the 80 percent LTV under three standard deviation assumptions. A number of key metrics are computed for different property values over the five-year period ranging from $250,000 (a 50 percent drop in property value from origination) to $500,000. Looking first at the 5 percent volatility scenarios, the distance-to-default (shown as d_2) for the $250,000 property value is −3.365, implying that a value of $250,000 is −3.365 standard deviations below the initial value of $500,000 and would be associated with a higher probability of default. This can be seen by looking at the value for this scenario of $N(-d_2)$, which is the default probability. In this case it is almost certain that this loan would default at a value of $250,000. Conversely, the distance-to-default for a scenario where value remains the same is 2.834 (notice the positive sign), and that is associated with a PD of .2 percent. Using Equation 5.9, the recovery rates and corresponding LGDs vary over the range of value outcomes from LGDs as high as 31 percent (for a value of $250,000) to 3.2 percent for values of $500,000. The ELs are easily computed for each value combination as are the credit spreads in the last column. The impact of embedded credit risk across scenarios on credit spreads is clear. For the scenario where values decline by 50 percent, credit spread is 7.4 percent, assuming a 5 percent volatility versus 0 percent for outcomes where value remains the same. The impact of doubling and tripling volatility can be seen in Table 5.1, which indicates there is slight variation in EL and credit spreads as volatility changes.

The effects of borrower equity on these scenarios are evident in comparing results across Tables 5.1–5.3. As LTV increases from 80 percent to 90 percent, there are material increases in EL and LGDs noticeable for the lowest property value scenarios. This explains the phenomena that mortgage default is driven to a large degree by negative equity, that is, when the value of the property falls below the value of the mortgage. In this case, the borrower exercises his or her default option and "puts" the mortgage back to the lender.

As LTVs move from 90 percent to 95 percent, EL and LGDs continue to show higher credit risk when borrowers put less down to finance the home. Compare the effects on credit spread between the 80 percent scenario of 7.4 percent and the 95 percent LTV scenario of 10.8 percent under the $250,000 property value decline outcome. While the Merton model provides an elegant way to think about how borrowers default in an option-theoretic framework, in reality borrowers do not "ruthlessly" exercise their default option. There may be friction costs associated with default such as the psychological attachment of the home that delays or puts off default or the possibility that the credit of the borrower will be damaged for some period. The Merton model nonetheless provides the risk analyst with a solid theoretical foundation from which to develop estimates of default that take other factors into account that describe default behavior.

TABLE 5.1 Merton Default Model Results for SifiMortgage LTV = 80 Percent

Property Value at Origination	$500,000
Loan Amount	$400,000
Original Loan-to-Value Ratio	80%
Risk-free Rate	2%
Time Horizon	5
Volatility	5%

Property Value	d_1	$N(d_1)$	d_2	$N(d_2)$	$N(-d_1)$	$N(-d_2)$ or (PD)	Recovery Rate	LGD	EL	Credit Spread
$250,000	-3.254	0.001	-3.365	0.000	0.999	0.9996	0.691	0.309	0.309	0.074
$300,000	-1.623	0.052	-1.735	0.041	0.948	0.959	0.819	0.181	0.173	0.038
$350,000	-0.244	0.404	-0.356	0.361	0.596	0.639	0.903	0.097	0.062	0.013
$400,000	0.950	0.829	0.839	0.799	0.171	0.201	0.941	0.059	0.012	0.002
$425,000	1.493	0.932	1.381	0.916	0.068	0.084	0.951	0.049	0.004	0.001
$450,000	2.004	0.977	1.892	0.971	0.023	0.029	0.958	0.042	0.001	0.000
$475,000	2.487	0.994	2.376	0.991	0.006	0.009	0.964	0.036	0.000	0.000
$500,000	2.946	0.998	2.834	0.998	0.002	0.002	0.968	0.032	0.000	0.000
Volatility 10%										
$250,000	-1.543	0.061	-1.767	0.039	0.939	0.9613	0.674	0.326	0.313	0.075
$300,000	-1.623	0.052	-1.735	0.041	0.948	0.959	0.819	0.181	0.173	0.038
$350,000	-0.244	0.404	-0.356	0.361	0.596	0.639	0.903	0.097	0.062	0.013
$400,000	0.950	0.829	0.839	0.799	0.171	0.201	0.941	0.059	0.012	0.002
$425,000	1.493	0.932	1.381	0.916	0.068	0.084	0.951	0.049	0.004	0.001

$450,000	2.004	0.977	1.892	0.971	0.023	0.029	0.958	0.042	0.001	0.000
$475,000	2.487	0.994	2.376	0.991	0.006	0.009	0.964	0.036	0.000	0.000
$500,000	2.946	0.998	2.834	0.998	0.002	0.002	0.968	0.032	0.000	0.000

Volatility 15%

$250,000	-0.935	0.175	-1.271	0.102	0.825	0.8981	0.635	0.365	0.328	0.080
$300,000	-1.623	0.052	-1.735	0.041	0.948	0.959	0.819	0.181	0.173	0.038
$350,000	-0.244	0.404	-0.356	0.361	0.596	0.639	0.903	0.097	0.062	0.013
$400,000	0.950	0.829	0.839	0.799	0.171	0.201	0.941	0.059	0.012	0.002
$425,000	1.493	0.932	1.381	0.916	0.068	0.084	0.951	0.049	0.004	0.001
$450,000	2.004	0.977	1.892	0.971	0.023	0.029	0.958	0.042	0.001	0.000
$475,000	2.487	0.994	2.376	0.991	0.006	0.009	0.964	0.036	0.000	0.000
$500,000	2.946	0.998	2.834	0.998	0.002	0.002	0.968	0.032	0.000	0.000

TABLE 5.2 Merton Default Model Results for SifiMortgage Loans: LTV = 90 Percent

Property Value at Origination	$500,000
Loan Amount	$450,000
Original Loan-to-Value Ratio	90%
Risk-free Rate	2%
Time Horizon	5
Volatility	5%

Property Value	d_1	$N(d_1)$	d_2	$N(d_2)$	$N(-d_1)$	$N(-d_2)$ or (PD)	Recovery Rate	LGD	EL	Credit Spread
$250,000	-4.307	0.000	-4.419	0.000	1.000	1.0000	0.614	0.386	0.386	0.098
$300,000	-2.676	0.004	-2.788	0.003	0.996	0.997	0.736	0.264	0.263	0.061
$350,000	-1.297	0.097	-1.409	0.079	0.903	0.921	0.843	0.157	0.145	0.031
$400,000	-0.103	0.459	-0.215	0.415	0.541	0.585	0.908	0.092	0.054	0.011
$425,000	0.439	0.670	0.327	0.628	0.330	0.372	0.927	0.073	0.027	0.005
$450,000	0.950	0.829	0.839	0.799	0.171	0.201	0.941	0.059	0.012	0.002
$475,000	1.434	0.924	1.322	0.907	0.076	0.093	0.950	0.050	0.005	0.001
$500,000	1.893	0.971	1.781	0.963	0.029	0.037	0.957	0.043	0.002	0.000
Volatility				10%						
$250,000	-2.070	0.019	-2.293	0.011	0.981	0.9891	0.609	0.391	0.387	0.098
$300,000	-2.676	0.004	-2.788	0.003	0.996	0.997	0.736	0.264	0.263	0.053
$350,000	-1.297	0.097	-1.409	0.079	0.903	0.921	0.843	0.157	0.145	0.029
$400,000	-0.103	0.459	-0.215	0.415	0.541	0.585	0.908	0.092	0.054	0.011

$425,000	0.439	0.670	0.327	0.628	0.330	0.372	0.927	0.073	0.027	0.005
$450,000	0.950	0.829	0.839	0.799	0.171	0.201	0.941	0.059	0.012	0.002
$475,000	1.434	0.924	1.322	0.907	0.076	0.093	0.950	0.050	0.005	0.001
$500,000	1.893	0.971	1.781	0.963	0.029	0.037	0.957	0.043	0.002	0.000

Volatility 15%

$250,000	−1.287	0.099	−1.622	0.052	0.901	0.9476	0.584	0.416	0.394	0.100
$300,000	−2.676	0.004	−2.788	0.003	0.996	0.997	0.736	0.264	0.263	0.053
$350,000	−1.297	0.097	−1.409	0.079	0.903	0.921	0.843	0.157	0.145	0.029
$400,000	−0.103	0.459	−0.215	0.415	0.541	0.585	0.908	0.092	0.054	0.011
$425,000	0.439	0.670	0.327	0.628	0.330	0.372	0.927	0.073	0.027	0.005
$450,000	0.950	0.829	0.839	0.799	0.171	0.201	0.941	0.059	0.012	0.002
$475,000	1.434	0.924	1.322	0.907	0.076	0.093	0.950	0.050	0.005	0.001
$500,000	1.893	0.971	1.781	0.963	0.029	0.037	0.957	0.043	0.002	0.000

TABLE 5.3 Merton Default Model Results for SifiMortgage Loans: LTV = 95 Percent

Property Value at Origination	$500000
Loan Amount	$475000
Original Loan-to-Value Ratio	95%
Risk-free Rate	2%
Time Horizon	5
Volatility	5%

Property Value	d_1	$N(d_1)$	d_2	$N(d_2)$	$N(-d_1)$	$N(-d_2)$ or (PD)	Recovery Rate	LGD	EL	Credit Spread
$250,000	-4.791	0.000	-4.902	0.000	1.000	1.000	0.582	0.418	0.418	0.108
$300,000	-3.160	0.001	-3.272	0.001	0.999	0.999	0.698	0.302	0.302	0.060
$350,000	-1.781	0.037	-1.893	0.029	0.963	0.971	0.807	0.193	0.187	0.037
$400,000	-0.587	0.279	-0.699	0.242	0.721	0.758	0.886	0.114	0.086	0.017
$425,000	-0.045	0.482	-0.156	0.438	0.518	0.562	0.911	0.089	0.050	0.010
$450,000	0.467	0.680	0.355	0.639	0.320	0.361	0.928	0.072	0.026	0.005
$475,000	0.950	0.829	0.839	0.799	0.171	0.201	0.941	0.059	0.012	0.002
$500,000	1.409	0.921	1.297	0.903	0.079	0.097	0.950	0.050	0.005	0.001
Volatility	10%									
$250,000	-2.311	0.010	-2.535	0.006	0.990	0.994	0.579	0.421	0.419	0.109
$300,000	-3.160	0.001	-3.272	0.001	0.999	0.999	0.698	0.302	0.302	0.060
$350,000	-1.781	0.037	-1.893	0.029	0.963	0.971	0.807	0.193	0.187	0.037
$400,000	-0.587	0.279	-0.699	0.242	0.721	0.758	0.886	0.114	0.086	0.017

$425,000	−0.045	0.482	−0.156	0.438	0.518	0.562	0.911	0.089	0.050	0.010
$450,000	0.467	0.680	0.355	0.639	0.320	0.361	0.928	0.072	0.026	0.005
$475,000	0.950	0.829	0.839	0.799	0.171	0.201	0.941	0.059	0.012	0.002
$500,000	1.409	0.921	1.297	0.903	0.079	0.097	0.950	0.050	0.005	0.001

Volatility

15%

$250,000	−1.448	0.074	−1.783	0.037	0.926	0.963	0.560	0.440	0.424	0.110
$300,000	−3.160	0.001	−3.272	0.001	0.999	0.999	0.698	0.302	0.302	0.060
$350,000	−1.781	0.037	−1.893	0.029	0.963	0.971	0.807	0.193	0.187	0.037
$400,000	−0.587	0.279	−0.699	0.242	0.721	0.758	0.886	0.114	0.086	0.017
$425,000	−0.045	0.482	−0.156	0.438	0.518	0.562	0.911	0.089	0.050	0.010
$450,000	0.467	0.680	0.355	0.639	0.320	0.361	0.928	0.072	0.026	0.005
$475,000	0.950	0.829	0.839	0.799	0.171	0.201	0.941	0.059	0.012	0.002
$500,000	1.409	0.921	1.297	0.903	0.079	0.097	0.950	0.050	0.005	0.001

PORTFOLIO CREDIT RISK DYNAMICS

Beyond assessing the credit risk of individual borrowers, many times financial institutions need to assess credit risk in a portfolio over time. Economic and market conditions can and will affect a borrower's ability to repay an obligation and their own financial circumstances may change, in many cases tied to general fluctuations in the economy. Consequently, it is important to understand the dynamics of changes in borrower credit profile over time and equally important to assess how loans of differing characteristics affect portfolio credit risk in the aggregate.

This type of analysis was developed by J.P. Morgan and is called CreditMetrics™, although several other companies have established related methodologies. The CreditMetrics™ approach draws on concepts of credit risk migration, usually observed in bond ratings but with applicability to other asset types as well as portfolio diversification effects on credit risk.

SifiMortgage risk managers are interested in implementing a version of the CreditMetrics™ capability but focused on the SifiMortgage portfolio. To illustrate the concept to senior management for their buy-in, analysts apply the method to a $2 billion synthetic portfolio consisting of a $1 billion A-rated tranche of a prime mortgage CDO structure purchased by SifiMortgage and a $1 billion B-rated tranche of another prime mortgage CDO. As the performance of mortgages underlying the CDOs changes over time, it may be reflect changes in the ratings of the two CDO tranches. It is assumed that there are only two tranches in each CDO, that is, A- and B-rated components. This is clearly an oversimplification of a standard CDO, which typically has more than two tranches, however, this assumption greatly reduces the complexity of the problem for illustration purposes.

Given these assumptions, there are only three possible outcomes for the migration of credit risk of each tranche. The A-rated tranche could remain A-rated in the next period, it could be downgraded to B if conditions affecting the underlying mortgage change, or the mortgages could all default, which is an extreme assumption made to simplify the computations. Similarly, the B-rated tranche could remain the same in the next period, it could be upgraded to A if conditions improve for the collateral, or the loans could all default.

The migration of the credit quality of an asset to another category of credit quality over time is referred to as a **transition-state-analysis** and can be visualized in Figure 5.5. In this simple model, the changes in credit quality for a given asset such as a CDO can be estimated by computing the probability of observing each of the resulting outcomes shown by the arrows in the figure. Note that once an asset enters a default state D, it remains there in any subsequent period. The analyst must assume a time horizon over which the analysis will be conducted, which is one year in this case.

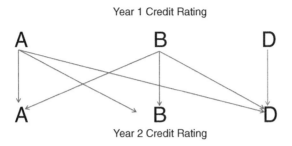

FIGURE 5.5 Simple One-Year Transition-State Model

Generalizing over time t, these relationships can be examined with the use of techniques such as **Markov chains**.[2] Historical information collected on the one-year ratings migration patterns of mortgage CDO tranches is used by SifiMortgage analysts. Knowing the total outstanding amount of each tranche at the beginning of each year and the amount of each tranche that moves from grade i to grade j in one year, a 1-year marginal mortality rate (MMR) for each migration can be computed as the following:

$$MMR_{ij}^1 = \frac{V_{ij}^1}{V_i^1}$$ 5.12

where V_{ij}^1 represents the dollar value of tranche i that migrates to a rating of j in one year and V_i^1 is the total dollar value of tranche i at the beginning of the year. Consider a dataset as shown in Table 5.4 for A-rated CDO tranches for each year from 2000 to 2010. The downgrades to B are shown in the table as well as each year's MMR. Since the MMRs will vary over time, an average of 8.65 percent could be used in the CreditMetrics™ analysis for this particular migration outcome. Other ratings transitions could be computed in a similar fashion. Once these transition probabilities have been computed, a transition rate matrix can be developed as shown in Table 5.5. Each transition rate or probability is shown in the table as p_{ij} representing the migration in one year from rating i to j. Looking at the table, it is clear that most of the time ratings remain the same over one year. For example, there is a 95.5 percent chance that the A-rated CDO tranche will

---

[2] A Markov chain describes the manner in which a group of variables with a set of outcomes in one period will migrate or transition to different states over time. This may be more formally represented as: $\Pr[Z_{n+1} = Y | Z_1 = Y_1, Z_2 = Y_2, \ldots Z_n = Y_n]$

TABLE 5.4 Calculations for a One-Year Transition Rate from A to B Rating

Year	Tranche A Outstandings	Downgrades to B	MMR (%)
2000	$250,000,000,000	$25,000,000,000	10.00
2001	$150,000,000,000	$10,000,000,000	6.67
2002	$400,000,000,000	$35,000,000,000	8.75
2003	$500,000,000,000	$42,000,000,000	8.40
2004	$300,000,000,000	$23,000,000,000	7.67
2005	$275,000,000,000	$20,000,000,000	7.27
2006	$425,000,000,000	$45,000,000,000	10.59
2007	$225,000,000,000	$19,000,000,000	8.44
2008	$550,000,000,000	$47,000,000,000	8.55
2009	$650,000,000,000	$60,000,000,000	9.23
2010	$575,000,000,000	$55,000,000,000	9.57
			8.65

remain A-rated the next year. In addition, the transition probabilities for each tranche should sum to 100 percent across each row. The sums in each column, however, will not equal 100 percent. The price of each tranche is dependent upon what rating it migrates to over the next year. If the A-rated CDO tranche remains A-rated in one-year, its price would reflect the underlying cash flows discounted at the prevailing forward rates for A-rated

TABLE 5.5 One-Year Transition Rates for Mortgage CDO Tranche Example

			To		
		A	B	D	
	A	pAA	pAB	pAD	
From	B	pBA	pBB	pBD	
	D	pDA	pDB	pDD	

			To		
		A	B	D	Sum
	A	0.955	0.035	0.010	1.000
From	B	0.125	0.725	0.150	1.000
	D	0.000	0.000	1.000	1.000

TABLE 5.6 Prices on CDO Tranches ($ per $100 of face amount)

		To		
		A	B	D
From	A	$100.80	$ 86.79	$70.00
	B	$101.00	$107.01	$70.00

bonds. In this case the price, P_{AA} sells at a slight premium of $100.80 of the face amount of the tranche (Table 5.6). If, however, the A-rated tranche were to realize a downgrade to B next year, it would be appropriate to take those same cash flows and discount them at the forward rates for a B-rated bond. Recall that credit spreads reflecting the underlying credit risk associated with an asset will be greater as expectations for credit risk increase and vice versa. In this case we would expect the price of the A-rated bond migrating to B, P_{AB}, to be lower due to effect of using the higher discount rates and in this example, P_{AB} is $86.79. In the case of any tranche that defaults to D in the next period, SifiMortgage would realize a loss severity of 30 percent, which translates into a recovery rate of 70 percent and hence an implied price of $70 for default outcomes. Bond pricing details, including the forward rates applied, are shown in Table 5.7.

In this two-CDO portfolio, an estimate of the combined set of transition rate outcomes is required to establish the portfolio's value. In this example, there are a total of nine possible portfolio outcomes: three A-rated outcomes times three B-rated outcomes, or more generally:

$$\sum_{i=1}^{n}\sum_{j=1}^{m} p_{ij}p_{ji} = 1 \qquad 5.13$$

Each of the products, that is, the $p_{ij}p_{ji}$, are referred to as a **joint migration probability** Ψ_{ij}, which is defined as CDO i and j's state next year. To clarify notation, if the A-rated tranche were to migrate to B and the B-rated tranche were to migrate to D in the next year, then the joint migration probability would be represented as $p_{AB}p_{BD} = \Psi_{BD} = (.035)(.15) = .5\%$. Using the individual CDO tranche probabilities from earlier, a three-by-three matrix of joint migration probabilities can be constructed as shown in Table 5.8. Note that the sum of the nine joint migration probabilities must be 100 percent.

The values of the two-CDO portfolio (V_{ij}) are similarly computed as shown in Table 5.9 for each set of outcomes. The highest value outcome is

TABLE 5.7 Bond Pricing Detail

Coupon	4%	6%
Term	5	6

	Cash Flows ($M)		Discount Rates		Bond A	Bond B	Bond A	Bond B
Year	Bond A	Bond B	A Quality	B Quality	Remains A	Remains B	Becomes B	Becomes A
1	$224,627,113	$203,362,628	3%	7.60%	$ 217,988,379	$188,479,780	$208,188,049	$ 197,352,354
2	$224,627,113	$203,362,628	3.25%	8.100%	$ 210,490,759	$172,947,959	$191,032,153	$ 190,564,502
3	$224,627,113	$203,362,628	3.50%	8.60%	$ 202,237,299	$157,116,997	$173,545,837	$ 183,092,361
4	$224,627,113	$203,362,628	3.75%	9.100%	$ 193,338,348	$141,314,900	$156,091,403	$ 175,035,836
5	$224,627,113	$203,362,628	4%	9.60%	$ 183,909,126	$125,837,417	$138,995,527	$ 166,499,238
6		$203,362,628	4.25%	10.60%	**$1,007,963,911**	$107,661,359	**$867,852,970**	$ 157,589,056
						$893,358,411		$1,070,133,349

TABLE 5.8   Joint Migration Probabilities for CDO Tranches Portfolio (%)

PaaPba = 11.94	PaaPbb = 69.24	PaaPbd = 14.33
PabPba = .44	PabPbb = 2.54	PabPbd = .53
PadPba = .13	PadPbb = .73	PadPbd = .15

the top left of the table at $2.08 billion, which is associated with the best possible result: the A-rated tranche stays A-rated and the B-rated tranche is upgraded to A. Conversely, the lowest value outcome is when both tranches default, resulting in just the recovery value of the tranches, or $1.40 billion. With the joint migration probabilities in Table 5.8 and the portfolio values in Table 5.9, the analyst can compute the expected value of the portfolio and its volatility as the following;

$$
\begin{aligned}
PV = \sum \Psi_{ij} V_i &= (11.9\%)(\$2.08B) + (69.2\%)(\$1.89B) \\
&+ (14.3\%)(\$1.71B) + (.4\%)(\$1.94B) + (2.5\%)(\$1.76B) \qquad 5.14 \\
&+ (.5\%)(\$1.57B) + (.1\%)(\$1.77B) + (.7\%)(\$1.58B) \\
&+ (.2\%)(\$1.40B) = \$1.88B
\end{aligned}
$$

Similarly the standard deviation for the portfolio, σ_P can be calculated as:

$$
\sigma_P = \sqrt{\sum \Psi_{ij} V_{ji}^2 - PV^2} = \$.105B \qquad 5.15
$$

The SifiMortgage analysts can use this information to characterize the credit risk profile of the portfolio. For example, the nine portfolio outcomes can be rank-ordered from the worst value (where both tranches next year default) to the best value (where the A-rated tranche stays A and the B-rated tranche is upgraded to A) as shown in Table 5.10 with their associated joint migration probabilities. The joint migration probabilities are then summed

TABLE 5.9   Values of 2-CDO Portfolio ($B)

PaaPba = 2.08	PaaPbb = 1.89	PaaPbd = 1.71
PabPba = 1.94	PabPbb = 1.75	PabPbd = 1.57
PadPba = 1.77	PadPbb = 1.58	PadPbd = 1.40

TABLE 5.10   Rank-Ordering of CDO Tranches Portfolio Outcomes

Scenario	V_{ij}	Ψ_{ij}	Cumulative Probability
1	1.40	0.002	0.002
2	1.57	0.005	0.007
3	1.58	0.007	0.014
4	1.71	0.143	0.157
5	1.75	0.025	0.182
6	1.77	0.001	0.183
7	1.89	0.692	0.875
8	1.94	0.004	0.879
9	2.08	0.119	0.998

sequentially from lowest value to highest, as shown in Table 5.10. While there are only nine distinct outcomes for this portfolio's value, it does provide a discrete distribution of portfolio value that can be used to establish an estimate of the portfolio's **credit VaR**. Instead of selecting a confidence level, as would be the case for estimating VaR from a continuous distribution, in this situation where there are only nine outcomes, the proxy for credit VaR would be to select a percentile of interest such as 1 percent. In other words, the credit VaR for this portfolio would be the scenario value of the portfolio that comes closest to the 1 percent level based on its cumulative probability. In this example, this would be a value of $1.58 billion for scenario 3. This just comes in under the 1 percent level but is the closest outcome.

Diversification benefits from having both CDO tranches in the portfolio can also be observed. The standard deviation of the A-rated or B-rated tranches using the data from earlier would be based on the following equation.

$$\sigma_i = \sqrt{\sum p_{ij} V_i^2 - \overline{V}_i^2}$$

5.16

where $\overline{V}_i^2$ is the mean value for tranche i. Applying this formula gives σ_A a value of $.0396 billion and an expected value of $.999 billion. For the B tranche the corresponding values are σ_B equal to $.096 billion and an expected value of $.873 billion. Note that the sum of individual tranche standard deviations is greater ($.136 billion) than the 2 CDO portfolio volatility of $.105 billion. This is due to the fact that the correlation between the two tranches is not perfect. This gives rise to a similar result from Modern Portfolio Theory that a diversified portfolio can lower risk.

The credit portfolio manager can also use the CreditMetrics™ results to conduct an assessment of the contribution of individual assets to portfolio risk. The idea is that the incremental or marginal risk of an asset to the portfolio can be compared with a portfolio without that asset. This concept leverages the portfolio deviation calculation by computing it with and without the asset of interest. This result can then be presented relative to the asset of interest's size or exposure. In this way, two important dimensions of an asset's contribution to portfolio risk, namely its volatility and exposure, are captured. The **marginal standard deviation** (MSD) computed in CreditMetrics™ is defined as:

$$MSD = \frac{\sigma_{P+i} - \sigma_P}{\mu_i} \qquad 5.17$$

where σ_{P+i} is the standard deviation of the portfolio including asset i, μ is the dollar size of asset i, and σ_P is the standard deviation of the portfolio without asset i. SifiMortgage analysts decide to evaluate 10 CDO tranches for consideration in a large portfolio of similar assets (σ_P) . The portfolio standard deviation of the portfolio without any of these 10 assets is $10.5 million. The computed MSDs for each asset are shown in Table 5.10. The

TABLE 5.11 SifiMortgage CDO MSD Calculations

Asset	σP+i	μi	$(\sigma$P+I $- \sigma$P$)/\mu i$
1	15.7	100	5.2
2	20.5	250	4.0
3	17.3	50	13.6
4	23.4	700	1.8
5	40.5	300	10.0
6	27.8	475	3.6
7	35.2	330	7.5
8	87.5	1,400	5.5
9	67.2	675	8.4
10	68.2	550	10.5

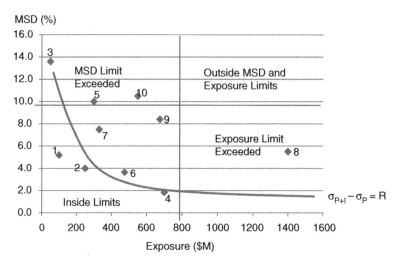

FIGURE 5.6   SifiMortgage CDO Portfolio Risk Limits and Asset Risk

results for MSD shown in the last column of the table can be depicted against company risk limits for MSD and exposure as shown in Figure 5.6. SifiMortgage's risk committee recently approved raising the limit on any individual exposure in its portfolio to $800M from $700M. In addition it also imposed a limit on MSD of 10 percent. The curved line indicates assets that have equal values of the MSD numerator. Most of the assets comply with both limits and thus would be acceptable risks for the portfolio. However, there are a number that pose risk beyond one or both limits. For example, tranche 8 exceeds the exposure limit of $800 million by $600 million even though its MSD is within tolerance. Alternatively, tranches 3 and 10 exceed the MSD limit even though their size is within the exposure limit. Using the CreditMetrics™ framework in this fashion thus provides the risk team with the ability to quickly determine how a target asset fits within the risk appetite of the bank. One of the crucial assumptions in the CreditMetrics™ framework is the transition rate for each asset migration scenario. These can change over time as observed in Table 5.5 and applying a simple average may not provide an accurate view of asset credit dynamics. The analyst should pay close attention to patterns or important shifts in the data suggesting a material change in how asset credit risk is changing. The simple two-asset example described in this section can be generalized to n assets, which adds some additional computational complexity to the risk assessment exercise.

ANALYTIC METHODS FOR CREDIT PORTFOLIO ASSESSMENT

As will be seen in Chapter 6, with sufficient data it may be possible to develop an empirical default or loss distribution. Techniques such as Monte Carlo simulation methods provide one such example, though these are typically computationally intensive. An alternative that may be able to provide insight into the shape of the default distribution under various assumptions, including what the tail of the distribution looks like, includes analytic methods such as the **Vasicek default model**.

The Vasicek model provides an easily implemented way to derive the default pdf of a portfolio given the correlation between assets and the expected default rate (EDR). Using estimates of these parameters, a default rate may be computed as below:

$$PD = N\left[\frac{N^{-1}(EDR) + \sqrt{\rho}N^{-1}(\Psi(PD))}{\sqrt{1-\rho}}\right]$$ 5.18

where ρ is the asset correlation parameter, $\Psi(PD)$ is the cumulative probability function for EDR, and N and N^{-1} are defined as before. To see how this works, assume that ρ is set at 15 percent and the PD of the portfolio is also 15 percent. If $\Psi(PD)$ is equal to 10 percent, the value of PD is then 4.82 percent. Alternatively, the cumulative distribution function may be computed as:

$$\Psi(PD) = N\left[\frac{\sqrt{1-\rho}N^{-1}(PD) - N^{-1}(EDR)}{\sqrt{\rho}}\right]$$ 5.19

Finally, if the pdf of the default distribution is desired, it can be computed as follows:

$$\varphi(PD) = \sqrt{\frac{1-\rho}{\rho}}e^{\left[.5\left((N^{-1}(PD))^2 - \left[\frac{\sqrt{1-\rho}N^{-1}(PD)-N^{-1}(EDR)}{\sqrt{\rho}}\right]^2\right)\right]}$$ 5.20

The results from two different scenarios on EDR and ρ are shown in Figure 5.7 using Equation 5.20. The tail of the 15 percent/15 percent distribution is much smaller than for the 25 percent/25 percent scenario. For example, the median default rate under the 15 percent/15 percent scenario is .066 percent versus .7 percent for the 25 percent/25 percent scenario. Moreover, using equation 5.18, the 95 percent PDs for scenarios 15 percent/15 percent and 25 percent/25 percent are 33 percent and 57 percent, respectively.

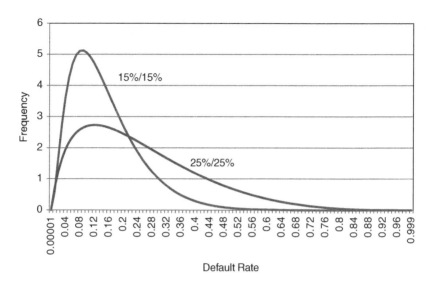

FIGURE 5.7   Default Distributions Derived from the Vasicek Default Model

COUNTERPARTY RISK

During the financial crisis of 2008–2009, counterparty risk came into focus for banks and regulators as institutions went bankrupt and were unable to perform on their obligations under the terms of a financial contract such as a CDS or other derivative. In this way, counterparty risk is different from standard credit risk in that it relates to the risk that a trading partner will not make good on a transaction. This is the most commonly observed form of counterparty risk; however, it may also take place with regard to loan partners that are used to expand the channel for a particular product. If the bank extends financing to the counterparty in advance of receiving the loans, in the event the counterparty becomes insolvent, the lender may be exposed to losses.

Counterparty risk may become compounded when correlations arise between the exposure to the counterparty and the likelihood of default of the counterparty. During the mortgage boom, mortgage portfolio lenders purchased insurance for portions of their portfolio from mortgage insurance companies that were highly dependent upon the performance of the mortgage industry (**monoline entities**). The purchase of credit protection from these companies was supposed to mitigate credit risk, however, once the crisis unfolded, a number of these firms became unable to pay claims at the very time they were most needed. This is an example of how counterparty risk can become exacerbated at different times and this type of risk is referred to as **wrong-way risk**.

Controlling counterparty risk consists of putting in place a set of dynamic processes and controls to understand not only the quality of the counterparty, but also where there may be weaknesses and to monitor changes on an ongoing basis. Within SifiInvestment Bank, for example, an entire department of counterparty risk experts prepare analyses and reports of new and existing counterparties. A counterparty risk policy exists that states the overall criteria in evaluating counterparties including establishing guidance on what the bank should look for in a strong counterparty. This would include the strength of any counterparty's financial profile as might be gleaned from publicly available information such as 10ks. However, such information is reported periodically and as seen during the financial crisis, a firm that appears financially stable one month could look very different the next month. Consequently, it is critical that counterparties be monitored with great frequency, although this can become extremely resource intensive. SifiInvestment Bank has established a triage approach for conducting counterparty reviews that is tied closely with the exposure the firm has to the company and the size and complexity of the firm, among other aspects of the relationship. Small counterparties might be reviewed once a year, for example, while the top 10 counterparties accounting for 75 percent of all of SifiInvestment Bank's trades would be reviewed monthly and even more frequently depending on market conditions, available information, and other factors.

Part of the counterparty assessment process includes establishing ratings that may be used to guide which counterparties will be permitted, what level of exposure will be allowed, and what collateral requirements or other criteria may be imposed on a counterparty. A counterparty assessment scorecard could be devised that relies on information gathered during the reviews. Rating agency information where available augmented by detailed financial analysis of the condition and performance of the counterparty are essential ingredients to such a scorecard. The scorecard could be based on expert judgment and weights assigned to important aspects of counterparty strength, For example, the scorecard might assign 20 percent of the weight of the counterparty score to rating, where ratings of A or better are assigned the most points. The counterparty policy may also stipulate that the bank will not do business with any counterparty that does not have at least two ratings of BBB (or equivalent) or better. A **watch list** is recommended to monitor adverse changes in marginal counterparties and to take action in advance of any potential problem affecting the integrity of the transaction. As in the case of other risk management activities, a counterparty database is essential to staying abreast of developments. Establishing limits and collateral requirement policies for counterparties is an effective way to manage exposure. Limits could be set to avoid significant concentrations of counterparty risk. And as conditions change, the bank should have a policy to ensure that additional collateral is available from the counterparty and to outline under what conditions that would occur for all parties.

Assessment of counterparty risk has taken on a new focus as accounting and regulatory requirements around counterparty risk have grown over the years. The Basel III capital standards, for example, establish methods for computing the amount of capital a bank should assign to counterparty risk. From an accounting perspective, a bank may need to take the potential default of a counterparty into account in computing income or marking a portfolio to market. The amount of the adjustment is described by the **credit valuation adjustment** (CVA) calculation. The CVA is defined as the expected loss associated with a counterparty and is a function of the exposure of the bank to the counterparty, the PD, and the LGD of a counterparty event. Taking these inputs together, CVA can be computed as follows:

$$CVA = \sum_{i=1}^{n} LGD \int_{0}^{T} PVE_t dPD_t \qquad 5.21$$

where PVE is the present value of exposure to the counterparty and PD is the probability of default of the counterparty. The calculation would be performed over n transactions with the counterparty over an interval of time T. To estimate PD, the bank would use the credit spread for the counterparty. The PVE variable could be computed over a range of possible outcomes using Monte Carlo simulation. In that way, the bank could derive a distribution of CVA outcomes on which capital requirements could be based. Clearly, computing CVA becomes computationally extensive when considering that a large counterparty may have many transactions with the bank. Once these computations have been performed, the bank could potentially use them to hedge counterparty risk since the option to default casts CVA in a similar light as other default options.

SUMMARY

This chapter introduces a number of key concepts that can be used to determine the default risk of an individual obligor or portfolio. Default can be described in an option-theoretic framework leveraging the Merton default model. The borrower's incentive to default is dependent on the relationship of the asset value at any point in time up to maturity to the obligation. In that sense it is easy to see that the borrower has a valuable put option allowing them to exercise their option to default when the value of the asset falls below the debt obligation. These relationships can be used to derive the probability of default (default frequency or PD) as well as loss severity (LGD). Estimates of expected loss are then possible to compute from PD and LGD. An important concept that accompanies the Merton model is the distance-to-default (DD), which measures how far an asset's value must fall before it defaults. This can be used to determine the expected default frequency (EDF) of the borrower.

The credit risk profile of an individual borrower or portfolio will change over time. Further, credit portfolios are subject to diversification effects that can be measured. Tools and techniques to handle credit risk dynamics in large portfolios are available, such as CreditMetrics™. These tools enable credit risk managers to use Markov chain analysis to develop transition probabilities from one credit state to another over time. Estimation of joint migration probabilities among loans within a portfolio further allow portfolio analysts to measure portfolio volatility and to provide a basis for performing various portfolio analyses including determination of the incremental contribution to portfolio risk from individual loans or pools.

While such methods are useful in some contexts for evaluating credit risk, analytic methods such as the Vasicek default model provide the ability to understand the shape of the default distribution in a parsimonious manner. Finally, assessment of counterparty risk is an area that requires considerable attention by banks, given the increased scrutiny by regulators on such risks.

QUESTIONS

1. Assume a company takes a loan out from ExBank of $10 million to buy land for a new manufacturing facility. ExBank requires the company to put down $2 million to buy this property. Based on the volatility of this property type, the asset value currently is estimated at $11.5 million. Describe the nature (i.e., what kind is it) of the option in this contract using the Merton default framework from the bank's perspective.

2. Using the Black-Scholes option pricing framework and the cumulative probability distribution, show what the importance of $N(-d_2)$ means for the borrower's option.

3. What is the estimated LGD for this loan assuming that $N(d_2) = .95$ and $N(-d_1) = .04$?

4. If the continuously compounded annualized risk-free rate is 2.5 percent and the term of the loan is five years, $N(d_2) = .95$, and $N(-d_1) = .04$, what is the expected loss on this loan?

5. Assuming a volatility of 10 percent, what is the estimated distance-to-default?

6. Using a graph, describe in words what distance-to-default means.
7. What is the estimated yield that the bank should expect on that investment, using what you have calculated in the above questions?

You have an investment portfolio consisting of two bonds, 1 and 2, that can migrate between each other, with 1 as the highest rating and default designated as 3. The probabilities associated with these transition outcomes are shown in the table below.

		To		
		1	2	3
	1	.9	0.07	0.03
From	2	0.1	0.7	0.2
	3	0	0	1

The forward rates associated with bond 1 are 2, 2.5, and 2.75 percent for Years 1, 2, and 3, respectively. The forward curve for bond 2 is 2.5, 2.75, and 3 percent for Years 1, 2, and 3, respectively. These rates can be viewed as discount rates. Bond 1 has a coupon rate of 2.5 percent paid annually and has a term of three years. Bond 2 also has a three-year maturity with a 3 percent coupon paid annually. The face amount of each bond is $1 million.

8. Produce the joint migration table for your portfolio and provide an interpretation of what these cells represent.
9. What are the associated values of your two-bond portfolio? If the bonds go into status 3 you recover 60 percent of the original value for each.
10. What is the expected value of your portfolio?
11. What is the volatility of your portfolio?
12. If the volatility of your overall portfolio today is $100,000 and you consider adding another asset with an exposure of $500,000 to it, that would now make portfolio volatility $150,000. How would you evaluate whether to add this asset to your portfolio, and what would you conclude about its relative risk?

CHAPTER 6

Consumer Credit Risk Measurement

OVERVIEW

Within the U.S. commercial banking sector, the consumer credit market comprises a variety of loan types, making up approximately 40 percent of loan portfolios (Figure 6.1). Considerable variation in consumer loan types exists across several dimensions including whether the loan is unsecured (e.g., credit card) or secured by underlying collateral (such as a residential mortgage) term, amortization schedule, and note rate, among others. These features can have profound impacts on the credit risk exposure of consumer loans. In measuring the credit risk of a consumer loan portfolio, the product features of each loan type along with borrower, collateral, and macroeconomic factors feature prominently in estimating credit risk. Techniques to estimate credit risk are comparable across consumer loan types, although over the years some product types adopted statistically driven measures earlier than others. Credit card businesses have relied upon sophisticated data mining techniques to stratify and estimate credit risk on their portfolios for many years, while the use of such models for mortgage loans accelerated in the mid-1990s with the advent of statistically based **automated underwriting systems** (AUS).[1] In this chapter, techniques to directly measure default incidence and loss severity will be highlighted across several consumer loan types, pointing out issues and approaches to handling unique aspects of each type.

---

[1] An AUS system includes a statistically based underwriting scorecard that generates a score for each borrower that is compared to a policy cutoff and rules to determine underwriting eligibility and approval.

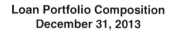

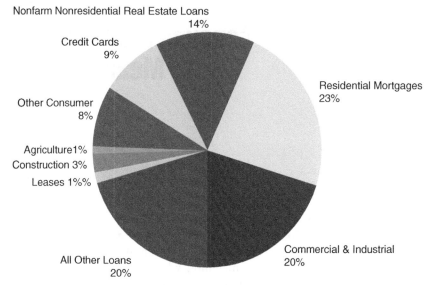

FIGURE 6.1   U.S. Commercial Bank Loan Composition
Source: FDIC Quarterly Banking Profile, December 31, 2013.

MEASURING PRODUCT EXPECTED LOSS

As profiled in Chapter 5, total dollar credit loss is defined by the product of **default probability** (PD), **loss severity** (LGD), and outstanding balance. Each of these components merits a separate approach to analytically deriving estimates for computing loss in the SifiBank consumer products division. In SifiBank in 2004, the CRO for the Consumer Products Group (CPG) had a portfolio of consumer loans of $20 billion. CPG has three separate business divisions, Auto Lending (ALD) ($2 billion portfolio), Credit Cards (CCD) ($8 billion portfolio), and Residential Mortgage (RMD) ($10 billion portfolio). Within RMD, the business is further split into first mortgage ($7 billion portfolio) and second mortgage ($3 billion). Inside the first lien mortgage portfolio are $5 billion in prime mortgages and $2 billion in subprime mortgages. Differentiating prime and subprime loans is largely based on a widely accepted industry definition of subprime loans as borrowers with credit scores below 620. These loans are expected to perform worse than prime mortgages and would be priced accordingly through higher rates and origination fees for subprime loans.

Second-lien mortgages lie in a subordinated position to first-lien mortgages and as a result are often thought of as having the loss severity characteristics of unsecured debt. This means that after a default, the holder of the second-lien mortgage lies in a lesser position with regard to claim on the property relative to the owner of the first lien. This has significant implications for calculating loss severities for the two second-lien product types: Home Equity Lines of Credit (HELOC) and Closed-End Second Liens (CES). HELOCs are essentially a line of credit that has a revolving feature much like a credit card. At the time of origination a line amount is established, say $100,000, of which some amount may be taken out with additional draws as needed up to the total line amount. Thus, the undrawn portion of the HELOC creates a *contingent exposure* for SifiBank that later on can pose additional credit risk should the economy deteriorate and borrowers look to the HELOC as a source of cash flow. CES products have a fixed loan balance at origination and thus resemble a standard first-lien mortgage but lie in a junior or subordinated position with respect to the first lien. To illustrate how the CES product works consider a borrower interested in taking out a $180,000 mortgage on a $200,000 home. To avoid paying mortgage insurance, which goes into effect at LTVs over 80 percent, the homeowner could take on a first-lien mortgage in the amount of $160,000 (80 percent) and add to it another second-lien CES for $20,000 (10 percent). These types of products were referred to as 80/10/10s and these were widely marketed during the housing boom. The CES product does not pose a contingent exposure issue for SifiBank in contrast to the HELOC that may have an undrawn line associated with it.

Each month, the CRO of SifiBank requests a set of management reports profiling the credit risk of CPG. An essential part of this reporting is to quantify both the actual performance of the portfolio as well as the expected losses of the division and how the risk of this portfolio changes over time. Note the distinction between historical losses and expected losses. Risk managers must always be forward-looking in their views and thus it is essential that tools be developed providing a window into the potential movement of credit risk. Specifically, it is critical to understand the degree to which the credit model is over- or underestimating credit risk over time. This issue of model risk will be explored in more detail in Chapter 15.

Fortunately, SifiBank has been originating consumer loans for more than a decade and through its loan servicing systems has retained considerable detail at the loan level for each of its products. SifiBank generates a set of delinquency metrics for each product type as shown in Table 6.1. **Delinquency status** is measured starting from the first date after which a scheduled payment is missed, defined as 30 days past due (30DPD), and extending for each late payment thereafter: 60DPD, 90DPD, 120DPD, 180DPD, and so forth.

TABLE 6.1 CPG Consumer Loan Portfolio Delinquency Rates (%)

Loan Type	30–59DPD	60–90DPD	90+DPD	Default
Credit Card	22.10	18.76	15.55	10.25
Prime Auto	10.75	8.63	7.45	5.50
1st Mortgage	8.30	6.22	5.15	3.00
2nd Mortgage	11.55	9.35	8.24	5.75

Typically once a loan moves to 90DPD or worse it is classified as **nonaccruing** and is considered **nonperforming**. The risk manager however has some latitude in defining what is considered to be a nonperforming loan in developing projections of future loss performance. It is important for internal comparisons that some benchmark delinquency state is used across portfolios when aggregating performance across the enterprise. Loan performance can exhibit movements back and forth between delinquency statuses. For example, a borrower could miss two payments, becoming 60DPD, and then make next month's scheduled payment plus one of the missed payments, in which case the loan would be reclassified in the next month as 30DPD. And in a number of instances, either through actions by the bank or the borrower, a loan may "cure," or return to a current status. In Chapter 8, how loss mitigation efforts can help cure loans in various stages of delinquency and thus lower the bank's loss exposure as a result of such actions taken will be explored.

The risk manager also must understand the difference between marginal and cumulative default rates. A marginal default rate is defined as the number or dollar weighted balances of defaults occurring within a specified period of time (e.g., one month), expressed as a percent of current outstanding balances adjusted for prepayments and defaults experienced up to that point.

A consideration in computing delinquency metrics is whether these rates are conditional (as in the example above) on other events such as prepayment or whether they are referenced to original or current unpaid principal balance (OUPB and CUPB) of the pool. It may be helpful, for example, to analyze the performances of specific origination years (vintages) from the perspective of OUPB as a means of comparing one cohort to another at a specific point in time. It is critical in doing so that the analyst controls for the amount of time since origination, as loan aging will result in differences in performance holding other factors constant. For example, in comparing performance as of July 2007 between mortgage loans originated in July 2002 to loans originated in July 2003, the analyst would need to adjust for the additional 12 months of time (60 months versus 48) over which the 2002 cohort could experience additional defaults. To see how this works, consider Table 6.2 for a subset of CPG's mortgage portfolio. The top part of

TABLE 6.2 Example 90+DPD Prime Mortgage Deliquency Rate Report

	OUPB	12	24	36	48	60	Lifetime
Jul-2002	$1,000,000,000	$10,000,000	$15,000,000	$25,000,000	$37,500,000	$42,500,000	$42,500,000
Jul-2003	$1,500,000,000	$22,500,000	$41,250,000	$56,250,000	$60,000,000		$60,000,000
Jul-2004	$ 800,000,000	$14,000,000	$16,000,000	$30,400,000			$30,400,000
Jul-2005	$ 750,000,000	$18,750,000	$28,125,000				$28,125,000
Jul-2006	$ 500,000,000	$21,000,000					$21,000,000
	$4,550,000,000						

Panel B: Annual 90+DPD Rates through each Period

	12	24	36	48	60	Lifetime
Jul-2002	1.00%	1.52%	2.56%	3.95%	4.66%	13.68%
Jul-2003	1.50%	2.79%	3.92%	4.35%		12.56%
Jul-2004	1.75%	2.04%	3.95%			7.73%
Jul-2005	2.50%	3.85%				6.35%
Jul-2006	4.20%					4.20%

the table displays the marginal dollar amount of 90+DPD prime mortgage loans originated in July 2002 and July 2003 in 12-month increments of seasoning since origination. The bottom part of the table displays the same information now in percentage terms of UPB adjusted for defaults occurring over time. To gain a better feel for how this table is constructed consider the marginal default rate computed for the 2003 vintage 48 months from origination. The default rate of 4.35 percent is computed as follows:

$$DR_{90DPD}^{2003}$$

$$= \frac{2003Defaults_{90DPD}^{48}}{OUPB^{2003} - 2003Defaults_{90DPD}^{36} - 2003Defaults_{90DPD}^{24} - 2003Defaults_{90DPD}^{12}}$$

Note that without controlling for the seasoning, or age of each vintage from its origination date, it is difficult to compare default performance. To see this, the lifetime, or cumulative default rates of the 2002 vintage is 13.68 versus 12.56 percent for the 2003 vintage. Now if we look at the 90+DPD rates by specific periods after origination, a different picture emerges, showing that the 2003 vintage exhibits worse performance at 12, 24, 36, and 48 months from origination than the 2002 vintage at the same point in time. The analyst can then perform additional forensic analysis about the characteristics of the loans to determine if this is a concern or not. Conducting basic vintage analysis is an important part of understanding where performance differences may arise. Performance differences in three vintages of CPG mortgages can be seen in Figure 6.2. Comparisons at a point in time are most appropriate (such as 36 months) as they control for seasoning of older vintages. In the figure, 2001 has much higher delinquencies than the other two vintages and this may be explained by more relaxed underwriting standards in that year, which saw high approval rates for risky borrowers.

Looking at the data in Table 6.1, differences in delinquency rates are clearly present between products and within delinquency categories as well. Earlier delinquency buckets such as 30DPD tend to be higher than the later stage delinquency buckets, reflecting the **time profile of default** as loans season. In estimating the expected loss of the portfolio in a given period of time, the risk manager must focus on developing an estimate of default incidence. The starting point for this exercise is deciding upon what the delinquency definition is (sometimes referred to as the bad definition, where loans in a current payment status are considered "good").

There is no convention on what definition of delinquency to use in estimating default rates; however, some general guidance can shape the decision. The delinquency measure should be one that reflects a general level of stability in its performance. Looking at 30DPD rates tend to be noisy and

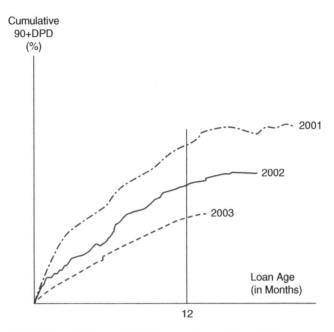

FIGURE 6.2   CPG 90+DPD Vintage Curves 2001–2003

thus not very representative of future long-term performance, since borrowers, for example, can miss a payment for reasons other than financial difficulty such as simply forgetting to mail a payment before heading off on vacation. Alternatively, management may not want to wait until the loan becomes nonperforming before having some indication of the direction and magnitude delinquencies will take. Also, the product itself tends to guide the delinquency definition. Products such as mortgages having longer terms than credit cards may warrant using later stage delinquency definitions such as 90DPD. Alternative definitions for the default outcome might include the number of times a borrower did not pay as agreed within some stated time period (e.g., over the past six months). Other considerations include the purpose for which the estimate is to be used. If the estimate will become part of an underwriting decision such as using an AUS scorecard, then the bad definition might reflect whether the borrower makes ultimate repayment versus timely repayment. A borrower might not make timely payments, but if you are the CRO of the credit card division, this may be a satisfactory business outcome since late fees and interest can be highly profitable. Alternatively, if the risk definition is that a borrower is technically in default after two missed payments, then that could serve as the basis of the default analysis.

CPG management in their 2004 strategic planning meeting decided to increase the amount of capital allocated to its subprime mortgage division, targeting an annual growth rate of 30 percent for these mortgages over the next three years based on favorable house-price appreciation, generally strong economic conditions, and low interest rates stemming from easy monetary policy by the Federal Reserve. SifiBank has historically originated fairly low credit risk mortgages by limiting the combinations of high-risk attributes. Risk management has been asked to work with the business areas to build a credit loss profile for the expanded business based on some relaxation of credit terms that the business is considering. The head of mortgage production has handed over product term sheets from two of its major competitors that recently launched a set of new mortgage products aimed at expanding profit margin by establishing loan parameters that are well outside the underwriting standards of the two housing agencies Fannie Mae and Freddie Mac, thus allowing these competitors to earn what management believes are returns well above the commoditized margins of loans sold to the two housing agencies. The risk management team has been applying a 90-days past due or worse (90DPD+) definition to estimating default incidence for its AUS scorecards.

Years before CPG built an extensive historical times series database of loan performance, it relied on simple comparisons of loan performance by loan product and risk attributes to guide its risk management decisions around products. For example, CPG would review its delinquency rates along various product segments such as fixed-rate versus adjustable rate mortgages, new versus used autos, and prime versus subprime credit cards. Within each product segment, risk management would further stratify performance along key risk attributes such as credit score (FICO), loan-to-value (LTV) for its mortgages, income, profession, length of time on job, and state. As more loan observations became available, the risk team was able to leverage statistical models to generate more accurate measures of credit performance.

In part, risk managers rely on the concept of **compensating factors**, as a way of making prudent risk trade-offs between borrower and loan attributes. Table 6.3 provides insight on this concept. Panel A depicts 90+DPD rates on prime first-lien mortgages by just two risk factors: FICO and LTV, with all others held constant. The baseline 90+DPD rate is for the 660 FICO/90 LTV loan, resulting in a 90+DPD rate of 2.5 percent. The relative risk of lower and higher FICOs to the 660 FICO are shown as risk multipliers in the far left column. Similarly, the 80 and 95 percent LTVs have risk multipliers of .6 and two times that of a 90 percent LTV, respectively, holding FICO and other attributes constant. Historically, CLG originated mortgages with LTVs of 90 percent and FICOs of 660 on average. If CLG

TABLE 6.3   Example of Risk-Layering for Prime First-Lien Mortgages (90+DPD %)

Panel A: FICO and LTV Impacts on Delinquency—Individual Factors

Risk Mutipliers		LTV		
		0.6	1	2
	FICO	80%	90%	95%
1.8	620	2.70%	4.50%	9.00%
1	660	1.50%	2.50%	5.00%
0.6	720	0.90%	1.50%	1.80%

Panel B: FICO and LTV Impacts on Delinquency-Interaction Effects Multipliers

	620	3.12	5.27	9.34
	660	1.75	3.23	5.86
	720	1.56	2.19	2.65

changed its credit policy to allow for lower creditworthy borrowers with 620 FICOs, then to maintain a comparable default rate as before requires a lower LTV to compensate for the lower FICO. While not an exact offset, the 620/80 percent loan combination results in a default rate closer (2.7 percent) to the baseline 660/90 percent loan.

As CLG relaxed its underwriting standards, it originated more loans with riskier combined attributes such as the 95 percent LTV/620 FICO combination that shows a 90+DPD rate that is 3.6 times that of the baseline loan originated under tighter credit policy. This illustrates the concept of **risk layering** where risk attributes are combined together in a loan that generates much higher default rates beyond just the additional risk formed by relaxing on the individual attributes alone. Risk-layered products may attract a different cohort of borrower whose behavior may differ from the bank's regular customers. This can lead to higher risk as shown in Panel B of Table 6.3. Without some analytical method for assessing the risk of these two attributes together, controlling for other factors contributing to default, the analyst cannot easily assess trade-offs among attributes.

Various statistical models are available to estimate such relationships, with the general class of model known as **binary choice**, an industry conventional approach.

Binary choice models deviate from standard regression models that allow for the dependent variable to be continuous. In a binary choice model, the dependent variable takes on a discrete value, for example either the loan is 90+DPD (= 1), or it is not (= 0). The reason why such models are favored by credit risk managers is first they allow for estimating a default probability in a way that ensures that it lies in an interval between 0 and 100 percent and it permits inclusion of multiple risk factors together (multivariate regression). A common form of binary choice model that ensures that default probabilities lie in the 0–1 interval is referred to as a **logistic** (or logit) regression model, which takes the following form:

$$F(z) = \frac{1}{1+e^{-z}} \qquad\qquad 6.1$$

Where $F(z)$ represents the probability of default for a loan. The variable z represents risk factors related to a loan. These risk factors: $\beta_0, \beta_1, \ldots, \beta_N$, are estimated parameters of the model and the X_i represent a set of loan characteristics (independent variables) likely to predict default risk. Further, the variable z is represented as a linear combination of the model parameters and loan characteristics:

$$z = \beta_0 + \sum_{i=1}^{N}\beta_i X_i \qquad\qquad 6.2$$

The logistic regression takes the functional form shown in Figure 6.3. The functional form represented by the curve ensures that the probability of default lies between 0 and 1 at all times, regardless of the combination of

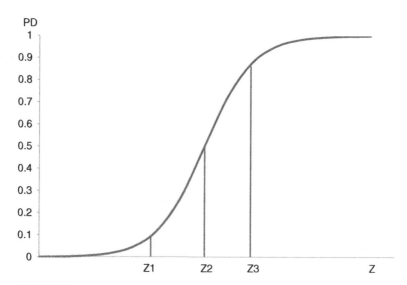

FIGURE 6.3   Illustrative Logistic Function

TABLE 6.4 Risk Factors for Default

Risk Factor	Expected Impact on Default
FICO	Higher FICO Scores tend to have lower probability of default
LTV	Higher LTVs tend to have higher probability of default
Debt-to-Income Ratio	Higher Debt-to-Incomes ratios tend to have higher probability of defaults
Documentation Type (Full, Low)	Low Doc loans tend to have higher probability of default
Product Type (ARM, Fixed-rate)	ARM loans tend to have higher probability of default
State	Certain states tend to have higher delinquency rates than others (e.g., California)
House Price Forecast	Rising house prices tend to have lower probability of default
Loan Age since Origination	As borrower circumstances change over time, defaults can reflect these changes

risk factors (Xs) specified in the model. A loan with attributes that are reflected by Z_1 has a lower default probability (about 10 percent) than either Z_2 (50 percent), or Z_3 (about 90 percent).

Looking at the first-lien mortgage portfolio, the risk management team settled on a set of risk factors it believes are predictive of mortgage default based on historical information in its database (Table 6.4).[2] Risk analysts often rely on insight from underwriters and other staff with extensive lending experience to provide input into what factors are appropriate to use. This may also include legal staff that has responsibility over compliance and regulatory issues. Certain risk factors may qualify for protected class treatment under certain laws such as the Equal Credit Opportunity Act (ECOA) Reg B provisions. These include age and race, which may not be permitted to be used in making lending decisions.

To complete the estimation, CPG risk management needs to select a sample of first-lien subprime mortgages from its historical database. For large institutions, pulling the entire loan population may not be operationally feasible, so a random or stratified sample of loans may be required. In

---

[2] Typical efforts to model default include more risk factors than that shown in Figure 6.4, but the underlying estimation process remains fundamentally identical to the example for SifiBank.

the case of CPG, a sample of 100,000 loans originated between January 1, 2000, and June 2004 are selected. In the case of mortgages, several years' worth of performance may be necessary in order to obtain sufficient seasoning of the loans to provide a sufficient number of bad loans to estimate the model. For other assets with shorter loan performance windows such as credit cards the estimation of default rates may be done using more recent vintages. Once the data are scrubbed for missing values, incomplete or inaccurate information, the modeling effort can begin.

Standard econometric packages are available to estimate such models and have the added feature of providing a variety of diagnostic statistics regarding the predictiveness of the default model. Using the data for the risk factors described above the CPG risk management team generates a logit model predicting the likelihood that a first-lien mortgage will be 90+DPD over a $3\frac{1}{2}$-year period. Note that the logit results generate default rates that are not lifetime (instead they reflect the seasoning of the development sample used to build the model) and subsequently will need to be scaled to reflect a 30-year lifetime default rate. The logit model can be enhanced to accommodate loan seasoning as will be described later in this chapter. A number of risk factors such as FICO, LTV, and DTI are presented as linear variables over a range of values.

Interpretation and evaluation of the default model requires assessment of the overall level of predictiveness of the model, the statistical significance of the estimated parameters, and that they have the expected signs, among other aspects of good model performance. In the CPG model, all coefficients as shown in Table 6.5 are significant at the 5 percent level. We would expect that as FICO score increases, the likelihood of default declines, in which case the coefficient should be negative. Alternatively, as the LTV increases, borrowers have less "skin-in-the-game" via their downpayment on the home and so we would expect default rates to rise, suggesting a positive coefficient in the estimated model. In some instances, the independent variables take on a binary form. This is seen by the loan documentation variable where the loan is originated under a full verification of income standard (= 0) or not (= 1). Low documentation, all else equal, should generate higher default risk than a fully documented loan and so its sign would be expected to be positive (i.e., higher default risk). Sometimes geographic location, local, regional macroeconomic conditions, or a combination of the three may enter into the model as control variables. Some states exhibit greater swings in defaults over time due to a variety of factors including demographic patterns and local economic conditions. In the case of mortgage loans, a variable for house price appreciation that is often included in mortgage default models as an important trigger event for default is whether the borrower experiences negative equity (i.e., loan balance greater than home value).

TABLE 6.5 Logit Default Model Results

Risk Factor	Parameter Name	Coefficients Default	Odd Ratios Default	Low Default Risk Loan Attributes	High Default Risk Loan Attributes
Intercept		-4.5000	0.5000		
FICO <620	Credit Score <620	0.0953	1.1000	0.0000	1.0000
FICO 620–660	Credit Score 620–660	0.0000	1.0000	0.0000	0.0000
FICO >660	Credit Score >660	-0.0202	0.9800	1.0000	0.0000
LTV <80%	Loan-to-Value Ratio <80%	-0.0513	0.9500	1.0000	0.0000
LTV 80–90%	Loan-to-Value Ratio 80%–90%	0.0000	1.0000	0.0000	0.0000
LTV >90%	Loan-to-Value Ratio >90%	0.2624	1.3000	0.0000	1.0000
DTI <36%	Debt-to-Income Ratio <36%	0.0000	1.0000	1.0000	0.0000
DTI ≥36%	Debt-to-Income Ratio ≥36%	0.0488	1.0500	0.0000	1.0000
LDOC	Loans not fully documented	0.4055	1.5000	0.0000	1.0000
ARM	Product type	0.5596	1.7500	0.0000	1.0000
California	Property Location	0.8109	2.2500	0.0000	1.0000
Loan Age 0–3 Years	Seasoning	-0.1054	0.9000	1.0000	0.0000
Loan Age 3–5 years	Seasoning	0.0000	1.0000	0.0000	1.0000
Loan Age >5 Years	Seasoning	-0.0513	0.9500	0.0000	0.0000
Annual House Price Appreciation Rate	House Price Effect	-0.3567	0.7000	0.1000	0.1000
Current Interest Rates	Interest Rate Effect	0.0400	1.0408	0.0500	0.0500
Probability Default P(D)				0.0089	0.0870

Interpreting the coefficients from a logit default model is also an important exercise for conveying relative risks of specific factors to management and other interested parties. In the CPG default model presented, management has been interested in expanding the underwriting guidelines for low documentation loans given competitive moves in the industry and the risk management team can provide empirical insight into this issue. The management team conducted their own analysis and found that of all the first-lien mortgages defaulting, the 90+DPD rate for fully documented loans was 3.75 percent and that of less than fully documented loans was 5 percent. Their analysis suggested that the relative risk of low documentation loans is thus 5/3.75 percent, or low documentation loans are 33 percent more likely to default than fully documented loans. Based on that result, the production team recommends that risk management expand the credit underwriting policy to allow for more of these mortgages while increasing their pricing for the higher risk. However, CPG risk management knows that this assessment is flawed. The production team did not control for the other risk factors associated with the loan. That means that the 90+DPD rates presented for both groups do not isolate the incremental risk due solely to documentation, controlling for all other risk factors. As described above, the CPG default model controls for other risk attributes and generates an estimated coefficient b for documentation effects of +.41. Given that the logistic regression represents each coefficient as the natural log of the **odds ratio** (a relationship expressing the relative risk of one risk factor to another—for example, low documentation to fully documented loans)—to derive the odds ratio, the parameter for documentation type is exponentiated: that is, $e^{+.41}$, which equals approximately 1.5. Formally, the odds ratio is described as follows:

$$\Psi = e^{\beta_i} \qquad\qquad 6.3$$

It measures how much more likely a borrower will be to enter default, in this case from having been originated as a low documentation loan versus the baseline of full documentation.

The CPG risk team communicates their findings that the incremental risk of low documentation underwriting is really 50 percent greater than that of fully documented loans (the baseline for this risk factor implying an odds ratio of 1.0 for fully documented loans). With regard to the desire to allow low documentation loans, such an expansion of risk in the view of the risk team is seen to be excessive and they recommend not relaxing underwriting standards for documentation. The CPG Credit Committee, which includes the CPG, CFO, and head of production as voting members, outvotes the CRO and concludes that business needs outweigh the marginal risks that they see based on very low 90+DPD rates on recent vintages.

Despite this setback, the risk management team forges ahead to quantify the expected risk of mortgages with the characteristics of each loan underwritten with the expanded documentation type. To do so requires taking the coefficients of the model shown in Table 6.5 and computing the default probability (in percent) using the logit formula $1/(1+e^{-Z}) = Pr(\text{Default})$ where:

$$Z = \beta_0 + \beta_1 * FICO + \beta_2 * LTV + \beta_3 * DTI + \beta_4 * LDOC + \beta_5 \\ * CA + \beta_6 * ARM + \beta_7 * AGELE3 + \beta_8 * AGE35 + \beta_9 \qquad 6.4 \\ * AGEGT5 + \beta_{10} * HPI + \beta_{11} * INTRATE$$

Note that in Table 6.5 two loans are presented with their risk factors. One loan has strong risk factors, leading it to have a low estimated default rate of 89bps, or .89 percent. In contrast, the second loan is riskier along several characteristics including FICO, LTV, and documentation type. This loan as a result is estimated to have a default rate of 8.7 percent.

By combining risk factor upon risk factor, this resulting risk layering can amplify the default propensity of a loan well beyond one with standard underwriting characteristics. Risk layering can be a silent killer to banks that do not guard against it. It will often occur in cases where a high degree of competition takes place in the market for loan products during a period of relatively good credit performance, hence hastening calls for relaxation of underwriting criteria. But without solid historical performance to back up risk management concerns over risk layering, it may be difficult to rein in. This is where a strong risk culture and governance structure can weigh in.

The logit model results for these loans provide an estimated 90+DPD delinquency rate over about a 3½-year period. Risk managers often like to know what the lifetime default rate is on an asset. For long-lived assets such as mortgages, it is impractical to collect performance data for 30 years (the usual term of most mortgages). For other asset types with shorter maturities such as credit cards or auto loans, lifetime default rates can be constructed using actual data with far less effort than for mortgages. One method used to derive estimates of the entire time profile of default including a cumulative default rate is based on survival analysis. Used in a variety of disciplines including epidemiology, survival analysis applied to loan default aims to understand the likelihood of a pool of loans surviving to some point conditional on some defaults occurring before that time. In this case the survival rate $S(t)$ may be computed. Related to the survival rate is the hazard rate $h(t)$

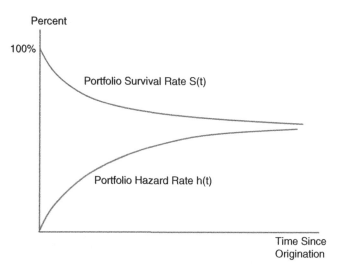

FIGURE 6.4   Frequency of Defaults

which defines the default rate between two periods of time conditioned on no defaults leading up to that time.

For a mortgage portfolio, an example of a survival and hazard curve could be plotted from estimates derived from a survival analysis as depicted in Figure 6.4. Figure 6.4 also shows the cumulative percentage of defaults in a given year after loan origination. For the mortgage pool example, by year 10 more than 95 percent of defaults that occur during the life of these mortgages would be realized. In other words, only a small percentage of defaults occur after year 10 for this mortgage pool.

INCORPORATING BORROWER OPTIONS INTO RISK VIEWS AND COMPETING RISK ASSESSMENT

The risk management team of CPG understands that measuring mortgage default rates is complicated by a couple of factors. First, many loans pay back principal at some regular schedule referred to as amortization. Second, mortgages are among the most complex consumer assets to value given their optionality. As Chapter 5 discusses, default can be viewed as a put option, and in the case of mortgages, this put option is exercised whenever the value of the home falls below that of the mortgage. The borrower would be in a negative equity position, providing an economic incentive to default.

Consumer assets also have another option feature in the form of loan prepayment. This option (a call option) in the case of a mortgage carries no premium, thus making it a potentially valuable feature to the borrower as interest rates change. This issue is of particular interest in Chapter 9 as mortgage prepayments present interest rate risk to financial institutions. However, its significance in understanding credit risk is recognizing that it acts as a competing risk to default. To illustrate this concept, assume that a mortgage loan has a note rate of 6 percent. If prevailing mortgage rates for the same loan are at or above 6 percent, the borrower has no economic incentive to refinance his or her loan and will thus continue to make payments as agreed. However, should interest rates decline such that current mortgage rates are at 5 percent, the borrower now has an incentive to refinance into a new loan at the lower rate. If that occurs, the bank holding that loan in its portfolio (or the investor in a mortgage-backed security) would face the loss of income represented by the difference of the original and new loan rates. From the standpoint of interest rate risk exposure, this can also reduce the value of the mortgage. However, loans that prepay clearly cannot default, and importantly, understanding loan default comes down to assessing the conditional risk that it presents, taking into account loan prepayments. Further, the risk attributes that drive prepayment may be inversely related to default and vice versa. The concept of **competing risks** and its impact on default and prepayment is shown in Figure 6.5. In this figure, the left-hand graph depicts the baseline cumulative default rate under a normal set of interest rate conditions (represented

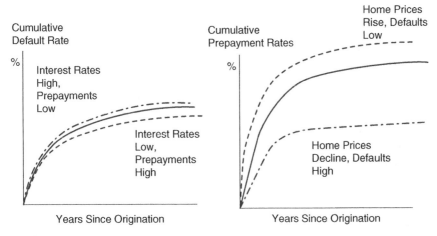

FIGURE 6.5 Competing Risks between Default and Prepayment for a Mortgage

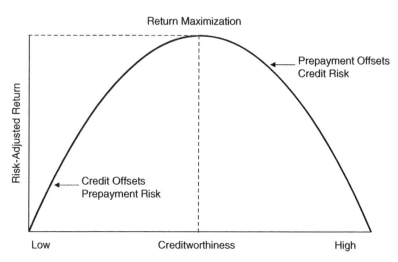

FIGURE 6.6 Return Maximization

by the solid curve), whereas if interest rates decline, prepayments accelerate, which tends to pull down default rates. Likewise, the right-hand graph illustrates what happens to prepayments when home prices change along with default rates. As home prices decline, defaults rise, which leads to lower prepayments.

In Figure 6.6, holding all else constant, borrowers that have better creditworthiness as represented by high credit scores would be more likely to prepay their mortgage than borrowers with low scores. This would tend to lower the value of a mortgage to a bank due to the prepayment, or interest rate risk exposure. Alternatively, loans with low credit scores are unlikely to be in a position to refinance their mortgages should rates be attractive to do so and so the value of the mortgage should be higher, absent default risk. We would expect low credit scores to present higher default risk and vice versa, suggesting a lower value of the mortgage, putting aside prepayment risk for the moment. When taking both risks into account, the risk-adjusted return profile of the mortgage may appear concave. This reflects the fact that mortgage values associated with low credit scores are driven more by loan default whereas mortgage values for high credit scores are pulled down due to prepayments. Somewhere in between these scores, mortgage return is optimized.

CPG risk managers leverage enhanced versions of binary choice models to tackle the competing risk problem for consumer assets such as mortgages. A typical methodology is referred to as a **generalized logistic**

regression model. This model extends the simple logit default model by recognizing that there are more than two outcomes for the mortgage. In this case, the mortgage can remain active and not default (the dependent variable Z equals 0), or the loan defaults (Z equals 1), or the borrower prepays (Z equals 2). This type of model could be estimated with risk factors changing over time. An example would be credit scores that migrate through time reflecting changes in the borrower's credit profile, or house price changes reflecting underlying market conditions. Other risk factors remain static, such as product type, and these would be reflected in the specification of the model. Such models are referred to as discrete-time models as they assess risk over individual time periods such as month or quarter. Continuous-time variations of these models are also used but in the case of consumer loans where payments are made at regular intervals, a generalized logit may align better with the discrete payments in the data. Separate regression models are estimated for default and prepayment using the set of risk attributes predictive of both risk types. An example of the generalized logit for the mortgage portfolio of CPG is shown below:

$$Z_{Default} = \alpha_D + \beta_{1D}FICO + \beta_{2D}LTV + \beta_{3D}DTI + \beta_{4D}DOCTYPE \\ + \beta_{5D}PRODUCT + \beta_{6D}HPI + \beta_{7D}STATE + \beta_{8D}RATE + \varepsilon \qquad 6.5$$

$$Z_{Prepay} = \alpha_D + \beta_{1P}FICO + \beta_{2P}LTV + \beta_{3P}DTI + \beta_{4P}DOCTYPE \\ + \beta_{5P}PRODUCT + \beta_{6P}HPI + \beta_{7P}STATE + \beta_{8P}RATE + \varepsilon \qquad 6.6$$

$$\Pr(\text{Default}) = z_D = \frac{e^{\sum_{i=1}^{N}\beta_{1i}X_i}}{1 + e^{\sum_{i=1}^{N}\beta_{1i}X_i} + e^{\sum_{i=1}^{N}\beta_{2i}X_i}} \qquad 6.7$$

$$\Pr(\text{Prepayment}) = z_{PP} = \frac{e^{\sum_{i=1}^{N}\beta_{2i}X_i}}{1 + e^{\sum_{i=1}^{N}\beta_{1i}X_i} + e^{\sum_{i=1}^{N}\beta_{2i}X_i}} \qquad 6.8$$

Each of the Xs above represent a risk factor explaining default or prepayment as illustrated in Table 6.6. As with the logit model (that treated prepayments the same as active paying loans), estimated probabilities of default and prepayment can be computed as shown in the companion spreadsheet for this chapter. As before, a low and high default risk

TABLE 6.6 Competing Risk Model: Default and Prepayment

Risk Factor	Definition	Coefficients		Odds Ratios		Low Default Risk Loan Attributes	High Default Risk Loan Attributes
		Default	Prepayment	Default	Prepayment		
Intercept		-4.5000	-1.0000	0.5000	0.2500		
FICO <620	Credit Score <620	0.0953	-0.3567	1.1000	0.7000	0.0000	1.0000
FICO 620–660	Credit Score 620–660	0.0000	0.0000	1.0000	1.0000	0.0000	0.0000
FICO >660	Credit Score >660	-0.0202	0.4055	0.9800	1.5000	1.0000	0.0000
LTV <80%	Loan-to-Value Ratio <80%	-0.0513	0.5596	0.9500	1.7500	1.0000	0.0000
LTV 80–90%	Loan-to-Value Ratio 80%–90%	0.0000	0.0000	1.0000	1.0000	0.0000	0.0000
LTV >90%	Loan-to-Value Ratio >90%	0.2624	-0.3567	1.3000	0.7000	0.0000	1.0000
DTI <36%	Debt-to-Income Ratio <36%	0.0000	0.0000	1.0000	1.0000	1.0000	0.0000
DTI ≥36%	Debt-to-Income Ratio ≥36%	0.0488	-0.0202	1.0500	0.9800	0.0000	1.0000
Low Documentation	Loans not fully documented	0.4055	-0.0834	1.5000	0.9200	0.0000	1.0000
Adjustable Rate	Product type	0.5596	0.4055	1.7500	1.5000	0.0000	1.0000
California	Property Location	0.8109	0.6931	2.2500	2.0000	0.0000	1.0000
Loan Age 0–3 Years	Seasoning	-0.1054	-0.0513	0.9000	0.9500	1.0000	0.0000
Loan Age 3–5 years	Seasoning	0.0000	0.0000	1.0000	1.0000	0.0000	1.0000
Loan Age >5 Years	Seasoning	-0.0513	-0.0305	0.9500	0.9700	0.0000	0.0000
Annual House Price Appreciation Rate	House Price Effect	-0.3567	-1.0498	0.7000	0.3500	0.1000	0.1000
Current Interest Rates	Interest Rate Effect	0.0400	-0.9163	1.0408	0.4000	0.0500	0.0500
					Pr(D)	0.0050	0.0630
Probability					Pr(P)	0.4387	0.2668

loan are presented to illustrate the differences in default and prepayment rates from the model. The low default risk loan has an estimated default probability of .5 percent versus the high default risk loan of 6.3 percent. However, the effect of the competing risk from prepayment is observed by the corresponding prepayment rates. The low default risk loan has characteristics that while they make the loan attractive from a credit risk perspective, actually increase the interest rate risk profile as indicated by higher prepayment rates: 43.9 percent versus 27.7 percent for the higher default risk loan. This is due in part to the fact that borrowers with good credit are more easily able to refinance their loans and hence prepay earlier than expected.

To better understand the nature of how prepayment and defaults relate to each other consider Table 6.7. Applying the estimates for prepayment and default on a hypothetical mortgage with a FICO of 726 and LTV of 74 percent, the table shows each estimate of the quarterly default and prepayment hazard rates derived from the prepayment and default generalized logistic regression models as well as the estimated marginal and cumulative default and prepayment rates. The estimated default and prepayment rates are computed for each quarter as:

$$
\begin{aligned}
DR(t) &= h_D(t)S(t-1) \\
PP(t) &= h_{PP}(t)S(t-1)
\end{aligned}
\qquad 6.9
$$

The survival probability in each quarter $S(t)$ is defined as:

$$
S(t) = S(t-1)[1 - h_D(t) - h_{PP}(t)] \qquad 6.10
$$

Finally, the cumulative default and prepayment rates are computed for any period t as:

$$
\begin{aligned}
DR_C(t) &= \sum_{t=1}^{T} DR(t) \\
PP_C(t) &= \sum_{t=1}^{T} PP(t)
\end{aligned}
\qquad 6.11
$$

Once default rates are computed using some methodology such as a competing risk model, the risk management team needs to understand the loss potential of the mortgage portfolio. Deriving estimates of loss severity for consumer loan products is critical as these tend to vary from product to product based on whether the loan is secured by collateral or not as well as the characteristics of the collateral when present.

TABLE 8.7 Calculating Marginal and Cumulative Default and Prepayment Rates in a Competing Risk Model

Quarter	Original Credit Score	Original LTV	Default Z	Prepayment Z	Default Hazard Rate	Prepayment Hazard Rate	Survival Probability	Estimated Period t Defaults	Estimated Period t Prepayments	Cumulative Defaults	Cumulative Prepayments
0							1				
1	726	74	-5.803	0.668	0.000	0.013	0.987	0.000	0.013	0.000	0.013
2	726	74	-5.803	0.668	0.000	0.030	0.957	0.000	0.030	0.000	0.043
3	726	74	-5.803	0.668	0.001	0.040	0.918	0.001	0.038	0.001	0.081
4	726	74	-5.803	0.668	0.001	0.049	0.872	0.001	0.045	0.002	0.126
5	726	74	-5.803	0.668	0.001	0.055	0.823	0.001	0.048	0.003	0.174
6	726	74	-5.803	0.668	0.002	0.060	0.772	0.001	0.049	0.004	0.223
7	726	74	-5.803	0.668	0.002	0.062	0.723	0.001	0.048	0.006	0.271
8	726	74	-5.803	0.668	0.002	0.061	0.677	0.002	0.044	0.008	0.315
9	726	74	-5.803	0.668	0.003	0.056	0.638	0.002	0.038	0.010	0.353
10	726	74	-5.803	0.668	0.003	0.056	0.600	0.002	0.036	0.012	0.388
11	726	74	-5.803	0.668	0.003	0.053	0.566	0.002	0.032	0.013	0.420
12	726	74	-5.803	0.668	0.003	0.053	0.534	0.002	0.030	0.015	0.450
13	726	74	-5.803	0.668	0.003	0.051	0.505	0.002	0.027	0.017	0.478
14	726	74	-5.803	0.668	0.004	0.055	0.475	0.002	0.028	0.019	0.506
15	726	74	-5.803	0.668	0.004	0.055	0.447	0.002	0.026	0.021	0.532
16	726	74	-5.803	0.668	0.004	0.051	0.423	0.002	0.023	0.022	0.555
17	726	74	-5.803	0.668	0.004	0.047	0.401	0.002	0.020	0.024	0.575
18	726	74	-5.803	0.668	0.004	0.046	0.381	0.002	0.018	0.026	0.593
19	726	74	-5.803	0.668	0.004	0.040	0.365	0.001	0.015	0.027	0.608
20	726	74	-5.803	0.668	0.004	0.043	0.348	0.002	0.016	0.028	0.624
21	726	74	-5.803	0.668	0.004	0.043	0.331	0.001	0.015	0.030	0.639
22	726	74	-5.803	0.668	0.004	0.040	0.317	0.001	0.013	0.031	0.652

23	726	74	−5.803	0.668	0.003	0.041	0.303	0.001	0.013	0.032	0.665
24	726	74	−5.803	0.668	0.004	0.045	0.288	0.001	0.014	0.033	0.679
25	726	74	−5.803	0.668	0.003	0.049	0.273	0.001	0.014	0.034	0.693
26	726	74	−5.803	0.668	0.004	0.049	0.259	0.001	0.013	0.035	0.706
27	726	74	−5.803	0.668	0.004	0.050	0.245	0.001	0.013	0.036	0.719
28	726	74	−5.803	0.668	0.003	0.053	0.231	0.001	0.013	0.037	0.732
29	726	74	−5.803	0.668	0.003	0.062	0.216	0.001	0.014	0.038	0.746
30	726	74	−5.803	0.668	0.003	0.060	0.203	0.001	0.013	0.038	0.759
31	726	74	−5.803	0.668	0.002	0.056	0.191	0.000	0.011	0.039	0.771
32	726	74	−5.803	0.668	0.003	0.054	0.180	0.001	0.010	0.039	0.781
33	726	74	−5.803	0.668	0.004	0.054	0.170	0.001	0.010	0.040	0.791
34	726	74	−5.803	0.668	0.003	0.057	0.160	0.000	0.010	0.040	0.800
35	726	74	−5.803	0.668	0.003	0.061	0.149	0.001	0.010	0.041	0.810
36	726	74	−5.803	0.668	0.003	0.062	0.140	0.000	0.009	0.041	0.819
37	726	74	−5.803	0.668	0.004	0.066	0.130	0.001	0.009	0.042	0.828
38	726	74	−5.803	0.668	0.002	0.057	0.122	0.000	0.007	0.042	0.836
39	726	74	−5.803	0.668	0.003	0.051	0.116	0.000	0.006	0.042	0.842
40	726	74	−5.803	0.668	0.005	0.056	0.109	0.001	0.007	0.043	0.848
41	726	74	−5.803	0.668	0.004	0.047	0.103	0.000	0.005	0.043	0.854
42	726	74	−5.803	0.668	0.002	0.032	0.100	0.000	0.003	0.044	0.857
43	726	74	−5.803	0.668	0.003	0.044	0.095	0.000	0.004	0.044	0.861
44	726	74	−5.803	0.668	0.003	0.036	0.091	0.000	0.003	0.044	0.865
45	726	74	−5.803	0.668	0.005	0.051	0.086	0.000	0.005	0.045	0.869
46	726	74	−5.803	0.668	0.000	0.035	0.083	0.000	0.003	0.045	0.872
47	726	74	−5.803	0.668	0.000	0.036	0.080	0.000	0.003	0.045	0.875
48	726	74	−5.803	0.668	0.004	0.045	0.076	0.000	0.004	0.045	0.879
49	726	74	−5.803	0.668	0.000	0.033	0.074	0.000	0.003	0.045	0.881

LOSS SEVERITY

In the context of a consumer loan portfolio, loss severity represents the percentage of a loan that is not recovered by the lender after the loan has defaulted. For unsecured loans such as credit cards and some personal loans, loss severities are typically figured to be 100 percent since there is no collateral behind the loan that can be taken back by the lender to offset the loss on the outstanding loan amount. For collateralized loans such as mortgages, loss severities are usually much lower, for example a prime first-lien mortgage historically might have a loss severity of 25–35 percent, whereas a subprime mortgage loss severity could be 50+ percent. These differences reflect a number of risk factors and costs associated with selling the property. For CPG's mortgage group, the loss severity (LS) can be represented as the following:

$$LS = \frac{PVALUE_t - UPB_t - COSTs_t}{UPB_t}$$

6.12

where PVALUE represents the value of the property in t, UPB represents the unpaid principal balance in period t, the time at which the loss is observed, and COSTS reflect lost interest and other transactions costs of the property and loan. Cost components of loss severity vary by asset type, and for the CPG mortgage portfolio are comprised of several parts. Properties taken over by a lender after a default become part of the **real estate owned** inventory (REO) and present a number of challenges and costs to the bank selling that property. Costs include any rehabilitation to the property needed to make it presentable to prospective buyers, marketing and real estate transactions, expenses, legal fees, and lost interest. In addition, the bank may attempt to forestall costly and protracted foreclosure and REO outcomes by entering into one of several types of foreclosure alternatives with the borrower. This could include a short sale where the borrower and bank agree to a selling price on the home that is less than what is owed on the property, among other alternatives. Since foreclosure alternatives can affect the sales price of the property, they should be factored into loss severity analysis. Historical costs associated with defaulted loans are usually a good source of information for developing loss severity estimates. With sufficient loan level detail, accounting and statistical models of loss severity can be developed and used in some combination.

Two approaches to modeling loss severity by CPG are provided. The first is a purely statistical model using historical loan level data on actual losses sustained on individual mortgages over the past 10 years. The second approach combines an accounting model of costs incurred by the bank once the loan has entered default with a statistical model estimating the sales price value of the underlying property. Determining which approach to use is really up to the analyst, although use of accounting and statistical models together offers the advantage of combining direct estimation of costs on an accounting basis with less easily observable data such as property sales price which can be a function of many factors and estimated in a statistical model.

In estimating loss severity under the first approach, the dependent variable is defined as the percent of unpaid principal balance that is not recovered, net of disposition of the property, and/or any settlements with the borrower. Notice that this can also be modeled using the logit specification. An example of a loss severity model is represented below as:

$$LS = \alpha + \beta_1 STATE1 + \beta_2 STATE2 + \beta_3 STATE3 + \beta_4 CONDO$$
$$+ \beta_5 INVESTOR + \beta_6 CASHOUT + \beta_7 SUBPRIME + \beta_8 LSIZE \qquad 6.13$$
$$+ \beta_9 AGELT3 + \beta_{10} AGE35 + \beta_{11} AGEGT5 + \beta_{12} HPI$$

where *STATE1*, *STATE2* and *STATE3* are groupings of different states reflecting differences in the foreclosure process. States that require a court proceeding (judicial states) tend to have longer foreclosure timelines than nonjudicial states that allow a property sale to take place without a court order, as long as the chain of documentation to the property is in order. The robo-signing problems of large banks after the mortgage crisis underscore the needs for strong operational controls, an issue that we will visit in Chapter 14. In CPG's example, states with foreclosure timelines averaging less than six months are placed into the *STATE1* category, or if they have an average timeline between 6 and 12 months, they are classified as *STATE2* and for all others as *STATE3*. The longer the foreclosure timeline, the more cost the bank may incur as a result of property expenses, lost interest incurred on the mortgage, and other expenses. Other risk factors such as property type and ownership type can affect severities. Condos and investor-owned properties, for example, may have higher loss severities than single family and owner-occupied properties. Similarly, loan purpose, such as cashout refinance loans, may be associated with greater loss severity than loans where the borrower is just buying the home (purchase money loans). Subprime loans and larger loans may also exhibit higher loss severities. The age of the loan may also exhibit differential severities as do local house price movements. Actual severity models may have additional variables and greater complexity than the simple model used by CPG.

Table 6.8 provides results for loss severity for CPG's mortgage portfolio. Five representative loans from CPG's portfolio are provided. Estimates

TABLE 6.8 Mortgage Loss Severity Model Results

Statistically-Based Loss Severity Model	Coefficient	Loan				
		1	2	3	4	5
State Type 1	0.05	0	0	1	0	1
State Type 2	0.1	1	0	0	1	0
State Type 3	0.25	0	1	0	0	0
Condo	0.05					
Investor	0.035					
Cashout Refinance	0.02	0	1	1	1	0
Subprime Loan	0.25	0	1	0	1	0
Loan Size at Origination ($)	0.005	$100,000	$100,000	$250,000	$50,000	$150,000
Loan Age: 0–3 years	0.025	0	1	1	0	1
Loan Age: 3–5 years	0.05	1	0	0	0	0
Loan Age: >5 years	0.075	0	0	0	1	0
House Price Appreciation	−1	−5%	−10%	−10%	−40%	5%
Estimated Loss Severity		25.76%	75.26%	30.71%	98.41%	8.46%

of loss severity based on each loan's individual characteristics are shown. For example, Loan 1 has a severity rate estimated to be nearly 26 percent as compared to Loan 4 or Loan 5, which have a 98.4 and 8.5 percent loss severity, respectively. Drivers of differences in severity rates for these three loans include the house price appreciation (or depreciation where negative) variable, state type and loan, and property characteristics.

Turning to the second approach for estimating severities, consider Table 6.9. The statistical model now has as its dependent variable the change in the value of the underlying property between sale and origination prices expressed as a percentage of the original sales price. A number of new factors enter this model including the type of foreclosure alternative and property location. Other variables are common to the loss severity model as discussed earlier. An accounting model augments the sales price model and features estimates of various costs incurred by the bank. These include realtor and legal fees, maintenance costs and other carry costs. Carry costs are expenses incurred by the bank over the period between the time the bank takes possession of the property and its sale. These include property taxes and hazard insurance. Table 6.9 illustrates how the estimated sales price and accounting estimates of other expenses can be applied against the loss severity formula provided earlier in this section.

GENERATING CREDIT LOSS ESTIMATES

With an estimate of loss severity, default probability, and a **transition, or roll rate** from 90+ to foreclosure available for each loan, the risk management team is able to generate loan level estimates of credit loss on their first-lien mortgage portfolio. This information can then be communicated to senior management or risk committees and additional analysis can be performed on weaker spots of the portfolio for potential risk management actions such as reinsurance or asset sales on portions of the portfolio. The CPG risk management team prepares a set of loss estimates for each of the major segments of the first- and second-lien mortgage portfolio as follows in Table 6.10.

Loss estimates based on a relatively benign economic environment as used by CPG can severely underestimate losses when market conditions worsen. CPG is fortunate that it has sufficient historical data and analytical resources to deploy statistically based loss models on its consumer portfolio, however, in the absence of such capabilities, other techniques can be used and applied to estimate credit risk for the **allowance for loan and lease losses** (ALLL), a critically important function for the risk team.

TABLE 6.9 Loss Severities Computed from Accounting-Based Approach

	Coefficients					
Unpaid Principal Value at Default		$ 95,000	$100,000	$225,000	$ 45,000	$175,000
Years Since Default		2	3	4	5	6
Discount Rate	2%					
State Foreclosure Timelines (in months)						
State Type 1		6	0	6	0	6
State Type 2		12	0	0	12	0
State Type 3		24	24	0	0	0
Estimated Months in in Default		12	24	6	12	6
Property Value Statistical Model (% Change in Value)						
Condo	−0.05	0	1	1	1	0
Investor	−0.075	0	0	0	1	0
Default Alternatives						
Real-estate Owned (REO)	−0.25	1	0	0	1	0
Short Sale	−0.4	0	1	0	0	0
Deed-in-Lieu	−0.05	0	0	1	0	1
Property Location						
Urban	−0.1	1	0	0	0	1
Suburban	−0.15	0	1	0	1	0
Rural	−0.23	0	0	1	0	0
House Price Appreciation	1	−5%	−10%	−10%	−40%	5%
Original Property Value		$140,000	$120,000	$300,000	$100,000	$200,000
Estimated Property Value		$ 84,000	$ 36,000	$171,000	$ 7,500	$180,000

Accounting Cost Estimates	Monthly Cost					
Realtor Fees (% of property value)	6%	$ 5,040	$ 2,160	$ 10,260	$ 450	$ 10,800
Legal Fees (% of unpaid principal balance)	4%	$ 3,800	$ 4,000	$ 9,000	$ 1,800	$ 7,000
Maintenance Expenses (% of property value/month)		$ 8,400	$ 7,200	$ 8,550	$ 750	$ 9,000
Home Value >$250000	0.17%					
Home Value <$250000	0.83%					
Other Carry Costs (% property value)	0.13%	$ 1,260	$ 1,080	$ 1,283	$ 113	$ 1,350
Total Expenses		$ 18,500	$ 14,440	$ 29,093	$ 3,113	$ 28,150
Estimated Loss Severity		29.85%	73.92%	34.12%	81.74%	11.75%

TABLE 6.10 Estimated Credit Losses on CPG Portfolio

Risk Segment	Outstanding Balance ($B)	PD (%)	LS (%)	Roll Rate	Loss Rate (%)
1st Lien					
Prime	50	3.0*	30*	.8 =	0.72
Subprime	80	12.0*	50*	.9 =	5.4
2nd Lien	50	20.0*	100*	.95 =	19

LOAN LOSS RESERVING AND FORECASTING

The ALLL is an accounting entry that reflects the losses underlying a portfolio that are incurred but not yet realized. The idea is that some loans will eventually default some point in the future based on their risk profile yet have not done so. In that regard, the accounting rules that apply under the **Generally Accepted Accounting Principles** (GAAP), referred to as Financial Accounting Standard 5 (FAS 5) do not permit estimates of expected losses to be used in determining the ALLL. In other words, the reserve is not a forward-looking statement of loss. Rather, the estimates must be "probable" and "reasonably estimable," as well as charged to income and disclosed on the institution's financial statements. Loan loss reserve practices permit the use of statistical estimates to determine the inherent losses associated with a homogeneous pool of loans (e.g., prime mortgages) over some specified period of time (the **loss confirmation period**). A variety of techniques and considerations can be taken into account when developing this portion of the ALLL, including migration patterns of delinquency states, market conditions, and borrower and loan risk factors. The accounting provisions do not suggest a specific loss confirmation period, however, regulatory agencies have indicated that 12 months may be appropriate for consumer loan portfolios based on seasoning and other considerations.

A common technique used in lieu of statistical default models is the **roll rate** method. This methodology simply measures the percentage of loans in a particular state of delinquency (e.g., 30DPD) that ultimately "roll" to default. Loans that are ultimately charged-off net of recoveries (**net charge-offs**, or NCOs) on defaulted loans provide a basis for establishing the size of the ALLL. The risk management team can stratify the portfolio along important segments as shown in Table 6.11 within each roll rate "bucket."

The table depicts the percentage of loans of each status type, for example, current roll rates that subsequently roll or transition to the same or

TABLE 6.11   One-Period Roll Rates for CPG Mortgages

| | | | This Month | | | | | | |
Last Month	Prepay	Current	30–59	60–89	90+	FCL	REO	Default	Total
Current	2%	97%	1%	0%	0%	0%	0%	0%	100%
30–59	1%	21%	33%	37%	8%	0%	0%	0%	100%
60–89	0%	9%	9%	33%	40%	7%	1%	0%	100%
90+	0%	6%	1%	1%	81%	11%	1%	0%	100%
FCL	0%	1%	1%	0%	4%	92%	2%	0%	100%
REO	0%	0%	0%	1%	0%	1%	85%	13%	100%

different status in the next period. Note that reading across each row, the total percentage adds up to 100 percent. So, of all loans designated as 30–59 days past due in the previous month, 33 percent remain 30–59DPD in the current month, while 37 percent migrate into the 60–89DPD bucket, and the remainder are shown to either improve or worsen their status. A bank's portfolio constantly changes and as a result of seasoning, differences in economic environments, and a host of other drivers, the monthly roll rates will not remain static. In fact, they may remain relatively stable over a benign economic period, but start ramping up quickly when economic conditions worsen. Staying ahead of the acceleration in defaults is important for forecasting and loan loss reserving exercises. Consequently, various methodologies to build in more recent information into roll rates can be accomplished by using moving average models. These can be weighted or unweighted by loan balances. A simple moving average model for determining 30–59DPD roll rates could be described as the following:

$$RR^{30-59DPD} = \frac{RR_{t-1}^{30-59DPD} + RR_{t-2}^{30-59DPD} + ...RR_{t-n}^{30-59DPD}}{t} \qquad 6.14$$

In estimating the current month's roll rates, the analyst would remove the oldest roll rate $t - n$ and replace it with the latest month's estimate, thus reflecting any new changes that may be going on in portfolio delinquencies.

Technically, roll rate analysis is subsumed under the broader analysis of transition rates and can be modeled using Markov chain processes as well as statistical models. Understanding how delinquent loans migrate over more than a single period can be estimated using the concept of a joint transition or migration probability. To illustrate this using a two-month stylized roll rate matrix, Table 6.12 provides two one-month transition probability matrices: one looking at how loans in period $t - 1$ transition to period t and the

TABLE 6.12   Example Transition Rate Matrix

From $t-1$	To t		
	Current	Default State 1	Default State 2
Current	$\pi 11$	$\pi 12$	$\pi 13$
Default State 1	$\pi 21$	$\pi 22$	$\pi 23$
Default State 2	$\pi 31$	$\pi 32$	$\pi 33$
From $t-2$	To $t-1$		
	Current	Default State 1	Default State 2
Current	$\gamma 11$	$\gamma 12$	$\gamma 13$
Default State 1	$\gamma 21$	$\gamma 22$	$\gamma 23$
Default State 2	$\gamma 31$	$\gamma 32$	$\gamma 33$

other examining movement from period $t - 2$ to $t - 1$. Using simple matrix algebra, to assign the joint probability that a current loan will remain current two periods hence is calculated as:

$$\Pr(Current) = \pi_{11}\gamma_{11} + \pi_{12}\gamma_{21} + \pi_{13}\gamma_{31} \qquad 6.15$$

Using this same approach, each cell in this example 3 × 3 two-period joint transition rates could be computed. Table 6.13 expands on this concept for CPG mortgages for each of the delinquency states. Take the estimated two-period roll rate of 93.01 percent for loans staying current over the two periods, which is derived as the sum of the products of the probability of migrating from current to another state between September and October and October and November.

A projection of a portfolio's delinquency profile in the next period can be developed from a transition or roll rates analysis. Table 6.14 depicts this type of analysis. CPG analysts in November 2004 know what the delinquency states for a subset of its portfolio are as shown in the first two columns expressed as a percent as well as in actual numbers of loans. To generate the December forecast of defaults by delinquency status, CPG analysts use the most recent transition rate matrix shown in the second section of Table 6.14 applied against the number of loans in each category for November to come up with an estimate of December's delinquencies, taking into account that some loans prepay over the period and hence are removed from the loan population. Analysts can tune the expected delinquencies based on qualitative and quantitative adjustments such as changes in home prices, interest rates and other macroeconomic factors relevant to loan performance. In

TABLE 6.13 Two-Period Roll Rate Estimation for CPG Mortgages

	November						
October	Current	30–59	60–89	90+	FCL	REO	Total
Current	97.50%	1.50%	0.75%	0.25%	0.00%	0.00%	100.00%
30–59	22.20%	32.95%	37.05%	7.50%	0.20%	0.10%	100.00%
60–89	8.50%	9.30%	33.50%	40.40%	7.30%	1.00%	100.00%
90+	5.50%	0.80%	1.10%	80.80%	10.75%	1.05%	100.00%
FCL	0.95%	0.60%	0.30%	3.80%	92.25%	2.10%	100.00%
REO	0.00%	0.12%	0.50%	0.30%	13.00%	86.08%	100.00%

	October						
September	Current	30–59	60–89	90+	FCL	REO	Total
Current	95.00%	2.50%	1.25%	1.00%	0.25%	0.00%	100.00%
30–59	21.00%	33.50%	37.70%	7.40%	0.30%	0.10%	100.00%
60–89	7.50%	9.70%	33.50%	40.50%	7.80%	1.00%	100.00%
90+	7.00%	0.50%	0.70%	79.50%	11.25%	1.05%	100.00%
FCL	0.80%	0.70%	0.25%	3.90%	91.15%	3.20%	100.00%
REO	0.00%	0.10%	0.60%	0.25%	12.50%	86.55%	100.00%

	2-Month Transition Probability						
	Current	30–59	60–89	90+	FCL	REO	Total
Current	93.01%	3.01%	2.04%	1.59%	0.33%	0.01%	100.00%
30–59	31.31%	15.23%	25.17%	23.64%	4.08%	0.57%	100.00%
60–89	15.43%	6.83%	15.14%	46.75%	13.99%	1.86%	100.00%
90+	11.22%	0.99%	1.34%	65.22%	19.12%	2.11%	100.00%
FCL	2.06%	0.92%	0.61%	6.80%	84.80%	4.81%	100.00%
REO	0.19%	0.27%	0.76%	1.17%	22.68%	74.93%	100.00%

theory, with sufficient data to model each outcome, separate statistical models could be developed that estimate each transition rate's probability. For instance, taking just one of transition states, 30DPD to 60DPD, the transition probability (TP_{30-60}) can be estimated from:

$$TP_{30-60} = \alpha + \beta_1 FICO + \beta_2 CLTV + \beta_3 PriorDel + \varepsilon \qquad 6.16$$

where a variety of borrower risk attributes enter the model along with prior delinquency history. Using a logit model described earlier, where the binary

TABLE 6.14 Forecast of CPG Mortgage Default Rates

Number of original loans 2000	November 1000		December Forecast 970.63	
	%	#	%	#
30–59DPD	0.30%	3.00	0.619	6.01
60–90DPD	0.20%	2.00	0.434	4.21
90+DPD	0.15%	1.50	0.483	4.69
FCL	0.10%	1.00	0.127	1.23
REO	0.05%	0.50	0.049	0.47
DEFAULT	0.02%	0.20	0.008	0.08
Prepaid (1-month)	2.92%	29.17	1.987	19.29
Current and Active	96.26%	962.63	96.293	934.65

Last Month	This Month								
	Prepay	Current	30–59	60–89	90+	FCL	REO	Default	Total
Current	2%	97%	1%	0%	0%	0%	0%	0%	100%
30–59	1%	21%	33%	37%	8%	0%	0%	0%	100%
60–89	0%	9%	9%	33%	40%	7%	1%	0%	100%
90+	0%	6%	1%	1%	81%	11%	1%	0%	100%
FCL	0%	1%	1%	0%	4%	92%	2%	0%	100%
REO	0%	0%	0%	1%	0%	1%	85%	13%	100%

November	December								
	Prepay	Current	30–59	60–89	90+	FCL	REO	Default	Total
Current	19.25	933.75	4.81	2.41	2.41	0.00	0.00	0.00	962.63
30–59	0.02	0.64	0.99	1.12	0.23	0.01	0.00	0.00	3.00
60–89	0.00	0.17	0.19	0.66	0.81	0.15	0.01	0.01	2.00
90+	0.00	0.08	0.01	0.02	1.21	0.16	0.01	0.00	1.50
FCL	0.00	0.01	0.01	0.00	0.04	0.92	0.02	0.00	1.00
REO	0.00	0.00	0.00	0.00	0.00	0.00	0.43	0.07	0.50
	19.28	934.65	6.01	4.21	4.70	1.24	0.47	0.08	970.63
Rate for December (%)	1.987	96.293	0.619	0.434	0.483	0.127	0.049	0.008	1

Can use a multiperiod moving average model to update roll rates

dependent variable is whether the loan migrates from 30DPD to 60DPD or not, the transition probability could be expressed as a function of several predictor variables such as borrower credit score, current LTV, and prior payment history. Once the transition rates have been established, a loss forecast can be generated. Using transition state models requires greater care to ensure that the effort is focused on only the relevant transition states. For example, if coming up with an estimate for the ALLL is the objective of the exercise, then the intermediate states such as 30DPD to 60DPD may not be required and may only complicate the analysis. This can be made even more complex should the explanatory variables in each of the transition states vary, which is quite likely. Applying such models then becomes a trade-off between complexity and accuracy with the ultimate objective guiding the approach.

The quantitative approaches described above may need to be augmented with qualitative adjustments reflecting management judgment regarding factors not otherwise included in the analysis due to a lack of information or changes to important relationships that cannot be picked up quickly in the models. An example of this would be changes in underwriting practices that cause the underlying quality of the loans to change. Alternatively, the model over successive periods can be seen to over- or underestimate loss on a systematic basis. Re-estimating models is usually a time-consuming process and so an interim solution may be to assign a qualitative adjustment factor to the empirical estimate that can be documented in the ALLL procedures based on observable historical performance. If, for example, the model for 90+DPD delinquencies was showing systematic underestimation of defaults by 10 percent compared to actual performance, risk management may apply a 1.1 factor to these estimates until the models can be re-estimated. Constant attention to model performance as discussed later in Chapter 15 is imperative to maintaining vigilance over estimated performance metrics. To further stabilize the estimates, the roll rates are generated off of a three-month moving average. CPG has established a 12-month loss confirmation period and while there is no requirement to establish an amount of reserves that covers a certain number of months' worth of credit losses, risk management has determined that they want to maintain the ALLL to a level of at least 12 months coverage of loan losses on the portfolio as probable losses on the portfolio should manifest themselves over a one-year period.

The ALLL thus stands at $2.4 billion on the $180 billion mortgage portfolio, or 1.33 percent on this portfolio. The risk team understands the model does not reflect the fact that CPG management has decided to significantly relax the underwriting standards of the mortgage products, which should result in higher credit losses in the future since the underlying roll rates only reflect the historical underwriting of the mortgage business. The risk team thus believes it needs to capture this incremental risk through an additional qualitative adjustment to the model. Drawing from other publicly available data on the relative performance of loans from a large competitor that has a similar set of mortgages with relaxed underwriting terms, the risk team compares the relative 90DPD+ rates between the historical CPG product and the competitor's and finds that the competitor product performs 1.5 times worse than CPG. They realize that the 90DPD+ rates are not the same as a loss rate but the competitor's product has only been in existence for a year or two, limiting the availability of sufficient loss rate information from which to draw a robust estimate. The risk team also knows that economic conditions appear to be slowing down as reported in their latest portfolio leading indicators assessment, however, they believe that with only a month or two of deterioration, they cannot justify adding a qualitative adjustment for economic conditions until more information is observed for at least one or two more months. Losses over the last year for the mortgage portfolio in CPG have averaged $3.5 billion, thus leaving the coverage ratio for the ALLL under the target 12 months. While this result falls short of their coverage ratio, it remains compliant with GAAP requirements but this will be watched closely. At the end of the month, CPG management and the CFO review the risk team's ALLL recommendation. Immediately, they take issue with the application of a qualitative factor for underwriting, pushing back that CPG needs to employ a better process to review the underlying loan quality of the competitor and suggest that no such factor should be applied unless there is better empirical information. Due to a lack of definitive empirical support for the 1.5 multiplier, CPG risk management revises their ALLL projection downward to $2.4 billion taking into consideration other qualitative information on the loan process. This revision generates just over eight months of coverage. As part of their regular monitoring activities, the risk team tracks the months of ALLL loss coverage and observes the trend over the last year shown in Figure 6.7.

Coverage steadily rises, peaking out over 10.5 months, then steadily falling back below 8 months in the most recent period. The risk team knows that various economic indicators have been softening, including GDP, unemployment, and consumer confidence. Housing prices have also started to crest and in the past few months credit losses have started to increase. The ALLL methodology, being based on a three-month moving average of historical data remains relatively flat over the period. The decrease in monthly coverage is somewhat concerning and has also caught the attention of SifiBank's primary regulator who requests that the bank revisit their methodology and raise their ALLL to at least 12 months of loss coverage. The risk team is caught between the regulatory issue and GAAP

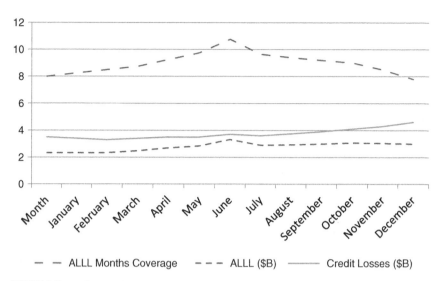

- — ALLL Months Coverage   - - - ALLL ($B)   ———— Credit Losses ($B)

FIGURE 6.7   SifiMortgage ALLL Trends

accounting principles that do not allow a strict policy of increasing the ALLL to achieve a target coverage level. Shortly after reaching a decision to maintain the ALLL at its current level, the housing market undergoes a sharp correction, declining 15 percent over the next year. Delinquencies and then credit losses rise sharply and the bank finds itself in a position of raising reserve levels each month to keep pace with the acceleration in losses. Credibility of SifiBank among its regulators, customers, and investors becomes an issue that the bank must contend with. While the bank wrestles with increasing its reserve levels during the crisis, to do so sharply lowers its net income during the downturn, putting more pressure on the bank. Of additional concern to key stakeholders is the level of capital held by the bank.

Reserving processes tend to be procyclical in nature; that is, reserves tend to accelerate when losses are peaking and slow down when losses are low. To gain a better sense of the timing and variability of the reserving process over different periods of time, consider Figure 6.8. This chart shows the ratio of the ALLL for FDIC-insured banks to nonperforming loans (i.e., 90+ days past due or worse)—ALLL/NPA. This ratio reached a low point around the third quarter of 2002 at 120 percent, just after the end of the 2001 recession, and then rose to 173 percent during the second quarter of 2005. Since that time, the ratio sharply declined to about 64 percent in the 3rd quarter

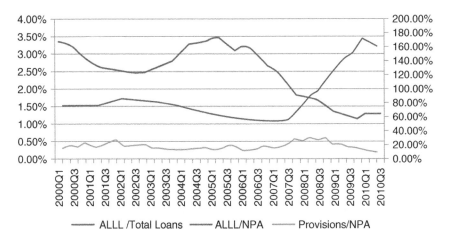

FIGURE 6.8 ALLL and Loan Loss Provision Trends, 2000–2010
Note: Lefthand scale references ALLL/Total Loans; right-hand scale references ALLL/NPA and Provisions/NPA.
Source: FDIC Call Report Data.

of 2010. At first blush, if one were to look only at the ALLL/NPA ratio over time, the ratio appears to follow a countercyclical pattern. This is only partially true, however. A truly countercyclical loss reserving methodology would involve a high ratio of Provisions/NPA during good times when NPAs are at a cyclical low point and a low ratio of Provisions/NPA during bad times when NPAs are rising rapidly. The Provisions/NPA line in Figure 6.8 shows exactly the opposite—with the loss provisioning rate peaking during the recessions of 2001 and 2008–2009, at the same time that NPAs are skyrocketing and bottoming out during good economic times between the two recessions. During the time period between the 2001 and 2008–2009 recessions when credit delinquencies were low, reserve levels as a percentage of loans (ALLL/Total Loans) hovered around 1–1.5 percent but in 2008 and afterward ALLL/Total Loans rose to more than 3.5 percent of total loans as FDIC-insured banks were now forced to ramp up reserves due to rising loss rates and inadequate reserving during good times.

During the financial crisis, many financial institutions began to implement the expected loss-reserving model, even though in so doing it conflicted with the incurred loss methodology prescribed by FAS 5. These changes brought reserving practices into closer alignment with the loss estimation methodology embedded in the Basel II capital requirements framework. Bank regulators were supportive of these changes and the SEC has neither endorsed nor objected. More recently, FASB and the International Accounting Standards Board (IASB) drafted a proposal that would permit the expected loss concept to be applied to loss reserving. Details of how the expected loss concept should be applied have yet to be worked out. Thus, there has been some progress in adopting practices that should reduce the procyclicality of loss reserving in the future, but until accounting rules are explicitly revised, uncertainty will remain.

UNEXPECTED LOSS

Thus far, the CPG risk team has developed point estimates of losses based on historical performance over the past several years. The team understands that formulating these estimates does not result necessarily in expected loss, or the exposure that is most likely to occur on the portfolio. If the historical performance has been during a growth part of the business cycle when economic conditions are most favorable and losses low, it may not appropriately characterize future credit losses under a different environment. Statistically based methodologies to measure credit risk are limiting in this regard, requiring risk managers to look beyond recent history to develop forward-looking views of credit risk. Moreover, risk teams must not ignore the distributional aspects of their portfolios. Credit losses tend to be distributed in a lognormal fashion and so the underlying distribution to be simulated should reflect that experience. Expected losses while important to understand do not provide insight into concentration of risk in the tail of the distribution. Other techniques must be employed to approximate the portfolio's distribution.

To generate a loss distribution for a portfolio of loans requires developing a set of scenarios that propagate losses over some time period based on key risk triggers. In the case of CPG's mortgage portfolio, an important credit risk trigger is negative equity or, in the case of the prepayment option, the refinance incentive for the borrower. For mortgage credit risk, house price changes are an important driver of negative equity, as are interest rates for mortgage refinance incentives. Each of these variables typically enters mortgage default and prepayment models and other variables may influence risks in nonmortgage loan portfolios such as unemployment rates for credit cards. A **Monte Carlo** methodology is a standard approach used to simulate the behavior of these key risk factors. Full treatment of the mathematics and operational implementation of this approach is beyond the focus of this book, however, basic concepts of how such a simulation can be developed follow.

At the heart of the simulation is the need to define a **stochastic process** for a risk factor (for mortgage credit risk, house price movements) that allows the factor to evolve over time randomly based on the factor's direction (**drift**) and volatility. A simple house price process can be represented by the following:

$$dHPI_i(t) = \ln \frac{P_i(t)}{P_i(t-1)} \qquad\qquad 6.17$$

$$dHPI_i(t) = \mu HPI_i(t)\Delta t + \sigma HPI_i(t)\Delta z \qquad\qquad 6.18$$

Where $dHPI_i(t)$ represents the house price change for the *ith* housing market (e.g., $P_{\text{Los Angeles}}$) in period t. It is assumed that house price movements are lognormally distributed as shown with an average rate of change of μ over some period of time and the volatility of price movements are measured by σ. The second expression above characterizes house price movements in terms of a **Weiner stochastic process**, where a random variable, Δz is assumed to have a mean of 0 and a variance that is proportional to Δt or alternatively its standard deviation is equal to $\sqrt{\Delta t}$. It may be more formally defined as $dz = e\sqrt{dt}$ where e is a random variable drawn from the standard normal distribution. With, for example, 500 estimates of changes in home prices drawn from the stochastic process, these results would be inputs to the default models reviewed earlier via the HPI variable where 500 different estimates of default would be generated. This is conceptually depicted in Figure 6.9.

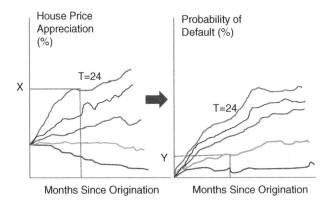

FIGURE 6.9   Home Price Simulation and Default Distribution

The implications for such results can be considerable. With a default or loss distribution generated for the entire portfolio, the risk team proceeds to produce an estimate of risk, or economic capital associated with the portfolio. As described in Chapter 4, economic capital defines the buffer required to cover unexpected losses up to some designated tolerance. The economic capital assigned to an individual loan varies according to its unique risk profile. The team then decides that it wants to set a threshold for setting aside capital to cover itself in the event that an adverse scenario affects the portfolio. To do so, the CRO in consultation with management and the Board establishes a level of risk capital equal to losses associated with the worst 5 percent of the loss distribution. In other words, the risk team wants to ensure that they are 95 percent confident that credit losses would not exceed that threshold. Such an approach to setting risk capital defines **credit value-at-risk** (C-VaR). In this example, a mortgage loan is estimated to have lifetime expected losses of 1.75 percent. Figure 6.10 also illustrates the relative subjectivity involved with establishing a level of risk capital. The 99th percentile worst loss outcome at 7.75 percent is selected in this case as a more risk-averse CRO might prefer holding that level of

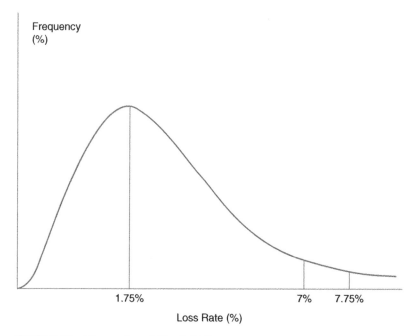

FIGURE 6.10   Illustration of Credit VaR

risk capital than one with a more frequent (e.g., 95 percent level) but lower loss (7 percent).

As in any implementation of a risk model, care must be taken in blindly using the estimates from the simulation process. Empirical estimates of home price drift and volatility, for instance, are reflections of the historical data and may not reflect future outcomes well. For example, SifiMortgage risk analysts had developed their house price model from home price data reflecting the period 1980–2002. While there had been some regional events where home prices declined significantly, at a national level home prices were relatively stable. Applying such estimates of home price drift and volatility severely underestimated the amount of credit risk in the bank's portfolio as it led to a tight clustering of home price paths that were centered on a relatively favorable long-term house price trend. Instead, the home price paths should have been more disperse over time, thus reflecting the potential for some years to produce significant declines in home prices at a regional and national level that would have reflected outcomes experienced after 2008. Calibration of simulation parameters against other modeled outcomes or results could help guide parameterization of such models, however, in the end underlying correlations between home prices in different markets can and will change, requiring vigilance on the part of the risk analyst in monitoring the results from such models.

If the model incorporates other risk such as from prepayments, a stochastic process describing interest rate movements over time can be estimated and used to drive simulated prepayment paths from models described earlier. In this case, the analyst would need to make an assumption regarding the correlation between interest rates and home prices. Historical data can provide some guidance on this, but as before such relationships are dynamic.

In discussing the concept of risk capital with senior management and the Board, the CRO realizes the challenge in conveying an abstract concept such as C-VaR. Expressing very technical quantitative risk management methods to such individuals is difficult and trying to explain what a 5 percent loss scenario looks like is itself challenging. In such cases it is useful to provide realistic benchmarks to illustrate the relative impact of simulation-based results. As seen earlier, estimates of risk capital have many uses including providing management with tools for allocating capital across the enterprise and establishing risk-adjusted return targets.

In general, the risk team adds to its arsenal of credit analysis a variety of stress tests performed on its portfolios. Such stress tests are meant to expose the portfolio under a number of potential shocks. In the case of the mortgage portfolio, this includes combinations of adverse house price (default) and interest rate scenarios (prepayment). The team knows that in the early

TABLE 6.15 Mortgage Default Stress Test Scenarios

Scenario	Home Prices	Interest Rates
Baseline	Current house price forecast holds	Current rate forecast holds
Severe Housing Market Decline	Home prices fall 15% next year	Current rate forecast holds
Housing Market Decline/Recession	Home prices fall 15% next year	Rates decline 50bps
California Housing Market Decline	CA home prices decline 15%, non-CA flat	Current rate forecast holds
Strong Refinance Market/Stable Housing	Current house prices forecast holds	Rates decline 300bps

1990s, the LA housing market collapsed in part due to defense industry downsizing. As a result, one of the stress tests includes this specific event in terms of its impact on home prices and credit losses. Stress tests can be performed on the ALLL as well, shocking the portfolio in various ways, such as evaluating the reserves for the mortgage portfolio should house prices fall 10 percent over the next year. Providing a set of scenarios that can be repeated on a periodic basis reflecting the inherent risks of the portfolio is a useful practice for risk managers. Such stress tests need to be designed to be informative and realistic to the individual portfolios, sufficiently flexible to incorporate various aspects of the firm's exposures across the enterprise, forward looking, and easily replicated. The CPG risk team has set the following scenarios as shown in Table 6.15.

These scenarios capture a range of credit and prepayment risk combinations that have either occurred in the past or are stylized representations. Each is benchmarked against expected conditions (baseline scenario) in order to provide a reference point to management on the severity of the outcomes. The prepayment, default and loss severity models can be used to conduct the stress test. Critical macroeconomic factors such as house price appreciation and interest rates that are included in the models as seen earlier can be adjusted for specific stress cases of interest. Their impact holding other risk factors constant can then establish the level of credit risk for a particular scenario. Credit and interest rate risk impacts are then produced for management review. A limitation of the analysis is that establishing a probability of each scenario is somewhat difficult, but subjective assessments to real events can be offered to better sensitize management to the relative likelihood of a set of outcomes.

SUMMARY

Consumer credit risk management has become more quantitatively oriented over the past decade or more with advances in computing power, statistical methodologies and software and data management tools. Still, risk analysts must be mindful that each decision along the way in building a quantitative view of credit risk is fraught with pitfalls. The data underlying credit estimates requires care in attending to the quality of the information, establishing a realistic historical performance period from which to establish loss estimates, determining what constitutes a bad credit outcome, and applying solid judgment and experience when statistical measures produce results that appear out of line with reasoned intuition.

The building blocks of understanding the credit risk of a consumer loan portfolio begin with assessing default risk. Producing robust estimates of the probability of default and loss severity of a loan portfolio ideally starts by dissecting a loan population into various risk cohorts described by such attributes as product type, term, geography, and origination period (vintage), among others. Combining these elements allows the risk analyst to produce an estimate of credit loss, which can be presented in percentage of outstanding, origination balance, or dollars depending upon the application including establishing a loan loss reserve, one of the most visible activities performed by the risk team.

Profiling a portfolio's credit risk potential also requires assessing both expected and unexpected losses. This requires establishing a set of risk factors that reflect the most likely set of outcomes over a period of time for setting expected loss as well as an adverse outcome that represents management's view of unexpected losses. Various methodologies exist to establish such estimates including statistically based logistic regression and survival models. Such techniques cannot be mindlessly applied without turning to how the results compare to expectations about the future. Admittedly subjective, good analytical risk management practices leverage experience and intuition in complementing quantitative rigor.

By implementing concepts reviewed in Chapter 5 with a set of robust empirical models, the risk manager can readily quantify credit risk in a loan or portfolio. In order to generate a reasonable view of credit risk over a variety of scenarios a loan or portfolio may be exposed to, techniques such as Monte Carlo simulation may be used. These methods provide a way to generate a loss distribution based on the underlying characteristics of the loan or portfolio. Further, by introducing stochastic processes for key risk factors, the impact of default can be observed over a wide variety of outcomes. As with any analysis, it is critical that the analyst understand how the results from the modeling exercise comport with reality and be prepared to augment the quantitative exercise with expert judgment when appropriate.

QUESTIONS

You are looking at two segments of mortgage loans in your bank portfolio that were originated in different parts of the country. You have estimated some home price process models for these loans as follows:

Geography 1: $\Delta HPI(t) = .05dt + .25dz$

Geography 2: $\Delta HPI(t) = .045dt + .28dz$

Where $dz = e\sqrt{dt}$

The home price index currently for geography 1 and 2 are 105 and 110, respectively. A value, for example, of 105 means that home prices are 5 percent higher than the base index value established in period X. Assume you want to generate next month's projection of home prices for loans on an annualized basis in each geographic area.

1. What would your estimates of home prices for each area be on this one randomly generated path?
2. How would you interpret this answer to your management?
3. Suppose that you have used this information to originate and hold mortgages in your portfolio. In five years you have put $100 billion in mortgages on the books from both geographies; Geography 1 accounts for $75 billion and Geography 2 for the rest of the new portfolio. Since originating these loans you have found that the volatility of home prices in Geography 1 is now .5. How would that affect your view of portfolio credit risk?
4. How might you respond to the situation described in question 3?

You have estimated a default model for your credit card portfolio and have the following table of information on two credit card customers. You have imposed a credit standard that you will not grant credit to any loan with an estimated default rate over 40 percent.

	Estimates	Borrower 1	Borrower 2
Credit Score	−0.027	680	700
Credit Balance to Limits	20	0.75	0.85
Loan Payment to Income	4	0.5	0.45
Number of Open Credit Lines	0.02	5	7

5. How would you estimate the default risk of each borrower and who would you grant credit to?

6. If in your credit policy you stipulated that you would allow customers to have up to 10 open credit lines as long as they had a minimum credit score of 750, what term would you use to describe this policy and what is its rationale?

7. After two years, the credit card business has expanded the program after several years of very low loss experience. Changes in the credit policy of the program look as follows:

	Year 1	Year 3
Minimum credit score	660	620
Maximum credit balance to limits	0.85	0.95
Maximum payment to income ratio	0.5	0.6
Maximum number of open credit lines	7	10

How would you describe the changes in policy over time and do you have any response to this change? Provide a supporting argument if so.

You have the following results on your portfolio's performance over the past five years. Defaults in dollars are shown for one, two, three, four, and five years after origination where applicable.

	OUPB	12	24	36	48	60	Lifetime
Vintage 1	$100,000,000	$ 850,000	$ 1,000,000	$ 1,125,000	$ 1,000,000	$750,000	$ 750,000
Vintage 2	$400,000,000	$ 6,000,000	$11,000,000	$15,000,000	$16,000,000		$16,000,000
Vintage 3	$650,000,000	$25,000,000	$20,000,000	$30,000,000			$30,000,000
Vintage 4	$850,000,000	$35,000,000	$40,000,000				$40,000,000
Vintage 5	$250,000,000	$ 700,000					$ 700,000

8. What are the marginal default rates for each vintage for each year after origination?

9. What inference might you draw across vintages that would be helpful to understand credit performance over time?

You have the following information on credit performance of your mortgage portfolio.

	March						
February	Current	30–59	60–89	90+	FCL	REO	Total
Current	90.00%	5.00%	2.50%	1.25%	0.75%	0.50%	100.00%
30–59	30.00%	25.00%	37.05%	7.75%	0.15%	0.05%	100.00%
60–89	10.00%	7.50%	30.00%	42.50%	8.50%	1.50%	100.00%
90+	4.00%	3.00%	5.00%	75.00%	10.00%	3.00%	100.00%
FCL	1.00%	2.00%	3.00%	3.00%	85.00%	6.00%	100.00%
REO	0.00%	0.50%	1.00%	1.50%	25.00%	72.00%	100.00%

	February						
January	Current	30–59	60–89	90+	FCL	REO	Total
Current	95.00%	2.50%	1.25%	1.00%	0.25%	0.00%	100.00%
30–59	21.00%	33.50%	37.70%	7.40%	0.30%	0.10%	100.00%
60–89	7.50%	9.70%	33.50%	40.50%	7.80%	1.00%	100.00%
90+	7.00%	0.50%	0.70%	79.50%	11.25%	1.05%	100.00%
FCL	0.80%	0.70%	0.25%	3.90%	91.15%	3.20%	100.00%
REO	0.00%	0.10%	0.60%	0.25%	12.50%	86.55%	100.00%

10. What are the two-month transition rates for each category for this portfolio?

CHAPTER 7

Commercial Credit Risk Overview

A common denominator in estimating credit risk on commercial and consumer loans is that both require estimates of the probability (or, frequency) of default (PD) and loss given default (LGD). When applied against the notional value of a loan at default—that is, the exposure at default (EAD)—an estimate of expected loss can be made on the loan or a portfolio of loans. However, commercial loans also have a number of characteristics that require a somewhat different approach to estimating losses.

Commercial loans can be categorized broadly into two groups: **commercial and industrial (C&I)** loans are loans made to businesses large and small to support their operations. These can include standard loan contracts secured by collateral such as plant and equipment, or receivables and inventory, or may include unsecured lines of credit. Another type of commercial loan is for real estate lending—**commercial real estate,** or CRE—such as for office space, apartments, shopping centers, hospitals, and other commercial buildings.

Commercial loans to small and in some cases medium-sized businesses, may have sufficient uniformity and scale to allow the bank to use statistical techniques such as underwriting scorecards to assess credit risk. Large commercial loans are characterized by their general lack of uniformity and size, which limits the application of standard modeling to estimating losses associated with such loans. Commercial risk management commonly requires assigning ratings to each loan, taking into consideration its unique risk characteristics, including the financial health of the borrower, collateral quality, and guarantees, if any, among other factors. Ratings provide banks with a systematic way to assess credit risk across different borrowers and loan types and, where consumer lending has become heavily driven by advanced risk modeling, commercial loan assessment relies heavily on underwriting judgment and fundamental analysis.

In part the lumpiness of commercial loan portfolios heightens the need for good risk controls around managing loan exposures. Buildups of risk concentrations in certain geographic regions, sectors, and borrowers can lead to excessive exposures to market conditions that could be mitigated through portfolio diversification strategies augmented with risk limits. Understanding how SifiBank underwrites, assesses, and manages commercial loan exposures is the subject of this chapter.

SIFICOMMERCIAL LENDING DIVISION

SifiCommercial Lending Division currently has a portfolio of $130 billion, as shown in Table 7.1, comprising both C&I and CRE loans. The two lending departments have separate staff involved in sourcing, underwriting, and loan production, along with customer and asset management duties. In addition, an important control function in the process is conducted by an independent group referred to as **loan review,** in which a group of ex-underwriters perform periodic reviews of loans, including their risk ratings. Loan officers are highly involved with the loan process as understanding their customer's needs; the market they serve and business are important indicators of the future performance of any credit extended by the bank. SifiCommercial Lending operates primarily on the East Coast, having been acquired by SifiBank in the purchase of a regional bank primarily engaged in lending in New England. Loan officers are located in 10 offices across New England as well as in three offices in California, as the bank recently acquired a small commercial bank in that state. A profile of the portfolio is shown in Table 7.2.

The CRE portfolio has an average loan size of $6 million and 7,500 borrowers. The portfolio is divided across several markets (sectors) from 25,000–50,000 square-foot office buildings to multifamily apartments, 100,000 square-foot or larger manufacturing facilities, and smaller strip-mall shopping centers. In 2001, SifiCommercial experienced major losses in its CRE portfolio as the effect of a nationwide recession reverberated across New England. Manufacturing and retail businesses were particularly hard hit and this was reflected in the losses sustained in the portfolio. Even so, the head of risk management of SifiCommercial has expressed concerns about an overconcentration in lending in New England, where 75 percent

TABLE 7.1 SifiCommercial Loan Portfolio

Commercial Loan Type	Portfolio ($B)
CRE	45
C&I	
Small & Medium Business	25
Large Corporate	60

TABLE 7.2 SifiCommercial Portfolio Characteristics

	CRE	Small & Middle Segment	Large Customer Segment
Number of Loans	$ 7,500	$ 100,000	$ 5,000
Average Size	$ 6,000,000	$ 250,000	$12,000,000
Smallest Loan	$ 5,000,000	$ 50,000	$ 5,000,000
Largest Loan	$15,000,000	$ 5,000,000	$50,000,000
Average Term	7	2.5	5
% Unsecured	0	50	25
% Guarantees	25	10	40
Obligor Concentration	30	35	5
Geographic Concentration (%)	75	25	30
Sector Concentration (%)	35	12	50

of the portfolio exists, as well as in small shopping centers, which appear to have given way to centers co-located with large prominent retail businesses. Another concern with the CRE portfolio is that 30 percent of the portfolio lies with the 10 largest customers. These customers fortunately have in general exhibited strong financial performance over the past several years and all were able to weather the recession of 2001; however, recent analysis has shown that two of these customers focused on retail space have experienced a worrisome increase in vacancy rates, as economic conditions following the recession of 2008–2009 linger.

All CRE loans are secured by the underlying property and a quarter of them have some form of financial guarantee. These typically come in the form of bank letters of credit or other third-party guarantees. In some cases financial guarantees are provided by the parent company of the borrower, where the parent entity enjoys a higher credit rating.

The C&I lending department is divided into two groups: one focused on small and middle market commercial lending (SMM) and the other dedicated to larger corporate loans (LC). A major differentiator between the two groups is the size of their customer base. Loans for the SMM business tend to average $250,000 while large corporate loans average $12 million. The stakes are certainly higher for LC lending as a single loan default can have a material impact on SifiCommercial portfolio's performance. While borrower concentrations are small for SMM, given average loan size against the portfolio, for LC there is greater concentration in the portfolio among the 10 largest customers. Loan terms for C&I range between three and five years and are a mix of variable and fixed-rate loans. For LC, large corporate customers have external credit ratings that allow SifiCommercial to augment their underwriting process with additional insights from one or more of the rating agencies. For SMM, most of these companies do not have an external rating, and therefore reliance on understanding the financials of the company is critical to the underwriting decision. While these simple statistics shed light on some aspects of the portfolio, to understand the amount of credit risk contained in the SifiCommercial loan portfolio requires a discussion of the commercial loan risk rating process.

DEVELOPING RISK RATINGS

To assess the credit risk of its commercial loan portfolio, SifiCommercial needs to develop some form of risk-rating methodology. There are a number of ways to construct such ratings but all require an assessment of the loan structure and terms (the **facility**) and the creditworthiness of the borrower (**obligor**). A simple risk-rating matrix might look like the one shown in Table 7.3. The basic components of any risk rating are a set of grades, some description of their general risk profile, an estimate of expected default, and some mapping to external ratings where possible. Establishing the number of risk grades is somewhat subjective, guided by the risk profile of the specific portfolio as well as regulatory guidance. For instance, in Table 7.3 the bottom four grades—**Special Mention, Substandard, Doubtful,** and **Loss**—would be expected by the regulator to be a part of any risk-grading exercise.

TABLE 7.3 One-Dimensional Risk Rating Matrix

Grade		1-Year EDF	Approximate External Rating
1	Negligible Risk	0.01	AAA
2	Very Low Risk	0.05	AA
3	Low	0.10	A
4	Moderate	0.50	BBB
5	Average Risk	1.25	BB
6	Marginal Risk	5.50	B
7	Special Mention	25.00	CCC
8	Substandard	50.00	CC
9	Doubtful	90.00	C
10	Loss	100.00	D

Grades above Special Mention are described as **Pass** and their number is in part a function of the complexity and size of the portfolio and level of sophistication for the bank. With a large portfolio and number of loans, it might be possible to identify more than six Pass grades based on performance. A finer gradation of risk could better inform the loan loss reserving and capital determination processes, for instance, as well as loan pricing; however, it may increase reporting and other portfolio management activities as complexity rises. In the matrix shown in Table 7.3, the six Pass grades correspond to external ratings representing better performing credits. Note that the ratings start with the highest quality credits and decline in sequence to the worst. This is seen both by the expected default frequency (EDF) as well as by the external rating assigned to the risk grade.

Establishing what risk measure to apply to risk grades is important and while EDF is shown in Table7.3, the firm could choose to use expected loss by leveraging information on the loss severity of the facility. Gathering historical information that provides a reliable indicator of expected risk in the portfolio is difficult for many commercial banks, given data limitations and other constraints, and so leveraging performance history from external ratings is a useful exercise.

Selection of an appropriate time horizon for defaults or losses is required although a common standard is one year. Commercial rating agencies typically rely on an average one-year default rate over a long time horizon as the estimate of expected defaults. An important consideration in setting a loan's rating is whether to evaluate it at a **point-in-time** (PIT) or **through-the-cycle** (TTC). In a PIT assessment, a bank will look at assigning a loan to a risk grade based on its expected performance at a point-in-time. If the rating was conducted when economic conditions were favorable and therefore result in a lower expected default rate for a borrower, it might be rated as a 3, but when conditions worsen and default rates increase, it could be downgraded to a 4. Applying such a methodology could lead the bank to under- or over estimate defaults by not taking into consideration both good and bad environments. By using the TTC approach that assesses default risk in all economic scenarios, the bank's potential for misstating risk in the portfolio can be reduced.

For banks wishing to obtain even more sophistication around their risk ratings, rather than create a combined view of risk based on the facility and obligor risk factors, it can create a split, or **dual rating**, structure that establishes separate risk grades for the facility and obligor and then combines them across grades. An example of such a structure and final mapping to a one-year expected loss is found in Table 7.4. In this structure 10 grades each are used to assign facility and obligor ratings. The number of facility and obligor grades does not need to be the same and it may be that the

TABLE 7.4 Facility and Obligor-Based Rating Matrix

Panel A:

Obligor Grade	1-Year EDF/LGD (%)	Facility Grade									
		1	2	3	4	5	6	7	8	9	10
1	0.01	0.0005	0.001	0.0015	0.0015	0.0025	0.0035	0.005	0.0075	0.0095	0.01
2	0.05	0.0025	0.005	0.0075	0.0075	0.0125	0.0175	0.025	0.0375	0.0475	0.05
3	0.1	0.005	0.01	0.015	0.015	0.025	0.035	0.05	0.075	0.095	0.1
4	0.5	0.025	0.05	0.075	0.075	0.125	0.175	0.25	0.375	0.475	0.5
5	1.25	0.0625	0.125	0.1875	0.1875	0.3125	0.4375	0.625	0.9375	1.1875	1.25
6	5.5	0.275	0.55	0.825	0.825	1.375	1.925	2.75	4.125	5.225	5.5
7	25	1.25	2.5	3.75	3.75	6.25	8.75	12.5	18.75	23.75	25
8	50	2.5	5	7.5	7.5	12.5	17.5	25	37.5	47.5	50
9	90	4.5	9	13.5	13.5	22.5	31.5	45	67.5	85.5	90
10	100	NA	NA	NA	NA	NA	NA	NA	NA	NA	100

Panel B:

Final Rating	1-Year EL (%)
1	.0005–.0015
2	.0015–.0125
3	.0125–.1000
4	.1000–.2500
5	.2500–1.2500
6	1.2500–5.5000
7	5.5000–10.0000
8	10.0000–25.0000
9	25.0000–90.0000
10	90.0000–100.0000

facility ratings fit into a smaller number of categories. Before getting into the details of what factors are included in these ratings, there are EDF and LGDs assigned to each risk grade. Each of the table cells show the product of each facility's EDF and obligor's LGD rating. In this example, there are potentially 100 different expected loss scenarios. For example, if an obligor was rated as 4 and the corresponding facility was rated as 5, the one-year estimated expected loss would then be .125 percent. Managing a set of 100 individual risk grades would be too cumbersome and so the bank needs to shrink this down to a much smaller set of expected loss risk grades. What it can do is establish ranges of expected loss across risk grades that the 100 expected loss categories can be mapped into. The highest quality loans would be rated as 1 with expected losses ranging between .0005 and .0015 percent. Other combinations of EDF and LGD outcomes would similarly be grouped into a common expected loss range and grade as shown in the bottom table.

One benefit of using a dual rating process is that it provides greater flexibility with regard to rating the individual obligor and facility. If the characteristics of the facility were to remain the same over a period of time while the condition of the obligor deteriorated, it would allow the rater of the credit to downgrade the obligor rating while maintaining the facility at its current rating. This provides better transparency around the drivers of ratings that can assist management in understanding the dynamics of the portfolio over time.

SifiCommercial has established a dual rating process as described above and the results of this ratings approach are shown in Figure 7.1. Ideally, the ratings should conform to general distributions observed in external ratings processes. This would imply that the percentage of very high or very low quality credits is much lower than middle-rated credits. This is somewhat

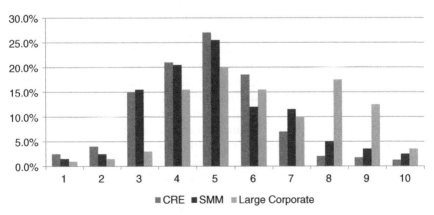

FIGURE 7.1 SifiCommercial Risk Ratings Distribution

evident for the ratings of each loan type. For the CRE portfolio, 81.5 percent of the portfolio is found in risk grades 3–6 with 6.5 percent allocated to grades 1 and 2. About 12 percent of CRE credits are contained in the problem asset categories 7–10.

In comparison, the large corporate portfolio appears to have higher risk as seen by the heavier portion of loans falling into the problem asset categories. Of particular concern is the fact that 20 percent of the portfolio falls into grades 8 and 9, which is indicative of major difficulties in loan repayment. Further attention of this outcome would be required by the risk and business teams to understand the drivers of the large corporate risk-grading outcomes. Finally, the SMM portfolio risk grades are closer to the CRE portfolio distribution, though a higher portion of the portfolio is found in the problem asset grades than for CRE.

Another aspect of establishing a risk-rating process is determining the criteria by which loans will be rated in a consistent fashion that provides a representative view of the risk across many different borrower, loan, and collateral types. In addition, since ratings are developed by individuals rather than by models, the need to clarify the exact criteria and due diligence analysis is great. SifiCommercial requires the loan officer (relationship manager) to develop the risk ratings for all portfolios with the credit staff assigned to the business unit required to approve the final rating before being entered into the system of record. Clearly there are incentives for the relationship managers to grade their credits more favorably in part since their compensation is performance driven. Having a second check on validating the rating results by the credit staff embedded in the business can mitigate some of that problem; however, it may be the case in some circumstances that even the credit staff might not be sufficiently conservative given their alignment with the business rather than the risk organization. This is why an independent loan review function is critical to ensuring the integrity of the risk grading process. The individual heading SifiCommercial's loan review function reports directly to the board of director's Risk Committee and administratively to the Chief Credit Officer.

A risk rating process needs to be able to address a number of questions regarding the quality of the obligor and facility. For the obligor it is essential that the bank gain a detailed understanding of the financial position and health of the borrower. This would include performing a financial analysis on the obligor looking at the balance sheet and income statement for evidence of strength of the borrower's ongoing ability to repay the obligation. Determining the obligor's leverage and debt are essential to the analysis, as are detailed cash flow projections of the firm. Understanding sources of revenues and their volatility and susceptibility to market conditions is an important part of this exercise. In addition, the analysis should look at operating expenses and overhead, the company's profitability and inventory turnover, among other items of interest. For CRE loans, additional information will be required, such as knowledge of vacancy rates, absorption rates and **debt service coverage ratios** (DSCRs). Developing a set of peer metrics can help establish relative performance against benchmarks for the particular industry the borrower is in. Specific details of how these risk factors are used in assessing commercial loan risk are reviewed later in this chapter. Gathering information on the quality of the borrower's audit process can also be useful in understanding the quality of the financials under review. As part of this assessment, obtaining an external rating for the borrower is critical. For smaller credits, an external rating on the business may not exist, and in these cases it may be necessary to obtain a credit report on the owners of the company, if it is privately held.

If the bank has an ongoing relationship with the borrower, this can provide good insight into how the loan may perform. Previous loan history is an important predictor of default and such historical information can provide details on the borrower that might be more difficult to ascertain if this were a new loan. Cultivating a relationship with the borrower can yield intimate details about the company that might not otherwise be available through secondary sources.

SifiCommercial requires an assessment of the quality of the borrower's management team as an input to the rating process. Success or failure of an enterprise is highly dependent on the abilities of management. The number of years the company has been in business, the experience level of the management team and their business and management turnover provide key information on this important rating factor. The more information can be obtained on the culture of the company, its risk appetite and governance structure, the more that will help round out the profile of the borrower's management team and structure.

Another assessment category for the risk rating process is industry and market analysis. To what extent is the business vulnerable to business cycles? Is it a market leader or follower in its sector and what is its market share? How diversified is the product mix? Is the business in a mature market or is it relatively new? Having too dominant a position in the industry could be as detrimental as being a marginal player. Understanding what is important for a specific business sector requires experience and judgment, thus making commercial credit risk rating very different from some consumer model-driven risk assessments. Geography also is important to understanding commercial credit risk. Does the borrower have broad geographic coverage or is it focused on a certain area? Local market conditions clearly will affect a commercial borrower's business more if it is in a single, specific location than if it has greater access to other markets. Understanding supply chain dynamics can likewise be an important consideration in rating risk. For example, if the borrower has access to only one provider of a key input of production, how vulnerable is the business to disruptions in supply and/or unexpected price adjustments?

Other considerations in the process include assessing the quality of underlying collateral, the impact of any financial guarantees, and the terms of the facility. For secured loans, it is important to carefully assess and appraise the value of the underlying collateral. In commercial real estate lending, property classifications such as Class A designate the quality of properties and can help guide decisions based on these designations. The strength of any financial guarantee can also be a major determinant of whether the loan is made or not, as well as how it grades. This should include an assessment of the guarantor's financial health, the type of guarantee provided, and the extent of the guarantee.

RISK-RATING SCORECARD PROCESS

Putting all of these pieces of information together in a systematic fashion that can be used by relationship managers and credit officers across the organization is challenging. How does one weigh the importance of management experience against company leverage ratios? This is where the skill of an experienced business and risk team comes in to enrich the quantitative information with knowledge of observed performance over time. One way to introduce consistency in the assessment process is to describe in some detail the expected features of loans rated in a particular category. This can be as simple as establishing specific thresholds or ranges for key metrics. For example, the bank could establish that a minimum threshold for a Pass credit must be that the debt service coverage ratio is at least 1.1. And specific thresholds for individual risk grades could be established as well. A more complicated way to ensure consistency in the risk grading process would be to develop a **risk-grading scorecard**. Such scorecards would not necessarily be statistically based, but developed from expert opinions regarding the drivers of loan performance and their associated impacts. A benefit from using a heuristic scorecard is that it provides a consistent rank ordering of the components underlying different loans. Over time, as additional information is obtained on loan performance, adjustments to risk drivers and their weights can be made.

At the highest level, the use of a risk-rating scorecard can be designed in a number of ways, but to illustrate the concept, a scorecard used to assign the risk grade for one of SifiCommercial's SMM customers, National Communications Device, Inc. (NCD), is shown in Table 7.5. NCD is a producer of a type of telecommunication device specific to the trucking industry. The

TABLE 7.5 SifiCommercial Obligor Risk-Rating Scorecard

Name	National Communications Device Inc.			
Address	100 Main Street, Smithtown, New York			
Business Sector	Manufacturing			
Business Specialty	Telecommunications			

	Weight	Assessment	Score	Weighted Score
Obligor Rating Business & Market				
Market Conditions	0.15	Average and Improving	3	45
Product Diversification	0.25	Low Diversification	1	25
Company Competitive Position	0.20	Moderate	3	60
Years in Business	0.40	7	3	120
Subtotal	1.00			250
Management				
Quality of Management	0.40	Good Experience and Strategic Focus	3	120
Company External Credit Rating	0.25	B-	2	50
Quality of Operations	0.20	Good Controls and Processes	3	60
Quality of Financial Reporting & Audit	0.15	Sound Practices	3	45
Subtotal	1.00			275
Financials				
Current Ratio	0.10	2.208	4	40
Quick Ratio	0.10	1.195	4	40
Inventory Turnover Ratio	0.10	1.858	4	40
Gross Profit Margin/Assets	0.10	0.139	2	20
Expense Ratio	0.10	0.076	2	20
Return on Assets	0.10	0.015	1	10
Debt/Equity	0.10	1.130	1	10
Cash Flow Coverage Ratio	0.10	0.524	2	20
Sales Growth Rate	0.10	0.075	2	20
Net Worth to Assets Ratio	0.10	0.300	2	20
Subtotal	1.00			240
Total Score				765

(*continued*)

TABLE 7.5 *(Continued)*

Cash Flow-at-Risk	1.00	Within CFaR Tolerance	3	150
		Maximum Score = 250		
Facility Rating				
Collateral Type	0.50	Unsecured	1	50
Loan Tenor	0.15	Two years	4	60
Loan Terms	0.15	Appropriate for Risk	3	45
Guarantees	0.20	None	1	20
	1.00		Total	175

Maximum Score = 500

global positioning communicator, or GPC, allows trucking companies to track and locate where each of their trucks is at any point enroute, allowing shipments to be tracked online by customers. The company had sales in 2014 of $1.3 million and requested a $250,000 loan from SifiCommercial to add new equipment to their production process. SifiCommercial has had an established relationship with NCD for two years that includes all of its business banking. Prior to that NCD had banked with one of SifiCommercial's major competitors for 10 years.

In order to understand the risk of this new loan to the bank, SifiCommercial's relationship manager for NCD has put together the scorecard shown in Table 7.5 for NCD. The relationship manager is also required to put together a facility rating scorecard that is described below. The NCD obligor scorecard has several components: the business and market conditions section, management quality, and financials and cash flow analysis. Behind each section of the scorecard are a number of metrics that are required for any evaluation. To maintain consistency in the rating process, scorecard drivers and weights are identical for C&I lending risk ratings. Conceptually, in each of the three sections of the scorecard, a set of risk factors are identified, such as market conditions under the business and market section. Each risk factor is assigned a weight that is fixed for any obligor and assigned a score from 1 to 5, with 1 representing the worst outcome and 5 the best. The relationship manager performs his analysis of each risk factor and then enters the results into the assessment and score columns of the rating tool. For example, under market conditions, the overall economy has remained stable and is slowly improving compared to the past few years. The score is set at 3, which is average for this factor. Since market condition carries a 15 percent weight for this section, the weighted score is .15 * 100 * 3 = 45. Note that the weights for each section add up to 100 percent.

From a product diversification perspective, the GPC is the only product NCD produces. Consequently it is highly dependent on the success of this product, making it vulnerable to downturns in the shipping industry. The relationship manager originally had this rated as a 3, arguing that because NCD has broad product diversification to hundreds of customers that it has average diversification. Upon further review and approval by SifiCommercial's credit officer, this was overturned and put into the assessment with a score of 1 as shown, as it was felt by the credit team that the customer diversification did not provide sufficient offset to the single product risk. The relationship manager must be careful about putting too high a rating on a credit, as SifiCommercial usually takes actions against those who assign an overly favorable rating.

Another factor in assessing the business and market risk for NCD is its competitive position within its industry. The GPC is somewhat of a niche product in the telecommunications industry and NCD has five major competitors that offer similar technologies. Three of these companies are diversified multinational technology companies. NCD has produced the GPC product for five years, although the company has been around for seven years. The products competing with GPC from the three large competitors have been in the market for six years, although NCD has innovated beyond each of them in several important ways that make it a more expensive, though more reliable and accurate product. Taking all of these considerations into account, NCD is assigned a score of 3 for its competitive position. Taking all of these market and business factors together results in a weighted score for NCD of 250 out of a maximum of 500 points.

Turning next in the scorecard to management quality, the relationship manager has been able to interview the management team on various aspects of how their business is run. An important consideration is the experience of the management team in the telecommunications business. It turns out that the President and CEO, the CFO, and the Head of Production and Sales had worked at senior levels at one of their large competitors for several years prior to starting their own company. However, none of them was a technical specialist in the development of the GPC device and they had to recruit talent from other firms to produce it. The company had been able to secure an external rating from a reputable ratings company that specializes in small business ratings. The rating obtained for last year was a B-, which on this rating scale is considered below average. The relationship manager also spent time looking into the operations of NCD including R&D, production, sales, and even quality control. The findings from this on-site review suggested that NCD is well-controlled for its size in general, although a few deficiencies in its production process were identified.

The financial and accounting processes of NCD were also reviewed in some detail to ensure the integrity of the data used to assess financial strength as well as to corroborate how well NCD follows standard financial and accounting practices. It was determined that the company adheres to good practice and that its external audits were complete and in order for the past five years, with no significant findings.

Taking all of this information into account led the relationship manager to give NCD a score of 275 out of 500 on its management quality section. The third section of the rating scorecard requires a detailed analysis of NCD's financials and cash flows. Such an analysis should not rely on only the most recent year's information, and so the relationship manager pulls the past five years of financial statements and related information. A summarized view of key financial data from the balance sheet is provided in Table 7.6. Looking at the last five years of NCD's performance reveals a lot about the company's experience. In 2010 and 2011, the company had amassed significant short- and long-term debt resulting from its startup in 2009. For 2010 and 2011, this debt burden created a drag on earnings that negatively affected retained earnings. After 2011, the company was able to make significant strides in retiring that debt and with increased sales was able to increase retained earnings. By 2014 NCD had built $168,000 in retained earnings. NCD's income statement over this period provides more insight into the drivers of their performance and this is shown in Table 7.7. NCD has shown steady improvement in sales over the past five years, a sign that the GPC product has been well received in the market. Taking the cost of goods sold into account, NCD's gross profit also increased significantly over the past five years. By 2012, earnings before interest and taxes (EBIT) were positive, as was net income for the past three years.

This information, while useful in forming a general picture of the overall health of the company, requires further analysis to assess the company's financial strength including profitability, liquidity leverage, and debt burden, among other factors. A common approach to such analysis is to perform a ratio analysis that takes selected information from the balance sheet and income statement along with other data and computes a set of key financial ratios that can then be compared to established benchmarks such as peer ratios over a common time period. Such analysis can be quite comprehensive, covering numerous ratios and metrics. Ratio analysis is a useful tool for measuring important trends and the condition of obligors, but care must be taken in over relying on such information. At times, companies can take actions to make it appear as though their performance is better than it actually is. Most data-driven analyses are backward looking. That is why augmenting a financial ratio analysis with a cash flow analysis that provides

TABLE 7.6 NCD Selected Balance Sheet Information ($)

	Operating Year				
	2014	2013	2012	2011	2010
Cash & Other Liquid Assets	223,452	210,112	194,732	172,132	165,158
Accounts and Receivables	524,000	515,893	556,992	523,202	495,672
Inventories	518,345	573,127	623,923	672,123	756,122
Total Current Assets	1,265,797	1,299,132	1,375,647	1,367,457	1,416,952
Property, Buildings, and Equipment	351,854	325,904	303,862	297,452	286,459
Accumulated Depreciation	(112,943)	(101,224)	(93,285)	(91,023)	(85,392)
Total Fixed Assets	238,911	224,680	210,577	206,429	201,067
Short-Term Debt	111,673	156,382	215,689	315,284	325,674
Accounts Payable	235,565	276,292	285,622	319,324	333,952
Accruals	101,264	110,453	115,374	124,126	131,274
Current Liabilities	448,502	543,127	616,685	758,734	790,900
Long-Term Debt	175,292	263,122	253,923	267,834	275,193
Total Liabilities	623,794	806,249	870,608	1,026,568	1,066,093
Common Stock	474,247	476,832	484,274	482,375	485,268
Retained Earnings	167,756	16,051	20,765	(141,486)	(134,409)
Total Liabilities and Equity	1,265,797	1,299,132	1,375,647	1,367,457	1,416,952

forward-looking estimates of cash flows should be an important part of a commercial risk-rating process.

The SifiCommercial relationship manager is required by the scorecard to produce a specific set of ratios, as shown in Table 7.8. The relationship manager is required to compute and validate these measures using an average of the past five years, data.

Alongside that estimate, the relationship manager, in conjunction with the credit staff, has prepared a set of peer company results for each ratio

TABLE 7.7 NCD Summarized Income Statement ($)

	Operating Year				
	2014	2013	2012	2011	2010
Production Sales (Net)	1,354,598	1,163,295	1,189,720	973,924	974,464
Cost of Goods Produced	965,414	964,254	973,943	953,285	941,394
Gross Profit	389,184	199,041	215,777	20,639	33,070
Operating Costs	77,384	79,476	85,392	87,395	91,234
Depreciation	52,843	48,372	45,067	43,294	41,295
Earnings Before Interest and Taxes	258,957	71,193	85,318	(110,050)	(99,459)
Interest Expense	11,167	15,638	21,569	31,528	32,567
Income Taxes	56,321	15,662	18,770	(24,211)	(21,881)
Net Income	191,469	39,892	44,979	(117,367)	(110,145)
Stock Dividends	23,712	23,842	24,214	24,119	24,263
Net to Retained Earnings	167,756	16,051	20,765	(141,486)	(134,409)

TABLE 7.8 Selected Financial Ratios

Ratio	Definition
Current Ratio	Current Assets/Current Liabilities
Quick Ratio	(Cash & Accounts Receivable/Current Liabilities)
Inventory Turnover Ratio	Sales/Inventory
Gross Profit Margin	Gross Profit/Sales
Expense Ratio	Operating Costs/Sales
Return on Assets	Net Income/Assets
Debt/Equity	Total Debt/(Total Equity + Retained Earnings)
Cash Flow Coverage Ratio	Operating Cash Flows/Debt Service
Sales Growth Rate	$(\text{Sales}(t) - \text{Sales}(t-1))/\text{Sales}(t-1)$
Net Worth to Assets Ratio	(Equity + Retained Earnings)/ (Current Assets + Fixed Assets)

TABLE 7.9 NCD Ratio Analysis Results

Ratios (%)	Operating Year					5-Year Average	5-Year Peer Average
	2014	2013	2012	2011	2010		
Current Ratio	2.82	2.39	2.23	1.80	1.79	2.21	2.50
Quick Ratio	1.67	1.34	1.22	0.92	0.84	1.19	1.50
Inventory Turnover Ratio	2.61	2.03	1.91	1.45	1.29	1.86	2.10
Gross Profit Margin	0.29	0.17	0.18	0.02	0.03	0.14	0.20
Expense Ratio	0.06	0.07	0.07	0.09	0.09	0.08	0.05
Return on Assets	0.80	0.18	0.21	-0.57	-0.55	0.02	0.15
Debt/Equity	0.45	0.85	0.93	1.71	1.71	1.13	0.45
Cash Flow Coverage Ratio	1.40	1.20	0.51	-0.25	-0.24	0.52	1.30
Sales Growth Rate	0.16	-0.02	0.22	0.00	0.01	0.07	0.15
Net Worth to Assets Ratio	0.43	0.32	0.32	0.22	0.22	0.30	0.45

over a five-year period for comparability. Taking a closer look at each of these ratios provides more insight into the drivers of NCD's financial performance. The results of the NCD ratio analysis are reported in Table 7.9. The current ratio estimates the company's solvency over the short term as well as its ability to service its debt. The ratio is above 1 across all years, indicating that NCD remained solvent over the period and is assigned a score of 4 in the rating scorecard. Note that the risk management function would have established specific thresholds for defining the scoring for each ratio. Nevertheless, care must be taken not to conclude too much based on a simple ratio, given that many factors may drive the results as well as the corresponding peer ratios. The quick ratio may be viewed as a measure of company liquidity, specifically looking at liquid assets compared to liabilities. In this case a higher ratio is indicative of greater liquidity and the increasing trend is a positive sign for the company although the five-year average ratio was lower than the peer average. Once again, the score for this attribute was 4.

To get a perspective on how well NCD manages its inventory levels, the inventory turnover ratio measures the number of times its inventory turns over relative to its sales. A low turnover ratio may create a drag on earnings as high relative levels of inventory are not being put to productive use. The inventory turnover ratio has been increasing over time for NCD and has outperformed the industry on this metric. As a result, NCD scores a 4 on this ratio.

A couple of profitability measures are included in the analysis: gross profit margin to assets and return on assets. Both measures have steadily improved over time, although they underperform their peers over the past five years. It is important to note that NCD struggled in 2010 and 2011, which clearly affects the average ratio. A more sophisticated analysis might look at weighting the results by sales or some other appropriate measure of firm size. This may also be an opportunity for the relationship manager to put a qualitative statement about NCD's performance into the record and could be used to support upgrading the scores beyond their simple results in the scorecard. This might be an area of improvement for future modification of the SifiCommercial risk rating scorecard and illustrates the importance of balancing quantitative and qualitative results in assessing risk.

Cash flow analysis, as mentioned earlier, is an essential ingredient in sound assessment of commercial credit risk. This entails making projections of the company's cash flows based on various assumptions about the market, operations, pricing, and other drivers of performance. Ideally the analysis should evaluate the company's cash flows over a number of scenarios. Various approaches to cash flow analysis exist in the industry, such as **Uniform Credit Analysis**; however, risk ratings are not bound by use of a particular framework. Instead, this approach provides an accurate portrayal of company cash flows and is applied consistently across risk ratings. Some software packages provide the ability to generate cash flow simulations that can be used in developing expected cash flow estimates, as well as a variation on VaR referred to as **cash flow at risk** (CFaR). The variability of cash flows as measured by the standard deviation can be used along with the mean cash flow to establish the distribution. From this information, the analyst could determine the level of cash flow that places the company at risk of insolvency. This could be based on actual historical information on firms of similar size and sector for example. Taking this information into account, a confidence level could be developed that establishes a risk boundary that the company must not exceed. The analyst performing the cash flow simulation can then determine whether the company stays within the VaR limit or not based on the analysis. In Figure 7.2, deterioration in cash flows below CF_I would likely force the company into some level of severe financial distress. Understanding the drivers of that stress would be important to the analyst as it could provide insight into what aspects of the company's financial picture may pose risk sometime in the future. The cash flow simulation for NCD established that its cash flows would remain within the CFaR threshold, and as a result it was assigned a score of 3.

One other ratio deserving special attention is the cash flow coverage ratio. The cash flow coverage ratio measures the number of times the

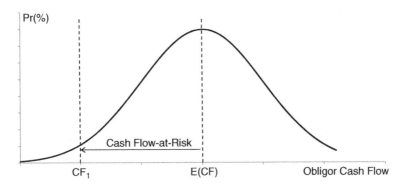

FIGURE 7.2 Conceptual Depiction of Obligor Cash Flow at Risk

company's cash flows cover its debt service and so provides an indicator into the ability of the firm to service its debt. Although different standards of performance may apply, a cash flow coverage ratio below 1.2 signals potential problems by the firm to satisfactorily service its debt from operating cash flows. Only in the past two years has NCD been able to generate cash flows that support its debt service by a factor of at least 1.0. Not unlike some of the other ratio results, there is both a good and bad news story for NCD. In its early years it faced significant financial problems, that while leaving it technically solvent call into question its long-term ability to repay its obligations. During that period it is important to note that the company never approached its creditors with a request to restructure its debt or become delinquent. Conversely, the company exhibited a resiliency to improve its financial condition over time, and in fact for many of the ratios actually outperforms the industry currently. These conflicting views of NCD illustrate the importance of having an experienced relationship manager and credit team that can take all of these considerations into account. The twin dangers for the business and risk teams are making a decision to deny the loan when in fact the obligor is able to make the payments, or just the reverse, making a loan to NCD when they are unable to repay.

Having taken all of NCD's financial information into account and loading the scores into the risk rating scorecard, NCD receives a total score of 240 points out of a maximum of 500 possible. This completes the obligor part of the rating scorecard process and the total obligor score reflecting the sum of the market and business, management quality, and financial performance sections is 915 points (765 for business and market, management, financials and 150 points for CFaR) out of a total of 1,750. This final score will be used in assigning NCD an obligor risk rating, but before that occurs the relationship manager must develop a facility score for the NCD loan request.

Where the obligor rating was intended to determine the likelihood of default by NCD, the facility rating is meant to ascertain the loss given default (LGD). Factors that contribute to the LGD are the structure and terms of the loan, the existence and extent of financial guarantees, and quality of collateral if required.

For NCD, the request is for a $250,000 unsecured loan for purchasing additional production equipment. NCD has two other unsecured loans outstanding with SifiCommercial over the past two years that have been paid as agreed. While SifiCommercial usually requires some form of collateral such as inventory or plant and equipment as collateral, an exception was made by management to relax this policy in order to obtain NCD's complete banking business. The decision to take this risk was approved by SifiCommercial's CRO, who was swayed by the past loan performance history of the company and its more recent financial performance.

Other factors considered in the analysis are the loan's maturity or tenor and specific terms. The loan has a two-year tenor with a 6 percent note rate and a fixed term payable monthly. The approximately $11,000 per month payment of interest and principal is reasonable given NCD's current debt and income stream. Finally, the loan does not have any guarantees associated with it. When all of these factors are taken into consideration collectively, the facility scores as 175 out of a total of 500.

SifiCommercial risk management has mapped facility and obligor scores into the rating matrix based on a combination of historical performance data and alignment with other external rating sources for these kinds of credits. The relationship of scores to final obligor and facility risk ratings is shown in Table 7.10. As a result of this mapping, the obligor rating is set as 4 and the facility rating is 7. This dual rating is then finally mapped into the overall risk rating based on an estimated one-year expected loss rate of .25 percent for the NCD loan applying estimates of obligor and facility EDF and LGD, respectively, from Panel A of Table 7.4. This results in a final rating classification of 4.

LOAN REVIEW PROCESS

Once a loan has been approved and an initial rating assigned, this does not mean that SifiCommercial's oversight of the loan is concluded. In fact the bank has put in place an important function to maintain independent oversight of ratings over time. The Loan Review group is charged with conducting periodic reviews of credits. Part of the function of the group is to ensure

TABLE 7.10 Mapping of Risk Rating Scores to Final Ratings

Obligor Score to Risk Rating Mapping

		Obligor Score Range
1	Negligible Risk	> 1350
2	Very Low Risk	1150–1349
3	Low	1000–1149
4	Moderate	850–999
5	Average Risk	750–849
6	Marginal Risk	500–749

Facility Score to Risk Rating Mapping

	Facility Score Range
1	> 450
2	400–449
3	350–399
4	300–349
5	250–299
6	200–249
7	150–199
8	100–149
9	50–99
10	0–49

alignment of the risk rating process across commercial units at the bank and to bring attention to ratings that appear out of line with credit policy.

In addition to its work in examining ratings, the Loan Review group holds regular meetings between risk and business unit management and their teams to review specific deals and to discuss changes in policy and/or market conditions that could affect ratings. In fact, the ratings are not static but should be changed to reflect material changes in the components of the risk rating. Take, for example, the NCD loan. After a year has gone by, some developments have occurred that began affecting NCD's financial situation. An announcement was made by one of the primary competitors that it had developed a new technology that was both faster and cheaper than any existing product on the market including NCDs and as a result sales over the past few months for the GPC product declined 10 percent. This reaction negatively affected NCD's cash flows and at about this time the head of production and sales voluntarily left to take a position with a competitor. In addition, inventory levels have been rising at NCD since the announcement. There was also an article in the local newspaper that indicated that company management may have established a hostile work environment, based on a pending class action lawsuit brought on behalf of six workers at the main production facility of NCD. The lawsuit is requesting damages of $20 million.

The relationship manager has been watching these developments closely and is expected to make adjustments to the rating every six months as needed. To guide that process, the relationship manager puts another risk rating scorecard together for NCD, with results as shown in Table 7.11. A number of risk factors have been changed as a result of the new information on NCD. For example, the management quality rating was lowered as a result of the loss of the head of production and sales, as it was determined that that individual was instrumental to the boost in NCD sales over the past two years. Likewise the quality of operations score was lowered, reflecting the pending issues with the class action lawsuit. In addition, some of the financial ratios were adjusted based on expectations of lower sales due to the new product entering the market. Taking these factors into account results in a downgrade of the NCD obligor rating from 4 to 5. The facility rating remains the same as before and so the combined rating is downgraded to 5 based on a revised one-year expected loss rate of .625 percent.

Another important part of the risk-rating process for SifiCommercial is the **Watch List** process. The Watch List is a special designation for transactions that merit close attention for some reason, such as having undergone a significant change in risk profile resulting in a downgrade. A number of factors go into designating a transaction to the Watch List including size of the deal, potential exposure, reclassification frequency. The SifiCommercial risk management organization has established the criteria for the bank's Watch List and because the transaction is only a year old and has already undergone a one-grade movement, it is selected for review at the upcoming Loan Review Committee meeting where the relationship manager is required to present to the members the rationale behind the deal and subsequent rating.

At the meeting, a senior loan review officer who has also been reviewing the NCD file presents an independent view of the risk of the deal. During the meeting it is revealed that the Loan Review team believes the NCD transaction should be rated two notches below where it currently stands as a 6 based on the number of significant negative issues affecting the company.

TABLE 7.11 NCD Risk Rating Scorecard 1 Year After Origination

Name	National Communications Device Inc.
Address	100 Main Street, Smithtown, New York
Business Sector	Manufacturing
Business Specialty	Telecommunications

	Weight	Assessment	Score	Weighted Score
Obligor Rating Business & Market				
Market Conditions	0.15	Average and Improving	3	45
Product Diversification	0.25	Low Diversification	1	25
Company Competitive Position	0.20	Moderate	3	60
Years in Business	0.40	7	3	120
Subtotal	1.00			250
Management				
Quality of Management	0.40	Good Experience and Strategic Focus	2	80
Company External Credit Rating	0.25	B-	2	50
Quality of Operations	0.20	Good Controls and Processes	2	40
Quality of Financial Reporting & Audit	0.15	Sound Practices	3	45
Subtotal	1.00			215
Financials				
Current Ratio	0.10	2.208	4	40
Quick Ratio	0.10	1.195	4	40
Inventory Turnover Ratio	0.10	1.858	3	30
Gross Profit Margin/Assets	0.10	0.139	2	20
Expense Ratio	0.10	0.076	2	20
Return on Assets	0.10	0.015	1	10
Debt/Equity	0.10	1.130	1	10
Cash Flow Coverage Ratio	0.10	0.524	2	20
Sales Growth Rate	0.10	0.075	1	10
Net Worth to Assets Ratio	0.10	0.300	2	20
Subtotal	1.00			220
Total Score				685

(*continued*)

TABLE 7.11 *(Continued)*

Cash Flow-at-Risk	1.00	Outside CFaR Tolerance	2	100
Facility Rating				
Collateral Type	0.50	Unsecured	1	50
Loan Tenor	0.15	Two years	4	60
Loan Terms	0.15	Appropriate for Risk	3	45
Guarantees	0.20	None	1	20
	1.00		Total	175

Maximum Score = 500

The relationship manager presents his case for why it should be rated as 5 instead of 6 and a debate ensues at the committee regarding the facts of the deal. At the end of the discussion the head of Loan Review decides that the rating should be downgraded to a 6. Normally, at SifiCommercial when a two-grade decline in risk rating occurs, the relationship manager is removed from the deal and may face other disciplinary action including a haircut of their bonus. In this case, the relationship manager is not formally disciplined but is warned not to let this happen again.

RATING CRE LOANS

The risk-rating process is essentially the same for C&I and CRE loans, however, some of the risk attributes differ among loan types. In the case of CRE loans, where the quality of the property and its ability to generate cash flows is critical, close attention to key metrics that can shed light on these items is prudent in the course of the risk rating process. Table 7.12 provides a list of some of the more useful metrics for assessing CRE loan risk.

One of the more important ratios to consider in rating CRE loans is the **debt service coverage ratio** (DSCR). It describes the level of net operating income against debt service and therefore is an important indicator of the property's ability to cover debt service costs. It can be defined more formally as:

$$\text{DSCR} = (\text{Annual Net Income} + \text{Amortization/Depreciation} $$
$$+ \text{Interest Expense} + \text{Other Noncash Items}) \qquad 7.1$$
$$/(\text{Principal Repayment} + \text{Interest} + \text{Lease Payments})$$

TABLE 7.12   Key CRE Risk Attributes

Attribute
Absorption Rate
Property Sales Price
Contingency Reserves
Rental Rate
Vacancy Rate
Interest Rates
Loan-to-Value Ratio
Debt Service Coverage Ratio

A DSCR below 1 indicates that there is insufficient income to cover debt costs and while banks vary in terms of what an appropriate DSCR is, a general rule of thumb is that DSCRs between 1.15 and 1.35 are deemed adequate.

Another important metric is the **absorption rate**. This metric describes the rate at which properties or units with similar features are absorbed by the market over some time interval. Take the following example to illustrate the metric. Suppose SifiCommercial is evaluating a CRE loan to a customer for a 500-unit apartment complex. The absorption period was set at six months and the number of units leased out during that period in the complex was 100. In this case the absorption rate is 100/500, or 20 percent over six months. Higher ratios are indicative of better market absorption, and lower estimates could indicate trouble for the property owner. Many factors could affect this ratio such as location, market conditions, and competition, so it is important for the analyst to understand the dynamics facing the property to gain a more complete picture of the risk.

COMMERCIAL LOAN SYNDICATION

SifiCommercial usually has no trouble in meeting customer loan requests on its own. However, there have been circumstances, particularly on the C&I side where very large loans have come to their attention but are well outside the comfort level of the bank to take on by themselves from an exposure perspective. In these cases, a **loan syndication** might make sense. Suppose SifiCommercial has a major customer who is interested in taking out a $250 million loan. SifiCommercial might form a syndicate with several other banks interested in participating in the loan. The loan might be priced at prime +2 percent on a floating basis with an 8 percent cap and 3 points upfront. SifiCommercial might take $25 million of the deal and allocate the remainder among five other banks. In its lead role, SifiCommercial would earn a portion of the interest on $25 million as well as some upfront fees. In addition, it would be required to handle payment disbursements, conduct underwriting due diligence and perform any collections activities on the transaction.

SifiCommercial could turn around and find itself in the role as one of several partners in a syndication where it is not in the lead position. There can be a number of issues affecting the risk of such a transaction, which the participating banks must consider. One of these issues relates to potential agency costs that can arise between the lead bank and participating banks. Since the lead bank is primarily responsible for conducting due diligence and monitoring of the loan, it can clearly impact the risk on participating institutions. Understanding how well the lead bank conducts its assessment is critical for any bank wishing to participate in such a structure. In addition, clauses over cash flow control and repayment should default occur need to be closely reviewed by participating banks to make sure adequate protections are in place to obtain collateral or other repayments expected as part of the structure.

SUMMARY

Over the years, consumer credit risk management has evolved into more of an analytically driven exercise with improvements in data collection and computer technology. In part the relative smaller size and homogeneity of consumer loans facilitated the use of automated underwriting and credit risk measurement tools. For commercial credit risk, the movement toward quantitative risk models has occurred more slowly, a reflection of the heterogeneity of commercial loans and their larger sizes, which has limited the development of large databases from which to build analytic risk models. The mortgage crisis reminds us that over-reliance on models at the expense of strong underwriting processes can lead to significant losses in the future. In this regard, commercial credit risk management with its emphasis on underwriting judgment augmented with quantitative metrics has some advantages in leveraging the best of both worlds.

While commercial credit risk analysis requires considerable experience in understanding the business sector of the customer, their market and other aspects of the business, some structure is required to assign risk estimates to these loans. The centerpiece in any commercial risk management department is the risk rating process. Risk ratings come in many different forms, however, the objectives remain the same; i.e., to assign a risk rating that reflects the underlying credit risk, measured in default rate or losses over some time interval such as one year. Risk ratings rely on a number of key inputs such as market and business conditions, management quality, financial performance of the obligor and cash flow analysis, along with an assessment of the underlying collateral in the deal.

Risk Ratings are intended to be dynamic and thus must be monitored closely for material changes that could occur. Loan Review functions and Watch Lists also are an essential part of a well-run commercial credit organization. Risk ratings should be re-evaluated on a periodic basis to keep up with material changes in risk and reviewed by the independent Loan Review staff. Such processes ensure that risk is being evaluated on a consistent basis across the organization regardless of loan type. Moreover, loan review allows the risk management team to reinforce expectations on relationship managers and others in the business unit regarding the level of acceptable risk to the organization.

QUESTIONS

You have the following commercial credit risk ratings.

	Obligor Score Range
Negligible Risk	>1,350
Very Low Risk	1,150–1,349
Low	1,000–1,149
Moderate	850–999
Average Risk	750–849
Marginal Risk	500–749
	Facility Score Range
	>450
	400–449
	350–399
	300–349
	250–299
	200–249
	150–199
	100–149
	50–99
	0–49

Facility Grade	EDF (%)	Obligor LGD(%)
1	1	2.5
2	10	5
3	20	25
4	25	35
5	35	45
6	40	55
7	55	65
8	65	75
9	85	90
10	100	100

Final Rating	One-Year EL
1	.0005–.0015
2	.0015–.0125
3	.0125–.1000
4	.1000–.2500
5	.2500–1.2500
6	1.2500–5.5000
7	5.5000–10.0000
8	10.0000–25.0000
9	25.0000–90.0000
10	90.0000–100.0000

1. In performing a credit analysis of a commercial C&I loan that was made recently, what type of information would you require and what would you do with it?
2. In your commercial scorecard you determine that the facility rating scores as 200 and the obligor score is 1,158. Suppose further that according to the commercial credit risk policy, loans must be pass grades, that is, 6 or better.

   How would you evaluate the overall risk of this loan?
3. Suppose in your analysis you discover that the bank providing a standby letter of credit as a guarantee to your borrower has experienced a major liquidity crisis and it appears that the firm will shortly be forced into receivership. The terms of the contract make it clear that in such events the guarantee is no longer in force. How would that affect your view of the loan?

4. You have been provided the following information on two commercial loans your bank is considering. Which one would you prefer based on this information?

	Loan 1	Loan 2
Annual Net Income	$ 900,000	$ 875,000
Amortization	$ 300,000	$ 400,000
Interest Expense	$ 600,000	$ 700,000
Other Noncash Items	$ 100,000	$ 75,000
Principal Repayment	$ 750,000	$ 900,000
Interest	$ 850,000	$ 925,000
Lease Payments	$ 150,000	$ 250,000

5. You are looking at two apartment complex loans. Complex 1 has 1,000 units available and Complex 2 has 700. Over the past year, Complex 1 leased out 200 units while Complex 2 leased out 150. Based on this information which loan do you prefer and what is this based on?

6. Your bank has established a strategic priority to grow its commercial business next year from an exposure of $10 million to $50 million. You do not have time to materially increase staffing given the time-frame and level of expertise needed. What would be one way to meet the objective and what considerations would you make in pursuing this strategy?

7. During a recent Commercial Risk Management Committee meeting you were shown a distribution of risk ratings on the portfolio (see figure).

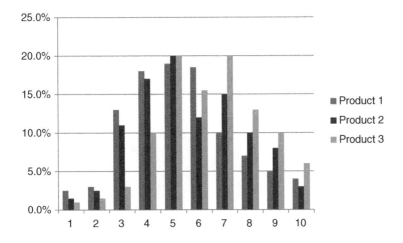

How would you think about the output from this figure relative to the commercial credit risk profile and what it means about the risk evaluation process?

8. You have observed that over the past 10 years commercial borrower 1 has had an expected cash flow of $1 million on a monthly basis with a volatility of $250,000. Borrower 2 has an expected cash flow of $2 million and a volatility of $500,000. You forecast that next year's cash flow for borrower 1 is $550,000 and for borrower 2 is $1,300,000. You have a credit policy that an obligor's projected cash-flow must not breach the 95 percent confidence level, using 1.65 as the volatility factor. What is your conclusion about these two loans?

9. What considerations do you have in the time horizon of a risk rating?

10. A commercial loan officer originated a $500,000,000 loan last year that was rated as a 3, or Low Risk on the bank's combined commercial risk rating system. For the commercial loan portfolio this is a very large exposure and merits close attention. Some preliminary analysis also suggests that in that year, the risk rating may have migrated to a 5 rating. How would you handle this loan—specifically, what process would you follow?

CHAPTER 8

Credit Risk Mitigation

OVERVIEW

While identifying and measuring risk are critical activities for any risk management function, understanding how to use that information to shape the amount of risk exposure in a portfolio is equally important. Specifically, as loans or transactions build up in a portfolio, whether it is market, credit, or interest rate risk, the risk manager will want to maintain that the risk exposure lies within the bank's risk tolerance as measured by VaR or other metrics. Understanding what tools are available to the risk manager in such cases is the focus of the next several chapters, beginning with this chapter on credit risk mitigation.

In the specific case of credit risk, there are a number of techniques and activities that the risk manager can undertake to manage the risk exposure of the credit portfolio. At the front end, credit policies, underwriting guidelines, concentration limits on certain risk attributes, and other restrictions define the general and specific contours of credit quality to be allowed into the portfolio. These criteria screen out unwanted credit risks early in the process, and as long as the bank applies strong controls on the process and has an effective way of monitoring loan quality coming into the portfolio on an ongoing basis, this is an important way to maintain the balance of credit risk to expectations. However, the mortgage boom ending in 2007 and leading to the mortgage crash following this period was in part facilitated by a widespread relaxation of prudent underwriting standards brought on by aggressive competition among mortgage lenders.

Once loans have come into the portfolio, the risk manager has a variety of other tools to use to limit or expand the amount of credit risk consistent with risk policy. One strategy entails applying business rules on the treatment of borrowers entering different stages of delinquency. Such account management processes have a number of applications for marketing as well as risk management, among others. For managing credit risk exposure, even after a loan has been originated, its performance can be influenced by actions taken by the bank. Before a borrower enters a later stage of delinquency, such as 60 or 90 days past due, the bank can proactively address issues by applying differential treatments to borrowers. For example, for some borrowers who have never been late in making a payment, their loan history might call for a simple automated call from the servicing center to the borrower gently reminding them to make their payment. For more serious and chronic delinquencies, protocols may warrant letters, multiple calls by a customer service agent, or even an onsite visit, depending on the circumstances. The use of statistical models much like those used for automated underwriting have become integral parts of many large servicing operations. Such initiatives can have a material impact on lowering default rates by understanding which borrowers are likely to fall further behind in their payments and designing effective strategies to cure these loans.

Conceptually, a variety of agreements and structures have been developed over the past several years that allow institutions to leverage capital markets for credit risk transfer activities. **Risk transfer** describes the process by which one institution enters into a contract with one or more institutions for the purpose of selling or buying exposure to some reference pool of collateral. In the case of credit risk, it might be a set of loans such as mortgages that could default over some period of time and thus expose the owner of those loans such as a bank to credit risk that it may no longer have an appetite for. Such transactions can be one-off arrangements between counterparties, or standardized structures that could be traded in an open market. Since these structures rely on the underlying collateral for settlement, these arrangements broadly are referred to as **credit derivatives**. Examples of credit derivatives include **credit default swaps** (CDS), **collateralized debt obligations** (CDOs), and **credit-linked notes** (CLNs). In addition, credit portfolio managers may look to obtain coverage on a portion of the credit exposure via standard insurance and reinsurance contracts. In the case of mortgage portfolios, the availability of mortgage insurance has been a staple for decades in managing the level of credit risk. Insurance products can be arranged on an individual loan basis or on a pool of new or existing loans.

Whatever type of credit risk transfer mechanism is used—credit derivative or insurance product—the risk manager must be able to accurately quantify the credit risk exposure in the structure in order to determine the financial benefit obtained by entering the contract. This requires using the techniques discussed in Chapter 6 to assess the losses that could be expected on the pool. Guarding against adverse selection in credit risk transfer structures is critically important because if the estimates of credit risk turn out to be lower than actual experience, and other counterparties have better capabilities for assessing credit risk, the institution may find itself unknowingly taking on an excessive amount of credit risk.

This chapter focuses on the experience of the SifiMortgage division to illustrate how different credit risk mitigation techniques are used and valued. To understand SifiMortgage's experience in credit risk mitigation requires stepping back into the years leading up to the financial crisis of 2008–2009 and examining their portfolio at the time. In 2004, SifiMortgage had $10 billion in mortgages held in its portfolio. The portfolio was comprised of $5 billion in prime residential first-lien mortgages, $2 billion in subprime first-lien mortgages, and $3 billion in second-lien mortgages, otherwise known as home equity lines of credit (HELOCs).

SifiMortgage had historically been a small part of SifiBank activities. Initially, as the bank began to ramp up its mortgage purchases in 2004 because it saw significant expected returns on originating and holding mortgages in its portfolio, it did not engage in any form of credit enhancement to its loan portfolio. This was largely due to the fact that credit losses over the preceding years had been negligible and the housing market had been robust. Housing prices had remained strong and interest rates low, contributing factors to continued strength in housing and the overall economy.

By 2005, the risk team of SifiMortgage had observed that 35 percent of its portfolio had originated within the past three years and mostly in California, Arizona, and Nevada, causing some concern as to whether it was exposing itself to excessive concentration in a few origination years and in states where underwriting standards had been significantly relaxed. At the same time the risk team had been tracking unusual house price appreciation trends in these areas and became alarmed when home prices in several cities had jumped by more than 25 percent in a single year.

INSURANCE CONTRACTS

At the first SifiMortgage Credit Risk Management Committee Meeting in 2005, the head of SifiMortgage risk management made several recommendations to limit potential credit risk in the mortgage portfolio. The first recommendation was to establish a set of **soft markets concentration limits** that would restrict the amount of mortgages that could be purchased from certain states and cities that were experiencing abnormally high house price appreciation rates. This strategy entailed extensive monitoring of local housing market data on a monthly basis. Secondary data gathered on macroeconomic and local housing market trends such as inventory levels, sales price trends, number of months' supply, and other related information helped determine the relative health of the housing market. Reviewing this data over a period of time allowed the risk managers to form a baseline of performance as well as establish thresholds for when certain actions to limit exposure would take place. The information gathered for each market was aggregated in such a way that each market was assigned a rating. Based on this rating, SifiBank decided how it would allocate assets into its portfolio, limit the amount of loans from a market coming into the portfolio, or in some cases, halt loan production from certain soft markets.

The second set of recommendations centered around obtaining **pool mortgage insurance policies** for certain segments of the SifiMortgage portfolio on an ongoing basis. Mortgage insurance companies have historically offered to absorb credit losses on mortgages for a price. Any mortgage with an LTV above 80 percent is required to have a mortgage insurance policy in order for it to be sold to either Fannie Mae or Freddie Mac. Such insurance is considered to be loan level coverage versus pool coverage on a portfolio of loans. In both instances, mortgage insurance is in a first loss position, absorbing losses up to some stipulated amount before reverting to the lender. In return, the mortgage insurance company receives a periodic insurance premium from the lender. Usually loan level insurance policies establish a per incident coverage such as 25 percent for loans between 85 and 90 percent LTVs. Suppose a loan was made by SifiBank for $90,000 on a property originally worth $100,000. If after several years, the property declines in value to $80,000, resulting in a negative equity position (112.5 percent LTV) for the borrower and consistent with option-theory as reviewed in Chapter 6, the borrower defaults. At this point the lender would present a claim to the mortgage insurance company for the unpaid principal of the loan plus allowable expenses and the insurance company would compensate the lender for up to 25 percent of that total.

Perhaps of more interest to SifiMortgage risk managers is the use of pool insurance contracts. Absent such a contract, SifiMortgage would assume all credit losses on its portfolio shown in the top panel of Figure 8.1. In the event that the bank entered into a loan level mortgage insurance contract, the loss allocation would look as represented in the bottom panel of Figure 8.1. In this case, the insurance company shares in a portion of credit losses across the loss distribution. By contrast, a pool level insurance agreement would have a loss-sharing structure more like the one shown in Figure 8.2. In this example, the arrangement calls for the insurance company (counterparty 1) to take on losses on the pool up to a stated percentage of the pool of loans. So if the contract established the insurance coverage to be at 2 percent and losses experienced on the pool wind up at 1.5 percent, then the insurance company absorbs all losses. Alternatively, if losses over the contract period were 3 percent, then the insurance company would take

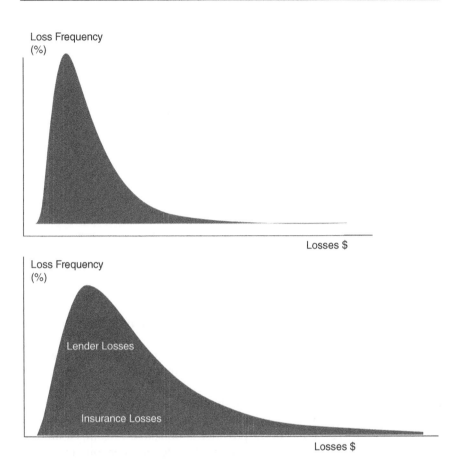

FIGURE 8.1 SifiMortgage Held-for-Investment Mortgage Portfolio Credit Losses versus Loan Level Insurance Coverage

the first 2 percent and SifiMortgage (counterparty 2) would be responsible for absorbing losses thereafter, or 1 percent.

The risk team solicited bids from three mortgage insurance providers. The process entailed putting a loan level data tape together containing a variety of borrower and loan risk attributes for the insurance companies to evaluate. Each company developed their own models based on similar loans that they had insured over time and for which they had actual loan performance information. In addition, the SifiMortgage risk team provided the insurance companies with their credit policy and underwriting guidelines for their review.

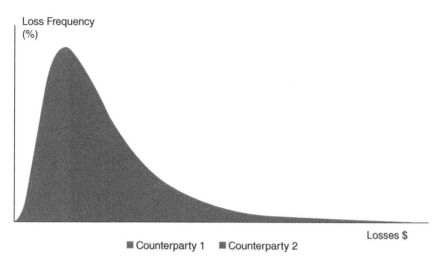

FIGURE 8.2 Pool Insurance Example

In return, SifiMortgage received from each insurance company a set of premiums that the bank would be charged on the pools as well as a set of stipulations, or **pool "stips,"** that establish what loan attributes would be acceptable to be covered under the policy and in what concentrations. Similar to other forms of insurance such as automobile or health insurance, mortgage insurance is structured such that the buyer (SifiMortgage) pays an insurance company a periodic premium on the outstanding loan balance of the pool. In return, the insurance provider is obligated to compensate the buyer for losses on mortgages sustained in the reference portfolio up to any limits when presented with a claim that meets the terms and conditions of the contract. In some cases, insurance providers may elect to deny or rescind coverage altogether on a policy should there be some form of misrepresentation or fraud committed in underwriting the loan. For the buyer and the seller, determining a fair premium to be charged for this insurance is complicated because of the borrower's ability to freely prepay their mortgage when interest rates fall below their mortgage contract rate. Loans that prepay reduce the number of loans that could potentially default in the future and as a result, this borrower behavior needs to be incorporated into the insurance pricing model.

Another consideration in pricing this insurance is considering over what period of time payouts are to be made. In other words, is this insurance in force for the first five years after loan origination, 10 years, or over the life of the loan? Moreover, if insurance payments are made as loans default over time with some lag between the incidence of default and the payment, what

TABLE 8.1 Mortgage Insurance Premiums and Pool Stips

Mortgage Insurance Provider	Lifetime Premium (%)	CA, AZ, NV (%)	Pool Limits Investor-owned (%)	DTI >40%	Weighted Average	
					FICO	LTV
1	4.25	25	5	10	660	80
2	5.15	50	10	15	640	85
3	4.95	30	8	12	650	90

is the appropriate discount rate to use? What is the event that actually triggers payment? Some loans that enter default after 180 days delinquent might be classified as a default event, whereas an alternate definition could be that default occurs only when the borrower is foreclosed on. The ramifications can be significant for both parties in terms of the present value of cash flows from the policy and thus knowing exactly what the event of interest that triggers a claim is critical to the contractual process. Before entering a mortgage insurance contract or any other credit risk transfer structure the risk team at SifiMortgage must develop their own views of what they believe the distribution of credit losses looks like, using models described in Chapter 6.

Contractually, the mortgage insurance policy requires the buyer to make a periodic payment, the premium to the insurer, instead of a lump sum on the original balance. Assuming an annual premium payment, the lifetime loss estimate could be divided by an estimate of the expected life of the loan as measured by its duration, or other appropriate measure of estimating the expected time over which payments will occur. The SifiMortgage team has determined that the subprime pool has a weighted average duration of five years. As a result, the fair premium SifiMortgage expects to pay is 100bps on the original unpaid principal balance each year. SifiMortgage provides three different mortgage insurers with the loan details for this 5,000 loan subprime pool and in return receives their premium estimates and terms as shown in Table 8.1.

Mortgage insurer 1 would charge a lifetime/annual premium of 4.25 percent/.85 percent on the original pool balance but limits the pool concentration of California, Nevada, and Arizona mortgages to 25 percent. In addition, they require the weighted average FICO and LTV on the pool to be 660 and 80 percent, respectively. They also limit the percentage of investor-owned properties and debt-to-income ratios over 40 percent to 5 and 10 percent, respectively. Insurer 2 would charge a lifetime premium of 5.15 percent on the original balance but while its premium suggests that it has priced itself out of the business for this insurance request, it also has more favorable terms on the pool characteristics. Specifically, they allow up to 50 percent of the pool from California, Arizona, and Nevada, and their weighted average FICO and LTVs are more favorable than insurer 1 as well, at 640, and 85 percent, respectively. The third insurer presents a premium between the other two providers and their pool stips are generally between the other two insurers. The key question for SifiMortgage is how to optimize the allocation of pool insurance across each provider. Due to concerns that a downturn in the economies in California, Nevada, and Arizona would expose SifiMortgage to significant losses beyond their original expectations, the business would like to get as much of the portfolio covered with pool insurance as possible. The reason for the variation in premiums and pool stips among insurers is due to differences in each of their proprietary loss models and risk appetites. This presents itself as a classic linear programming problem where SifiMortgage can minimize the cost of insurance across the three insurers, as well as the option to self-insure, based on the premiums and SifiMortgage's internal estimates of what it believes the fair premium should be; that is, the 500bps estimate. This becomes a constrained optimization problem since it minimizes costs subject to the pool stips of each insurer. The model can be set up with the following structure:

$$MIN$$

$$\sum_{i=1}^{5,000} \sum_{j=1}^{4} X_{ij} p_j$$

$$st$$

$$0 \leq \sum_{j=1}^{4} X_{ij} \leq 1$$

$$X_{ij} = 0,1$$

$$\sum_{i=1}^{N} X_{i1} FICO_{i1} \frac{UPB_{i1}}{\sum_{i=1}^{N} UPB_{i1}} \leq 660 \qquad\qquad 8.1$$

$$\sum_{i=1}^{N} X_{i2} FICO_{i2} \frac{UPB_{i2}}{\sum_{i=1}^{N} UPB_{i2}} \leq 640$$

$$\sum_{i=1}^{N} X_{i3} FICO_{i3} \frac{UPB_{i3}}{\sum_{i=1}^{N} UPB_{i3}} \leq 650$$

$$\sum_{i=1}^{N} X_{i1} LTV_{i1} \frac{UPB_{i1}}{\sum_{i=1}^{N} UPB_{i1}} \leq 80$$

$$\sum_{i=1}^{N} X_{i2} LTV_{i2} \frac{UPB_{i2}}{\sum_{i=1}^{N} UPB_{i2}} \leq 85$$

$$\sum_{i=1}^{N} X_{i3} LTV_{i3} \frac{UPB_{i3}}{\sum_{i=1}^{N} UPB_{i3}} \leq 90$$

$$\frac{\sum_{i=1}^{m} X_{i1} State_i \frac{UPB_{i1}}{\sum_{i=1}^{n} UPB_{i1}}}{\sum_{i=1}^{N} X_{i1}} \leq .25$$

$$\frac{\sum_{i=1}^{m} X_{i2} State_i \frac{UPB_{i2}}{\sum_{i=1}^{N} UPB_{i2}}}{\sum_{i=1}^{N} X_{i2}} \leq .50$$

$$\frac{\sum_{i=1}^{m} X_{i3} State_i \frac{UPB_{i3}}{\sum_{i=1}^{N} UPB_{i3}}}{\sum_{i=1}^{N} X_{i3}} \leq .30$$

$$\frac{\sum_{i=1}^{m} X_{i1} Investor_i \frac{UPB_{i1}}{\sum_{i=1}^{N} UPB_{i1}}}{\sum_{i=1}^{N} X_{i1}} \leq .05$$

$$\frac{\sum_{i=1}^{m} X_{i2} Investor_i \frac{UPB_{i2}}{\sum_{i=1}^{N} UPB_{i2}}}{\sum_{i=1}^{N} X_{i2}} \leq .10$$

$$\frac{\sum_{i=1}^{m} X_{i3} Investor_i \dfrac{UPB_{i3}}{\sum_{i=1}^{N} UPB_{i3}}}{\sum_{i=1}^{N} X_{i3}} \leq .08$$

$$\frac{\sum_{i=1}^{m} X_{i1} DTI_i^{>40\%} \dfrac{UPB_{i1}}{\sum_{i=1}^{N} UPB_{i1}}}{\sum_{i=1}^{N} X_{i1}} \leq .10$$

$$\frac{\sum_{i=1}^{m} X_{i2} DTI_i^{>40\%} \dfrac{UPB_{i2}}{\sum_{i=1}^{N} UPB_{i2}}}{\sum_{i=1}^{N} X_{i2}} \leq .15$$

$$\frac{\sum_{i=1}^{m} X_{i3} DTI_i^{>40\%} \dfrac{UPB_{i3}}{\sum_{i=1}^{N} UPB_{i3}}}{\sum_{i=1}^{N} X_{i3}} \leq .12$$

The structure of the optimization model formalizes the premiums and pool stip information provided by the insurers. Note that the objective function is expressed to minimize the cost of insuring the portfolio including the possibility of SifiMortgage self-insuring the loan. There are four decision variables (X_i) in the model, one for each insurer plus a fourth reflecting self-insurance by the bank. The Xs are binary (i.e., either 0 or 1 only). While such a model can be extended to capture correlations between loans, for purposes of exposition it is assumed that the correlations are 1. The p_i factors represent the premiums for each insurer plus SifiBank's loss estimate as the cost of self-insuring loan i. Each pool stip is determined on a weighted basis using each loan's unpaid principal balance as the weight.

Once the model premiums and stips have been put into the model, each loan in the pool will be designated according to its least cost disposition given each insurer's constraints on the insured portfolio. In this case, it is determined that 35 percent of the loans are allocated to insurer 1, 15 percent to insurer 2, and 30 percent to the 3rd insurer, leaving 20 percent self-insured by SifiMortgage. This is a feasible solution meeting each of the pool stips.

CREDIT DERIVATIVES AND RISK MITIGATION

In the second half of 2006, SifiMortgage risk management became increasingly apprehensive over the direction of house prices across the country. Although it felt that its purchase of pool insurance for its subprime portfolio was adequate, it began rethinking whether it ought to have some sort of protection for the prime first lien and HELOC portfolios as well. It could secure insurance for these loans as well, but the team was concerned that it might build up an excessive counterparty exposure to these insurers should mortgage losses rise sharply. After all, none of the insurers had an external credit rating above A and these were "monoline" insurers, meaning that their business was focused on a single industry. In this case their specialization in mortgage insurance amplifies their risk in a downturn given their exposure to this industry.

The risk team began looking into alternative credit risk mitigation strategies focusing on credit derivative instruments. Credit derivatives had been in existence for a number of years and increasingly new instruments were being developed and traded more actively in the market. This ability to buy and sell credit risk at will in the open market was appealing to the risk team as it would provide them greater flexibility to react to market conditions by transacting in areas of the market that were more developed, that is, where trading activity was greater. Markets characterized by relatively strong trading between buyers and sellers support better price discovery. Since this would be their first real attempt at trading credit derivatives, the head of risk wanted to impose some limitations on the amount of credit derivatives that would be bought or sold by SifiMortgage.

The risk team had been looking at three types of credit derivatives. The first are credit default swaps (CDSs) that bear some similarities to insurance products in that for a premium against a reference pool of collateral, a buyer of credit protection (SifiMortgage) would receive payments from the seller on defaults that had occurred according to the definitions of a default event in the contract. CDSs are among the most traded credit derivatives, with many different underlying reference assets available, including mortgages.

The second type of credit derivative evaluated by SifiMortgage was credit-linked notes, or CLNs. CLNs resemble fixed-income instruments in that payments of principal and interest are made periodically to the holder of the CLN (the CLN buyer or investor). A reference entity or asset underlies the payment stream that is assumed to have some default propensity for which the seller of the CLN would seek some credit protection. As payments on the reference pool (in this case mortgages) come in to SifiMortgage, they would be reduced by any defaults during that period and these payments would be passed along to the CLN buyer.

The third structure considered by SifiMortgage was the collateralized debt obligation (CDO). A CDO allows various investors to share credit risk on a reference pool according to designated levels of losses on the pool. These structures establish a priority by which investors receive their payments and defaults. Investors in a position in the CDO structure that requires them to take losses before any other investor (referred to as a **first loss position**) are subordinate or junior to others. Investors next in line are referred to as **mezzanine investors** and those last in line to receive losses are in the **senior position**. Those investors in the junior position and thus more likely to absorb losses are compensated with higher yields on their tranche of the CDO compared to senior tranche investors.

In exploring the potential application of these three credit derivatives to protecting SifiMortgage against mortgage losses, the risk team established some criteria to guide them in the assessment process. First, the underlying reference pool for the evaluation was a $1 billion randomly selected pool of their jumbo prime first-lien business. According to SifiMortgage credit models, lifetime losses on this pool were estimated to be 2 percent. These are loans that are otherwise outside the underwriting guidelines of Fannie Mae and Freddie Mac but are higher loan amounts (jumbo loans) than what the two agencies can accept. The pool's duration was also estimated to be four years. In addition, SifiMortgage wanted a transaction that could be traded easily in the market and minimized regulatory and accounting-related reporting issues. The structure also needed to be operationally tractable in that SifiMortgage did not want to invest a lot of resources in developing new infrastructure for tracking performance, reporting, and disbursement.

As the team explored its options, it discovered that while it could enter into various transactions with interested counterparties directly using its jumbo prime subportfolio as the reference pool, this would be a more customized type of transaction that would not be able to be traded on the market easily given its features. Alternatively, consideration was given to the fact that rather than use the reference portfolio itself, SifiMortgage could buy credit derivatives in the market such as CDSs that were tied to reference assets such as mortgage pools similar in composition and other features as SifiMortgage's jumbo prime portfolio. With these considerations in mind the suitability of each of these three credit derivatives to protect SifiMortgage from losses was investigated.

CREDIT DEFAULT SWAP MECHANICS

CDS instruments are widely used instruments that efficiently allow investors to take positions in credit risk without having to actually hold the asset in a portfolio, as in the case of SifiMortgage for its prime mortgage portfolio.

Instead, an investor seeking to sell credit protection can enter into a CDS with a buyer of credit protection. In SifiMortgage's situation, a traded CDS index, PrimeFR30 (fixed rate 30-year mortgages) CDI (credit default swap index) exists on prime first-lien jumbo mortgages. The reference pool for the index specifically are mortgage-backed securities (MBS) composed of qualifying jumbo loans. The underlying pool of mortgages for the MBS in effect makes the CDSs a derivative of a derivative. The mortgages are vintages comparable to that of SifiMortgage's portfolio but are not perfectly aligned with it. As a result, there will be some basis risk between the underlying mortgages and the CDS contract. The Prime FR30 CDI credit default swap was created to provide standardization in trading mortgage credit risk synthetically.

SifiMortgage decides that it wants to accept the interest rate risk associated with holding the mortgages on its balance sheet but needs to offset the credit risk on these loans. Consequently it decides to enter into a four-year CDS on this index for a notional amount of $1 billion (remember that the risk team is only willing to put on a CDS up to this amount and so does not offset the entire amount of risk on the portfolio). To enter into this contract as the buyer, it will make quarterly payments of 12.3bps (referred to as the credit swap spread and expressed as an annual rate) on the $1 billion notional over the course of the four-year contract period. The four-year period coincides with the duration of the underlying pool of mortgages and so aligns well with the timing of when credit protection is most likely to be needed. In the event that no defaults occur on the mortgages underlying the MBS, the seller of the CDI (SifiMortgage's counterparty) would not make any default payments. Conceptually the structure of the contract is as shown in Figure 8.3.

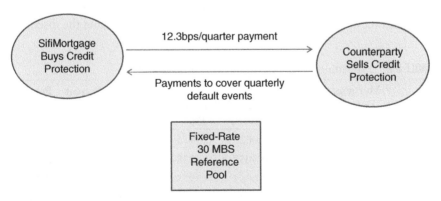

FIGURE 8.3 Prime FR30 CDI Credit Default Swap Contract for SifiMortgage as Buyer

When a default event occurs, the contract calls for the buyer to stop making its payments to the seller and in return the seller makes a default payment to SifiMortgage. This specific structure requires the buyer payments to be made at the end of every quarter and default payments likewise are made at the end of the quarter by the seller. A key question is how the 49.2bps annual credit default spread is determined. As can be imagined, the spread is dependent upon the defaults expected on the pool of mortgages underlying the reference MBS. In particular it can be thought of as the amount that would need to be paid against the present value of expected payments by the buyer's net of defaults over the period to equal the present value of the expected payouts for default by the seller. This is expressed more formally as the following:

$$PV_{Payments}CS = PV_{Default} \qquad 8.2$$

where CS represents the credit spread that would be paid by the buyer to the seller. The credit spread can be viewed as an annual average loss rate on the reference pool represented by the expected default rates multiplied by the loss severity rate. Defaults occur throughout the contract period and are estimated based on methods described in earlier chapters on computing hazard rates. In addition, loss severity models can be used in estimating the amount of losses sustained once loans default. Table 8.2 presents these estimates for the MBS collateral. The risk-free rate is assumed to be 3 percent, which is used to generate the discount factors for each year. Default rates are shown for each year based on the loan level attributes of the loans underlying the MBS. These are one-year default rates. The cumulative four-year default rate is 2 percent. Likewise the severity rate on this pool is 25 percent. The product of the default rate and severity rate for each year of the contract defines the expected loss in a given year. Applying the discount

TABLE 8.2 Estimating Credit Spread for SifiMortgage CDS

Contract Year	Mortgage Default Rate	Mortgage Severity Rate	Expected Loss	Remaining Pool	Discount Factor	Present Value Payments	Present Value Defaults
1	0.01	0.25	0.0025	0.9975	0.970874	0.9684	0.0024
2	0.015	0.25	0.0038	0.9938	0.942596	0.9367	0.0035
3	0.025	0.25	0.0063	0.9875	0.915142	0.9037	0.0056
4	0.03	0.25	0.0075	0.9800	0.888487	0.8707	0.0065
			0.0200			3.6796	0.0181

TABLE 8.3 Estimated Credit Spreads for SifiMortgage CDS Assuming Default Rates Double

Contract Year	Mortgage Default Rate	Mortgage Severity Rate	Expected Loss	Remaining Pool	Discount Factor	Present Value Payments	Present Value Defaults
1	0.02	0.25	0.0050	0.9950	0.970874	0.9660	0.0048
2	0.03	0.25	0.0075	0.9875	0.942596	0.9308	0.0070
3	0.05	0.25	0.0125	0.9750	0.915142	0.8923	0.0112
4	0.06	0.25	0.0150	0.9600	0.888487	0.8529	0.0128
			0.0400			3.6420	0.0358

factors to the remaining pool balances and to the expected losses leads to a total present value of $3.68 against $.0181 of present value default payments. Applying the relationship above, the credit spread SifiBank would be expected to pay is 49.2bps.

To see how higher estimates of default would affect credit default spreads, assume that the default rates double from what was shown in Table 8.2. Table 8.3 shows the impact this has on the present value of payments and defaults. Using the calculation for credit default spread from the original example results in a spread of 98.3bps.

Note that mortgage prepayments would affect the analysis by reducing default rates as borrowers that refinance their mortgages are no longer in the pool that could default later on. This can be seen in Table 8.4 from the results assuming that 10 percent of the pool balance prepays each year. In this example, the present value of defaults is lower: 1.38 versus 1.81 percent, since there are fewer loans that can default on the pool as loans prepay. This manifests itself in the form of a lower credit default spread as well. In this example, the estimated credit spread is 37.4bps, or 11.8

TABLE 8.4 Credit Spreads for SifiMortgage CDO Assuming 10 percent Prepayments

Contract Year	Mortgage Default Rate	Mortgage Severity Rate	Expected Loss	Remaining Pool	Discount Factor	Present Value Payments	Present Value Defaults
1	0.01	0.25	0.0025	0.9981	0.970874	0.9691	0.0018
2	0.015	0.25	0.0038	0.9953	0.942596	0.9382	0.0027
3	0.025	0.25	0.0063	0.9907	0.915142	0.9066	0.0043
4	0.03	0.25	0.0075	0.9851	0.888487	0.8752	0.0050
			0.0200			3.6891	0.0138

basis points lower than the 0 percent prepayment base case. Clearly, while estimating the amount of credit risk inherent in the reference pool is critical, when valuing mortgage-related CDS, it is also important to accurately reflect prepayments.

The example above vastly oversimplifies the reality of using a CDS to offset the risk of an underlying credit exposure as exemplified by SifiMortgage's prime mortgage portfolio. It would be impossible to match a CDS reference pool's default performance exactly with that of the underlying pool and as such a certain amount of basis risk will exist between the underlying asset and the hedge instrument. For example, suppose that Sifi-Mortgage had entered into a CDS on prime FR30 jumbo mortgages for a notional amount equivalent to their prime jumbo portfolio. If losses on the reference pool were 1.5 percent, the compensation received by SifiMortgage once defaults occurred would not cover the 2 percent losses expected on the portfolio. In theory it might be possible to construct a hedge ratio based on differences in credit risk between the portfolio and reference pool as well as any correlations that could be determined between the two sets of collateral and adjustments made to increase or decrease the size of the CDS notional amount accordingly. It may not be possible to conduct a detailed estimation of these differences in risk and their correlations due to a lack of detailed loan level information on the reference collateral. This could lead to difficulties in creating a stable hedge.

CREDIT-LINKED NOTE MECHANICS

Although buying into a CDS contract allows SifiMortgage to directly offset some portion of its credit risk without having to sell the asset, it does have its limitations in terms of providing SifiMortgage with a good hedge. An alternative arrangement to the CDS would be to rely on the prime jumbo loans as a reference pool directly. In the case of a CLN, SifiMortgage would issue a note through a trust or special purpose entity that would provide par value to the investor in the CLN if no defaults on the reference pool occur (Figure 8.4). The CLN can be structured to pay a fixed or floating rate to the buyer of the note over a specified term. Assume that SifiMortgage creates a CLN on a $1 billion notional of prime jumbo mortgages in its portfolio and issues a five-year 5.5 percent coupon CLN. If the pool were to realize losses, the CLN investor's cash flows received from the trust would be reduced by the amount of defaults experienced by the reference asset. As in the case of the credit default swap, the underlying coupon paid to the investor would reflect the inherent default risk of the reference assets. This in turn would be captured as a spread over a comparable duration risk-free bond. Just as

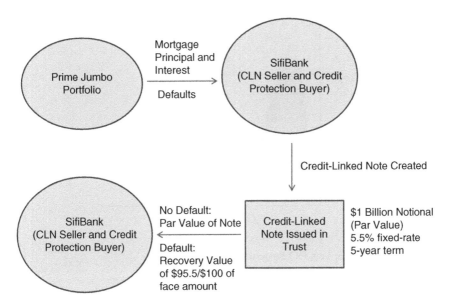

FIGURE 8.4 CLN Issued by SifiBank Using Prime Jumbo Portfolio as Reference Asset

in the case of the CDS, estimates of default risk would need to be computed along with loss severity for determining the amount of credit spread the investor should receive. Assuming the losses on the reference pool were such that the present value of the underlying collateral were $955 million, the CLN investor would realize that value on their investment.

The CLN provides an efficient way to transfer SifiMortgage's credit risk to investors. This type of structure may be difficult to execute for a smaller firm or one with a poor credit rating since it is not a standard type of product and is backed by the underlying collateral of the reference asset. It may also present SifiMortgage with a number of regulatory reporting issues if the transaction triggers certain rules that designate its treatment as a "commodity pool" under the Commodity Futures Trading Commission rules. That could lead to a significant regulatory reporting burden that could influence the bank's willingness to issue CLNs on an ongoing basis as a hedge instrument.

COLLATERALIZED DEBT OBLIGATION MECHANICS

The third structure evaluated by SifiMortgage risk managers was a CDO. The structure of the CDO effectively slices up a loss distribution for some reference assets according to a prioritized schedule. This differs from a CDS

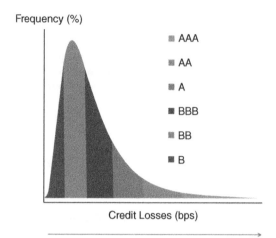

FIGURE 8.5   Illustrative CDO Structure

where the CDS seller winds up absorbing the credit losses in the transaction. In some cases an investor in credit risk may not wish to take the first losses on a pool due to higher capital requirements imposed on such investments. Alternatively an investor seeking yield may be interested in taking the riskier first or mezzanine positions to augment their overall investment portfolio's performance.

The idea behind the CDO can be seen in Figure 8.5. This hypothetical structure shows six credit risk tranches ranging from the highest risk (B-rated) to the lowest risk (AAA-rated). The shape of the loss distribution depicted directly reflects the reference assets used in putting the CDO together. Losses that materialize from the reference pool are borne first by the B tranche until it exhausts their notional amount, and then sequentially losses greater than tranche B's level go to each of the other tranches. Only when the other tranches have been wiped out would AAA CDO investors absorb losses. The B tranche may also be referred to as a first-loss position, or the junior investor in the CDO. Tranches BB-AA would be intermediate investors in the CDO and are referred as mezzanine positions. The AAA tranche is referred to as the senior tranche in the CDO.

To gain a better perspective on the relative magnitude of losses for different tranches, consider that the expected loss would occur somewhere around the BB tranche. In that case the single B and some part of the BB tranche would most likely incur losses. In order to be induced to take that risk, these investors would require to be compensated by higher yields relative to the more senior investors. Conversely, investors in the higher-rated tranches expect to have little or no losses and as a result are willing to take lower yields.

In the past CDO structures received external ratings as shown in Figure 8.5 and these ratings provided investors with information on the risk associated with these tranches. For example, a AA-rated tranche might correspond with a level of credit losses that occurs only 1 percent of the time. Understanding the level of losses and their likelihood is critical in pricing a CDO. As the financial crisis of 2008–2009 unfolded, however, it became increasingly clear that ratings assigned to subprime mortgage CDOs were not accurately picking up the credit risk in mortgages, resulting in huge losses sustained not only for the junior and mezzanine positions but also for the senior tranche-holders. Since these tranches were not expected to take losses, these outcomes reverberated throughout the capital markets leading to a collapse in investor confidence in these investments. One lesson from the crisis is the importance of understanding the accuracy of modeled views of credit risk, which will be examined in Chapter 15.

To construct a CDO using SifiMortgage subprime loans as the reference portfolio, the bank works with a Wall Street dealer specializing in these securities. The proposed security would have six tranches, as represented in Figure 8.5, built around a $1 billion pool of subprime mortgages the bank has originated for which it does not want to hold all of the credit risk. The allocation of each tranche is shown in Table 8.5. The column labeled **loss subordination** refers to the amount of credit losses that would be absorbed before a tranche would have to incur loss. In this CDO, the B tranche that stands in the first loss position would absorb the first 5 percent of credit losses that occur on the subprime mortgage reference pool.

Similarly, the BBB tranche has a loss subordination of 7 percent, reflecting the fact that the B-rated tranche takes the first 5 percent of losses

TABLE 8.5 SifiMortgage Subprime CDO Composition

Reference Pool	$1,000,000,000 Tranche Size	Percent of CDO	Loss Subordination (%)	Attachment Point (%)	Detachment Point (%)
AAA	$ 890,000,000	89	11	11	
AA	$ 20,000,000	2	9	9	11
A	$ 10,000,000	1	8	8	9
BBB	$ 10,000,000	1	7	7	8
BB	$ 20,000,000	2	5	5	7
B	$ 50,000,000	5	0	0	5
	$1,000,000,000	100			

followed by the BB tranche that takes the next 2 percent of credit losses. Another way of characterizing the risk boundaries of a given tranche is by referring to its attachment and detachment points. In the case of the BBB tranche, it begins to take losses once losses reach 7 percent of the reference pool (**attachment point**) and stop once they reach 8 percent (**detachment point**). In all, the BBB tranche would absorb a total of 1 percent of the reference pool's losses. Note that in this CDO structure, the senior tranche (i.e., AAA) attaches at 11 percent but then would absorb all losses thereafter. On a pool where losses are expected to be 1 percent, for example, the probability for the AAA tranche to take losses should be very low.

The size of each tranche is directly related to the amount of loss subordination. For example, since the B-rated tranche takes on the first 5 percent of credit losses, it represents 5 percent of the CDO. Likewise, for the BB-tranche it represents 2 percent of the CDO based on the amount of losses (difference between detachment and attachment points) it would absorb. Based on this approach the AAA tranche winds up comprising the vast majority of the CDO, in this example 89 percent. Establishing where the attachment and detachment points are is based in part on the rating methodology that is in part assessing the likelihood of credit events and their severity based on historical experience of similar collateral over long periods of time. Given that the underlying collateral is mortgages, the valuation of the CDO would take into account the effect of prepayments. Recall that in a competing risk environment, loans that prepay would reduce the number of loans that could default over time. Understanding the effects of prepayment would therefore be an important consideration in establishing the pricing for this type of security. For ease of exposition, however, it will be assumed that there are no loan prepayments.

To determine how to price the CDO and each tranche requires having some idea of the likelihood of loss events on the underlying collateral. Ideally, having a model that could describe the loss distribution depicted in Figure 8.5 would provide a way to assign weights (frequency of loss outcomes) to each payoff scenario for a tranche. For sophisticated applications, the loss distribution could be generated from a Monte Carlo simulation as described in Chapter 6. Suppose a simple form of such a model has been developed and produces 10 loss paths described in Table 8.6. Along each path an estimate of the unpaid principal balance, weighted average probability of default, and severity rate are produced, which provides estimates of loss for the pool for that particular scenario. In addition, the simulation results produce a scenario probability. In Table 8.6, for example, the scenario that results in a lifetime loss of .5 percent of SifiMortgage's subprime collateral occurs 45 percent of the time while in the scenario that yields losses of 12 percent would occur only 1 percent of the time. Note that the sum of all

TABLE 8.6 SifiMortgage Subprime Pool CDO Loss Scenarios

Loss Outcomes	Frequency (%)	Loss (bps)
1	45	50
2	17	100
3	10	200
4	7	300
5	6	400
6	5	500
7	4	600
8	3	800
9	2	1000
10	1	1200
	100	

10 scenarios must be 100 percent. These scenario losses and probabilities are used in allocating losses to the CDO tranches as well as for determining their price and corresponding yields.

As stated earlier, each tranche in the CDO is allocated losses according to a prioritized schedule. Each tranche is priced based on its share of the payout from the CDO adjusted for losses it expects to incur over time. To understand how tranches take credit losses according to this schedule, consider Table 8.7. The top panel of Table 8.7 shows the 10 loss scenarios along with the losses sustained by each tranche. The rule for loss allocation for this CDO is as follows:

$$TL_i = Min\left(Notional_i, LS_m - \sum_{j=1}^{J} TL_j \right) \qquad 8.3$$

where TL_i is the loss associated with tranche i, $Notional_i$ is the notional dollar amount of tranche i, and LS_m is the loss associated with scenario m. Applying this expression to tranche BB for loss scenario 1, for example, the losses of $5 million would be allocated entirely to tranche B and thus the BB-rated tranche incurs no loss on that scenario. However, for loss scenario 7, $50 million of the $60 million in losses are absorbed by tranche B up to its notional amount of $50 million. In other words a tranche cannot lose more than its notional amount. The remaining $10 million in credit losses would be allocated to tranche BB. None of the higher rated tranches would experience losses in scenario 7. For loss scenarios 8–10, tranche BB is

TABLE 8.7 Schedule of Losses and Payouts for SifiMortgage CDO Tranches

Loss Scenario	Scenario Loss Amount ($)	Tranche Losses					
		B	BB	BBB	A	AA	AAA
1	$ 5,000,000	$ 5,000,000	–	–	–	–	–
2	$ 10,000,000	$ 10,000,000	–	–	–	–	–
3	$ 20,000,000	$ 20,000,000	–	–	–	–	–
4	$ 30,000,000	$ 30,000,000	–	–	–	–	–
5	$ 40,000,000	$ 40,000,000	–	–	–	–	–
6	$ 50,000,000	$ 50,000,000	–	–	–	–	–
7	$ 60,000,000	$ 50,000,000	$ 10,000,000	–	–	–	–
8	$ 80,000,000	$ 50,000,000	$ 20,000,000	$ 10,000,000	–	–	–
9	$ 100,000,000	$ 50,000,000	$ 20,000,000	$ 10,000,000	$ 10,000,000	$ 10,000,000	–
10	$ 120,000,000	$ 50,000,000	$ 20,000,000	$ 10,000,000	$ 10,000,000	$ 20,000,000	$ 10,000,000

Loss Scenario	Scenario Loss Amount ($)	Tranche Payoffs					
		B	BB	BBB	A	AA	AAA
1	$ 5,000,000	$45,000,000	$20,000,000	$10,000,000	$ 10,000,000	$ 20,000,000	$ 890,000,000
2	$ 10,000,000	$40,000,000	$20,000,000	$10,000,000	$ 10,000,000	$ 20,000,000	$ 890,000,000
3	$ 20,000,000	$30,000,000	$20,000,000	$10,000,000	$ 10,000,000	$ 20,000,000	$ 890,000,000
4	$ 30,000,000	$20,000,000	$20,000,000	$10,000,000	$ 10,000,000	$ 20,000,000	$ 890,000,000
5	$ 40,000,000	$10,000,000	$20,000,000	$10,000,000	$ 10,000,000	$ 20,000,000	$ 890,000,000
6	$ 50,000,000	–	$20,000,000	$10,000,000	$ 10,000,000	$ 20,000,000	$ 890,000,000
7	$ 60,000,000	–	$10,000,000	$10,000,000	$ 10,000,000	$ 20,000,000	$ 890,000,000
8	$ 80,000,000	–	–	–	$ 10,000,000	$ 20,000,000	$ 890,000,000
9	$ 100,000,000	–	–	–	–	$ 10,000,000	$ 890,000,000
10	$ 120,000,000	–	–	–	–	–	$ 880,000,000

wiped out and even some of the higher rated tranches must then absorb the remaining losses. Note that for the AAA tranche only for scenario 10 does it take any losses. And even in this scenario they are small compared to the size of the AAA tranche.

The bottom panel of Table 8.7 shows the payouts for each tranche and loss scenario as simply the difference between the notional amount of the tranche less losses. Once the schedule of losses is established for each tranche and loss scenario, an estimate of the fair price of the CDO can be developed by weighting the payouts against the scenario probability. The pricing formula for the SifiMortgage CDO tranche is given as the following:

$$P_i^{CDO} = e^{-r} \left[\sum_{m=1}^{10} p_m Payoff_m \right] \qquad 8.4$$

where p_m and $Payoff_m$ are the probability and payoff for tranche i associated with the mth loss scenario and r is the risk-free rate. The prices for each CDO tranche are shown in Table 8.8. Corresponding with each CDO tranche price is its yield. The calculation of the CDO tranche yield is:

$$y_i^{CDO} = \ln \frac{Notional_i}{P_i^{CDO}} \qquad 8.5$$

The CDO process clearly reflects the impact of credit losses in the structure. For example, while each tranche price is lower than its notional value, some are considerably lower. Tranche B has a price of $31 million as compared to its $40 million notional value. This is because tranche B

TABLE 8.8 SifiMortgage CDO Tranche Prices and Yields

Tranche	Tranche Price ($)	Tranche Yield (%)
AAA	$863,599,480.30	3.01%
AA	$ 19,020,732.46	5.02%
A	$ 9,413,321.68	6.05%
BBB	$ 9,122,188.02	9.19%
BB	$ 17,856,197.82	11.34%
B	$ 31,102,779.35	47.47%

absorbs losses in every scenario and in five of them it actually is entirely wiped out. Contrast that with the AAA tranche that experiences losses in only scenario 10, which happens with low probability. The effects of differential risk-taking by CDO investors can also be observed in the yields on each tranche. The AAA CDO tranche has a yield just slightly over the risk-free rate while the B tranche has a yield of nearly 48 percent, reflecting the substantial losses expected to be experienced by this tranche.

Such structures thus make it easy for investors to take positions in credit risk without having to actually be in the mortgage business. For SifiMortgage it provides a potential outlet for credit risk that might not otherwise exist. In that regard, the CDO structure makes an appealing credit derivative for both buyers and sellers of credit risk. However, as an investor there is the potential that sellers of credit risk could offload significant credit risk onto unsuspecting investors unable to peer into the quality by which the loans in the reference pool were underwritten. This issue came to pass during the financial crisis, where many mortgage securities experienced higher-than-expected losses due to shoddy underwriting practices. Because a number of mortgage originators did not retain an interest in the credit performance of loans in CDOs, they did not have an incentive to ensure these processes were robust until well after the crisis developed. As a result, regulators have issued new rules requiring lenders to retain a 5 percent interest in the credit risk of the transaction if the loans do not meet certain quality criteria.

CREDIT HEDGING OUTCOMES

By late 2007, severe problems in the mortgage market were evident. The secondary mortgage market that dealt in various mortgage securities had effectively shut down on news that several subprime securities had taken significant losses. The fair value estimates that had been established using the methods described earlier for valuing mortgage securities had underestimated the defaults that ultimately occurred. The implications of decisions SifiMortgage management made in 2005 came back to affect their business several years later.

Although SifiMortgage risk management had recommended that pool insurance be obtained on a $1 billion subset of the subprime portfolio, senior management decided against putting any insurance on the portfolio. The recommendation to pursue pool insurance, while approved by the SifiMortgage Credit Risk Committee, was overturned at the Executive Committee. SifiMortgage's head of production and CFO expressed concern that obtaining mortgage insurance was a waste of money based on their observation that defaults over the past five years had been minimal and manageable. Despite signs in 2005 of accelerating house price appreciation and deterioration in borrower quality, management felt it had sufficiently priced that risk into their models. In management's opinion, buying insurance would create an earnings drag for the company during a period in which investors were expressing concern about SifiMortgage's ability to sustain their double-digit return performance. Despite the risk team's analysis showing that optimizing disposition of mortgage insurance would be in the best interest of the company, management disputed the validity of loss projections used in the analysis as being abnormally pessimistic. Eventually, a compromise ensued and management agreed to obtain insurance for a $500 million segment of the portfolio.

Ultimately, as the secondary market began unraveling, borrower default rates soared in the industry so that by 2007, SifiMortgage realized that it was in the midst of an emerging default crisis. To get a better sense of how this was unfolding for the bank, consider Figure 8.6. Originally, the risk team had used its modeled projections shown in Figure 8.6 to develop its pool insurance optimization. Management had believed in coming to their decision not to obtain insurance that defaults would be more like past experience as

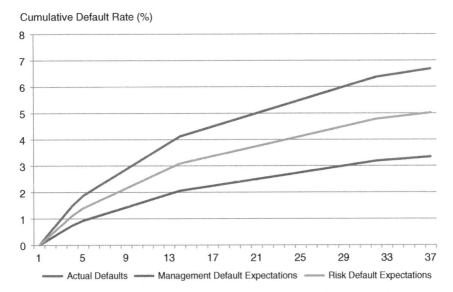

FIGURE 8.6 Cumulative Default Rates and Expectations for 2005 SifiMortgage Originations

shown by their estimates in Figure 8.6. Neither group was right in this case as actual defaults turned out to be double what management expected and about a third higher than what the risk team projected.

Obtaining mortgage insurance for even the $500 million portion of the portfolio was a wise choice for the most part, even though the other $500 million that was recommended to have insurance experienced direct lifetime losses of approximately $30 million for SifiMortgage, taking into account prepayment. To get a sense of the savings had SifiMortgage obtained insurance for this $500 million portion that did not get credit protection, Table 8.9 presents the estimated cost of insurance and losses to self-insure for a $500 million pool of SifiMortgage loans. The payments made over the course of three years for the pool are shown in the last column along with the estimated lifetime losses experienced on the portion of the portfolio Sifi-Mortgage would self-insure. Note that the loss rates for each of the insurers differs from SifiMortgage's loss rate. These reflect differences in the pool stips provided by each insurer. For example, insurer 2 due to an aggressive market share strategy had more liberal pool stips, leading to higher risk loans being insured by that company. Consequently, its loss rate of 8 percent is much higher than insurer 1's loss rate since it had more stringent pool requirements. On an undiscounted basis, total costs of insuring the portfolio plus self-insurance losses were $14.5 million. Had SifiMortgage insured the remaining $500 million requested by the risk team, it would have saved approximately $15.5 million, that is, the difference between the unhedged losses of $30 million and the $14.5 million in the hedged outcome using insurance.

Even with this insurance, SifiMortgage was exposed to counterparty risk. SifiMortgage was not the only portfolio that the insurance companies had insured during the period. In fact, during that period, insurance companies had embarked on an aggressive market share campaign that after 2007

TABLE 8.9 Summary of Insurance Costs and Losses to Self-Insure SifiMortgage $500 Million Portfolio

Insurer	Allocation	Premium/Loss	Loss Rate	Payment
1	0.35	0.0255	0.0650	$ 3,567,769
2	0.15	0.0309	0.0800	$ 1,852,841
3	0.3	0.0297	0.0700	$ 3,058,088
Self-Insured	0.2	0.0669	0.0669	$ 6,018,750
				$14,497,448

wound up causing two of the three insurers that SifiMortgage had done business with to file for bankruptcy. A contributing factor to the demise of these companies was their underestimation of premiums that were based more on competitive pricing than on actuarial analysis of default. While some claims were paid before the 2009–2010 dates when these companies filed for bankruptcy protection, SifiMortgage would have to file legal claims to try and recover unpaid amounts. In addition, all three companies had vigorously pursued strategies to rescind or deny coverage on the insurance policies, claiming that a significant amount of misrepresentation and fraud had occurred in the loan origination process, thus creating a breach in the insurance contract terms. This further created added legal expense for Sifi-Mortgage as it worked to assert its claims against insurers.

SifiMortgage did experience some success on other fronts to hedge credit risk using derivative products. It entered into a $1 billion Prime FR30 four-year CDS with a counterparty in 2005 using the assumptions shown in Table 8.4. Losses sustained on SifiMortgage's portfolio over the period were approximately $16 million. SifiMortgage incurred approximately $1.3 million over the four-year contract. However, because the reference pool was on a similar but not exact pool as SifiMortgage's loans, the contract payments for defaults compensated SifiMortgage over the four years for all but $2 million in losses sustained. Further, since the contract extended for only four years, once it expired SifiMortgage was unhedged for the remaining life of its portfolio and as a result incurred post-CDS losses of $4 million. The CDS thus had a net effect of saving SifiMortgage approximately $8.7 million, as shown below in Table 8.10. While the CDS did not completely offset SifiMortgage's credit risk in its portfolio, it did provide significant protection. It might have improved the credit hedge by entering into another following expiration of the original transaction. By that time CDS premiums would have risen substantially, however, so it would have eroded the net financial benefit from entering into the agreement.

TABLE 8.10   Savings to SifiMortgage from CDS

	Cost
Lifetime Losses on SifiMortgage Prime FR30 Portfolio	$16,000,000
Premiums Paid by SifiMortgage on CDS	$ 1,300,000
Losses Not Covered in Years 1–4 on CDS	$ 2,000,000
Losses Following CDS Expiration	$ 4,000,000
	$ 8,700,000

SifiMortgage elected not to enter into a CLN on a portion of its portfolio. In hindsight, moving forward with the transaction instead of the CDS could have provided a more direct way to have hedged its portfolio credit risk since it would have used the mortgages in the portfolio as reference collateral for the CLN structure. Further, it could have set the structure to have a longer term, for example, 10 years, that would have covered the vast majority of losses.

Finally, SifiMortgage did create a CDO on a $1 billion portfolio of its subprime portfolio using the assumptions from earlier in the chapter. With losses sustained on this reference portfolio of 8 percent, scenario 8 was realized, resulting in all but the A, AA, and AAA tranches taking complete losses. Similar losses were sustained by other CDOs that were issued in the market at the time. Holders of these securities were forced to write down the value of these securities to their market value, which had declined due to the massive losses hitting these structures. What had been a CDO worth approximately $950 million in 2005, turned out to have a market value in early 2008 of $893 million. Further losses on the reference assets would force even further reductions in value over time and as investors fled the market.

SUMMARY

Hedging credit risk is not a perfect science. Despite the need for advanced analytics to guide the risk manager, oftentimes experience and judgment are necessary ingredients for effective credit risk management. In the case of SifiMortgage, the risk team used its modeling capabilities and historical data to develop loss projections that, while higher than what had been experienced over the previous five years, were well below actual experience during the mortgage crisis that began in 2007.

The use of insurance contracts and credit derivative instruments can be effective tools for hedging credit risk as seen by SifiMortgage's experience. Insurance contracts require understanding the nature of the collateral; in this case the fact that mortgages can prepay will reduce the amount of losses that will be experienced. Consequently it is critical to have an informed view of this behavior even though it is not a form of credit risk. Further, by optimizing the disposition of insurance across different insurers and an option to self-insure, SifiMortgage was able to minimize its overall costs of credit risk (premiums plus self-insured loss). However, despite the efforts to estimate its exposure and develop an effective insurance program, senior management limited the effort to half of the recommended amount. Once again, SifiMortgage management exhibited short-sighted behavior reinforced by their own pecuniary benefits in the form of annual bonus and an incentive structure that contributed to this behavior.

A number of credit derivatives were also explored by SifiMortgage. The company executed a CDS used to offset some of the credit risk of its portfolio. It turned out to be an incomplete hedge for several reasons. First, the underlying reference pool was closely but not perfectly correlated with the actual portfolio SifiMortgage was looking to hedge. Second, the CDS had a four-year term, and while that provided significant credit protection, once it expired, SifiMortgage remained unhedged against credit risk exposure. Sifi-Mortgage could have used a CLN instead to have hedged its portfolio risk directly by using the loans as the reference portfolio. This would have avoided the issues of basis risk in using the CDS. However, it may have come with an additional regulatory reporting burden and potentially higher costs, since this would have been a structure not easily tradable in the open market. Lastly, the CDO structure offered considerable flexibility to a wide range of investor risk appetites using the actual SifiMortgage loan pool as the reference portfolio. The pricing of each credit derivative requires a sophisticated understanding of the shape of the underlying collateral loss distribution. Therefore static, one path loss analysis is insufficient to portray the full dimension of potential credit loss scenarios. As a result, simulation-based methodologies as may be used in mortgage product risk assessment must also take on a competing risk framework that includes both defaults and prepayments.

QUESTIONS

1. The table below shows the tranche size for each tranche in a CDO.

Reference Pool	$1,000,000,000 Tranche Size	Percent of CDO
AAA	$500,000,000	90
AA	$ 10,000,000	2
A	$ 5,000,000	2
BBB	$ 4,000,000	1
BB	$ 6,000,000	2
B	$ 15,000,000	3
	$540,000,000	100

What is the loss subordination level for each tranche and what does that mean for the BBB tranche specifically?

2. What are the losses for each tranche given in the table of scenarios below?

Loss Outcomes	Frequency (%)	Loss (bps)
1	50	50
2	27	100
3	6	200
4	5	300
5	4	400
6	3	500
7	2	600
8	1	800
9	1	1000
10	1	1200
	100	

3. What are the payoffs for each tranche?
4. What are the prices for each tranche?
5. What is the yield for each tranche?
6. You are evaluating a mortgage pool and want to understand what the credit spread implied by the underlying loans should be. Annual default frequencies are shown. LGD is 40 percent and the risk-free rate is 2.5 percent. What is the implied credit spread on the pool?
7. Now assume that in years 1 and 2 the annual prepayment rate is 40 percent and that it is 30 percent for years 3 and 4. How would that affect your answer in question 6?

You have the following information available about a set of loans. You can decide to retain all of the loans or else obtain insurance on them from Provider 1 and Provider 2 for any loan. You face the following pool stips for each provider and your bank also observes the characteristics of each loan and assigned premium for insuring the loss or placing the loan in the bank's portfolio.

Risk-Free Rate	0.025						
Contract Year	Mortgage Default Rate	Mortgage Severity Rate	Expected Loss	Remaining Pool	Discount Factor	Present Value Payments	Present Value Defaults
1	0.03	0.4	0.012	0.9928	0.975609756	0.9686	0.007
2	0.04	0.4	0.016	0.9833	0.951814396	0.9359	0.0091
3	0.05	0.4	0.02	0.9695	0.928599411	0.9003	0.013
4	0.06	0.4	0.024	0.9532	0.905950645	0.8636	0.0152
			0.072			3.6683	0.0444
Credit Spread	0.0121						

8. Provide a structure for how you might decide to allocate these loans.
9. Which party, Provider 1, Provider 2, or the bank gets each loan?
10. If over time you were to observe that the bank's loss estimates were consistently lower than any other insurance provider, what would you make of that outcome?

CHAPTER 9

Interest Rate Risk

OVERVIEW OF SIFIBANK'S INTEREST RATE RISK EXPOSURE

SifiBank's Fixed Income Division (SFID) was established within the Treasury office of SifiBank to invest excess cash from the bank in fixed-income securities. SFID is permitted to invest only in high-quality sovereign, government-sponsored, or corporate debt with at least AA-ratings according to two **nationally recognized statistical rating organizations** (NRSROs) such as S&P. Currently SFID has a portfolio of $62 billion allocated in the investments shown in Table 9.1. SFID's investments are largely a buy-and-hold strategy so the bank is not concerned about price or market risk, as would be the case in SifiBank's trading division. However, SFID is exposed to interest rate risk. Interest rate risk arises from a mismatch in the maturity between the assets and liabilities. This imbalance can have negative effects on the income stream of the firm as well as on the market value of assets and liabilities. In the case of fixed-income instruments like Treasury securities that do not have any embedded options such as prepayment, the price of a bond moves inversely with its yield. As interest rates rise, this lowers the price of the bond and the maturity of the bond plays a significant role in determining how much of a decline in value is realized. It is this change in market value dimension of interest rate risk that SFID is most concerned about since it does not have liabilities to directly manage. If it did, the difference in income accruing to its assets and liabilities could be greatly affected by whether interest rates rise or fall, thus leading to unexpected fluctuations in its income stream. And while this has important implications for the ongoing profitability and financial health of the company, SFID's major concern is guarding against significant declines in the market value of its portfolio due not to changes in market prices, as would be the concern of a trading organization, but the impact that changes in interest rates have on portfolio value.

TABLE 9.1 SFID Portfolio Allocation

Fixed-Income Investment	Coupon Rate (%)	Portfolio Allocation ($B)
1 year AAA Corporate Bonds	0.12	12
5 year AAA Corporate Bonds	0.71	15
10 year AAA Corporate Bonds	1.74	17
15 year AAA Corporate Bonds	2.35	8
30 year AAA Corporate Bonds	2.91	10

Duration Models

At its simplest level the relationship between bond price and yield can be derived from the following standard coupon bond pricing formula:

$$B_{PV} = \sum_{t=1}^{T} F(C)e^{-rt} + Fe^{-rT} \qquad 9.1$$

where B_{PV} signifies the present value of the bond in dollars, given its face amount F (in dollars), C the coupon rate, an appropriate discount factor r at time period t. Relating the change in price B for a change in yield r, results in the following relationship:

$$\frac{dB}{dr} = -\left[\sum_{t=1}^{T} tF(C)e^{-rt} + TFe^{-rT} \right] \qquad 9.2$$

We can define the relationship further for discrete changes in yield movements as the following:

$$\Delta B = -\Delta r \frac{dB}{dr} \qquad 9.3$$

or, dividing both sides by B and substituting dB for equation 9.2 yields,

$$\frac{\Delta B}{B} = -\Delta r \frac{\sum_{t=1}^{T} tF(C)e^{-rt} + TFe^{-rT}}{B} = -D\Delta r \qquad 9.4$$

In this expression, D is defined as **Macaulay duration,** an important measure of the sensitivity of a bond's price to changes in interest rates. Note that only in the case of a zero coupon bond, where a single cash flow is received at maturity, is the maturity of a bond equal to its duration. In all

TABLE 9.2   SFID Portfolio Durations

Fixed-Income Investment	Duration
1 year AAA Corporate Bonds	1
5 year AAA Corporate Bonds	4.9
10 year AAA Corporate Bonds	9
15 year AAA Corporate Bonds	12.4
30 year AAA Corporate Bonds	19.1

other cases, duration will be less than the bond maturity. Duration may be expressed in years or as the percentage change in the bond's price for a unit change in r. To see this consider Table 9.2, which provides the durations for each of the bond positions for SFID. The bonds all pay an annual coupon. In the case of the one-year bonds, the duration equals the bond's maturity since these are essentially zero-coupon bonds. For all other bonds in the portfolio, the durations are less than maturity. Further, an important property of duration illustrated in Table 9.2 is that it increases at a decreasing rate.

To better understand the significance of duration as a measure of interest rate risk, consider the five-year bond's duration of 4.9. For this portfolio alone, if interest rates were to rise by 1 percent it would cause the value of this portfolio to decline by 4.9 percent or on a dollar basis, the portfolio of five-year bonds would decline by $.74 billion. Note that by comparison, the 30-year bond portfolio exhibits much greater risk to the market value of the portfolio for the same 1 percent increase in interest rates. In this case, a 1 percent increase leads to a 19.1 percent decline in value, or $1.9 billion. Clearly the risk of holding 30-year bonds is much greater than that of any of the other positions. We can then state that the longer the duration of the bond, the greater the interest rate risk is to the portfolio.

Once a portfolio's duration is computed it is easy to determine the relative impact on the portfolio's value for any change in interest rates, making it a handy metric among fixed income professionals. However, its compact representation of interest rate risk has some limitations. Among these is the fact that as a linear approximation of the true change in bond price for a given change in interest rate, it loses accuracy for large movements in interest rates. To see this consider Table 9.3, which shows the estimated impact on each of SFID's bond portfolios using the duration approximation for a range of changes in interest rates along with the actual change in bond price for the same changes in interest rates using the bond pricing formula. What is immediately evident from the results is that across bond portfolios,

TABLE 9.3 Duration Model Compared to Bond Present Value Cash Flows

BOND DATA

Principal ($M)	Coupon	Maturity (years)	Spot Rate	PV	Duration (D)	Convexity (CX)
$12,000	0.17%	1	0.12%	$11,985.62	1.00	2.00
$15,000	0.79%	5	0.71%	$15,058.74	4.92	28.97
$17,000	1.86%	10	1.74%	$17,185.76	9.22	95.31
$ 8,000	2.50%	15	2.35%	$ 8,150.23	12.72	183.18
$10,000	3.14%	30	2.94%	$10,395.07	20.07	502.57

Interest rate changes (bps) Duration Approximation

Bond	-300	-200	-100	-50	50	100	200	300
1 Year	N/A	N/A	N/A	N/A	-0.50%	-1.00%	-2.00%	-3.00%
5 Year	N/A	N/A	N/A	2.46%	-2.46%	-4.92%	N/A	-14.77%
10 Year	N/A	N/A	9.22%	4.61%	-4.61%	-9.22%	9.22%	-27.67%
15 Year	N/A	25.43%	12.72%	6.36%	-6.36%	-12.72%	12.72%	-38.15%
30 Year	N/A	40.14%	20.07%	10.03%	-10.03%	-20.07%	20.07%	-60.21%

Interest Rate Changes (bps) Bond Present Value Cash Flows

Bond	-300	-200	-100	-50	50	100	200	300
1 Year	N/A	N/A	N/A	N/A	-0.50%	-0.99%	-1.96%	-2.91%
5 Year	N/A	N/A	N/A	2.50%	-2.42%	-4.78%	-9.27%	-13.46%
10 Year	N/A	N/A	9.70%	4.73%	-4.49%	-8.75%	-16.54%	-23.38%
15 Year	N/A	29.10%	13.63%	6.59%	-6.13%	-11.80%	-21.77%	-29.91%
30 Year	N/A	50.19%	22.58%	10.66%	-9.41%	-17.56%	-30.09%	-37.59%

the duration approximation of bond price changes is comparable to the true price change for small changes in interest rates, for example, 50bps, but for large interest rate changes the duration model deviates significantly from what would result from the bond's actual cash-flow impacts. Note that the duration estimates of price change are symmetric for the same positive or negative changes in interest rates although the errors will not be.

Table 9.3 compares what the value would be for each bond given an upward or downward adjustment in market interest rates against the original spot rate. In addition, it also shows what the duration model would predict the bond's price to be for the same rate change. Some entries in the table are represented as N/A since the interest-rate change scenario would result in a negative interest rate in this example. Referring to the five-year bond, a 50bps increase in rates would result in a 2.46 percent decline in the bond's value, according to the duration model as compared to a 2.42 percent decrease in price using the standard bond pricing formula. The resulting error due to the duration model is relatively small. However, for larger rate shocks, the duration model error widens. Take for example what happens if spot rates rise by 300bps. The actual change in the five-year bond's price will be a decline of 13.46 percent while the duration model expects the price to be 14.77 percent lower. Moreover, the error in the duration model as maturity increases is seen in any column of rate changes.

These results are explained by the fact that the duration model is only a linear approximation of an otherwise nonlinear relationship between price and yield as expressed by the bond pricing formula. This nonlinearity is referred to as **convexity**. An adjustment to the duration model that accounts for convexity can be represented as the following:

$$CX = \frac{\dfrac{d^2B}{dr^2}}{B} = \frac{\displaystyle\sum_{t=1}^{T-1} t^2 F(C) e^{-rt} + T F e^{-rT}}{B} \qquad 9.5$$

Using this definition, the adjustment to the duration model for convexity is the following:

$$\frac{\Delta B}{B} = -\Delta r D + \frac{1}{2}(CX)\Delta r^2 \qquad 9.6$$

With this change, the results from Table 9.3 can be recalculated and compared with the actual movement in bond prices for the same change in rate. The results in Table 9.3 correcting for convexity and Figure 9.1 (for the 30-year bond) clearly show that by correcting for nonlinearity, the duration-convexity approximation is much closer to the actual price change.

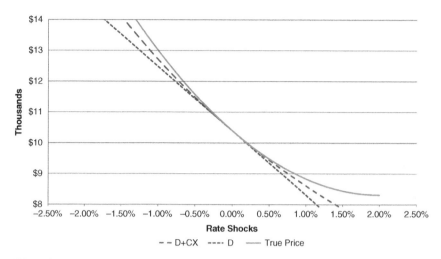

FIGURE 9.1 Impact of Duration and Convexity on Bond Price

And while the adjustment for convexity provides greater accuracy to the standard duration approximation model for large interest rate movements, it still suffers from an inability to handle more complicated movements in the yield curve.

Thus far, the interest scenarios depicted in the above tables assume rates shift in a parallel up or down fashion along the entire yield curve. Moreover, to this point, the underlying assumption of a constant interest rate r implies that the yield curve is flat. Although a discussion on theories describing the shape of yield curves (**term structure determination**) are beyond the scope of this book, interest-rate risk analysis must be able to handle a variety of shapes and movements of the yield curve.

Extensions of the Duration Model

The simple assumption of a common static shift in interest rates across the entire term structure equally can mislead the risk analyst into making the wrong decisions on how to hedge various assets and liabilities. To accommodate the possibility that different parts of the yield curve will experience different rate effects at a specific time, an extension to the traditional duration model is to refine the model by estimating a set of **key rate** or **partial durations** that would reflect differences in yield curve shifts. Key rates can be thought of as reference points along the yield curve against which changes in interest rates can be allocated across specific segments of the yield curve. We can in effect deconstruct the duration measure from above into separate durations associated with specific interest rate changes along the term structure. This can be represented more formally as the following:

$$D_i = \frac{\frac{dB_i}{dr_i}}{B} \text{ and } D = \sum_{i=1}^{I} D_i \qquad\qquad 9.7$$

where i represents a particular location on the yield curve, for example, the one-year rate. Conceptually, the impact on bond prices as a result of changes in yield across the term structure can be assessed without the restrictive assumption that all rate changes are the same.

Selection of key rates directly affects the degree of complexity introduced in the key rate duration calculation exercise. SFID analysts have selected key rates of 1, 2, 3, 5, 7, 10, 20, and 30 years. To illustrate the concept, assume that SFID analysts want to understand the incremental effects from a 1bp increase in rates over some short period of time for each key rate analyzed.

The spot rate at each time period is adjusted by the selected key rate effect. So, the spot rate is adjusted for the 1bp increase in the one-year key rate across all 30 time periods. Similar adjustments to the spot rate are then made for the remaining key rates.

The key rate duration model assumes that this interest rate effect decreases over each period in a linear fashion toward the next key, eventually reaching zero at that next key rate. A linear interpolation method can be used to spread these rate effects across the term structure.

With these estimated rate shocks allocated across key rates, the key rate duration for each key rate can be determined by estimating the present values at each period using the spot rates adjusted for the key rate shifts as discount rates. This process is shown in Table 9.4 for the 30-year key rate. The original spot rates are shown in the second column along with the present values (labeled DCF for discounted cash flow) for the 10-year instrument. The associated price is $10,951 and the duration of the 30-year bond is computed as 19.656. For each key rate (only 1 and 30 are shown in Table 9.4 for brevity, but the calculations are comparable for the other key rates between 1 and 30 shown in the table), the new present value of the 30-year bond using the new discount rates is extremely close applying the one-year key rates given the 1bp increase. The resulting one-year key rate duration is .029 and the 30-year key rate duration is estimated at 13.082.

The results for all key rates across SFID's five different bonds are shown in Table 9.5. As indicated in the table, the duration of any of the bonds in the portfolio should be approximately equal to the sums of the key rate durations. As a result, this provides a way to decompose changes in interest rates across the term structure on specific instruments. In the example provided

TABLE 9.4 Example Calculation for 10-Year Key Rate Duration

Principal	$10,000
Coupon	3.14%
Maturity	30

		Present Value $10,951	Duration 19,656		Key Rate – 1 Year	Present Value $10,951	Duration 19,656	Key Rate Duration −0.029		Key Rate – 30 Year	Present Value $10,936	Duration 19,643	Key Rate Duration −13.082	
t	Spot Rate	DCF	(DCF*t)/PV		Key Rate Shift 0.01%	DCF	Key Rate (DCF*t)			Key Rate Shift 0.01%	DCF	(DCF*t)/PV		
1	0.16%	$313	0.029		0.17%	$313	0.029			0.16%	$313	0.029		
2	0.26%	$312	0.057		0.26%	$312	0.057			0.26%	$312	0.057		
3	0.38%	$310	0.085		0.38%	$310	0.085			0.38%	$310	0.085		
4	0.58%	$307	0.112		0.58%	$307	0.112			0.58%	$307	0.112		
5	0.77%	$302	0.138		0.77%	$302	0.138			0.77%	$302	0.138		
6	1.00%	$296	0.162		1.00%	$296	0.162			1.00%	$296	0.162		
7	1.22%	$288	0.184		1.22%	$288	0.184			1.22%	$288	0.185		
8	1.41%	$281	0.205		1.41%	$281	0.205			1.41%	$281	0.205		
9	1.60%	$272	0.224		1.60%	$272	0.224			1.60%	$272	0.224		
10	1.79%	$263	0.240		1.79%	$263	0.240			1.79%	$263	0.240		
11	1.86%	$256	0.257		1.86%	$256	0.257			1.86%	$256	0.258		
12	1.94%	$249	0.273		1.94%	$249	0.273			1.94%	$249	0.274		
13	2.01%	$242	0.288		2.01%	$242	0.288			2.01%	$242	0.288		
14	2.09%	$235	0.301		2.09%	$235	0.301			2.09%	$235	0.301		
15	2.16%	$228	0.312		2.16%	$228	0.312			2.16%	$228	0.313		
16	2.23%	$220	0.322		2.23%	$220	0.322			2.23%	$220	0.323		
17	2.31%	$213	0.331		2.31%	$213	0.331			2.31%	$213	0.331		
18	2.38%	$206	0.338		2.38%	$206	0.338			2.38%	$206	0.338		
19	2.46%	$198	0.344		2.46%	$198	0.344			2.46%	$198	0.344		
20	2.53%	$191	0.348		2.53%	$191	0.348			2.53%	$191	0.348		
21	2.57%	$184	0.353		2.57%	$184	0.353			2.57%	$184	0.354		
22	2.61%	$178	0.358		2.61%	$178	0.358			2.61%	$178	0.358		
23	2.65%	$172	0.361		2.65%	$172	0.361			2.66%	$172	0.361		
24	2.69%	$166	0.364		2.69%	$166	0.364			2.70%	$166	0.364		
25	2.74%	$160	0.365		2.74%	$160	0.365			2.74%	$160	0.365		
26	2.78%	$154	0.366		2.78%	$154	0.366			2.78%	$154	0.366		
27	2.82%	$148	0.366		2.82%	$148	0.366			2.82%	$148	0.366		
28	2.86%	$143	0.365		2.86%	$143	0.365			2.87%	$142	0.365		
29	2.90%	$137	0.363		2.90%	$137	0.363			2.91%	$137	0.364		
30	2.94%	$4,324	11.846		2.94%	$4,324	11.846			2.95%	$4,312	11.827		

Repeat for Remaining Key Rates Across Term Structure

TABLE 9.5 Key Rate Duration Results

Maturity	1 year	5 year	10 year	15 year	30 year
1	-0.998	-0.008	-0.018	-0.024	-0.029
2	0.000	-0.016	-0.036	-0.047	-0.057
3	0.000	-0.039	-0.090	-0.116	-0.140
5	0.000	-4.821	-0.175	-0.225	-0.273
7	0.000	0.000	-0.302	-0.388	-0.471
10	0.000	0.000	-8.414	-6.210	-1.741
20	0.000	0.000	0.000	-5.398	-3.333
30	0.000	0.000	0.000	0.000	-13.082
Sum KRD	-0.998	-4.883	-9.036	-12.408	-19.125
Duration	-1.000	-4.922	-9.196	-12.668	-19.656

in Table 9.5, the duration of the 10-year bond of 9.196 is about equal to the sum of the key rate durations noted in the table. For the 10-year bond, the majority of the risk from rising rates would be felt in the intermediate part of the term structure (around 5–10 years) and far less from changes in the short-end of the curve. To gain a better sense of these effects, consider Figure 9.2, which depicts the impact of rate changes on the term structure affecting the 10-year bond.

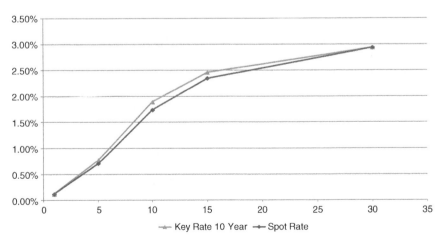

FIGURE 9.2 10-Year Adjusted Key Rates Compared to Original Spot Curve

Another way to assess the impact of a nonparallel shift in rates as described in the example is to use the key rate durations as a measure of bond price or portfolio value sensitivity to the entire shift in rates. For example, the 10-year key rate duration of 9.036 suggests that a 1bp increase in the 10-year key rate would result in a -9bps ($-D_{10}$1bps) decline in value. The total effect on the 10-year bond from the changes in interest rates in the example would be:

$$\Delta P_{10} = -D_1 \Delta r_1 - D_2 \Delta r_2 - D_3 \Delta r_3 - D_5 \Delta r_5 - D_7 \Delta r_7 - D_{10} \Delta r_{10}$$
$$- D_{20} \Delta r_{20} - D_{30} \Delta r_{30} = -9.036\% \qquad 9.8$$

Importantly, key rate durations illustrate the need to evaluate the differential impact of rate changes across the term structure rather than relying on an overly simplistic assumption of a parallel shock to the yield curve.

PRINCIPAL COMPONENTS ANALYSIS

While calculation of key rate durations enhances the ability to assess more realistic changes in the yield curve, computationally, it can become quite burdensome over each spot curve. For example, in the previous section many calculations were required to establish adjusted spot rates for the eight key rates. A more efficient approach to understanding more complicated changes in the yield curve would be to take advantage of the correlations in yields over the term structure. It may be the case, for instance, that changes in the 10- and 15-year yields move with a high degree of correlation. **Principal components analysis** or PCA employs a statistical methodology to determine what factors are most important in explaining changes in the shape of the yield curve, such as a parallel shift in the yield curve, a change in its slope, or changes in the curvature of the yield curve, among others. For the purposes of interest-rate risk assessment, these three changes tend to account for the vast majority in variation in rates.

The first step in conducting a PCA analysis involves taking a sample of interest rate data such as daily rates for 2012 for 1-, 2-, 3-, 5-, 7-, 10-, 20-, and 30-year Treasuries. From this time series, daily changes in interest rates are computed as: $\Delta r^n_{t-1} = r^n_t - r^n_{t-1}$ for each maturity, or tenor n in the term structure for each period t. From this series of daily rate changes a variance-covariance matrix with dimensions 8×8 (representing each of the eight tenors in this example) can be computed as shown below in Figure 9.3, where the variance terms appear on the diagonal and the covariances in daily rate changes appear in the off-diagonal.

$$
\begin{vmatrix}
\sigma_{1yr}^2 & \sigma_{1yr,2yr} & \sigma_{1yr,3yr} & \sigma_{1yr,5yr} & \sigma_{1yr,7yr} & \sigma_{1yr,10yr} & \sigma_{1yr,20yr} & \sigma_{1yr,30yr} \\
 & \sigma_{2yr}^2 & \sigma_{2yr,3yr} & \sigma_{2yr,5yr} & \sigma_{2yr,7yr} & \sigma_{2yr,10yr} & \sigma_{2yr,20yr} & \sigma_{2yr,30yr} \\
 & & \sigma_{3yr}^2 & \sigma_{3yr,5yr} & \sigma_{3yr,7yr} & \sigma_{3yr,10yr} & \sigma_{3yr,20yr} & \sigma_{3yr,30yr} \\
 & & & \sigma_{5yr}^2 & \sigma_{5yr,7yr} & \sigma_{5yr,10yr} & \sigma_{5yr,20yr} & \sigma_{5yr,30yr} \\
 & & & & \sigma_{7yr}^2 & \sigma_{7yr,10yr} & \sigma_{7yr,20yr} & \sigma_{7yr,30yr} \\
 & & & & & \sigma_{10yr}^2 & \sigma_{10yr,20yr} & \sigma_{10yr,30yr} \\
 & & & & & & \sigma_{20yr}^2 & \sigma_{20yr,30yr} \\
 & & & & & & & \sigma_{30yr}^2
\end{vmatrix}
$$

FIGURE 9.3   Variance-Covariance Matrix for Principal Components Analysis

With the variance-covariance matrix constructed, the principal components of the yield curve can be derived. Essentially, the process entails deriving a set of values describing how interest rate changes across the term structure as a function of the variability among rates as described by the variance-covariance matrix. One set of values, actually a vector of $n \times 1$, is associated with each tenor in the term structure, in this case 8×1. The elements in the vector are determined by solving the following relationship:

$$
\begin{bmatrix} k_1 \\ k_2 \\ ... \\ k_n \end{bmatrix} \rightarrow
\begin{bmatrix} m_1 \\ m_2 \\ ... \\ m_n \end{bmatrix} =
\begin{bmatrix} \sigma_{11}^2 & \sigma_{12} & ... & \sigma_{1n} \\ & \sigma_{22}^2 & ... & \sigma_{2n} \\ & & ... & ... \\ & & & \sigma_{nn}^2 \end{bmatrix}
\begin{bmatrix} k_1 \\ k_2 \\ ... \\ k_n \end{bmatrix}
\qquad 9.9
$$

where for each tenor n a linear combination of the variance-covariance elements and the vector k can be defined as the following:

$$
m_i = \sigma_{i1}k_1 + \sigma_{i2}k_2 + ... \sigma_{in}k_n = \sum_{j=1}^{n} \sigma_{ij}k_j \qquad 9.10
$$

We can define a value λ such that the following relationship holds; $\Omega k = \lambda k$ where Ω is the variance-covariance matrix. The vector k is defined to be the **eigenvector** of the matrix Ω and λ is the **eigenvalue**. Eigenvector and

TABLE 9.6 Principal Component Factors by Tenor (bps)

Tenor	Eigenvectors k1	k2	k3	k4	k5	k6	k7	k8
1	0.219	−0.529	0.801	−0.159	0.069	−0.001	−0.010	0.001
2	0.320	−0.499	−0.266	0.515	−0.555	−0.048	0.032	−0.025
3	0.362	−0.310	−0.346	0.086	0.705	0.350	0.131	0.091
5	0.393	−0.071	−0.241	−0.361	0.099	−0.570	−0.523	−0.208
7	0.395	0.111	−0.102	−0.484	−0.235	−0.139	0.655	0.289
10	0.388	0.249	0.037	−0.221	−0.309	0.677	−0.424	0.052
20	0.367	0.363	0.186	0.248	0.077	−0.004	0.284	−0.742
30	0.349	0.405	0.251	0.476	0.150	−0.268	−0.137	0.558

eigenvalue computations are beyond the scope of this discussion, however, for the example their values are displayed in Table 9.6. The 8 k vectors in Table 9.6 each characterize a specific impact to the term structure. The first vector k_1 is associated with a parallel shift in the yield curve. Each element (**factor loading**) in that vector describes the impact a parallel shift in the yield curve has on each tenor. For example, for the five-year tenor, a parallel increase in interest rates will increase the five-year rate by .393bps for a one-unit change in the first principal component. The second vector principal component k_2 is associated with a change in the slope of the yield curve. Thus a change in the slope of the yield curve would lower the five-year rate by .071bps for a one-unit change (e.g., one standard deviation) in k_2.

The impact of each principal component in explaining the variability in changes to the yield curve can be directly measured by comparing the standard deviations for each principal component to the total variance associated with changes in the yield curve. One attribute of PCA analysis is that the principal components are uncorrelated and independent from each other. The variance of the factors are referred to as the eigenvalues, or λ described earlier. The total variation in the term structure for the example can be computed as:

$$\sum_{i=1}^{n} \lambda_i^2 = 8 \qquad 9.11$$

As shown in Table 9.7, 75.1 percent of the total variation in the term structure is attributed to the first principal component reflecting a parallel

TABLE 9.7 Principal Component Contribution to Total Variation in Term Structure

	k1	k2	k3	k4	k5	k6	k7	k8
Eigenvalues (λ)	6.006	1.154	0.601	0.147	0.049	0.020	0.012	0.012
Standard deviation	2.451	1.074	0.775	0.383	0.221	0.142	0.110	0.108
Proportion of Variance	0.751	0.144	0.075	0.018	0.006	0.003	0.002	0.001
Cumulative Proportion	0.751	0.895	0.970	0.988	0.995	0.997	0.999	1.000

shift in the yield curve. A change in the slope of the yield curve accounts for 14.4 percent of the variation in the term structure and 7.5 percent is attributed to the curvature effect. In all, 97 percent of the variation in the yield curve is due to the first three principal components. While this example illustrates the utility of the PCA approach at reducing the dimensionality problem associated with changes in term structure given that the majority of the variation in the yield curve can be explained using these three factors, usually the total contribution from the first three principal components is 90–95 percent. To gain additional insight into the effect these first three principal components have on the yield curve, consider Figure 9.4. A parallel shift in the yield curve is shown to be flatter than the other factors while the factor relating to a change in slope exhibits a positive slope consistent with most yield curves. Finally, the curvature effect is pronounced at about the two-year maturity bucket.

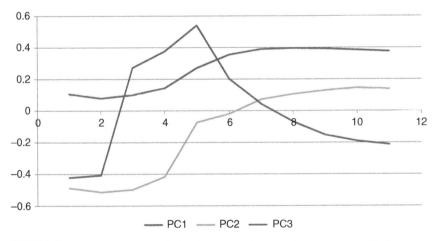

FIGURE 9.4 Effect of Parallel Shift, Change in Slope, and Curvature on Yield Curve

ANALYTIC VAR MEASUREMENT OF INTEREST RATE RISK

Leveraging the discussion on key rate duration and PCA, an analytically tractable measurement of interest rate risk exposure for the SFID portfolio can be accomplished.[1] Bringing both concepts together enables the risk manager to determine SFID's interest rate value-at-risk (IVaR). Conceptually, changes in interest rates will impact the value of SFID's portfolio much as changes in market prices of various assets affect the value of the trading division's portfolio value. Changes in interest rates as described in the previous section are much more complicated than simple parallel shifts in the yield curve. Consequently, the use of PCA can be instrumental in incorporating additional changes in the yield curve such as slope and curvature effects.

At its most basic level, the impact to a bond's value for a given change in interest rates is measured by its duration. Expanding on this concept further, the impact of rate changes attributed to shift, slope, and curvature yield curve movement can be allocated to each principal component. In turn, the effect of each principal component on a bond or portfolio's value could be assessed using a set of key rate durations. The measure of VaR for over a time interval t at a P level of confidence in this case would be defined as follows:

$$IVaR_t^P = \sqrt{\sum_{i=1}^{3}\left[\sum_{j=1}^{11} \Delta r_{ij} D_j^\$ \right]^2} \qquad 9.12$$

where Δr_{ij} represents a stressed rate change associated with the first three principal components, and $D_j^\$$ is the key rate dollar duration (equal to $D_j P_j$, where P_j is the original price of bond j) for each of the eight tenors in the previous example. The definition of Δr_{ij} is given as:

$$\Delta r_{ij} = k_{ij}^S \sigma_j^{\Delta r} R_{T,j} \qquad 9.13$$

where k_{ij}^S represents the stress principal component, $\sigma_j^{\Delta r}$ is the standard deviation in periodic interest rate changes (weekly for this example), and $R_{T,j}$ is the most recent term structure interest rates. Finally, the stress principal component is defined as:

$$k_{ij}^S = \sigma_{ij} \lambda \Phi^{-1} \qquad 9.14$$

---

[1] Marco Folpmers and Niels Eweg, "How to Estimate and Calibrate Analytical VaR for Interest Rate Risk," *Risk Professional*, June 2000, pp. 46–52.

where σ_{ij} is the covariance between rates among parts of the term structure i and j, λ is the standard deviation of the principal components, and $\Phi^{-1}$is the inverse of the standard normal distribution. Applying the values on key rate durations and PCA from the earlier sections, a 99 percent, one-week IVaR would be $180M on the portfolio assuming a 1bp increase in interest rates across the term structure. The interpretation of this result would be that SFID over a one-week period could lose $180 million or more 1 percent of the time as a result of changes in interest rates owing to a parallel movement in rates, a change in the slope of the yield curve or changes in its curvature. While the analytic VaR method for interest rate risk is complex, it has the advantage of not having to generate a set of interest rate paths using a stochastic interest rate process. Such Monte Carlo simulation-based methods can be computationally burdensome as well as require considerable attention to the reliability and specification of the underlying parameters describing the behavior of interest rates over time. Despite these and other drawbacks, simulation-based methods still find considerable utility among interest-rate risk managers.

MONTE CARLO VAR INTEREST RATE RISK METHODS

An alternative approach to the analytic-based methods in the previous section is to develop a Monte Carlo simulation of interest rates, bond prices, and ultimately bond portfolio value. In developing a simulation-based interest-rate risk VaR for the SFID portfolio, the risk managers build a distribution of the portfolio's values. In order to generate a sufficient number of outcomes, a large number of simulations of interest rate scenarios are required. These interest rate scenarios can then be used in calculating each bond's value in the portfolio. These bond values are then aggregated across all rate scenarios, resulting in a distribution that can be used to establish the portfolio's VaR. An advantage in simulating interest rates is that the analyst can actually generate many different specific rate scenarios along which bond prices can be computed. Such approaches provide great flexibility to explore the effects of rate changes on portfolio value; however, interest rate risk simulation methods must be used with great care as their results are highly dependent on underlying assumptions and parameterization of interest rate models.

In the example of SFID's portfolio using a set of key rate durations, only a limited set of rate outcomes could be evaluated. A Monte Carlo simulation will allow many alternative interest rate scenarios to be used in valuing the portfolio. A first step in development of the simulation is to create a model of the term structure. While many such models are available and the theory and assumptions behind each is beyond the scope of this chapter, the risk managers for SFID have opted to use a standard model of short-term zero coupon interest rates called the **Cox-Ingersoll-Ross (CIR) model.**

Conceptually the entire term structure can be modeled based on the short-term rate. These type of models rely on a stochastic process that describes how variables such as interest rates evolve over time under uncertainty. A type of stochastic process called a **Markov process** assumed to underlie movements in financial asset prices and applied to interest rate movements has the characteristic of generating rates that are independent from historical experience. The manner in which interest rates change over time are a function of the average movement in rates (**drift**) and the variance of rate movements. Conceptually, if short-term interest rates follow a pattern reflective of both the mean and variance of historical experience, its path over time might take the following as shown in Figure 9.5 driven by these parameters. While the level of drift over time moves with certainty, the variance does not. The degree of randomness in interest rate movement over a period of time in Figure 9.5 reflects this variability component of the interest rate process. With this basic concept describing interest rates, the CIR interest rate model can be described more formally as the following:

$$dr = \alpha(\beta - r)dt + \sigma\sqrt{r}dz \qquad\qquad 9.15$$

This type of model is referred to as a **one-factor term structure model** since it has only one stochastic process. More complicated models of the

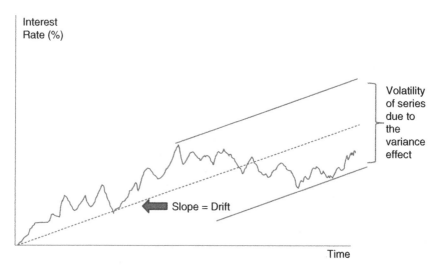

FIGURE 9.5   Illustrative Short-Term Interest Rate Stochastic Process

term structure can incorporate two or more factors to address some of the shortcomings of one-factor models. But this comes at the expense of introducing significant complexity into the modeling of interest rates. The CIR model belongs to a class of interest rate models called equilibrium models that impose certain economic conditions that explain interest rate movements. One of the potential limitations of such models is that they may not be reflective of the existing term structure, which can be problematic for traders needing to price fixed-income securities in financial markets.[2]

For the CIR model dr represents a small change in the short interest rate, dt represents a small change in time, dz is referred to as a **Weiner process** describing the movement of a variable z over time, α is the drift in interest rates, β is a base or historic level to which rates revert over time and σ is the volatility of rates. We can further define dz as:

$$dz = \varepsilon\sqrt{dt} \qquad\qquad 9.16$$

where ε represents a standard normal random variable with a mean of 0 and standard deviation of 1. An important property of the CIR model is that interest rates revert to their historical mean over time, implying that if interest rates get too high or too low relative to what their historic levels have been, they eventually revert back to those normal levels. The parameters for drift, volatility, and level of rates described in the CIR model can be estimated using historical data.

The CIR model generates a value for the short-term interest rate in a given term structure scenario or path. However, generating the entire term structure requires establishing a relationship between the price on zero coupon bonds of various terms to the modeled short-rate, $r(t)$. In particular, for the CIR model, zero coupon bond prices are given by the following:

$$P(t,T) = A(t,T)e^{-B(t,T)r(t)}$$

$$B(t,T) = \frac{2(e^{\gamma(T-1)} - 1)}{(\gamma + \alpha)(e^{\gamma(T-1)} - 1) + 2\gamma}$$

$$A(t,T) = \left(\frac{2\gamma e^{(\alpha+\gamma)(T-t)/2}}{(\gamma + \alpha)(e^{\gamma(T-1)} - 1) + 2\gamma} \right)^{2\alpha\beta/\sigma^2} \qquad 9.17$$

$$\gamma = \sqrt{\alpha^2 + 2\sigma^2}$$

---

[2]Another class of interest rate model known as no-arbitrage models better aligns with the existing term structure and actually uses the current term structure as an input to the modeling framework.

Finally, the interest rate for any term can then be computed as:

$$R(t,T) = -\frac{1}{T-t}\ln P(t,T) \qquad\qquad 9.18$$

With these parameters, a set of randomly generated values for ε can be developed using readily available functions in software packages such as Excel to generate $r(t)$ for any number of interest rate paths. In generating random variables, a typical approach begins with applying a uniform distribution, designated as $U(0,1)$ with mean 0 and standard deviation of 1. These randomly generated variables can then be transformed using the normal distribution ($N(\mu,\sigma)$). These εs can then be used in calculating the initial short-rate in the CIR model. Once these short-rates are computed, the price of an associated zero coupon bond is calculated using the formula above $P(t,T)$, and the associated rates along the entire term structure can then be evaluated using $R(t,T)$. The SFID risk managers opt to run 500 interest-rate scenarios using the CIR model framework. An example of the simulation mechanics is shown in Table 9.8 for the first 10 trials.

Once the 500 interest rate paths have been generated, each of the bonds in the SFID portfolio can be valued using the rates given in each path. As a result, a total of 500 prices would be computed for each bond in the portfolio. For each of the 500 interest rate paths, a new estimate of the SFID bond portfolio's value would be calculated based on the sum of all the bond values in the portfolio (Table 9.9).

Once the bond values have been determined, the cumulative distribution of portfolio value can be generated. Such a distribution is shown in Figure 9.6. At the 99th percentile SFID would be expected to lose $104M over a one-week period 1 percent of the time. Risk managers would use this VaR as an important risk metric in managing SFID's interest rate risk exposure to SifiBank's risk tolerance.

MODELING INTEREST RATE RISK OF MORE COMPLEX INSTRUMENTS

The relative simplicity of SFID's fixed income portfolio of AAA-rated corporate bonds greatly reduced the complexity that would be needed to evaluate interest rate risk on assets with embedded options such as mortgages. Moreover, many instruments have floating rate payment features tied to some index such as the **London Interbank Offer Rate**, or *LIBOR*. And because SFID's bond portfolio was entirely high-quality corporate bonds, issues relating to default risk were omitted from the analysis. In previous chapters assessment of credit risk was reviewed as it related to measuring the spread

TABLE 9.8 SFID Simulated Bond Prices and Portfolio Value

Bond Portfolio

Principal ($M)	$12,000	$15,000	$17,000	$8,000	$10,000				
Coupon	0.17%	0.79%	1.86%	2.50%	3.14%				
Maturity (years)	1	5	10	15	30				
Trial						Portfolio Value	Gain/Loss (M)	Gain/Loss (M)	Percentile
0	$12,006	$15,062	$17,282	$8,290	$10,927	$63,567			
1	$12,006	$15,058	$17,267	$8,285	$10,898	$63,514	−52.5058	−53	7.0%
2	$12,006	$15,062	$17,281	$8,308	$10,920	$63,577	10.42533	10	58.8%
3	$12,006	$15,066	$17,277	$8,313	$10,970	$63,633	66.44783	66	95.6%
4	$12,006	$15,057	$17,279	$8,306	$10,890	$63,537	−29.0999	−29	21.8%
5	$12,006	$15,061	$17,262	$8,292	$10,929	$63,550	−16.8161	−17	30.0%
6	$12,006	$15,059	$17,280	$8,298	$10,948	$63,591	24.50007	25	73.6%
7	$12,006	$15,064	$17,299	$8,299	$10,963	$63,631	64.27966	64	94.8%
8	$12,006	$15,067	$17,298	$8,279	$10,911	$63,561	−5.15019	−5	43.4%
9	$12,006	$15,056	$17,262	$8,272	$10,929	$63,524	−42.0327	−42	12.4%
10	$12,006	$15,066	$17,299	$8,283	$10,937	$63,591	24.09447	24	72.6%

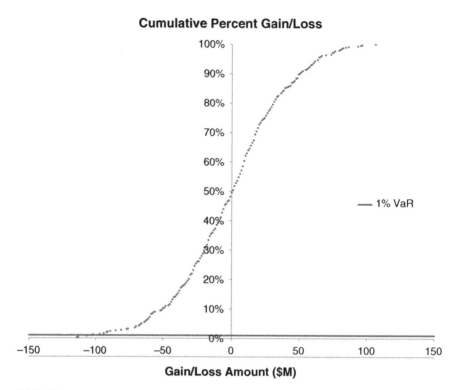

FIGURE 9.6 SFID Bond Portfolio Value Cumulative Distribution and VaR

TABLE 9.9 Monte Carlo Simulation of Term Structure (500 Trials)

Cox-Ingersoll-Ross				
Δt	0.004			
Number Days	5			
Maturity	Drift (a)	Mean Level (β)	Volatility (σ)	r^0
1	0.001	0.12%	0.05%	0.12%
5	0.001	0.71%	0.54%	0.71%
10	0.001	1.74%	0.68%	1.74%
15	0.001	2.35%	0.71%	2.35%
30	0.001	2.94%	0.69%	2.94%

in rates between risk-free and risky debt of comparable maturity and so this aspect of bond valuation is set aside for this chapter on interest rate risk. However, since a variety of debt instruments have embedded options, understanding how to handle these features in measuring interest rate risk exposure is important.

An example of an embedded option is debt that may be **callable** by the issuing company. Imagine a company that issues three-year debt at a fixed rate of 5 percent that pays annual coupons on a $100 million issuance of bonds. If rates remain at 5 percent next year, then the bond is priced at par value or $100 of face amount. If, however, if interest rates decrease to 4.5 percent next year, the issuer is locked into higher financing costs than what prevails in the current market. The value of the bond would price at a premium of $101.37. But what if the issuer could add a feature to the bond that allowed them to buy back the bond at par value? The issuer would be able to effectively cancel the 5 percent bonds, pay the investor and go back into the market and issue new bonds at the lower rate of 4.5 percent. In effect the company has issued a call option that allows them the right but not the obligation to "call" the bond back.

Another example of a bond-like instrument that has an embedded call option is a mortgage. Mortgages actually have two embedded options: a default and a call option. The default option is discussed in Chapter 6 on SifiBank's consumer loan portfolio. However, the call option is related to interest rate risk. When a mortgage is originated, a borrower has a valuable and free call option. This option allows them the opportunity to freely refinance (or prepay) their mortgage when market rates fall below the borrower's mortgage rate. In this case they can "call" the mortgage back, replacing it with a lower cost loan. While valuable to the borrower, this prepayment option poses interest rate risk to the lender or holder of the loan. When interest rates fall, the value of a mortgage with a prepayment option tends to fall once rates decline to a certain level. Thus, the inverse price/yield relationship that applies to bonds without call features is offset by the prepayment effect of the embedded option. This can be visualized in Figure 9.7. At rates above X (the borrower's mortgage rate), the mortgage acts much like a standard bond as the borrower continues to pay on the loan. But as rates fall below X, the borrower is incented to prepay the mortgage, which has a dampening effect on the loan's value, eventually pulling the value down even as interest rates fall. This portion of the curve thus exhibits negative convexity.

Valuation of mortgages is complicated by the existence of the prepayment option as well as the borrower's default option. Putting aside the default option for the time being, how would you approach assigning a value to the mortgage? First, if the jumping-off point in determining the rate on a mortgage is a comparable duration risk-free rate such as a five-year

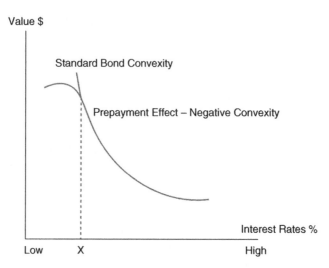

Value $

Standard Bond Convexity

Prepayment Effect – Negative Convexity

Interest Rates %

Low X High

FIGURE 9.7 Standard Bond Value Compared to Mortgage Value with Embedded Call Option

Treasury, we know that since the Treasury does not have a prepayment feature, a mortgage investor must be compensated for bearing that additional risk in the form of additional yield. In other words:

$$y_M = y_T + C(y,t) \qquad 9.19$$

where y_M is the yield on the mortgage, y_T is the yield on a comparable duration Treasury and $C(y,t)$ is the call value of the prepayment option, often referred to as the **option-adjusted spread**, or **OAS**. The price of a mortgage then may be expressed as the following:

$$P_M = \sum_{n=1}^{N} \sum_{t=1}^{T} \frac{E(CF_t)}{(1 + r_t^n + OAS)^t} \qquad 9.20$$

where P_M is the price of the Treasury instrument, $E(CF_t)$ is the expected cash flow in time t, r_t^n is the spot rate at time t for Monte Carlo simulation trial n, and OAS is the option-adjusted spread. Note that the OAS is a constant spread over time that when added to all the rates used to discount the mortgage's cash flows will make the expected (average across interest rate paths) present value cash flows of the mortgage equal to its market price across all paths. Also note that the numerator in the above expression differs from that in a standard coupon bond. The expectation operator reflects the fact that a mortgage may be prepaid at any point in time and this must be taken into account in pricing the loan. When a borrower has the incentive to refinance their loan, the investor receives the remaining balance of the mortgage back in that period and the mortgage is extinguished. It is necessary that the analyst have an ability to measure the borrower's prepayment propensity.

Statistically based loan level prepayment models can be developed alongside the default models described in Chapter 6. Such a model defines two possible outcomes: the loan continues to pay as agreed or the borrower prepays. Just as in the credit risk-modeling example, a logistic regression model (binary choice or limited dependent variable) may be specified using borrower risk attributes and other loan and market characteristics important in determining the likelihood of prepayment. An example of such a model would be the following:

$$\Pr(P) = \frac{1}{1 + e^{-X\beta}} \qquad 9.21$$

where the probability of prepayment P is a function of a set of predictor variables X and estimated parameters β. An example of such a model is given below as:

$$\Pr(P) = \beta_0 + \beta_1 INCENT + \beta_2 HP + \beta_3 CLTV + \beta_4 SCORE + \beta_5 OAMT \qquad 9.22$$

where $INCENT$ is the refinance, incentive for the borrower defined as (Mortgage Rate – Market Rate), HP is house price appreciation rate $CLTV$ is the current loan-to-value (LTV) ratio for the property, $SCORE$ is the borrower's credit score, and $OAMT$ is the origination amount in dollars.

Using monthly estimates of the probability of prepayment, the expected cash flows of any mortgage can be determined as the scheduled principal payment plus interest accruing during the month plus any unscheduled payments (prepayments) occurring that month. Note that although an individual borrower will either prepay or not in a period, making it a discrete event, in actuality since many loans are being evaluated together in a portfolio or pool, the cash flow analysis assumes a percentage of loans prepay over time rather than 0 or 100 percent.

In addition to its corporate bond portfolio, SFID also has a $15 billion mortgage-backed securities (MBS) portfolio that has as its underlying collateral 75,000 mortgages. The mortgages in this MBS all have a 4 percent coupon rate and they are fixed-rate 30-year amortizing mortgages with a free prepayment option. Since this is a mortgage-backed security guaranteeing investors against credit losses, there is a 25bps guarantee fee deducted from the coupon that goes to the credit guarantor and another 25bps that goes to the servicer of the loans. Thus, the rate that is passed-thru to SFID as the investor is 3.5 percent. Net interest payments are based on this rate. (These securities are held for investment and the risk team is interested in generating a one-week 99 percent VaR for the MBS portfolio.) The CIR interest rate model, used for the analysis and previous work to calibrate the OAS between modeled and market MBS prices, has established the OAS for the analysis at 50bps. The mortgage contracts require the borrower to make monthly amortizing payments split into principal and interest as follows:

$$PMT_t = UPB_{t-1} \left(\frac{\frac{r}{12}\left(1+\frac{r}{12}\right)^{n-t+1}}{\left(1+\frac{r}{12}\right)^{n-t+1} - 1} \right) \qquad 9.23$$

where UPB_t is the unpaid principal balance of the loan at time t, r is the mortgage rate and n is the number of months of payments on the loan (for this example $n = 360$). The amount of interest allocated to the payment decreases over time and is computed as:

$$INT_t = UPB_{t-1}\left(\frac{r_t}{12}\right) \qquad 9.24$$

With these relationships, Figure 9.8 displays the monthly allocation to interest and principal under a situation where there are is no prepayment.

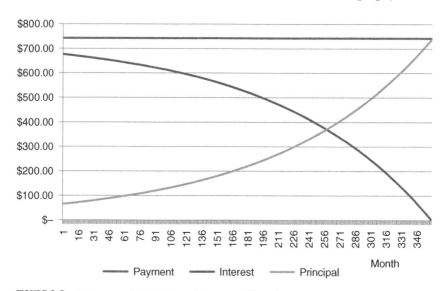

FIGURE 9.8 Mortgage Principal and Interest Allocation

When considering a pool of mortgages as underlying SFID's MBS, we need to account for expected prepayment over the life of the pool. A simplified industry model can be used to illustrate the impact on the value of the MBS as prepayments change. The **Public Securities Association** (PSA) model establishes a baseline annual conditional prepayment rate (CPR) of .2 percent for month 1, increasing .2 percent per month until month 30, where it caps out at 6 percent per year thereafter. This is referred to as 100 percent PSA. A monthly prepayment rate, called the **single monthly mortality rate** (SMM) is used to compute a monthly prepayment rate based on the CPR. This calculation is given as:

$$SMM = 1 - (1 - CPR)^{\frac{1}{12}} \qquad 9.25$$

Under the PSA model, multiples of the 100 percent PSA describe relative prepayment scenarios. For example, a 125 percent PSA describes a prepayment scenario where prepayments occur at a rate 1.25 times faster than the 100 percent PSA assumptions. Similarly, a 75 percent PSA assumption refers to a prepayment scenario that is 75 percent of the 100 percent baseline rate. To illustrate the effect of prepayment under different scenarios, consider Figure 9.9 on the SFID MBS portfolio. Prepayment peaks early in the life of the mortgages and then declines thereafter at different rates. The rate

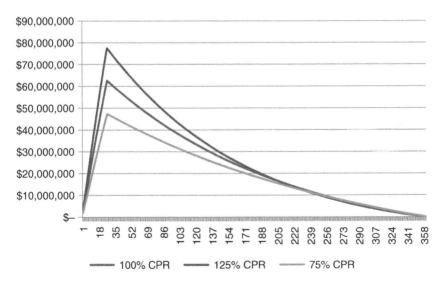

FIGURE 9.9 Prepayment Schedule for 100, 125, and 75 Percent CPR Scenarios

TABLE 9.10   Macaulay Duration and MBS Price under Alternative CPRs

CPR (%)	Duration (Years)	Price ($ 000's of face Amount)
0	13.03	106.62
75	9.66	104.87
100	8.85	104.45
125	8.14	104.09

at which prepayments decline affect the cash flows in any period. Taking SFID's MBS portfolio under the same prepayment scenarios and assumptions, the differences in duration and price can be observed from Table 9.10. Not surprising, as prepayments accelerate, an investor will get fewer interest payments later in the life of the security. This tends to offset the benefit of lower rates, accelerating cash flows to the investor from a price perspective. This is clearly seen in Table 9.10, as faster CPRs reduce duration and MBS price. This simple approach to incorporating prepayments into a cash flow model of MBS can be replaced with a statistical prepayment model that estimates the monthly prepayment rate based on the unique characteristics of each loan supporting the MBS. Using an estimated prepayment model described above, SFID risk management applies this model to its Monte Carlo simulation of interest rates and generates a distribution of cashflows for each mortgage in the MBS. The analysts then discount these cashflows adjusted for prepayment each month with the term structure associated with each path. The present value of each mortgage cash flow is summed across all mortgages in the pool resulting in 500 different MBS values. Using this information, the risk team develops a distribution on MBS portfolio values and derives a one-week 99 percent VaR of $80M.

SUMMARY

Interest rate risk can be a significant exposure to financial institutions with rate sensitive assets and liabilities. In addition to issues relating to repricing and reinvestment risk associated with adverse movements in interest rates given the composition and relationship of assets and liabilities, understanding the impact interest rates have on the value of the portfolio and individual assets and liabilities is critical in forming a view of the overall effect of interest rate risk on both the income statement and balance sheet of the firm.

In this chapter, the focus was on understanding the impact on SFID's portfolios from changes in interest rates. Duration provides an effective measure of the interest sensitivity of fixed-income instrument prices and is quite useful for small changes in interest rates. Under volatile interest rate conditions, the duration model breaks down due to its linear form and cannot be relied upon by itself to provide an accurate measure of the price impact on a bond or portfolio without a convexity adjustment for the price-yield curvature effects in bond valuation.

Beyond the duration model, simple assumptions that the yield curve shifts in a parallel fashion are useful starting points for understanding immediate shocks in the term structure but are relatively naïve constructs, as they do not reflect the more complicated nature of yield curve movements which allow for shifts, changes in slope, and curvature of the yield curve. Consequently, the application of key rate durations that allow the analyst to explore the effect of differential rate effects are an extension of the simple uniform shift in rate assumption handled by the standard duration approach.

Just as in the case of market risk, VaR models can be applied to understanding the interest rate risk exposure of the firm. An analytical method leveraging key rate duration and PCA analysis permits development of an interest rate risk VaR without the computational burden required in a Monte Carlo simulation. PCA analysis reduces the "curse of dimensionality" problem that results in analyzing the term structure of interest rates across rate change scenarios. Instead, PCA is an effective approach at reducing the number of factors driving changes in the yield curve. Typically 90–95 percent of the variation in the yield curve is associated with three factors: a parallel shift in yields, a change in the slope of the yield curve, and a change in its curvature.

If computational burden is not an issue, the use of Monte Carlo simulation to develop a distribution of portfolio values under alternative interest rate scenarios can be a useful technique in assessing interest rate risk. Key to the development of such a process is selection of a model describing the term structure of interest rates. A wide variety of models exist relying on varying economic assumptions. Some of these models generate a theoretical term structure that may not tie to the existing term structure. Others can be developed that better align with prevailing rate conditions. However, a simulation-based VaR requires considerable attention to underlying assumptions regarding interest rate movements historically as well as the parameterization of the interest rate model, which could lead to results not consistent with likely outcomes. Nonetheless, simulation-based VaR can be an effective approach to modeling complex interest rate dynamics on portfolio value.

All of these interest rate risk techniques can be applied against plain vanilla fixed-income instruments that do not have embedded options, default risk, or floating rate payments. Cash flow modeling and credit analysis can easily address default risk and floating rate payment structures, however, additional analysis is required in evaluating bonds with embedded options such as mortgages. A mortgage instrument is characteristic of bonds with embedded call options. When interest rates fall, a mortgage borrower has an incentive to refinance the loan at a lower rate, hence they can exercise their option to call the loan and replace it with one having a lower interest rate. Modeling this prepayment behavior can be handled in various ways, from industry standard prepayment benchmarks such as PSA to empirically estimated prepayment models. Once a prepayment model is developed, the cash flows can be modified to reflect the timing of when unscheduled principal payments are made which have important effects on the value of the individual mortgage or mortgage securities. In addition, the interest rate risk exposure of complicated interest-sensitive instruments such as mortgages or MBS can be assessed using duration and VaR methods described earlier.

QUESTIONS

You have a bond with a face value of $100 in your portfolio with a maturity of five years. The bond makes an annual coupon payment of 3 percent. Yields are 4 percent.

1. What is the duration of this bond?
2. If rates rise by 50bps, what is the resulting error in the price between the duration approximation and the standard discounted cash flow approach?
3. How could you correct the duration approximation and what would the result be now?
4. Assume that instead the five-year bond had even (level) cash flows in each year. What would the duration be? What explains the difference from the result in question 1?

You have the following information on the first three principal components for a 10-year rate. The total variation in term structure is 9 for all components.

	Factors	Eigenvalues	σ
k1	0.35	5.29	2.3
k2	0.22	1.21	1.1
k3	0.05	0.64	0.8

5. What would be the effect on 10-year rates from a one-unit change in k_1?

6. How much do each of the three principal components explain rate movements in general? What do each of these represent in terms of yield curve movements?
7. You are provided the following key rate durations associated with a 30-year bond

Maturity	KRD
1	−0.010
2	−0.050
3	−0.150
5	−1.000
7	−2.500
10	−2.500
20	−6.500
30	−14.000

How would you assess the impact of rate movements on this bond?

8. You have been provided the following key rate shifts for a five-year bond

t	Spot Rate	Key Rate Shift
1	0.16%	0.16%
2	0.26%	0.26%
3	0.38%	0.38%
4	0.58%	0.58%
5	0.77%	0.77%
6	1.00%	1.00%
7	1.22%	1.22%
8	1.41%	1.41%
9	1.60%	1.60%
10	1.79%	1.79%
11	1.86%	1.86%
12	1.94%	1.94%
13	2.01%	2.01%
14	2.09%	2.09%

(continued)

t	Spot Rate	Key Rate Shift
15	2.16%	2.16%
16	2.23%	2.23%
17	2.31%	2.31%
18	2.38%	2.38%
19	2.46%	2.46%
20	2.53%	2.53%
21	2.57%	2.57%
22	2.61%	2.61%
23	2.65%	2.66%
24	2.69%	2.70%
25	2.74%	2.74%
26	2.78%	2.78%
27	2.82%	2.82%
28	2.86%	2.87%
29	2.90%	2.91%
30	2.94%	2.95%

What is the estimate for the 30-year key rate duration for this five-year bond assuming a 1bp increase in rates across the term structure?

9. You are provided the following information. What would your estimate of the change in interest rates be?

Input	Value
α	0.001
β	3.25%
σ	0.69%
r	3.00%
dt	0.004

10. You have been provided the following information on two five-year mortgage bonds. The first bond does not allow for prepayment and its annual cash flows are shown in millions of dollars. The second bond allows for prepayment and its cash flows are shown in millions of dollars.

The yield on the no prepay bond is 5 percent. What should the yield be for the bond that allows prepayment if market yields are 5 percent assuming discrete compounding?

		Bonds	
t	CF	No Prepay	Prepay
1	CF1	$11.50	$15.00
2	CF2	$11.50	$18.00
3	CF3	$11.50	$12.00
4	CF4	$11.50	$ 5.50
5	CF5	$11.50	$ 5.50

CHAPTER 10

Market Risk

SifiBank reported $180 billion of trading account assets against $72 billion in trading account liabilities last year in their Capital Markets Division (CMD). CMD provides investment services for a variety of corporate and institutional customers serving as a market maker and earning commissions and fees for service. In its capacity as a market maker for its clients, SifiBank seeks to maintain a neutral stance in the market, using a variety of hedge instruments to offset long/short positions for its clients.

In addition, SifiBank maintains a relatively small proprietary trading department, Trading Services Department (TSD) within CMD that trades a variety of financial instruments with the objective of generating an additional source of profits for SifiBank. TSD has been operating since 2010 and is focused on trading fixed-income, equities, U.S. Treasury futures, and options contracts. TSD grew out of a part of CMD that had a proven track record in understanding relative market movements in commercial banking and fixed income markets, particularly during times of market uncertainty as experienced in the years following the financial crisis of 2008–2009. TSD's trading positions are shown in Table 10.1. The bank realizes that over time it will need to shift its trading focus into areas that will allow it to comply with the Volcker Rule prohibition on proprietary trading. Despite having returned in excess of 20 percent on capital deployed to its activities, SifiBank's CEO is increasingly concerned that he does not have a complete picture of the risk posed by TSD on an ongoing basis. Trading billions of dollars of complex financial instruments exposes SifiBank to significant trading losses if markets go against TSD positions. These losses occurring due to pricing fluctuations on trading positions create market risk for SifiBank. The Corporate Risk Office of SifiBank has employed a VaR methodology, as described in Chapter 4, to assess its market risk exposure.

To illustrate how VaR methods could be used to assess the market risk of an individual stock, consider a simple example for a single bank stock where by tracking the daily returns of that stock over time we would be able

TABLE 10.1 TSD Trading Position

Trading Position	$ Billions
Fixed-income Securities	1.50
US Treasury Futures	2.25
US Treasury Options	1.75
Commercial Bank Equities	
Citigroup (C)	0.50
JP Morgan Chase (JPM)	1.00
Bank of America (BAC)	0.75
Wells Fargo (WFC)	1.50
US Bancorp (USB)	1.25

to compute the mean daily return and standard deviation for that stock and generate a probability distribution of stock prices. If we wanted to know the worst daily loss on this stock position that we could experience with 99 percent confidence, we would calculate $2.32\sigma\sqrt{t}$ where t is the time horizon measured in days (in this example one day) and define that amount as VaR for this stock. VaR in this example can thus be interpreted simply as the worst loss for the stock's value at a certain level of confidence over a specified time period. That does not mean that losses cannot still be experienced in the portfolio, just that at a 99 percent level of confidence this is the highest loss that may occur. If we assume the mean daily change in the stock's price is 0 (a conventional assumption for short time horizons), and its standard deviation is .3 percent, then on a stock portfolio valued at $250 million, the 99 percent one-day VaR would be defined as:

$$P_V(2.32)(\sigma)\sqrt{t} = \$250M(2.32)(.003)(1) = \$1.74M \qquad 10.1$$

In other words, 99 percent of the time we should not lose more than $1.74 million over one day on our $250M stock portfolio. While our hypothetical stock example illustrates the concept of VaR, we can easily extend the concept for multiple assets in a portfolio context.

CALCULATING VAR FOR A PORTFOLIO

Calculating a portfolio-level VaR can be accomplished in several ways and the method presented below is referred to as the **variance-covariance** approach. At its core portfolio VaR requires an estimation of the portfolio's volatility as shown below:

$$\sigma_P^2 = \sum_{i=1}^{n} \omega_i^2 \sigma_i^2 + 2 \sum_{i=1}^{n} \sum_{j \neq i,}^{m} \rho_{ij} \omega_i \omega_j \sigma_i \sigma_j \qquad 10.2$$

where ω represents the share of asset i in the portfolio, and ρ_{ij} is the correlation between returns on asset i and j. Portfolio theory instructs that if correlations are equal to 1 there is no diversification benefit from multiple assets in the portfolio, however, when returns are not perfectly correlated the portfolio's risk as measured by its volatility can be reduced. Since the relationship between correlation and covariance is established as: $\rho_{ij} = \frac{\sigma_{ij}}{\sigma_i \sigma_j}$ an alternative way of expressing the portfolio variance σ_P^2 is shown below:

$$\sigma_P^2 = \sum_{i=1}^{n} \sum_{j \neq i}^{m} \sigma_{ij} \omega_i \omega_j \qquad 10.3$$

where σ_{ij} represents the covariance in returns between asset i and j. For a portfolio with $n + m$ assets, a variance-covariance matrix can be constructed as follows:

$$\begin{vmatrix} \sigma_{11}^2 & \sigma_{12} & \sigma_{13} & \sigma_{1n} \\ \sigma_{21} & \sigma_{22}^2 & \sigma_{23} & \sigma_{2n} \\ \sigma_{31} & \sigma_{32} & \sigma_{33}^2 & \sigma_{3n} \\ \sigma_{n1} & \sigma_{n2} & \sigma_{n3} & \sigma_{nn}^2 \end{vmatrix}$$

The elements on the diagonal of the variance-covariance matrix represent the variances of each asset in the portfolio and the elements off the diagonal represent the covariance terms. Standard financial software can easily compute these statistics.

With this information, a 99 percent portfolio VaR can be calculated as follows:

$$VaR_P^{99\%} = P_V (2.32) \sigma_P \sqrt{t} \qquad 10.4$$

Despite the ease by which financial software applications can provide variance and covariance estimates, as the number of assets in a portfolio increases it adds substantial computational requirements to the problem. Techniques are thus required to simplify the calculations while ensuring an adequate level of accuracy in computing portfolio VaR. This process is referred to as "**cash flow mapping**" and entails reducing the number of calculations by grouping asset cash flows into a smaller number of categories. This technique can be illustrated for equities by using the bank stocks of the TSD proprietary trading portfolio.

Although this TSD portfolio is only comprised of five bank stocks, computing the variance-covariance matrix becomes more difficult as TSD's stock portfolio increases. As a result, the risk management unit takes advantage of the **Single-Index Model** given by the following relationship:

$$R_i = \alpha_i + \beta_i R_M + \varepsilon_i \qquad 10.5$$

Where R_i is the return for asset i, R_M is the market return (e.g., S&P 500 index) and β_i represents the ith asset's **Capital Asset Pricing Model (CAPM) beta** which describes the **systematic (undiversifiable) risk** of the ith asset. Stock betas may be derived statistically by estimating the above relationship. The CAPM model gives the following relationship for a stock's volatility as:

$$\sigma_i = \sqrt{\beta_i^2 \sigma_M^2 + \sigma_{ei}^2} \qquad 10.6$$

or, $\sigma_i = \beta_i \sigma_M$ since the risk specific to each stock (σ_{ei}) can be diversified away. This can be generalized for a portfolio of stocks as:

$$\sigma_P = \beta_P \sigma_M \qquad 10.7$$

where $\beta_P = \sum_{i=1}^{n} \omega_i \beta_i$

To illustrate how to calculate a portfolio VaR for TSD's bank stock portfolio by mapping cash flows using the Single Index Model approach, the risk office has collected return data over the three years for each of the five bank stocks and estimated the individual bank stock betas as shown in Table 10.2.

TABLE 10.2   TSD Bank Stock Characteristics

Stock	β	ω
Citigroup	2.56	10%
JP Morgan Chase	1.58	20%
Wells Fargo	1.45	30%
Bank of America	2.79	15%
US Bancorp	1.35	25%

Using this information, the portfolio beta for TSD, $\beta_{TSD}^{BankStocks}$ would be calculated as:

$$\beta_{TSD}^{BankStocks} = \omega_C\beta_C + \omega_{JPM}\beta_{JPM} + \omega_{WFC}\beta_{WFC} + \omega_{BAC}\beta_{BAC} + \omega_{USB}\beta_{USB} \qquad 10.8$$

or,

$$\beta_{TSD}^{BankStocks} = .1(2.56) + .2(1.58) + .3(1.45) + .15(2.79) + .25(1.35) = 1.763$$

The 99 percent VaR for TSD's bank stock portfolio would be calculated as the following assuming σ_M equals .5 percent (based on the S&P 500 index's performance):

$$VaR_{TSD}^{BankStocks} = P_{TSD}^{BankStocks}\beta_{TSD}^{BankStocks}2.32\sigma_M = \$5B(1.763)(2.32)(.005)$$
$$= \$102,254,000$$

This would mean that over a one-day period, TSD could lose as much as $102,254,000 1 percent of the time.

Cash flow mapping can be applied to other financial assets in TSD's portfolio such as bonds, futures, and options. Within TSD's bond portfolio are hundreds of different government and corporate bonds of various maturities and cash flow payments. For standard coupon bonds, prices move inversely with changes in interest rates. Drawing on relationships featured in Chapter 9, changes in bond prices for a given change in interest rates (yield) can be defined as:

$$\frac{\delta P_{Bond}}{P_{Bond}} = -D\delta r \qquad 10.9$$

Where D is the duration of the bond and δr is the change in the interest rate. **Duration** is a measure of the bond's interest elasticity, or the change in price for a unit change in interest rate. We can define the volatility of a bond i's price as $D_i\sigma_{dr}$ where σ_{dr} represents the standard deviation of movements in interest rates over some time period. In turn, the 99 percent VaR for this bond would be defined as:

$$VaR_{Bond}^{99\%} = P_{Bond}2.32D_i\sigma_{dr} \qquad 10.10$$

But to calculate this across hundreds of individual bonds taking into account the possibility of different coupon payments and timing for each would make the computations more extensive. As a result, the cash flows for each coupon period could be converted into equivalent positions in zero coupon bonds in order to simplify and consolidate the various bond cash

TABLE 10.3 Example VaR Calculations for Bonds

Term	Market Value	Duration	σ_{dr}	VaR$_i$
1	$ 425,000,000	0.75	0.12	$ 887,400.00
5	$ 350,000,000	4.85	0.15	$ 5,907,300.00
10	$ 325,000,000	8.60	0.18	$11,671,920.00
20	$ 275,000,000	16.45	0.11	$11,544,610.00
30	$ 125,000,000	27.55	0.09	$ 7,190,550.00
	$1,500,000,000			

flows in the portfolio. A set of standard coupon periods could be established by the risk team along with a set of standard deviations and correlations of bond returns for these coupon periods.

For simplicity, assume a bond portfolio is comprised of bonds with a single coupon payment in the following maturities shown in Table 10.3. The market values, durations, and daily standard deviations in the relevant spot rates for each bond are shown along with their resulting 99 percent VaRs. For instance, the 99 percent VaR for the one-year maturity bond is calculated using the formula above as $425M(.75)(.0012)$ $(2.32) = \$887,400$. For coupon bonds with multiple coupon payments, the approach would be extended to account for each discounted coupon payment across periods. Futures contracts on fixed-income instruments would follow a similar cash-flow mapping exercise and set of VaR calculations.

In the case of option contracts, the measure of price sensitivity of an option (O) relative to changes in the underlying asset price (A) is the **delta** (Δ) **of the option,** or dO/dA which is defined as $\sigma_A A \Delta$. In this case the calculation of VaR would be presented as the following:

$$VaR_{Option}^{99\%} = 2.32 A \Delta \sigma \qquad 10.11$$

The standard deviation in option prices is given as σ_{dO} which can be derived from standard relationships underlying the Black-Scholes option pricing model.

To calculate the 99 percent VaR for TSD's entire portfolio, the following calculation would need to be made:

$$VaR_P^{99\%} = \sqrt{\sum_{i=1}^{N} VaR^2_i + 2\sum_{i=1}^{N}\sum_{j\neq i}^{N} \rho_{ij} VaR_i VaR_j} \qquad 10.12$$

TABLE 10.4 TSD VaR Results

| Asset Type | 99% VaR | Correlations | | | |
		Stocks	Bonds	Futures	Options
Stocks	$102,254	1	−0.25	0.13	0.65
Bonds	$ 65,777		1	0.77	−0.55
Futures	$ 59,231			1	0.32
Options	$ 67,883				1
Sum	$295,145				
	Portfolio VaR	$183,837			

Applying the correlation estimates found in Table 10.4, the 99 percent VaR for TSD's portfolio is found to be $183,837,000. This would be interpreted as that there is a 1 percent chance that TSD's portfolio could lose $183,837,000 or more in a single day. Note that the portfolio VaR is lower than the sum of the individual asset VaRs. Since assets in the TSD are not perfectly correlated, there is a diversification effect that reduces the overall portfolio's VaR from what it would be otherwise.

SIMULATION ANALYSIS AND VAR

An alternative methodology to the variance-covariance approach is to use Monte Carlo simulation to generate the asset or portfolio return distribution. While a full treatment of Monte Carlo simulation (MCS) is beyond the scope of this book, its application to risk management warrants some discussion as it relates to market risk for SifiBank. Underlying MCS are important statistical properties describing the movement of asset prices and returns over time. Prices for financial assets such as stocks are not perfectly predictable over time, and this uncertainty in intertemporal asset price changes can be described using what is called a **stochastic process**. Specifically, it can be shown that for each of TSD's bank stock investments that their price change over time is related to the expected rate of return of each stock (μ_i) and standard deviation of the stock's return (σ_i). More formally, the change in stock price over time t is shown to be the following:

$$dP_i = \mu_i P_i dt + \sigma_i P_i \varepsilon \sqrt{dt} \qquad 10.13$$

Where the term $\varepsilon\sqrt{dt}$ describes how a stock price behaves over time with ε randomly drawn from a standard normal distribution (i.e., where $\mu = 0$ and $\sigma = 1$). It can be shown that changes in a random variable z are equal to $\varepsilon\sqrt{dt}$ according to a concept called **Geometric Brownian Motion (GBM)**. This process thus provides a way to characterize the apparent random movements in stock prices. To gain a better sense of how a stochastic process relates to an asset price, consider Figure 10.1. This figure presents the components of an asset's price reflected by a GBM process. The trend line represents the drift or mean level of the asset's price over a small period of time, dt. The variability of the asset's price movements over time is captured by the dZ component which reflects the random effects, e. Finally, both components can be put together as shown in Figure 10.1.

For some assets such as equities, prices are lognormally distributed. For equity price P, it has a lognormally shaped distribution if lnP is normally distributed. The volatility of lnP turns out to be $\sigma\sqrt{t}$. Finally, it can be shown that the price of an equity over some period dt may be written as:

$$P_{dt} = P_t e^{\mu dt + \sigma Z\sqrt{dt}} \qquad\qquad 10.14$$

Implementing this model over a 45-day period defines dt as the daily change over a year (1/250 business days) as .004. Assuming a stock price in t of \$50, μ equal to 15 percent, and σ equal to 50 percent, Figure 10.2 displays the daily prices.

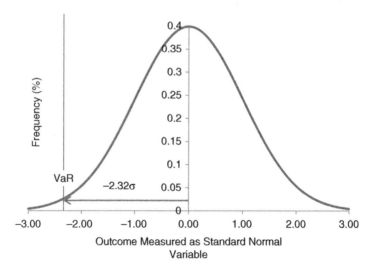

FIGURE 10.1   Decomposing a Stochastic Process

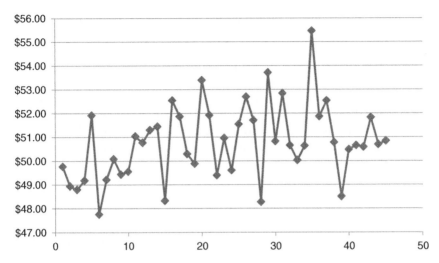

FIGURE 10.2 Lognormally Distributed Stock Prices Generated by a Stochastic Process

Using this relationship to describe the movement of TSD's bank stocks, an estimate of TSD's VaR for its bank stock portfolio can be derived. The returns for each bank stock can be expressed as the following, assuming the prices are lognormally distributed and the expected returns μ_i are zero:

$$r_{it} = \ln\left(\frac{P_{it}}{P_{it-1}}\right) = \sigma_i \varepsilon_i \sqrt{dt} \qquad 10.15$$

Since TSD has five bank stocks in its portfolio, we assume that the underlying distribution is multivariate normal since we have five random variables of interest, z_i.

As a result, the following correlation matrix for each combination of assets needs to be determined:

$$
\begin{vmatrix}
\rho_{C,C} & \rho_{C,JPM} & \rho_{C,BAC} & \rho_{C,WFC} & \rho_{C,USB} \\
\rho_{JPM,C} & \rho_{JPM,JPM} & \rho_{JPM,BAC} & \rho_{JPM,WFC} & \rho_{JPM,USB} \\
\rho_{BAC,C} & \rho_{BAC,JPM} & \rho_{BAC,BAC} & \rho_{BAC,WFC} & \rho_{BAC,USB} \\
\rho_{WFC,C} & \rho_{WFC,JPM} & \rho_{WFC,BAC} & \rho_{WFC,WFC} & \rho_{WFC,USB} \\
\rho_{USB,C} & \rho_{USB,JPM} & \rho_{USB,BAC} & \rho_{USB,WFC} & \rho_{USB,USB}
\end{vmatrix}
$$

Taking daily historical prices for each stock over a period of time believed by the risk analysts to be representative for the analysis, the standard deviations for each stock and the correlation matrix from above are calculated.

Using this information, a distribution of returns for each stock is generated by estimating 5,000 different returns using the return relationship above. A standard random number generator produces 5,000 different results for ε_i. A five-day VaR is of interest; thus, we will assume $t = 5$ for this exercise. These returns are then converted to 5,000 bank stock prices five days from now by solving the return relationship above for price five days from now as:

$$P_{i5} = P_{i0}e\left(\sigma_i\varepsilon_i\sqrt{dt}\right) \qquad 10.16$$

Once these 5,000 different prices for each bank stock are computed, the dollar value for each price outcome can be calculated by multiplying each price by the original number of shares of each stock in the portfolio. Taking the portfolio value for each stock over the next five days over each of the 5,000 trials, Π_{i5}^{τ} where τ represents a trial, the combined portfolio value over five days for an individual trial τ would be calculated as:

$$\sum_{i-1}^{5}\Pi_{i5}^{\tau} \qquad 10.17$$

The change in TSD's bank stock portfolio between today and five days from now is simply the difference in the portfolio value computed above and that at time 0. With 5,000 estimates of the change in the value of TSD's bank stock portfolio, a distribution could be generated that allows the risk team to empirically determine the VaR associated with this portfolio. This is shown in Figure 10.3 where the changes in portfolio value are normally distributed. The cumulative normal distribution is shown by the curve, which is associated with the right-hand vertical axis. If the risk team were interested in selecting a 99 percent VaR for this portfolio, the area to the left starting at 0 on the frequency axis up to a point on the cumulative distribution at 1 percent would indicate the worst 1 percent changes in TSD's stock portfolio over a five-day window. This turns out to be a value of approximately –$386 million, or there is a 1 percent chance of observing a loss in the portfolio of approximately $386 million or more over five days.

POSITION LIMITS POLICIES

The methods applied above to measure market risk provide risk management with useful tools to monitor trading behavior at an aggregate level as well as at the individual trading level since a consistent set of metrics can be

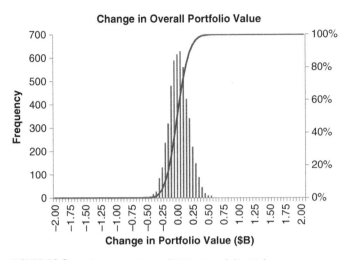

FIGURE 10.3 Change in Overall TSD Portfolio Value

applied across the entire trading organization. To visualize how this might be set up for TSD, consider Table 10.5. In this configuration, the corporate risk office has assigned the following risk limits across TSD. A house limit using the portfolio VaR is set as well as individual VaRs for each of the four segments of the portfolio. The portfolio VaR was developed based on correlations between asset classes in TSD. Methods to allocate VaR following the discussion in Chapter 4 assuming linear homogeneity of the portfolio could be used to assign VaR limits to each trader. Note again that the sum of the trader VaRs in a TSD segment in Table 10.5 are greater than the VaR associated with each segment, reflecting cross-correlation effects that are different from 1.

The head of the options trading unit faces a position limit for her group of $67,883,000 each day. The three traders in that unit likewise are required to maintain a VaR limit shown in Table 10.5. Trader 16 over the past two years has posted a consistent string of good annual contributions to TSD's overall profitability by buying put options on a number of bank stocks with heavy concentrations in Greece and Italy that the trader believes will decline over the next 12 months based on his assessment of overseas economic conditions and that of these target banks. Over time, the trader restructures the options portfolio, increasing the position on purchased put options.

Each month, a TSD positions limit report is put out that is used in the TSD Market Risk Review Committee meeting, which is chaired by the head of TSD. Other attendees include the head of each trading unit and the head of

TABLE 10.5   TSD House and Trader VaR Limits Existing Model ($000s)

House(TSD)	$183,837
Equities	$102,254
Trader 1	$ 23,518
Trader 2	$ 27,404
Trader 3	$ 15,338
Trader 4	$ 31,699
Trader 5	$ 35,789
Bonds	$ 65,777
Trader 6	$ 23,680
Trader 7	$ 17,760
Trader 8	$ 23,680
Trader 9	$ 13,155
Trader 10	$ 12,498
Futures	$ 59,231
Trader 11	$ 23,682
Trader 12	$ 20,731
Trader 13	$ 26,654
Options	$ 67,883
Trader 14	$ 25,796
Trader 15	$ 27,153
Trader 16	$ 28,511

business risk who reports to the head of TSD. On occasion TSD has witnessed a few isolated breaches in trader limits, but each time they have been able to bring the position back in line with the risk limits. Over the past six months, however, Trader 16's risk exceeded the VaR limit by more than 25 percent on 5 different days. Discussions at each of the monthly Market Risk Review Committee Meetings centered at first on understanding the position and the trader's strategy and the Committee determined that no change in the positions were warranted. Instead, an examination of the internal VaR model's assumptions was conducted and a recommendation was made for the TSD market risk team to update the VaR model using data more reflective of current market conditions that had been moderating over the past year. In fact, the head of the options trading unit had shown that the underlying volatilities of option prices had indeed come down such that if those numbers had been used, Trader 16 would have breached the limits in only one instance. The market risk officer objected to these demands for a change to the TSD VaR model, arguing that a longer-term data time series for options was more likely to pick up a broader array of market conditions, both favorable and unfavorable. The head of TSD acknowledged the market risk officer's concerns but at the end of the meeting instructed the risk team to redevelop a new VaR model using the more benign option pricing data from the last year.

One month later the TSD Market Risk Committee met to go over the new market risk limit report as well as the new VaR model used in setting those limits. The new model's effects on trading are shown in Table 10.6.

TABLE 10.6 House and Trader Exposures Versus VaR Limits

	New VaR Model Limits	% of Old Limit
House (TSD)	$163,615	89
Equities	$ 88,961	87
Trader 1	$ 21,167	90
Trader 2	$ 23,568	86
Trader 3	$ 13,498	88
Trader 4	$ 28,212	89
Trader 5	$ 32,568	91
Bonds	$ 57,226	87
Trader 1	$ 20,029	87
Trader 2	$ 15,806	89
Trader 3	$ 19,891	84
Trader 4	$ 11,445	87
Trader 5	$ 11,498	92
Futures	$ 52,123	88
Trader 1	$ 20,139	85
Trader 2	$ 18,658	90
Trader 3	$ 23,455	88
Options	$ 59,737	88
Trader 1	$ 22,442	87
Trader 2	$ 24,166	89
Trader 3	$ 24,519	86

The new VaR model, taking into account the new data lowered the percent of TSD's exposure as a percent of the VaR limit by about 10 percent from what it had been under the original model. This greatly reduced the chances that a trader would breach their limit as a result. The Committee approved the change to the new TSD VaR model but the changes were never shown to SifiBank's Corporate Market Risk Office. As a result, the corporate risk office was unaware that any material change to the TSD model had occurred.

One consequence of this change in limits was to effectively lower the risk for the TSD organization and traders, thus enabling the group to take on additional risk in their positions from what the previous model had indicated. Over the ensuing six months, TSD continued to build its positions with the new VaR model results in place. Shortly thereafter market volatility in European markets sharply rose due to concerns about the health of European banks, which led to a massive sell-off in U.S. bank stocks. TSD's positions in these securities sustained major losses as a result and over the next 60 days saw its market value decline by 23 percent. The fallout from these losses led to an internal investigation as well as a targeted examination by the OCC that ultimately led to the removal of the head of TSD and several traders involved in putting on some of the riskier positions.

VAR LIMITATIONS AND ISSUES

Heavy dependency on statistical theory and assumptions makes VaR a powerful tool in assessing market risk but also exposes the model to significant error should those outcomes not be realized. Therefore, it is essential that model builders gain an understanding of how representative the data being used to build the VaR model is to the business environment in which it will be applied. As seen in the above section, data drawn from a stable economic environment will yield much different model results than from a period marked by extreme fluctuations in asset prices. At their core, VaR models usually assume an underlying distribution for some random variable Z (or in some cases $\ln(Z)$ for a lognormal distribution) that is normal. In cases where the tails of the distribution turn out to be heavier or larger than assumed under the normal distribution, the VaR model will underestimate the amount of risk that exists. A graphic representation of this concept is shown in Figure 10.4.

In Figure 10.4, the standard normal distribution is compared to another distribution where the standard deviation is 1.25. The area under this distribution and to the left of the vertical line is larger than that of the normal distribution. Hence this distribution exhibits a fatter tail than the standard normal. Had a risk analyst developed a VaR model based on the underlying

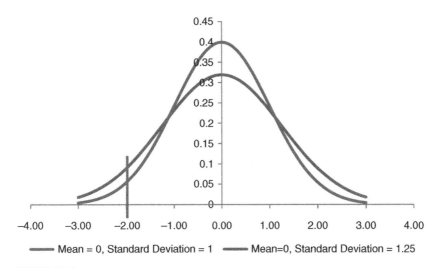

0.45
0.4
0.35
0.3
0.25
0.2
0.15
0.1
0.05
0

-4.00   -3.00   -2.00   -1.00   0.00   1.00   2.00   3.00   4.00

━━━ Mean = 0, Standard Deviation = 1   ━━━ Mean=0, Standard Deviation = 1.25

FIGURE 10.4   Fat-Tailed Risk and VaR Estimates

standard normal distribution when the actual results are borne out by the fat-tailed distribution, the model would have underestimated the amount of risk observed at a level beyond that indicated by the selected percentile.

One way of handling these issues is to develop VaR using an approach called **historical backsimulation.** The method entails obtaining estimates of the values for each position and computing the changes each period in value over a specified timeframe, for instance, daily changes for one year. The changes in the portfolio's value (gain or loss) would be tracked over time. The results from these daily portfolio changes could be rank-ordered from highest loss to lowest and a cutoff applied for a specified VaR, for example, 5 percent worst loss. This approach avoids the need to make assumptions regarding the shape of the underlying loss distribution which can lead to risk assessment errors if market conditions deviate from normality.

SifiBank's risk team can estimate a 99 percent one-day VaR using the historical backsimulation for TSD's bank stock portfolio using the historical daily data used in the Monte Carlo VaR simulation above. Daily prices from February 2, 2012, to January 31, 2013, were drawn for each of the five stocks as shown in Table 10.7. For each daily stock price, an adjusted price is computed, benchmarked against the current period price (January 31, 2013, for this example). This may be calculated as:

$$P_i^s = P_i^0 \, \frac{P_i^t}{P_i^{t-1}} \qquad\qquad 10.18$$

TABLE 10.7 TSD Bank Stock Prices

Date	C	JPM	BAC	WFC	USB
2/1/2012	31.60	37.60	7.36	29.89	28.56
2/2/2012	31.99	37.55	7.45	29.90	28.57
2/3/2012	33.54	38.28	7.84	30.63	29.20
2/6/2012	33.30	38.14	7.97	30.20	29.16
2/7/2012	33.07	37.87	7.85	30.26	29.45
2/8/2012	34.23	38.30	8.13	30.63	29.63
2/9/2012	33.66	37.86	8.18	30.58	29.34
2/10/2012	32.93	37.61	8.07	30.26	29.01
2/13/2012	32.88	38.30	8.25	30.62	29.18
2/14/2012	32.08	37.92	7.98	30.42	29.00
2/15/2012	31.72	37.40	7.78	30.17	28.63
2/16/2012	32.71	38.00	8.09	30.37	29.08
2/17/2012	32.92	38.47	8.02	31.09	29.35
2/21/2012	33.36	38.46	8.11	30.96	29.12
2/22/2012	32.36	38.07	7.95	30.59	28.81
2/23/2012	32.71	38.49	8.02	30.65	28.99
2/24/2012	32.35	38.28	7.88	30.18	28.73
2/27/2012	32.93	39.06	8.04	31.03	29.30
2/28/2012	33.48	39.21	8.12	31.37	29.17
$\cdots$	$\cdots$	$\cdots$	$\cdots$	$\cdots$	$\cdots$
1/31/2013	42.16	47.05	11.32	34.83	33.10

where P_i^s represents the adjusted price for simulation s occurring in time period t for the ith asset. An adjusted price for each bank stock in the TSD portfolio is computed in a similar fashion for each day in the sample period except for February 1, 2012. These results are shown in Table 10.8.

The portfolio values for each bank stock in the current period are then recomputed over each simulated period as follows:

$$V_i^s = V_i^0 \frac{P_i^s}{P_i^0} \qquad 10.19$$

TABLE 10.8 TSD Bank Stock Adjusted Prices

| Date | Adjusted Prices | | | | |
	C	JPM	BAC	WFC	USB
2/2/2012	42.68	46.99	11.46	34.84	33.11
2/3/2012	44.20	47.96	11.91	35.68	33.83
2/6/2012	41.86	46.88	11.51	34.34	33.05
2/7/2012	41.87	46.72	11.15	34.90	33.43
2/8/2012	43.64	47.58	11.72	35.26	33.30
2/9/2012	41.46	46.51	11.39	34.77	32.78
2/10/2012	41.25	46.74	11.17	34.47	32.73
2/13/2012	42.10	47.91	11.57	35.24	33.29
2/14/2012	41.13	46.58	10.95	34.60	32.90
2/15/2012	41.69	46.40	11.04	34.54	32.68
2/16/2012	43.48	47.80	11.77	35.06	33.62
2/17/2012	42.43	47.63	11.22	35.66	33.41
2/21/2012	42.72	47.04	11.45	34.68	32.84
2/22/2012	40.90	46.57	11.10	34.41	32.75
2/23/2012	42.62	47.57	11.42	34.90	33.31
2/24/2012	41.70	46.79	11.12	34.30	32.80
2/27/2012	42.92	48.01	11.55	35.81	33.76
2/28/2012	42.86	47.23	11.43	35.21	32.95
. . .	. . .	. . .	. . .	. . .	. . .
1/31/2013	42.37	46.97	11.26	34.69	33.06

The value of the five-stock portfolio in a given simulation period s is as follows:

$$P^s_{BankStock} = \sum_{i=1}^{5} V^s_i \qquad 10.20$$

The results of these calculations for each simulated period are shown in Table 10.9. For example, taking the simulated period corresponding to February 1, 2012 (designated as simulated period 1), the values for each bank stock in period 1 are shown in Table 10.10. The Citigroup portfolio rises in

TABLE 10.9   TSD Simulated Portfolio Values

Outcome	Value	Gain/Loss	Gains/Losses
1	$5,014,951,810	$ 14,951,810	$(247,276,680)
2	$5,147,114,763	$ 147,114,763	$(240,727,335)
3	$4,982,431,029	$ (17,568,971)	$(163,620,269)
4	$4,993,586,564	$ (6,413,436)	$(138,935,657)
5	$5,081,625,893	$ 81,625,893	$(137,890,137)
6	$4,970,115,464	$ (29,884,536)	$(121,924,499)
7	$4,942,711,580	$ (57,288,420)	$(119,731,110)
8	$5,059,486,024	$ 59,486,024	$(113,914,484)
9	$4,935,859,146	$ (64,140,854)	$(111,425,950)
10	$4,933,603,263	$ (66,396,737)	$(107,700,184)
11	$5,091,123,272	$ 91,123,272	$(107,089,264)
12	$5,056,256,279	$ 56,256,279	$(106,996,121)
13	$4,998,771,700	$ (1,228,300)	$(105,593,366)
14	$4,928,841,675	$ (71,158,325)	$(104,444,210)
15	$5,033,795,920	$ 33,795,920	$(103,912,564)
16	$4,941,736,470	$ (58,263,530)	$(101,002,692)
17	$5,111,615,435	$ 111,615,435	$(100,621,606)
18	$5,030,543,612	$ 30,543,612	$ (98,961,167)
19	$4,990,551,651	$ (9,448,349)	$ (93,956,505)
20	$5,080,232,372	$ 80,232,372	$ (92,848,521)
21	$4,976,047,039	$ (23,952,961)	$ (78,948,134)
22	$4,942,753,762	$ (57,246,238)	$ (78,843,539)
23	$4,861,064,343	$(138,935,657)	$ (74,961,878)
24	$5,090,454,213	$ 90,454,213	$ (73,653,443)
25	$5,098,966,141	$ 98,966,141	$ (73,032,696)
. . .	. . .	. . .	. . .
250	$4,989,337,343	$ (10,662,657)	$ 291,383,981

this period to $506,170,886 or an increase of $6,170,886. For the five-stock portfolio there is an overall increase of $14,951,810.

Looking at Table 10.9, the final step in the process is to take each of the gains or losses for the five-stock portfolio for each simulated period (250 in all, corresponding to each day in the sample period less the first

TABLE 10.10 Period 1 TSD Portfolio Stock Prices

	Stock Position Value	Change from Period 0 Value
C	$ 506,170,886	$ 6,170,886
JPM	$ 998,670,213	$ (1,329,787)
BAC	$ 759,171,196	$ 9,171,196
WFC	$1,500,501,840	$ 501,840
USB	$1,250,437,675	$ 437,675
Total	$5,014,951,810	$14,951,810

day (February 1, 2012)) and rank order the losses from highest to lowest as shown in the last column of the table. Choosing a cutoff percentile of 10 percent, this would correspond with the 25th worst path out of the approximately 250 simulated outcomes. This loss is shown to be $73,032,696 for TSD's bank stock portfolio.

A variation on the historical backsimulation approach and required for compliance with Basel risk-based capital standards is for firms to perform a stress VaR exercise. In this case, a one-year period of time that the bank experienced significant stress in its portfolio serves as the test period for the analysis. A 10-day VaR at a 99 percent level of confidence could be computed following a similar procedure as the standard historical backsimulation method. One of the limitations of the historical backsimulation method is that it relies on a discrete sample of outcomes which can result in mismeasurement of the standard errors or percentiles of the distribution. The accuracy of the estimates drawn from such an approach improves with the square root of the sample size used.

One problem with VaR is that by establishing an absolute risk limit without recognizing the possibility of extremely low probability events that produce massive losses well beyond the VaR limit, traders may be incented to take on riskier positions and still be able to maintain technical compliance with the imposed risk limit. Consider two traders, each facing a 99 percent VaR limit of $5 million. Most of the time both traders are in technical compliance with the VaR limit. Now assume that the other 1 percent of the time the average loss for Trader 1 is $10 million while for Trader 2 it is $25 million. Clearly, the risks of these two portfolios are much different due to the magnitude of average losses in the tail beyond the VaR limit. Unfortunately, VaR is unable to capture these differences in expected losses in the tail and this can lead to potential gaming by traders. In the example above, Trader 2 can stay within the VaR limit while taking considerably more risk than Trader 1. An approach to address this situation is to apply a variation of VaR referred to as the **mean expected shortfall method (MES)** or **conditional VaR**. Conceptually, the risk analyst would compute the expected loss among portfolio loss outcomes beyond VaR. Suppose in our example, in developing the original VaR limits the risk analytics team had determined that the expected one-day losses beyond the 99 percent level are $15 million. Applying this metric to both traders, Trader 1 would remain in compliance with the expected shortfall requirement while Trader 2 would have breached the limit by $10 million and would be forced to make changes in the risk profile of the portfolio.

SUMMARY

A number of techniques are available to risk managers in measuring market risk in a trading portfolio. VaR models have become the industry standard for such measurements owing to advances in analytics, data, and computational power. Among the methods used today, historical back-simulation is perhaps the easiest to implement as it is far less dependent on more advanced analytic methods and detailed asset pricing information. And while one of its advantages is that it avoids the strict normality assumptions of other techniques, its accuracy will be in part dependent on the sample size drawn and over what period of time. Other methods such as variance-covariance and Monte Carlo simulation-based VaR methodologies are supported by rigorous statistical and financial theory, but during the crisis, such methods were found to be woefully deficient in estimating extreme losses when market conditions worsened. Key statistical assumptions such as normality can pose serious limitations to the risk manager in the presence of nonnormal outcomes. Ongoing validation and model assessment is therefore a critical part of any market risk assessment program.

QUESTIONS

You oversee the trading division's risk of your bank and have three trading groups for equities, bonds, and call options. Relevant information on the positions of each of these groups is found in the tables below. In addition you know the volatility of the overall equity market is 25 percent.

Bond	Market Value	Duration	σ_{dr}
Term 1	$200,000,000	0.75	0.04
Term 2	$100,000,000	1.75	0.12
Term 3	$250,000,000	2.75	0.09
Term 4	$500,000,000	3.50	0.13

Stock	Position ($)	β	ω
Stock 1	$400,000,000	1.1	0.432
Stock 2	$200,000,000	0.75	0.216
Stock 3	$150,000,000	1.25	0.162
Stock 4	$175,000,000	1.85	0.189

Call	Δ	σ_{dO}	Position
1	0.25	0.05	$ 100,000,000
2	0.76	0.12	$ 150,000,000
3	0.55	0.09	$ 75,000,000
4	0.12	0.15	$ 50,000,000

1. What is the 99 percent VaR of the equity group and what is this approach called?
2. Given the information above and correlations in the table below, what is the 99 percent VaR for the Call Options trading group? How does this result compare to a portfolio where correlations are all 1?

Option	1	2	3	4
1	1	0.35	0.65	0.37
2		1	0.45	0.15
3			1	0.4
4				1

3. Given the information above and correlations in the table below, what is the 99 percent VaR for the fixed-income trading group?

Bond	Term 1	Term 2	Term 3	Term 4
Term 1	1	–0.25	0.13	0.65
Term 2		1	0.77	–0.55
Term 3			1	0.32
Term 4				1

4. Given the information above and correlations below, what is the 99 percent portfolio VaR for the trading group?

	Call Options	Bonds	Stock
Options	1	–0.25	0.7
Bonds		1	–0.5
Stock			1

5. If, due to a structural shift in the market, the correlations between assets were to all move in the same direction, how would that affect the VaR estimate in question 4?
6. You have taken some historical data on a stock and computed its mean return to be 25 percent with a volatility of 15 percent. For a stock with a price of $100 today, produce a graph showing the evolution of this stock's price over 12 months. The time interval of interest is monthly on an annual basis.
7. You have simulated the prices of five stocks in your portfolio over 30 trials as shown in the table below. Using the information provided, produce a table showing the portfolio value and gain or loss associated with each trial.
8. Produce a table showing the 90 percent VaR for this portfolio.
9. What are some limitations to VaR models?
10. What alternatives do you have to using a standard VaR methodology?

$ Value Trial	Stock 1 $500,000,000.00	Stock 2 $1,000,000,000.00	Stock 3 $750,000,000.00	Stock 4 $1,500,000,000.00	Stock 5 $1,250,000,000.00
Initil Price	$42.16	$47.05	$11.32	$34.83	$33.10
1	$42.68	$46.99	$11.46	$34.84	$33.11
2	$44.20	$47.96	$11.91	$35.68	$33.83
3	$41.86	$46.88	$11.51	$34.34	$33.05
4	$41.87	$46.72	$11.15	$34.90	$33.43
5	$43.64	$47.58	$11.72	$35.26	$33.30
6	$41.46	$46.51	$11.39	$34.77	$32.78
7	$41.25	$46.74	$11.17	$34.47	$32.73
8	$42.10	$47.91	$11.57	$35.24	$33.29
9	$41.13	$46.58	$10.95	$34.60	$32.90
10	$41.69	$46.40	$11.04	$34.54	$32.68
11	$43.48	$47.80	$11.77	$35.06	$33.62
12	$42.43	$47.63	$11.22	$35.66	$33.41
13	$42.72	$47.04	$11.45	$34.68	$32.84
14	$40.90	$46.57	$11.10	$34.41	$32.75
15	$42.62	$47.57	$11.42	$34.90	$33.31
16	$41.70	$46.79	$11.12	$34.30	$32.80

17	$42.92	$48.01	$11.55	$35.81	$33.76
18	$42.86	$47.23	$11.43	$35.21	$32.95
19	$41.96	$47.09	$11.11	$34.74	$33.36
20	$43.18	$48.40	$11.53	$35.11	$33.45
21	$42.12	$47.35	$11.33	$34.54	$32.61
22	$41.64	$46.78	$11.10	$34.48	$32.68
23	$40.21	$45.79	$10.95	$33.86	$32.49
24	$43.63	$47.80	$11.78	$35.18	$33.42
25	$43.12	$47.63	$11.38	$35.96	$33.70
26	$42.41	$47.74	$11.31	$35.12	$33.74
27	$42.27	$46.49	$11.24	$34.66	$33.06
28	$44.82	$50.36	$12.03	$36.84	$34.58
29	$40.73	$47.26	$11.79	$34.87	$33.60
30	$43.43	$48.26	$11.83	$35.56	$33.31

Liquidity Risk Management

A major contributing factor to the global financial crisis of 2008–2009 was a massive liquidity crisis that transpired in 2007–2008 and a liquidity bubble that grew during the years leading up to 2007. Two important events during this period helped shape what would eventually become one of the worst financial catastrophes in history. In the United States, the housing market had undergone an enormous transformation, expanding into a variety of new and more exotic mortgage products that helped fuel extraordinary demand for mortgages. During this time, banks increasingly moved away from putting these mortgages into their own portfolios to packaging them up for sale as mortgage-backed securities, or MBS. To fund this highly profitable mortgage securitization activity, firms increasingly relied upon shorter-term financing instruments and over time turned their attention to nonbank funding sources via the **shadow banking system** such as asset-backed commercial paper (ABCP) and term repos. Funding with ABCP instruments having maturities of one year or shorter and collateralized by mortgages permitted banks to enhance their profitability by boosting the spread between the income earned on longer-term assets and expense on shorter-term liabilities. Banks could face liquidity risk if their access to ABCP was cut off, thus preventing them from rolling over their debt. Hence, lines of credit extended to banks, called **liquidity backstops**, were common during the time. Likewise, term repos, or repurchase agreements, where investment banks sell collateral to another counterparty today with a promise of buying it back at a later date, were a good source of cheap funding during this period. And over time, this funding became even cheaper.

In February 2007, cracks in the booming subprime mortgage market materialized with credit losses sustained on some mortgage securities. This began an eventual liquidity death spiral, triggering numerous ratings downgrades of securities of issuing companies by the credit rating agencies over the next six months. During this period, spreads in the ABX market for credit default swaps spiked, indicating a significant increase in the cost of insuring mortgages due to higher credit losses. The secondary mortgage market for mortgage securities also stopped working as investors pulled away from these securities and prices plummeted. This triggered additional negative announcements from a number of prominent financial institutions over the next several months with regard to their earnings and write-downs for credit losses.

About this time a number of large U.S. mortgage-specializing financial institutions began realizing liquidity problems as their ability to securitize mortgages abruptly stopped due to the pullback by investors in the mortgage secondary market. One of these firms, IndyMac—a thrift institution that relied heavily on securitization and without a way to sell mortgages in their pipeline—would have to bring these loans onto their balance sheet quickly. Credit losses also mounted and these events drained the company's capital. Depositors, fearing a loss of access to their accounts began lining up at IndyMac branches to withdraw their money. This event also affected other large firms such as Washington Mutual, the largest thrift and sixth largest depository institution in the United States. In about two weeks in mid-July, Washington Mutual lost about $10 billion in deposits from unexpected withdrawals, and another $2.3 billion in a three-day period in September 2008 after having their credit rating downgraded to junk status. Another company, Countrywide Financial Corporation, the largest mortgage company in August 2007, had to draw on its entire $11.5 billion line of credit from banks in order to stay in operation as it could no longer sell or borrow against its loans. Counterparty risk concerns blew across financial markets, creating a liquidity crunch that prevented all but the highest quality firms from accessing funding markets outside of Federal Reserve emergency liquidity programs. Eventually, all three institutions went out of business, either falling into conservatorship (IndyMac), receivership (WaMu) or sale to another company (Countrywide to Bank of America). Poor liquidity risk management at many institutions sealed their doom, a lesson unfortunately learned at a very heavy cost to taxpayers, investors, and depositors.

SIFIBANK'S EXPOSURE TO LIQUIDITY RISK

In order to meet its financial obligations to customers, vendors, debtholders, and other counterparties in a timely and cost-effective manner, SifiBank must have sufficient funds available to it when such needs arise. Liquidity defines this process for the bank and is the lifeblood of the institution. If SifiBank is unable to pay depositors on time, for instance, it poses liquidity risk to the company. Liquidity arises from both sides of the balance sheet, thus the bank must carefully manage its assets and liabilities together to meet expected and unexpected cash demands. Consequently, effective liquidity risk management must take into consideration a wide variety of factors such as the composition, dollar position, and duration of its assets and liabilities, the level and sensitivity of financial instrument prices, the volatility of cash flows, credit and market risks of its assets and liabilities, derivatives contracts, and, most importantly, the reaction of customers and markets to perceived and real adverse outcomes for the bank.

Characteristics giving rise to bank liquidity risk include a lack of diversification in funding sources, unpredictable and volatile cash flows, over-concentration in a particular asset type and/or sector, an over-reliance on assets that have limited marketability, and dependence on funding that is acutely credit and rate sensitive. If, for example, the bank were entirely funded by wholesale deposits and lines of credit, any material adverse change in the bank's condition could result in credit lines being withdrawn and/or funding costs to skyrocket, at the very worst possible time for the firm. Likewise, asset sales could be used to generate liquidity during stress events, but if the firm has built up an overconcentration in assets that have no observed market prices, it could greatly limit the attractiveness and use of this potential source of liquidity. The Office of the Comptroller of the Currency (OCC) provides a good representation of how various assets on a bank's balance sheet contribute to liquidity, as shown in Figure 11.1. Assets

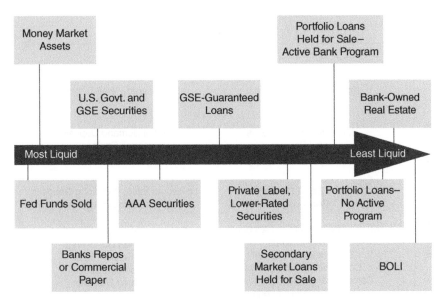

FIGURE 11.1   Continuum of Financial Asset Liquidity
Source: Office of the Comptroller of the Currency, Liquidity, Comptroller's Handbook, June 2012.

that can be turned over quickly without significant pricing impacts provide banks with the most liquidity. These include instruments such as money market mutual funds (MMMF), various U.S. securities, and other instruments of the highest credit quality and marketability. In determining their optimal asset composition, each asset's contribution to the bank's liquidity profile should be considered in the evaluation process along with profitability and other risks.

On the other side of the balance sheet, the composition of a bank's liabilities affects the company's liquidity. More stable liabilities allow for greater predictability in cash flows with stability a function of many factors including the risk profile of the bank and the use of federally insured deposits. The sensitivity of various bank liabilities to credit and interest rate risk is profiled in Figure 11.2. Wholesale deposits such as brokered deposits are more credit risk sensitive than retail insured deposits since the latter are protected by the FDIC. Similarly, certificates of deposit tend to exhibit greater sensitivity to changes in interest rates than retail demand deposits. Developing an ability to understand how different liabilities and assets affect the liquidity profile of the bank is important.

Liquidity risk may lead the institution into insolvency before other risks such as credit risk have an opportunity to generate enough losses

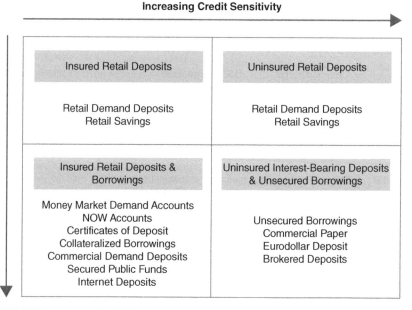

FIGURE 11.2   Financial Liabilities Credit and Rate Sensitivity Matrix

to drain reserves and capital. At times, adverse press from a credit or regulatory event at the bank can lead bank depositors and debtholders to act ruthlessly to protect their deposits or investments to the detriment of the bank's long-term viability. The outset of the financial crisis of 2008–2009 was associated with a severe liquidity crunch on financial institutions and many firms were unable to weather that event. What began as fundamentally a credit risk problem among mortgage lenders quickly cascaded into a full-blown destabilizing event that led to a number of high profile bank runs and disequilibrium in various wholesale funding markets such as commercial paper and tri-party repurchase agreements. Consequently, having in place a strong liquidity risk management program is essential for best practice financial risk management. Similar to other areas of risk management such as credit, market, and interest rate risk, analytic models for liquidity risk management have evolved over time but remain dependent on management judgment regarding adverse events that could trigger a liquidity crisis for the firm. However, increasing use of statistically based models of depositor behavior as well as credit and interest rate risk models for various assets has been made by best practice institutions. In some cases even more advanced analytic capabilities such as stochastic liquidity risk models are available to the sophisticated liquidity risk manager.

SifiBank incorporated a set of liquidity risk management practices into its Asset-Liability Management (ALM) process that includes an assessment of the net funding requirements for the firm over specified time periods, managing the composition, profile, and volatility of its assets and liabilities, and adopting various contingency plans in the event a liquidity problem arises.

SIFIBANK'S APPROACH TO LIQUIDITY RISK MANAGEMENT

Building a Static Maturity Ladder

The ALM risk management group for SifiBank adopted the use of a **static maturity ladder** for profiling the bank's liquidity condition over a 30-day period. Knowing that this practice is well established in the industry and recognized as an important tool by regulators in managing liquidity, SifiBank designed its maturity ladder to measure the difference in cash inflows and outflows arising on a daily basis over a one-month period. While the selection of the length of period for the maturity ladder—for example, daily, monthly, quarterly—is up to the risk manager, typically a short-term horizon is selected since liquidity risks emerge over short

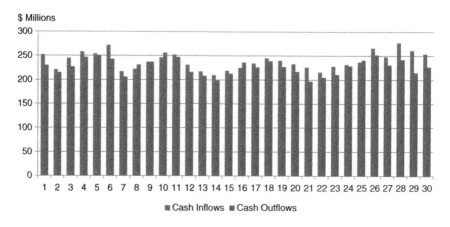

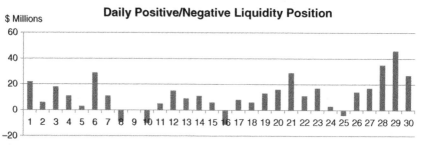

FIGURE 11.3 Simple 30-Day Static Maturity Ladder

periods of time. Banks with significant settlement and transactional activities would likely implement an intraday liquidity analysis as part of its short-term liquidity assessment processes. Conceptually, an example of a 30-day ladder where a bank's cash inflows and outflows are tallied up is shown in Figure 11.3.

Cash inflows and outflows are accumulated from both sides of the balance sheet. Assets maturing in the time period of interest, for example, would represent an inflow of cash to the bank. Conversely, maturing liabilities such as a certificate of deposit would constitute a cash outflow. The risk manager would need to account for all such movements in cash flows in each time period of the maturity ladder. This would include interest income and expense accruals, asset sales, drawn lines of credit and changes in derivatives positions, deposit runoff, loan prepayment, and credit losses incurred. In Figure 11.3, cash inflows and outflows are shown on a daily basis as well as their net position in the lower panel. On days 8, 10, 16, and 25, the bank shows a net negative gap in cash inflows and outflows, suggesting that steps would need to be taken in order to ensure that sufficient cash and collateral exist to cover expected liquidity needs for the next 30 days. This might entail adjusting rates on short-term deposits to raise the level of deposit inflows in the days where funding deficits are expected, reassessing the time when asset sales are conducted and the magnitude of such sales, among a variety of other strategies, that would enter into the bank's contingency planning strategy.

SifiBank risk managers have carefully looked over the balance sheet and have developed a baseline average daily maturity schedule as shown in Table 11.1. Mechanically, SifiBank risk managers would use this schedule to compute the net liquidity position of the bank each day over the next 30 days. For ease of exposition, the schedule in Table 11.1 depicts an average of the cash flows expected to occur each day. The same analysis would be used, however, to construct each day's ending liquidity position.

Table 11.1 breaks down SifiBank's cash flows by on- and off-balance sheet assets and liabilities and associated components generating cash inflows and outflows. On-balance sheet assets have been grouped into mortgage and nonmortgage assets in order to highlight some of the modeling differences used in constructing SifiBank's liquidity position. The bank's mortgage portfolio of $120 billion over time generates cash flows in a variety of ways. Mortgage loans can be retired by borrowers after reaching their final payment, and borrowers in some circumstances may choose to pay off their mortgage early. Moreover, mortgage defaults can affect cash flows by reducing the amount of interest that would otherwise accrue on these loans. SifiBank would need to determine the amount of inflows and outflows from these sources using a combination of experience and judgment augmented with analytic tools where data may be available. For instance, the default risk models described in Chapter 6 for mortgages could be used to determine lifetime expected losses. Those estimates could be converted into annualized default rates based on estimates of the mortgage portfolio's duration, another metric leveraged from the bank's interest rate risk management analysis. In turn these annual default rates could easily be recomputed into daily default rates. The practicality of allocating credit losses on a daily basis for a maturity ladder may be limited depending on asset type. Mortgage loans, for example, tend to have a lengthy seasoning pattern to default than shorter-lived assets such as credit cards and so building up day-specific estimates could be of less utility than applying an average daily default estimate to the analysis. Prepayment models could also be applied in determining additional cash inflows accruing to the bank from this activity. New loan estimates might be obtained from production units based on flow contracts and information. SifiBank would need to estimate the amount of mortgages

TABLE 11.1 SifiBank Average Daily Net Funding Profile for Static Maturity Ladder

CASH INFLOW SOURCES	Average Daily Baseline
On-Balance Sheet	
Mortgage Assets	$119,997,573,233
Loans Maturing	$ 1,643,836
Loans Defaulting	$ (1,053,597)
Loans Prepaying	$ 68,222,485
New Loans	$ (68,493,151)
Mortgages Sold	$ 16,438,356
Interest & Fee Income	$ 19,725,628
NonMortgage Assets	$879,553,972,603
Assets Maturing	$ 36,164,384
Assets Prepaying	$ 361,643,836
Assets Defaulting	$ (96,438,356)
New Loans	$ (48,219,178)
Assets Sold	$ 24,109,589
Interest & Fee Income	$ 180,730,268
Off-Balance Sheet	
Lines of Credit Draws by Bank	$ 5,178,082
Derivative Instrument Activity	$ 6,213,699
TOTAL	$ 603,357,834
CASH OUTFLOW SOURCES	
On-Balance Sheet	
Core Retail Deposits	$247,500,000,000
Deposits Maturing	$ 135,616,438
Deposit Runoff	$ 48,529,412
New Deposits	$ (33,904,110)
Interest Expense	$ 7,797,945
Non-Core Retail Liabilities	$247,500,000,000
Liabilities Maturing	$ 96,868,885
Liability Runoff	$ 126,309,494
New Deposits	$ (67,808,219)
Interest Expense	$ 15,256,849

TABLE 11.1 *(Continued)*

CASH OUTFLOW SOURCES	Average Daily Baseline
Other Liabilities	$333,000,000,000
Liabilities Maturing	$ 152,054,795
New Liabilities	$ (18,246,575)
Interest Expense	$ 13,684,932
Off-Balance Sheet	
Lines of Credit Draws by Customers	$ 22,260,274
Derivative Instrument Activity	$ 8,837,260
TOTAL	$ 507,257,379
Net Liquidity Position	$ 96,100,455

remaining, net of mortgages sold, defaults, prepayments, and losses in order to determine interest income and fees accruing to the mortgage book.

Nonmortgage asset cash flows would be determined in similar fashion for each asset type and then aggregated on the maturity ladder. Net cash inflows are determined for the bank by netting loan defaults and new loans (drains on cash flow) from total mortgage and nonmortgage asset cash inflows. Off-balance sheet items can also contribute to liquidity risk if not properly recognized. For example, SifiBank has $12.6 billion in lines of credit available to it from various counterparties. Over the course of time, the bank has drawn on these lines as additional sources of funding and has historically estimated that it has drawn 15 percent of these lines annually. Additional insight from SifiBank's Treasury activities might provide even more detail on the daily draws over the next 30 days. While recognized as a cash inflow for purposes of assessing liquidity risk, if SifiBank ran into difficulties, financially or otherwise, it could lead counterparties to curtail these lines according to contractual terms, and/or significantly price future lines at much higher rates. Both outcomes would add to SifiBank's cash outflows.

The bank's derivatives activities could also pose liquidity risk. Counterparties on various over-the-counter (OTC) derivatives contracts such as swaps and options may require the bank to unwind the contract in order to mitigate credit exposure to the counterparty if the bank had experienced some form of distress. The lack of a clearinghouse function in the OTC market that would otherwise provide a measure of protection against counterparty risk raises the prospect of such requests that can exacerbate liquidity problems. As shown in Table 11.1, derivative positions can also contribute to cash inflows for the bank based on the bank's experience in unwinding contracts with potentially risky OTC counterparties.

In determining cash outflows, SifiBank risk managers will also need to focus on the liability side of the balance sheet. Similar to the simple categorization for mortgage and nonmortgage assets, Table 11.1 simplifies the liquidity assessment process by focusing on retail non-core deposits, wholesale deposits, and all other liabilities. **Core deposits** represent the most stable form of funding for a commercial bank like SifiBank, as they include demand deposits (checking) and other accounts that are less sensitive to interest rate fluctuations and what may be characterized as "sticky" with respect to their movement. Retail deposits such as savings accounts, certificate of deposits and other interest rate sensitive products may be subject to runoff based on a number of factors unique to the depositor base as well as deposit pricing conditions between the bank and its competitors. Wholesale deposits offer another source of funding to the bank such as through brokered deposits that trade openly in markets. Other liabilities from the bank's balance sheet are also referenced in Table 11.1 for construction of the liquidity profile.

Calculating the amount of deposits and other liabilities that will mature over the 30-day window is a rather straightforward process that can be obtained from ALM reports on the tenor (maturity) of the bank's liabilities. As in the case of its assets, where loan prepayments and defaults were estimated, the bank needs to have some understanding of the behavior of its customers to withdraw deposits over time. With sufficient historical data on their depositor base, SifiBank has been able to construct estimated cash flows for its core and noncore retail deposits. To provide a sense of what such models entail, consider SifiBank's modeling of retail certificate of deposit (CD) cash flows. For each CD instrument, the bank will incur servicing costs on these CDs, pay interest on the CD to the holder, experience early withdrawals and have some CDs that rollover into a new CD. The cash flows of these CDs can be represented as the following:[1]

$$CF_t = NIC_t + BEW_t + (B_t - BROLL_{t+1}) \qquad 11.1$$

where NIC represents noninterest expenses associated with servicing the CD, BEW is the dollar balance of early withdrawals by customers in period t, B is the dollar balances of CDs in t, and $BROLL$ is the dollar amount of CDs that rollover into a new CD with the bank at period $t + 1$. Estimates of early withdrawal rates and rollover rates can be derived from

---

[1]Office of Thrift Supervision, Net Portfolio Value Model, Detailed Description of Methodologies, January 2000.

statistical models that usually include factors representing macroeconomic conditions, institution- and borrower-specific characteristics, along with measures reflecting the relative attractiveness of the bank's deposit pricing to the market's. A rollover model applying historical parameterization is as follows:

$$BROLL_t = B_t \left(\frac{r_t}{R_t}\right)^{\mu} e^{[q+a(s-q)/t]} \qquad 11.2$$

where: B_t = deposit balance at end of month t

e = base of the natural logarithm = 2.7183

q = industry-wide rollover parameter = -1.834

s = institution-specific rollover parameter for institutions

a = convergence factor representing the speed by which the bank's deposit rollovers converge to the industry

r_t = projected interest rate on retail CDs, in annual percentage form

R_t = implied-forward secondary-market CD rate in month t, in annual percentage form

μ = interest rate sensitivity parameter = 0.237

T = reported remaining maturity

TR = maturity of balances that are rolled over

In addition an equation defining the early withdrawal rate EW is shown as:

$$EW_t = 1 - \left(1 - \frac{C1 + C2\,Arctan\left(C3\left(C4 - \frac{Gain_t}{Cost_t}\right)\right)}{100}\right)^{1/12} \qquad 11.3$$

where C1–C4 are estimated parameters, arctan is the arctangent function, *Gain* is the amount of interest a bank CD customer would earn from early withdrawal and *Cost* is the foregone interest from early withdrawal at month-end. Completing the cash flow model, we have the following:

$$BEW_t = (EW_t)B_{t-1}$$
$$IC_t = BROLL_t(r_t) \qquad 11.4$$
$$B_t = BROLL_t + IC_t - BEW_t$$

where r is the prevailing rate on CDs and all other terms are previously defined.

Expected deposit rates can be derived similarly from interest rate models used for ALM analysis. Simplified versions of such models drive the cash outflow results for the core and noncore deposit entries in Table 11.1. These models aim to estimate the amount of deposits retained over time at the bank or, conversely, they may be expressed to represent the amount of runoff, that is (1 − retention rate) in deposits the bank could experience. In the specification for Table 11.1, as rates offered on deposits by SifiBank increase relative to the market rate, the retention/runoff rate rises/falls monotonically. The models have estimated that based on relative deposit rates expected over the next 30 days, the average daily retention rates are approximately 93 and 81 percent for core and noncore retail deposits, respectively. Demand deposit balances could be estimated from historical experience using similar factors as those included in estimating deposit retention profiles.

$$B_t = B_{t-1} \cdot (a + b \cdot \arctan(d + c \cdot r_t \ / \ R_t)^{1/12} + e \cdot rt \qquad 11.5$$

where: B_t = demand deposit balance at end of month t

arctan = arctangent function

r_t = interest rate offered on deposits in month t by reporting institution (in annual, percentage form).

The parameters $a, b, c, d,$ and e are set based on deposit type from historical experience

R_t = implied-forward three-month LIBOR in month t (in annual, percentage form)

Similarly, estimates of new demand deposit balances can be developed from models as the one presented below:

$$B_t \ / \ (B_{t-1}) = L \cdot rr_0 + (1 - L) \cdot RR_t \qquad 11.6$$

where: $L = 1/t$

rr_0 = institution's retention rate parameter

RR_t = retention rate in month $t = (a + b \cdot \arctan(d + c \cdot r_t/R_t))^{1/12} + e \cdot r_t$ and all other terms are defined as before.[2]

Such models are parameterized by the analyst with interest rate data over a relevant time period of interest. With sufficient time and data, retention rate and demand models could be estimated with greater granularity.

---

[2] OTS, NPV Model.

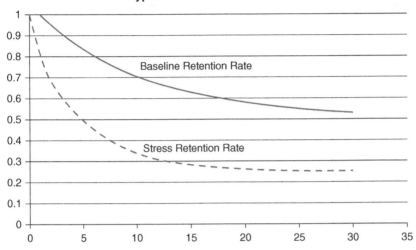

FIGURE 11.4 Hypothetical Retention Rate

Likewise, models describing runoff patterns of other liabilities including wholesale deposits would be used and the results aggregated across liability types as shown in Table 11.1. Although the exercise for SifiBank has been simplified to an average daily perspective, in actuality the risk manager will want to estimate various liability and asset changes over a time window of some predetermined length. Deposit retention models, for example, would be estimated to account for changes in the time profile of customer runoff. Customer response to an adverse event at their bank may fall off fast initially and then stabilize over time as depicted in Figure 11.4. Under the normal or baseline retention rate model, customer runoff starts to shallow out around month 15, whereas under a scenario where the bank encounters some form of stress, customer reaction is more severe, resulting in a higher/lower runoff/retention rate.

Having completed this exercise, SifiBank risk management determines that net cash inflows on an average daily basis over the next 30 days will be $603 million against a net cash outflow for the same period of $507 million. In other words, SifiBank is in a net positive liquidity position of $96.1 million. While this suggests that on average over the next 30 days the bank has sufficient liquidity to meet its obligations, on any given day it may wind up in a negative position with the bank needing to address any such deficiency in its contingency plan. As a result, the risk managers would need to expand the analysis in Table 11.1 for each day of their 30-day horizon.

STRESS TESTING THE LIQUIDITY PROFILE

The results from Table 11.1 provide important insights into the bank's liquidity profile under baseline, or normal market conditions. Understanding how SifiBank's liquidity position fares under a variety of extreme conditions would allow the bank to better prepare for unexpected outcomes that could put the firm in jeopardy should access to liquidity dry up. Similar to stress tests performed in managing credit risk, liquidity risk managers should develop a number of alternative scenarios depicting situations severely restricting access to liquidity and/or depleting the bank's liquidity. These scenarios could be built around three types of outcomes: a systemic event such as the financial crisis of 2008–2009 that affected the entire financial industry, sectoral or product events such as the thrift crisis of the 1980s, or institution-specific events isolated to the unique circumstances of SifiBank. Scenario analysis has long been used by risk managers as an effective way to assess the risk impacts to the bank under a set of specific assumptions. However, as in the case of credit risk stress tests, it is difficult for management to understand the likelihood of the event occurring. This is a significant issue as the costs associated with addressing liquidity gaps found in such an extreme scenario could be quite high and management would want to have a better understanding of the trade-offs being made under those circumstances.

In the case of a systemic event scenario, problems originating with one large systemically important institution or sector could lead to contagion effects across the industry. In 2008 for example, with the deterioration of the subprime mortgage market and associated banking institutions such as Lehman Brothers, investor sentiment toward the banking sector turned sour with a sharp decline in lending in repo and asset-backed commercial paper (ABCP) markets. The liquidity crisis that ensued provides risk managers with a useful, if extreme scenario to apply against the bank's liquidity position. Understanding how the various funding sources may dramatically shrink or evaporate altogether provides SifiBank management with critical information on liquidity gaps that could put the firm at risk as an ongoing concern.

A sectoral event affecting a certain region or market may not present as large a problem potentially as a systemic event, but could pose liquidity challenges for the bank due to asset quality issues or adverse publicity associated with the bank and its activities in this market, for example. Likewise, understanding the effects of bank-specific events that could lead to liquidity difficulties is important since any number of issues adversely affecting the bank, such as a regulatory consent decree, operational risk breakdown, a large class-action lawsuit, or performance issues could negatively affect depositor and investor behavior.

SifiBank risk management realizes that it should stress test its liquidity position and decides to develop three scenarios. The first scenario assumes an extreme systemic risk event occurs similar to the liquidity crisis of 2007–2008. The second scenario assumes a significant sectoral event occurs, in this case a downturn in the housing market that leads to large credit losses in the portfolios of commercial banks. The third scenario assumes some bank-specific event has occurred for SifiBank that causes a major disruption in its access to liquid funding over the next 30 days. The details behind each of the scenarios are shown in Table 11.2. For each scenario a

TABLE 11.2 SifiBank Liquidity Stress Scenarios

Definitions	Assumed Effects	Model Factor Adjustment
Stress Scenario 1—Systemic Crash		
Severe market downturn	3 Ratings Downgrade	Undrawn Lines to Bank goes to 0
2007–2008 style liquidity crisis	Massive credit losses	Asset default rates increase 5X
Pan-financial crisis ensues	Bank runs	
	Capital market tightening	Runoff rates increase by 30%
	Low interest rate environment	Wholesale deposit rates increase 50%
	Asset prices plummet	No New Liabilities available (Repos and CP)
		Asset prices drop 25%
Stress Scenario 2—Institution Specific		
Bank-specific stress	2 Rating Downgrade	Undrawn lines fall by 30%
Earnings problems, ratings downgrade	Negative exam downgrade	Runoff rates increase by 15%
	Isolated Bank run	
Stress Scenario 3—Sectoral Specific and Recession		
High credit losses sustained	Default rates spike	Mortgage Loan losses increase 2X
	Interest rates low	Runoff Rates increase by 10%
	Isolated Bank runs	Undrawn lines to bank fall by 20%

set of adverse events is assumed that would limit access to liquidity and/or increase cash outflows over the next 30 days. The basis for the assumptions could be a combination of bank-specific historical experience over similar events and judgmentally driven assumptions depending upon the desired severity of the scenario.

Scenario 1: Systemic Risk Event

In the case of Scenario 1, it is assumed that SifiBank has experienced a three-rating downgrade of its external credit rating to a notch above junk status—an outcome that would significantly affect its ability to raise debt in the capital markets. The rating downgrade is assumed to result in outstanding credit lines for SifiBank going completely away. The drop in SifiBank's credit rating also causes the cost of wholesale deposits such as brokered deposits to rise 50 percent over baseline rates. Access to repo and ABCP markets also dries up completely for SifiBank. Concurrently it is assumed that asset default rates increase fivefold over baseline rates. At the same time, bank runs at smaller banks begin, leading to a run on deposits at SifiBank where deposit runoff rates increase 30 percent above baseline runoff. Widespread unexpected credit losses across consumer, commercial, and even sovereign sectors lead to significant uncertainty in loan pricing, resulting in a 25 percent haircut in asset prices across the board.

The impact of Scenario 1's assumptions on SifiBank's average daily liquidity position over the next 30 days is shown in Table 11.3 alongside the baseline result as well as Scenarios 2 and 3. The impacts to SifiBank under Scenario 1 are indicated. The first takeaway from Scenario 1 is that it results in a negative liquidity position for SifiBank. Driving this outcome is the increase in cash outflows by more than $100 million while cash inflows decline by about $15 million. The bank's risk managers working with the Treasury office would want to develop a contingency plan in the event this scenario materialized. A detailed discussion of contingency planning is taken up in a later section. Decomposing the changes in outflows and inflows is easily accommodated in Table 11.3, where over half of the change in cash outflow from base case levels is attributed to retail and liability deposit runoff. SifiBank's relative limited use of lines of credit turns out to greatly help it navigate market disruption, although it may want to consider diversifying its counterparties as a way of limiting its exposure to credit line cancellation to a few counterparties. By knowing the sensitivity of the bank's liquidity position to movements in its liability structure, SifiBank can begin to adjust the composition of its liabilities in such a fashion as one way to reduce some of these negative effects.

Scenario 2: Sector-Specific Risk Event

Scenario 2's sector-specific event is clearly less severe than Scenario 1. SifiBank remains in a positive liquidity position although its liquidity has been cut by about 45 percent. Again as in Scenario 1, the biggest driver is deposit runoff. It is clear from all scenarios that the assumptions regarding loan prepayment are critical inputs to determining cash inflow given that prepayments account for a large share of cash inflow in the examples. To provide more insight into the specification of a prepayment model, a model of the **constant prepayment rate** (CPR) for mortgages is provided below:

$$cpr_{n,t} = seasoning_t \times seasonality_t \times refi_{n,t} \qquad 11.7$$

where $seasoning_t$ is the seasoning factor that reflects the number of months after the loan was originated, and $seasonality_t$ is the monthly seasonality factor reflecting the fact that borrowers pay off their loans due to relocation or other factors at greater frequency at different times over the year, $refi_{n,t}$ is the prepayment rate resulting from the refinancing incentive on path n which reflects the relationship between their contractual note rate and prevailing market rates.[3]

The **seasoning factor**, $seasoning_t$, has a value of .0333 for a new mortgage and increases linearly with mortgage age by a value of one at month 30, and remains constant thereafter. Each of these components of CPR can further be estimated as follows.

$$Seasonality_t = 1 + .2Sin\left\{1.571\left[\frac{month + (t-3)}{3}\right] - 1\right\} \qquad 11.8$$

Where *Sin* is the sine function, and *month* represents the number of months of the year for which the analysis is performed,

$$refi_{n,t} = .2406 - .1389 \arctan\left[5.952\left(1.089 - \frac{c}{m_{n,t-3}}\right)\right] \qquad 11.9$$

where: c = coupon of the mortgage

$m_{n,t-3}$ = simulated mortgage refinancing rate (lagged three months)

arctan = arctangent function

The combination of these factors drives the CPR rate in any given period to between 0 and 100 percent. The arctangent function mathematically ensures the CPR rates are bounded between 0 and 1 as shown in

---

[3] OTS, NPV Model, Detailed Description of Asset Methodologies, March 2000.

TABLE 11.3 SifiBank Baseline and Stress Scenario Comparisons (Figures reported in dollars)

CASH INFLOW SOURCES	Average Daily Baseline	Average Daily Stress Scenario 1	Average Daily Stress Scenario 2	Average Daily Stress Scenario 3
On-Balance Sheet				
Mortgage Assets	$119,997,573,233	$119,993,358,844	$119,997,573,233	$119,996,519,636
Loans Maturing	$ 1,643,836	$ 1,643,836	$ 1,643,836	$ 1,643,836
Loans Defaulting	$ (1,053,597)	$ (5,267,986)	$ (1,053,597)	$ (2,107,194)
Loans Prepaying	$ 68,222,485	$ 68,222,485	$ 68,222,485	$ 68,222,485
New Loans	$ (68,493,151)	$ (68,493,151)	$ (68,493,151)	$ (68,493,151)
Mortgages Sold	$ 16,438,356	$ 12,328,767	$ 16,438,356	$ 16,438,356
Interest & Fee Income	$ 19,725,628	$ 19,724,936	$ 19,725,628	$ 19,725,455
NonMortgage Assets	$879,553,972,603	$879,168,219,178	$879,553,972,603	$879,457,534,247
Assets Maturing	$ 36,164,384	$ 36,164,384	$ 36,164,384	$ 36,164,384
Assets Prepaying	$ 361,643,836	$ 361,643,836	$ 361,643,836	$ 361,643,836
Assets Defaulting	$ (96,438,356)	$ (482,191,781)	$ (96,438,356)	$ (192,876,712)
New Loans	$ (48,219,178)	$ (48,219,178)	$ (48,219,178)	$ (48,219,178)
Assets Sold	$ 24,109,589	$ 18,082,192	$ 24,109,589	$ 24,109,589
Interest & Fee Income	$ 180,730,268	$ 180,651,004	$ 180,730,268	$ 180,710,452
Off-Balance Sheet				
Lines of Credit Draws by Bank	$ 5,178,082	$ –	$ 3,624,658	$ 4,142,466
Derivative Instrument Activity	$ 6,213,699	$ 6,213,699	$ 6,213,699	$ 6,213,699
TOTAL	$ 603,357,834	$ 587,962,808	$ 601,804,409	$ 602,302,228

CASH OUTFLOW SOURCES

On-Balance Sheet				
Core Retail Deposits	$247,500,000,000	$247,500,000,000	$247,500,000,000	$247,500,000,000
Deposits Maturing	$ 135,616,438	$ 135,616,438	$ 135,616,438	$ 135,616,438
Deposit Runoff	$ 48,529,412	$ 63,088,235	$ 55,808,824	$ 53,382,353
New Deposits	$ (33,904,110)	$ (25,428,082)	$ (28,818,493)	$ (23,732,877)
Interest Expense	$ 7,797,945	$ 7,797,945	$ 7,797,945	$ 7,797,945
Non-Core Retail Liabilities	$247,500,000,000	$247,500,000,000	$247,500,000,000	$247,500,000,000
Liabilities Maturing	$ 96,868,885	$ 96,868,885	$ 96,868,885	$ 96,868,885
Liability Runoff	$ 126,309,494	$ 164,202,342	$ 145,255,918	$ 138,940,443
New Deposits	$ (67,808,219)	$ (50,856,164)	$ (57,636,986)	$ (47,465,753)
Interest Expense	$ 15,256,849	$ 15,256,849	$ 15,256,849	$ 15,256,849
Other Liabilities	$333,000,000,000	$333,000,000,000	$333,000,000,000	$333,000,000,000
Liabilities Maturing	$ 152,054,795	$ 152,054,795	$ 152,054,795	$ 152,054,795
New Liabilities	$ (18,246,575)	$ —	$ (18,246,575)	$ (18,246,575)
Interest Expense	$ 13,684,932	$ 20,527,397	$ 13,684,932	$ 13,684,932
Off-Balance Sheet				
Lines of Credit Draws by Customers	$ 22,260,274	$ 22,260,274	$ 22,260,274	$ 22,260,274
Derivative Instrument Activity	$ 8,837,260	$ 8,837,260	$ 8,837,260	$ 8,837,260
TOTAL	$ 507,257,379	$ 610,226,174	$ 548,740,064	$ 555,254,968
Net Liquidity Position	$ 96,100,455	$ (22,263,366)	$ 53,064,345	$ 47,047,260

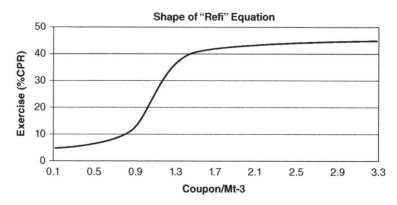

FIGURE 11.5 Shape of "Refi" Equation

Figure 11.5. This model does not need to be estimated at the loan level; however, greater accuracy in the prepayment estimates may be obtained by specifying the model at a more granular level which would leverage borrower and loan specific attributes such as credit profile and mortgage product type. Ideally, the risk management team preparing these scenarios would leverage the suite of statistical prepayment models used in conducting its interest rate risk management assessment. Another major consideration for SifiBank in preparing their stress tests would be the yield curve environment facing the bank during the scenario. Depending on the scenario, adjustments to the baseline curve, either up or down could be used to drive the other factors such as deposit runoff, loan prepayment and interest income and expense. While SifiBank technically remains in a positive liquidity position under Scenario 2, managers would still want to consider whether any contingencies in funding and asset management should be made.

Scenario 3: SifiBank-Specific Risk Event

The SifiBank-specific risk event depicted in Scenario 3 is just one of many alternative scenarios that the bank could explore and in all likelihood further analysis would be performed to understand the sensitivities on the liquidity position from incremental changes in key stress scenario assumptions. For example, while the inputs to Table 11.2 scenarios are simple multipliers against baseline results, the level of rigor of the analysis could be enhanced by modeled outcomes. But as in all situations where modeled outcomes and key assumptions are used, testing these assumptions over a range of inputs is critical to understanding how robust the stress test results may be.

For Scenario 3 specifically, the net liquidity position of SifiBank is smaller than under Scenario 2. This is largely due to the assumption that new deposit formation is significantly lower in Scenario 3. This might be attributed to historical experience where an event such as a publicly known security breach of depositor information led to a chilling effect by prospective and current depositors. Pulling together such events from the operational risk management and business teams would be useful in constructing realistic bank-specific scenarios where actual outcomes could be applied to the analysis.

LIQUIDITY CONTINGENCY PLANNING

Liquidity contingency planning is expected to complement the liquidity risk assessment process. Contingency planning prepares the bank for emergency situations where sources of funding available to the bank during normal times drop or altogether disappear. In those instances, the bank must prepare for how it will respond to these different liquidity scenarios. Planning thus involves identification of alternative funding sources such as backup lines of credit or brokered CDs, the reliability of such funding access under alternative stress scenarios and their magnitude, the set of protocols the bank would need to set in motion to respond to the crisis, and the communication plan needed for messaging the bank's situation and timely response to external constituents, employees and the board.

SifiBank has put together its own contingency funding plan using the baseline and stress scenarios from its liquidity risk assessment process described earlier. SifiBank's Treasury Office has worked on identifying a number of alternative funding sources as shown on Table 11.4 in working with various counterparties. From this exercise, the bank has identified $10 million in unpledged assets that could be sold at market prices under current, or baseline conditions. However, those same assets under the three stress liquidity scenarios are less available to SifiBank depending on the severity of the scenario. This is also evident in the other contingency funding sources highlighted by SifiBank in Table 11.4. For example, the bank has made plans to deepen its access to wholesale deposits and CDs such as brokered deposits, however, during Scenario 1 which entails a systemic risk, access to wholesale deposits is not possible. In fact, access to other borrowing lines and loans available for securitization fall to zero in Scenario 1 but are available in varying amounts in the other two stress scenarios. In the case of securitization, experience by SifiBank with the financial crisis of 2008–2009 is relied upon where the private label securitization market for mortgages evaporated, requiring the bank to brings all of these mortgages onto its balance sheet.

TABLE 11.4 Contingency Funding Sources and Liquidity Scenarios (All Figures in Millions of Dollars)

Contingency Liquidity Sources	Baseline	Scenario 1	Scenario 2	Scenario 3
Unpledged Assets Available for Sale	10	3	5	7
Unsecured Fed Funds Lines	3	2	3	3
Wholesale Deposits and CDs	5	0	3	3
FHLB Advances	5	3	5	5
Other Borrowing Lines	10	0	2	5
Loans Available for Securitization	15	0	10	5
TOTAL	48	8	28	84
Net Liquidity Position	96.1	−22.263	53.064	47.047
Net Liquidity After Contingency Funding	144.1	−14.263	81.064	131.047

SifiBank total sources of contingent liquidity sources are summed across all funding types as shown on Table 11.4 and then added to the net liquidity position shown in Table 11.3 for each scenario. Since the Baseline and Scenarios 2 and 3 resulted in a positive liquidity position for SifiBank, the addition of the contingent liquidity sources further adds to that position as shown in the last row of Table 11.4. Only for the most severe scenario, Scenario 1, does the net liquidity position, including contingent funding sources, remain negative. In this situation, SifiBank would be outside its liquidity policy tolerance of remaining in a positive liquidity position across all scenarios. SifiBank would communicate this result to its Board of Directors and make recommendations for how it would get the bank into compliance for this scenario.

In addressing its liquidity shortage for Scenario 1, the management team in consultation with the Board embarks on a strategic initiative to fully investigate the diversification of its asset and funding base. Diversification in this case focuses on the composition of its assets and liabilities as well as the maturity or tenor of assets and funding types. The process for optimizing the mix of assets and liabilities transcends the isolated exercise of liquidity risk management as adjusting the balance sheet has implications for projected profitability, credit, interest rate, and market risk, among other considerations. Ideally SifiBank needs to take these issues into consideration while restructuring its balance sheet to ensure it meets all of its prescribed liquidity policy targets. For example, one way it might choose to address its Scenario 1 liquidity shortage is by actively expanding its use of core deposits and targeted focus on customer segments that are known to be much more "sticky" in their account withdrawals compared under adverse liquidity events. Analysts at the Bank found that retirees were 40 percent less likely to withdraw their accounts even under economic stress than nonretirees and so SifiBank plans on implementing a new campaign to attract new deposits from this cohort using a variety of promotional and pricing inducements. The Bank decides that it will raise savings deposit rates by 25bps over peer market average in its retail branches as well as raise the rate on CDs with maturities less than one year by 15bps. It has estimated that the response to such rate moves would ensure sufficient new deposits that would runoff more slowly than its current deposits and that on balance this would place SifiBank in a net positive liquidity position for Scenario 1.

As part of its evaluation of its funding sources, the bank would want to strengthen the relationships it has with current and prospective providers of funding since maintaining reliable access to markets is critical during stress events. At the same time, SifiBank would need to strengthen its understanding of what factors and conditions are most likely to drive funding providers to withdraw, reduce, or terminate these sources to the bank. In turn, the bank would need to monitor changes in these metrics to provide an early warning to potential changes or shifts in funding access. This might include the credit ratings of the bank, vendor-supplied bank performance indices, asset growth rates, and changes in credit quality. Increasingly, advances in social media permit banks to monitor the amount of positive and negative perceptions of customers and the general public via sentiment analysis that leverages technologies designed to "scrape" text-based information citing bank-specific commentary off various social media websites. Such information could be invaluable to detecting any material shifts in customer sentiment that could tip off the bank to a bank run or other adverse funding event.

Another course of action SifiBank pursues as part of its board-initiated liquidity management strategy is to ensure it has sufficient liquid assets to meet various liquidity needs. Again, this strategy must take into consideration a range of impacts on the bank's profitability and risk exposures. Certainly a bank that is highly concentrated in mortgage loans would potentially face greater challenges in managing a liquidity crisis than an institution with a more diversified and shorter-tenor asset mix. In addition to managing the mix and tenor of its assets, SifiBank also needs to identify that group of assets that are otherwise unencumbered by legal, regulatory, or other contractual obligations. For example, as part of its arrangement with the Federal Home Loan Bank of San Francisco (FHLBSF), it has committed $25 billion of its mortgage portfolio as collateral for its access to the FHLB's advances, a form of loan available to SifiBank. These mortgage loans pledged as collateral to the FHLBSF would not be available to the bank for sale easily should

SifiBank need to tap assets to support unexpected liquidity needs. Moreover, SifiBank needs to take into account the quality of its assets in putting its liquidity plan together. Assets of the highest credit quality such as U.S. Treasury securities would be most salable with a reasonable pricing event during stress events and facilitate SifiBank's access to repo and other markets when it needs. However, returns on Treasuries and related high-quality instruments come at the expense of lowering the bank's overall return if it were substituting higher risk and higher return assets for these more liquid assets.

SifiBank's complex balance sheet and risk management issues may lead the bank to develop a formal balance sheet optimization capability. While discussion of SifiBank's balance sheet optimization model is beyond the scope of this chapter, the basic structure of the framework would entail maximizing the bank's risk-adjusted profitability or other appropriate performance metric subject to a variety of constraints. These constraints could take the form of policy limits such as specific liquidity targets, minimum regulatory requirements such as risk-based capital ratios, and other market, business, or risk requirements. The decision variables could include asset and liability types. Inputs to parameterize the model could include such items as interest rates on assets and liabilities, fees, risk weights, and expected and unexpected loss estimates, along with other important characteristics of the bank's cash inflows and outflows.

LIQUIDITY MEASUREMENT

Along with its liquidity policies and procedures and scenario analysis, SifiBank has developed a set of liquidity metrics to help it monitor changes in key factors affecting its liquidity profile. While many different indicators of liquidity risk exist, it is important that the analyst identify a few that are most reflective of the bank's liquidity risk profile and then monitor these metrics frequently over time. As part of its asset-liability management process, SifiBank has also set a number of policy thresholds on these metrics to ensure ongoing compliance.

Specifically, SifiBank is required to adopt one short-term measure of liquidity and chooses to also adopt another metric originally proposed by the Basel Committee to strengthen bank liquidity. These ratios are referred to as the **Liquidity Coverage Ratio** (LCR) and **Net Stable Funding Ratio** (NSFR). The LCR is intended to measure the bank's short-term liquidity requirements over a 30-day stress scenario. Conceptually, the LCR measures the ratio of the stock of high-quality liquid assets to net cash outflows arising over an upcoming 30-day period. The LCR must be maintained at a ratio at or above 100 percent. Included in the numerator of the LCR are such assets as cash and reserves held at central banks, U.S. Treasuries and other instruments with U.S. backing, and other public sector and Agency securities. Assets counting toward inclusion in the numerator must be traded in a deep liquid market.

In calculating the denominator of the LCR, cash outflows from on- and off-balance sheet commitments, payments of principal and interest, and contingent liabilities such as lines of credit would be included. Cash outflows are computed under various stress scenarios such as the bank experiencing a multinotch downgrade in its credit rating, a partial run on deposits, a loss on secured funding on all but the most liquid collateral, increased draws on committed lines, and associated derivatives impacts.

The contribution of each liquid asset and cash outflow category to the numerator and denominator of the LCR are weighted by a set of prescribed factors proposed by the Basel Committee. SifiBank's calculation of the LCR is found in Table 11.5 in simplified form. The calculation of the numerator first begins by categorizing assets by the Basel Committee designated Level 1 and Level 2 as shown. Level 1 assets carry a 100 percent weight compared to Level 2's 85 percent factor and reflects the greater quality of Level 1 assets. The dollar balances of each asset are then weighted by the appropriate factor and those products summed over all asset classes. The result is a $268 million liquid asset base over the next 30-day period.

Calculating the denominator of the LCR requires computing expected cash outflows and inflows assuming the stress impacts noted above. For example, the LCR requires SifiBank to assume that stable and less stable retail deposits runoff at 5 and 10 percent, respectively. Other assumptions are reflected by the factors presented in Table 11.5 under cash outflows. Similarly cash inflows are accounted for but with similar weights assigned as shown. Cash inflows are limited to no more than 75 percent of cash outflows according to the LCR requirements. Since the cash inflows exceed cash outflows, they are limited to $837.3 million. The difference between cash outflows and this amount of inflows is shown in Table 11.5 as $279.1 million. The ratio of liquid assets to net cash outflows thus is 96 percent which is under the minimum target LCR of 100 percent. The shortfall of $11.1 million would thus need to be made up by SifiBank by making readjustments to its balance sheet as described earlier.

In addition to a short-term measurement of liquidity such as the LCR, SifiBank also measures the stability of its liquidity over a longer-term period. As part of the Basel regulatory capital framework the NSFR may become a key metric for banks to use in estimating the stability of their liquidity over a horizon of one year. In part, the NSFR is designed to ensure that banks do not focus solely on short-term funding but also maintain stability in their liquidity profile over time. Similar to the LCR, the NSFR assigns weights (Availability Factors) to specific sources of funding and assets (both

TABLE 11.5 Liquidity Coverage Ratio Calculation for SifiBank

Numerator—Liquid Assets	Balance ($B)	Weight	Balance × Weight
Level 1 Assets		100%	
Cash and Central Bank Reserves	13.5		13.5
U.S. Treasuries and Fully Guaranteed Securities of the U.S. Federal Government	75.2		75.2
Level 2 Assets		85%	
Obligations of Fannie Mae or Freddie Mac	4.5		3.8
Fed Funds Sold	150.7		128.1
Corporate and Municipal Bonds with Ratings Better than AA-	17.3		14.7
Commercial Paper	25.4		21.6
Mortgage-backed Securities of Fannie Mae or Freddie Mac	28.7		24.4
TOTAL	315.3		268.0
Denominator—Cash Outflows			
Stable Retail Deposits	3467.5	5.0%	173.4
Less Stable Retail Deposits	1965.2	10%	196.5
Stable Commercial Deposits	1325.7	7.5%	99.4
Less Stable Commercial Deposits	1661.9	25%	415.5
Undrawn Committed Credit Facilities	189.3	5%	9.5
Other Undrawn Commitments	222.1	100%	222.1
TOTAL	8831.7		1116.4
Denominator—Cash Inflows			
Loan Prepayments	456.8	0%	0.0
Loans Maturing	1887.9	50%	944.0
Investments Prepaying	175.3	50%	87.7
Investments Maturing	28.4	100%	28.4
TOTAL	2548.4		1060.0
Cash Outflows less Inflows (Max 75% of Outflows)			279.1
Liquidity Coverage Ratio			96.0%
Target Ratio			100.0%
LCR Excess/(Shortfall)			−11.1

on- and off-balance sheet) in computing the ratio. Specifically, the NSFR is computed as follows:

NSFR = Available Amount of Stable Funding/Required Amount   11.10
       of Stable Funding >= 100%

Sources of funding with the highest weights are recognized as the most stable or reliable to the bank over a one-year period. For example, Tier 1 and Tier 2 capital along with secured and unsecured borrowings receive a 100 percent weight on these amounts. At the other extreme, SifiBank's remaining liabilities and equity are assigned zero weight. The amount of stable funding sources is compared to SifiBank's stable assets. Assets that have the highest chance of being liquidated during a stress event carry a zero weighting. This would include cash and securities with maturities less than one year among other types. Conversely, assets with the least liquidity that would need to be supported with stable funding sources carry the highest required stable funding factors. For example, loans with terms beyond one year in term would be assigned a 100 percent weight.

SifiBank's calculation of the NSFR is shown in Table 11.6. The balances of SifiBank's assets, liabilities and equity used in computing the numerator and denominator of the NSFR are allocated across each of the risk-weighted categories. SifiBank's NSFR of 100.5 percent is just above the minimum required threshold of 100 percent indicating that SifiBank's medium- to long-term funding stability is adequate. No further actions would be required for the bank at this point unless the ratio were to slip below the threshold.

Advanced Liquidity Analytics: Probability-Based Liquidity Modeling

To this point, the approach to measuring SifiBank's liquidity risk exposures has been based on deterministic analysis that does not reflect a probability-based approach. These static analyses provide important insights into SifiBank's liquidity adequacy under normal and stress environments. However, there are in theory an infinite number of different outcomes that would directly affect the bank's liquidity position. Having some ability to understand the distribution of outcomes requires a more sophisticated analysis.

One technique that has gained in popularity among liquidity risk managers is **liquidity-at-risk** (LVaR) which is based on establishing a distribution for the net liquidity position computed in the earlier maturity ladder example for SifiBank. Conceptually, liquidity-at-risk is analogous to other value-at-risk measures already discussed, where the bank determines its worst acceptable level of liquidity over a specified time period (e.g., 30 days) with

TABLE 11.6   Net Stable Funding Ratio Calculation for SifiBank

Denominator—Required Stable Funding	Balance $B)	Weight	Balance × Weight
Cash and Money Market Instruments	50.6		0.0
Securities with maturities < 1 year	78.3	0%	0.0
Loans to financial entities < 1 year	45.4		0.0
		5%	
Unencumbered marketable securities to sovereigns, other quasi-governments ≥ 1 year	6.2		0.3
		20%	
Unencumbered Corporate bonds AA or higher and ≥ 1 year	35.8		7.2
		50%	
Gold	2.4		1.2
Loans to non-financial corporate clients < 1 year	100.0		50.0
		85%	
Loans to retail customers < 1 year	57.3		
		100%	
All other assets	624.0		624.0
TOTAL	1,000.0		682.7
Numerator—Available Stable Funding		100%	
Tier 1 and Tier 2 Capital	100.0		100.0
Securities and unsecured borrowings and liabilities (including term deposits) > 1 year	215.3		215.3
		85%	
Stable Retail Deposits < 1 year	220.3		187.3
Stable unsecured wholesale funding < 1 year	175.3		149.0
		70%	
Less stable nonmaturity retail and term deposits < 1 year	23.7		16.6
Less stable unsecured funding < 1 year	17.4		12.2
		50%	
Unsecured wholesale funding, nonmaturing deposits and term deposits < 1 year by nonfinancial corporate clients	11.3		5.7
		0%	
All other liabilities and equity	136.7		0.0
TOTAL	900.0		686.0
Net Stable Funding Ratio			100.5%

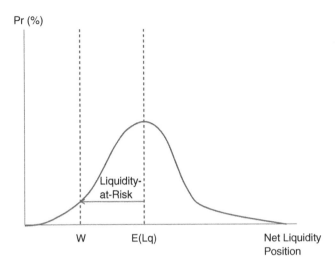

FIGURE 11.6 Liquidity-at-Risk Concept

a certain level of confidence (e.g., 95 percent). A depiction of this process is shown in Figure 11.6. A net liquidity position distribution is shown where SifiBank's expected liquidity position is denoted $E(Lq)$ and W represents a level of net liquidity associated with an x percent probability of observing a net liquidity position of that size or worse over 30 days. LVaR is defined as:

$$\text{LVaR} = E(Lq) - z\sigma \qquad 11.11$$

where z is a value based on the standard normal distribution, and σ is liquidity volatility. SifiBank would determine a level of confidence and time horizon over which it would establish its liquidity VaR. The bank would then establish policy limits to ensure that it remains within the policy's upper limit of the net liquidity position and would monitor adherence to this limit as a part of its regular ALM reporting process.

To generate the net liquidity position distribution requires incorporating an ability to simulate the impact on the drivers of cash inflows and outflows used in determining the net liquidity position of the bank. For example, in computing cash inflows, the bank would need to know what its level of mortgage and nonmortgage loan prepayments would be in the period. Statistical models estimating the amount of mortgage prepayments would include such factors as interest rates which would be determined based on a stochastic interest rate process as would be used to construct a VaR analysis. A key driver of a borrower's likelihood of refinancing their mortgage is the spread between their mortgage rate and prevailing mortgage rates which are in turn determined by interest rates. The interest process used in asset-liability modeling exercises described in Chapters 12 and 13 allow the risk analyst to generate a distribution of prepayments, which would be used to establish a distribution of cash flows for SifiBank, reflecting the underlying prepayment outcomes. Estimating prepayment outcomes for one asset is just one of many similar exercises that could be included in simulating the cash flows and liquidity position of SifiBank over different economic and market scenarios. For example, in constructing estimates of cash inflows and outflows arising from the liability-side of SifiBank's balance sheet, the analyst may develop models of deposit runoff that include both economic (e.g., interest rates) and behavioral (e.g., response to bad financial news for SifiBank) scenario drivers. Historical information augmented by industry data and other information could be used to shape the simulation analysis for these additional component models for estimating SifiBank's cash flows and liquidity.

SUMMARY

The financial crisis of 2008–2009 sensitized SifiBank to the need to incorporate robust liquidity risk management practices. Many firms during the crisis went out of business due to the liquidity crisis that occurred. Maintaining adequate sources of liquidity on balance sheet to withstand normal and severe liquidity environments is essential to the long-term viability of the bank. Banks should utilize a variety of techniques for measuring and managing their liquidity exposures including static maturity ladders or liquidity gap analysis of periodic cash inflows and outflows on a daily basis and over longer periods of time. Banks can gain more precision around estimating cash flows using historical information and modeling customer and counterparty behavior under different market and interest rate environments.

More recently, regulators have strengthened requirements around bank liquidity management by imposing the LCR rules on large banking institutions. Such rules standardize liquidity quality and thus may force many institutions to rebalance their liquidity profiles. In addition to such requirements, banks should undertake exercises to examine how their liquidity profile performs under a variety of different stress scenarios. And more advanced institutions may be able to draw on efforts to compute VaR for other risk types and apply those techniques to generating liquidity VaR estimates.

QUESTIONS

You have the following information available to you.

CASH INFLOW SOURCES	Average Daily Baseline
On-Balance Sheet	
Mortgage Assets	$119,997,573,233
Loans Maturing	$ 1,643,836
Loans Defaulting	$ (1,053,597)
Loans Prepaying	$ 68,222,485
New Loans	$ (68,493,151)
Mortgages Sold	$ 16,438,356
Interest & Fee Income	$ 19,725,628
NonMortgage Assets	$879,553,972,603
Assets Maturing	$ 36,164,384
Assets Prepaying	$ 361,643,836
Assets Defaulting	$ (96,438,356)
New Loans	$ (48,219,178)
Assets Sold	$ 24,109,589
Interest & Fee Income	$ 180,730,268
Off-Balance Sheet	$
Lines of Credit Draws by Bank	$ 5,178,082
Derivative Instrument Activity	$ 6,213,699
TOTAL	$ 603,357,834
CASH OUTFLOW SOURCES	
On-Balance Sheet	
Core Retail Deposits	$247,500,000,000
Deposits Maturing	$ 135,616,438
Deposit Runoff	$ 48,529,412
New Deposits	$ (33,904,110)
Interest Expense	$ 7,797,945

(continued)

(Continued)

CASH OUTFLOW SOURCES	Average Daily Baseline
Non-Core Retail Liabilities	$247,500,000,000
Liabilities Maturing	$ 96,868,885
Liability Runoff	$ 126,309,494
New Deposits	$ (67,808,219)
Interest Expense	$ 15,256,849
Other Liabilities	$333,000,000,000
Liabilities Maturing	$ 152,054,795
New Liabilities	$ (18,246,575)
Interest Expense	$ 13,684,932
Off-Balance Sheet	$
Lines of Credit Draws by Customers	$ 22,260,274
Derivative Instrument Activity	$ 8,837,260
TOTAL	$ 507,257,379

1. What is the net liquidity position of your bank?
2. The CPR in your mortgage portfolio is defined as:

$$CPR = \frac{1}{1 + e^{2-30(Original\ Coupon - Market\ Mortgage\ Rate)}}$$

If market rates are 3.8 percent and the weighted average origination coupon is 3 percent, what impact does this have on your bank's net liquidity position? Remember to adjust outstanding mortgage balances by the daily CPR. What is the CPR and how does that compare to when origination coupons are 6 percent?

Suppose that you have built a retention model for noncore retail liabilities with the following specification:

$$RR = .02 + .7(Current Rate / Deposit Rate)^{.5}$$

3. The weighted average deposit rate is 1.75 percent and current rates are 3.25 percent. What are your expected retention rates and what effect do you think this will have on the net liquidity position?

4. Suppose annual projected interest rates on retail CDs are 2.5 percent and the implied forward CD rate is 2 percent. Also the value of $a(s - q)/t = 1$. If current CD balances are $100 million, what do you estimate the dollar amount of rollover balances to be?

5. If the gains-to-cost ratio for a CD holder is one and you have the following table of values, what is the expected early withdrawal rate on your retail CDs?

Parameter	Value
C1	.3062
C2	−1822
C3	8.49
C4	1.273

6. If current rates are 2 percent, what is the expected interest cost and month-end balance on your CDs?

7. If you found that your net liquidity position was short over the next 30 days what type of assessment process would you want to go through and what are some examples of criteria you would be looking for in this process?

8. You have calculated your bank's cash outflows at $180 billion and cash inflows at $150 billion. Your liquidity profile is comprised of $25 billion in U.S. Treasuries and $20 billion in Freddie Mac MBS. Are you in compliance with LCR?

9. What actions, if any, would be warranted to ensure compliance with LCR?

10. Your bank's expected cash flow over the past 10 years has been $100 billion. You have measured the volatility of cash flows at $25 billion. You want to maintain a level of liquidity that never falls below the 95th percentile. What would that threshold need to be, what is it called, and how would you respond if current liquidity levels were at $60 billion?

CHAPTER 12

Market Risk Hedging

OVERVIEW

In Chapter 10, the Trading Services Department (TSD) is noted for its proprietary trading activities in fixed-income instruments and bank equities. The trading activities of this group are monitored by SifiBank's Corporate Risk Office, which has established a set of position limits and VaR tolerances for the company that it expects to be followed by each of the divisional and departmental risk offices. The sole purpose of TSD is to take positions in various investments in order to generate a profit for the bank. In this regard TSD's objectives are quite different from other divisions that trade on behalf of customers or are market makers. These entities do not wish to take a particular view of the market and thus rely on various hedging strategies to maintain a neutral position. For TSD, hedging is a strategy for maintaining the portfolio's risk tolerance within the stated daily VaR limit.

TSD's head of risk management was hired by the head of TSD several years earlier, as both had worked together in TSD, where the risk officer had been one of the better traders on the desk. The primary oversight of TSD's activities, including adherence to VaR and position limits, is by the TSD risk office. This group develops its own VaR models for TSD and applies the 99 percent confidence level daily VaR tolerance established by SifiBank risk management to the TSD portfolio. The TSD Risk Committee reviews the VaR on a monthly basis, although management and the risk office monitor daily changes in VaR as part of their procedures. For the corporate risk office, any breach in VaR is viewed as an event requiring a report from the senior business risk officer with an explanation for the breach and a description of what actions have been taken to address the breach under the bank's risk limits policy.

Over the past 24 business days, the TSD risk unit has discovered that on several separate occasions TSD has breached their VaR limit, as shown in Figure 12.1. These results made their way up to the corporate risk office, which became alarmed at the frequency and materiality of the breaches. The

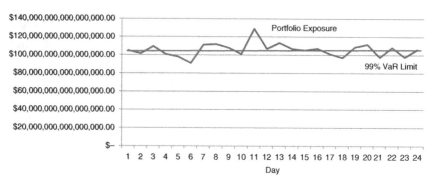

FIGURE 12.1   TSD 24-Day VaR Trends

head of TSD was summoned to the CRO's office along with the head of TSD risk management and were informed that corrective actions would need to be taken in the next week to address this problem. At one point the CRO informed the head of TSD that without material change in this situation, the CRO would have no choice but to require that TSD reduce its trading activity by 20 percent as a measure to ensure the trading activity would remain inside the stated limits.

During the TSD VaR review, it was revealed that the group did not engage in any type of hedging activity that would allow TSD to manage its VaR to within the designated limit. Traders in the bank equity unit, for example, simply bought and sold individual bank stocks without any hedging taking place. When pressed on why no hedging plan had been implemented, the head of TSD stated that it preceded the introduction of the VaR limits and that they had always been able to successfully manage the portfolio's market risk by smart transactions. The CRO objects to this explanation, stating that an unhedged position, no matter how smart the trader, will at some point result in an unacceptable portfolio loss.

The head of TSD noted that the division's strategy of opportunistically buying selected bank stocks affected by the downturn in the financial sector that had occurred in 2009 had been highly profitable for the bank, in fact at one point compensating for losses taken in the consumer portfolio in recent years. The CRO countered that the financial environment was different from what it had been over the past few years so maintaining the same strategy unhedged might not work out so well going forward. The counterargument made by the head of TSD was that hedging could be costly and that most of the breaches were immaterial and that insisting that TSD adhere strictly to the VaR limit would wind up jeopardizing the profitability of the department, which would be felt throughout the bank.

The CRO finished the meeting by requiring TSD to establish a plan to ensure the department would stay within the VaR limits. TSD after some discussion came back with a plan to reduce risk by adhering to daily limits that could be accomplished by a combination of asset sales and hedging. Since TSD was an investor in bank stocks, it holds a long position that could be offset from time to time by selling its portfolio. An alternative strategy to reduce risk for the TSD bank stock portfolio and the focus of this chapter would be to hedge the portfolio using a variety of hedge instruments such as options and futures contracts. While a full treatment of the pricing, market, and structure of such derivative instruments is beyond the scope of this book, some discussion of options and futures contracts is necessary in order to understand the principles of hedging.

HEDGING PRINCIPLES AND BASICS

Conceptually, the use of a financial instrument to offset the profit or loss of another position can be regarded as a hedge. Simple hedges may be established on a particular position or instrument. An example of this for TSD would be to hedge the risk that one of its bank stocks could fall in value by purchasing an option on that same stock that pays off when the stock declines in value. Hedging an entire portfolio increases the complexity of the risk mitigation strategy as it can entail using a variety of hedge instruments at various times depending upon the nature of the exposure being hedged.

At the most fundamental level, hedging requires the risk manager to have an understanding of the risk exposure from leaving the position or portfolio unhedged. If as in the case of TSD the portfolio consists of bank stocks that have been purchased, the position is **long** and would suffer a decline in value should the price of these stocks decline. Alternatively, if the unhedged position were **short** (as associated with selling), it would mean that the risk is from price increases since a short position does better when the asset's price declines and vice versa. Once an understanding of what the unhedged position's exposure to price movements is, then the hedge strategy can begin to develop.

The use of derivatives, that is, financial instruments whose value are determined by some underlying asset for hedging, is analytically complex; however, it is far from a pure science. In fact there as many qualitative aspects involved in establishing an effective hedge strategy as there are quantitative models for valuing the hedge position. Such considerations as selecting the appropriate time horizon for the hedge, the types of instruments to be used, and determining how much to hedge are among the important questions in designing a hedge strategy. These may be based on quantitative outcomes; however, there remains a great deal of judgment in the process as well.

For TSD, one of its larger bank stock exposures is to JP Morgan Chase (JPM). Historically the company performed well during the financial crisis as it had avoided originating most of the riskier mortgage products that contributed to the mortgage meltdown. However, in the years afterward, the bank encountered one series of legal problems after another including the highly publicized "London Whale" derivatives trading incident where the bank lost over $6 billion. In addition, the U.S. Department of Justice and several other civil cases over mortgage securities fraud issues had in recent years dented the company's otherwise sterling reputation in risk management. TSD had been buying up JPM stock since the crisis at an accelerated rate based on its analysis that among large banks, JPM was expected to outperform its competitors and if that scenario was realized, TSD would stand to gain significant profits. However, the stock price had been declining over the past year as JPM's legal woes continued to be front page news. As a result, TSD profits from its JPM holdings were slipping away as the price of JPM stock declined.

HEDGING USING FUTURES CONTRACTS

One way TSD could hedge the risk of JPM stock would be to take an offsetting position in a futures contract on JPM. TSD would enter into a three-month **futures contract** to sell JPM stock at a prearranged price today for delivery at a date in the future. Since TSD owns JPM stock, TSD would need to sell futures at a futures price that generated a profit for the department that offsets losses if JPM stock price declines. Figure 12.2 presents this hedge using JPM futures contracts in the same amount of stock held in portfolio for a one-year contract with a futures price of $50, the current price of TSD holdings of stock in the portfolio. As shown in the figure, this simple hedge would completely offset the risk of holding JPM stock across all possible prices, leaving the combined position of owning the stock and selling the futures contract at a net profit of zero, absent transactions costs. TSD's risk is not from price increases in JPM, however, and the futures contract does not provide the flexibility to TSD to only provide an offset when JPM price declines and still allow TSD to earn a profit as the price rises for the long position. For that strategy, an options contract would be preferred and is examined in more detail later in this chapter.

This simple hedge example provides a perfect hedge against losses that could be sustained on the long position should JPM stock price drop. If for some reason JPM futures contracts were not available to TSD, an alternative futures contract could be used but would need to be adjusted for the fact that the price of the underlying (**spot** or **unhedged asset**) does not move

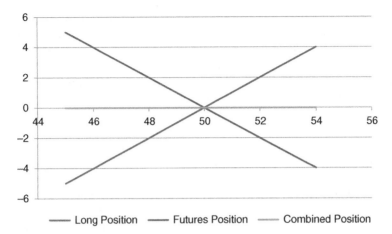

FIGURE 12.2 Futures Contract to Hedge JPM Long Position

perfectly with that of the futures price used to hedge. Consider TSD's dilemma where it cannot buy a three-month JPM futures contract for the period over which it anticipates JPM stock price volatility. Instead it finds that there is a three-month contract for Citigroup stock. This is referred to as a **cross-hedge**. Technically a cross-hedge exists when the derivative instrument has an underlying asset that is not the same as the asset to be hedged. Looking at a historical weekly price series of JPM and Citigroup three-month futures prices, TSD finds the relationship shown in Figure 12.3.

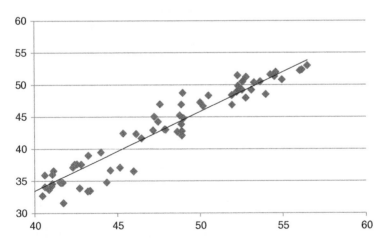

FIGURE 12.3 Weekly JPM Spot Price and Three-Month Citigroup Futures Price Relationship

There is a distinct relationship between both prices; however, they are not perfectly correlated. A simple regression line can be estimated from the two time series as shown in Figure 12.3 where JPM spot prices and Citigroup futures prices represent the dependent and independent variables, respectively. The slope of that line or β represents the change in the spot price for JPM stock for a unit change in the price of the three-month Citi futures price. Figure 12.4 presents the summary results of this regression using Excel.

The β for this relationship is .77, meaning that a $1 increase in the three-month Citi futures price would lead to a $.77 increase in JPM stock. This information is critical in establishing a hedge strategy using the three-month Citi futures contract. If TSD was interested in offsetting the entire amount of JPM stock (20 million shares) they could enter into a short futures contract. The problem is that in using the three-month Citi futures contract, the number of contracts to sell is dependent on not only the number of shares per contract but also the **basis** of the position. The basis is simply the difference between the spot price for the unhedged position and the futures price of the contract used in the hedge. In TSD's specific situation where it owns JPM stock, the profit from short hedging would be as follows:

$$\Pi_H = (S_t - S_{t+1}) + \beta(F_t - F_{t+1}) \qquad 12.1$$

where S_t and F_t are the spot and futures prices at time t. In the case of a perfect hedge there is no basis risk and β is 1. In the hedge using Citigroup three-month futures, with $\beta = .77$, there is a degree of basis risk that needs to be reflected in the number of Citigroup futures contracts to sell.

It can be shown that β is also referred to as the **optimal hedge ratio,** H^O and may be defined by the following:

$$H^O = \rho \, {}^{\sigma_S}\!\big/\!{}_{\sigma_F} \qquad 12.2$$

where ρ is the correlation between the spot JPM price and the Citigroup futures price, σ_S is the standard deviation of JPM stock price and σ_F is the standard deviation of Citigroup stock futures price. The hedge ratio is defined then as the ratio of the unit size of the futures position to the unit size of the spot position.

To illustrate how basis risk influences the hedge, consider a situation in which TSD is concerned that over the next three months JPM stock will be battered by bad press surrounding a number of regulatory and legal actions taken against the company. In this scenario TSD ignores β and assumes it to be 1. Today, JPM stock price is $50 and TSD owns 20 million shares, for a

SUMMARY OUTPUT

Regression Statistics	
Multiple R	0.85
R Square	0.71
Adjusted R Square	0.70
Standard Error	1.35
Observations	25

ANOVA

	df	SS	MS	F	Significance F
Regression	1	104.48	104.48	57.49	0.00
Residual	23	41.80	1.82		
Total	24	146.28			

	Coefficients	Standard Error	t Stat	P-value	Lower 95%	Upper 95%	Lower 95.0%	Upper 95.0%
Intercept	1.57	6.74	0.23	0.82	−12.37	15.51	−12.37	15.51
X Variable 1	0.77	0.14	5.51	0.00	0.65	1.13	0.65	1.13

FIGURE 12.4 Regression Output for JPM and Citigroup Stock Price Analysis

current period value of $1 billion. The number of futures contracts that TSD would need to sell is determined by:

$$N = \beta \frac{V_U}{C_F} \qquad 12.3$$

where V_U is the value of the JPM unhedged portfolio in the current period ($1 billion) and C_F is the dollar size (units) of one Citigroup three-month stock futures contract. One futures contract for this example is 104 shares and Citi spot stock price at time 0 is $48, or C_F equal to about $5,000. Given the other inputs, TSD plans on selling approximately 200,000 three-month Citigroup futures contracts.

The price for the three-month Citigroup futures contract today is determined by the futures pricing formula:

$$F_t = S_t e^{(r-\delta)T} \qquad 12.4$$

where r is the risk-free rate, δ is the dividend on the underlying stock, and T is time. Assuming the annualized risk-free rate is 1 percent, Citigroup pays no dividends, and the spot price for Citigroup stock is $48, the current period three-month futures price for Citigroup is:

$$\$48e^{.01(4/12)} = \$48.16 \qquad 12.5$$

Table 12.1 summarizes the impacts from this hedge. The unhedged portfolio declines by $77 million with the drop in JPM stock, however, the futures position gains $107.5 million by TSD agreeing to sell approximately 200,000 Citigroup futures contracts in three months at a futures price of $48.16 per share or $5,009 per contract. The spot price is $43 at time T and the payoff to the short futures position is $F_0 - S_T$ times the dollar size of the position. The number of contracts is computed as: $1,000,000,000

TABLE 12.1 Summary of TSD Short Futures Hedge ($\beta = 1$)

	Spot JPM Position		Futures Citigroup Position	
S_0	$	50	F_0	$	48.16
S_T	$	46.15	S_T	$	43.00
$V_{U\,t=0}$	$1,000,000,000		$V_{H\,t=0}$	$1,003,338,895
$V_{U\,t=3}$	$ 923,000,000		$V_{H\,t=3}$	$ 895,833,333
Profit	$ (77,000,000)		Profit	$ 107,505,562
Hedge Profit	$ 30,505,562			

TABLE 12.2 Summary of TSD Short Futures Hedge ($\beta = .77$)

	Spot JPM		Futures Citi
S_0	50.00	F_0	48.16
S_T	46.15	F_T	43.00
$V_{U\,t=0}$	\$1,000,000,000	$V_{U\,t=0}$	\$772,570,949
$V_{U\,t=3}$	\$ 923,000,000	$V_{U\,t=3}$	\$689,791,667
Profit/Loss	–\$ 77,000,000	Profit/Loss	\$ 82,779,283
Net Profit/Loss			\$ 5,779,283

(the current value of the JPM portfolio) times β (1) divided by the current price of Citigroup stock (\$48) times 104 (the size of each Citigroup futures contract). Hedge profit from this exercise is \$30.5M versus a loss of \$77M unhedged. However, even with this large profit TSD would be overhedged since it did not take into account the hedge ratio.

If TSD had instead hedged a short futures position by taking into account the hedge ratio estimated earlier of $\beta = H^O = .77$, the results would be quite different, as shown in Table 12.2. The first thing to notice is that TSD requires fewer futures contracts to hedge. Before, TSD sold about 200,000 Citigroup's futures contracts. Now, assuming a hedge ratio of .77, it needs to sell only 154,247 contracts based on the definition of N above. Consequently, the profit from the futures position is now \$82.8 million and the net profit from the combined hedged and unhedged position is \$5.8 million. The position where β was assumed to be one was significantly overhedged, since TSD did not take into account the fact that price volatility for JPM was less than that for Citigroup. As a result, TSD would require fewer futures contracts to hedge.

A practical consideration for TSD in executing the futures hedge includes estimating β. Since historical prices were used to estimate β, it is possible that hedge ratios will change over time as underlying relationships between the spot and futures prices change. Selecting a period of time for the sample prices in the regression model is important. The hedge manager must also consider periodically updating the hedge ratio as new data becomes available. Figure 12.5 for example, shows the daily times series for a stock price. The three lines represent different periods over which a regression model could be estimated and how the slopes of each model differ depending on the time interval used for the estimation. Using a shorter window at different periods could wind up having a materially different estimate of β than say a longer window of time. This is where experience and judgment play an important role in deciding on what data to use.

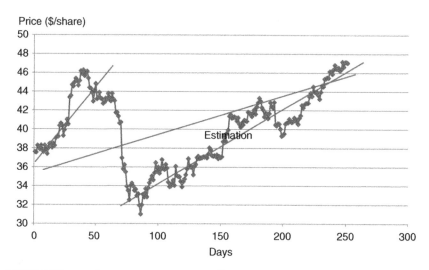

FIGURE 12.5   Stock Price Time Series and β Estimation

Another consideration in hedging a position is making sure the hedge complies with hedge accounting rules. **Financial Accounting Standard 133, Accounting for Derivative Instruments and Hedging Activities,** requires institutions to mark their derivatives transactions to market; otherwise known as **fair value accounting treatment.** The use of hedge accounting can significantly reduce the volatility of the bank's income. The TSD example presented should be defined as a cash flow hedge for accounting purposes since the risk of the unhedged JPM stock portfolio is hedged using a derivative position. The derivative's fair value would be entered onto the balance sheet at this value. The gain or loss from the change in value of the derivative would then be recorded in an entry referred to as **Other Comprehensive Income** (OCI). FAS133 also splits the hedge performance into a component that is effective and another that is ineffective. The ineffective component could be viewed as not contributing to the hedge and if large enough could be considered speculative. The effective component of the hedge would be reported as OCI and deferred from being reported in the income statement. The portion that is considered ineffective would be reported immediately as income which presents an unexpected volatility to the firm's earnings. As a general guideline, hedges are deemed effective when the percentage of the unhedged risk reduced from the hedge is between 80 and 125 percent. It turns out that the statistic describing hedge effectiveness is R^2 or **coefficient of determination.** The R^2 from Figure 12.4 is .71, suggesting that the hedge is ineffective. TSD should consider using another hedge instrument in order to take advantage of FAS 133 hedge accounting rules.

ROLLING HEDGES AND RISKS

In hedging its portfolio using futures contracts, the earlier discussion highlights the need to align the hedge with the unhedged position. Beyond the issue of cross-hedging where the same underlying asset for the derivatives is not available or at a high cost, the hedge strategy also needs to account for the potential for creating alternative forms of price risk. In the most basic case, if TSD does not hedge its position, it introduces the potential for **spot price risk**; that is, in a long position, the price of JPM stock declines from the current period over time. However, there are other price risks that TSD can face such as **futures price risk,** where price changes in the futures contracts move adversely to the bank's position, or even **basis risk** as described earlier.

Let's assume that TSD has entered into a forward contract with a counterparty, requiring it to sell 100,000 shares of Citigroup stock every month for the next three months at a price of $42.5. At the same time, TSD buys a one-month futures contract on Citigroup stock in month 1, closing out the position and entering a new one-month period in month 2 and then doing so again in month 3. The results from this **rolling three-month hedge** are shown in Table 12.3. Under these spot, forward, and futures price assumptions, the three-month forward contract makes a profit of $150,000 and the rolling hedge loses $150,000 to make net profit under this scenario 0. If TSD had

TABLE 12.3   TSD Three-Month Rolling Hedge Example

Prices	Month 1	Month 2	Month 3
S	$ 40.00	$ 42.00	$ 44.00
F (1 month)	$ 40.25	$ 42.50	$ 44.75
F (3 month)	$ 42.50		
Transactions			
Sell 100,000 Shares Citigroup Stock in Forward Contract			
Installment 1	$250,000		
Installment 2		$ 50,000	
Installment 3			$(150,000)
Buy 100,000 Shares in Futures Market			
Contract Month 1	$ (25,000)		
Contract Month 2		$(50,000)	
Contract Month 3			$ (75,000)
	$225,000	$–	$(225,000)
		Net Profit	$ –

remained unhedged but spot prices in Month 2 and 3 were instead $44 and $46, the three-month forward contract would have lost $250,000. In this case an unhedged position is exposed to spot price risk.

Now assume that the rolling hedge faces a new futures price in months 2 and 3 of $43 and $45, respectively. In this scenario, the rolling hedge now loses $225,000 causing the net profit for the combined position to be −$75,000. In this instance, TSD is exposed to futures price risk as prices rise. An alternative to the rolling hedge would be for TSD to enter into a **stack and roll hedge**. This hedge would require TSD to buy 300,000 shares of Citigroup stock in a one-month futures contract, close out that position at the end of the month, and buy a new one-month futures contract on 200,000 shares in month 2. Then, after that contract closes out, TSD would enter into another one-month contract in month 3 for 100,000 shares. The structure of a rolling hedge compared to a stack and roll hedge are shown in Figure 12.6. The width of the long position decreases over the three-month

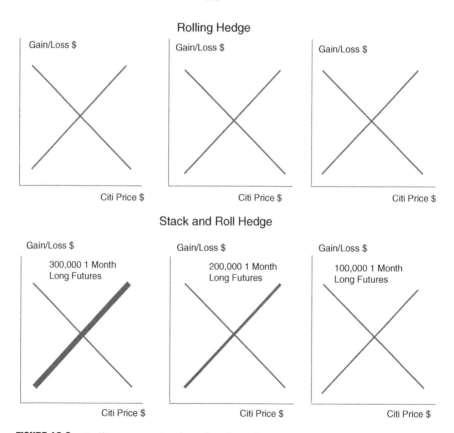

FIGURE 12.6 Rolling versus Stack and Roll Hedge

TABLE 12.4　TSD Three-Month Stack and Roll Hedge Example

Prices	Month 1	Month 2	Month 3
S	$ 40.00	$ 42.00	$ 44.00
F (1 month)	$ 40.25	$ 43.00	$ 44.50
F (3 month)	$ 42.50		
Transactions			
Sell 100,000 Shares Citigroup Stock in Forward Contract			
Installment 1	$250,000		
Installment 2		$ 50,000	
Installment 3			$(150,000)
Buy 100,000 Shares in Futures Market			
Contract Month 1	$ (75,000)		
Contract Month 2		$(200,000)	
Contract Month 3			$ (50,000)
	$175,000	$(150,000)	$(200,000)
		Net Profit	$(175,000)

period of the hedge reflecting the successive reduction of the hedge amount in shares each month as one contract for 100,000 shares expires. The gains and losses from such a position are shown in Table 12.4.

Here it is assumed that month 2 and 3 futures prices are instead $43 and $44.5, respectively. The basis in months 1, 2, and 3 is then $.25, $1, and $.5. In this scenario, the net position loses $175,000 due to the fact that the value of the stack and roll hedge loses $325,000 versus $150,000 when the basis was constant at $.25. In this case the stack and roll hedge is exposed to basis risk as the futures prices vary over the contract period.

HEDGING USING OPTIONS

A flexible way that TSD could insulate itself from further declines would be to use option contracts. Option contracts come in two basic forms: calls and puts. A **purchased call option** gives the holder of the option the right but not the obligation to buy the underlying asset at a prespecified price (the exercise or strike price). Conversely, a **put option** provides the holder with the right but not the obligation to sell the underlying asset at a prespecified price. In both cases the buyer of a call or a put option must pay a premium to the seller. The seller of a call or put option has a profit that is a mirror image of the purchased option holder's. The option seller (writer) receives the premium from the option buyer. Profits for the four basic option contracts are as follows:

$$\text{Purchased Call: } MAX((S - K,0) - c \qquad 12.5$$

$$\text{Written Call: } -MAX((S - K),0) + c \qquad 12.6$$

$$\text{Purchased Put: } MAX((K - S),0) - p \qquad 12.7$$

$$\text{Written Put: } -MAX((K - S),0) + p \qquad 12.8$$

where K is the exercise price, S is the price of JPM stock at period T, and c and p are premiums for call and put options, respectively. In terms of TSD, among the four option types, only the purchased put provides protection in the event of a price decline. This type of position is also referred to as a floor.

Assume TSD had decided to buy 100,000 put option contracts on JPM stock with a strike price of $50 and the option expires in one year. Over the next 12 months, if TSD were concerned that JPM stock price would fall, it would benefit from the increase in the option's payoff as shown in Figure 12.7. The unhedged position in JPM stock would steadily decline in a linear fashion, and the option would have no payoff should JPM prices

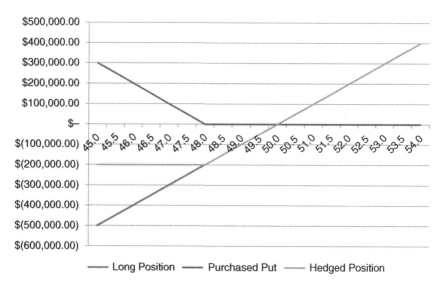

— Long Position — Purchased Put — Hedged Position

FIGURE 12.7 TSD Hedge of JPM Stock Using Purchased Put Options

rise above $50, but would show a positive payoff should JPM stock price decline. In effect, by purchasing a put option on JPM stock, TSD could immunize itself against price declines over the year. The combined position of the JPM stock and options provides upside potential should JPM stock go above $50 per share. The option thus has an advantage over the futures contract in this respect; however, the option contract is not costless given that TSD would have to pay the premium on the put options at the time of purchase. The optionality that TSD has in purchasing the put option must be reflected in the premium in order for there not to be an arbitrage opportunity between the futures contract and the option contract. If each option cost $1.25, then TSD would wind up paying $125,000 on the purchase which would reduce the company's profitability across the board for the hedged position. This would imply that even when the option is profitable (in-the-money) and the combined position is offset, TSD would still realize a loss due to the premiums paid.

One way TSD could reduce its hedging costs would be to buy put options that are **out-of-the-money**: options that would not be economical to exercise at the moment. Buying an option with a strike price that is lower than the $50 strike price in the example reduces the value of the option and correspondingly the put premiums. But lower premiums come at the expense of the lower strike put option being further out-of-the-money, compared to the $50 strike option.

In designing the hedge for JPM stock, another way of reducing option cost is to adjust the time horizon or maturity of the option contract. Longer dated American-style options tend to be more expensive; however, they offer the portfolio a longer period of protection against downturns. Determining an appropriate time horizon must factor in the expectations for holding the asset and market conditions over which losses could arise. Later on in the chapter a discussion of dynamic hedging and rollover risk will provide additional details on how to construct an effective hedge over time by rolling over hedge positions successively and maintaining a hedge as the position changes in value.

Aside from using single contracts to execute the hedge, TSD could also use a strategy that combines option contracts to offset risks from the long position over a range around a particular price of JPM stock. Two such strategies are called **spreads** and **collars**. In the case of spreads, these are formed by either using all call or put options. For TSD either a call or put **bear spread** would be a potential hedge strategy against the long JPM position. In a call bear spread, the combination of a written call with a purchased call on JPM stock with the strike price of the written option lower ($48) than the purchased option ($52) is shown in Figure 12.8.

The written call option earns TSD a premium that can be used to offset the premium it must pay on the purchased call. The net profit from both

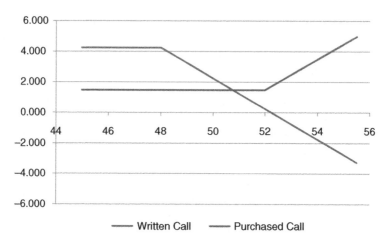

FIGURE 12.8   TSD Hedge of JPM Stock Using Purchased Put Options at Lower Strike Price

options over the range of $45 to $54 is shown in Figure 12.9 along with the net position from the spread and the long unhedged position in JPM stock. The bear spread benefits when prices move from $52 to $48, helping to offset losses from the unhedged long position in that range. When paired with the unhedged position, it is easy to see how the bear spread can soften

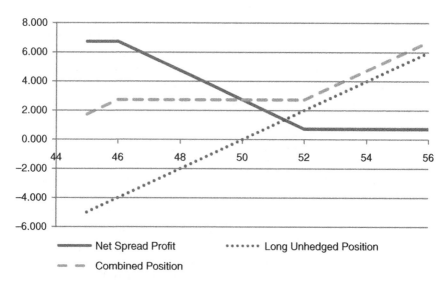

FIGURE 12.9   Call Bear Spread Hedge Strategy

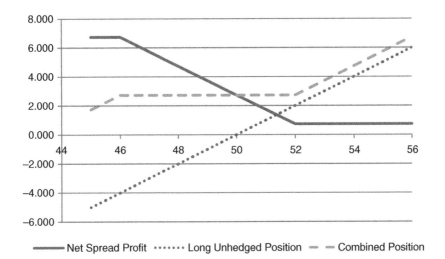

FIGURE 12.10 Spread Position and Combined Position for JPM Portfolio for $46 Strike Call

the losses to holding JPM stock while also dampening gains when the price rises within a price range.

It should be evident from these figures that establishing the strike prices for the two options is an important consideration in designing the hedge strategy. The price of both options is a function of several factors such as the price and volatility of JPM stock, the time to maturity for the options, dividends, and the risk-free rate.[1] In addition, the strike price also influences option pricing and so this must factor into hedge design weighed against such issues as what price risk TSD is trying to guard against as well as the cost of the hedge. For call options, a lower strike price leads to a higher option price, all things equal. For instance, setting a strike price at $46 instead of $48 would result in the combined position, as shown in Figures 12.10 and 12.11.

While the focus in this example was on a call bear spread, the exact hedge outcome could be obtained by using put options instead. A written put option as in the original example with a strike price of $48 could be

---

[1]The Black-Scholes option pricing model, while beyond the scope of this discussion provides an analytical solution to pricing call and put options using the factors described in this section.

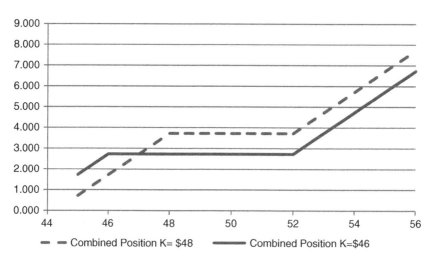

FIGURE 12.11 Combined Positions for Call Bear Spreads at Strike Prices of $46 and $48

combined with a purchased put with a strike price of $52 to achieve the same net position as the $48–$52 bear call spread. In the case of where a short unhedged position exists, TSD could have employed a **call or put bull spread** where the only difference from the bear spread is that the lower strike option is the purchased call or put for the bull spread.

An alternative hedge strategy for TSD from the bear spread is to execute a collar. A collar involves both call and put options, unlike spreads. A **purchased collar** would be appropriate for TSD given their long position in JPM stock. TSD would purchase a put option and write a call option where the strike price on the call is greater than that for the put. Both options would be on JPM stock as in the spread example and also would have the same time to expiration.

Assume that TSD decides to investigate a purchased collar that has the same width and price range as the combined position in Figures 12.9 and 12.10. The **collar width** is determined as the difference between the two strike prices, or $4 ($52–$48). TSD could buy a put option with a strike price of $48 and write a call option on JPM stock at a strike price of $52. The resulting combined position from this purchased collar is shown in Figures 12.12 and 12.13.

Notice that over the same range of strike prices, the collar is flat, whereas the spread position declines in profit as prices rise. In the case of the spread, the combined hedged and unhedged position shown in Figure 12.9

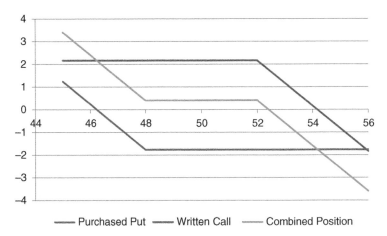

FIGURE 12.12   Purchased Collar to Hedge JPM Stock Portfolio

winds up being flat in the range between the two strike prices. Contrast that to the combined collar and long stock position shown in Figure 12.13. The collar-long position results in having the overall position flatten out for prices beyond each strike price while allowing the position to benefit from gains in stock price in the strike price interval. In other words, TSD would give up some profit when JPM stock prices rise above $52 but mitigates losses it would face when prices drop below $48.

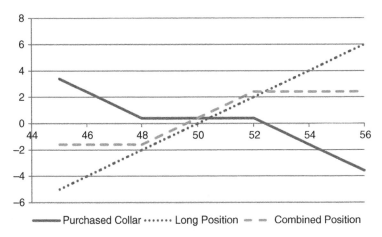

FIGURE 12.13   Purchased Collar, Long Position, and Combined Outcome

Under the call bear spread example the bank would realize a small but constant profit within the strike price range, but then profit from price increases above \$52 and suffer losses below \$48. These losses would still be less than the unhedged position. Clearly the TSD management team has many factors to consider in determining which hedge strategy is best suited for their problem.

DELTA HEDGING

Hedging is typically a dynamic exercise taking into account changes in the value of the unhedged and hedged positions. In the specific case of options used to hedge a portfolio, hedging TSD's JPM portfolio exposure can be accomplished by taking advantage of an important concept in option pricing known as the **replicating portfolio**. Conceptually, it can be shown that one purchased call option is equivalent to purchasing delta shares of the underlying asset plus borrowing to buy the stock. More formally this is represented as:

$$P_C = \Delta P_A - e^{rt} B \qquad 12.9$$

where P_C is the price of one call option, Δ is the delta of the call option, P_A is the price of the underlying asset, and B is the amount borrowed. To illustrate the ideas behind delta hedging, suppose TSD wanted to immunize its long position over some price level. The department could leverage their knowledge about the replicating portfolio by writing call options on JPM stock over this period since they want a hedge asset that will offset the performance of the long stock portfolio over some price range in the event JPM's stock price declines. As shown earlier, TSD holds 20 million shares of JPM stock that has a current (Week 0) price of \$50 per share. Using a Black-Scholes option pricing model, a one-year call option on JPM stock having a strike price of \$50 that has a standard deviation of 10 percent, no dividend, a 1 percent annual risk-free rate, and the call price is \$2.243. The call delta is defined as the following:

$$\Delta = \frac{\partial C}{\partial S} = e^{-\delta(T-t)} N(d_1) \qquad 12.10$$

where the term on the right-hand side of the above formula is derived from the Black-Scholes expression. Specifically, for an equity option, δ is the dividend yield on the stock. The delta of a put option may be similarly derived. The **call delta** may be interpreted as the change in the price of the option for a \$1 increase in the stock price. Using the inputs to the Black-Scholes option pricing model above for week 0, the call delta is approximately .56.

This would mean that a $1 increase in JPM stock would lead to a $.56 increase in the value of the option. Since the payoff to the call option is defined as *Max(S–K,0)*, as *S* increases, the value of the call must also increase, but typically does not do so at a one-to-one ratio. A call delta is bounded between 0 and 1, whereas a put delta ranges between –1 and 0. Note that intuitively a put delta must be negative given its relationship to the put and stock price. For a call option, the option is increasingly in-the-money as it moves from 0 to 1 and vice versa for a put option.

To employ the delta hedging strategy, TSD must determine how many call options it needs to sell. This can be determined as the following:

$$N_C = \frac{N_S}{\Delta_C Q_C} \qquad 12.11$$

where N_S is the number of shares of JPM stock in the portfolio, and Q_C is the number of shares of JPM stock per call option contract. Using the call delta from above, TSD needs to sell 357,387 call options on JPM stock. At an option price of $2.243, each option contract is priced at $224.3, making the value of the call portfolio $80.1 million.

Over the course of week 1, JPM stock moves up to $50.71. As a result, the call price has changed for two reasons affecting the Black-Scholes option pricing model: The stock price has increased and the time to expiration of the option (one year) is now one week closer to maturing. The model would then use the new JPM price and a time to expiration of 51/52. This yields a new call price of $263.5 per contract and likewise the call delta has increased to .6144. Given the change in the call delta, TSD would need to rebalance the hedge portfolio by decreasing the number of call options it sells to 325,496. Over this one-week period, the JPM long stock portfolio makes $14.2 million, while the call option value declines by just over $14 million. Remember that the call portfolio declines as call value increases since it is a short position. These results can be seen in Table 12.5. Over the week, the borrowing costs associated with maintaining the stock portfolio have cost TSD about $176,909 leaving a net profit of $13,521, a negligible amount relative to the JPM portfolio value. This exercise is played out over the next 11 weeks in periods where the stock price goes up and down. Net profit over the period remains relatively negligible throughout the hedge period.

There is a reason that the net profit over the hedge period is as small as it is. Embedded in the example was an assumption that JPM stock prices moved each week by 1 standard deviation. In another path-breaking analysis, Black and Scholes demonstrated that if a stock's price changes by one standard deviation up or down, then delta-hedging a portfolio will realize

TABLE 12.5 Delta Hedging of TSD JPM Stock Portfolio over a 12-Week Period

Week	0	1	2	3	4	5
JPM Price	$ 50.00	50.71	50.02	49.34	50.04	49.36
Shares of JPM	20,000,000	20,000,000	20,000,000	20,000,000	20,000,000	20,000,000
JPM Portfolio Value	$1,000,000,000	$1,014,200,000	$1,000,425,017	$ 986,837,128	$1,000,809,870	$ 987,216,754
Required Number of Written Call Options	357,387	325,496	357,093	397,235	356,774	397,747
Option Price	$ 224.30	$ 263.50	$ 220.60	$ 182.00	$ 216.80	$ 178.10
Call Portfolio Value	$ 80,161,904					
Call Delta	0.5596	0.6144	0.560	0.5035	0.5606	0.5028
Gain/Loss on JPM Portfolio		$ 14,200,000	$ (13,774,983)	$ (13,587,889)	$ 13,972,742	$ (13,593,116)
Gain/Loss on Call Portfolio		$ (14,009,570)	$ 13,963,778	$ 13,783,790	$ (13,823,778)	$ 13,807,154
Net Gain		$ 190,430	$ 188,796	$ 195,901	$ 148,964	$ 214,038
Financing		$ (176,908.95)	$ (195,057.22)	$ (192,407.93)	$ (189,794.62)	$ (192,481.94)
Hedged Profit		$ 13,521	$ (6,261)	$ 3,493	$ (40,831)	$ 21,556
Hedge Profit as % of JPM Portfolio Value		0.0013	-0.0006	0.0004	-0.0041	0.0022

Week	6	7	8	9	10	11	12
JPM Price	50.06	49.38	48.71	48.05	47.39	46.75	46.12
Shares of JPM	20,000,000	20,000,000	20,000,000	20,000,000	20,000,000	20,000,000	20,000,000
JPM Portfolio Value	$1,001,194,871	$ 987,596,526	$ 974,182,875	$ 960,951,410	$ 947,899,656	$935,025,172	$ 922,325,551
Required Number of Written Call Options	356,424	398,281	452,601	523,993	620,852	750,718	933,672
Option Price	$ 212.90	$ 174.20	$ 140.20	$ 110.60	$ 85.20	$ 64.40	$ 47.30
Call Portfolio Value							
Call Delta	0.5611	0.5022	0.4419	0.3817	0.3221	0.2664	0.2142
Gain/Loss on JPM Portfolio	$ 13,978,117	$ (13,598,345)	$ (13,413,651)	$ (13,231,465)	$ (13,051,754)	$ (12,874,484)	$ (12,699,621)
Gain/Loss on Call Portfolio	$ (13,841,596)	$ 13,793,609	$ 13,541,554	$ 13,396,990	$ 13,309,422	$ 12,913,722	$ 12,837,278
Net Gain	$ 136,522	$ 195,263	$ 127,903	$ 165,524	$ 257,668	$ 39,238	$ 137,657
Financing	$ (189,867.63)	$ (192,555.99)	$ (189,940.67)	$ (187,360.88)	$ (184,816.12)	$ (182,305.92)	$ (179,829.82)
Hedged Profit	$ (53,346)	$ 2,707	$ (62,038)	$ (21,837)	$ 72,852	$ (143,068)	$ (42,173)
Hedge Profit as % of JPM Portfolio Value	−0.0053	0.0003	−0.0064	−0.0023	0.0077	−0.0153	−0.0046

367

a net profit of zero when considering financing costs.[2] More precisely, the **Black-Scholes partial differential equation** (PDE), not to be confused with the Black-Scholes option pricing formula from which the call delta was derived above, shows mathematically that such a portfolio should only earn the risk-free rate. This is represented as the following:

$$rC_t = \Theta + r\Delta S_t + .5\sigma^2 S_t^2 \Gamma_t \qquad 12.12$$

where C_t is the call option premium, σ is the volatility of the stock price, Θ is the theta of the call option representing the change in the call value as the option moves through time toward expiration, and Γ_t is the option's **gamma**, or the change in delta as the underlying stock price changes.

Mathematically, gamma is just the second order condition on the call delta. Gamma for a purchased call option will be greater than or equal to zero. Delta, gamma, and **theta** (reflecting option price sensitivity to changes in time) are an important subset of the "**Greeks**" often discussed alongside the Black-Scholes option pricing model.

TSD's hedge managers could employ a useful short-cut in delta hedging their portfolio by applying an approximation for delta in their analysis. In spirit this is akin to the use of duration approximations in fixed income analysis as will be seen shortly. Under this approach an estimate of the call value in the following week could be derived by the following:

$$C_{t+1} = C_t + \Delta_t (S_{t+1} - S_t) \qquad 12.13$$

If TSD applied this approach to estimating the call value for week 1, it would determine the value of the call option as:

$$\$2.6403 = \$2.243 + .5596(\$50.71 - \$50)$$

The fair value of the call option from the Black-Scholes pricing model is $2.635. The error has to do with the fact that the delta approximation is a simple linear computation and hence ignores the nonlinearity of the call option's value that is due to gamma. This is analogous to the duration concept in fixed income analysis which is a linear approximation of the impact of changes in yield on bond price. A convexity correction factor may be used to improve the error of the duration approximation to the bond's true price. The analogy to the option value problem can be observed

---

[2]Note that the example shown in Table 12.3 results in small positive and negative profits over the 12-week period which are due to rounding and other simplifying assumptions.

from Figure 12.14. In the diagram, the relationship between option price and stock price is nonlinear, and when movements in stock price are small around the initial price, the delta approximation works reasonably well. However, for large movements up or down in stock price, the delta approximation results in more error. One way to reduce that error is to add a gamma correction factor to the delta approximation. This may be represented as the following:

$$C_{t+1} = C_t + \Delta_t(S_{t+1} - S_t) + .5(S_{t+1} - S_t)^2 \Gamma \qquad 12.14$$

Turning back to the original example, the call gamma is computed as:

$$\Gamma = \frac{e^{-\delta T} N'(d_1)}{S\sigma\sqrt{T}} \qquad 12.15$$

where $N'(d_1)$ is the standard normal probability density function. The value of gamma for the call option at week 0 is .076. Making this adjustment to the delta approximation yields an estimate for the call option of:

$$\$2.6595 = \$2.243 + .5596(\$50.71 - \$50) + .5(\$50.71 - \$50)^2(.076)$$

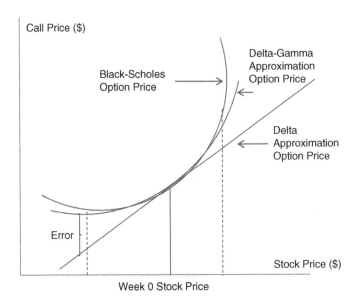

FIGURE 12.14 Delta, Delta-Gamma Approximations Compared to Fair Option Pricing

This is almost exactly equal to the call price of $2.66. A correction for theta could be applied to further true up the approximation to the fair price. In the case of TSD, the price changes each week were relatively small, making the delta approximation reasonable for computing the hedge. However, had there been large changes in JPM price, relying on a delta approximation could have introduced hedging errors.

One approach to accounting for large swings in the price of the unhedged position is to augment the option position with a set of options that leave the gamma of the position neutral. In the case of the written $50, one-year call options, TSD would need to offset the gamma of these options by purchasing a set of call options. In this case, suppose it selects some out-of-the money JPM call options with a strike price of $53 and 6 months to expiration. The gamma in this case is .07. For every call option it writes, it would need to buy .076/.07, or 1.086 $53 strike call options to leave it in a gamma neutral position. This can be shown as:

$$-.076 = .07(1.086)$$

Note that gamma for the written option is negative while for the purchased position it is positive. These positions when applying the ratio of the two gammas then offset each other.

SUMMARY

While constructing a hedge using a derivative instrument is a fairly straightforward exercise, there are a multitude of considerations involved that make hedge strategy a complicated activity. Deciding on which derivative instruments to use depends upon a number of issues including the ultimate aim of the hedge strategy, pricing and market liquidity of the derivatives, duration, and amount of exposure to hedge, availability of instruments, and accounting issues. Option contracts require the buyer to pay and the seller to receive a premium for the right but not the obligation to exercise the option. Options can thus provide cash flow when sold and provide upside potential with downside protection, which make them attractive in many instances to hedge.

An important factor in hedging is having a view of what could potentially happen to the portfolio. This might be as simple as developing a forecast of likely outcomes for a portfolio or asset or as complex as developing a market VaR limit that must be complied with by management. In Chapter 10, for instance, VaR limits form the basis for determining the outer boundary for acceptable risk in the portfolio, and when these are breached actions must be taken to bring them back into tolerance. Hedging provides management with an effective way to stay within the VaR limits while not having to engage in costly portfolio sales or rebalancing exercises that can undermine the strategic value of the portfolio in the first place. Hedging, however, is not without a cost, and so will affect the bottom line of the operating unit. As a result, in some cases it can be difficult to gain management consent to a costly hedge strategy, particularly when profits and market share targets are under pressure. Nonetheless, portfolio hedging is a staple of the risk manager's risk mitigation toolkit and understanding both the mechanics and strategy of hedging arms the analyst with the right combination of abilities to maintain risk exposure of the firm within stated objectives.

QUESTIONS

1. You have a long position in Stock 1 and would like to hedge it using a three-month futures contract on Stock 2. A series of daily prices is provided below. What is the hedge ratio for this transaction?

Day	Stock 1	Stock 2
1	51.94	48.4
2	52.24	48.89
3	52.8	51.21
4	52.59	50.49
5	52.56	49.22
6	50.53	48.33
7	52.32	49.83
8	53.29	50.35
9	54.52	51.32
10	56.49	53
11	56.05	52.21
12	56.16	52.35
13	54.97	50.81
14	53.99	48.53
15	52.79	47.97

(*continued*)

(*Continued*)

Day	Stock 1	Stock 2
16	51.96	46.87
17	53.13	49.22
18	54.27	51.6
19	54.59	51.99
20	53.66	50.52
21	52.3	51.45
22	48.96	48.75
23	47.57	46.97
24	48.88	46.92
25	47.23	45.03

2. You have a $500 million long portfolio in Stock 1 that has a current price of $55 per share, the risk-free interest rate is 2 percent, and there are no dividends. The size of each three-month futures contract is 250 shares. The current price of Stock 2 is $45 and at time T it is $43.9 per share. What are the number of contracts needed to implement this hedge?
3. Produce a table like that shown in Table 12.2. What position do you take in the three-month futures contract (long or short), and what is the net hedge profit?
4. You have been provided the following information. Produce a table similar to Table 12.3 where you enter into a forward contract to sell 250,000 shares of stock for the next three months at the price shown in the table below and you also enter into a rolling three-month hedge.

Prices	Month 1	Month 2	Month 3
S	$25.00	$27.00	$30.00
F (1 month)	$26.00	$28.00	$31.00
F (3 month)	$28.50		

5. Repeat the above, but now instead of the rolling hedge you implement a stack and roll hedge.
6. In a graph and table, demonstrate what a put bull spread looks like. What type of position would this provide a hedge for, that is, long or short?

7. In a graph and table, demonstrate what a written collar looks like. What type of position would this provide a hedge for, that is, long or short?

The price of an underlying nondividend paying stock today is $100. Using a Black-Scholes option pricing model you calculate d_1 to be .5. The risk-free interest rate is 2 percent. A one-year call option premium on this stock is $3.

8. What is the delta for this option and what can you infer about whether it is more likely in- or out-of-the-money?
9. How much would you need to borrow to establish a replicating portfolio for the call option?
10. This stock has a price a day later of $101. The value of the standard normal PDF evaluated at d_1 is .6 and the volatility of the stock is .3. What would you predict the next day's call option price to be and how did you arrive at that conclusion?

CHAPTER 13

Hedging Interest Rate Risk

OVERVIEW

An integral part of SifiMortgage's business is its activities in the mortgage secondary market. The bank has the benefit of either originating and holding whole mortgage loans in its portfolio (referred to as the held-for-investment, HFI portfolio), or delivering loans to the secondary market, principally through loan sales to Fannie Mae and Freddie Mac. The primary mortgage market describes the process by which a borrower obtains a mortgage loan from a lender. The lender, in this case SifiMortgage, may find for a number of reasons that selling the loan into the secondary market rather than holding it is a preferred strategy economically.

There are a number of processes SifiMortgage must go through before a loan can be packaged up with other loans and sold to Fannie Mae or Freddie Mac. A borrower first will approach a lender about obtaining a **loan commitment** from the lender to have a loan at a prearranged interest rate today for settlement of the home sometime in the future. Usually such a commitment ranges from 30 to 90 days in length, during which the lender agrees to "lock in" the interest rate for the borrower. This takes away considerable uncertainty about the direction of interest rates for the borrower while the closing process works its way through, however, it also creates substantial interest rate risk for the lender.

The accumulation of mortgage commitments over time is referred to as the mortgage pipeline. The pipeline does not consist of actual loans but rather commitments to borrowers to provide funding at prescribed mortgage rates sometime in the future. Once commitments close, they turn into inventory that is placed into a virtual mortgage warehouse that SifiMortgage will use for a short period while it determines where to eventually place the loan (sell or retain). The timeline for a loan is represented in Figure 13.1. The commitment period extends for 1–3 months followed by a short period in the warehouse, at which point it becomes a loan that is eventually retained

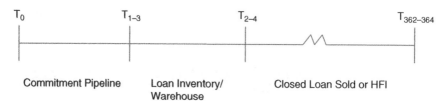

T_0	T_{1-3}	T_{2-4}	$T_{362-364}$
Commitment Pipeline	Loan Inventory/ Warehouse	Closed Loan Sold or HFI	

FIGURE 13.1 SifiMortgage Mortgage Loan Lifecycle

by SifiMortgage, sold for cash or for an MBS (securitized). Mortgage commitments have features that act very much like a standard bond in the sense that commitment prices move inversely with interest rates under most conditions. However, the rate lock provision for the borrower can be viewed as an option provided to the borrower that will be exercised when it is in the borrower's financial interest to do so. Suppose that SifiMortgage enters into a loan commitment with a borrower today at 4 percent on a fixed-rate 30-year loan of $200,000. As long as the borrower closes the loan in three months, the 4 percent note rate is what the borrower will pay on the loan amount. If rates on mortgages were to rise to 4.5 percent in 90 days, the borrower exercises the option to close the loan as agreed with SifiMortgage. Alternatively, if interest rates decline to 3.5 percent over the next 90 days, the borrower would be less likely to close. The act of not closing on the loan is referred to as pipeline fallout and is a variation on the concept of mortgage prepayment for an actual mortgage. From the borrower's perspective, the rate commitment is like a purchased put option that is free to the borrower. The 4 percent interest rate can be viewed as the strike price, or alternatively the current price of the commitment (let's assume it is valued at par or $200,000). Figure 13.2 illustrates the nature of this option. By being in a long position with these commitments, the lender faces interest rate risk from rate increases as the value of the commitments will decline. The lender can mitigate some of this risk by shorting an appropriate hedge instrument but if the firm does not account for the embedded option of the commitment it could wind up over- or underhedged as a result.

SifiMortgage has a monthly mortgage pipeline of fixed-rate 30-year amortizing loan commitments with interest rates varying between 4 and 4.5 percent over the year. For this hedging exercise, one month's production in the pipeline of $100 million in commitments with rates of 4 percent represent the unhedged position for the mortgage company. One way for SifiMortgage to avoid the rate and subsequent price uncertainty would be to enter into a forward agreement with Fannie Mae or Freddie Mac to sell these loans. If interest rates rise over the period, SifiMortgage would

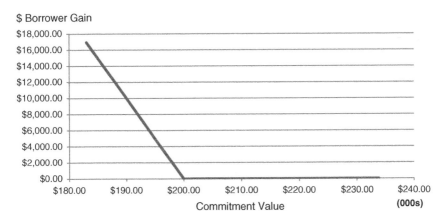

FIGURE 13.2 Borrower Rate Commitment as Put Option

gain the amount of the difference between the forward contracted price (e.g., $200,000) and the prevailing mortgage price (e.g., $187,000). Similarly if rates decline, the value of the short forward contract to SifiMortgage declines.

The problem for SifiMortgage is determining exactly how many commitments will close and hence turn into loans. If SifiMortgage were to sell 1,000 loans forward to Fannie Mae in 90 days, and rates remain the same, then 1,000 loans will actually close (we will disregard the fact for the moment that in reality there will be some borrowers who will fall out for various reasons), matching the number of loans in the forward sale agreement. However, if interest rates decline, it could be that SifiMortgage closes only 700 loans, in which case it has overhedged its interest rate risk via the forward sale since it did not correctly take into account fallout risk. Alternatively, if interest rates were to rise, and SifiMortgage expected 900 loans to close (there will always be some amount of fallout even if rates rise) and entered into a forward sale on 900 loans but 950 turned out to close as a result of even higher than expected interest rates in the period, SifiMortgage would be underhedged. To gain a better perspective on the relationships involved in managing mortgage pipeline risk, consider Table 13.1. Given the fluctuation in interest rates over time, SifiMortgage needs to hedge the pipeline taking fallout into account.

The remainder of this chapter focuses on the various hedge instruments available to SifiMortgage in hedging its mortgage pipeline, what issues and considerations SifiMortgage must take into account when establishing its hedge strategy including basis risk, the impact of time on

TABLE 13.1 Interest Rate Impacts on Mortgage Prices and Fallout

Rate Scenario	Mortgage Price Impact	Fallout Impact
Rise	Decrease	Lower
Flat	No change	Very low
Decline	Increase	Higher

the value of the hedge position, and liquidity and transactions costs. An effective hedge strategy is likely to incorporate multiple hedge instruments and analytically sophisticated risk managers could develop a hedge optimization capability to determine what combinations of hedge instruments are required to immunize the pipeline from interest rate risk over a variety of rate scenarios.

HEDGE INSTRUMENT ALTERNATIVES

To hedge the mortgage pipeline, SifiMortgage has a number of alternative hedge instruments from which to use. These include Treasury and MBS futures contracts, as well as call and put option contracts. Each of these instruments will be evaluated against a set of criteria assessing their strengths and weaknesses as viable hedge instruments, specifically, the effects of basis risk, time decay on options, and liquidity and costs.

Futures and Forwards

At the simplest level, SifiMortgage could enter into a short 10-year Treasury futures contract to hedge the interest rate risk on the effective long position it has in the mortgage pipeline. The 10-year Treasury futures contract is selected based in part on the need to have a hedge instrument that has a comparable duration with the unhedged position. The coupon bond nature of the 10-year Treasury implies that the duration of the underlying Treasury note is less than 10 years depending on yields and the Treasury's coupon rate. Similarly, due to prepayment risk and the monthly cash flows of the mortgage, a mortgage will have a duration well below its 30-year maturity. From a liquidity perspective, using Treasury futures to hedge the commitment pipeline might make sense as it could be a relatively inexpensive way to hedge this risk. However, doing so ignores the impact of prepayment and fallout on the mortgage and commitment. This divergence is presented in Figure 13.3.

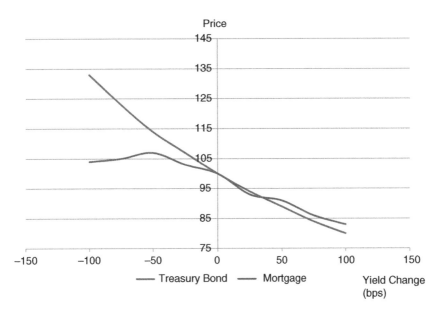

FIGURE 13.3 Treasury and Fannie Mae MBS Pricing Relationships

In Figure 13.3, the price of the mortgage and Treasury bond are well-aligned up to a point. As interest rates decline to some level below the note rate on the mortgage or commitment, borrowers will prepay causing this option to become more valuable to the borrower. This price compression as yields decline for mortgages is referred to as **negative convexity** and illustrates the problem associated with hedging mortgage-related contracts using instruments such as Treasuries that do not have this embedded option. Hence a hedge using short Treasury futures would not provide a sufficient offset to losses on long mortgage positions across all interest rate scenarios, particularly those at relatively lower rates. This can be seen in Figure 13.4, which graphs a short Treasury futures contract against a long position in a mortgage.

In this situation, although price for the mortgage rises to a point as rates fall, it does not keep up with the change in Treasury futures price, leading to a loss in the hedge position under low rate scenarios. This difference in price movement between the mortgage and Treasuries leads to basis risk. Preferably, SifiMortgage would want to construct a hedge strategy that leaves the net position relatively flat to any changes in interest rates over the period in question.

To avoid basis risk from using Treasury futures to hedge the mortgage position, SifiMortgage could sell forward contracts on mortgage-backed

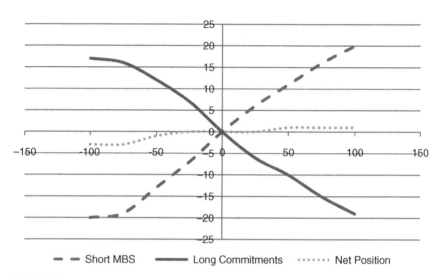

FIGURE 13.4 Short MBS Futures Hedge and Long Mortgage Position

securities (MBS). Such instruments will reflect the embedded optionality of the underlying mortgages in the security and thus avoid the outcome shown in Figure 13.3. However, the hedge manager must take into consideration the liquidity of such MBS futures contracts. Liquidity becomes an issue in determining what hedge instruments to use as the cost of hedging must be controlled. In fact the objective function of the hedge manager should be the following:

$$\sum_{i=1}^{R}\left(V_i^U - V_i^H + C_i\right) = 0 \qquad 13.1$$

where V_i^U and V_i^H represent the change in value for the unhedged and hedged position under rate scenario i, and C_i represents the costs associated with hedging rate scenario i.

Hedging costs can become quite expensive when using purchased option contracts to execute the hedge. In the case of futures contracts, the transactions costs associated with entering and then eventually unwinding contracts are affected by the **bid-ask spread** of the futures contract of interest. The wider the spread between what the hedge manager will pay to enter into the contract (**ask**) and unwind the contract (**bid**), generally the less liquidity there is in the contract and thus the costlier it will be to use in the hedge strategy. In the case of MBS forwards versus Treasury futures contracts, the hedge manager will need to assess differences in bid-ask spreads as a criterion for determining which futures contract to use.

Options

Even though using MBS forward contracts would address basis risk concerns, they would not be able to successfully hedge fallout risk in the pipeline. Recall that fallout is effectively like granting the borrower a free put option, and as a result this optionality would need to be offset in SifiMortgage's hedging strategy. In this regard, SifiMortgage's hedge strategy becomes a bit more complicated as it needs to decompose the types of risks it has in the pipeline. In looking at its historical pipeline performance over a variety of interest rate cycles, SifiMortgage is aware that 50 percent of its loans regardless of interest rate conditions will turn into closed loans. From this perspective, selling Treasury futures contracts on this portion of the pipeline would be an appropriate hedge strategy since they know that a portion of the pipeline will always close. In addition, the data also inform SifiMortgage analysts that on average 10 percent of the pipeline always falls out; no hedge is required on this portion of the pipeline. For the remaining 40 percent of the portfolio there is some likelihood that the commitments will not close (i.e., will fall out), and for these commitments option contracts would be a likely hedge instrument.

A central concept in understanding the likelihood that the borrower put option will be exercised is the option delta. The delta of an option measures the change in the value of the option (i.e., its premium) for a $1 change in the price of the underlying asset; specifically the mortgage (prepayment option) or commitment (close option) for this chapter. It can be derived formally from the Black-Scholes option pricing model as the first-order condition:

$$\Delta_P = \frac{\partial P}{\partial M} = -e^{-T} N\left(-\frac{\ln(M/K + (r + .5\sigma^2)T)}{\sigma\sqrt{T}} \right) \qquad 13.2$$

where $N(.)$ is the standard normal distribution, M is the mortgage (or commitment) price, K is the strike price, r is the risk-free rate, σ is the volatility of the mortgage price, and T is the expiration period (commitment period) of the rate lock. For a put option, the value of the premium moves inversely with the price of the underlying asset. As a result, the put delta ranges between 0 and -1.[1] A depiction of the borrower's put delta over a range of mortgage prices is found in Figure 13.5. For a loan commitment, delta measures the likelihood that the borrower will close the loan at the end of the

---

[1] For implementation purpose, the negative sign on the put delta will be ignored.

commitment period. Conversely, $1 - \Delta$ is referred to as the fallout rate. Consider an extreme scenario where interest rates decrease by 100bps during the commitment period. In this situation, the price of the mortgage would rise, notwithstanding prepayment effects, and the borrower would have an economic incentive to fallout of the pipeline and enter into a lower commitment rate. In this circumstance, the put option to close the loan has no value to the borrower and the option expires effectively out-of-the-money. In others words, there is a negligible probability that the commitment will go to closing. At the other extreme is a scenario where interest rates rise 100bps during the commitment period. In this situation, the price of the mortgage declines as rates rise and the option is deep in-the-money for the borrower. If rates lead to a mortgage price that is reflected at the lower left side of Figure 13.5, then for every $1 *decrease* in the price of the mortgage, the put option *increases* by $1.

In this case there is a very high likelihood that the commitment will close. Calculating this put delta then becomes an integral part of the pipeline hedging exercise for commitments where there is some uncertainty over the closing of these commitments.

The option delta is also referred to as the hedge ratio of the option as it may be used in determining how many option contracts to use against the unhedged portion of the pipeline subject to fallout risk. There are a few

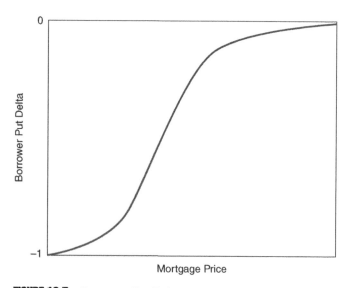

FIGURE 13.5 Borrower Put Delta

ways to estimate the put delta from very simplistic to more complicated. A simple approach would be to calculate the ratio of commitments that close to total commitments over a given period. Such an approach provides some general indication of the fallout propensity; however, it ignores a variety of factors that could differentiate closing potential. For example, a key driver of a borrower's likelihood of falling out would be current interest rates. Thus, constructing a variable that compares the difference between the borrower's commitment rate to prevailing mortgage rates could be used in gaining more precision on the incentive to close the loan. Other factors influencing the fallout decision include borrower characteristics such as income, age, and occupation, as well as the state where the property is located, product features, season, and channel in which the loan was sourced. Fortunately, SifiMortgage has accumulated this information into a commitment level historical fallout database that allows it to estimate a statistically based fallout model predicting the likelihood that a commitment will close based on these characteristics. Such models are similar to the binary choice default and prepayment models described elsewhere in this book where in the case of fallout, the dependent variable is coded as 1 if the commitment closes and 0 otherwise. It should be clear by now that even if the put option is in-the-money, some borrowers for whatever reason will not exercise the option. In theory, whenever the option is economically attractive to exercise, the borrower should ruthlessly exercise. This outcome is also referred to as **efficient exercise of the option.** However, other factors influence the exercise decision. Some examples include life events such as a divorce, illness, or unemployment that occur during the commitment window, or even indecision or inertia, which hold borrowers back from exercising the option.

By now it should also be expected that the hedge manager's job is complicated by the dynamic nature of the option delta. In other words, merely putting in place a set of options to offset the fallout risk would be overlooking the fact that as rates change, borrower fallout risk will change, and as a result the hedge should adjust to reflect such movements in the position's value. Using the concept of put delta, SifiMortgage hedge managers can construct a "delta hedging" strategy that can offset its pipeline fallout risk.

The first thing that the hedge managers must establish is the nature of the fallout risk to be hedged as it will inform them of what type of options positions to use as hedge instruments for this portion of the pipeline. In this case, SifiMortgage has written put options to the borrower and so should offset that risk by purchasing options either directly in the market or synthetically. For comparability, these put options should be on similar asset types such as MBS, but Treasuries, due to their liquidity, may also be used.

Since SifiMortgage would need to purchase options to offset its fallout risk, they would need to pay premiums on these options. Buying options can be an expensive proposition across such a large portfolio and minimizing hedge costs would certainly be an important consideration in determining hedge strategy. An alternative approach to buying put options outright would be to synthetically create the cash flows of a purchased put option by entering into a combination of futures and call option contracts that mimic the put option.

This approach relies on an important option pricing principle known as **Put-Call Parity**. Essentially it can be demonstrated that under no arbitrage conditions, the cost of a long forward position in an underlying asset must be equal to buying a call option and writing a put option on the same underlying asset where both options have the same strike price and time to expiration. More formally this may be represented as follows:

$$e^{-rT}F = C - P + e^{-rT}K \qquad\qquad 13.3$$

where F represents the futures (or forward) price, C and P are the call and put premiums and K is the strike price on both options. Note that in this relationship, the negative sign on the put option implies it is a written option. Graphically, Put-Call Parity is described in Figure 13.6. As is seen in Figure 13.6, the net cost of the written put plus purchased call option mimics the cash flows of the long forward contract. We can use this information then to synthetically create a long put option contract without having to

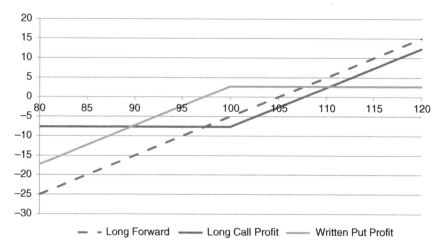

FIGURE 13.6 Put-Call Parity Relationships

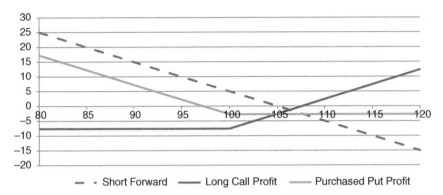

FIGURE 13.7   Synthetic Purchased Put Creation Leveraging Put-Call Parity

actually buy the option. Mathematically, we can rearrange the Put-Call Parity formula as follows:

$$P = C - e^{-rT}(F - K)$$ 13.4

In this form a purchased put option is equivalent to buying call options while simultaneously selling forward contracts on the underlying asset. This is shown in Figure 13.7.

Now applying this to mortgage pipeline hedging, SifiMortgage still would be required to pay premiums on these call options where the underlying asset could be U.S. Treasuries given market liquidity. Concurrent with the purchase of these options, SifiMortgage could sell Treasury forward contracts consistent with Put-Call Parity conditions above. The combination of the call and futures contract given the current rates and prices of Treasuries (designated as the strike price *K*), would generate the same cash flows as a purchased put on Treasuries.

Delta Hedging

As mentioned earlier, an effective strategy SifiMortgage could use to manage its pipeline risk is obtained by delta hedging. In this case, the hedge managers would estimate the delta of the fallout option by using a model such as the one previously described and over the commitment period enter into a short forward contract equal to the notional amount of the pipeline multiplied by the delta. This strategy effectively replicates a purchased option without having to actually buy the option in the market. To reinforce the effect of this strategy, consider Table 13.2. SifiMortgage's $100 million pipeline is

TABLE 13.2　SifiMortgage Realized Mortgage Pipeline Exposure

Rate Scenario	Change in Mortgage Price (bps)	Delta	Pipeline Gain/Loss
−100	265	0.2	$ 530,000
0	0	0.5	$ 0
100	−575	0.9	−$5,175,000

subject to interest rate risk under three rate scenarios: +100bps, flat (baseline), and −100bps. The change in price for each mortgage in the pipeline is shown along with the delta of the borrower put option, which reflects the percentage of commitments that will close into loans. The value of this long position is shown in the last column, indicating that in the event of a large spike in interest rates, most borrowers will exercise their option and close. Given that prices have fallen, SifiMortgage would be subject to significant losses in selling the loans into the market.

A way to hedge that risk is to employ a delta hedging strategy. In Table 13.3, SifiMortgage estimates what the put delta associated with borrower commitments should be and these are shown for the three interest rate scenarios in the third column. Since SifiMortgage uses Fannie Mae MBS futures to hedge, there is a slight difference between price effects across rate scenarios for the short futures position and mortgage commitments in Table 13.2. The underlying loans of the MBS are close but not exactly the same as those in the pipeline and so we should expect some small differences in rates and close rates as a result. Beyond that, another difference between the commitments and hedge position is in the impacts associated with fallout. Differences between the realized close rates in Table 13.2 and the estimated close rates in Table 13.3 are explained by deviations in SifiMortgage's statistical fallout model, another potential risk that is examined elsewhere in the book.

Taking the delta hedge position with the long commitments yields a net hedged position shown in Table 13.4. Under both the −100 and +100 bps

TABLE 13.3　SifiMortgage Estimated Delta Hedge Exposure

Rate Scenario	Change in Short MBS Price (bps)	Estimated Delta	Pipeline Gain/Loss
−100	−270	0.15	−$ 405,000
0	0	0.45	$ 0
100	580	0.95	$5,510,000

TABLE 13.4 Net Hedged Position from Delta Hedging

Rate Scenario	Net Hedged Position	% of Notional
−100	$125,000	0.00125
0	$ 0	0
100	$335,000	0.00335

rate scenarios the bank shows a small profit but effectively the bank is well hedged. The net hedged position as a percent of the pipeline notional amount is between .125 and .335 percent. This example assumed that SifiMortgage applied an estimate of the borrower's delta in hedging its risk at the inception of the commitment. However, as indicated in Table 13.4, the put delta will change as the underlying mortgage price and rates changes. If SifiMortgage does not account for changes in delta over the commitment period, it could wind up being over- or underhedged.

Consider, for example, that the hedge managers anticipate that at the beginning of the commitment period, SifiMortgage assigns a delta of .45 under the baseline rate scenario and holds that delta throughout the period. If interest rates rise by 100 bps, the bank will wind up suffering a loss of $2.57 million as shown in Table 13.5. In this case while the bank technically employed a delta hedge strategy, because it did not adjust or the change in delta at inception of .45 to .95 the delta over time, it wound up costing SifiMortgage.

Use of Multiple Hedge Instruments

Between developing a hedge strategy that employs only put options that may effectively offset fallout risk but is expensive and a pure delta hedging strategy using short forwards, SifiMortgage could use a combination of short forwards and option contracts to achieve the desired hedge outcome. To illustrate this approach, assume now that SifiMortgage enters into a forward agreement to sell $100 million in loans in 90 days that coincides

TABLE 13.5 Static Delta Hedge Example

Position	Price Change	Delta	Gain/Loss
Commitments	−575	0.9	−$5,175,000
Hedge Position	580	0.45	$2,610,000
Net Hedged Position			−$2,565,000

TABLE 13.6   Short Forward and Long Mortgage Commitments Net Position Gains and Losses Example

Rate Scenario	Change in Mortgage Price (bps)	Estimated Fallout	Short Forward Gain/Loss
−100	785	0.8	−$6,280,000
0	0	0.2	$ 0
100	−835	0.1	$ 835,000

with the point at which the commitments will close. The sensitivity of mortgages and associated hedge instruments such as Treasury or MBS futures to changes in interest rates introduce a complexity to the hedge strategy due to prepayment differences (negative convexity for mortgages and MBS) that lead to designing the pipeline hedge to take a more holistic perspective. As mentioned earlier, the objective of the pipeline hedge is to leave the hedged position neutral, taking into account hedging costs. In this example, where SifiMortgage has established a short forward as a natural hedge upfront on the commitments, a decrease in rates will actually lead to a loss on the short forward position adjusted for fallout of nearly $8 million. This is because the short forward payout is defined as (forward price − spot price). If the forward price were established at $101.5 per $100 of face amount of mortgages, and spot prices were now $109.35 as interest rates fall by 100bps, then SifiMortgage would experience a loss before taking fallout into account of $100 million multiplied by ($101.50 − $109.35), or −$7.85 million. However, since 20 percent of the loans close, the loss is somewhat offset by the gain in price that SifiMortgage will obtain as these long commitments turn into loans. In other words, SifiMortgage will expect a gain of about 785bps under the down 100bps rate scenario on those commitments that actually become loans. Thus, the loss on the short forward adjusted for fallout, as this is the portion of the short forward loss not offset by commitments that become loans, would be −$7.85 million multiplied by .8, or −$6.28 million (see Table 13.6). This is so because the net position consists of the change in value of the short forward $(F - S)V$, where V is the value of the pipeline, and the long commitments times the close rate, or delta of the borrower put option $(S - F)V$. Mathematically this can be shown as:

$$(F - S)V + (S - F)V\Delta = V(F - S)(1 - \Delta) \qquad 13.5$$

Applying the same rational to a +100bps rate scenario, the short forward would gain only $835,000, since 90 percent of the loans go to closing in this scenario and the long commitment position turns a loss from a large percentage of commitments becoming loans when prices fall. Graphically, these relationships across a range of rate scenarios can be seen in Figures 13.8 and 13.9. The first thing that is apparent from Figure 13.8 is the shape of the long mortgage curve. Unlike a long position in Treasuries, the curve is nonlinear, with noticeable flattening occurring as interest rates fall. This effect reflects the negative convexity in mortgage prices due to accelerated prepayment reducing the value of the mortgages. In this respect, using Treasuries as a hedge instrument could expose SifiMortgage to basis risk. Later on we will explore the trade-offs in using Treasuries and MBS futures contracts in establishing the hedge from both the impact of basis risk and cost to hedge. In an effort to offset the risk of these commitments, SifiMorgage enters into a short forward contract to deliver closed loans to Fannie Mae. If 100 percent of loans closed across all interest rate scenarios, SifiMortgage would be able to completely offset the interest rate risk of its positions by delivering the closed loans to meet the short forward delivery commitment. However, we know that the close rate on commitments drops with interest rates during the commitment period, as shown in Figure 13.9.

Note that while the put delta technically should be in the 0 to −1 range, the option is displayed in the positive domain as the estimated closing rate.

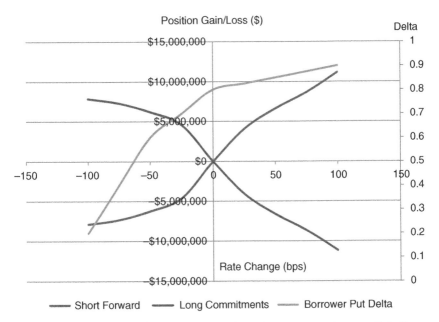

FIGURE 13.8 Short Forward and Fallout Adjusted Long Commitments Gain/Loss

With the put delta effectively changing with rate changes, it factors directly into the effectiveness of the hedge since the size of the long commitments for delivery changes dramatically for SifiMortgage. This is shown in depiction of the net position taking the put delta into account in Figure 13.9. In the extreme scenario where rates decline 100bps, the dollar value of the long commitments increases, however, only 20 percent close. Ordinarily, with all loans closing SifiMortgage could have offset its losses on the short forward with the long commitments; however, with 20 percent fewer commitments turning into loans, SifiMortgage loses an amount equal to the difference in the forward and spot prices multiplied by the 80 percent fallout rate since SifiMortgage would need to make up that difference in the market at the higher prevailing mortgage price in order to meet the terms of the short forward delivery. The effect of the borrower put option is clear in Figure 13.9. The long-short position does badly as rates decline due to the fallout issue described above, while as the option is well out-of-the-money for rate increases, gains are limited.

The example of hedging interest rate risk for a single rate scenario using a single hedge instrument oversimplifies the hedging problem. From a risk management perspective, banks would prefer to remain relatively protected under a wide range of rate scenarios. To do so may involve using

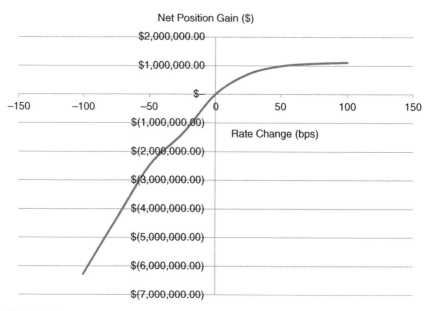

FIGURE 13.9   Net Position from Long Commitments and Short Forwards

TABLE 13.7 Treasury Futures Prices Under –100bps Interest Rate Scenario

| | Rate Scenario | | |
| | –100 bps | Baseline (Flat) | |
Treasury Futures Prices	Dollar Price	Dollar Price	Price Change
2-year Contract	110.95	109.35	1.6
5-year Contract	123.75	119.15	4.6
10-year Contract	131.25	123.85	7.4

different hedge instruments under different scenarios. To see this, consider what sort of combination hedge would offset the short forward-long commitment fallout adjusted losses (referred to as the unhedged position) under a –100bps rate scenario. For purposes of this analysis, SifiMortgage considers hedging its pipeline with three Treasury futures contracts: the 2-year, 5-year, and 10-year, as well as six purchased option contracts reflecting call and put options on each of the three Treasury futures contracts. Details on prices for the futures and options contracts are shown in Tables 13.7 and 13.8. The size of each Treasury futures and option contract is $100,000. Price changes are also shown for each hedge instrument from baseline current rate levels. Note the comparative differences in prices and price changes for the call and put options. Call options increase in price normally with the

TABLE 13.8 Treasury Option Contract Prices under –100bps Interest Rate Scenario

| | Rate Scenario | | |
| At-the-Money Purchased | –100 bps | Baseline (Flat) | |
Treasury Options Prices	Dollar Price	Dollar Price	Price Change
2-year Contracts			
Calls	1.35	0.75	0.6
Puts	0.05	0.25	–0.2
5-year Contract			
Calls	3.85	1.15	2.7
Puts	0.15	0.55	–0.4
10-year Contract			
Calls	5.55	1.75	3.8
Puts	0.35	0.85	–0.5

Note: All options have three-month expirations.

price of the underlying asset, as would be expected under the rate decline scenario depicted. Conversely, put options gain value as the price of the underlying asset declines, hence the negative values for the put options shown in Table 13.8.

Hedge Optimization Techniques

The hedge manager could formalize a strategy about which hedge instruments to use by performing a linear optimization analysis. A number of objectives could be established, such as ensuring the net position from both the unhedged and hedged positions is close to zero or some target risk tolerance. In addition, hedge costs should be minimized. In terms of hedging costs, purchased options can be expensive hedge instruments, since the option buyer for both puts and calls winds up paying the premiums for the options. By contrast, futures contracts do not require a premium; however, futures trading will entail a cost that reflects the difference in bid and ask prices in the market. As hedge managers look to enter and unwind hedge transactions, they will face different bid-ask spreads that reflect inherent liquidity in a hedge instrument. The greater the amount of transactions taking place in the market between buyers and sellers, the greater the liquidity and the narrower the bid-ask spreads. Treasuries and their associated futures contracts are highly liquid compared with other contracts, such as futures on Fannie Mae MBS. Recall that due to the potential for borrowers to prepay their mortgages when interest rates decline, mortgages and MBS prices will depart from Treasuries when rates fall. As a result, this sets up the potential for basis risk in using Treasury futures contracts; their cost may be very low compared with comparable duration MBS futures.

For SifiMortgage, the hedge constrained optimization is defined as the following:

$$\text{Min} \sum_{i=1}^{N} n_i c_i \qquad 13.6$$

Subject to

$$R_L \leq \frac{V_{UH} + \sum_{i=1}^{N} n_i V_i}{P_0} \leq R_U$$

$$n_i \geq 0$$

where n_i is the number of contracts for the ith hedge instrument, c_i is the cost associated with one contract for the ith hedge instrument, V_{UH} and V_i

are the dollar values of the unhedged position and the ith hedge instrument, respectively, P_0 is the original dollar value of the unhedged position, and R_L and R_U are upper and lower risk tolerances on the net hedge position relative to the original unhedged position. For example, risk management might set target risk tolerances of +/–5 percent for the net position across each rate scenario. This means that the net gain or loss from the combined hedged and unhedged positions could not deviate more than 5 percent from the original unhedged dollar position in either direction.

Using the set of hedge instruments described above and a risk tolerance of 1 percent, such a model may be implemented easily in Excel using the Solver function. Bid-ask spreads for the two-, five-, and one-year Treasury futures contracts are assumed to be 10, 15, and 25 bps respectively and are used in establishing the hedge costs for these contracts shown in Table 13.9, which also provides the results of this hedge optimization. Since this example focuses on only a single rate scenario and the model is linear in hedge costs and value, only one hedge instrument is used in the strategy. It turns out that using 1,148 five-year Treasury futures contracts minimizes hedge costs to $172,174 while ensuring that the net hedged position meets the established risk tolerance of 1 percent. SifiMortgage management argues that imposing such a tight risk tolerance on the net hedge position is overly conservative to such a degree that it materially affects the profitability and business model of the division. They conduct their own sensitivity analysis shown in Table 13.10, whereby loosening the tolerance to 5 percent would

TABLE 13.9 Hedge Optimization Results for –100bps Interest Rate Scenario

Treasury Futures	Per Contract Hedge Value ($)	Per Contract Cost ($)	Number of Contracts
2-year Contract	$1,600	$ 100	0
5-year Contract	$4,600	$ 150	1,148
10-year Contract	$7,400	$ 250	0
2-year Calls	$ 600	$ 750	0
2-year Puts	–$ 200	$ 250	0
5-year Calls	$2,700	$ 1,150	0
5-year Puts	–$ 400	$ 550	0
10-year Calls	$3,800	$ 1,750	0
10-year Puts	–$ 500	$ 850	0
Total Hedge Cost		$172,174	

TABLE 13.10 Hedge Optimization Risk Tolerance Sensitivity for −100bps Interest Rate Scenario

Risk Tolerance	Number of Contracts	Hedge Cost
0.1	0	0
0.05	278	$ 41,739
0.01	1148	$172,174

significantly reduce the number of five-year Treasury futures contracts and with it total hedge costs. Note that if the risk tolerance was loosened further to 10 percent, no hedge would be required since the value of the unhedged position under a −100bps rate scenario would fall within the tolerance. SifiMortgage's risk management office would ultimately decide to stay with the 1 percent risk tolerance despite protests from SifiMortgage business management.

Taking the concepts from this single rate scenario and applying them to a range of rate scenarios is rather straightforward. The impact on the long commitment pipeline can be seen in Table 13.11. As described above, the borrower put option creates an asymmetry in gains and losses for the net short forward-long commitment adjusted position, potentially requiring more than one type of hedge instrument. The impact on the three Treasury futures contracts and six Treasury option contracts is shown in Tables 13.12 and 13.13. Finally, the hedge costs for each potential hedge instrument by

TABLE 13.11 Multiple Interest Rate Scenario Effects on Mortgage Pipeline

Mortgage Pipeline	Rate Scenario in bps						
	−100	−50	−25	0	25	50	100
Mortgage Price ($)	107.85	106.15	102.75	100	97.75	96	91.65
Price Change from Par	7.85	6.15	2.75	0	−2.25	−4	−8.35
Estimated Close Rate	0.2	0.4	0.6	0.8	0.85	0.9	0.9
Expected Pipeline Gain/Loss	$6,280,000	$3,690,000	$1,100,000	$0	−$337,500	−$400,000	−$835,000

TABLE 13.12 Treasury Futures Price Impacts Across Multiple Interest Rate Scenarios

| | | | | | Rate Scenario in bps | | | | | |
Treasury Futures	−100	−50	−25	0	25	50	100
2-year Contract							
Price	110.95	110.35	109.85	109.35	108.9	108.5	107.8
Change from Baseline	1.6	1	0.5	0	−0.45	−0.85	−1.55
Per contract Hedge Value	1600	1000	500	0	−450	−850	−1550
5-year Contract							
Price	123.75	121.75	120.95	119.15	118.6	118.2	117.5
Change from Baseline	4.6	2.6	1.8	0	−0.55	−0.95	−1.65
Per Contract Hedge Value	4600	2600	1800	0	−550	−950	−1650
10-year Contract							
Price	131.25	128.85	126.25	123.85	123.25	122.86	122.1
Change from Baseline	7.4	5	2.4	0	−0.6	−0.99	−1.75
Per Contract Hedge Value	7400	5000	2400	0	−600	−990	−1750

TABLE 13.18 Treasury Futures Option Price Impacts Across Multiple Interest Rate Scenarios

At-the-Money Purchased Treasury Options	Rate Scenario in bps						
	−100	−50	−25	0	25	50	100
2-year Contracts							
Calls							
Price	1.35	1.15	1.05	0.75	0.55	0.25	0.05
Price Change from Baseline	0.6	0.4	0.3	0	−0.2	−0.5	−0.7
Per Contract Hedge Value	600	400	300	0	−200	−500	−700
Puts							
Price	0.05	0.125	0.175	0.25	0.65	1.05	1.4
Price Change from Baseline	−0.2	−0.125	−0.075	0	0.4	0.8	1.15
Per Contract Hedge Value	−200	−125	−75	0	400	800	1150
5-year Contracts							
Calls							
Price	3.85	2.25	1.85	1.15	0.85	0.35	0.125
Price Change from Baseline	2.7	1.1	0.7	0	−0.3	−0.8	−1.025
Per Contract Hedge Value	2700	1100	700	0	−300	−800	−1025
Puts							
Price	0.15	0.25	0.425	0.55	1.75	2.95	4.05
Price Change from Baseline	−0.4	−0.3	−0.125	0	1.2	2.4	3.5
Per Contract Hedge Value	−400	−300	−125	0	1200	2400	3500

10-year Contracts

Calls

Price	5.55	3.65	2.75	1.75	1.05	0.65	0.25
Price Change from Baseline	3.8	1.9	1	0	-0.7	-1.1	-1.5
Per Contract Hedge Value	3800	1900	1000	0	-700	-1100	-1500

Puts

Price	0.35	0.55	0.715	0.85	1.65	3.15	5.75
Price Change from Baseline	-0.5	-0.3	-0.135	0	0.8	2.3	4.9
Per Contract Hedge Value	-500	-300	-135	0	800	2300	4900

TABLE 13.14 Hedge Costs for Candidate Hedge Instruments

	Rate Scenario in bps						
	(100)	(50)	(25)	–	25	50	100
2-year Contract	100	100	100	100	100	100	100
5-year Contract	150	150	150	150	150	150	150
10-year Contract	250	250	250	250	250	250	250
2-year Treasury Calls	1,350	1,150	1,050	750	550	250	50
2-year Treasury Puts	50	125	175	250	650	1,050	1,400
5-year Treasury Calls	3,850	2,250	1,850	1,150	850	350	125
5-year Treasury Puts	150	250	425	550	1,750	2,950	4,050
10-year Treasury Calls	5,550	3,650	2,750	1,750	1,050	650	250
10-year Treasury Puts	350	550	715	850	1,650	3,150	5,750

rate scenario are found in Tables 13.14. Using these inputs, SifiMortgage hedge managers perform a similar optimization as before but now extend the constraints on the net hedge position for all rate scenarios. They now apply a risk tolerance of +/–1 percent as before but now for every scenario the optimization results require the use of 718 10-year futures contracts and 79 five-year Treasury put option contracts to meet the constraints. This results in a total hedge cost of $223,072. Note that this is higher than the single scenario result due to the addition of the put options. And while there are some short forward-long commitment scenarios that result in a gain, the purpose of the hedge from a risk management perspective is to leave the net position effectively immunized across scenarios regardless of outcome. In this case the put options result in a gain offsetting the losses from the 10-year futures contracts for these rate increase scenarios. It should also be pointed out that the hedge value associated with the option positions is not the same as the intrinsic value of the option. Recall that in the case of a purchased put option, the intrinsic value is defined as $MAX(K - M, 0)$ where K is the put option strike price and M is the price of the underlying asset. However, options also exhibit time value, owing to the probability that over time an option may come into the money before expiration. Consequently, the hedge values are reflecting this aspect of the options.

Cost Considerations

Since SifiManagement is closely monitoring the costs associated with hedging activity, one course of action the hedge managers could take to maintain compliance with the risk tolerances would be to add out-of-the-money

TABLE 13.15 Hedge Value and Costs for ATM and OTM Put Options

Put Options	Rate Scenario in bps							Hedge Cost
	−100	−50	−25	0	25	50	100	
OTM	−115	−100	−45	0	350	600	900	125
ATM	−200	−125	−75	0	400	800	1,150	550

options (OTM) in addition to the at-the-money (ATM) options in the original hedge strategy. The trade-off between using OTM and ATM options are cost and value. As options go further out-of-the-money, their value declines but so does their cost. Hedge managers therefore can establish effective hedges by mixing in the use of OTM options that are relatively cheap hedges. Their lower contribution to hedge value implies that more contracts would have to be put on relative to ATM options; however, the value-to-cost relationship between ATM and OTM options drives the decision for which to use in hedging. To illustrate the effects of OTM options, SifiMortgage decides to include five-year Treasury put option contracts among the candidate hedge instruments. The range of hedge values and each option's cost are shown in Table 13.15. These options have a per contract hedge value of $125 versus the $550 hedge value for the ATM five-year Treasury put options at the beginning of the hedge period (baseline). Also note that the hedge value for the OTM options is lower.

Rerunning the optimization now including these OTM put option yields a total hedge costs of $218, 246, a bit lower than the original result using ATM put options. More OTM options contracts are used than ATM options (127 versus 79) reflecting the lower incremental hedge value of the OTM options that require SifiMortgage hedge managers to use more contracts to achieve compliance with the original risk tolerance.

Addressing Basis Risk

Earlier the issue of basis risk regarding the Treasury futures hedge instruments and the underlying mortgage pipeline was discussed. Recall that mortgages are like a fixed income instrument coupled with a prepayment option. Thus, the prices between Treasuries and MBS will deviate, as shown in Figure 13.2. This gives rise to basis risk if Treasuries are used in hedging the pipeline. But Treasuries enjoy greater market liquidity and hence the bid-ask spreads for Treasuries are lower. To see the effect of using Fannie Mae MBS forward contracts in the hedge optimization, consider the range of hedge values for Fannie Mae MBS forwards with a weighted average coupon (WAC) comparable to the mortgages in the pipeline shown in Table 13.16. Also, hedge costs are assumed to be $275 per contract. Applying this information

TABLE 13.16 Fannie Mae MBS Forwards Hedge Values by Rate Scenario

	−100	−50	−25	0	25	50	100
Fannie Mae MBS Hedge Value	8,150	(50,000)	(25,000)	–	(550)	(1,000)	(1,650)

to the optimization model yields a total hedge cost of $212,552, but now the hedge strategy calls for using 267 OTM five-year Treasury put options and 652 Fannie Mae MBS forward contracts. Although the cost of the MBS forwards is higher than the 10-year Treasury futures contracts used in the earlier hedge, the hedge value owing to the improved basis risk makes the MBS forwards a preferred choice in the pipeline hedge.

Effects of Option Time Decay (Theta)

It was shown earlier that the option delta is dynamic, changing with interest rates. Option value also changes as options move closer to expiration. Calls and puts tend to exhibit a reduction in value as they approach expiration and this has consequences for hedging. As options approach expiration, the decline in value may accelerate. This can affect the value the option brings to the hedge strategy if not properly accounted for. The hedge examples discussed thus far assumed that the candidate option contracts have an expiration (90 days) matching the pipeline. But over that 90-day period, the value of the options will erode and therefore the value of the hedge. To gain a better sense of the impact of time decay on options for the SifiMortgage hedge, consider the results in Table 13.17. Theta is the

TABLE 13.17 Effect of Time Decay on 90-day Put Options over Multiple Rate Scenarios

90-day Expiring Options	−100	−50	−25	0	25	50	100
5-year Put Current Price	0.15	0.25	0.425	0.55	1.75	2.95	4.05
90-day Value of Time Decay (Theta)	0.075	0.135	0.225	0.25	0.275	0.255	0.125
Put Price in 90 days	0.075	0.115	0.2	0.3	1.475	2.695	3.925

TABLE 13.18   Effect of Time Decay on 120-day Put Options over Multiple Rate Scenarios

120-day Expiring Options	−100	−50	−25	0	25	50	100
5-year Put Current Price	0.2	0.3	0.475	0.6	1.8	3	4.1
90-day Value of Time Decay (Theta)	0.04	0.065	0.09	0.12	0.14	0.15	0.12
Put Price in 90 days	0.16	0.235	0.385	0.48	1.66	2.85	3.98

greek letter associated with an option's time decay and more formally is measured as the rate of change of the option when the time to expiration declines by one day. Theta for the put options shown results in lower option values across the board with some differentiation by rate scenario. An approach to managing the effects of time decay for options in the hedge would be to select options that have a longer time to expiration, for example, 120-day put options. The effects of time decay over 90-day and 120-day puts are shown in Table 13.18. The 120-day options have a higher value as options with longer times to expiration and otherwise identical characteristics are more valuable. Notice, too, that time decay after 90 days has less of an effect for the 120-day puts than for the 90-day puts based on the fact that the 90-day options lose more value as expiration approaches while the 120-day options have a month of expiration left. The associated differences in hedge value for these two options is shown in Table 13.19. Just as in other earlier examples, there are trade-offs to be made in using longer-dated options that include the higher premiums associated with the options and the hedge value that comes with using options that are less affected by time decay during the hedge window.

TABLE 13.19   Hedge Value Differences for 90- and 120-day Put Options

Impact of Time Decay on 5-year ATM Puts	(100)	(50)	(25)	–	25	50	100
Hedge Value Ignoring Time Decay after 90 days	(400)	(300)	(125)	–	1,200	2,400	3,500
Hedge Value with Time Decay	(475)	(435)	(350)	(250)	925	2,145	3,375
Hedge Value of 120-day Put	(390)	(315)	(165)	(70)	1,110	2,300	3,430

SUMMARY

Hedging interest rate risk is not simply a matter of choosing a set of hedge instruments that offset the unhedged exposure. As seen in the example of SifiMortgage's mortgage pipeline hedging problem, hedging is not a static exercise as the value of the mortgage commitments changes with interest rates. SifiMortgage can enter into a short forward delivery of closed loans at the expiration of the commitment period as a way of mitigating interest rate risk; however, the problem is not straightforward due to the existence of a put option freely granted by SifiMortgage to the borrower. That option changes the complexion of the hedge strategy since the borrower can choose to fall out of the pipeline should interest rates fall. Conversely, by locking in an interest rate 30–90 days ahead of their closing date, the borrower has the option to close at the contracted rate. As interest rates rise over the commitment period, the value of that put option increases as the probability that it expires in-the-money rises. The change in the option's value as the underlying mortgage price changes due to changes in interest rates is known as the delta of the option. For that reason, the option delta can be used as a hedge ratio in forming a hedge strategy that changes as the underlying asset values change.

A variety of hedge strategies and hedge instruments can be deployed by SifiMortgage to offset the pipeline's interest rate risk. Typically a sound hedging strategy will make use of a variety of hedge instruments including futures, forwards, and options. The choice of hedge instruments is driven by a number of factors including cost and effectiveness of the hedge. Futures contracts offer greater liquidity than forwards and purchased option contracts carry a premium. However, along a continuum of rate scenarios, one type of hedge instrument is unlikely to do an adequate job at maintaining a robust hedge. When certain hedge instruments are either unavailable or too expensive in the open market, the use of Put-Call Parity can help establish synthetic cash flows that provide a useful hedge outcome. Difficulty comes in designing the hedge strategy across many candidate hedge instruments. Treasury futures contracts of various types exist, for instance, as do forward contracts on mortgage derivatives such as Fannie Mae MBS. Again, trade-offs in cost and basis risk offer insights into which instruments ultimately are used to construct a viable hedge. This is where the use of more sophisticated hedge analytical tools can play an important role. The use of optimization techniques that minimize hedge cost subject to constraints on risk tolerance provide hedge managers the flexibility to include a multitude of hedge instruments in the course of designing the optimal hedge. In the case of option contracts, differences in hedge value and cost exist between in-the-money, at-the-money, and out-of-the-money options. Likewise, time decay can affect the contribution of options to the strategy and this aspect of option value dynamics also needs to be accounted for in the hedge strategy. Finally, hedging is not a static exercise. An effective hedge strategy is one that clearly articulates the need for hedging, the amount of risk the company is willing to take, the window of time over which the hedge will be in place along with oversight, accountability, and processes and controls in monitoring, adjusting, and unwinding the hedge.

QUESTIONS

Suppose you are a lender that has made a loan commitment to a borrower. The value of the commitment is $500,000 made today for a 90-day rate lock at 4.5 percent. 45 days into the lock of the commitment, the value falls to $450,000. The volatility of commitments is 30 percent, or .3. and five-year Treasuries, a benchmark for the risk-free rate, have a coupon of 1.5 percent.

1. Provide a conceptual description of the components of the loan commitment.
2. From a financial instrument perspective, how should the borrower be thinking about this loan commitment?
3. From the lender's perspective, what risk do they face and what estimate can be placed on this risk using the information given above? Make sure to take into account that it is on an annualized basis.

Suppose purchased 90-day put options on five-year Treasuries are priced at $5 per option with a strike price of $118 and you would like to use put options to hedge your mortgage pipeline. Prices on five-year Treasury futures are $120 per contract. Your supervisor looks over your recommended hedge and thinks there may be a less expensive way to construct the hedge without using puts.

4. Are you buying or writing put options in your strategy to use puts? Explain your answer relative to the pipeline risk.
5. Using only what you know in the information provided above, how could you still implement your strategy? What is this called? What is the price you would pay for this?
6. You manage a $25 million pipeline of jumbo mortgages (loan amounts greater than those Fannie Mae or Freddie Mac will accept) with a commitment period of 60 days. A simple internal model estimates the fallout percent in your pipeline as the following:

$$\text{Fallout\%} = .5 + .15(\text{WAC} - \text{Market Rate})$$

WAC stands for the weighted average coupon of the pipeline, which is 4.5 percent. If the market rate in 60 days moves up to 4.5 percent, commitment prices for this rate are $99.5 per $100 of face value, and at a WAC of 4 percent for the pipeline are valued at par. What amount would need to be established as a hedge for this?

7. Suppose that you could use five-year Treasury or Fannie Mae MBS futures contracts to hedge this risk. What are some issues you would note between these two instruments?

8. Suppose now you want to also hedge against rates moving up to 5 percent. Assume you do not change your fallout rate assumption. What impact will this have on your results?

You have a menu of put options including options with 30, 60, and 90 days to expiration that you may use to hedge your pipeline.

9. What factors would you consider in making a decision to use options in your pipeline hedging strategy?

10. Under what circumstances would you consider using optimization as a part of the hedge strategy?

CHAPTER 14

Operational Risk Management

OVERVIEW

Ten years ago SifiBank made the headlines after a computer glitch in its retail banking processing system shut down access to 90 percent of its ATM machines and 65 percent of branch office customer accounts for three consecutive days. During this period virtually all customer transactions at the affected locations came to a standstill. Customers naturally were frustrated with being unable to access their funds when needed. Check-cashing services, payment reconciliation, and basic processing activities were not possible during this time. The event made the national television news each evening, further putting SifiBank in an unfavorable light. Once the problem in the processing software was found and fixed, the bank was able to address the backlog of customer processing requests; however, by that time SifiBank had determined that the cost of this business interruption was about $250 million, a large portion of which was attributed to lost business revenue during the period as well as deposit withdrawals afterward attributed to poor customer service. At the next board of directors meeting, this event was discussed by management and a recommendation to establish a separate and independent office for operational risk management was made.

According to the Bank for International Settlements, operational risk is defined as the "risk of direct or indirect loss resulting from inadequate or failed internal processes, people, or systems, or from external events."[1] In SifiBank's retail banking shutdown, it experienced costs associated with a breakdown in systems. Operational risk in many ways is more difficult to identify and manage than other risks such as credit risk as it manifests in many different ways throughout the organization. Financial institutions have tended to focus more on measuring and managing traditional bank risks such

---

[1]Basel Committee on Banking Supervision, Consultative Document, Operational Risk, January 2001.

as credit or market risk, in part due to the development of better data and analytics to assess those risks and the overall impact of such risks. One study found, for example, that 86 percent of a sample of large bank risk-weighted assets were attributed to credit risk while market and operational risk comprised 7.5 and 6.5 percent, respectively.[2] Processes differ across business units such that when operational risk events materialize they reflect the unique activities of these businesses. This in turn implies that the business units represent the front-line of defense against unwarranted operational risks as they are most familiar with the specific processes deployed in that particular business unit. However, risk management organizations are essential partners to facilitate collection, aggregation, and analysis of operational risk data, assessment and communication of the state of operational risk readiness across the enterprise, and coordination of mitigation activities to address deficiencies.

It is important to distinguish operational risk from other risk types. For example, consider a bank loan officer who receives cash bonuses for originating mortgages and then changes borrower information on mortgage applications to ensure the loans are approved. This internal fraud in many instances results in a high incidence of borrower default as shortly after the loans close many borrowers find out they do not have the financial wherewithal to continue making payments. Such losses that accrue to Sifibank due to this fraud should be counted as operational losses and not credit losses if identified. Qualified loan review functions in this case should be able to conduct root cause analysis following default to identify the circumstances that may have contributed to borrower default. If employee fraud is identified, what may have been counted as a credit loss would be reassigned as an operational risk.

There are situations, however, where operational weaknesses could lead to substantial credit losses over time. In these cases, depending on the circumstance, the losses may still be designated as credit events. Take for example, the case of two banks originating the same exact type of mortgages. In Figure 14.1, lender A has developed a strong set of processes and controls around its mortgage origination business while lender B has invested elsewhere in the company, and thus its operational controls in its mortgage business are weak. This manifests itself in the form of higher default risk controlling for other borrower, loan, and collateral risk attributes. In the case of loan X, holding all characteristics of the loan constant, the only difference in the exact same loan made by lenders A and B are the processes used in underwriting the borrower. It could be that the underwriters for lender B do not properly check required loan documentation for income or assets, which help determine the borrower's capacity

---

[2]Vanessa Le Leslé and Sofiya Avramova, Revisiting Risk-Weighted Assets, IMF Working Paper, WP/12/90, March 2012.

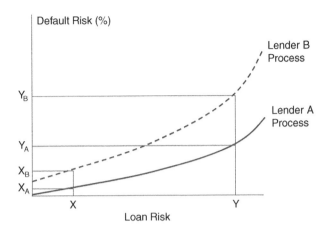

FIGURE 14.1 How Operational Processes Affect Credit Risk

to repay the mortgage obligation. Over time this could lead to a higher default rate for loans, such as X originated by lender B relative to lender A. This difference in default risk attributed to operational quality of the two lenders is defined by the difference $X_B - X_A$. Similarly, as the risk profile of the loan increases due to additional risk features being layered together, the divergence in default risk exposure increases between lenders as defined by $Y_B - Y_A$. Technically, relative weaknesses in the underlying origination process for lender B drive incrementally higher defaults compared to lender A and this would be an indirect way that operational risk could expose lender B to additional losses.

Specific guidance on the types of operational risk events has been provided to banks by the Basel Committee in facilitating bank compliance with Basel risk-based capital standards. The seven event categories identified are shown along with their subcategories in Table 14.1. Given SifiBank's size, its operational risk activities are driven substantially by the Basel protocols. For purposes of categorizing its operational risk events by business activity, it elects to follow a proposed Basel mapping as described in Table 14.2. SifiBank has organized its operational risk management team accordingly around its Investment Banking, Banking, and Retail Brokerage and Asset Management groups. Each business unit and subunit participates in the assessment of operational risk by engaging in a number of activities designed to identify operational risks on an ongoing basis, assess the strength of operational processes and controls, collect data on specific operational events, develop analytic models to quantify the level of operational risk to the bank, and develop action plans for addressing deficiencies.

TABLE 14.1 Operational Risk Event Categories

Event Category	Event Subcategory
Internal Fraud	Unauthorized Activity
	Theft and Fraud
External Fraud	Theft and Fraud
	Systems Security
Employment Practices and Workplace Safety	Employee Relations
	Safe Environment
	Diversity and Discrimination
Clients, Products, and Business Practices	Suitability, Disclosure, and Fiduciary
	Improper Business or Market Practices
	Product Flaws
	Selection, Sponsorship, and Exposure
	Advisory Activities
Damage to Physical Assets	Disasters and Other Events
Business Disruption and System Failures	Systems
Execution, Delivery, and Process Management	Transaction Capture, Execution, and Maintenance
	Monitoring and Reporting
	Customer Intake and Documentation
	Customer/Client Account Management
	Trade Counterparties
	Vendors and Suppliers

Sifibank's experience with its mortgage business highlights important issues and challenges in managing operational risk, although each business unit at the bank encounters its own unique circumstances. During the period from 2002–2007, Sifibank embarked on a major acquisition spree of smaller mortgage banking units across the industry to broaden its presence and market share in the mortgage business, which expanded significantly during this period due to a variety of factors, including a period of low interest rates and rising home prices. Sifibank had historically been a traditional retail mortgage originator, largely making loans eligible for sale to Fannie Mae or Freddie Mac or for its own portfolio that would be considered prime

TABLE 14.2 Mapping of SifiBank Business Activities for Operational Risk Assessment

Business Unit	Subunit	Activity
Investment Banking	Corporate Finance	Corporate Finance Government Finance Merchant Banking Advisory Services
	Trading and Sales	Sales Market Making Proprietary Positions Treasury
Banking	Retail Banking	Retail Banking Private Banking Card Services
	Commercial Banking	Commercial Banking
	Payment and Settlement	External Clients
	Agency Services	Custody Corporate Agency Corporate Trust
Others	Asset Management	Discretionary Fund Management Non-Discretionary Fund Management
	Retail Brokerage	Retail Brokerage

mortgages of high credit quality. SifiBank's CEO and Board were pressing each business unit to find growth opportunities during this period and the head of SifiMortgage presented a business plan to enter the highly profitable subprime and near-prime mortgage business. However, since SifiMortgage was not set up to originate these types of loans, which required more specialized underwriting and servicing practices, it decided to make a number of strategic acquisitions. With the Board's approval SifiBank made five notable acquisitions, one a subprime originator and four others engaged largely in near-prime mortgage originations. Near-prime mortgages included products not otherwise eligible for sale to the GSEs, such as stated-income, or no income documentation mortgages and option adjustable rate mortgages that provide the borrower with several payment options each month for their mortgage.

SifiBank operated each acquisition as a separate subsidiary that rolled into SifiMortgage for reporting purposes. That meant that each unit maintained its own underwriting systems and had responsibility for managing personnel in each of its offices. There was some integration with SifiBank policies and procedures but for the most part during this period the 5 new units had relative autonomy to build their businesses with limited oversight from SifiMortgage.

By late 2006 and early 2007, the consolidated market share of SifiMortgage including the 5 new business units had vaulted the company to number 3 in market share and the bank enjoyed double-digit return on equity throughout much of the period. SifiMortgage Enterprise Risk Management had engaged SifiMortgage business and risk management personnel to participate in its development of a comprehensive operational risk management process in 2005 to get ahead of anticipated requirements for Basel risk-based capital determination. SifiBank ERM provided SifiMortgage with its expectations on establishing processes to assessing the level of operational risk throughout its organization, including the five new business units. This included development of a set of new **Risk Control Self-Assessments** (RCSA), expected to be produced each quarter by SifiMortgage and reviewed at the executive committee and risk committees of the company and business unit level. These RCSAs were a variant of a process that SifiBank already had in place called **COSO**, for the Committee of Sponsoring Organizations of the Treadway Commission that enabled the bank to systematically capture and qualitatively assess its various processes and controls across the company. Up to that point, SifiMortgage had not spent any time capturing data on actual operational events it experienced over the past 10 years, and so it needed to initiate a new data collection process that would be used to build quantitative models of SifiMortgage's expected and unexpected loss potential to operational events. The SifiMortgage team struggled with the exercise and was only able to identify fewer than 50 instances that they believed met the criteria in Table 14.1 for operational risk events in the business. When they went back to determine loss experience, the team found that 45 of these events resulted in losses averaging $200,000 or less and that in only three instances were losses higher: a branch office fraud incident in one case resulted in losses of $10 million and two others were systems-related issues, each totaling about $2 million. By the time June 2007 arrived, SifiMortgage was beginning to experience heavier than expected losses on its mortgage portfolio. Particularly worrisome were its losses from loans originated in its five acquired mortgage units, which by 2007 accounted for nearly half of its held-for-investment (HFI) portfolio and loan securitizations. The operational risk initiative yielded little benefit to management at that point as it had yet to be fully implemented in the business.

In 2007, mortgage losses on SifiMortgage loans began increasing at an alarming rate as the housing boom turned to bust and investors fled private-label securities, some of which were created by SifiBank. As borrower defaults mounted, SifiMortgage's servicing unit, which had experienced under-investment in technology and staff for year, came under extreme pressure to handle the wave of default and collection activity. To expedite foreclosure on defaulted loans, SifiMortgage servicing took a number of processing shortcuts that allowed thousands of mortgages to proceed to foreclosure with hardly any review on the material facts or extenuating circumstances associated with the loan. Many borrowers had not even entered default and others were provided little or no ability to work with the bank before having their home taken away. This activity became known as **robo-signing** in the industry, and subsequently led to a deluge investigations from regulators and states' attorneys general. In the wake of these events, SifiBank became embroiled in a number of class action lawsuits brought on behalf of affected borrowers. In addition, a number of states filed suit, as did the federal government, resulting in several high-profile settlements. In all, the cost associated with robo-signing for SifiBank was estimated to be $15 billion.

As the details surrounding the mortgage crisis emerged, it became evident that the industry had engaged in a number of underwriting practices that, in hindsight, had put many borrowers at risk of default. The lack of proper documentation of income and assets to confirm the borrower's capacity to repay their loan was one such problem, among many others that favored market share over strong process. Many of the low documentation loans originated by SifiMortgage during the 2005–2007 period defaulted at rates 5 times that of fully documented loans. As the crisis wore on, SifiBank became a prime target of numerous lawsuits, regulatory actions, and civil money penalties. In addition, SifiMortgage was involved in a number of loan repurchase requests from mortgage insurance companies and trustees of their mortgage-backed securities that experienced heavy credit losses due to breaches in a number of contractual **representations and warranties** (R&Ws) in their underwriting. It was estimated that deficiencies in its underwriting processes cost SifiBank a total of $20 billion. In hindsight, if SifiMortgage had implemented a robust operational risk management process, it may not have prevented some problems from arising, but it would likely have greatly reduced the severity of the underwriting and servicing problems that occurred by identifying and addressing many of the more serious practices.

Having learned a costly lesson during the crisis, SifiBank mandated the requirement to focus with greater scrutiny on controlling operational risk for all business units. Most of the top management of SifiMortgage and SifiBank were swept out immediately following the crisis and the new management team was acutely sensitive to the need to drive operational excellence among all the business units. Implementing SifiBank's new operational risk management process fell to the Enterprise Chief Risk Officer. At the same time, the bank's General Auditor, at the direction of the SifiBank Board of Director's Audit Committee to which she reported, requested that the bank also establish a strong internal control assessment process. At the highest level, bank activities across operating units identified as shown in Table 14.2 were identified in order to capture essential functions that could pose operational risk to the firm.

INTERNAL CONTROLS ASSESSMENT

The chairman of the bank's Audit Committee had known about best practices in internal control assessment as described by COSO. COSO provides a framework for companies of any kind to assess the sufficiency of internal controls along a number of dimensions. Over time variations on such structures to evaluate the quality of internal processes and controls have come in different forms such as RCSAs. Regardless of form, these assessment processes typically have the following components: process and key activity identification, key risk identification, control inventory, process assessment, risk assessment, and response.

Any good internal control assessment framework requires a comprehensive list of core processes associated with the development of a product or service. Development of a complete list of processes critical to the business activity prevents gaps in the assessment process. Each business unit within Sifibank would be required to develop their own RCSA from a template provided by the Internal Audit Group (IAG). Each quarter business management is required to update their RCSA and provide it to IAG for their review. Self-identification of control weaknesses should be encouraged across the organization. A sign that management is not taking the RCSA process seriously would be consistent assessments showing few or no control weaknesses identified by management over time. Most processes require constant improvement reflecting changes in market conditions, business, and technology. Such actions by management and their teams to ferret out potential weaknesses are positively reinforced by senior management at the bank via compensation structures, career advancement opportunities and other means rather than by disciplinary measures.

For SifiMortgage, a list of these core processes are shown in Table 14.3 as developed by their management team. Each process is made up of a collection of activities that involve subprocesses, staff, and various technologies and systems. The management team must further drill down into the core

TABLE 14.3 SifiMortgage Core Internal Processes

SifiMortgage Core Process
Sourcing and Production
Loan Pricing
Underwriting
Collateral Valuation
Loan Processing
Custodial Services
Risk Management
Servicing

processes to identify these specific activities. For SifiMortgage Risk Management, these subprocesses are identified in Table 14.4. Once these processes and activities have been identified, management would need to perform an assessment of the risks associated with each one. For example, under counterparty risk, a breakdown in the process for evaluating suitable correspondent lenders could lead to material credit losses in the event a lender does not comply with SifiMortgage's underwriting standards, and/or goes out of business. Each business is required to assign a risk level to each activity risk representing potential operational risk exposure; satisfactory for risks with losses/costs less than $5 million; needs improvement for risks with losses/costs between $5 million and $25 million, and unsatisfactory for losses/costs

TABLE 14.4 SifiMortgage Risk Management Activities

Activity
Counterparty Management
Credit and Collateral Policy
Exception Processing
Monitoring and Reporting
Loan Reserving
Portfolio Management
Quality Control

above $25 million. These estimates are based on a combination of historical experience and judgment by management. Once activities and their potential risk exposure have been determined, management must outline what controls it has put in place to address potential risks in its processes. An example of a control under the risk management counterparty risk activity would be for risk management to perform a periodic assessment of the financial condition of each counterparty along with an annual on-site due diligence of their loan underwriting process. Each control is assessed for its effectiveness for mitigating risk. Finally, for each process rated as needing improvement or unsatisfactory, management would need to develop a remediation plan describing the action steps and timing required to address the issue. An assessment of management's progress against that plan should also be incorporated into the RCSA, with accountable personnel identified. Finally, the quality of RCSAs, including the scope of activities, self-assessment, and remediation plans should form a noticeable component of management and staff annual performance plans. An abbreviated example of SifiMortgage Risk Management's RCSA appears in Tables 14.5a, 14.5b, and 14.5c.

SifiMortgage risk management has determined that the largest potential risk to the organization is associated with its credit and collateral valuation policies. Development of poor policies can lead to high credit and operational losses. For example, the development of loan products where borrowers were allowed to state their income rather than provide documentation for it resulted in widespread fraud losses for the bank. Note that other than for a few activities, potential risk across the risk organization caused by poor processes and controls is medium to high. For each activity identified, a set of controls are listed. For brevity, details on each control are limited for this high-level RCSA summary but would be found in the complete report.

In Table 14.5b, management provides their assessment of each control. In the case of the risk management unit, all but one of these controls is assessed as satisfactory or needing improvement. In the case of the portfolio management activity risk data warehouse, the process is deemed to be unsatisfactory. Such a finding along with the potential risk of the activity would be important in prioritizing resources for remediation.

For each process deficiency, a remediation plan is required, as shown in Table 14.5c. In a number of cases the remediation plan may impose dependencies with other corporate or business units as seen in several instances for SifiMortgage risk management. The information technology (IT) department of SifiBank is identified as a dependency by risk management for several systems and data-related enhancements. Managers from both the relevant risk and IT units responsible for addressing the control weakness should be identified on the RCSA. An assessment of where the remediation project stands against implementation deadlines is also shown. For projects

TABLE 14.5A SifiMortgage Risk Management RCSA Template

Activity	Potential Risk	Controls
Counterparty Risk Management		
Evaluation of Third-Party Originators	Needs Improvement	Counterparty scorecards evaluated every quarter
Evaluation of Mortgage Insurers	Needs Improvement	MI financial assessment undertaken each year
Risk Management Vendor Evaluation	Needs Improvement	Major vendors evaluated annually
Credit & Collateral Policy		
Development of Credit Policy	Unsatisfactory	Delegation of authority matrix used for loan approval
Development of Appraisal Policy	Unsatisfactory	Appraisers do not report to loan production officers
Automated Underwriting Scorecards	Unsatisfactory	Scorecards, cutoffs, and overrides approved by risk
Loan Exception Processing	Needs Improvement	Loan exception approval policy developed by risk
Risk Modeling		
Scorecards	Needs Improvement	Statistically-based scorecard validated annually
Reserving Models	Needs Improvement	Reserve models undergo independent audit annually
Economic Capital Models	Needs Improvement	Economic capital models reviewed annually
Loan Loss Reserving		
Policies and Procedures	Needs Improvement	Formal policies and procedures in place
Systems	Needs Improvement	Separate system for reserve calculations and output developed
Data	Needs Improvement	Transaction level detail retained for last 5 years
Portfolio Management		
Insurance Activities	Needs Improvement	Multiple insurance providers allocated
Management Reporting	Needs Improvement	Monthly risk reporting performed and presented
Risk Data Warehouse	Needs Improvement	Historical loan level detail maintained for analysis
Market Analysis	Satisfactory	Economic analysis performed each month
Quality Control		
Policies and Procedures	Needs Improvement	Formal policies and procedures exist
Systems	Satisfactory	Separate QC system used to generate samples and for archiving
Reporting	Satisfactory	Monthly management reporting conducted

TABLE 14.5B SifiMortgage Risk Management RCSA Template

Activity	Remediation Plan	Progress	Accountable Manager
Counterparty Risk Management			Smith
Evaluation of Third-Party Originators	New risk-based scorecard in development	On Schedule	
Evaluation of Mortgage Insurers	Quarterly assessment process under development	On Schedule	
Risk Management Vendor Evaluation			
Credit & Collateral Policy			Jones
Development of Credit Policy			
Development of Appraisal Policy	Appraisal rotation process developed & deployed	Completed	
Automated Underwriting Scorecards	Cutoff analysis underway and to be presented for approval	Behind Schedule	
Loan Exception Processing	Exception policy being rewritten and current exceptions stopped	On Schedule	
Risk Modeling			White
Scorecards	Outside vendor to be retained for model validation	On Schedule	
Reserving Models			
Economic Capital Models	Quarterly assessment process in development	On Schedule	
Loan Loss Reserving			Roberts
Policies and Procedures			
Systems	IT to develop single system for reserving	Behind Schedule	
Data	IT to work with Risk on developing reserve data warehouse	Behind Schedule	
Portfolio Management			Williams
Insurance Activities			
Management Reporting	New set of risk management reports in development	On Schedule	
Risk Data Warehouse	IT working with Risk on new database	Behind Schedule	
Market Analysis			
Quality Control			Johnson
Policies and Procedures			
Systems	IT developing new QC system		
Reporting		No plan yet	

TABLE 14.5C SifiMortgage Risk Management RCSA Template

Activity	Process Assessment	Process Finding
Counterparty Risk Management		
Evaluation of Third-Party Orginators	Needs Improvement	Scorecards based only on production not risk
Evaluation of Mortgage Insurers	Needs Improvement	MI assessments need to be conducted quarterly
Risk Management Vendor Evaluation	Satisfactory	
Credit & Collateral Policy		
Development of Credit Policy	Satisfactory	No random process in place for assigning appraisals
Development of Appraisal Policy	Needs Improvement	Credit risk rising yet same cutoffs in place for 5 years
Automated Underwriting Scorecards	Needs Improvement	Many exceptions being allowed than expected
Loan Exception Processing	Needs Improvement	
Risk Modeling		
Scorecards	Needs Improvement	Independent validation no performed
Reserving Models	Satisfactory	
Economic Capital Models	Needs Improvement	Model results should be assessed each quarter
Loan Loss Reserving		
Policies and Procedures	Satisfactory	Multiple systems tied together poses risk
Systems	Needs Improvement	Data inconsistent across origination platforms
Data	Needs Improvement	
Portfolio Management		
Insurance Activities	Satisfactory	Insufficient detail in reporting found
Management Reporting	Needs Improvement	Data errors and inconsistencies found
Risk Data Warehouse	Unsatisfactory	
Market Analysis	Satisfactory	
Quality Control		
Policies and Procedures	Satisfactory	Excel-based systems need replacing
Systems	Needs Improvement	
Reporting	Satisfactory	

417

behind schedule or where no plan exists, further explanation would be warranted to management.

The RCSA process provides a foundation for developing a robust assessment of internal controls and processes; however, it alone would be insufficient to establish a best practice operational risk management capability. For instance, an RCSA is unlikely to provide a quantitative assessment of operational risk, and so methods to leverage and enhance the utility of such a framework consistent with regulatory expectations such as Basel can improve the ability to identify, measure, and manage operational risk. One such enhancement of the RCSA process is to develop a scorecard that rank-orders the quality of an organization's processes. This will be reviewed in some detail in Chapter 16.

QUANTITATIVE ASSESSMENT OF OPERATIONAL RISK

Advancements in the quantification of operational risk have come about over the past 10 years; however, great care must be taken in understanding the implications of key assumptions about modeling operational losses. This is partly a result of the relative paucity of empirical data for a typical financial institution from which to model operational risk events with a high degree of reliability. In addition, the different types of operational risk events as shown in Table 14.1 may generate different loss distributions, imposing even further complexity on the analysis. Complicating that analysis is the fact that aggregating operational losses across event types and business units presents its own analytic challenges. The point of this discussion is not to provide an exhaustive treatment of operational risk modeling but to delve into the essential features and issues associated with this topic.

To illustrate these issues, consider SifiMortgage risk management's efforts to estimate operational losses in this division of the bank. The first step in developing the analysis is to determine what data is available internally and what might be missing. SifiBank had not done a particularly good job at building a historical database of operational risks; however, the bank did initiate such a data collection effort, anticipating it would need to comply with Basel capital requirements for operational risk. For analytic purposes, the bank decided to cull its records for events falling into one of the seven operational risk categories identified in Table 14.1. Records included the date of an event, its type, and an explanation for the event (e.g., rogue trader, branch office security breach), and the dollar amount of loss or cost to the bank associated with the event.

The loss of an operational risk event is defined as the product of its frequency of occurrence and the severity of the loss once it occurs. Differences in losses between types of operational risk events may be attributed to variations in frequency and loss severity outcomes. Some events may be characterized by a relatively high frequency of homogeneous outcomes, such as cases of mortgage fraud as experienced during the subprime mortgage crisis. Such events are typically associated with relatively low loss severities compared to other operational risks. In contrast, some events such as a cyber-attack on the payments system might be rare in occurrence but high in loss severity. These differences drive how the risk analyst thinks about specifying the right model that best reflects the differences in frequency and loss severity.

SifiMortgage fortunately has retained considerable information on its operational risk events; consequently the bank does not have to fill in any data gaps by obtaining that information from external operational data consortia. Such organizations maintain comprehensive repositories of operational risk events experienced by participating banks over time. This data can then be used to build loss profiles adjusted for characteristics of the firm. An example of an adjustment would be that a small institution might need to scale loss exposures provided from external sources that reflect the experience of larger institutions. In addition, the use of scenarios based on expert judgment can be used to evaluate low frequency–high severity risk events due to the rarity of their occurrence. Scenarios would be developed to reflect the likelihood of occurrence of particular events and these proxies for event frequency would then be used as key assumptions in operational risk models.

SifiMortgage risk analysts pulled together event data for all seven operational risk events. For internal fraud, the bank was able to collect event data from the last 25 years, including the all-important financial crisis and boom period. Mortgage fraud committed by employees during the last 25 years was found largely in a number of individual retail branches of the bank. It was found that there were 200 separate instances of mortgage fraud occurring over the past 25 years. On this basis it is estimated that SifiMortgage would experience an average of eight internal mortgage fraud cases per year. With operational events occurring in a discrete fashion over time, discrete distributions measuring event frequency are typically chosen, of which the Poisson distribution is a common type. The Poisson probability distribution across k losses per year can be represented as:

$$f(k,\lambda) = \frac{(\lambda T)^k e^{-\lambda T}}{k!} \qquad 14.1$$

where λ represents the mean number of risk (loss) events each year, and k is the number of loss events in a given time period T. Usually, a period of one

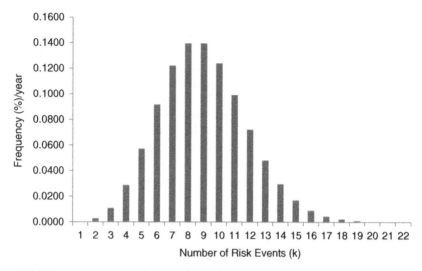

FIGURE 14.2 Distribution of Internal Fraud Losses at SifiMortgage

year is assumed for such analyses. Using as the estimate for λ of eight mortgage fraud events per year, a distribution of internal mortgage fraud across k different loss scenarios is shown in Figure 14.2 using the Poisson formula. The probability of 11 events occurring in one year as shown in Figure 14.2 would be computed according to 14.1 as:

$$Pr(11,8) = (8(1)^{11}e^{-8(1)})/11! = (8.589B)(.00034)/39.917M = 7.22\% \quad 14.2$$

Next, estimates of the severity associated with each loss event k can be computed as the following:

$$X = e^{\mu+\sigma N^{-1}(Z)} \quad 14.3$$

where μ and σ is the mean and standard deviation of the log of losses and Z is a random number between 0 and 1. SifiMortgage has categorized its losses as shown in Table 14.6 based on historical information and computed μ and σ.

The bank was able to estimate the amount of loss it experienced due to the fraud and to generate the following histogram of losses in Figure 14.3. Note that shape of this loss distribution is not normal or symmetric. Just as in the case of the frequency distribution, a number of alternative forms could be used to represent the data; however, the lognormal distribution

TABLE 14.6   Estimates of Loss Severity μ and σ

Fraud Amount $	Midpoint	Log of Midpoint
$		
0–25000	$ 12,500	9.43
25000–50000	$ 25,000	10.13
50000–75000	$ 37,500	10.53
75000–100000	$ 50,000	10.82
100000–125000	$ 62,500	11.04
125000–150000	$ 75,000	11.23
150000–175000	$ 87,500	11.38
175000–200000	$100,000	11.51
200000–225000	$112,500	11.63
225000–250000	$125,000	11.74
250000–275000	$137,500	11.83
275000–300000	$150,000	11.92
	Mean of Log Loss	**11.10**
	S.D of Log Loss	**0.76**

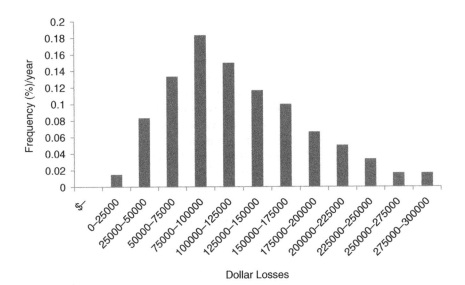

FIGURE 14.3   Histogram of SifiMortgage Mortgage Fraud Losses

reviewed in Chapter 6 for credit risk applications is commonly applied to assessing the severity of operational risk events.

Combining the frequency and severity loss distributions allows the risk management team to generate the loss distribution for SifiMortgage internal fraud operational risks. An assumption that many institutions apply in this process is that the frequency of a risk event and its severity are independent from each other. That may be true in some cases but be an oversimplification in other circumstances. For example, poor internal controls on tracking employee access and changes to loan documents could lead to both higher loss frequencies as well as higher loss severities once fraud has been committed. Methods exist to accommodate distributional dependency; however, treatment of them here is beyond the scope of this discussion.

Mathematically, the combined annual loss distribution for SifiMortgage internal fraud losses could be described as follows:

$$P(L_{IF}) = \sum f(k, \lambda) * g(x \mid k) \qquad\qquad 14.4$$

where $f(k, \lambda)$ is the frequency distribution and $g(x \mid k)$ is the severity distribution conditional on an event k occurring. Analytic and simulation-based methods may be used to combine the distributions, however, care is required in using analytic methods given data issues described earlier. SifiMortgage risk analysts instead decide to use a Monte Carlo simulation approach at combining the distributions for internal fraud losses.

Such an approach requires generating a set of random numbers that will be used to estimate n possible internal fraud frequency outcomes. SifiMortgage elects to generate 500 trials. For each trial, an estimate of event frequency is generated by comparing the random number Z_0 (ranging between 0 and 1) to the Poisson estimated probability sequentially for each of k events in the distribution. If the random number Z_0 is greater than the Poisson probability for event k, an estimate of loss is determined based on the loss severity estimate from Figure 14.3, otherwise loss is set to 0. The Poisson probability is compared to the random number Z_0 for the next event, $k + 1$, and if it is greater than Z_0, the loss is computed as given in Equation 14.3.

To make this more concrete, for trial 1, assume that the value for Z_0 is .0096. For k equal to 1, the Poisson probability for a loss event of $k - 1$, or 0, is .000335 for $\lambda = 8$. Since Z_0 exceeds .000335, the loss is estimated at $\exp(11.1 + N^{-1}(Z(k))(.76))$, or \$45,337, where $Z(k)$ is another randomly generated number between 0 and 1 for event k. For k equal to 2, the frequency of $2 - 1$, or 1 event is .003 and again, Z_0 is greater than .003 and so the severity amount is computed as \$49,096 applying equation 14.3. For all values of k greater than 2, Z_0 is less than the Poisson probabilities and so severity is 0 for remaining events greater than 2. This is repeated for each trial. Within each trial, the set of estimated losses are summed across k events to generate total losses for trial n. For this trial, total operational losses are estimated at $94,433, the sum of k equal to 1 and 2. For internal fraud, over 500 trials the average loss is $671,851 and the standard deviation is $291,864.

The mean and standard deviation of internal fraud losses can then be used in combination with similar estimates for the other six operational risk types using a similar simulation methodology in SifiMortgage to generate a complete view of operational risk losses. Table 14.7 displays the standard deviations for each of the seven operational risk event types (1 = Internal Fraud).

Aggregation of operational risks for SifiMortgage across each of the seven risk types can be accomplished in one of several ways. By making the assumption that the composite loss distribution from all seven distributions is normally distributed, the following expression may be used:

$$\sigma_{Composite} = \sqrt{\sum_{i=1}^{n}\sum_{j=1}^{n}\sigma_i\sigma_j\rho_{ij}} \qquad 14.5$$

where σ_i and σ_j are the standard deviations of risk type i and j and ρ_{ij} represents the correlation between risk types i and j. Critical to the determination of the composite standard deviation is the correlation matrix. Obtaining detailed information about correlations between risk types may be difficult empirically, however, such a matrix with available data as in the case of SifiMortgage is shown in Table 14.8.

Using the results in Tables 14.7 and 14.8 to compute the composite standard deviation yields a result of $1.22 million. Note that in the absence

TABLE 14.7   Standard Deviations for SifiMortgage Operational Risk Types

Risk Type	Standard Deviation
1	$277,410
2	$450,234
3	$104,892
4	$619,375
5	$318,037
6	$277,936
7	$147,372

TABLE 14.8   SifiMortgage Operational Risk Type Correlation Matrix

Risk Type	1	2	3	4	5	6	7
1	1.00	0.00	0.10	0.25	0.12	0.15	0.17
2	0.00	1.00	0.05	0.15	0.09	0.19	0.16
3	0.10	0.05	1.00	0.21	0.14	0.23	0.20
4	0.25	0.15	0.21	1.00	0.13	0.18	0.26
5	0.12	0.09	0.14	0.13	1.00	0.23	0.12
6	0.15	0.19	0.23	0.18	0.23	1.00	0.09
7	0.17	0.16	0.20	0.26	0.12	0.09	1.00

of data, a simple assumption that all seven risk types are perfectly correlated would result in a substantially higher standard deviation of loss. Again, the reliability of the correlation data will be a primary determinant of its use in estimating operational risk losses.

Armed with this composite estimate of operational risk, SifiMortgage risk analysts can calculate what their economic capital would be for operational risk. Leveraging the previous discussions in earlier chapters on VaR, assuming a 99.9 percent worse-case outcome as the target level for VaR, the amount of economic capital the bank would need to hold would be measured as approximately $3.77 million, or $1.22 million multiplied by the 99.9 percent factor 3.09.

REGULATORY STANDARDS

The Basel risk-based capital standards have heightened the need for banks to pay more attention to operational risk analysis than ever before. As mentioned previously, over the years banks have traditionally focused on credit, market, and interest rate risk management, and so the data and tools for banks to properly measure operational risk have been lacking in the industry. Basel has evolved over time and with it the way in which banks are required to compute operational risk capital. Three methods for calculating operational risk capital are used in Basel: the **Basic Indicator Approach**, the **Standardized Approach**, and the **Advanced Measurement Approach** (AMA).

Under the simplest approach, the Basic Indicator method, gross income serves as a proxy for operational risk and banks using this method would be required to hold 15 percent of their gross income for operational risk capital. This method, while simple from a computational perspective, is only a crude approximation of capital for operational risk and does not take into consideration operational differences across and within financial institutions. Along with that simplicity the Basic Indicator method may set a higher level of capital for a bank than if it used the other Basel methods in order to incent larger institutions to gravitate toward developing more robust measurement systems.

Under the Standardized Approach, the gross income concept is extended to individual business lines within the company against which separate capital charges (betas) are assigned. Table 14.9 summarizes the differences in capital charges under the Standardized Approach. The gross income for each business unit would be multiplied against the beta for that line of business. The three-year average of the sum of capital charges across each business line would constitute the capital assigned for the bank for its operational risk.

The AMA approach is reserved only for those institutions with certain controls and processes in place to develop the data and analytics for empirical measurement of operational risk. First, it must demonstrate that it has proper oversight by the board of directors and senior management, that it has a system in place for operational risk management and that resources exist within the business units and firm to conduct this analysis. Using a combination of internal and external data and scenario analysis where appropriate, banks can then build their own models following the **Loss Distribution Approach** (LDA), which requires that a loss frequency and severity distribution be constructed as illustrated in the previous section for SifiMortgage.

TABLE 14.9 Basel Standardized Approach for Operational Risk

Business Line	Beta
Corporate Finance	0.18
Trading and Sales	0.18
Retail Banking	0.12
Commercial Banking	0.15
Payment and Settlement	0.18
Agency Services	0.15
Asset Management	0.12
Retail Brokerage	0.12

CYBER-SECURITY RISK

Over the years, a relatively new and sophisticated operational risk impacting commercial banks has come in the form of various types of **cyber-security threats.** Cyber attacks on banking systems have increased with advances in technology. Banks have become attractive targets for would-be hackers as access to private customer data, financial records, and funds has become highly lucrative. Although the banking industry has spent considerable resources to harden critical IT systems and data, technology continues to evolve and with it the prospect for significant cyber-attacks that could expose banks to significant losses as well as reputational risk. Further, this is relatively unknown territory for risk managers who have had to come up the learning curve quickly with their IT counterparts in assessing the likelihood and extent of risk as well as how to protect company and customer assets from such threats.

One of the features that make protecting against cyber-attacks difficult is the variation in types of attacks. Table 14.10 summarizes types of cyber-threats to banks along several impact areas. **Distributed denial of service** (DDoS) attacks aim to prevent the use of bank systems and applications by customers or other users and have been on the rise. Installation of various types of malware to insert viruses that destroy, alter, or steal sensitive information are also among the more common types of cyber-attacks facing banks on nearly a daily basis. Many of these types of attacks, while frequent in nature, have tended to be low severity events, fortunately; however, it may be only a matter of time before more extensive and coordinated attacks could come against one or more banks or financial market utilities and exchanges. The Office of Financial Research (OFR), the analytical arm of the **Financial Stability Oversight Council** (FSOC), in charge of overseeing systemic risk to the financial sector in the United States, has identified cyber-security threats as an emerging systemic risk to the industry. Likewise, the OCC has called attention to cyber-security in its regular assessment of

TABLE 14.10 Types of Cyber-Threats to Commercial Banks

Info Security	Financial Attack	Access	Reputation
Password Cracking	EFT Fraud (e.g., ATMs, Gas Stations)	Denial of Service	Malicious Spread of Misinformation
Keystroke Tracking	Malware	Malware	Website Defacement
Malware	Botnet Attacks	Botnet Attacks	
Phishing/Pharming			

banking risk. In the past few years the industry has come together to conduct large cyber attack war game exercises (e.g., Quantum Dawn 2) featuring scenarios that span across multiple institutions and markets.

The motives behind cyber attacks are varied but offer some insight into the potential for such risk and why it may be on the rise. Cyber threats can come from inside the organization by a disgruntled employee seeking personal gain or retribution against the firm. While such threats can be destructive and costly, they tend to be very low frequency events. However, the sensational breach by Edward Snowden of highly sensitive National Security Agency data is an example of how the actions of a single employee, or contractor in this case, can have devastating effects for the firm. Other attacks from outside the organization are no less threatening in their effect. Over the past few years, the potential for rogue governments, paramilitary groups, terrorists, and criminal organizations to exploit vulnerabilities in corporate systems and data have become more apparent. Attacks on large retail companies, universities, and other sources of confidential information have become all too familiar. Whether these organizations stand to enrich their members financially or are motivated by politics or ideology, cyber attacks should not be underestimated in their risk to the bank. Establishing a corporate mindset that cyber-risk is of paramount importance throughout the firm can inculcate the kind of cyber-aware culture needed to fend off potential attacks.

Once the firm recognizes the importance of managing cyber-security risk, the bank must establish a governance process around it. While the CRO must play a key role in monitoring and managing this risk he must also work closely with the Chief Information Officer (CIO), given their expertise in this area. It must be acknowledged that cyber-security risk is first and foremost a business imperative and not simply an IT-centric solution.

Other considerations in establishing a cyber-security risk management process entail establishing a communications plan in the event a breach occurs, both for internal and external constituents. In addition, the company should be ready with a playbook in the event a cyber-attack occurs. This would include deployment of a team of cyber-risk specialists to minimize loss of data or resources from the attack. Measures aimed at mitigating cyber-risk include increasing the staffing for cyber-security specialists, training of employees on cyber risk, enhancement of cyber-threat detection and response, and regular assessment of threat vulnerabilities to systems and data. While putting in place such reactive measures as firewalls and enhanced data encryption technologies are essential to cyber risk planning, other proactive steps should augment these activities.

Some of these would include penetration assessment tests that should be performed periodically. They might entail the use of personnel hired specifically to try and hack into the company's systems or data infrastructure. Participation in war-gaming exercises at the firm or industry level can maintain readiness and spot weaknesses before events occur. Other measures could include structural responses such as walling off critical data and systems from other parts of the company to prevent the potential for a breach in one area to infect other critical infrastructure. Cyber-security risk presents yet another variation on operational risk to the firm that is evolving. Cyber-risks of the past featuring DDoS, malware, and phishing attacks, for example, may be overshadowed by more coordinated and bold attacks designed to disrupt, dismantle, or destroy financial assets and markets. Banks need to enhance existing processes for addressing cyber threats and make required investments to forestall major losses.

SUMMARY

Operational risk management activities at financial institutions blend art and science in establishing the potential exposure firms have from a wide variety of operational breakdowns in people, processes, and systems. For years measurement of operational risk has been handicapped by access to solid historical information from which to build measurement systems. With the advent of Basel capital standards, banks have increasingly been working to develop both usable data and models to estimate operational risk exposures.

Methodologies for operational risk measurement range greatly in their degree of complexity; however, expectations for the largest commercial banks are that they will need to comply with AMA standards. A combination of analytical and simulation-based methods may be used in constructing loss frequency and severity distributions and a wide variety of functional distributions may apply based on the fit of the data against specific types of operational risk.

Great care must be taken in developing these models as any number of assumptions can easily change results. Therefore it is important that the risk analyst charged with developing these capabilities understand the limitations of the data, assumptions, and methods being used to construct operational risk estimates.

QUESTIONS

1. As the head of operational risk for your bank, how might you categorize different operational risk events?

2. You have been shown the RCSAs for the capital markets division. Back office reconciliation of trade reporting has appeared as satisfactory on the RCSA for the past two years, meaning that this process is considered by management to be well-controlled. Last year, however, there was a trading loss of $45 million that was due to a rogue trading incident. How might a conversation with the head of capital markets go with regard to their RCSA?

3. Between 2000 and 2007, your bank observed 49 operational events. From 2008–2013, the bank grew considerably and as a result, your bank has seen the number of operational risk events climb to 150. How might you compare the relative operational risk from the 2000–2007 period to the 2008–2013 period?

4. What is the probability of observing five operational risk events in a single year for the 2000–2007 period?

   Assume that you have $\lambda = 5$, the mean and standard deviation of the log losses are $100,000 and $10,000, respectively, and $Z_0 = .5$ for simulation trial n.

5. Calculate the frequency distribution of operational events.

6. What would be the estimate of loss for any given loss event k?

7. What would be the total loss for simulation trial n?

8. Given the following standard deviations of risk type 1 and 2 of $200,000 and $300,000 along with their associated correlations shown below, what would the composite standard deviation be for these risks?

Risk Type	$200,000 1	$300,000 2
1	1	0.15
2	0.15	1

9. If z for the 95 percent level of confidence is 1.65, what is the 95 percent operational risk VaR and what does that mean?

10. How would you differentiate an operational risk from a credit risk?

CHAPTER 15

Model, Regulatory, Legal, and Reputational Risk Management

OVERVIEW

Beyond managing traditional bank risks such as credit, market, liquidity, and operational risk, SifiBank cannot afford to ignore a host of ancillary risks that may result in significant losses associated with lost business and customer relationships, costly penalties, and restrictions on bank activities, among other negative outcomes. Four risks of particular interest are model, regulatory, legal, and reputational risk. What makes these risks somewhat different from the other risks facing SifiBank is that they do not lend themselves to easy quantification of their overall contribution to Sifibank aggregate risk exposure. For that reason, SifiBank risk management must rely more on effective processes and controls than on development of sophisticated analytics.

Further, these risks may come together under certain conditions to amplify risk exposure for the firm. For example, introduction of a new product for which the bank has limited to no experience might lead to a vast underestimation of credit risk due to model misspecification that could lead to higher than expected credit losses. In turn, poor operational controls on this product could lead to greater regulation and legal battles with customers, investors, and counterparties, and the ensuing negative publicity could damage the reputation of the company in the eyes of these same constituencies. Building in checkpoints allowing management to gauge the level of these risks on an ongoing basis throughout the business provides an effective mechanism for incorporating these risks into the firm's overall risk assessment process.

SifiMortgage's experience before and after the financial crisis of 2008–2009 provides a basis for understanding how these risks can unfold, how they can hurt the bank, and what can be done to account for these risks. In

2004, SifiMortgage embarked on a strategy to expand the business away from standard mortgage products that could be sold to either Fannie Mae or Freddie Mac and into a set of nontraditional mortgage products. As Fannie and Freddie increased their presence in the mortgage secondary market, profits earned by originators such as SifiMortgage would shrink as the business became more commoditized.

The bank seized on the idea of originating products called option adjustable rate mortgages (ARMs) that provided borrowers with considerable flexibility in selecting one of several monthly payment options. These included making either the fixed-rate 30-year amortizing payment, a fixed-rate 15-year amortizing payment if the borrower wanted to accelerate paying off their loan, an interest-only payment (where the borrower pays only the interest portion of the payment) or a minimum payment using a below note rate or "teaser rate." Borrowers making this minimum payment would experience negative amortization where the difference between the amount that should be paid using the note rate and the teaser rate would be added onto the remaining loan balance. This could lead to circumstances where borrowers would find that their mortgage balance would eventually be larger than when the loan was taken out. These loans also introduced payment shock to the borrower by imposing a requirement that five years after origination the loan would reset to a rate that could be much higher than what it had been at origination.

SifiMortgage had no prior experience with these mortgages and as a result had little empirical data on which to build default models for pricing and loan loss reserving activities. The bank did have product guidelines on similar products originated by its key competitors and had considerable loan level data on mortgages somewhat similar in nature except for the payment options and rate reset features. This data became the basis for the analytical models used in developing the program.

Concurrent with the model development exercise, SifiMortgage product managers came to the business CRO with their competitor's underwriting guidelines requesting that risk management endorse matching their product guidelines. One institution had been originating this product for 20 years and had been successful managing its credit, interest rate, and operational risk performance in all business environments. This company further had elected to retain these option ARMs for its portfolio rather than packaging them up into a private label mortgage security that it could issue directly. Since this bank knew it would own all of the risk, it needed to make sure that the product was designed well and had strong controls in place to manage the credit, interest rate, and operational risk. In doing so, this bank originated these loans only to financially sophisticated borrowers that needed the payment flexibility to align with uneven income streams. High-income professionals with large down payments, excellent credit, and demonstrated capacity to repay the mortgages were the primary customers for this product. Furthermore, the bank also placed tight controls around the types of properties that would qualify and allowed only bank employees to conduct appraisals rather than outsourcing them to appraisal vendors.

SifiMortgage risk management had studied this program for many months and believed it offered the best opportunity as a portfolio product; however, the head of production and SifiMortgage's CFO were displeased with the credit guidelines proposed by the risk team for this new product. The risk management team had decided that the new option ARM product should remain focused on borrowers with demonstrated abilities to handle the complex payment features. Moreover, the risk management team decided that only in-house appraisals could be performed. The risk team contended that these program parameters and requirements would allow SifiMortgage to rollout the product on a limited basis, test its performance over time, and gradually relax various credit requirements as experience with the product evolved consistent with target risk levels. The product was taken to the Credit Risk Committee of SifiMortgage and was approved. The product's parameters were significantly relaxed over a short amount of time by the business over the objections of the CRO to better align with the competition and risk management was effectively relegated to a monitoring role. These events greatly affected the models used to assess risk, and invited considerable regulatory, legal, and reputational risk to SifiMortgage and SifiBank during the financial crisis.

MODEL RISK

Model risk for SifiMortgage came in three ways. First, since the bank did not have any experience with option ARMs, it faced limitations on the data used to build its models. Second, poor specification of mortgage default of option ARMs could lead to under- or overestimation of credit risk. A third issue affecting model risk emerged from the key assumptions used in analytic models. Model risk can lead to two types of outcomes: the risk that the models underestimate the actual losses of a portfolio or just the opposite, an overestimation of risk. In the case of an individual loan it manifests itself in statistics such as **Type I** and **Type II** errors. Suppose SifiMortgage has developed a model that predicts the likelihood that an option ARM will default or not. Comparing the results on a particular loan to what actually happens to the loan can be seen in Figure 15.1. In this binary outcome example, that is, default or no default, there are four combinations of actual versus modeled (expected) outcomes. Two of the four boxes are where

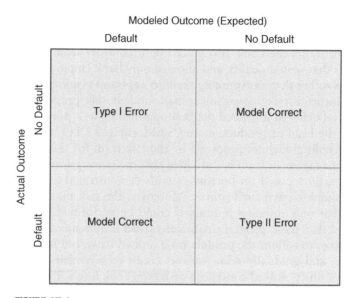

FIGURE 15.1   Type I and Type II Model Errors

the model correctly predicts a default or no default outcome. But the other two boxes show a Type I and Type II error. A Type I error is where the null hypothesis H_0 is true but is rejected. In this example, the model determines that the borrower will default, when in fact he does not (otherwise known as a false positive). In the case of a Type II error, the null hypothesis is false but is not rejected by the model. Here the model expects no default when in fact it does occur. From a business perspective, a model that has a high level of Type II error introduces more credit risk to SifiBank by approving more risky borrowers than warranted. Conversely, a model that contains a high degree of Type I errors may reject more qualified loan applicants and in the process reduce the amount of business the bank may conduct. The bank may trade off Type I and Type II errors in setting credit cutoffs that demarcate which borrowers will receive a loan based on the modeled default probability. To grasp the nature of these trade-offs graphically, consider Figure 15.2. The data used by SifiMortgage to develop its default risk model of option ARMs contains 98,000 nonoption ARM loans that never defaulted (i.e., 90+ days past due of worse) against 2,000 loans that went into default over a five-year interval. The data included mortgages originated between 1998 and 2003. While there had been a recession in 2001, for the most part the period in the data was marked by relatively favorable economic growth, low interest rates, and strong home price appreciation—all elements contributing to relatively low default rates during the sample period. The statistical

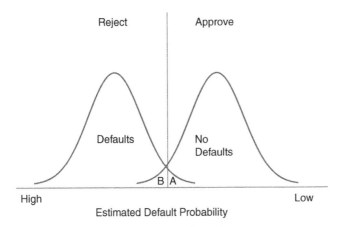

FIGURE 15.2   Type I and Type II Error Trade-Offs in Risk Models

models developed rely on borrower, loan, and economic factors to generate a predicted default probability for each loan in the sample. Figure 15.2
displays the distribution of loans that did not default in the sample by the
modeled default probabilities (rightmost distribution) along with the distribution of loans that did default (leftmost distribution). A perfect model
would be one where the two distributions do not overlap. While such an
outcome is highly unlikely in actual modeling efforts, there is an expectation that the default and no default distributions will overlap. The higher
the overlap, the worse the accuracy of the model to predict default. If Sifi-
Mortgage imposes a credit cutoff shown as the vertical line in Figure 15.2,
expressed as the marginal default probability that is acceptable to the bank,
it implicitly makes a trade-off on the amount of Type I and Type II errors it
will encounter. The amount of Type I error in this example is shown as the
area under the no default curve to the left of the cutoff labeled B. Conversely
the area under the default curve to the right of the cutoff designated as A is a
Type II error. Moving the cutoff to the left or right will increase or decrease
Type II and Type I errors, respectively.

DATA ERRORS

Good modeling starts with good data. The most sophisticated model specifi-
cations are only as good as the data on which the model is built. In the case
of SifiMortgage, the bank was fortunate to have a talented group of PhD
modelers with expertise in mortgage default modeling. Knowing that they
would need to generate a view of expected and unexpected losses on the

new option ARM portfolio, the risk modeling team developed a simulation model of default and prepayment with two stochastic variables: home prices and interest rates.

The types of loans in the sample included mortgages where the borrower was not required to provide income or asset information to the borrower. These low and no doc loans were coded differently from fully documented loans in the data; however, their inclusion led to misspecification errors in the default model with respect to a key measure of the borrower's capacity to repay the mortgage, namely the debt-to-income (DTI) variable. Borrowers knew, as did their brokers, that stating an income on their loan application higher than what they earned would increase the chances of being approved for the loan. By allowing this program, SifiBank unknowingly sabotaged its own data. Loans where incomes were overstated showed up in the data as having low DTIs, which historically would be associated with lower default rates. However, with increasing numbers of borrowers misstating their incomes, the DTI-default relations became distorted for SifiBank, as shown in Figure 15.3. Using data where incomes are fully documented, the DTI-default relationship is steeper than when using data where incomes are not verified. Even after controlling for other factors in the model, the DTI effect is flatter in the data where some incomes are stated rather than verified by the lender, leading to the incorrect conclusion that it may not be as important a factor in mortgage underwriting as traditionally thought. This would lead SifiMortgage production managers to lobby risk management to raise its credit policy on eligible DTIs from 40 to 50 percent. Fortunately,

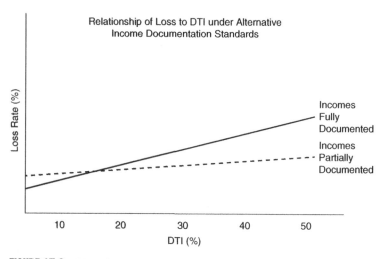

FIGURE 15.3 How Data Errors Contribute to Model Errors

the risk management team recognized the issue and augmented their statistical estimates from their original sample with DTI estimates drawn from a sample of loans consisting of only fully documented loans.

Another trouble spot for SifiMortgage modelers was around investor-owned properties. Over the years, SifiMortgage had found statistical evidence that investor-owned properties were riskier than owner-occupied loans. As a result, an upfront fee of 1 percent of the loan balance was imposed on the borrower at closing for being an investment property. Human nature being what it is, many investors avoided paying the fee by stating that they would occupy the property, while knowing full well that they would not. The bank had limited ability to verify the occupancy status of the borrower after the fact and over time, SifiMortgage unknowingly had 20 percent of investors claiming to be owner-occupants. This error in the data led to SifiMortgage underestimating the risk of investor-owned properties while overestimating the risk for owner-occupants.

On top of these data issues, SifiMortgage also experienced problems in estimating LTVs, one of the most statistically predictive factors explaining mortgage default. The LTV variable, unlike occupancy status, is a constructed variable from the loan balance and appraised property value. Property appraisals can be an art in their own right and require a significant amount of experience with local property markets to make objective valuations. To ensure the integrity of the appraisal process, appraisals should be conducted independent of the production unit incentivized with bringing the loan in the door. In the case of SifiMortgage, the appraisal unit was captive to the production unit, allowing production managers to control the process. Appraisers that did not provide valuations that would meet LTV credit standards were not called back in new transactions. As a result, this process led to considerable inflation of property values, which in turn led to much lower LTVs. These data errors would manifest in the SifiMortgage default model by underestimating the impact of LTVs on default, particularly at the highest and therefore riskiest levels of this variable. Each of these data errors on their own was troublesome, but their collective impact would not show up until the crisis, although the model team's validation against the development and holdout sample showed that the default model held up well against that data.

MODEL ASSUMPTIONS

The data used by SifiMortgage to estimate its default models would eventually come back to haunt it and almost all of its competitors originating option ARM loans. For one, while the data did go back five years, it did not span a complete business cycle, and more importantly it was from a period of time that experienced better than average default performance. At the time the model was developed, the risk team had generated a number of simulated paths of defaults based on the trajectory of home prices and interest rates. The paths generated by these stochastic processes were believed to be too compressed and tilted downward over the life of the loan, implying that the estimated defaults were lower than they ought to be. From that analysis, the risk team found a period of time where significant defaults had occurred, but it was for a specific region and not nationally representative. Nevertheless the risk team used the simulated values based on interest rates and regional home prices in generating a default rate distribution that was more dispersed and resulted in default rate projections that were about double the original estimates. The risk team did not believe that the new option ARM products should be expected to have default rates comparable to those of ARM products that did not have the potential for payment shock reflected in the model's development sample. Looking at aggregate default statistics of option ARMs compared to traditional ARM products from other lenders, the risk team had expected to find the new products to perform two times worse. With their revised model generating results that seemed consistent with the aggregate performance in the industry, SifiMortgage risk analysts presented the results to the credit risk committee for approval as their loan loss reserve and pricing model. Once again the risk management group faced stiff opposition from the business and finance area that contended the models were judgmentally overridden rather than allowed to rely on the actual experience of the loans. Instead, the original models (with lower loss estimates) not based on the regional data were approved. The CRO of the business unit refused to sign off on the reserve process and eventually resigned from the company.

Even though the risk team recognized important differences in the new option ARM products versus those in the development sample that would lead eventually to higher than expected defaults, there was a blindspot in the analysis that assumed correlations in home prices across housing markets would remain relatively the same in all economic environments. In the United States, with thousands of individual local markets for housing, a portfolio comprised of mortgages representative of the overall market provided a diversification effect to the holder of those loans. That was largely the result of home prices in one market such as Los Angeles not being perfectly correlated with Boston. If home prices dropped in Los Angeles due to eroding economic conditions, they might be picking up in Boston for just the opposite reason. Thus higher defaults in Los Angles due to a crash in home prices and other events might be muted by the favorable conditions in other markets in the bank's portfolio. In the years before the crisis, this diversification benefit would work well as an effective portfolio strategy. But as home prices began rising, the relationship of home prices across markets changed. Over time nearly all markets started to experience higher than normal home price appreciation, as a period of strong economic growth and low interest rates super-charged housing markets. As a result, house prices across markets started to become more correlated. Once the housing market bubble burst, home prices tumbled across markets and that same high degree of correlation showed up in SifiMortgage's portfolio as excessive losses. This can be seen in Figure 15.4. At the time SifiMortgage developed its estimates of mortgage losses, it relied on estimates of housing market correlations that reflected the relatively benign period leading up to the crisis. Those correlations would lead SifiMortgage to believe that the loss distribution for its mortgage portfolio would resemble the distribution labeled *diversified*. However, as correlations changed during the housing boom and markets became more correlated over time, losses would eventually manifest as the *undiversified* distribution in Figure 15.4. As shown in that figure, as markets became more correlated, the tail of the distribution became heavier, implying that the likelihood of realizing a loss level of X or greater as shown in the figure was higher than what SifiMortgage estimated using the historical correlations. Assuming housing market correlations would remain relatively constant in all environments was a major error in the end. Spotting important changes in the relationship of key variables and

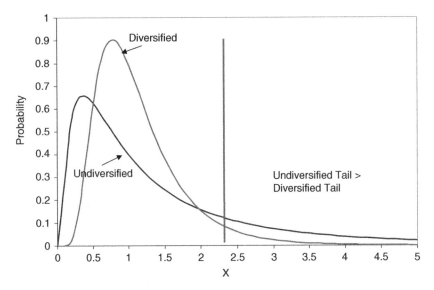

FIGURE 15.4   Impact of Changing in Correlation Structure on Stress Loss Events

adjusting risk levels to those changes is an important part of the model assessment and management process.

RISK LAYERING

One of the more insidious ways that models can go awry for risk managers is by incrementally changing a product's features over time. This has the effect of rendering the underlying data used to construct model risk estimates less relevant as the product features in the original data no longer provide an accurate view of borrower behavior under the new product characteristics. During a boom period when competition for borrowers is high and default experience low, banks tend to relax underwriting standards for loan products in ways that, if the bank is not careful, will morph into product sets that little resemble what the bank based its original loss estimates on.

SifiMortgage experienced this problem, called **risk layering**, over the years leading up to the crisis on its option ARM product. When the product was first rolled out, its option ARM program was oriented toward financially sophisticated borrowers with at least 720 FICOs, putting a 20 percent downpayment on the property with fully documented income and with DTIs no greater than 36 percent. This worked out well in the first couple of years for SifiMortgage as originations expanded in the relatively new nontraditional mortgage market. But as the program matured and competition began chipping away at their market share, SifiMortgage decided to make fundamental changes in the product by relaxing its credit standards across most aspects of the product. By the time the product was in full swing, FICO score minimums had been dropped to 620, borrowers were allowed to put only 5 percent down on the home, and incomes no longer were required to be verified. While SifiMortgage management justified these actions based on low default experience and a need to offer the borrower a more efficient application experience, what the bank did not realize was that it was radically changing the type of borrower it was attracting. Essentially the product strayed from its roots as a specialty product that worked for a certain type of borrower; it became mass marketed and thereby changed the risk profile of the product.

SifiMortgage did not have much empirical history with FICOs less than 720 on the option ARM product from which to develop robust estimates of default. For that matter it did not have experience with any of the features it would eventually allow. Moreover, SifiMortgage unknowingly compounded its risk exposure by relaxing features across the board. Initially, risk management had allowed a reduction of some features such as lower FICO scores as long as the borrower had a higher downpayment. This would provide the bank with a **compensating factor** that would offset the risk of relaxing a credit standard. But over time, the SifiMortgage product team took control of the product and elected to broadly relax credit terms without regard to compensating factors. This decision would eventually play out in the form of extensive model error when borrowers encountered financial stress. The models, which were tuned to a completely different type of borrower, were unable to pick up important behavioral shifts underlying the individual credit attributes of the borrower and, importantly, the compound effects of broad relaxation of credit standards exacerbated the credit risk for the bank. The models were not able in their original specification to assess the compound effect of low FICO with high LTV and low documentation. Individually, each attribute was accounted for in the model, but thin or no data for some features would reduce the accuracy of the model for riskier credit segments. The absence of interaction effects of certain risk attributes also meant that the models could not pick up the impact of broad relaxation of credit terms. The effect from this model error was that SifiMortgage drastically underestimated the amount of credit risk it would realize after the crisis. It had mispriced the product, underestimated the amount of its loan loss reserve and hemorrhaged credit losses for several years.

GUARDING AGAINST MODEL RISK

Model risk can be mitigated through implementation of a strong governance process, periodic model validation exercises, and effective controls on product development. Bank regulators have increased their expectations on model risk over the years. One of the most critical components of a robust model development program is the oversight of models. In the aftermath of the crisis, SifiMortgage completely overhauled its model development process across the company making it a leader in model management among its large bank peers.

The first action the bank took was to create a Model Governance Committee headed up by a new position reporting to SifiBank's CRO, the Deputy CRO for Model Risk Management. The committee was composed of representatives from each of SifiBank's model development areas. The composition of the committee needed to strike the right balance between technical expertise and independence for model review. The committee was formalized by a charter outlining the specific objectives, tasks, and rules for how models would be developed, validated, deployed, and reported on throughout the company. An important aspect of the model committee is that it would set clear criteria for when a model would be ready for deployment, when it would need to be revised or replaced, and the establishment of a periodic validation schedule for each model. All models in the company would fall under the requirements of the committee and in that way assure SifiBank that it was applying consistent practices across the firm. The company also created a model policy document outlining the specific steps in each phase of a model's development, validation, deployment, and performance reporting that would be expected from each model group.

In terms of development, the model policy outlined data management processes used in acquiring, processing and using datasets for modeling. Understanding the quality, limitations, and gaps of data used for modeling exercises is a critical task that must be performed well in advance of any modeling. Part of this exercise would include development of a data dictionary containing detailed information on data and any constructed variables, as well as variable names and related pertinent information. In addition, the model development team would be required to compile a comprehensive set of documentation on the model including the specification, the justification for the model, variables and theoretical relevance, estimation results, and associated model code. This is necessary to create a living document that prevents key person dependencies in the event of staff turnover.

From a model development standpoint, a set of model performance metrics, minimum thresholds, and tolerances would be established around when models are ready for deployment. These would vary from model to model depending on the type. If SifiMortgage were developing a new underwriting scorecard for its mortgage business, it might rely on such econometric techniques as logistic regression as discussed in Chapter 6. In the case of such binary choice models, model diagnostics such as the **Kolmogorov-Smirnoff test** (KS) may be used along with other comparable tests of model performance.[1] Reliance on a single measure of a model's **goodness-of-fit** may not provide a sufficient all-around perspective on how well the model is performing. The model committee might require that before any scorecard can be deployed it must have a minimum KS of some level. Results from such tests as illustrated in Figure 15.5 are useful in making decisions on when a model may be ready for deployment or not. Against a minimum KS standard of 30, SifiMortgage would not be allowed to deploy the model shown in Figure 15.5 since the KS statistic was lower than the model policy threshold. A consideration in testing the model's performance is where

---

[1]KS is one measure of the performance of models with binary choice outcomes such as logistic regression models that are commonly used in building automated underwriting scorecards. A KS ranges between 0 (nonpredictive) and 100 (perfectly predictive) measures the separation between good and bad outcomes in a population. It is usually measured at the maximum distance between the two empirical distributions.

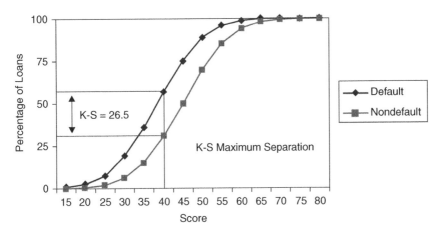

FIGURE 15.5 Representative Model Diagnostics for SifiMortgage Mortgage Scorecard

to measure the KS. The model, for example, may appear to perform well against KS measured at the maximum point between the good and bad loan distributions, but may be weak around where the model is actually used, that is, the policy cutoff for approve or reject.

Once a model has been developed, it must undergo extensive validation. During the development phase the model builders will perform their own validation of how well the new model (challenger) works, typically compared with an existing model (champion). Validation against the development sample used to build the model provides an important baseline against which to gauge a model's specification and performance. However, validation must go further, requiring that the model be tested against samples not used in the development of the model. Validations performed against a holdout sample or out-of-sample test should serve as the basis for gauging whether the model should be deployed or not. These could include separate holdout samples: a subsample of the original development database not used in the model building exercise and/or an out-of-sample test that includes running the model on a different time period or related cohort that will test the model's flexibility outside of its original period. Important to this effort, however, is the need for the model to be validated independently from the group building the model. Reporting to the new head of model risk management is a model validation team whose purpose is to provide independent validation of all of SifiBank's models. They report to the model committee and provide a recommendation on the performance of the model. The committee members then vote on whether to deploy the model or place additional requirements on it before it can be released.

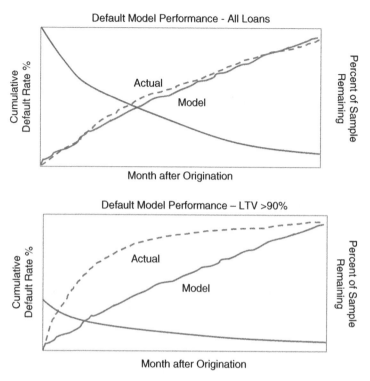

FIGURE 15.6 SifiMortgage Error Tracking Analysis

The committee also requires the model validation team to provide regular reporting on the performance of models. A variety of techniques can be used to make such assessments, and in addition to computing a number of key model metrics, the validation team also needs to track the model's expected outcomes against actual performance. One example of this type of error tracking is shown in Figure 15.6. In this example, the overall performance of the credit default model is shown over time in the top figure as mortgages age in months after origination. The model also shows the percent of loans in the dataset over time as a way to gauge whether a sufficient sample size exists to provide a robust estimate of default.

This should not only be done at the aggregate level but also for important subsets of the portfolio, transactions, or originations. The model could very well hold up well on average, as it appears in the top figure, but on certain subsets under- or overestimate the amount of risk to the firm. To see this consider the bottom figure in Figure 15.6. In this figure the model is compared against actual defaults on only loans with LTVs above 95 percent. Note that the model on this segment significantly overpredicts default. In addition, the sample size is much smaller, an indication that the model may suffer from not having sufficient observations on high LTV loans from which to generate a statistically reliable estimate of default. Understanding how the model was developed including how much data for each subset existed from which to build the model is important.

Over time it is expected that model performance will deteriorate. Some of this can occur as business strategy changes or as the underlying mix of business shifts. A model could continue to hold up well if the underlying conditions on which it were built and composition of risk attributes remains relatively the same as the data on which the model were developed. However, if the mix of business were to materially change along with a shift in underlying economic conditions, it could lead to significant errors in the model. That is why tracking changes in the portfolio of interest along with market conditions should be an integral part of any ongoing model validation process. While not technically part of the model validation process, one way to assess and manage risk shifts which could introduce model error is by developing metrics that identify changes in the portfolio's composition. One example would be to set a threshold for a certain level of risk as the percentage of loans each month that are originated with expected default rates more than 2 standard deviations over the mean default rate. Each month SifiMortgage collects data on the characteristics of its monthly originations. This information is then fed into its default models and for each loan an estimate of lifetime default risk is generated. A distribution of default rates is created as shown in Figure 15.7. SifiMortgage might set a tolerance that no more than 5 percent of its monthly originations should have a default risk estimate greater than 5 percent, which is 2 standard deviations over the average from when it began the program. This would allow the bank to identify important risk concentrations and get ahead of them before they become unmanageable. When risk concentrations begin closing in on the threshold, the bank would begin analyzing the drivers of these shifts and could respond by requesting changes in credit guidelines or other program adjustments to bring the risk back in line with expectations. Doing so would also help maintain the applicability of the default model to recent originations.

At times models may be observed to enter a phase where their performance has deteriorated to a level where redevelopment will be required. However, development is a protracted process and should not be rushed. Interim modifications may be warranted ahead of a full-blown re-estimation exercise. For instance, it might be observed that a model has

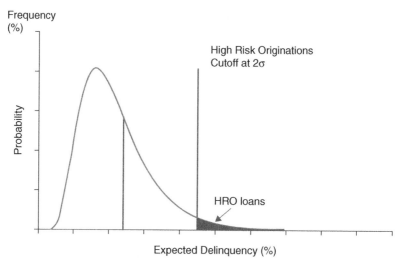

FIGURE 15.7　High-Risk Loan Monitoring

not deteriorated below pre-specified model performance thresholds but has exhibited a systematic underestimation of default over the past six months. In particular the validation team estimates that actual defaults are coming in 5 percent higher than what is predicted by the model. Since the model is also being used in estimating the loan loss reserve for this product, a determination would be made to adjust the model by a factor of 1.05 as an interim change to improve the alignment of the model with actual experience. This would be documented as an interim change to the model and included as part of the loan loss reserve documentation as well. The model committee would review this change and also vote on its adoption. Along with that change, the committee would impose any stipulations on how long the change could remain in place and establish the prioritization for redevelopment of the model. Once the new model has been developed it would be vetted through the same review and approval process and be staged for deployment.

REGULATORY RISK

By virtue of the bank charter, depository institutions enjoy advantages over nonbanking institutions, such as subsidized deposit insurance, which affords banks a funding advantage over nonbanks. In return for these advantages, banks are exposed to significant regulation. With that come a variety of risks that can be subsumed under a general category called regulatory risk. Regulatory scrutiny of the banking system tends to ebb and flow with market cycles. In the years preceding the thrift crisis of the 1980s or the financial crisis of 2008–2009, regulatory intensity was much lower than in the years following each of these events. This is a natural outcome during booms and busts to expect variations in regulatory focus. Beyond the regulatory dynamics affecting the industry lie specific risks that each institution faces as a regulated entity.

Regulatory agencies such as the OCC, the Federal Reserve, and FDIC have at their disposal a number of policy tools varying in their effect on the firm that it can use to enforce compliance with bank regulation. In severe cases, regulators can shut down an institution, even before it becomes technically insolvent due to provisions under federal banking **Prompt Correction Action** regulations in order to avoid a costlier outcome for the FDIC as well as the industry. In the course of the examination process, regulatory authorities can impose restrictions on banking activities such as mergers and acquisitions, or expansion into new products depending on the materiality of their findings of deficiencies in the bank. Clearly such an outcome could reduce the profitability of the firm for a period of time and lose competitive advantage that it might otherwise enjoy, absent a regulatory action.

In the years leading up to the crisis SifiMortgage faced relatively lax regulatory oversight in the development of its nontraditional mortgage business strategy. Regulators were well-informed by the company as to its products and strategy and while there were some concerns expressed at times by the bank's OCC examination team on payment shock potential and risk layering of these products if a stress event were to occur, the agency did not prevent the bank from increasing its portfolio of these assets.

As mass marketing of its option ARM products continued, the bank continued to use disclosure documents describing the terms and conditions of its products that were relatively difficult for the lay person to understand, particularly for products with as much complexity as the bank's option ARMs. Many borrowers had trouble understanding that they would face the potential for negative amortization should they make the minimum payment each month for their mortgage and the prospect of payment shock in the future if interest rates moved higher. The bank continued to use the standard disclosure documents until 2006, at which point it decided to revamp the disclosure by providing specific examples of what negative amortization and payment shock could do to monthly payments.

Concurrent with its introduction of the option ARM product, a boom in mortgage originations occurred, owing in large measure to a low interest rate environment engineered by the Federal Reserve that brought a period of strong economic growth and low unemployment. Lenders such as

SifiMortgage could not keep up with the demand for mortgages and began hiring loan originators and underwriters from all walks of life. People who had no previous background in underwriting became the frontline of defense in making sure the quality of its originations were consistent with the credit profile expected by risk management. More importantly, underwriters were part of the SifiMortgage production unit and as a result were given bonuses based on the number of loans they could underwrite and approve in a month. These underwriters reported to loan production officers that likewise had large upside potential for bonuses tied to production goals. This compensation structure thus placed extraordinary pressure on SifiMortgage underwriters to approve loans, which led to significant lapses in validating borrower application information such as incomes that under the program could be stated rather than validated by paystubs or other means. While this greatly increased the number of borrowers approved for loans, it came at a major price.

Each month the risk management team's quality control unit performed a monthly random audit of loans originated in the previous month. The QC team specified that the sample should provide a 95 percent level of confidence in results. In addition, the team under the direction of the CRO would conduct target audits of new or high-risk products to understand the quality of the loan manufacturing process. The QC team would look at how well the underwriters adhered to credit guidelines including the accuracy of such key attributes as income and property appraisals, among other components of the assessment process.

At one point, SifiMortgage conducted a QC audit of 500 recently originated option ARMs and reported its findings to the CRO. Since the program had begun, the percentage of loans where income was fully documented declined from 80 percent to 50 percent in just two years. But once the QC team began pulling IRS tax documents that verified what incomes borrowers were actually making, it was clear that SifiMortgage had significant breakdowns in their underwriting process. For the more recent three months of originations, the QC team found that nearly half of the loans where borrowers were allowed to state their incomes, income reported on their applications was 40 percent higher than what was reported to the IRS. This result was reported at the next Corporate Credit Committee Meeting and SifiMortgage Credit Committee Meeting and also sent along to other senior management.

Senior production management dismissed the results coming from the corporate QC team as unreliable since that group had been viewed as obstructionist for some time against the production unit. The QC unit assigned to the production team was asked to conduct their own assessment, and while it confirmed some of the corporate QC's findings, it claimed that much of the original findings could be dismissed due to differences in what was included as income, which exaggerated the income deviations found. Based on these findings, the corporate risk management results and recommendations to scale the program back were ignored. The option ARM program continued to grow until early 2007 when the first mortgage losses on private label mortgage-backed securities emerged.

By 2008, with SifiMortgage experiencing unprecedented losses, attention began turning back to the way the company had originated mortgages in the years leading up to the crisis. Eventually this led to intense regulatory scrutiny by the OCC and other regulators. On top of that Congress acted swiftly to enact the **Dodd-Frank Wall Street Reform and Consumer Protection Act,** which ushered in hundreds of new rules and regulations spanning nearly every corner of banking. Among the new rules affecting SifiMortgage directly were prohibitions on certain types of mortgages; a brand new agency, the **Consumer Financial Protection Bureau** (CFPB), charged with overseeing consumer financial protection; and tighter rules on fair lending as well as what interest rates and fees lenders could charge borrowers. On top of that, the regulatory agencies required all large banks to provide monthly loan level data on the performance and characteristics of their originations.

SifiMortgage's regulatory issues were just a microcosm of what SifiBank faced following Dodd-Frank. As a newly designated **systemically important financial institution** (SIFI), the bank had to comply with new reporting requirements on its activities and exposures as well as additional capital requirements. SifiBank was inundated with requests for information and analysis from the Federal Reserve, the OCC, the FDIC, the New York Fed, and the CFPB. SifiBank's systems, data, and personnel were not well situated to handle the increased regulatory burden. Given that the regulatory agencies had come under fire by Congress after the crisis for a lack of oversight, their interactions with bank management became increasingly demanding with little tolerance for delays and gaps in responding to their requests.

Caught off-guard by the new regulatory environment, the bank initially was forced into hiring a number of consultants to help them build a new regulatory risk and compliance function within the corporate division of SifiBank. This wound up costing the bank more than $100 million in the first year of this initiative as well as the hiring of several hundred compliance officers whose job it would be to manage regulatory requests and compliance with new regulations across the firm. In addition, the bank wound up spending nearly $750 million on Project Advance, an effort to streamline, modernize, and integrate the bank's multiple information and reporting systems. All in the bank estimated that the ongoing annual cost of compliance was going to be between $50 million and $75 million.

SifiBank's neglect in taking regulatory risk into account not only directly led to credit, reputational, and legal risks but also contributed to the systemic risk of the banking sector that was followed by a period of heavy regulation. Taking stock of these deficiencies, the new management team at SifiBank wanted to reflect on what it should have done to mitigate its exposure in order to better manage regulatory risk going forward.

The CRO and General Auditor were charged with conducting a comprehensive assessment of the failings of the firm to manage regulatory risk before the crisis. After six months of looking over various documents such as **risk control self-assessments** (RCSAs) containing management's periodic assessment of their vulnerabilities and risk mitigation activities, management and risk committee meeting minutes and documents as well as policies and procedures in force before the crisis and after countless discussions with management and staff, seven recommendations were made to the bank's Executive Committee. The findings were as follows:

1. Direct assessment of regulatory risk exposure to the firm was not consolidated into a single executive with accountability; instead, regulatory risk was managed diffusely across businesses and in an inconsistent fashion.
2. Management embraced an environment at the time that created an adversarial posture with key regulators.
3. Regulatory risk was not factored into product development and portfolio management strategy discussions.
4. Data and management reporting systems were unable to provide timely responses to management and regulatory requests or at a level of disaggregation to flexibly respond to multiple and myriad requests for information.
5. Management and staff were not well versed in regulatory risk, and concerns raised by regulators about bank activities had limited exposure across the company.
6. RCSAs were not taken seriously by management and were viewed as more of a paperwork issue than as an effective risk management tool.
7. SifiBank was woefully understaffed in regulatory and compliance staff.

In response to these major findings, the bank's CEO requested that bank management implement the following recommendations from the CRO and General Auditor for strengthening the bank's regulatory risk capabilities. They centered on principles of identification, assessment and mitigation of potential regulatory risk. The major changes to the bank's focus on regulatory risk included the following eight actions:

1. The CRO was formally charged with leading the bank's regulatory risk activities with support from the General Counsel's office. While compliance and regulatory risk activities are commonly found reporting to the

legal division, the bank sought to take a holistic view toward managing all bank risks under one roof.

2. The CRO created a consolidated function from other areas of the company to lead the bank's regulatory and compliance function. A Deputy CRO position was created and compliance officers assigned by the corporate operating division. Compliance officers were embedded with each operating unit directly reporting back to the Deputy CRO, but with indirect reporting to each operating unit CEO.

3. The RCSA process was overhauled to include regulatory risk as a new category. In addition, senior management along with their teams now had 25 percent of their incentive compensation and performance evaluations based on the quality of their RCSA assessments, mitigation strategies, and regulatory and compliance findings.

4. Product development and other business strategies were required to directly take regulatory risk into account in their processes. The CRO was inserted as a control point to review and approve large exposure regulatory risks with delegations of authority for lesser exposures assigned to other risk managers.

5. Employees from business units were incented to elevate concerns about irregularities they found in bank activities that could lead to regulatory risk and a campaign was started to raise awareness of regulatory risk across the company.

6. The CEO and his direct reports embarked on a new engagement strategy with regulators that was based on professional respect, transparency, and trust.

7. Project Advance became a major initiative for the firm involving every business unit. SifiBank created a new IT infrastructure architected around the concept of transaction level reporting and analysis. Specifically, each transaction's details including attributes and risk profile over time were captured with a common lexicon applied across the company allowing the bank to aggregate not only at an operating unit level, but also across portfolios and subportfolios as needed. The ability to data mine was a paramount objective supporting a myriad of bank regulatory and business activities such as regulatory stress test and capital management exercises along with ALM and risk management activities.

8. The bank implemented a regulatory rules engine through Project Advance that tracked compliance with regulations and laws over all operating units. A plug-and-play capability was designed into the rules engine allowing compliance officers to update and edit rules and modify management reports that tracked compliance with these regulations.

LEGAL RISK

SifiMortgage's sloppy underwriting practices left SifiBank in the years following the crisis a major target of civil and criminal litigation from state governments, federal agencies, investors, customers, and other parties. The litigation principally centered on SifiMortgage's underwriting and loan servicing activities during the boom years. Examples of the type of litigation it faced included the following:

1. Multibillion-dollar class-action lawsuits from multiple state attorneys general over deceptive and fraudulent mortgage practices that displaced hundreds of thousands of borrowers who were unable to make their mortgage payments and eventually went into foreclosure.
2. Multibillion-dollar demands for loan repurchase from Fannie Mae, Freddie Mac, mortgage insurance companies, and other investors for defective loans that violated the contractual terms of transactions with these counterparties.
3. Department of Justice and CFPB civil class-action fair-lending case charging SifiMortgage with engaging in discriminatory pricing and underwriting practices against certain borrower protected classes.
4. A variety of multibillion-dollar civil class action cases from investors in SifiBank private label mortgage securities and stock claiming damages against reckless business practices that led to massive losses for investors.
5. A variety of criminal investigations of executive management by the Department of Justice during the boom years.

By 2008, the amount of litigation confronting SifiBank overwhelmed the General Counsel's office, requiring the bank to retain a number of prominent law firms to represent them in these various cases. As cases piled up for the bank, it quickly adopted a strategy to aggressively defend against these cases to a point at which a reasonable settlement could occur. Nevertheless, the cost of outside counsel and legal settlements would reach more than $50 billion by 2014.

Beyond the legal expenses incurred, the seemingly unending litigation was fodder for the media, creating significant reputation risk for the bank. The adversarial nature of the litigation also stymied the bank's strategy of cultivating a better relationship with its regulators. As with the initiative launched by the CEO to conduct a postmortem on the bank's regulatory risk practices before the crisis, he also commissioned the General Counsel to conduct an internal investigation of how it failed to anticipate such large legal risk exposure.

After several months, the General Counsel reported back to the Executive Committee and Board of Directors with the following four major findings:

1. When product and business strategies were under review, legal risks rarely entered into the discussion. In fact, as SifiMortgage's option ARM product was first developed or afterward, there was no evidence that management ever questioned whether the product posed any legal risk to the company.
2. Evidence of widespread mortgage fraud coming from within certain origination branch offices of SifiMortgage as well as through mortgage brokers selling loans to SifiMortgage was detected by the bank's loan review team which reported to the corporate CRO. However, while these findings were reported both to management and the board, little action was taken to address the issues until the crisis.
3. The incentive compensation structure of the bank at the time created perverse incentives to allow lax processes and controls throughout the company and promoted actions that unintentionally exposed the firm to legal risk. One example cited in the investigation was a SifiMortgage sanctioned process to streamline borrowers in the mortgage underwriting queue. This process effectively allowed exceptions to the underwriting criteria to be overridden, thereby allowing riskier borrowers to gain loan approval faster for a price. This practice not only exposed the firm to eventual repurchase risk of bad loans it sold to various counterparties or sought insurance on but also created fair lending risk exposure since a disproportionate share of the borrowers in this streamlined process were protected classes who were charged upfront fees that were 2–3 percent higher than similarly situated white borrowers. Bank management and staff were compensated on volume with no accountability for risk management on their performance evaluation.
4. RCSAs were found to have little reference to potential legal risks or mitigation strategies.

In the aftermath of SifiBank's investigation of legal risk management practices it put forward a set of recommendations that were endorsed by the CEO, the Board, and the Executive Committee. Going forward, SifiBank would establish the following five practices to guard against legal risk:

1. Incentive compensation structures would have a long-term component for legal costs incurred by the bank over an established threshold. Given the bank's high profile and nature of its business, it was expected that there would be some "normal" level of legal risk; however, beyond

that level, management was taking a zero tolerance posture that would directly cost management over time by reducing their bonuses and in more significant circumstances lead to dismissal from the company.

2. As with the regulatory risk investigation, the company established a whistleblower "See Something Say Something" campaign designed to allow employees to report potential legal risks to management without fear of retribution.
3. Legal risk was featured as a new category in SifiBank's RCSAs and management was expected to take potential legal risk into consideration in all of its business practices.
4. The bank retained outside counsel to conduct an annual legal risk review of the company that would be presented to the Board and the Executive Committee.
5. The General Counsel was given veto authority on any product or business activity that it believed could put the company at significant legal risk. Bank management would be allowed to make their case to the General Counsel but they would no longer be able to go directly to the CEO and plead their case without the General Counsel being present. A formal Business Legal Risk Review Committee was created to elevate legal risk from across the company and vet these potential risks.

REPUTATION RISK

By now it was evident to SifiBank that a catastrophic failure to effectively manage its business processes and controls coupled with a lack of strong risk governance practices not only exposed the bank to massive credit losses after the crisis, but also subjected the firm to extraordinary levels of regulatory and legal risks. But as mentioned earlier, SifiBank's size and scope of operations made it a favorite target for media stories on its latest regulatory or legal gaffe.

Reputational risk is a "softer" type of risk management in that, unlike other risk types such as credit or market risk, it does not lend itself to easy measurement. Nonetheless, it can have damaging effects across the bank in the form of funding instability, a decline in demand for bank products and make it more difficult for the bank to enter new markets or expand existing businesses.

If the bank effectively manages its other risks, it reduces the chances that some form of reputational event forms. However, the bank should be constantly assessing the views of consumers, investors, and counterparties toward the bank as a way of detecting any signs of potential reputational risk.

In today's increasingly social media-oriented society, a bad experience by a single customer can go viral in real-time before the bank has had a chance to react and respond to the claim. In that environment the bank must build processes, data and analytic tools that allow it to observe trends in customer experience, investor sentiment or counterparty assessment of bank activities on a daily basis.

SifiBank established a corporate office for reputational risk assessment, bringing in a number of Silicon Valley programmers and social media marketing and technical personnel who created a new tracking process designed to browse social media websites looking for references to SifiBank. Negative, positive, and neutral responses to SifiBank were captured in the daily data download. Reports were created allowing management to see where the bank stood from a sentiment analysis perspective as well as over time and compared to its peers. A sample of one of the reports is shown in Figure 15.8. The report displays a variety of information on customer sentiment and events that could lead to reputational risk over various time periods. The data is presented in a number of ways, including the percent positive and negative sentiment at a point in time as well as the sources for information on SifiBank. In addition, the percent of negative responses for specific "events" are depicted. Over the past several months, SifiBank experienced a significant security breach in customer data, a new product rollout issue that prevented customers from accessing their accounts, and a regulatory "cease and desist" order. The security breach resulted in significant negative reaction, and the regulatory order was the least impactful on the bank's reputation in this instance. Capturing such information is important as the potential for certain events and sentiment to "stick" over time could present problems to the bank in that they may create lingering negative publicity that the bank would need to defend against. By highlighting the trends over time the bank can determine which areas require immediate attention by its public relations area as well as communicating reputational risk "hot spots" to business units where issues have shown up, such as a foreclosure on an elderly customer.

Figure 15.9 presents a timeline of SifiBank sentiment results taken from various public websites of an event that occurred on day 0. The top panel presents analysis of changes in consumer sentiment in the days leading up to the event as well as in the period afterward. In addition, SifiBank tracks sentiment against other large peer institutions as a way of gauging whether there could be any competitive fallout. Again, such analysis can help the bank get ahead of issues as they form. Such analysis, while still a relatively new area in risk management, provides much promise in anticipating important trends that can lead to reputational problems for the bank later on.

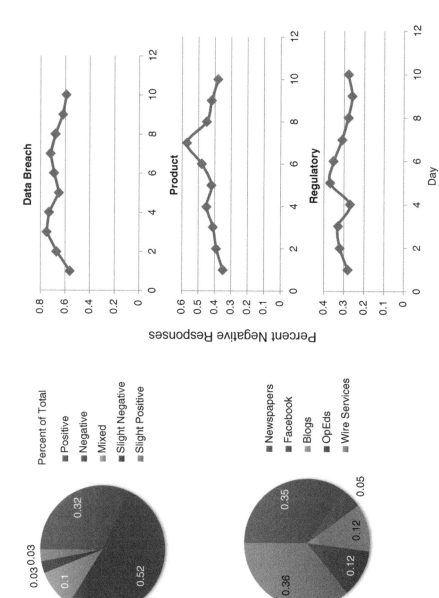

FIGURE 15.8 SifiBank Sentiment Analysis Dashboard

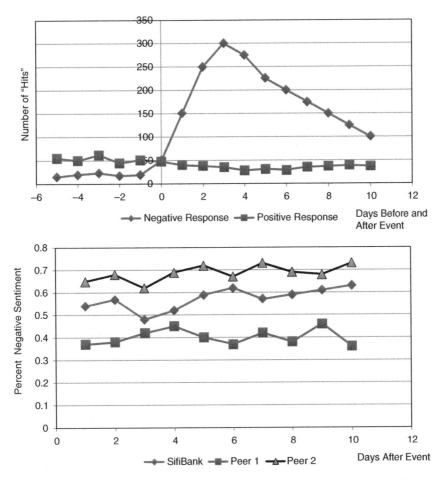

FIGURE 15.9 SifiBank Sentiment Analysis: Number of Positive and Negative "Hits" and Peer Comparisons

SUMMARY

With the evolution of risk management at SifiBank at a relatively immature stage before the crisis, the bank was crippled after the crisis by a host of risks that could have been significantly reduced had the bank recognized their importance and put in place a plan for identifying emerging threats, and establishing processes and controls throughout the company to manage and mitigate these risks.

Model risk was a real threat to SifiBank that led to it taking in much more credit risk than it was willing to accept. In part this risk was amplified by the false sense of security that management had in its models and analytic capabilities. As a result, it found itself well behind in loan loss reserving when credit losses started to mount since its models had vastly underestimated incoming credit losses over the next five years. This was exacerbated by the procyclical nature of the loan loss reserving process discussed in Chapter 6. These losses ate into the bank's income to such an extent that for several years it remained unprofitable. The amount of income derived from its risky loan products was insufficient to offset credit losses and this was also a result of model error. Errors due to data deficiencies, application of data from time periods not representative of future periods or the products being modeled, poor model specification of underlying behavior, an inability to incorporate important macroeconomic factors, product risk layering, and breakdowns in model governance can be major contributing factors to model risk. Models, like any other business practice, must be well-controlled and governed in a way that allows models to be used when they have demonstrated a minimum level of accuracy and be replaced when they have deteriorated below target levels.

Regulatory risk presents a host of challenges for banks in the postcrisis era as heightened scrutiny of bank activities and a flurry of new regulations have left the industry reeling. Regulation is an important part of a bank's day-to-day activity and cannot be underestimated as a critical process to manage. Strengthening overall processes and controls surrounding business activities can mitigate regulatory risk. SifiBank realized, for instance, that its compensation packages incented the wrong type of behavior and thus exposed the firm to significant regulatory, legal, and reputational risk. The bank strengthened its oversight and control of regulatory risk by first repairing a broken relationship with its regulators that had gone on for years. Once management realized that regulatory oversight was important to manage, the bank took steps to put in place an organization and infrastructure to consistently manage and mitigate regulatory risk exposure.

The bank's massive legal tab after the financial crisis was another major expense that sapped the company's ability to turnaround its financial fortunes. The legal risk it faced was preventable. In the years leading up to the crisis, the bank had opportunities to stem activities that would eventually lead to large legal settlements but these were largely ignored. Again, poor executive compensation arrangements and a culture promoting growth at nearly all costs over prudent risk management put the firm in grave danger. Moreover, its legal problems cast the bank in a poor light for many years with the public, leading it to become one of the most "unlikable" institutions in the industry. Once again, SifiBank's failure to recognize that risk of one type can lead to other risks brought the bank to near-insolvency. An almost reckless abandonment of operational controls in its mortgage business led to unprecedented credit losses, legal costs, a withdrawal of its customer base, and a number of limitations on its business for several years from its regulators. While model, regulatory, legal, and reputational risk are not as easy to measure as other risks, their focus and attention by business and risk management is absolutely critical to the long-term health of the institution.

QUESTIONS

As the head of your model validation group, you are presented with a model that is being used to approve customers for a new "Platinum" credit card oriented toward the highest credit quality customers. You have established a model deployment KS threshold of 35. The overall KS of the model has been tested at 42 against the development sample and 36 on an out-of-sample basis according to the model development group. The model validation group presents results showing the model has a KS of 36 out-of-sample and 32 at around where the credit policy cutoff for approval would be set.

1. Should you approve the model for deployment or not?
2. Suppose additional information is made suggesting that for your best customers, the model KS is 40. How would you react to this information?
3. The Platinum Card model as it is known is showing that 25 percent of customers that have never been delinquent on a credit-card payment would be rejected for a Platinum card. What kind of error is this?
4. It is also established through the validation exercise that 15 percent of customers having gone at least 30 days past due over the past six months in their credit card payments would be approved by the model. What type of error is this?
5. During the model review discussion at the Model Validation Committee, the development team reveals that to build the model they used data from their subprime credit card customer base. Moreover, the data that they used was from the past two years, in which GDP has been 4 percent per year and unemployment rates 4 percent. Over the next year, the Fed projects that a mild recession is likely to take place. How would you react to this information?

Your head of derivatives trading has embarked on a new trading strategy that will profit from trading on a basket of option contracts intended to generate large profits for the company over the next year. There has been a noticeable spike in cigarette use by young people in a number of underdeveloped countries and several tobacco firms are looking to make handsome profits on this new market segment over the next several years. The strategy is to buy options on companies engaged in this activity. The head of trading believes they can demonstrate to the regulators that the strategy conforms to a qualified hedge under the Volcker Rule ban against proprietary trading. Meanwhile the trader that will execute the trades expects to establish a formal hedge that is in place for the first six months; afterward he expects to significantly reduce the hedge portion of the transaction but continue to report it as a full hedge.

6. Would there be any issues with regulatory risk with this transaction?
7. Are there any legal risks associated with the trades?
8. Is there any reputational risk apparent in the strategy?
9. How might you get a handle on customer reaction to the strategy?
10. What steps should you take before considering whether to roll out this strategy?

CHAPTER 16

Toward Integrated Risk Management

OVERVIEW

SifiBank's near-death experience wound up having a transformative effect on the way the bank and its subsidiary companies identified, measured, and managed its various risks. It embraced robust risk governance and established a risk culture that permeated the entire organization. Throughout the bank's hallways were banners stating, "Risk Management Is Everyone's Responsibility!" Those five words had an empowering effect on management and employees and expectations surrounding that motto were clearly identified in all performance and incentive compensation evaluations.

The CEO and CRO had even bigger plans for risk management. Although the quality of the risk management function had increased significantly after the financial crisis, there appeared to be gaps in the way the bank processed all of the information it was gaining from these capabilities. Specifically, the risk management teams within each business unit still operated in a silo mentality. That is, organizational challenges limited SifiBank's ability to leverage its risk units beyond its individual business unit risk functions. The risk departments of each operating unit of the bank were largely organized around individual risks, for example, credit, market, and operational risks. While this approach recognizes the need for specialization it limits the bank's understanding of how risks intersect and their implications on the business. Information flows were coming from each business risk unit and were then aggregated at the corporate risk level and communicated to the Bank Corporate Risk and Executive Committees; however, it became apparent that when questions arose regarding whether issues in one risk area could affect others, no one seemed to have an answer.

The CRO flagged this as a significant gap and embarked on a strategy to develop an integrated risk management framework within the bank. But first, management needed to define what it meant by integrated risk management. To some in the organization, it simply meant that the bank would improve its ability to aggregate risk across the organization by leveraging analytical solutions such as copula-based methods for aggregating VaR measures within each business unit and risk type. However, that was not what the CRO had in mind.

DEFINING INTEGRATED RISK MANAGEMENT

Integrated risk management entails elevating the interaction between and among the business and risk areas. This includes creating a regular line of communication and information flow between areas and the corporate risk office. It implies a level of decision making about business and risk issues that is more participatory among business and risk areas than is typically the case. For example, a decision to purchase a separate loan servicing platform in the capital markets division for loans underlying asset-backed securities should take into account the existence of a loan servicing system in the consumer loan division before making a decision to have multiple systems within the bank. This affects not only the cost to the bank but the way it manages and reports its risks.

There are several goals associated with building an integrated risk management capability. First, it provides for a comprehensive view of the risk facing the organization that it would not be able to experience otherwise. Decisions to manage risk of one type in an operating unit, for instance, could impose significant costs on another area unless these functions are looking at risk exposure together. Consider SifiBank's experience in managing its rising risk to HELOCs during the crisis. The consumer credit risk area in 2008 became concerned that its $30 billion in undrawn lines of credit to homeowners would be tapped as borrowers came under financial stress. As a result, the credit department decided to curtail line draws for customers that had experienced deterioration in their credit scores by more than 60 points in the past six months. While the risk team had checked with the legal department to make sure that this new policy would not violate the original HELOC contract, what they failed to recognize was a host of other noncredit issues arising from this decision. Within a week of the policy's execution several major newspapers were running front-page articles on how SifiBank was locking borrowers out of their HELOCs. Some of these stories focused on particularly vulnerable borrower segments, such as the case of an elderly widower who was on the verge of financial ruin if she was unable to draw $1,000 on her HELOC. This created a backlash for SifiBank that was felt in other consumer areas, especially in the retail deposit side where there was a noticeable spike in account closures for a 30-day period. While this did not pose a serious liquidity risk to the bank, it was unexpected and caught the Treasury unit off-guard. It also created significant reputational risk to the bank and increased its scrutiny from the CFPB and OCC during a delicate period of time when the bank was trying to gain regulatory approval for a set of new bank products. In addition, the General Counsel's Office began noticing an increase in legal filings against the bank from HELOC customers affected by the new credit policy. Had SifiBank put in place its new integrated risk management framework, other business and risk units would have had an opportunity to weigh in before the new policy was rolled out. A decision to move forward with the HELOC curtailment program would have had to be approved at the corporate risk level after all other feedback had been obtained.

Another advantage from pursuing integrated risk management is that it improves the accuracy of risk outcomes. Consider for example SifiBank's mortgage portfolio investment strategy before the crisis. SifiMortgage had built a held-for-investment mortgage portfolio by cherry-picking its origination pipeline for the best credit quality loans. The strategy from a pure credit risk management perspective made sense because SifiMortgage held 100 percent of the credit risk on these loans. However, this decision wound up adversely affecting the bank's interest rate risk exposure for a time and the pricing from its sale of private label mortgage-backed securities. By selecting the best credit quality assets for its portfolio, the bank inadvertently raised the prepayment speed on this portfolio. Borrowers with good credit profiles have better access to credit to refinance their loans and tend to be more sensitive to refinance opportunities than less creditworthy borrowers. Faster prepayment translated into lower income over time as loans prepaid away from the bank and new loans were at lower note rates than before. In addition, SifiBank did not realize that its decisions would also affect the capital markets division. By retaining the best quality loans, the MBS issued by the capital markets division was of lower credit quality. Investors realized that compared to other similar MBS security issuances from other banks, SifiBank MBS was materially worse and this was reflected in its pricing. At the time, a favorable economic environment masked much of the eventual credit risk that would manifest during the crisis. By not looking at the total risk picture across business units and risk types, SifiBank collectively could not gain an accurate picture of the risk exposure it faced.

Other benefits from integrated risk management include improved clarity and speed of decisions, establishment of regular feedback loops across the organization, and consistency in the process. All business and risk units operated under a set of controls for informing each other of risk issues and this process consistency helped the company avoid isolated but potentially debilitating risk outcomes. The new integrated risk process also allowed SifiBank to be more adaptive to new or evolving business conditions by enabling management and risk teams to evaluate risk issues quicker and with more information than before.

KEY RISK INTEGRATION POINTS

The activities of SifiBank can be thought of as a system as opposed to a set of independent operating units. Thinking of the bank as a system helps in designing a structure that weaves its risk management processes throughout its myriad activities. As seen above, it is critical that SifiBank develop processes that allow the operating units to see what is going on in other business areas and to provide a forum for elevating potential business and risk issues emanating from other areas outside their division. This can become tricky to manage if business owners' interests are not aligned collectively.

This is where integrated risk management must also include developing an incentive compensation structure that ensures business owners are accountable for performance in their areas and are also compensated on being good corporate citizens. In the years leading up to the crisis, the heads of SifiBank and SifiInvestment Bank became arch enemies as decisions over which businesses to grow became highly contested given the size of the bonuses at stake between these areas. At one point, the incoming CRO of SifiBank was briefed on the need to take an adversarial position with Sifi Investment Bank as a matter of standard operating practice—a dictum coming directly from the CEO of SifiBank. This "us versus them" mentality created enormous roadblocks in allowing the bank to focus on emerging risks as the crisis unfolded.

Under the new integrated risk management approach, incentive compensation schemes for the business areas comprised several key performance elements:

- Risk-adjusted performance results for the specific business unit using corporate risk management sanctioned models for determining economic capital
- Risk-adjusted performance results applied across the organization
- Demonstrated efforts to advance a strong risk culture

The new executive compensation process was intended to be actionable: easy to implement, easy to communicate, and supportive of a balanced short- and long-term focus on prudent growth opportunities.

Bonus payouts for a particular year were not paid out in full but rather allocated over time based on measurable risk-adjusted return targets. So, for example, an executive would receive 30 percent of their target bonus if their year-end goals were met. The remaining 70 percent would be paid out over the next two years (35 percent each year) upon meeting the second and third years' performance targets. In this fashion, managers know up front that decisions they make now will have long-term consequences not just for company but also for their bonus. Going back to Chapter 3, SifiBank's new incentive compensation plans provide a mechanism for reducing the potential for excessive risk-taking. By basing performance on risk-adjusted metrics, it aligns risk and return in a way that is a more accurate reflection of the risk-taking of the firm vis a vis its risk tolerance. It also significantly reduces the incentive to work on an isolated basis as 30 percent of everyone's bonus is based on how well the company performs over time.

Incentive compensation plans for SifiBank's risk management teams resemble the business performance plans with some important exceptions. The business risk units maintain largely the same objectives as the business teams since effective management of both risk and return is critical to the long-term competitive viability of the business. A risk team that is compensated solely on managing risk can hamper the business. Conversely, a risk team compensated on business metrics clearly poses significant risk to the firm. The risk-adjusted performance metrics for the business risk teams comprise a significant percentage of the total plan targets and include a separate weight on building a strong risk infrastructure.

The corporate risk office compensation plans have a lower weight assigned to the risk-adjusted performance part of their evaluation than the business team. The corporate risk function is largely compensated on its ability to actively promote the integrated risk management program and its ability to monitor and control risks throughout the organization as reflected by a combination of short and long-term risk performance metrics. This difference in the composition of performance criteria between business and corporate risk units reflects the fact that the corporate office is charged with carrying out the implementation of the board's risk appetite for the company though the governance, policy and other control processes deployed across the firm. The structure of the incentive compensation plan thus reflects an integration of risk and return that is tailored to business and risk units.

Another point of risk integration relates to the way SifiBank structures its risk management organization. It maintains both corporate and business units risk functions that are tied closely to each other as well as with the business units. The enterprise CRO adopted a risk triangulation framework whereby senior risk officers were established along business, geographic and product lines. This approach to organizing risk units begins to fulfill the vision of abandoning a structure built on managing risks in strict silos by risk type. Instead, risk teams are organized by the business (e.g., commercial lending), their region (e.g., Asia-Pacific), and product (e.g., real estate). Risk officers situated with the business have a solid reporting line to the corporate risk office and a dotted line to the head of the business, thus reinforcing the integration between business and risk functions while also aligning incentives for the business risk team toward balanced risk and return outcomes. Senior risk officers with a geographic or product focus report directly back to the corporate risk office and provide subject matter expertise about markets and products that augment the business risk team's expertise. This may include development of analytic models and data management but also consulting on new products and services from a risk management perspective. An important benefit from this risk triangulation approach is that it provides additional pairs of eyes and input on risk in a business area. The business risk teams for example, could be limited in their ability to seeing an emerging risk that could threaten its business. For example, SifiBank's US real estate experience during the housing boom and bust would become an important lesson for business risk teams operating in overseas markets. During one Asia-Pacific credit risk committee meeting, for instance, the business risk team in China presented a recommendation to relax its underwriting standards citing strong economic and housing market growth that was a risk mitigant in their opinion. The SifiBank Real Estate senior product officer provided evidence from the US mortgage experience before and after the crisis that the China housing market could be experiencing a housing bubble. In that environment, relaxing credit standards would be potentially risky. Hearing both sides, SifiBank's CRO denied the request to expand loan program guidelines on China real estate loans. Business risk teams included credit, market and operational risk expertise where relevant and were augmented with regulatory compliance, legal and reputational risk expertise.

Achieving better integration between quantitative and qualitative aspects of risk management was also an important objective for the SifiBank CRO. As discussed in Chapter 15, overreliance on quantitative models can lull risk and business management into a false sense of security. Recognizing that market conditions can change faster than models at times, SifiBank strengthened the way the modeling teams interacted with risk policy and quality control teams. As models were developed for products with limited performance history, management required regular random samples of loans by risk management QC staff to provide input on their findings to model developers. In one case, the mortgage unit of SifiBank Australia embarked on a new low documentation program. The modeling team had estimated the relative risk of the low documentation feature to be a multiple of 1.5 times that of a fully documented loan controlling for other risk attributes. This estimate was actually leveraged from U.S. low documentation experience rather than Australian mortgages due to a lack of data. Knowing this, the product was rolled out slowly into the market while monthly QC samples were gathered and reviewed. The findings from the QC team were surprising as it showed that more than half of low documentation borrowers were overstating their incomes by 40 percent or more. The risk multiplier assigned by the modeling team to these loans for loan loss reserving and pricing was based on products where only 10 percent of the borrowers were found to overstate their incomes, and when they did it was by an average of 15 percent. These QC findings on Australian low documentation loans helped the modeling team impose a qualitative adjustment to their risk multiplier, raising it to 3 from 1.5. Further adjustments would be watched closely based on the ongoing QC findings.

Quantitative results can be as helpful for developing credit policy as qualitative information can support modeling exercises. For instance, in setting up credit policy guidelines for a new mortgage product, the risk policy team wanted to demarcate three policy zones: Streamline Approve, Conditional Approve, and High Risk. The Streamline Approve would be only for those borrowers with a very low likelihood of default; that is, those within the top 5 percent of all applicants. Such loans would be allowed to go through only an automated underwriting scorecard with limited review by an underwriter other than standard validation of application information. The vast majority of borrowers are expected to be Conditional Approves, meaning that after running through an underwriting scorecard, the borrower's application must be reviewed by an underwriter and approved. Loans designated as High Risk are unlikely to be approved based on their characteristics and are expected to comprise about 10 percent of the applicant pool. SifiBank risk managers and business believe that setting credit policy in this fashion will not only bring the best loans to the bank, but also help drive efficiency gains in underwriting. However, in setting up the criteria the credit policy group has no way of understanding, except at an aggregate level, what the performance of specific loan parameters might be. This is where a fusion of modeling and qualitative judgment makes the best combination of credit policy development.

Once informed of the desired outcome for the loan policy, the modeling team begins to assess the default risk of loans representative of the applicants under the new loan program. The results from this analysis can be used to segment borrowers into the three classes based on their expected default propensity taking into account the risk attributes of each borrower.

Once the three groups have been identified, the modeling team can look more closely at attributes of the borrowers right at the margin between Streamline Approve and Conditional Approve. The policy team and modelers then work together to create credit risk standards for each credit zone. This is an iterative process as credit standards usually are expressed as a table or matrix of eligible criteria. SifiMortgage's credit policy matrix for this program is found in Figure 16.1.

The underwriting criteria for Streamline Approve and Conditional Approve loans are based on a combination of the underwriting scorecard outcome and individual risk attributes on loan documentation, credit score, and LTV. For all Streamline Approve loans, the underwriting score must be over 125, where higher values signify lower credit risk. In addition, the minimum FICO and maximum LTV allowed under that credit zone depends upon whether the loan is fully documented or not. Loans where borrower incomes, assets, and employment can be fully verified are allowed to have

Streamline Approve SifiMortgage Score greater than 125 AND				
			Maximum LTV	
	Minimum FICO Score	80	85	90
Full Documentation	620			Ineligible
	680		Eligible	
	720			
Low Documentation		80	85	90
	620		Ineligible	
	680	Eligible		
	720			
Conditional Approve SifiMortgage Score of 100-125 AND				
			Maximum LTV	
	Minimum FICO Score	80	85	90
Full Documentation	620		Ineligible	
	680		Eligible	
	720			
Low Documentation		80	85	90
	620		Ineligible	
	680			
	720		Eligible	

FIGURE 16.1 SifiMortgage Credit Policy Matrix

lower FICOs and/or higher LTVs than low documentation loans. These criteria become more restrictive for Conditional Approve loans. While this example is for consumer credit risk applications, other risk types can benefit from an integrated analysis performed by the relevant modeling and policy staff. For example, analysis of market risk might leverage results from VaR models to establish concentration and other policy limits on trading and portfolio activity.

ALIGNING RISK INFRASTRUCTURE WITH RISK-TAKING

At times in SifiBank's past it ran into trouble when its appetite for risk-taking exceeded its ability to take such risks. This is a common theme in banking that can become accentuated during boom periods when risks are relatively low and competitive pressures are high. Complicating matters in balancing the quality of risk infrastructure against risk-taking is that methodologies to assess variations in infrastructure quality against risk are not well developed.

Consider the situation for SifiBank's new CRO hired right before the financial crisis. The CRO had been recruited from a major competitor of SifiBank and had been given the assignment to come back to the Executive Committee after three months and provide an assessment of the bank's level of risk infrastructure against its level of risk exposure. While the evaluation process would be based largely on interviews with staff across all business lines and management reports, it would mark the first time the bank had actually looked into this issue in a systematic way.

The CRO appeared at the next quarterly Executive Committee meeting and presented a diagram depicted in Figure 16.2. The figure is segmented into four combinations of risk infrastructure and risk exposure. Risk infrastructure is defined as the collection of activities, processes, technology, and people used to acquire and manage risk assets at the bank. The quality of risk infrastructure is classified as high or low, as is the level of risk at the firm. The CRO conducted the assessment on SifiBank's largest three divisions; SifiBank, SifiInvestment Bank, and SifiAsset Management. Each quadrant was given a name reflecting the type of institution exhibiting that combination of risk infrastructure and exposure.

For instance, institutions that do not take much risk and have a low level of risk infrastructure would be characterized as risk novices (shown in the upper left quadrant). These are firms that simply may be too small to build advanced risk infrastructure and ordinarily have a lower appetite for risk-taking. Firms that have high-quality risk infrastructure but tend to take lower levels of risk are designated as risk averse. The deadliest combination

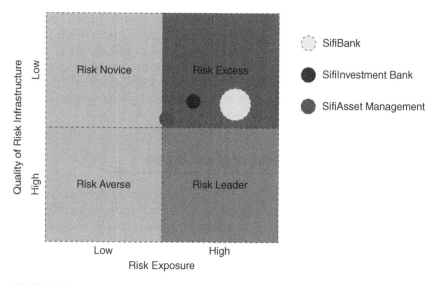

FIGURE 16.2   SifiBank Risk Infrastructure/Risk Exposure Matrix

of the four is found in the upper right quadrant, where the quality of risk infrastructure is low but risk-taking is high. Lastly, risk leaders would be found in the bottom right quadrant where risk infrastructure is high, enabling the bank to enter into higher risk areas with greater safety.

After much deliberation, the CRO superimposed the matrix with the three circles representing the Sifi operating divisions of interest. The size of each circle reflects the relative asset size of each unit, with SifiBank clearly the largest of the three. The assessment shocked senior management in that the CRO had designated each within the Risk Excess quadrant. SifiBank's CEO at the time shot back how the CRO could have come up with such a result and that more work would be required before management would be supportive of such an outcome.

With this feedback, the CRO quickly assembled his staff along with the business risk units to come up with a more structured way of thinking about assessing the bank. After much discussion and iteration, what was developed was a risk management scorecard (RMS) that, while not statistically based, provided management with a rank ordering of the quality of risk infrastructure in each division based on a set of standard criteria against risk processes. The scorecard consisted of more than 200 questions about various aspects of risk infrastructure such as reporting, data, analytics, policies and procedures, governance, staffing, and risk mitigation activities. A summarized version of the scorecard is depicted in Figure 16.3. The risk

Risk Scorecard Components	Weight (% of total)	Quality Score (1-10)	Weighted Score
		1 = Poor, 10 = Best Practice	
Risk Identification Capabilities			
Risk Data Warehouse	5	5	25
Risk Monitoring Systems & Technology	5	8	40
Risk Identification Human Capital	5	3	15
Risk Review Process & Controls	5	5	25
Risk Measurement Capabilities			
Risk Model Development & Deployment Process and Controls	5	6	30
Risk Metrics	5	3	15
Risk Measurement Human Capital	5	8	40
Risk Measurement Process and Controls	5	5	25
Risk Management Capabilities			
Risk Culture	15	7	105
Risk Governance	15	6	90
Policies & Procedures	10	4	40
Process and Controls	10	7	70
Risk Mitigation Activities	10	7	70
TOTAL Score	100		590

FIGURE 16.3   Risk Management Scorecard

team assigned weights for each component of a division's risk infrastructure categorized by risk identification, measurement, and management activities. These weights, while subjective, were meant to be reflective of the importance of each infrastructure component. The risk team for each component as shown assessed a quality score based on a 1–10 scale. The product of the risk component weight and the quality score resulted in a weighted score that when summed up over all scorecard components would provide a total RMS score for an operating division. An RMS score could range between 100 (poor) to 1,000 (high quality). An example of an RMS scorecard for SifiBank's Consumer Lending Division is shown as Figure 16.4. Although the general categories of risk infrastructure apply broadly across risk areas, the scorecard captures important distinctions specific to that area. The scorecard can be applied to specific risk types such as credit or market risk in an operating division depending on the preference of management. An example of such scorecard decomposition is found in Figure 16.5.

Armed with this information SifiBank has the ability to compare the relative quality of risk infrastructure across the lines of business and by risk type. The SifiBank risk management team could establish ranges of acceptable levels of infrastructure quality as follows: < 600, Unacceptable; 600–700, Marginally Acceptable; 700–800, Acceptable; and > 800, Exceptional.

Credit Risk Management - Consumer Lending Division	Weight	Quality Score	Weighted Score
Risk Identification			
Mortgage default and prepayment reporting	5	5	25
Mortgage data warehouse	5	6	30
Sufficiency, expertise and capability of mortgage risk reporting staff	5	4	20
Adequacy, frequency and quality of mortgage risk reporting	5	7	35
Risk Measurement			0
Mortgage automated underwriting scorecards	5	6	30
Automated collateral valuation models	5	7	35
Mortgage pricing models	5	8	40
Loan loss reserve models	5	5	25
Stress test/economic capital models	5	3	15
Modelling staffing and capabilities	5	8	40
Quality of risk-adjusted performance measurement	5	6	30
Risk Management			0
Stature of the mortgage risk function	10	6	60
Reporting structure of mortgage risk function	10	5	50
Adequacy of mortgage risk committee structure	5	7	35
Quality of credit and collateral valuation policies and processes	10	5	50
Adequacy of collections and default processes	5	6	30
Credit portfolio management capabilities	5	7	35
	100		**585**

FIGURE 16.4   SifiBank Consumer Lending Division RMS Scorecard

The categories of risk infrastructure quality can be further used to guide the bank's activities over some period. For instance, during SifiBank's annual strategic planning meetings with senior management, the CRO could tie business objectives to level of risk infrastructure. SifiBank's head of consumer lending proposes to grow the business by 15 percent next year by expanding into a number of new products. Applying the risk infrastructure quality ranges from above, the CRO recommends that the consumer lending division cannot grow beyond current year levels or into new products until

Business Line	Risk Management Score						Average Score
	Credit	Market	Operational	Liquidity	Interest Rate	Counterparty	
Consumer Lending Division	585	620	590	625	550	600	595
Commercial Division	625	600	575	640	585	630	609
Markets and Trading Group	700	725	735	750	720	715	724
Wealth Management Group	650	675	700	660	640	670	666
	640	655	650	669	624	654	

FIGURE 16.5   RMS Scorecard Results across Business Units and Risks

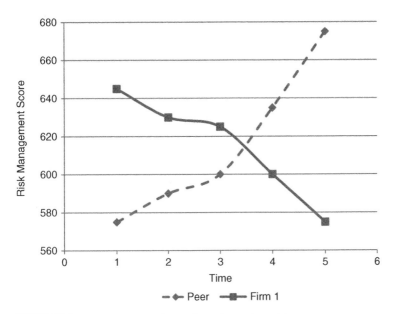

FIGURE 16.6   RMS Scorecard Trends and Benchmarking

it has achieved a risk infrastructure score over 700. Management could make enhancements to their business risk processes during the year and once validated by the corporate risk office would be allowed to pursue their planned strategy. In this fashion, the bank would not be able to enter riskier markets or grow their business until strengthening the quality of their risk infrastructure. To ensure consistency across business units, the CRO could establish annual risk infrastructure thresholds tied to growth and product targets allowed for each risk infrastructure category.

The risk infrastructure scorecard may also be used to benchmark changes in risk infrastructure over time for individual business units as well as across operating divisions as shown in Figure 16.6. The ability to assign a consistent score across business areas provides transparency and invites business and risk dialogue on areas needing improvement.

SUMMARY

SifiBank has come a long way in how it views and manages risk across the firm. One of the innovations it adopted to help it better manage risk across the firm is its integrated risk management framework. Integrated risk management is about improving the interaction among risk and business units in a way to reduce gaps in understanding the impact of various risk intersections. Within the firm are a number of integration points to take into account. These include integration between corporate and business risk functions, risk types, quantitative modeling and policy, and executive compensation plans and risk management, among others.

With risk integration comes accountability. Being able to establish a scorecard that provides an indication of the quality of the company's risk infrastructure enables constructive discussions between corporate, business risk, and business functions to take place. With proper rules of engagement identified at the outset and clear criteria set for what quality risk infrastructure looks like, the business and risk teams can leverage each other in a manner that prudently balances returns and risk for the bank.

QUESTIONS

1. How would you explain the concept of integrated risk management to the Executive Committee of your bank?
2. If you were to implement integrated risk management at your bank, what criteria would you be looking for?
3. Your bank has established a structural alignment between the business and risk management functions where the operating units are co-led by a business and risk executive. The risk head reports to the enterprise CRO. Is this an example of integrated risk management at work and are there any recommendations you have for this arrangement?
4. You are the head of credit card risk management and your analytics team has provided you with information suggesting that a major metropolitan area is likely to suffer a major decline in its economy with the announced withdrawal of two of the largest companies operating in that area. Your risk policy manager recommends in the latest Risk Management Committee meeting to impose limits on credit card usage and to sharply limit card approval to low- and moderate-income customers. The risk committee includes all of your direct reports, the CFO of the line of business, and the head of marketing. How would you characterize this scenario against the integrated risk management concept?

The head of the small business-lending group puts forth an initiative to grow its market share from 10 percent last year to 15 percent in the coming year. The group has been in operation for about five years and just last year hired its first risk officer who used to head one of the product lines. Management reporting has been very good at portraying the financial picture of the group. Reporting on credit performance has been slated for development in the coming year but has not been established beyond some very basic reports. This is a reflection of the underlying data that remains largely in Excel spreadsheets across the product lines. Business analytics has been very strong in identifying potential customers and leveraging these relationships for other small business products; however, there has been no use of analytics to forecast credit loss. The ALLL relies on simple roll rate methodologies and is heavily dependent on manual processing and qualitative adjustments.

5. How would you respond to this request?
6. What type of analysis could be used to support your case?
7. How would you go about building the analysis described in question 5?
8. The head of the aircraft leasing group of your bank is concerned about a material downturn in the airline industry globally that is likely to set its business back over the next one to two years. In addition, there has been a $1 billion commercial lending program to provide capital to a number of large airline companies. You, as the head of risk management, contacted the head of capital markets with this information and the two of you together decide to establish a hedging program to short airline stocks and buy put options on these stocks as a measure of protection for both the leasing and lending businesses. How would you characterize this scenario against the integrated risk management concept?
9. The risk executive for the commercial lending division who reports to the head of commercial lending and the corporate CRO jointly is having her performance objectives for the coming year established. Last year, this executive was paid a bonus that was 200 percent of her base pay based on a blended result that was 30 percent market-driven, 30 percent profitability driven, 20 percent business process development and the remainder driven by the year's overall credit performance. Are there ways to improve this structure for next year and what is your rationale supporting any changes?
10. The credit policy unit of the auto lending division has been asked to establish a new loan product for one-year-old cars used by rental companies that come up for sale each year. The auto lending department has acquired a loan level dataset of 40,000 used car loans with performance history over the past five years as well as a number of key credit performance attributes and characteristics of the cars. The credit policy unit has constructed an underwriting matrix that is virtually identical to the one used to originate new car loans that reflect more creditworthy borrowers. The auto analytics team has built a default model from the new dataset showing that borrower income, employment history and credit score are the most predictive variables determining default. How could you use this information consistently with the discussion on integrated risk management?

Answer Key

This Answer Key provides answers to even-numbered questions found at the end of each chapter. The full Answer Key is available on Wiley's Global Education Site for instructors only.

CHAPTER 1

2. The four key elements include setting the bank's risk appetite or tolerance for risk-taking, asset and liability generation, risk monitoring, and management of the firm's risk profile.

4. Banks use a variety of financial and nonfinancial inputs to maximize profit (the difference between interest and noninterest revenues and expenses). Alternatively, the bank might seek to minimize risk subject to some target rate of return. This is typically a constrained optimization problem for the bank in that it optimizes its objective function subject to a set of specific business constraints.

6. It should always be looking to avoid systems integration issues that prevent the firm from seamlessly creating the necessary risk data and analytics to allow it to identify, measure, and manage its risks across the firm.

8. The Volcker Rule is one of the important provisions of the Dodd-Frank Act that among other things places a ban on proprietary trading at banks. Under the rule banks are no longer allowed to engage in trading for profit.

10. Systemic risk refers to the potential for spillover effects from one firm or market into the entire financial system. This is due to increasing interconnectedness among firms and markets that heighten concerns of contagion effects caused by a single or several large SIFIs and markets that can result in a collapse of other firms and markets on a systemwide basis.

12. CAMELS is a regulatory rating process used to define the overall safety and soundness of a depository institution. It comprises an assessment of the bank's capital adequacy (C), asset quality (A), management quality (M), earnings (E), liquidity (L), and sensitivity to market risk (S).

CHAPTER 2

2. Since you are concerned only about the worst 5 percent of returns, you would want to use a factor of 1.65 standard deviations because that cuts off 5 percent in each tail of the distribution. In this case, $10\% - 1.65(3\%) = 5.05\%$ as the worst return associated with the 95 percent level.

4. There are two types of risks in this case. Model risk is present since the trading unit is exposed to large errors due to an outdated model. In addition, a rogue trader has committed fraud against the firm while at the same time stealing assets. This is operational risk.

6. As indicated in the above question, fixed-income instruments, market risk, and interest rate risk are considered to be analogous. More specificly, interest rate risk may be thought of as a subset of market risks. Other classes of assets and liabilities are not sensitive directly to interest rate fluctuations, but price movements of instruments for trading purposes would pose market risk.

8. You face liquidity risk as well as reputation risk. Liquidity risk may arise if bank customers begin to withdraw significant amounts of deposits over a short period of time and/or creditors decline to renew lines of credit or roll over short-term debt.

CHAPTER 3

2. You might think about specific events such as the prefinancial crisis era in which many banks were convinced that home prices could continue to rise. In this rapidly accelerating home price environment the risk management team must begin thinking about how to manage risk when the market may be experiencing an abnormal period of heightened competition, which could lead to greater risk. Pressures from overly aggressive business management could further influence your decisions and you must adapt to these changes. Product risk can also change over time and you should be closely monitoring such situations. This would mean adapting the risk management controls and processes to ensure even greater oversight during such periods.

4. A blended model, with both a corporate risk office combined with a business risk function embedded within the business, could provide the proper combination of independence, oversight, and responsiveness without compromising the integrity of the risk management function. This structure is more complicated to manage but has reasonable checks and balances.

6. He is exhibiting herd mentality since he is looking at what the competition is doing and pushing risk management to follow them in relaxing underwriting guidelines.

8.

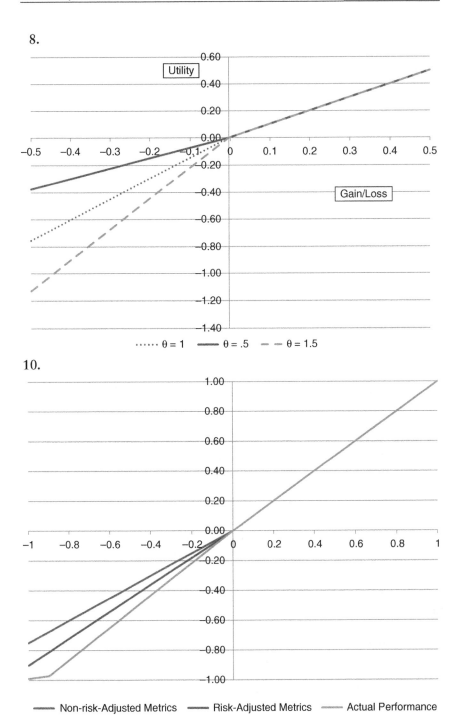

10.

CHAPTER 4

2. Daily Earnings at Risk is the worst return the company could observe in one day at a 95 percent level of confidence.

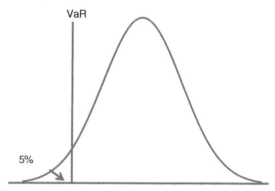

4. (.1+.06(1.96))SQRT(10) = .688 (Note: VaR in terms of expected default rate). Need to convert into dollars of loss, or .688*(1 − .65)*$500M = $120.4M

6. The VaR represents the worst losses at a given level of confidence that would be assessed against an asset or portfolio whereas risk capital deducts expected loss from that amount.

8. You could rely on copula methods to address the nonnormality by mapping those distributions into a normal distribution

10. Apply RaRoC calculation (NI/EC), or (R-OC-FC-EL)/EC. From an ROE perspective, P2 has the more attractive return at (100-10-30-45)/.04($1.125B) = 33.3%, versus 11% for P1. However, when applying RaRoC, a different result is obtained. RaRoC for P1 is $5M/$25M = 20%, thus meeting the hurdle rate, while RaRoC for P2 is $15M/$90M = 16.6%

12. To calculate the total VaR, compute the following using the formula in the chapter. So, SQRT(64 + 25 + 2(8)(5)(.666)) = $11.93B. Note the correlation is calculated as covariance divided by the product of the two volatilities, or .025/(.15*.25) = .666. Also, the total VaR is less than the sum of both division VaRs due to the correlation being less than 1.

CHAPTER 5

2. As d_1 increases, the value of d_2 also rises, which increase the likelihood the call option is in-the-money. Conversely, this reduces the likelihood that the put option is in-the-money. $N(-d_2)$ can thus be considered the risk neutral probability of default.

4. Given that PD = 1 – .95 = .05, EL = .05*.19 = .95%

6. The firm is more likely to default as *DD* decreases. It refers to the number of standard deviations that the property value must decline to before a default is triggered.

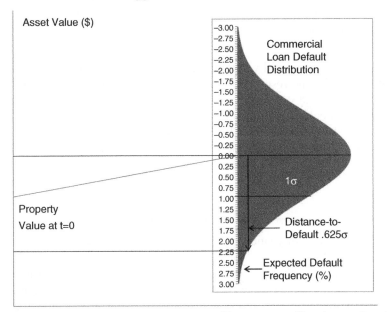

8. You need to calculate the product of each of the three possible combinations for 1 and 2 as shown below. Note each cell represents the movement from 1 outcome for each product to another over 1 period. The sum of the nine outcomes should equal 100 percent as indicated below.

p11p21	p11p22	p11p23	
p12p21	p12p22	p12p23	
p13p21	p13p22	p13p23	

0.09	0.63	0.18	0.9
0.007	0.049	0.014	0.07
0.003	0.021	0.006	0.03
			1

10. The combined portfolio values of the two bond portfolio for each outcome is as follows

$2,000,648	$1,993,469	$1,393,189
$1,993,549	$1,986,370	$1,386,090
$1,407,459	$1,400,280	$ 800,000

To calculate the expected value multiply the cell joint migration probability in Q8 by the respective portfolio value cell above. The answer should be $1,855,838.13.

12. You would calculate the marginal standard deviation MSD as shown in the text or $(150,000 - 100,000)/500,000 = 10$ percent. In this case the asset adds 10 percent to the risk of the portfolio for every dollar of that asset.

CHAPTER 6

2. We would expect a price increase of 5.18 and 5.38 percent, respectively, for G1 and G2.
4. You also have an imbalance in your portfolio with 75 percent of it in the high volatility geography. You may want to consider transferring that risk to other counterparties, sell some assets, and consider changing credit policy standards, among other activities.
6. This is an example of a compensating factor, which provides an offset to a risk factor such as number of credit lines that increases risk. Requiring a higher credit score lowers credit risk.
8. Note: These are computed based on adjustments to original balance for defaults in each year for each vintage:

	12	24	36	48	60
Vintage 1	0.85%	1.01%	1.15%	1.03%	0.78%
Vintage 2	1.50%	2.79%	3.92%	4.35%	0.00%
Vintage 3	3.85%	3.20%	4.96%	0.00%	0.00%
Vintage 4	4.12%	4.91%	0.00%	0.00%	0.00%
Vintage 5	0.28%	0.00%	0.00%	0.00%	0.00%

To illustrate this; the marginal default rate for Vintage 1 at month 60 is as follows:

$$\$750,000/(\$100,000,000 - \$850,000 - \$1,000,000 - \$1,125,000 - \$1,000,000) = .78\%$$

10. Using the approach outlined in the chapter you would find the following:

	Current	30–59	60–89	90+	FCL	REO	Total
	2-month Transition Probability						
Current	86.83%	4.18%	3.86%	3.31%	1.32%	0.50%	100.00%
30–59	37.07%	12.76%	22.27%	23.32%	4.05%	0.52%	100.00%
60–89	16.37%	5.95%	13.33%	46.93%	15.10%	2.32%	100.00%
90+	10.14%	2.04%	3.42%	62.31%	18.34%	3.76%	100.00%
FCL	2.49%	1.60%	2.04%	7.09%	78.81%	7.98%	100.00%
REO	0.49%	0.52%	1.03%	2.79%	32.04%	63.14%	100.00%

CHAPTER 7

2. According to the risk ratings, the facility rating would be 6 and the obligor rating a 2. Based on these results and given the EDF and obligor LGD, this loan would fall into the final risk-rating category of 3. That is, 40 percent EDF * 5 percent LGD = 2 percent loss, which falls into the 1.125 – 10 percent category 3 range, and this is a pass grade.

4. You should compute the debt service coverage ratio (DSCR) for each loan as shown in the chapter. This would result in a DSCR for Loan 1 of 1.09 and for Loan 2 of .99. Typically, banks have minimum DSCRs of at least 1, if not higher at 1.15, and on that basis, Loan 2 should not be made and Loan 1 is marginal.

6. You should look into the possibility of participating in a loan syndication where your firm could take an interest in the loan. However, care must be taken by the bank to conduct due diligence on the lead bank in the syndication and how well it performs its duties in addition to understanding the risk of the transaction.

8. You should compute each borrower's cash-flow-at-risk. For borrower 1 it would be:

$$CFaR = \$1M - 1.65(\$.25M) = \$.5875M$$

And for borrower 2 it would be:

$$CFaR = \$2M - 1.65(\$.5M) = \$1.175M$$

According to loan policy, borrower 1 breaches the cash flow trigger and thus should be remanded to the loan review group for additional analysis.

10. A decline of more than 1 risk rating in a short period of time is indicative of potential issues with the loan. It would require the loan be brought to loan review for further analysis. If the 2 rating downgrade is confirmed, it might warrant disciplinary action for the loan officer, or at least greater scrutiny on how loans are originated and additional training for staff.

CHAPTER 8

2.

Loss Scenario	Scenario Loss Amount ($)	B	BB	Tranche Losses BBB	A	AA	AAA
1	$ 2,700,000	$ 2,700,000	$ –	$ –	$ –	$ –	$ –
2	$ 5,400,000	$ 5,400,000	$ –	$ –	$ –	$ –	$ –
3	$10,800,000	$10,800,000	$ –	$ –	$ –	$ –	$ –
4	$16,200,000	$15,000,000	$1,200,000	$ –	$ –	$ –	$ –
5	$21,600,000	$15,000,000	$6,000,000	$ 600,000	$ –	$ –	$ –
6	$27,000,000	$15,000,000	$6,000,000	$4,000,000	$2,000,000	$ –	$ –
7	$32,400,000	$15,000,000	$6,000,000	$4,000,000	$5,000,000	$ 2,400,000	$ –
8	$43,200,000	$15,000,000	$6,000,000	$4,000,000	$5,000,000	$10,000,000	$ 3,200,000
9	$54,000,000	$15,000,000	$6,000,000	$4,000,000	$5,000,000	$10,000,000	$14,000,000
10	$64,800,000	$15,000,000	$6,000,000	$4,000,000	$5,000,000	$10,000,000	$24,800,000

4.

Tranche	Tranche Price ($)	Tranche Yield (%)
AAA	$484,815,179.65	3.08%
AA	$ 9,366,740.29	6.54%
A	$ 4,551,389.55	9.40%
BBB	$ 3,547,948.87	11.99%
BB	$ 5,065,725.69	16.93%
B	$ 8,728,187.13	54.15%
	$516,075,171.18	

6.

Risk-Free Rate   0.025

Contract Year	Mortgage Default Rate	Mortgage Severity Rate	Expected Loss	Remaining Pool	Discount Factor	Present Value Payments	Present Value Defaults
1	0.03	0.4	0.012	0.988	0.975609756	0.9639	0.0116
2	0.04	0.4	0.016	0.972	0.951814396	0.9252	0.0148
3	0.05	0.4	0.02	0.952	0.928599411	0.884	0.0177
4	0.06	0.4	0.024	0.928	0.905950645	0.8407	0.0202
			0.072			3.6138	0.0642

Credit Spread   0.017773

8. One could utilize a constrained optimization program where the cost associated with insurance or self-insuring is minimized—i.e., the premiums are minimized and subject to a set of policy constraints as indicated in the chapter example.

10. It could be telling you that the model is out of line with the market but that does not mean it should be adjusted. Other market participants could be mispricing the risk and if you had good empirical support for why your model is performing well, it should not be adjusted to align with the market. There is a possibility that the model could be off, however, and it would be necessary to perform additional validation work to decide whether to re-estimate the model or not.

CHAPTER 9

2. The differences are shown below:

Bond Price	+50bps Change
PV	92.984
D Only	92.957

4. The results would look as follows using the PMT function in Excel to compute the amortized annual cash flow.

	Coupon Bond			Amortized Bond		
t	PV	PVt		PMT	PV	PVt
1	2.868	2.868	2.868	21.835	20.97928	20.97928
2	2.742	5.484	10.967	21.835	20.15667	40.31333
3	2.621	7.863	23.590	21.835	19.36631	58.09894
4	2.506	10.023	40.093	21.835	18.60695	74.4278
5	82.247	411.236	2056.179	21.835	17.87736	89.3868
B	92.984	437.474	2133.698	109.177	96.98657	283.206
D	4.705		22.947	D	2.920	

The amortized bond has a much lower duration reflecting the fact that on a relative basis it receives its cash flows back sooner than the coupon bond.

6. The impact is measured for each principal component by dividing each component's eigenvalue by the total of 9. The proportions are shown below. So $k1$, for example, explains 58.8 percent of the variability in rate movements. $K1$ represents the impact of a parallel shift in rates, $k2$, a change in the slope of the yield curve, and $k3$, a change in the curvature of the yield curve.

Proportion	Cumulative Proportion
0.588	0.588
0.134	0.722
0.071	0.793

8. The results are shown below:

0.01%		
Present Value	Duration	Key Rate Duration
$10,936	19.643	−13.082

The differences in the spot and key rate adjusted rates are virtually the same given the 1bps assumption for rate change. However, there will be just enough difference in the present values to see some impact. You would compute the present value of the cash flows in each period using the spot rates, which would result in a value of $10,951. Repeating this process using the key rate shift rates provides a present value of $10,936. Estimated key rate duration for the 30-year would be (($10,951 – $10,936)/$10,951)/1bps or 13.082.

10. You should use the relationship in formula 9.20 to compute the OAS. The present value of the no prepayment bond is $49.79M. Using the formula you should find that the OAS that equates the present value of the prepayment and no prepayment bonds assuming a 5 percent discount rate should be about 1bp.

CHAPTER 10

2. The results should show the following:

Call Options	99% VaR	Corrrelations			
		1	2	3	4
1	$ 2,900,000	1	0.35	0.65	0.37
2	$31,737,600		1	0.45	0.15
3	$ 8,613,000			1	0.4
4	$ 2,088,000				1
Sum	$45,338,600				
	Portfolio VaR	$38,417,391			

4. The results should show the following:

Asset Type	99% VaR	Corrrelations		
		Call Options	Bonds	Stock
Call Options	38,417,390.52	1	–0.25	0.7
Bonds	5,851,947.79		1	–0.5
Stock	6,387,250.00			1
Sum	50,656,588.31			
	Portfolio VaR	41769439.59		

6. Applying the GBM approach to this stock assuming drift equals .25 and volatility is .15, a table of the next 12 months would like the following:

Time	RandNorm e	mdt	dS	lognormal P
1	–0.033739961	0.020833333	0.015772339	$101.59
2	–0.3948356	0.041666667	–0.017558673	$ 98.26
3	–0.128959486	0.0625	0.043156077	$104.41
4	–0.395600092	0.083333333	0.02399332	$102.43
5	–0.202191002	0.104166667	0.073838016	$107.66
6	0.325093167	0.125	0.173763975	$118.98
7	0.364856391	0.145833333	0.200561792	$122.21
8	–0.428420052	0.166666667	0.102403659	$110.78
9	0.062752873	0.1875	0.196912931	$121.76
10	0.151099261	0.208333333	0.230998222	$125.99
11	–0.006646438	0.229166667	0.228169701	$125.63
12	–0.052367755	0.25	0.242144837	$127.40

8. By rank ordering the gains and losses you would look for the third (Trial 28) lowest loss out of 30 (10 percent lowest loss).

Portfolio Value	Gain/Loss ($M)	Rank-ordered Gains/Losses ($M)	Outcome
$5,014,951,810	$ 14.95	$(247)	1
$5,147,114,763	$ 147.11	$(241)	2
$4,982,431,029	$ (17.57)	$(164)	3
$4,993,586,564	$ (6.41)	$(139)	4
$5,081,625,893	$ 81.63	$(138)	5
$4,970,115,464	$ (29.88)	$(122)	6
$4,942,711,580	$ (57.29)	$(120)	7
$5,059,486,024	$ 59.49	$(114)	8
$4,935,859,146	$ (64.14)	$(111)	9
$4,933,603,263	$ (66.40)	$(108)	10
$5,091,123,272	$ 91.12	$(107)	11
$5,056,256,279	$ 56.26	$(107)	12
$4,998,771,700	$ (1.23)	$(106)	13

Portfolio Value	Gain/Loss ($M)	Rank-ordered Gains/Losses ($M)	Outcome
$4,928,841,675	$(71.16)	$(104)	14
$5,033,795,920	$ 33.80	$(104)	15
$4,941,736,470	$ (58.26)	$(101)	16
$5,111,615,435	$ 111.62	$(101)	17
$5,030,543,612	$ 30.54	$ (99)	18
$4,990,551,651	$ (9.45)	$ (94)	19
$5,080,232,372	$ 80.23	$ (93)	20
$4,976,047,039	$(23.95)	$ (79)	21
$4,942,753,762	$ (57.25)	$ (79)	22
$4,861,064,343	$(138.94)	$ (75)	23
$5,090,454,213	$ 90.45	$ (74)	24
$5,098,966,141	$ 98.97	$ (73)	25
$5,053,026,040	$ 53.03	$ (73)	26
$4,974,994,118	$ (25.01)	$ (72)	27
$5,291,383,981	$ 291.38	$ (72)	28
$5,039,033,696	$ 39.03	$ (71)	29
$5,114,095,994	$ 114.10	$ (71)	30

10. Augmenting VaR models with appropriate stress tests can be a useful approach to managing risk. In addition, adopting variations in VaR models such as MES could reduce risk-taking.

CHAPTER 11

2. Applying the formula for CPR with the inputs given yields a CPR of 9.6 percent versus 20.75 percent in the results where the net liquidity position equals $96.1 million, assuming a coupon rate of 6 percent. A lower coupon should be expected to slow prepayments as observed between the two scenarios. Dividing this CPR by 365 days yields a daily prepayment rate of .000263, which applied against the mortgage balance of $120 billion yields a dollar amount of loans prepaying of approximately $31.6 million. This result lowers the net

liquidity position to $59.5 million since prepayments slow down as an inflow.

4. Applying the formula for rollover balances, BROLL, with the inputs as given in the problem yields a dollar amount of $45.8 million.

6. Use the equations to compute IC, BEW and B as provided in the chapter using the previous estimates for EW and BROLL. In this case, IC = $45.8M*2% = $.916M, BEW = $2.98%*$100M = $2.98M and then month-end balances should be B = $45.8M + $.916M − $2.98M = $43.74M.

8. LCR in this example equals (Level 1 Assets + qualified Level 2 Assets)/ Cash Outflows less Inflows. Inflows are only allowed up to 75 percent of cash outflows so net cashflow is $180M − $180M*.75% = $45M. Level 2 assets may only be counted up to 85 percent. So the numerator of the LCR is $25M + $20B*.85 = $42M. Thus the LCR = $42M/$45M = 93.3% and so the bank is not compliant with the requirement.

10. Using the formula for LVaR, you would assume a value of z of 1.65 for the 95th percentile and thus compute LVaR as $100B − $25*1.65 = $58.75M. The bank is in compliance with the LVaR tolerance and no changes would be warranted at that time.

CHAPTER 12

2. Using formula 12.3, with the information above yields 1.02756($500M)/ ($43.9*250), or $N = 45,671$

4. The table is as follows

Transactions			
Sell 250,000 Shares Citigroup Stock in Forward Contract			
Installment 1	$875,000		
Installment 2		$ 375,000	
Installment 3			$(375,000)
Buy 250,000 Shares in Futures Market			
Contract Month 1	$(250,000)		
Contract Month 2		$(250,000)	
Contract Month 3			$(250,000)
	$625,000	$ 125,000	$(625,000)
		Net Profit	$ 125,000

6. An example is below with assumed information. This position could be used to hedge a short position.

Price at T	Purchased Put $K = 80$	Written Put $K = 82$	Net Profit
	80	82	
70	10	–12	–2
73	7	–9	–2
76	4	–6	–2
79	1	–3	–2
80	0	–2	–2
82	0	0	0
85	0	0	0
88	0	0	0
91	0	0	0
94	0	0	0

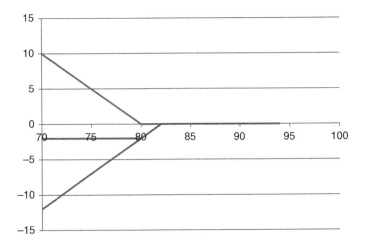

8. Using formula 12.10, you should get .691
10. Refer to formulas 12.14 and 12.15. Gamma is calculated as .6/$100(.3) (1) = .02. The new call premium should be about, $3 + .691(101–100) + .5(101 – 100)(101 – 100).02 = $3.701

CHAPTER 13

2. From the borrower's perspective they have the right to fall out of the pipeline without penalty, and in that regard it is as if they have a free put option. They can "put" or close the commitment at the contracted note rate. In this case they would likely exercise their close option.

4. You have effectively written put options to the borrower so you would want to buy put options on an underlying asset comparable to that of the mortgages in the pipeline.

6. You would apply formula 13.5. This would reflect both the long commitments adjusted for delta and the short forward. The estimated fall out for a 50bps increase in interest rates is .5 + .15(4–4.5) = .425. Now we know that the close rate is equal to 1 − fallout rate, or a close rate of .575. Using this information and formula 13.5 yields ($100 − $99.5).425($25M) = $.212($25M) = $5.3M that would need to be hedged.

8. It will lead to error in your hedge. If the rate change doubles while the fallout rate remains the same, the hedge will be insufficient to offset the continued loss on the commitments. This is why incorporating a dynamic hedging strategy is critical to the success of the hedge activity.

10. Optimization can be a useful tool in the hedge strategy when there are multiple hedge instruments of interest to consider as well as different interest rate scenarios to manage the risk across. One could minimize the cost of hedging subject to constraints on the net hedge position maintained within certain tolerances across rate scenarios, for instance.

CHAPTER 14

2. It would appear that the RCSAs for the capital markets division have not been kept up to date or have not been taken seriously in the business unit. They would need to be revised to a red with potential consequences on the division's operations potentially until it was to be remediated. A full remediation plan would be required.

4. Applying the Poisson formula for $k = 5$ and $\lambda = 7$, the probability is 12.77 percent

6. Note that your answers may be different due to the Rand() function changing each time but a representative table is shown below, applying formula 14.3 in the chapter.

k	Severity
0	$ 98,755.57
1	$ 100,220.78
2	$ 107,033.34
3	$ 94,211.22
4	$ 81,969.57
5	$ 94,182.45
6	$ 95,750.07
7	$ 79,624.99
8	$ 99,293.73
9	$ 101,700.44
10	$ 102,944.93
11	$ 101,784.39
12	$ 94,668.48
13	$ 91,906.46
14	$ 93,830.55
15	$ 100,109.51
	$1,537,986.48

8. You would need to use formula 14.4 in this case along with the information above to compute the following:

Risk Type			
1	$40,000,000,000	$ 9,000,000,000	
2	$ 9,000,000,000	$90,000,000,000	
	$49,000,000,000	$99,000,000,000	$148,000,000,000
			384707.6812

The composite standard deviation is computed as $384,707.

10. Operational risk could come in the form of fraud committed by an individual of the firm or external to the company that results in a default. The default, however, is not a credit loss since the reason why the borrower defaulted was due to the operational risk, or fraud in this case and should not be counted toward estimates of credit loss for the firm but should be captured as part of the company's fraud losses.

CHAPTER 15

2. While the scorecard appears to work well on the segment targeted for the card, the overall KS is not good enough at the policy cutoff to warrant moving the model into production.

4. This is an example of Type II error where the model approves loans that otherwise it should not.

6. If the strategy goes into place and over time the regulators determine that in pulling off the hedge the bank violated the Volcker Rule, it could be subject to significant penalties and regulatory orders.

8. There could be huge reputational risk if it were to be found out that the bank was in effect betting on the success of the tobacco companies' marketing strategy. For no other reason, the headline risk is large as it could paint the bank as insensitive to the outcomes of certain groups, even if they are abroad.

10. The bank should perform a thorough and comprehensive review across all relevant interests in the outcome of the strategy including risk management, compliance, legal, and public relations. The strategy should be benchmarked against the bank's corporate principles. In addition, the RCSA process should be reviewed to ensure that the trading would conform to all relevant regulations before moving it forward.

CHAPTER 16

2. An effective program of integrated risk management emphasizes regular lines of communication vertically and across the organization. It requires integration between analytic and policy units, alignment of incentive, and reporting structures for balanced risk and reward outcomes.

4. The risk committee does not include all of the parties needed to weigh in on this decision. Specifically, while the new limits would certainly mitigate potential credit risk exposure, it has a definite business impact as well as the potential for fair lending and other legal risks. Further, it could pose a reputational risk to the company once news on this position, should it move forward, hits the media. Representatives from legal, compliance, and production teams should be invited to this meeting. And the final decision may not rest with the CRO but could wind up at the Executive Committee level or higher.

6. Without supporting analysis, it is likely that the head of the small business unit and their executive management will put up significant opposition to the decision to limit their growth. You should develop a risk management scorecard not just for the small business group, but one that could be applied consistently across the organization and has been properly vetted with senior management well ahead of such strategic decisions.

8. This is a situation where insufficient communication across the organization takes place. By entering the hedging program, you potentially put the relationship with customers in the commercial lending division at risk if word gets out that the bank is betting against them. From a risk management perspective, this may be an appropriate risk mitigation strategy, but before it is implemented, an understanding of the effects on each business collectively should be established.

10. This is an example of a case where better integration between policy and analytics groups is required. In this case the credit policy group lacks hard evidence to determine where to establish credit policy boundaries and so may be setting up the business for failure early on by simply leveraging a set of policies that would significantly constrain the new program. However, in order to effectively manage the risk, the analytics team may be able to use its insights from the new data and model together in collaboration wth credit policy to set policy criteria that both manage risk and maintain a level of credit performance consistent with expectations. It may be that the team decides to establish a tighter set of underwriting criteria at first that can be relaxed gradually over time as performance aligns with established risk targets.

Index

Answer Key

CHAPTER 1

1. A SIFI refers to a systemically important financial institution. This definition is based on the size, complexity, and interconnectedness of the firm to other firms and markets. SIFIs are the largest financial institutions and their impact on markets, particularly during the 2007–2008 financial crisis, gave rise to a number of new regulations on these firms. These firms have oftentimes been referred to as Too-Big-to-Fail, as shutting these companies down may be more disruptive to markets than keeping them open. This creates a host of perverse incentives on behalf of management to take excessive risks, knowing the government may have limited appetite to force the company to close.

2. The four key elements include setting the bank's risk appetite or tolerance for risk-taking, asset and liability generation, risk monitoring, and management of the firm's risk profile.

3. The most notable difference is the financial intermediation function, which describes the process by which banks transform liabilities into earning assets. In addition, banks are heavily regulated entities that fund themselves largely by accruing federally subsidized deposits. These features have a large impact on the way the firms operate and are overseen by regulatory authorities.

4. Banks use a variety of financial and nonfinancial inputs to maximize profit (the difference between interest and noninterest revenues and expenses). Alternatively the bank might seek to minimize risk subject to some target rate of return. This is typically a constrained optimization problem for the bank in that it optimizes its objective function subject to a set of specific business constraints.

5. In a model where the bank maximizes the expected utility of profit, it can be shown that looking at the second-order conditions associated with the utility maximization problem, banks that are risk-takers experience higher levels of output. Greater risk-taking can lead to higher levels of asset generation and growth.

6. It should always be looking to avoid systems integration issues that prevent the firm from seamlessly creating the necessary risk data and analytics to allow it to identify, measure, and manage its risks across the firm.

7. It exhibited poor risk governance in the form of an executive management team that put growth ahead of risk; it relegated the CRO position to a lesser role than other important positions in the firm; it created a culture of risk-taking through poorly designed organization structures and incentive compensation schemes. It failed to recognize rising risk and product morphing due to risk layering.

8. The Volcker Rule is one of the important provisions of the Dodd-Frank Act that among other things places a ban on proprietary trading at banks. Under the rule banks are no longer allowed to engage in trading for profit.

9. While there are numerous metrics that are used in the industry today, many institutions and regulators focus on such measures as a bank's net interest margin (NIM) and the ratio of nonperforming loans to total loans or assets, among others.

10. Systemic risk refers to the potential for spillover effects from one firm or market into the entire financial system. This is due to increasing interconnectedness among firms and markets that heighten concerns of contagion effects caused by a single or several large SIFIs and markets that can result in a collapse of other firms and markets on a systemwide basis.

11. Risk layering occurs when individual risk attributes such as credit score and loan-to-value (LTV) ratio are combined in ways that materially raise the credit risk profile of the loan. For instance, allowing a lower credit score for a low-down-payment mortgage raises the likelihood of default for the loan beyond a loan that has both higher FICO and lower LTV (i.e., less risky).

12. CAMELS is a regulatory rating process used to define the overall safety and soundness of a depository institution. It comprises an assessment of the bank's capital adequacy (C), asset quality (A), management quality (M), earnings (E), liquidity (L), and sensitivity to market risk (S).

13. Following the financial crisis, Congress and the Administration came together to pass the most comprehensive legislation to affect the banking industry since the Great Depression, which was the Dodd-Frank Act (DFA). The Act touches virtually every aspect of banking and even sets out guidance for regulating nonbank SIFIs. Among key provisions of the Act are regulations regarding derivatives trading, such as over-the-counter (OTC) transactions, which includes CDS; securities that experienced significant losses during the crisis; a ban on proprietary trading by banks also known as the Volcker Rule; creation of a new Consumer Financial Protection Bureau (CFPB) and associated regulations on the mortgage industry; establishment of the Financial Stability Oversight Council (FSOC) and its analytics agency, the Office of Financial Research (OFR), charged with overseeing the buildup of sys-
financial sector, and establishing an orderly liqui facility for banks, requiring them to create their own "living

Printed and bound by CPI Group (UK) Ltd, Croydon, CR0 4YY

23/04/2025

wills" for how they would liquidate their operations under an insolvency, among other situations. The DFA also put the largest financial institutions, that is, those most likely to be too-big-to-fail, under a new set of regulations known as SIFI designation criteria that expose those firms to heightened supervision and other more stringent reporting and capital requirements.

CHAPTER 2

1. This is an example of situational risk awareness. The risk manager needs to understand that the environment in which the bank has taken risk is changing. At the same time management is pressuring the risk team to make changes that are contrary to what will be needed in the near future to effectively manage its risks.
2. Since you are concerned only about the worst 5 percent of returns, you would want to use a factor of 1.65 standard deviations because that cuts off 5 percent in each tail of the distribution. In this case, $10\% - 1.65(3\%) = 5.05\%$ as the worst return associated with the 95 percent level.
3. The contract is designed to remove the firm from credit risk exposure; however, it creates counterparty risk in the sense that the firm could find that the counterparty defaults on its obligation to cover credit losses in the event that it suffers financial distress.
4. There are two types of risks in this case. Model risk is present since the trading unit is exposed to large errors due to an outdated model. In addition, a rogue trader has committed fraud against the firm while at the same time stealing assets. This is operational risk.
5. This is technically interest rate risk since the decline in bond price is due to a rise in interest rates. Given that this results in a decline in valuation to the traded position, it could also be thought of as market risk.
6. As indicated in the above question, fixed-income instruments market risk and interest rate risk are considered to be analogous. More specificly, interest rate risk may be thought of as a subset of market risks. Other classes of assets and liabilities are not sensitive directly to interest rate fluctuations, but price movements of instruments for trading purposes would pose market risk.
7. You could sell a portion of your portfolio, for example, that might pose the greatest risk in a deteriorating market; you could try to enter into a reinsurance agreement with a counterparty willing to cover losses at some level in return for a stream of premiums or you may consider hedging a portion of your portfolio using derivatives by shorting stocks in auto companies that would suffer during a downturn.

8. You face liquidity risk as well as reputation risk. Liquidity risk may arise if bank customers begin to withdraw significant amounts of deposits over a short period of time and/or creditors decline to renew lines of credit or roll over short-term debt.

9. You should be concerned that the new CRO is not exhibiting a proper balance between quantitative and qualitative risk management. The company cannot effectively manage its risks through automation of its underwriting process. The human element remains essential in managing risk and experience can prove to be critical in times where models have limited empirical experience from which to generate robust estimates of risk exposure.

CHAPTER 3

1. ■ A supportive culture for risk management
   ■ An effective risk management team
   ■ Balanced risk management
   ■ Situationally aware risk organization

2. You might think about specific events such as the prefinancial crisis era in which many banks were convinced that home prices could continue to rise. In this rapidly accelerating home price environment the risk management team must begin thinking about how to manage risk when the market may be experiencing an abnormal period of heightened competition, which could lead to greater risk. Pressures from overly aggressive business management could further influence your decisions and you must adapt to these changes. Product risk can also change over time and you should be closely monitoring such situations. This would mean adapting the risk management controls and processes to ensure even greater oversight during such periods.

3. A centralized organization may provide greater independence in risk views and maintain better alignment across risk areas. The downside is that it may not be as responsive to business initiatives. This could constrain the business and opportunities for otherwise value-added products and services to be developed. A decentralized model, while providing greater engagement with the business, could suffer from becoming captive to the business unit and thus expose the firm to greater risk.

4. A blended model, with both a corporate risk office combined with a business risk function embedded within the business, could provide the proper combination of independence, oversight, and responsiveness without compromising the integrity of the risk management function.

This structure is more complicated to manage but has reasonable checks and balances.

5. *Herd mentality* describes a tendency to follow the competition, *ambiguity bias* refers to circumstances where management favor certain outcomes over uncertain ones, *confirmation bias* reflects conditions where management place greater weight on information supporting a point of view that they believe, and the *house effect* refers to conditions where management risk-taking is influenced more by recent events.

6. Exhibiting herd mentality since he is looking at what the competition is doing and pushing risk management to follow them in relaxing underwriting guidelines

7.

$$\theta(I_t) = \left\{ \begin{array}{ll} \Pi_{t+1} & \text{for } \Pi_{t+1} \geq 0 \\ \delta\Pi_{t+1} & \text{for } \Pi_{t+1} < 0 \end{array} \right\}$$

model $\qquad I_t = g(\overline{H}_t, A_t, \overline{HE}_t, G_t)$

This model describes how management utility is determined by incentive compensation arrangements that in turn are affected by a number of cognitive biases. Biases such as herd behavior can amplify management risk-taking and be reinforced by other biases such as confirmation and ambiguity bias.

8.

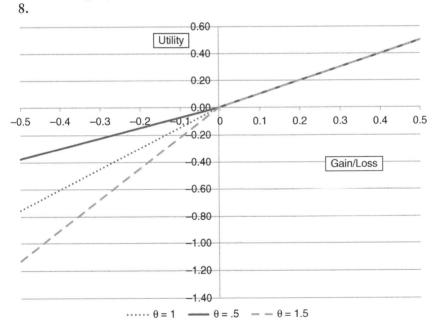

...... θ = 1　　—— θ = .5　　– – θ = 1.5

9. Ambiguity bias can affect management risk-taking and in part its impact would be driven by the stature of the risk organization as well as by the quality of data and accuracy of risk analytics.

10.

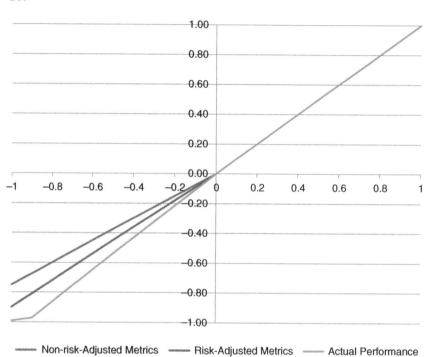

Non-risk-Adjusted Metrics — Risk-Adjusted Metrics — Actual Performance

CHAPTER 4

1. Using the VaR formula from the chapter $(.1 - (1.65)(.548)) * \$1B = \$.804M$

   Note: Use 1.65 as it cuts off 5 percent in each tail, since we are interested in the worst tail. Since this is a worst return distribution, need the minus sign.

2. Daily Earnings at Risk is the worst return the company could observe in one day at a 95 percent level of confidence.

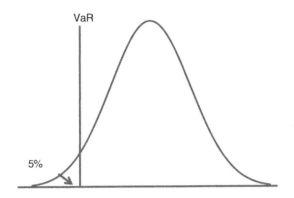

3. DEAR*SQRT(5) = $.804M*2.236 = $1.8M
4. (.1+.06(1.96))SQRT(10) = .688 (Note: VaR in terms of expected default rate). Need to convert into dollars of loss, or .688*(1 – .65)*$500M = $120.4M
5. Risk Capital RC = VaR – EL = $120.4M – (.1)(.35)($500M) = $102.9M
6. The VaR represents the worst losses at a given level of confidence that would be assessed against an asset or portfolio whereas risk capital deducts expected loss from that amount.
7. Since there is no accounting for correlations between risks, the estimate may be overly conservative and hence overstate the amount of risk, thus potentially allowing some otherwise profitable business opportunities to be foregone.
8. You could rely on copula methods to address the nonnormality by mapping those distributions into a normal distribution
9. This is a reverse stress test. The exercise aimed at finding what the risk factors had to be in order to cause the firm to become insolvent.
10. Apply RaRoC calculation (NI/EC), or (R-OC-FC-EL)/EC. From an ROE perspective, P2 has the more attractive return at (100-10-30-45)/.04($1.125B) = 33.3%, versus 11% for P1. However, when applying RaRoC, a different result is obtained. RaRoC for P1 is $5M/$25M = 20%, thus meeting the hurdle rate, while RaRoC for P2 is $15M/$90M = 16.6%
11. Define SVA = NI – HR*EC > = 0, or for P1, 5 – .15(25) = 1.25 versus for P2, 15 – .15(90) = –1.5. P2 thus destroys shareholder value while P1 increases value.

12. To calculate the total VaR, compute the following using the formula in the chapter. So, SQRT(64 + 25 + 2(8)(5)(.666)) = \$11.93B. Note the correlation is calculated as covariance divided by the product of the two volatilities, or .025/(.15*.25) = .666. Also, the total VaR is less than the sum of both division VaRs due to the correlation being less than 1.

13. Follow the discussion in the chapter for allocating capital in the table. With portfolio VaR given as \$12 billion, compute for D1 (12.5 − 12)/.05 as in the last column of the table in the text, or \$10 billion, and for D2 it would be (12.1 − 12/.05) = \$2B. This would line up to the total VaR of \$12 billion but provides an allocation across the two divisions based on their incremental usage of capital when exposures increase.

CHAPTER 5

1. From the bank's perspective, the loan is composed of two parts: a default-free fixed-income like instrument plus a free written put provided to the borrower as expressed as follows: $B = L - MAX[0, L - A_T]$

2. As d_1 increases, the value of d_2 also rises, which increase the likelihood the call option is in-the-money. Conversely, this reduces the likelihood that the put option is in-the-money. $N(-d_2)$ can thus be considered the risk neutral probability of default.

3. Applying the formula, $RR = \dfrac{A_T e^{-rT}\, \dfrac{N(-d_1)}{N(-d_2)}}{L}$ yields a recovery rate of about 81 percent, or an LGD of 1 − .81 = .19.

4. Given that PD = 1 − .95 = .05, EL = .05*.19 = .95%

5. Apply the formula $DD = \dfrac{\ln A_0 - \ln L + (r - 05\sigma^2)T}{\sigma\sqrt{T}}$ yields, (ln(11.5) − ln(10) + (.025 − .5(.10)^{2}5)/.1SQRT(5) = .625

6. The firm is more likely to default as DD decreases. It refers to the number of standard deviations that the property value must decline to before a default is triggered.

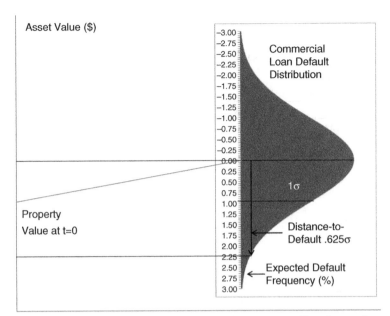

Asset Value ($)

Property
Value at t=0

-3.00	
-2.75	
-2.50	Commercial
-2.25	Loan Default
-2.00	Distribution
-1.75	
-1.50	
-1.25	
-1.00	
-0.75	
-0.50	
-0.25	
0.00	
0.25	
0.50	
0.75	1σ
1.00	
1.25	
1.50	Distance-to-
1.75	Default .625σ
2.00	
2.25	
2.50	Expected Default
2.75	Frequency (%)
3.00	

5 Years   Time (years after origination)

7. Specifically it can be shown that y is equal to $r + (1/T)(\ln(1/(1 - PD*LGD)))$. Alternatively the credit spread is defined as $y - r$. In this example problem, then, if $PD = .05$ and $LGD = .19$ percent, then $y = .025 + (1/5)*(\ln(1/(1 - .05*.19))) = .0269$ or 2.69%

8. You need to calculate the product of each of the three possible combinations for 1 and 2 as shown below. Note each cell represents the movement from 1 outcome for each product to another over 1 period. The sum of the nine outcomes should equal 100 percent as indicated below.

p11p21	p11p22	p11p23	
p12p21	p12p22	p12p23	
p13p21	p13p22	p13p23	

0.09	0.63	0.18	0.9
0.007	0.049	0.014	0.07
0.003	0.021	0.006	0.03
			1

9.

LGD	0.4	
T	3	
Face	$1,000,000	
Product	1	2
Coupon	0.025	0.03
Forward Rate		
Year		
1	0.02	0.025
2	0.025	0.0275
3	0.0275	0.03
NPV		
P11	$993,189	
P12	$986,090	
P13	$400,000	
P21	$1,007,459	
P22	$1,000,280	
P23	$400,000	

10. The combined portfolio values of the two bond portfolio for each outcome is as follows

$2,000,648	$1,993,469	$1,393,189
$1,993,549	$1,986,370	$1,386,090
$1,407,459	$1,400,280	$ 800,000

To calculate the expected value multiply the cell joint migration probability in Q8 by the respective portfolio value cell above. The answer should be $1,855,838.13.

11. $260,875

12. Would calculate the marginal standard deviation MSD as shown in the text or (150,000 − 100,000)/500,000 = 10 percent. In this case the asset adds 10 percent to the risk of the portfolio for every dollar of that asset.

CHAPTER 6

1. $dt = 1/12 = .0833$ = annualized monthly time interval of interest.

$$dHPI \text{ for } G1 = 105((.05*.0833) + .25*e*(sqrt(.0833)))$$
$$= 105(.0042 + .0722e) = 5.18 \text{ percent}$$

$$dHPI \text{ for } G2 = 105((.045*.0833) + .28*e*(sqrt(.0833)))$$
$$= 110(.00375 + .0722e) = 5.38 \text{ percent}$$

2. We would expect a price increase of 5.18% and 5.38 percent, respectively, for G1 and G2.
3. It is likely that such a change in volatility will result in a much different-looking distribution of defaults than what you originally developed. This could result in fat-tailed risk such that your unexpected losses will be higher for a given confidence level.
4. You also have an imbalance in your portfolio with 75 percent of it in the high volatility geography. You may want to consider transferring that risk to other counterparties, sell some assets, and consider changing credit policy standards, among other activities.
5. You need to use a logistic regression model of the form: $PD = 1/(1 + e^{\wedge} - Z)$
   Where $Z = -.027$(Credit Score) + 20(Credit Balance to Limits) + 4 (Loan Payment to Income) + .02(Number of Open Credit Lines) for each customer
   Estimates of PD are: $PD1 = 22.1$ percent; $PD2 = 51$ percent
   Would grant credit to borrower 1 only, given the policy
6. This is an example of a compensating factor, which provides an offset to a risk factor such as number of credit lines that increases risk. Requiring a higher credit score lowers credit risk.
7. This is an example of risk layering where the original product was changed significantly along every policy variable. This will result in much higher risk over time, which in part may be due to borrower selection issues. Less credit-worthy borrowers will be incented to take credit from the bank, which will also affect your portfolio's risk over time.
8. Note: These are computed based on adjustments to original balance for defaults in each year for each vintage:

	12	24	36	48	60
Vintage 1	0.85%	1.01%	1.15%	1.03%	0.78%
Vintage 2	1.50%	2.79%	3.92%	4.35%	0.00%
Vintage 3	3.85%	3.20%	4.96%	0.00%	0.00%
Vintage 4	4.12%	4.91%	0.00%	0.00%	0.00%
Vintage 5	0.28%	0.00%	0.00%	0.00%	0.00%

Note—these are computed based on adjustments to original balance for defaults in each year for each vintage:

To illustrate this; the marginal default rate for Vintage 1 at month 60 is as follows:

$$\$750,000/(\$100,000,000 - \$850,000 - \$1,000,000 - \$1,125,000$$
$$- \$1,000,000) = .78\%$$

9. The comparisons of cumulative default rates controlling for months after origination are more relevant as shown below. The cumulative default rates sum up the marginal default rates across time. Clearly vintages 2–3 are materially worse than vintage 1 at all comparable points across time after origination. Vintage 5 by comparison while only 12 months old appears to be of much better quality than any other vintage.

Marginal Default Rates	12	24	36	48	60
Vintage 1	0.85%	1.01%	1.15%	1.03%	0.78%
Vintage 2	1.50%	2.79%	3.92%	4.35%	0.00%
Vintage 3	3.85%	3.20%	4.96%	0.00%	0.00%
Vintage 4	4.12%	4.91%	0.00%	0.00%	0.00%
Vintage 5	0.28%	0.00%	0.00%	0.00%	0.00%
Cumulative Default Rates	12	24	36	48	60
Vintage 1	0.85%	1.86%	3.00%	4.04%	0.00%
Vintage 2	1.50%	4.29%	8.21% I	12.56%	
Vintage 3	3.85%	7.05%	12.00%		
Vintage 4	4.12%	9.03%			
Vintage 5	0.28%				

10. Using the approach outlined in the chapter you would find the following:

2-month Transition Probability						
	Current	30–59	60–89	90+	FCL	REO	Total
Current	86.83%	4.18%	3.86%	3.31%	1.32%	0.50%	100.00%
30–59	37.07%	12.76%	22.27%	23.32%	4.05%	0.52%	100.00%
60–89	16.37%	5.95%	13.33%	46.93%	15.10%	2.32%	100.00%
90+	10.14%	2.04%	3.42%	62.31%	18.34%	3.76%	100.00%
FCL	2.49%	1.60%	2.04%	7.09%	78.81%	7.98%	100.00%
REO	0.49%	0.52%	1.03%	2.79%	32.04%	63.14%	100.00%

CHAPTER 7

1. For the obligor part of the scorecard you should consider business and market factors such as competitive position, years in business, and economic conditions for the business, a management assessment

that includes external ratings where available, financial reporting and audit information and an assessment of the quality of management. Finally, a comprehensive financial analysis should accompany the scorecard.

2. According to the risk ratings, the facility rating would be 6 and the obligor rating a 2. Based on these results and given the EDF and obligor LGD, this loan would fall into the final risk-rating category of 3. That is, 40 percent EDF * 5 percent LGD = 2 percent loss, which falls into the 1.125 – 10 percent category 3 range, and this is a Pass grade.

3. Guarantees will improve the credit risk of the loan and in this case probably contributed to the rating that was received initially at origination. That the guarantee is about to come off the loan is troublesome in that, at the least, the loan should be re-evaluated from a risk-rating standpoint to determine if any change to the rating is in order.

4. You should compute the debt service coverage ratio (DSCR) for each loan as shown in the chapter. This would result in a DSCR for Loan 1 of 1.09 and for Loan 2 of .99. Typically banks have minimum DSCRs of at least 1 if not higher at 1.15 and on that basis, Loan 2 should not be made and Loan 1 is marginal.

5. You would need to compute the absorption rate on each property. In this case, it is 200/1,000 or 10 percent for Complex 1 versus 150/700 or 21 percent for Complex 2. Complex 2 has a better absorption rate, meaning that the property has a better chance of increasing its cash flows to service debt over time.

6. You should look into the possibility of participating in a loan syndication where your firm could take an interest in the loan. However, care must be taken by the bank to conduct due diligence on the lead bank in the syndication and how well it performs its duties in addition to understanding the risk of the transaction.

7. The distribution of risk ratings appears skewed more toward lower ratings, and ideally in establishing a risk rating system the ratings should have more of a normal distribution in general. The fact that a large percentage fall into the bottom 4 ratings that are associated with loans meriting special attention or watch is concerning and may point to either problems in the origination side of the business and/or issues in the risk rating process.

8. You should compute each borrower's cash-flow-at-risk. For borrower 1 it would be:

$$CFaR = \$1M - 1.65(\$.25M) = \$.5875M$$

And for borrower 2 it would be:

$$CFaR = \$2M - 1.65(\$.5M) = \$1.175M$$

According to loan policy borrower 1 breaches the cash flow trigger and thus should be remanded to the Loan review group for additional analysis.

9. Two alternatives are to use a point-in-time (PIT) or through-the-cycle (TTC) approach. Using a TTC ensures that the loan is observed over a range of outcomes in the business cycle than on one specific point. From a time horizon perspective, one year is a commonly used period for evaluation in a risk rating.

10. A decline of more than 1 risk rating in a short period of time is indicative of potential issues with the loan. It would require the loan be brought to Loan review for further analysis. If the 2 rating downgrade is confirmed, it might warrant disciplinary action for the loan officer or at least greater scrutiny on how loans are originated and additional training for staff.

CHAPTER 8

1. Loss subordination refers to the level of losses in a junior or subordinate position to the specific tranche of interest. So for B tranche, it is the first loss and hence has 0 subordination. BB has protection up to B's 3 percent losses, BBB has 5 percent subordination in light of B's 3 percent and BB's 2 percent, and so on.

Reference Pool	$1,000,000,000		
	Tranche Size	Percent of CDO	Loss Subordination (%)
AAA	$500,000,000	90	10
AA	$ 10,000,000	2	8
A	$ 5,000,000	2	6
BBB	$ 4,000,000	1	5
BB	$ 6,000,000	2	3
B	$ 15,000,000	3	0
	$540,000,000	100	

2.

Loss Scenario	Scenario Loss Amount ($)	Tranche Losses					
		B	BB	BBB	A	AA	AAA
1	$ 2,700,000	$ 2,700,000	$ –	$ –	$ –	$ –	$ –
2	$ 5,400,000	$ 5,400,000	$ –	$ –	$ –	$ –	$ –
3	$10,800,000	$10,800,000	$ –	$ –	$ –	$ –	$ –
4	$16,200,000	$15,000,000	$1,200,000	$ –	$ –	$ –	$ –
5	$21,600,000	$15,000,000	$6,000,000	$ 600,000	$ –	$ –	$ –
6	$27,000,000	$15,000,000	$6,000,000	$4,000,000	$2,000,000	$ –	$ –
7	$32,400,000	$15,000,000	$6,000,000	$4,000,000	$5,000,000	$ 2,400,000	$ –
8	$43,200,000	$15,000,000	$6,000,000	$4,000,000	$5,000,000	$10,000,000	$ 3,200,000
9	$54,000,000	$15,000,000	$6,000,000	$4,000,000	$5,000,000	$10,000,000	$14,000,000
10	$64,800,000	$15,000,000	$6,000,000	$4,000,000	$5,000,000	$10,000,000	$24,800,000

3.

Loss Scenario	B	BB	Tranche Payoffs BBB	A	AA	AAA
1	$12,300,000	$6,000,000	$4,000,000	$5,000,000	$10,000,000	$500,000,000
2	$ 9,600,000	$6,000,000	$4,000,000	$5,000,000	$10,000,000	$500,000,000
3	$ 4,200,000	$6,000,000	$4,000,000	$5,000,000	$10,000,000	$500,000,000
4	$ –	$4,800,000	$4,000,000	$5,000,000	$10,000,000	$500,000,000
5	$ –	$ –	$3,400,000	$5,000,000	$10,000,000	$500,000,000
6	$ –	$ –	$ –	$3,000,000	$10,000,000	$500,000,000
7	$ –	$ –	$ –	$ –	$ 7,600,000	$500,000,000
8	$ –	$ –	$ –	$ –	$ –	$496,800,000
9	$ –	$ –	$ –	$ –	$ –	$486,000,000
10	$ –	$ –	$ –	$ –	$ –	$475,200,000

4.

Tranche	Tranche Price ($)	Tranche Yield (%)
AAA	$484,815,179.65	3.08%
AA	$ 9,366,740.29	6.54%
A	$ 4,551,389.55	9.40%
BBB	$ 3,547,948.87	11.99%
BB	$ 5,065,725.69	16.93%
B	$ 8,728,187.13	54.15%
	$516,075,171.18	

5. See table in Question 4.

6.

Risk-free rate   0.025

Contract Year	Mortgage Default Rate	Mortgage Severity Rate	Expected Loss	Remaining Pool	Discount Factor	Present Value Payments	Present Value Defaults
1	0.03	0.4	0.012	0.988	0.975609756	0.9639	0.0116
2	0.04	0.4	0.016	0.972	0.951814396	0.9252	0.0148
3	0.05	0.4	0.02	0.952	0.928599411	0.884	0.0177
4	0.06	0.4	0.024	0.928	0.905950645	0.8407	0.0202
			0.072			3.6138	0.0642
Credit Spread	0.017773						

AU: we have set these two tables in 8.5pt

7.

Risk-free rate   0.025

Contract Year	Mortgage Default Rate	Mortgage Severity Rate	Expected Loss	Remaining Pool	Discount Factor	Present Value Payments	Present Value Defaults
1	0.03	0.4	0.0120	0.9928	0.975609756	0.9686	0.0070
2	0.04	0.4	0.0160	0.9833	0.951814396	0.9359	0.0091
3	0.05	0.4	0.0200	0.9695	0.928599411	0.9003	0.0130
4	0.06	0.4	0.0240	0.9532	0.905950645	0.8636	0.0152
			0.0720			3.6683	0.0444
Credit Spread	0.0121						

8. One could utilize a constrained optimization program where the cost associated with insurance or self-insuring is minimized—i.e., the premiums are minimized subject to a set of policy constraints as indicated in the chapter example.

9.

Rationale	Disposition
Violates P1's FICO limit, lower cost than P2	Bank
Lowest costs and meets P1 limits	P1
Lowest costs and meets P1 limits	P1
Lowest costs and meets P1 limits	P1
Violates P1's CA limit and bank's	P2

10. It could be telling you that the model is out of line with the market but that does not mean it should be adjusted. Other market participants could be mispricing the risk and if you had good empirical support for why your model is performing well, it should not be adjusted to align with the market. There is a possibility that the model could be off, however, and it would be necessary to perform additional validation work to decide whether to re-estimate the model or not.

CHAPTER 9

1. Using formula 9.2, the results are shown below as:

	Coupon Bond	
t	PV	PVt
1	2.882	2.882
2	2.769	5.539
3	2.661	7.982
4	2.556	10.226
5	84.329	421.646
B	95.198	448.275
D	4.709	

2. The differences are shown below:

Bond Price	+50bps Change
PV	92.984
D Only	92.957

3. You would add a convexity correction factor as calculated using formula 9.5. The results from this would now show:

	Coupon Bond		
t	PV	PVt	CX
1	2.882	2.882	2.882
2	2.769	5.539	11.077
3	2.661	7.982	23.947
4	2.556	10.226	40.903
5	84.329	421.646	2108.232
B	95.198	448.275	2187.041
D	4.709		22.974

Bond Price	+50bps Change
PV	92.984
D Only	92.957
D + CX	92.984

4. The results would look as follows using the PMT function in Excel to compute the amortized annual cash flow.

	Coupon Bond			Amortized Bond		
t	PV	PVt		PMT	PV	PVt
1	2.868	2.868	2.868	21.835	20.97928	20.97928
2	2.742	5.484	10.967	21.835	20.15667	40.31333
3	2.621	7.863	23.590	21.835	19.36631	58.09894
4	2.506	10.023	40.093	21.835	18.60695	74.4278
5	82.247	411.236	2056.179	21.835	17.87736	89.3868
B	92.984	437.474	2133.698	109.177	96.98657	283.206
D	4.705		22.947	D	2.920	

   The amortized bond has a much lower duration reflecting the fact that on a relative basis it receives its cash flows back sooner than the coupon bond.

5. A 1 unit change in this rate would be equal to a 1 standard deviation movement, or 2.3*.35, or .805bps higher rate.

6. The impact is measured for each principal component by dividing each component's eigenvalue by the total of 9. The proportions are shown

below. So $k1$ for example explains 58.8 percent of the variability in rate movements. $K1$ represents the impact of a parallel shift in rates, $k2$, a change in the slope of the yield curve, and $k3$, a change in the curvature of the yield curve.

Proportion	Cumulative Proportion
0.588	0.588
0.134	0.722
0.071	0.793

7. Most of the impact on the 30-year bond is in the longer-end of the term structure, particularly from five years and over.
8. The results are shown below:

0.01%

Present Value	Duration	Key Rate Duration
$10,936	19.643	–13.082

The differences in the spot and key rate adjusted rates are virtually the same given the 1bps assumption for rate change. However, there will be just enough difference in the present values to see some impact. You would compute the present value of the cash flows in each period using the spot rates, which would result in a value of $10,951. Repeating this process but using the key rate shift rates provides a present value of $10,936. Estimated key rate duration for the 30-year would be (($10,951 – $10,936)/$10,951)/1bps or 13.082.

9. Applying the CIR model, you should have an estimate close to .0017 percent.
10. You should use the relationship in formula 9.20 to compute the OAS. The present value of the no prepayment bond is $49.79M. Using the formula you should find that the OAS that equates the present value of the prepayment and no prepayment bonds assuming a 5 percent discount rate should be about 1bp.

CHAPTER 10

1. Using a cash flow mapping approach as shown in the chapter you would want to create a weighted average beta for the portfolio from which to compute VaR, that is, use $\beta_P = \sum_{i=1}^{n} \omega_i \beta_i$ and $VaR_{TSD}^{BankStocks} = P_{TSD}^{BankStocks} = \beta_{TSD}^{BankStocks} 2.32\sigma_M$ to yield

β (Bank Stocks)	1.190540541
VaR (Bank Stocks, $)	$6,387,250

2. The results should show the following:

		Corrrelations			
Call Options	99% VaR	1	2	3	4
1	$ 2,900,000	1	0.35	0.65	0.37
2	$31,737,600		1	0.45	0.15
3	$ 8,613,000			1	0.4
4	$ 2,088,000				1
Sum	$45,338,600				
	Portfolio VaR	$38,417,391			

3. The results should show the following:

		Corrrelations			
Asset Type	99% VaR	Term 1	Term 2	Term 3	Term 4
Term 1	139,200	1	−0.25	0.13	0.65
Term 2	487,200		1	0.77	−0.55
Term 3	1,435,500			1	0.32
Term 4	5,278,000				1
Sum	7,339,900				
	Portfolio VaR	5,851,948			

4. The results should show the following:

		Corrrelations		
Asset Type	99% VaR	Call Options	Bonds	Stock
Call Options	38,417,390.52	1	−0.25	0.7
Bonds	5,851,947.79		1	−0.5
Stock	6,387,250.00			1
Sum	50,656,588.31			
	Portfolio VaR	41769439.59		

5. Let's assume correlations to illustrate the concept off the diagonal are now .5. The results are shown below that the portfolio VaR will increase.

Portfolio VaR		Corrrelations		
Asset Type	99% VaR	Call Options	Bonds	Stock
Call Options	38,417,391	1	0.5	0.7
Bonds	5,851,948		1	0.5
Stock	6,387,250			1
Sum	50,656,588			
	Portfolio VaR	46439925.02		

6. Applying the GBM approach to this stock assuming drift equals .25 and volatility is .15, a table of the next 12 months would like the following:

Time	RandNorm e	mdt	dS	lognormal P
1	−0.033739961	0.020833333	0.015772339	$101.59
2	−0.3948356	0.041666667	−0.017558673	$ 98.26
3	−0.128959486	0.0625	0.043156077	$104.41
4	−0.395600092	0.083333333	0.02399332	$102.43
5	−0.202191002	0.104166667	0.073838016	$107.66
6	0.325093167	0.125	0.173763975	$118.98
7	0.364856391	0.145833333	0.200561792	$122.21
8	−0.428420052	0.166666667	0.102403659	$110.78
9	0.062752873	0.1875	0.196912931	$121.76
10	0.151099261	0.208333333	0.230998222	$125.99
11	−0.006646438	0.229166667	0.228169701	$125.63
12	−0.052367755	0.25	0.242144837	$127.40

7. See table shown in answer to question 8.

	Stock 1	Stock 2	Stock 3	Stock 4	Stock 5
$Value	$500,000,000.00	$1,000,000,000.00	$750,000,000.00	$1,500,000,000.00	$1,250,000,000.00
Trial Initial Price	$42.16	$47.05	$11.32	$34.83	$33.10
1	$42.68	$46.99	$11.46	$34.84	$33.11
2	$44.20	$47.96	$11.91	$35.68	$33.83
3	$41.86	$46.88	$11.51	$34.34	$33.05
4	$41.87	$46.72	$11.15	$34.90	$33.43
5	$43.64	$47.58	$11.72	$35.26	$33.30
6	$41.46	$46.51	$11.39	$34.77	$32.78
7	$41.25	$46.74	$11.17	$34.47	$32.73
8	$42.10	$47.91	$11.57	$35.24	$33.29
9	$41.13	$46.58	$10.95	$34.60	$32.90
10	$41.69	$46.40	$11.04	$34.54	$32.68
11	$43.48	$47.80	$11.77	$35.06	$33.62
12	$42.43	$47.63	$11.22	$35.66	$33.41
13	$42.72	$47.04	$11.45	$34.68	$32.84
14	$40.90	$46.57	$11.10	$34.41	$32.75
15	$42.62	$47.57	$11.42	$34.90	$33.31
16	$41.70	$46.79	$11.12	$34.30	$32.80
17	$42.92	$48.01	$11.55	$35.81	$33.76
18	$42.86	$47.23	$11.43	$35.21	$32.95
19	$41.96	$47.09	$11.11	$34.74	$33.36
20	$43.18	$48.40	$11.53	$35.11	$33.45
21	$42.12	$47.35	$11.33	$34.54	$32.61
22	$41.64	$46.78	$11.10	$34.48	$32.68
23	$40.21	$45.79	$10.95	$33.86	$32.49
24	$43.63	$47.80	$11.78	$35.18	$33.42
25	$43.12	$47.63	$11.38	$35.96	$33.70
26	$42.41	$47.74	$11.31	$35.12	$33.74
27	$42.27	$46.49	$11.24	$34.66	$33.06
28	$44.82	$50.36	$12.03	$36.84	$34.58
29	$40.73	$47.26	$11.79	$34.87	$33.60
30	$43.43	$48.26	$11.83	$35.56	$33.31

AU: we are set this table in 7pt

8. By rank ordering the gains and losses you would look for the third (Trial 28) lowest loss out of 30 (10 percent lowest loss).

Portfolio Value	Gain/Loss ($M)	Rank-ordered Gains/Losses ($M)	Outcome
$5,014,951,810	$ 14.95	$(247)	1
$5,147,114,763	$ 147.11	$(241)	2
$4,982,431,029	$ (17.57)	$(164)	3
$4,993,586,564	$ (6.41)	$(139)	4
$5,081,625,893	$ 81.63	$(138)	5
$4,970,115,464	$ (29.88)	$(122)	6
$4,942,711,580	$ (57.29)	$(120)	7
$5,059,486,024	$ 59.49	$(114)	8
$4,935,859,146	$ (64.14)	$(111)	9
$4,933,603,263	$ (66.40)	$(108)	10
$5,091,123,272	$ 91.12	$(107)	11
$5,056,256,279	$ 56.26	$(107)	12
$4,998,771,700	$ (1.23)	$(106)	13
$4,928,841,675	$(71.16)	$(104)	14
$5,033,795,920	$ 33.80	$(104)	15
$4,941,736,470	$ (58.26)	$(101)	16
$5,111,615,435	$ 111.62	$(101)	17
$5,030,543,612	$ 30.54	$ (99)	18
$4,990,551,651	$ (9.45)	$ (94)	19
$5,080,232,372	$ 80.23	$ (93)	20
$4,976,047,039	$(23.95)	$ (79)	21
$4,942,753,762	$ (57.25)	$ (79)	22
$4,861,064,343	$(138.94)	$ (75)	23
$5,090,454,213	$ 90.45	$ (74)	24
$5,098,966,141	$ 98.97	$ (73)	25
$5,053,026,040	$ 53.03	$ (73)	26
$4,974,994,118	$ (25.01)	$ (72)	27
$5,291,383,981	$ 291.38	$ (72)	28
$5,039,033,696	$ 39.03	$ (71)	29
$5,114,095,994	$ 114.10	$ (71)	30

9. VaR models are sensitive to model assumptions and could break down if normality conditions are violated. VaR models can also incent risk-taking. They can also be subject to fat-tailed risk outcomes, thus under-estimating the amount of risk exposure.

10. Augmenting VaR models with appropriate stress tests can be a useful approach to managing risk. In addition, adopting variations in VaR models such as MES could reduce risk-taking.

CHAPTER 11

1. Net liquidity position is defined as cash inflows minus cash outflows or in this case $96.1M.

CASH INFLOW SOURCES	Average Daily Baseline	Answer CPR Average Daily Baseline	Answer Non-Core Retail Deposits Average Daily Baseline
On-Balance Sheet			
Mortgage Assets	$119,997,573,233	$120,034,163,211	$120,034,163,211
Loans Maturing	$ 1,643,836	$ 1,643,836	$ 1,643,836
Loans Defaulting	$ (1,053,597)	$ (1,053,597)	$ (1,053,597)
Loans Prepaying	$ 68,222,485	$ 31,632,506.86	$ 31,632,506.86
New Loans	$ (68,493,151)	$ (68,493,151)	$ (68,493,151)
Mortgages Sold	$ 16,438,356	$ 16,438,356	$ 16,438,356
Interest & Fee Income	$ 19,725,628	$ 19,731,643	$ 19,731,643
Non Mortgage Assets	$879,553,972,603	$879,553,972,603	$879,553,972,603
Assets Maturing	$ 36,164,384	$ 36,164,384	$ 36,164,384
Assets Prepaying	$ 361,643,836	$ 361,643,836	$ 361,643,836
Assets Defaulting	$ (96,438,356)	$ (96,438,356)	$ (96,438,356)
New Loans	$ (48,219,178)	$ (48,219,178)	$ (48,219,178)
Assets Sold	$ 24,109,589	$ 24,109,589	$ 24,109,589
Interest & Fee Income	$ 180,730,268	$ 180,730,268	$ 180,730,268
Off-Balance Sheet			
Lines of Credit Draws by Bank	$ 5,178,082	$ 5,178,082	$ 5,178,082
Derivative Instrument Activity	$ 6,213,699	$ 6,213,699	$ 6,213,699
TOTAL	$ 603,357,834	$ 566,773,871	$ 566,773,871

AU: we have set this table from unedited docx file. Please check.

(continued)

CASH OUTFLOW SOURCES	Average Daily Baseline	Answer CPR Average Daily Baseline	Answer Non-Core Retail Deposits Average Daily Baseline
On-Balance Sheet			
Core Retail Deposits	$247,500,000,000	$247,500,000,000	$247,500,000,000
Deposits Maturing	$ 135,616,438	$ 135,616,438	$ 135,616,438
Deposit Runoff	$ 48,529,412	$ 48,529,412	$ 48,529,412
New Deposits	$ (33,904,110)	$ (33,904,110)	$ (33,904,110)
Interest Expense	$ 7,797,945	$ 7,797,945	$ 7,797,945
Non-Core Retail Liabilities	$247,500,000,000	$247,500,000,000	$247,500,000,000
Liabilities Maturing	$ 96,868,885	$ 96,868,885	$ 96,868,885
Liability Runoff	$ 126,309,494	$ 126,309,493.57	$ 17,671,363.42
New Deposits	$ (67,808,219)	$ (67,808,219)	$ (67,808,219)
Interest Expense	$ 15,256,849	$ 15,256,849	$ 15,256,849
Other Liabilities	$333,000,000,000	$333,000,000,000	$333,000,000,000
Liabilities Maturing	$ 152,054,795	$ 152,054,795	$ 152,054,795
New Liabilities	$ (18,246,575)	$ (18,246,575)	$ (18,246,575)
Interest Expense	$ 13,684,932	$ 13,684,932	$ 13,684,932
Off-Balance Sheet			
Lines of Credit Draws by Customers	$ 22,260,274	$ 22,260,274	$ 22,260,274
Derivative Instrument Activity	$ 8,837,260	$ 8,837,260	$ 8,837,260
TOTAL	$ 507,257,379	$ 507,257,379	$ 398,619,249
Net Liquidity Position	$ 96,100,455	$ 59,516,492	$ 168,154,622

2. Applying the formula for CPR with the inputs given yields a CPR of 9.6 percent versus 20.75 percent in the results where the net liquidity position equals $96.1 million, assuming a coupon rate of 6 percent. A lower coupon should be expected to slow prepayments as observed between the two scenarios. Dividing this CPR by 365 days yields a daily prepayment rate of .000263, which applied against the mortgage balance of $120 billion yields a dollar amount of loans prepaying of

approximately $31.6 million. This result lowers the net liquidity position to $59.5 million since prepayments slow down as an inflow.

3. The estimate of retention rate is 97.4 percent versus the original retention rate of 81.4 percent. This reduces liability runoff from $126 million to $17.6 million. In turn this increases the net liquidity position to $168.1 million.

4. Applying the formula for rollover balances, BROLL, with the inputs as given in the problem yields a dollar amount of $45.8 million.

5. Applying the formula for EW and parameters as given yields an early withdrawal rate of approximately 2.98 percent.

6. Use the equations to compute IC, BEW and B as provided in the chapter using the previous estimates for EW and BROLL. In this case, IC = $45.8M*2% = $.916M, BEW = $2.98%*$100M = $2.98M and then month-end balances should be B = $45.8M + $.916M – $2.98M = $43.74M.

7. You would want to conduct a liquidity contingency planning exercise. This would entail identifying alternative funding sources including the reliability of such funds under various scenarios, their magnitude, among other items.

8. LCR in this example equals (Level 1 Assets + qualified Level 2 Assets)/ Cash Outflows less Inflows. Inflows are only allowed up to 75 percent of cash outflows so net cashflow is $180M – $180M*.75% = $45M. Level 2 assets may only be counted up to 85 percent. So the numerator of the LCR is $25M + $20B*.85 = $42M. Thus the LCR = $42M/$45M = 93.3% and so the bank is not compliant with the requirement.

9. You could sell Freddie Mac MBS and buy Treasuries in order to bring the ratio into compliance. But you might run the risk of other banks having to do the same thing, resulting in potentially lower prices on Freddie securities being received.

10. Using the formula for LVaR, you would assume a value of z of 1.65 for the 95th percentile and thus compute LVaR as $100B – $25*1.65 = $58.75M. The bank is in compliance with the LVaR tolerance and no changes would be warranted at that time.

CHAPTER 12

1. You can estimate the relationship between the two series using a linear regression model to estimate β since it is also the hedge ratio. The results are shown below. The hedge ratio therefore is 1.0275.

SUMMARY OUTPUT

Regression Statistics

Multiple R	0.845
R Square	0.714
Adjusted R Square	0.702
Standard Error	1.348
Observations	25

ANOVA

	df	SS	MS	F	Significance F
Regression	1	104.482	104.482	57.494	0.000
Residual	23	41.797	1.817		
Total	24	146.280			

	Coefficients	Standard Error	t Stat	P-value	Lower 95%	Upper 95%	Lower 95.0%	Upper 95.0%
Intercept	1.571	6.739	0.233	0.818	−12.370	15.513	−12.370	15.513
X Variable 1	1.028	0.136	7.582	0.000	0.747	1.308	0.747	1.308

2. Using formula 12.3, with the information above yields $1.02756(\$500M)/(\$43.9*250)$, or $N = 45,671$

3. You take an offsetting short futures position and the net profit is $5.7 million versus a loss of $10.3 million on the unhedged position.

	Spot JPM Position			Futures Citigroup Position	
S_0	$	55	F_0	$	45.30
S_T	$	53.87	F_T	$	43.90
$V_{U\,t=0}$	$500,000,000		$V_{H\,t=0}$	$517,236,777	
$V_{U\,t=3}$	$489,724,000		$V_{H\,t=3}$	$501,240,444	
Profit	$ (10,276,000)		Profit	$ 15,996,332	
Hedge Profit	$ 5,720,332				

4. The table is as follows

Transactions			
Sell 250,000 Shares Citigroup Stock in Forward Contract			
Installment 1	$875,000		
Installment 2		$ 375,000	
Installment 3			$(375,000)
Buy 250,000 Shares in Futures Market			
Contract Month 1	$(250,000)		
Contract Month 2		$(250,000)	
Contract Month 3			$(250,000)
	$625,000	$ 125,000	$(625,000)
		Net Profit	$ 125,000

5. It now looks as follows

Transactions			
Sell 100,000 Shares Citigroup Stock in Forward Contract			
Installment 1	$ 350,000		
Installment 2		$ 150,000	
Installment 3			$(150,000)
Buy 300,000 Shares in Futures Market			
Contract Month 1	$(300,000)		
Contract Month 2		$(200,000)	
Contract Month 3			$(100,000)
	$ (50,000)	$ 50,000	$(250,000)
		Net Profit	$(250,000)

6. An example is below with assumed information. This position could be used to hedge a short position.

Price at T	Purchased Put $K = 80$	Written	
		Put $K = 82$	Net Profit
	80	82	
70	10	–12	–2
73	7	–9	–2
76	4	–6	–2
79	1	–3	–2
80	0	–2	–2
82	0	0	0
85	0	0	0
88	0	0	0
91	0	0	0
94	0	0	0

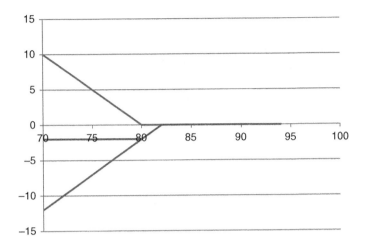

7. This position may be useful to hedge a short position

Price at T	Written Put $K = 80$	Purchased Call $K = 82$	Net Profit
	80	82	
70	−10	0	−10
73	−7	0	−7
76	−4	0	−4
79	−1	0	−1
80	0	0	0
82	0	0	0
85	0	3	3

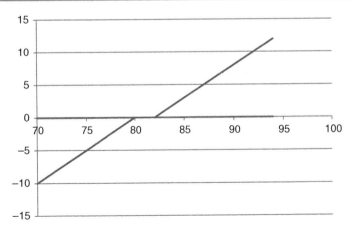

8. Using formula 12.10, you should get .691
9. You should use formula 12.9 for the replicating portfolio and solve for B given the other inputs and your answer for delta. Or, .691($100) + 1.0202(B) = 3, implies B = –64.79 which implies an amount borrowed by the negative sign.
10. Refer to formulas 12.14 and 12.15. Gamma is calculated as .6/$100(.3)(1) = .02. The new call premium should be about, $3 + .691(101–100) + .5(101 – 100)(101 – 100).02 = $3.701

CHAPTER 13

1. The loan commitment is composed of two parts, a bond-like set of cash flows where price changes are inversely related to changes in interest rates and an embedded written put option that allows the borrower to close the loan or not.
2. From the borrower's perspective they have the right to fall out of the pipeline without penalty, and in that regard it is as if they have a free put option. They can "put" or close the commitment at the contracted note rate. In this case they would likely exercise their close option.
3. They have written a put option to the borrower at no cost. You can use formula 13.2 for the delta of the put option. Using the inputs above and assuming time to expiration T is 45/365, yields a value of –.824. This would suggest that the option to the borrower is deep in the money for the borrower to exercise the option to close the loan. Note that this occurs because rates have moved up, causing the price of the commitment to go down. Higher rates incent the borrower to close.
4. You have effectively written put options to the borrower so you would want to buy put options on an underlying asset comparable to that of the mortgages in the pipeline.
5. You could synthetically create the cash flows of the purchased put by leveraging what you know about Put-Call Parity as described in formula 13.4. Specifically, by shorting a forward on Treasuries and purchasing a call option on five-year Treasuries you would synthetically create the same cash flows as a purchased put without having to actually buy it. You would still have to pay a premium for the call option, and you may find this to be a useful strategy if the put option is not available or is not traded much. Applying the formula

and solving for P, the put option value yields an estimate of C of $6.99016.

6. You would apply formula 13.5. This would reflect both the long commitments adjusted for delta and the short forward. The estimated fall out for a 50bps increase in interest rates is $.5 + .15(4–4.5) = .425$. Now we know that the close rate is equal to 1 – fallout rate, or a close rate of .575. Using this information and formula 13.5 yields $($100 – $99.5).425$25M = $.212($25M) = $5.3M$ that would need to be hedged.

7. Treasuries have better liquidity than MBS but could pose basis risk due to the lack of optionality in that instrument that does exist in the long commitments.

8. It will lead to error in your hedge. If the rate change doubles while the fallout rate remains the same, the hedge will be insufficient to offset the continued loss on the commitments. This is why incorporating a dynamic hedging strategy is critical to the success of the hedge activity.

9. Time decay should be a factor to consider, as option value declines with time to expiration. As value declines for options used for hedging it will require additional options to offset the loss in value. One way to address time decay would be to consider using longer-lived option contracts.

10. Optimization can be a useful tool in the hedge strategy when there are multiple hedge instruments of interest to consider as well as different interest rate scenarios to manage the risk across. One could minimize the cost of hedging subject to constraints on the net hedge position maintained within certain tolerances across rate scenarios for instance.

CHAPTER 14

1. Refer to Table 14.1 from the chapter.

2. It would appear that the RCSAs for the capital markets division have not been kept up to date or have not been taken seriously in the business unit. They would need to be revised to a red with potential consequences on the division's operations potentially until it was to be remediated. A full remediation plan would be required.

3. Between 2000 and 2007 there were 49 events in seven years, or seven events per year. For the period 2008–2013 there were 50 events in five years, or 10 per year. Using this information, we could demonstrate that

operational risk was greater in the 2008–2013 period by using a Poisson distribution. The distributions would look as follows:

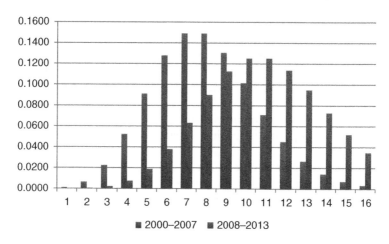

■ 2000–2007   ■ 2008–2013

4. Applying the Poisson formula for $k = 5$ and $? = 7$, the probability is 12.77 percent

5.

k	Poisson Frequencies
0	0.0067
1	0.0337
2	0.0842
3	0.1404
4	0.1755
5	0.1755
6	0.1462
7	0.1044
8	0.0653
9	0.0363
10	0.0181
11	0.0082
12	0.0034
13	0.0013
14	0.0005
15	0.0002

6. Note that your answers may be different due to the Rand() function changing each time but a representative table is shown below, applying formula 14.3 in the chapter.

k	Severity
0	$ 98,755.57
1	$ 100,220.78
2	$ 107,033.34
3	$ 94,211.22
4	$ 81,969.57
5	$ 94,182.45
6	$ 95,750.07
7	$ 79,624.99
8	$ 99,293.73
9	$ 101,700.44
10	$ 102,944.93
11	$ 101,784.39
12	$ 94,668.48
13	$ 91,906.46
14	$ 93,830.55
15	$ 100,109.51
	$1,537,986.48

7. Since Z0 exceeds each probability for each k, you would sum up all losses across the 15 event scenarios and have $1.58 million in losses.
8. You would need to use formula 14.4 in this case along with the information above to compute the following:

Risk Type			
1	$40,000,000,000	$ 9,000,000,000	
2	$ 9,000,000,000	$90,000,000,000	
	$49,000,000,000	$99,000,000,000	$148,000,000,000
			384707.6812

where the composite standard deviation is computed as $384,707
9. The operational VaR would be 1.65*$384,707, or $634,766 or the worst operational loss the bank should observe with a 95% level of confidence

10. Operational risk could come in the form of fraud committed by an individual of the firm or external to the company that results in a default. The default, however, is not a credit loss since the reason why the borrower defaulted was due to the operational risk, or fraud in this case and should not be counted toward estimates of credit loss for the firm but should be captured as part of the company's fraud losses.

CHAPTER 15

1. The threshold for determining whether to roll out the model or not should be based on the model validation team's results and not the model development group. In addition, the model tolerance should be based on a sample not used to develop the model. Additional information on how the model performs across key cohorts should be provided before making a decision. Strictly on the basis of the information provided above, the scorecard should not be approved given the 32 KS at which the model will be used most heavily.

2. While the scorecard appears to work well on the segment targeted for the card, the overall KS is not good enough at the policy cutoff to warrant moving the model into production.

3. The model makes a Type I error since it incorrectly rejects loans it should have otherwise made.

4. This is an example of Type II error where the model approves loans that otherwise it should not.

5. You should be concerned that the data do not reflect the type of customers that will be solicited and underwritten for the Platinum card. In addition, the data are unlikely to pick up a change in economic conditions, which could adversely affect the results for the business.

6. If the strategy goes into place and over time the regulators determine that in pulling off the hedge the bank violated the Volcker Rule, it could be subject to significant penalties and regulatory orders.

7. In this case there may not be any direct legal risks since the trades are technically legitimate, and the bank is not a direct participant in the marketing of potentially dangerous substances to people. However, it would be appropriate for the General Counsel's Office to weigh in on this strategy.

8. There could be huge reputational risk if it were to be found out that the bank was in effect betting on the success of the tobacco companies' marketing strategy. For no other reason, the headline risk is large as it could paint the bank as insensitive to the outcomes of certain groups, even if they are abroad.

9. If the strategy were to go into effect, it would be important to collect data on consumer and other market participant sentiment toward the bank and its strategy over time.

10. The bank should perform a thorough and comprehensive review across all relevant interests in the outcome of the strategy including risk management, compliance, legal, and public relations. The strategy should be benchmarked against the bank's corporate principles. In addition the RCSA process should be reviewed to ensure that the trading would conform to all relevant regulations before moving it forward.

CHAPTER 16

1. Integrated risk management is an inclusive concept that requires the collective attention of all parts of the organization, working together at reviewing different perspectives, information, and recommendations on important business initiatives and activities.

2. An effective program of integrated risk management emphasizes regular lines of communication vertically and across the organization. It requires integration between analytic and policy units, alignment of incentive, and reporting structures for balanced risk and reward outcomes.

3. The idea of shared leadership between risk and the business is a way of integrating risk more firmly in the business although it does introduce potential accountability issues by establishing more than one leader for each unit. That said, the reporting of the business risk leader to the enterprise CRO supports linkages in strong risk governance between business and corporate risk units that may be able to further reinforce culture and risk management best practices. The performance plans of both business and risk leaders of the operating units should have a balanced scorecard, where both have a sizable portion dedicated to long-term risk outcomes, although the proportions should be tilted heavier on that dimension for the business risk leader.

4. The risk committee does not include all of the parties needed to weigh in on this decision. Specifically, while the new limits would certainly mitigate potential credit risk exposure, it has a definite business impact as well as the potential for fair lending and other legal risks. Further, it could pose a reputational risk to the company once news on this position, should it move forward, hits the media. Representatives from legal, compliance, and production teams should be invited to this meeting. And the final decision may not rest with the CRO but could wind up at the Executive Committee level or higher.

5. The small business group appears to be ill-equipped to handle a large increase in its business. The infrastructure is simply not in place to identify, measure, and manage its risks. The data and reporting capabilities are weak as is the ALLL process and the risk expertise is underdeveloped at this point. The request should be denied until additional investment in core infrastructure is made.

6. Without supporting analysis, it is likely that the head of the small business unit and their executive management will put up significant opposition to the decision to limit their growth. You should develop a risk management scorecard not just for the small business group but one that could be applied consistently across the organization and has been properly vetted with senior management well ahead of such strategic decisions.

7. Such an effort would likely require the assistance of the risk units from across the company. A template should be developed that reflects a set of common processes, controls, and infrastructure required to perform the risk functions of each business organization. These processes should be assigned weights established by the risk team and a scoring system developed. Risk units would be engaged to assess each other's infrastructure quality and scores established for each operating unit. The scorecard should be vetted with the Executive Committee and approved for use in establishing annual strategic objectives.

8. This is a situation where insufficient communication across the organization takes place. By entering the hedging program, you potentially put the relationship with customers in the commercial lending division at risk if word gets out that the bank is betting against them. From a risk management perspective, this may be an appropriate risk mitigation strategy, but before it is implemented, an understanding of the effects on each business collectively should be established.

9. While there is a reporting line to the enterprise CRO, there is a potential misalignment in the focus of the business risk executive on risk objectives. With only 20 percent of their incentive compensation dependent on risk outcomes, the executive may be incented toward boosting their business-related objectives at the expense of long-term risk management. Both business and risk management should have clear risk-adjusted performance-based goals in their performance plans.

10. This is an example of a case where better integration between policy and analytics groups is required. In this case the credit policy group lacks hard evidence to determine where to establish credit policy boundaries and so may be setting up the business for failure early on by simply leveraging a set of policies that would significantly constrain the new program. However, in order to effectively manage the risk, the analytics

team may be able to use its insights from the new data and model together in collaboration wth credit policy to set policy criteria that both
manage risk and maintain a level of credit performance consistent with
expectations. It may be that the team decides to establish a tighter set of
underwriting criteria at first that can be relaxed gradually over time as
performance aligns with established risk targets.